LINGO
IN A NUTSHELL

A Desktop Quick Reference

LINGO
IN A NUTSHELL

A Desktop Quick Reference

Bruce A. Epstein

O'REILLY™

Cambridge · Köln · Paris · Sebastopol · Tokyo

Table of Contents

Preface

About This Book

You are holding in your hands one half of *Bruce's Brain in a Book*. The other half of my brain is in the companion book, *Director in a Nutshell*. These books are the distillation of years of real-life experience with countless Director projects plus many hours spent researching and testing Director 6's and 6.5's new features. While they can be used separately, they are ideally used as a single two-volume reference, which can be purchased together for less than most single Director books.

> *Lingo in a Nutshell* focuses on the abstract concepts in Lingo—variables, scripts, Behaviors, objects, mouse and keyboard events, timers, math, lists, strings, and file I/O. *Director in a Nutshell* focuses on the concrete aspects of Director—the Cast, the Score, Projectors, MIAWs, media (graphics, sound, digital video, text), Director's windows, GUI components (buttons, cursors, menus) and Shockwave.

If you already know a lot about Director or have been disappointed by the existing documentation, these are the books you've been waiting for. They address many of the errors and omissions in Macromedia's documentation and in many third-party books. There is no fluff or filler here, so you'll miss a lot if you skim. We are both busy, so let's get on with it.

What Are These Books and Who Are They for?

Director in a Nutshell and *Lingo in a Nutshell* are desktop quick references for Director and Lingo developers who are familiar with Director's basic operation and need to create, debug, and optimize cross-platform Director and Shockwave projects. These books are concise, detailed, respectful of the reader's intelligence, and organized by topic to allow quick access to thorough coverage of all relevant information.

Because Lingo and Director are inextricably linked, I have kept all information on a single topic within a single chapter rather than breaking it along the traditional Director versus Lingo lines (with the exception of the *Using Xtras* and *Lingo Xtras and XObjects* chapters). Don't be fooled by the titles of the books; both include a lot of Lingo, and they should be read in parallel.

Director in a Nutshell should not be confused with the third-party books that merely rehash the manuals, nor should it be considered an introductory book. It is exceptionally valuable for non-Lingo users but also covers Lingo related to those aspects of Director mentioned previously. *Lingo in a Nutshell* covers both the very basics of Lingo and its most advanced features. It is for both new and experienced Lingo programmers, which may sound impossible but isn't. Each book covers both Windows and the Macintosh.

To describe them as "beginner," "intermediate," or "advanced" would be misleading because they cover both the very basic foundation of Director and its very advanced usage. Strictly as a comparison to other books on the market, you should consider their *coverage* extremely advanced, but the text itself is accessible to Director users of all levels. *Lingo in a Nutshell* allows Director users to take full advantage of Lingo's power, and *Director in a Nutshell* helps users of all levels deal confidently with the spectrum of Director's media types and features.

What These Books Are Not

These books are not a rehash of the Director manuals or Help system but rather a complement to them; as such, they are unlike any other books on the market.

These books are not a celebration of Director as multimedia Nirvana. They are for people who know that Director has many quirks and some bugs and want to know how to work around them quickly and effectively.

These books are not courses in graphic design, project management, Photoshop, HTML, or JavaScript. They will, however, help you to integrate your existing skills and external content into Director's framework.

These books are not a Director tutorial; I assume that you are familiar with the basics of Director's Cast, Score, Stage, and menus. They are not for people who need hand-holding. They are for people who can apply general concepts to their specific problem and want to do so rapidly.

These books are not perfect—errors are inevitable—so use them as a guide, not the gospel. Although these books cannot anticipate all circumstances, they do provide the tools for you to confidently solve your specific problems, even in the face of erroneous or incomplete information.

Last, these books are not a static lecture. They are an ongoing conversation between you, the reader, and me, the author. Feedback from many customers, clients, and friends has already shaped their content. I have packed them with facts, but I also provide the tools to allow you to understand and debug any situation. Let us see if we can solve some problems in Director and learn something about ourselves along the way.

Lingo in a Nutshell

Lingo in a Nutshell covers the abstract aspects of Lingo that exist apart from its control over media elements, the Cast, and the Score. This book covers the spectrum from Lingo basics to advanced scripting with Lists, Behaviors, and Xtras. It is divided into five major sections.

Part I, *Lingo Basics*

Chapter 1, *How Lingo Thinks*, defines the Lingo language and its syntax including handlers, variables, and Lingo control structures. Refer also to Chapter 1, *How Director Thinks* in *Director in a Nutshell*.

Chapter 2, *Events, Messages, and Scripts*, explains where, when, and how to use various types of scripts to detect user and system events. It covers the new event and message passing in Director 6, including details on trapping events with Behaviors.

Chapter 3, *Lingo Coding and Debugging Tips*, helps you plan your Lingo and covers the Debugger, Message window, and Lingo error messages. See also Appendix E, *Error Messages and Error Codes*.

Chapter 4, *Lingo Internals*, is designed for experienced programmers and compares Lingo's syntax, commands, and structure to those of other languages. Refer also to the downloadable Chapter 20, *Lingo for C Programmers*.

Part II, *Lingo Data Types and Expressions*

Chapter 5, *Data Types and Expressions*, covers Lingo data types, implicit and explicit type conversion and coercion, type checking, logical expressions, comparison operators, and string operators.

Chapter 6, *Lists*, is a life-saving chapter covering the commands for linear lists, property lists, points, and rectangles in well-organized tables. It contains numerous examples including randomized and non-repeating lists.

Chapter 7, *Strings*, covers string expressions, concatenation, parsing, and manipulation, and chunk expressions (characters, words, items, lines, and fields). See also Chapter 12, *Text and Fields*, in *Director in a Nutshell*.

Chapter 8, *Math (and Gambling)*, covers arithmetic operators, math functions, exponentiation, geometry and trig functions, rounding and truncation, and random numbers.

Part III, *Lingo Events*

Chapter 9, *Mouse Events*, covers responding to mouse clicks and cursor movement, including how to make buttons with rollover and highlight states.

Chapter 10, *Keyboard Events*, covers responding to keyboard input and trapping various key combinations (including modifier keys, function keys, arrow keys, and the numeric keypad).

Chapter 11, *Timers and Dates*, covers timers, time-outs, dates, times, and unit conversion.

Part IV, *Applied Lingo*

Chapter 12, *Behaviors and Parent Scripts*, helps you make the most of Behaviors and other object-oriented scripting techniques.

Chapter 13, *Lingo Xtras and XObjects*, covers using Xtras and XObjects to extend Lingo's scripting language. See also Chapter 10, *Using Xtras*, in *Director in a Nutshell*.

Chapter 14, *External Files*, covers the *FileIO* Xtra for reading and writing files from within Director. It also covers commands that work with external Director-related files and non-Director documents and applications.

Chapter 15, *The MUI Dialog Xtra*, covers using the *MUI* Xtra to create basic Alert dialogs. Refer also to the downloadable Chapter 21, *Custom MUI Dialogs*, which provides painstaking detail on creating custom dialogs with the *MUI* Xtra.

Part V, *Lingo Command Reference*

Chapter 16, *Enumerated Values*, lists all the Lingo commands that accept or return numeric codes, symbols, or strings that indicate particular values, including transitions, ink effects, palettes, cursors, and window types.

Chapter 17, *Changed, Undocumented, and Misdocumented Lingo*, covers Lingo commands that are undocumented or misdocumented or behave differently in Director 6 than in prior versions of Director.

Chapter 18, *Lingo Keyword and Command Summary*, is a complete list of every command, function, symbol, and string recognized by Lingo, including a syntax example.

Chapter 19, *The Lingo Symbol Table*, explains the inner workings of the hidden Symbol Table and symbols in general. Refer also to the downloadable Chapter 22, *Symbol Table Archaeology*, for additional details.

Part VI, *Appendixes*

Appendix A, *ASCII Codes and Key Codes*

Appendix B, *Changes in D6 Through D6.5*

Appendix C, *Case-Sensitivity, Sort Order, Diacritical Marks, and Space-Sensitivity*

Appendix D, *The DIRECTOR.INI and LINGO.INI Files*

Appendix E, *Error Messages and Error Codes*

Glossary

The economics of print publishing precluded me from including everything in this book. The good news is that the material (plus many more examples) is available online in PDF (Acrobat) format (see *http://www.zeusprod.com/nutshell*).

Online Bonus Chapters:

Chapter 20, *Lingo for C Programmers*, is designed for experienced programmers and compares Lingo's syntax, commands, and structure to C. It picks up where Chapter 4, leaves off.

Chapter 21, *Custom MUI Dialogs*, covers the excruciating details of using the MUI Xtra to create custom dialog boxes. It expands on Chapter 15, which covers only the MUI Xtra's *Alert()* method.

Chapter 22, *Symbol Table Archaeology*, covers the history and hidden secrets of the Lingo Symbol Table and complements Chapter 19.

The companion volume, *Director in a Nutshell*, covers content development and delivery in Director. It also covers media and user interface elements and the Lingo to control them. Refer to the Preface in *Director in a Nutshell* for details.

Conventions Used in This Book

Typographical Conventions

- Lingo *keywords* (*functions*, *commands*, and *property names*) are shown in *italics* except in tables where they are italicized only when necessary to distinguish them from the surrounding text. Italics in tables usually indicate replaceable values.

- `Arguments`, `user-specified`, and `replaceable` items are shown in *italics* and should be replaced by real values when used in your code.

- New terms are shown in *italics* and are often introduced by merely using them in context. Refer to the Glossary for details.

- Menu commands are shown as `MenuName➤MenuItem`.

- Options in dialog boxes, such as the *Tab to Next Field* checkbox, are shown in *italics*.

- Constants, such as `TRUE`, `FALSE`, and `RETURN`, are shown in `Courier`.

- `#symbols` are preceded by the # character and shown in `Courier`.

- Optional items are specified with curly braces ({}) instead of the traditional square braces ([]) which Lingo uses for lists. For example:

  `go {to} {frame}` *whichFrame*

  means that the following all are equivalent:

  ```
  go whichFrame
  go to whichFrame
  go to frame whichFrame
  go frame whichFrame
  ```

- Allowed values for a property are separated by a " | ". The following indicates that *the alignment of member* property can be set to "left," "right," or "center":

  `set the alignment of member 1 = "left" | "right" | "center"`

Grammatical and Stylistic Conventions

- Most Lingo properties start with the word *the*, which can lead to sentences such as "The *the member of sprite property* can be changed at runtime." I often omit the keyword *the* preceding properties to make sentences or tables more readable, but you should include the *the* in your Lingo code.

- Lingo event handlers all begin with the word *on*, such as *on mouseUp*. I often omit the word *on* when discussing events, messages, and handlers or in tables where the meaning is implied.

- Be aware that some Director keywords are used in multiple contexts such as the *on mouseUp* event handler and the *the mouseUp* system property. The intended usage is discernible from context, or stated explicitly in ambiguous circumstances.

- I use terminology fairly loosely, as is typical among Lingo developers. For example, a "*mouseUp* script" is technically "an *on mouseUp* handler within a script." The meaning should be clear from the context.

- I capitalize the names of Director entities, such as the Score, the Stage, the Cast, and the Message window. I don't capitalize general terms that refer to classes of items, such as sprite scripts.

- Most handler names used in the examples are arbitrary, although handlers such as *on mouseUp* that trap built-in events must be named as shown. I use variable names like *myThing* or *whichSprite* to indicate items for which you should substitute your own values. When in doubt, consult Table 18-1, "*Lingo Command and Keyword Summary.*

- I use few segues and assume you will reread the material until it makes sense. As with a Dalí painting, you must revisit the text periodically to discover details that you missed the first time.

Examples

- Example code is shown monospaced and set off in its own paragraph. If a code fragment is shown, especially using the put command, it is implicit that you should type the example in the Message window to see the result. Any text following "--" is the output from Director or a comment from me:

```
set x = 5      -- Set the variable x to 5
put x          -- Display the value of x
-- 5
```

- Long lines of Lingo code are continued on the next line using the Lingo continuation character ([LC]) as shown here. This character is created using Opt-Return or Option-L (Macintosh) or Alt-Enter (Windows).

```
set the member of sprite (the currentSpriteNum) = ¬
    member "Hilighted Button"
```

- If you have trouble with an example, check for lines that may have been erroneously split without the Lingo continuation character (¬). Remember to use parentheses when calling any function that returns a value. Otherwise you'll either see no result or receive an error.

```
rollover          -- wrong
rollover()        -- wrong
put rollover      -- wrong
put rollover()    -- correct
```

- I sometimes use the single-line form of the *if...then* statement in an example for brevity. You should use multiline *if...then* statements in your code. See Chapter 1 for details on the *if* statement.

```
-- This will usually work
if (x > 5) then put "It's True!"
-- But this is more reliable
if (x > 5) then
    put "It's True!"
end if
```

- If a handler is shown in an example, it is implied that the handler has been entered into the appropriate type of script. Generally, mouse event handlers such as *mouseUp* belong in sprite scripts; frame events handlers such as *exitFrame* belong in frame scripts; and custom utilities belong in movie scripts. I often show a handler followed by an example of its use. Type the handler into an appropriate script, and then test it from the Message window. If I don't show a test in the Message window, either the handler does not output a visible result, or it is assumed that you will test it yourself.

```
-- This goes in a script, in this case a movie script
on customHandler
    put "Hello Sailor!"
end customHandler
```

```
-- This is a test in the Message window
customHandler
-- "Hello Sailor"
```

- The output shown may vary inconsequentially from the results you would see based on your system setup. Most notably, the number of decimal places output for floating-point values depends on your setting for *the floatPrecision* property.

- If the output of a handler is extremely long, the results will not be shown in their entirety or may not be shown at all.

- The examples are demonstrative and not necessarily robust, and they assume that you provide valid inputs when applicable. It is good practice to include type checking and error checking in your actual Lingo code, as described in Chapters 1 and 3. I often omit such checking to keep examples shorter and to focus on the main issue at hand.

- Some examples, particularly the tests performed from the Message window, are code *fragments* and won't work without help from the studio audience. You should ensure that any variables required by the examples (particularly lists) have been initialized with meaningful values, although such initialization is not shown. For example:

```
put count (myList)
```

The previous code fragment assumes that you have *previously* set a valid value for *myList*, such as:

```
set myList = [1, 7, 5, 9]
```

- Some examples allude to field cast members, such as:

```
set the text of field "Memory" = string(the freeBlock)
```
It is implied that you should create a field cast member of the specified name in order for the example to work.

- Screen shots may not match your platform's graphical user interface exactly.

- I present a simplified view of the universe whenever my assumptions are overwhelmingly likely to be valid. You can intentionally confuse Director by setting bizarre values for a property or performing malicious operations, such as deleting elements from a *rect* structure, but you do so at your own risk. I cover situations where errors might occur accidentally, but you should assume that all statements presented as fact are prefaced by, "Assuming you are not trying to screw with Director just for fun..." When they are likely to be relevant, I state my assumptions clearly.

- The myriad ways to perform a given task are shown when that task is the main topic of discussion but not if it is peripheral to the subject at hand. When it is incidental, I may show the most expedient or clearest method rather than the suggested method.

- Examples are usually self-contained, but they may rely on custom handlers shown nearby. If an example builds on previous examples or material cross-referenced in another chapter, it is assumed that the relevant handlers have been entered in an appropriate script (usually a movie script).

- What rightly belongs in one table sometimes is broken into two or three due to space constraints. Similar information may be organized in different ways in multiple tables to help you find what you want, especially in Chapter 6. The first column of each table contains the table's "key item" for which full details are provided. Subservient items, for which the table may not contain complete information, are relegated to other columns. For example, if a function is listed in the "*See Also*" column of a table, complete details on that command can be found in surrounding prose or other tables.

Refer to the Glossary for a complete list of definitions.

New Features in Director 6 and 6.5

Score, Sprites, Auto-Puppeting, and Paths

Director's new Score is *radically* different and includes a Sprite Toolbar and customizable views. Sprites receive several new messages (*beginSprite*, *endSprite*, *mouseEnter*, *mouseLeave*, etc.), allowing them to be managed much more easily. Refer to Chapter 3, *The Score and Animation*, in *Director in a Nutshell* and to Chapter 2 in *Lingo in a Nutshell*.

Help and Manuals

The new Help system includes a *lot* of information that is not in the manuals, plus many useful *Show Me* demonstration movies. Choose *Show Me* from the Help menu or from the Help *Contents* window for demonstrations of many of Director's new features.

New Behaviors, Messages, Cue Points, and Lingo

Behaviors allow you to easily add *multiple* scripts to a sprite. Director's message passing has been radically revised, and there are many new messages, including rollover events and error trapping. Refer to Chapter 2, 9, and 12. Director now supports cue points for synchronizing sounds with animation in the Score (see Chapter 15, *Sound and Cue Points*, in *Director in a Nutshell*).

Shockwave and Internet Improvements
Shockwave and Director now support streaming playback of Internet-based content. Many Director commands support linking to a URL, and linked cast libraries or streaming Shockwave audio can reside on the Internet. New commands (*frameReady*, *mediaReady*, *netDone*, etc.) support asynchronous operations in Director via the *NetLingo* Xtra. Refer to Chapter 11, *Shockwave and the Internet*, in *Director in a Nutshell*.

Shockwave Audio is now integrated with Director. Local sounds can be compressed as well as those on the Internet. See Chapter 15 in *Director in a Nutshell*. Shockwave-style movie compression is also available to make your local Director project use less disk space.

New Media Formats and Application Integration
Director 6.0 supports many new media formats.

 Using external media (including sounds) at runtime requires the *MIX Services* Xtra plus the support Xtra for that particular file type, such as *Sound Import Export*.

Refer to Chapter 4, *CastLibs, Cast Members and Sprites*, and Chapter 10, *Using Xtras*, in *Director in a Nutshell* for details on file import types and the required Xtras.

New Features in Director 6.5
Director 6.5 is the same as version 6.0.2 with the addition of many Xtras. See *http://www.macromedia.com/software/director/productinfo/newfeatures/* and refer to Appendix B, *Changes in D6 Through D6.5*. Refer also to *Director in a Nutshell*, especially to Appendix B, *New Features in Director 6.5*, and Chapter 16, *Digital Video*, which covers QuickTime 3.

Director Resources

The best thing about Director is the extended community of developers that you can torment for assistance. This book notwithstanding, Director is largely undocumented. Visit Macromedia's web site frequently, and plug into the broader Director community via mailing lists and newsgroups.

Director in a Nutshell and Lingo in a Nutshell

O'Reilly and Associates
http://www.oreilly.com/catalog/directnut/
http://www.oreilly.com/catalog/lingonut/

Home page for both books
  http://www.zeusprod.com/nutshell

Download example code
  http://www.zeusprod.com/nutshell/examples.html

Downloadable bonus chapters (PDF format)
  http://www.zeusprod.com/nutshell/chapters.html

Links page (all URLs in this book are available by chapter/topic)
  http://www.zeusprod.com/nutshell/links.html

Web Review—All things browser and web related
  http://www.webreview.com/

Macromedia

Macromedia home page and mirror sites
  http://www.macromedia.com

  http://www-euro.macromedia.com

  http://www-asia.macromedia.com

Director 6.5 update
  http://www.macromedia.com/software/director/productinfo/newfeatures/

  http://www.macromedia.com/software/director/upgrade/

Director Developers Center (searchable database of Tech Notes and tips)
  http://www.macromedia.com/support/director/

  http://www.macromedia.com/support/search/

  http://www.macromedia.com/support/director/how/subjects/

Shockwave Developer Center
  http://www.macromedia.com/shockwave/

  http://www.macromedia.com/support/director/how/shock/

Dynamic HTML and Shockwave browser scripting
  http://www.dhtmlzone.com/swdhtml/index.html

Director-related newsgroups
  http://www.macromedia.com/support/director/interact/newsgroups/

  news://forums.macromedia.com/macromedia.plug-ins

  news://forums.macromedia.com/macromedia.director.basics

  news://forums.macromedia.com/macromedia.director.lingo

Priority Access (fee-based) technical support
  http://www.macromedia.com/support/techsupport.html

  http://www.macromedia.com/support/director/suprog/

Beta program
  http://www.macromedia.com/support/program/beta.html

Director feature suggestions
  mailto:wish-director@macromedia.com

Phone support

MacroFacts (fax information) 1-800-449-3329 or 1-415-863-4409

Technical Support 1-415-252-9080

Main Operator: 1-415-252-2000

User groups

http://www.macromedia.com/support/programs/usergroups/worldwide.html

Developer Locator (find a Director or Lingo developer in your area)

http://www.macromedia.com/support/developer_locator/

Online services

CompuServe: Go Macromedia

AOL: The Macromedia forum on AOL no longer exists.

Macromedia User Conference (UCON), May 25–27 1999, in San Francisco, CA (There will be no UCON in the fall of 1998.)

http://www.macromedia.com/events/ucon99/

Web Sites and Xtras

Zeus Productions (my company) technical notes and Xtras

http://www.zeusprod.com

UpdateStage—monthly technical articles and the Director Quirk List and Xtras

http://www.updatestage.com

ftp://ftp.shore.net/members/update/

Director Online Users Group (DOUG)—articles, interviews, reviews

http://www.director-online.com

Maricopa Director Web—the mothership of Director information

http://www.mcli.dist.maricopa.edu/director/tips.html

ftp://ftp.maricopa.edu/pub/mcli/director

Lingo Behavior Database (example Behaviors) maintained by Renfield Kuroda

http://www.behaviors.com/lbd/

Peter Small's Avatars and Lingo Sourcery (far-out stuff)

http://avatarnets.com

Links to additional third-party web sites

http://www.mcli.dist.maricopa.edu/director/net.html

http://www.macromedia.com/support/director/ts/documents/tn3104-dirweb-sites.html

Third-Party Xtras

http://www.macromedia.com/software/xtras/director

FMA Online (Links to many Xtra developers)

http://www.fmaonline.com

Xtras developer programs

http://www.macromedia.com/support/program/xtrasdev.html

http://www.macromedia.com/support/xtras.html

QuickTime
> *http://quicktime.apple.com/*

Microsoft
> *http://support.microsoft.com/*

Mailing Lists

If you have the bandwidth, these mailing lists are often useful resources for Director, Shockwave, Xtras, and Lingo questions (see the Macromedia newsgroups). These mailing lists generate a *lot* of mail. Subscribe using DIGEST mode to avoid hundreds of separate e-mails each day.

DIRECT-L (Director and Lingo)
> Archives: *http://www.mcli.dist.maricopa.edu/director/digest/index.html*

> MailList: *http://www.mcli.dist.maricopa.edu/director/direct-l/index.html*

> Send the following in the *body* of an e-mail to *listserv@uafsysb.uark.edu*:

```
SUBSCRIBE DIRECT-L yourFirstName yourLastName
SET DIRECT-L DIGEST
```

Lingo-L (Lingo)
> *http://www.penworks.com/LUJ/lingo-l.cgi*

ShockeR (Shockwave)
> Archive: *http://ww2.narrative.com/shocker.nsf*

> MailList: *http://www.shocker.com/shocker/digests/index.html*

> Send the following in the *body* of an e-mail to *list-manager@shocker.com:*

```
SUBSCRIBE shockwave-DIGEST yourEmail@yourDomain
```

Xtras-L (Xtras for Director)
> *http://www.gmatter.com/xtras-l.html*

> Send the following in the *body* of an e-mail to *listserv@gmatter.com:*

```
SUB XTRAS-L yourFirstName yourLastName
```

Dedication

Lingo in a Nutshell is dedicated to my wife, Michele, whose love makes my life worthwhile.

Acknowledgments

I am indebted to many people, some of whom I've undoubtedly omitted from the list below. Please buy this book and recommend it to friends so that I can thank the people I've forgotten in the next revision.

My deep appreciation goes out to the entire staff at O'Reilly, whose patience, professionalism, and unwavering dedication to quality are directly responsible for bringing these books to market. Special thanks go to my editors, Tim O'Reilly, Katie Gardner, and Troy Mott, and to Edie Freedman, Sheryl Avruch, Frank Willison, Nancy Priest, Rob Romano, Mike Sierra, Paula Carroll, Nancy Kruse

Hannigan, Greg deZarn-O'Hare, and all the people who turn a manuscript into a book. My thanks also to the sales and marketing staff who ensure that my efforts were not in vain. Last, I want to thank all of the O'Reilly authors whose company I am proud to be in.

This project would not have happened without the efforts of my agent, David Rogelberg of Studio B Productions (*http://www.studiob.com*). He was instrumental in the development and genesis of both *Director in a Nutshell* and *Lingo in a Nutshell*, for which I am forever grateful. My thanks also to Sherry Rogelberg and to the participants of Studio B's Computer Book Publishing list.

The quality of the manuscript reflects my excellent technical reviewers, all of whom made time for this semi-thankless job despite their busy schedules: Lisa Kushins, who verified items to an extent that astounded me and provided feedback that improved every chapter she touched; Hudson Ansley, whose keen eye and unique perspective also improved the book immeasurably; Mark Castle (*http://www.the-castle.com*), who helped shape the style and content from the earliest stages; and Matthew Pirrone and James Terry (*http://www.kandu.com*), who both provided excellent feedback on Chapter 4, *Lingo Internals*, and Chapter 20, *Lingo for C Programmers*, (downloadable from the web site). My thanks also goes out to all my beta-readers who provided useful feedback, most notably Miles Lightwood and Birnou Sdarte.

I cannot begin to thank all the Macromedians who develop and support Director, many of whom provide technical support on their own time on various mailing lists. My special thanks goes to Buzz Kettles for all his feedback regarding Shockwave audio and to Michael Seery for being my inside connection at Macromedia all these years. My thanks also to Lalit Balchandani, David Calaprice, Jim Corbett, Landon Cox, Ken Day, Peter DeCrescenzo, David Dennick, John Dowdell, Mike Edmunds, John Embow, Eliot Greenfield, Jim Inscore, David Jennings, James Khazar, Leona Lapez, S Page, Bill Schulze, Karen Silvey, Joe Sparks, John Thompson, Karen Tucker, Anders Wallgren (expatriot), John Ware, Eric Wittman, Doug Wyrick, and Greg Yachuk, all of whom fight the good fight on a daily basis.

My thanks go out to the wider Director community, including but not limited to Stephen Hsu, Brian "Bam Bam" Johansen, Peter Fierlinger, Brian Gray, Roger Jones, Tab Julius, Irv Kalb, Kathy Kozel, Alan Levine, Gretchen Macdowall, Myron Mandell, Kevin McFarland, Hai Ng, Roy Pardi, Darrel Plant, Peter Small, Kam Stewart, Stephen Taylor, Andrew White, John Williams, Alex Zavatone, all the participants of the super-secret mailing lists that I cannot name, and all the users who have given me feedback over the years, including the AOL old-timers.

Thank you also to Caroline Lovell-Malmberg, who can now forgive her husband, Mark, for leaving her out of his acceptance speech. Perhaps he'll thank whomever I've inadvertently left out next time he wins an Oscar.

I'd like to thank you for taking the time to read this book. If I never get around to stand-up comedy, it is nice to know I still have an audience somewhere. If you enjoy the book, you owe a debt of gratitude to Professor David Thorburn, who taught me more about writing than anyone before or since.

Last, I want to acknowledge my entire family, whose sacrifices and support truly made this book possible. If this book saves you time that you can then devote to *your* family, my efforts will not have been in vain. Good luck in all your multimedia pursuits.

Bruce A. Epstein
May 1998
Franklin Park, NJ

"All the love that you miss...all the people that you can recall...do they really exist at all?" — Lowell George, anticipating Virtual Reality by 20 years

PART I

Lingo Basics

CHAPTER 1

How Lingo Thinks

So You're Too Busy to Learn Lingo

Do you really have time to read a book on Lingo when you're facing a deadline? The answer depends on how much time you waste struggling with Lingo and how often you've compromised your Director projects for lack of Lingo skills. If you make the investment now, this book will pay marvelous dividends. It may save you weeks otherwise spent flailing over relatively trivial Lingo problems, and it can help you to add snazzy new features and a professional polish to your Director projects.

 If you don't have a project to work on, pick one now. You will learn much more if you have a concrete goal and concrete problems to solve. You have been warned.

Learning to program is a process, not an event. Although this book is not a substitute for an introductory programming class, it covers basic, intermediate, and advanced topics. The material is very condensed, but the book also lavishes attention on topics that are omitted entirely from other Lingo books. Before proceeding, you should understand Director's Cast, Score, and media editing windows, as covered in Macromedia's *Using Director* manual. You might also want to skim Macromedia's *Learning Lingo* manual for a broad overview of Lingo.

Most books provide simple examples that leave you stranded when you try to accomplish your specific goals. This book teaches you how to do *anything* you want with Lingo, not just create simple clickable buttons. It provides a solid foundation instead of a house of cards, and it is for people who want to know more, not less. As such, this book explores many abstract concepts that may not be relevant to your immediate needs. You must exercise reasonable discretion by ignoring topics that don't interest you or are beyond your current level.

3

This chapter lays the groundwork for your Lingo-laden future, but the details of using Lingo to add interactivity are in later chapters (starting with Chapter 2, *Events, Messages, and Scripts*). You should first focus on understanding how Lingo itself "thinks." Lingo is a marathon, not a sprint, and the extra training will pay off in the long run. More practical examples are given in Chapter 9, *Mouse Events*, and Chapter 10, *Keyboard Events*. Refer to the companion book, *Director in a Nutshell*, for details on using Lingo to control and analyze cast members, sprites, sounds, digital video, MIAWs, fields, and memory.

You are not expected to understand the entirety of this book the first time you read it. Much of it will be meaningless until you've worked with Lingo for a few months and encountered specific problems that you wish to solve. At that time, you will recall enough to know what sections you need to reread. As in the film *The Karate Kid*, what may seem like meaningless manual labor is really your first step toward a black belt in Lingo. You should revisit this and other chapters periodically. They will reveal additional nuggets of knowledge as your experience and problems with Director and Lingo grow. Certainly, you should return to the appropriate chapter whenever you encounter a vexing problem, as the chances are high that the answer lies herein.

Even if Lingo is your first programming language, this chapter will help you to understand other people's Lingo code (which is the first step in creating your own). This chapter unavoidably introduces many new concepts that depend on other material not introduced until later (the old "chicken and the egg" problem). Skip around the chapter as necessary, and consult the Glossary whenever you feel queasy. Keep in mind that this chapter is intended to satisfy a broad range of users, some with much more programming experience than others. Skip the mind-numbing sections that don't have relevance for you yet (but revisit them later). Above all, do not lose heart. If you keep reading, you'll encounter the same concepts again, and they will eventually make sense. In the words of Owl, "Be brave, little Piglet. Chin up and all that sort of thing."

The example code used throughout this book is available from the download site cited in the Preface, but you should create a test Director movie file and type in the shorter examples by hand. Add the examples in each chapter to your test movie and use it like a lab notebook full of your experiments. This practice will make it much easier to write your own Lingo when the time comes. You might want to maintain a separate test movie for each chapter; start with a fresh movie (to eliminate potential conflicts) if an example doesn't seem to work.

 You must abandon the safety of spoon-fed examples and experiment. If at first you don't *fail*, try, try again. You will learn more from failure than from success.

Experienced programmers can skim most of this chapter but should read the sections entitled "*Recursion*," "*Dynamic Script Creation*," "*The Classic Three-Line If Statement*," "*Special Treatment of the First Argument Passed*," and "*Variable-Length Parameter Lists*." Also see Chapter 4, *Lingo Internals*.

Let us set our goals high and see if we can stretch our minds to reach them. Let us now commit ourselves not only to learning Lingo, but also to becoming true *Linguists*, as fluent in Lingo as we are in our own native tongues.

Like all experienced Linguists, you should first build a shrine to the Lingo Gods with an altar for burning incense to summon and appease them. Abandon all hope, ye who enter here, for there is no turning back.

"Do or not do. There is no try."—Yoda

Lingo Scripting Basics

Computer languages tend to be simpler and more rigid than human languages, but like any other language Lingo has a set of rules that control the structure (*syntax*) of your Lingo program. Just as languages have grammar, Lingo's *syntactical* rules restrict the spelling, vocabulary, and punctuation so that Director can understand your instructions.

 A *syntax error* or *script error* usually indicates a typographical error or the incorrect use of a Lingo statement.

Lingo's built-in *keywords* (or *reserved words*) make up Lingo's vocabulary and are the building blocks of any Lingo program. We'll see later how these keywords form the skeleton of your Director program, just as any language's words are the basis for sentences and paragraphs. It is crucial that you recognize which items in a Lingo script are built-in keywords versus those that are specified arbitrarily by the programmer. Refer to Chapter 18, *Lingo Keyword and Command Summary*, for a complete list of all Lingo keywords. The *PrettyScript* Xtra (*http://rampages. onramp.net/~joker/tools/*) is a $20 U.S. shareware tool that colorizes some items in your Lingo scripts to make them easier to recognize. The *ScriptOMatic Lite* Xtra, is available under `XtrasScriptOMatic►Lite`, colorizes a broader range of items, but it is crippled almost to the point of being useless. The full version is promised imminently from g/matter (*http://www.gmatter.com/products/scriptomatic/*) at press time.

Handlers and Scripts

A *handler* is a series of Lingo statements that tell Director to perform some useful function. Handlers are typed into *script* cast members in the Script window. ("Script" is also used loosely to refer to a handler within a script. "Code" is used both as a noun to indicate your Lingo scripts and as a verb, meaning "to program" or "to write Lingo scripts.")

The scripts in a Director movie control the action, just as real-life actors follow a script. There are several types of scripts (castmember scripts, movie scripts, sprite scripts, parent scripts, and Behaviors), which are covered in detail in the "*Lingo Scripts and Handler Types*" section of Chapter 2.

Hello World

As required by the International Programmers' Treaty of 1969, we'll start with an example that displays "Hello World." Open up a *movie script* cast member using Cmd-Shift-U (Macintosh) or Ctrl-Shift-U (Windows).

Enter Example 1-1 exactly as shown into the movie script window.

Example 1-1: Hello World

```
on helloWorld
  alert "Hello World"
end
```

The keyword *on* identifies the beginning of our handler, which we *arbitrarily* chose to name *helloWorld*. The keyword *end* signifies the end of our handler.

 The examples beginning with the word *on* are handlers that must be typed into a script, not the Message window.

With minor exceptions, your Lingo code for each handler goes between the *on handlerName* and *end* commands (see "*Where Commands Go*").

Handler names must be one word, but they are case-insensitive, so you can use capitalization to make them easier to read. Name your handlers descriptively so that you can remember what they do, and as a rule you should avoid naming them the same as existing Lingo commands (see Table 18-1).

A handler name must start with an alphanumeric character, not a digit, but it can contain digits, decimal points, and underscores. Only the first 260 characters of the name are significant.

Movie script cast members are simply repositories for our handlers and are not used in the Score (see Chapter 2 for details on score scripts).

Entering a handler into a script (as shown above) *defines* or *declares* the handler and is referred to as a *handler definition*. Defining (declaring) a handler makes it available for future use, but the handler doesn't execute until something tells Director to run it for you.

Close the Script window to *compile* it (that is, to prepare it to run). When the handler is run (*called*), Lingo will execute each line (that is, each *command*) in the order in which it appears in the handler. There is only one command in our *helloWorld* handler; the built-in *alert* command displays the specified text in an alert dialog box.

The *Message window* provides an area for printing messages from Lingo and testing Lingo scripts (see Chapter 3, *Lingo Coding and Debugging Tips*). A handler stored in a movie script can be executed (called) by typing its name in the Message window (or by using its name in another handler).

Open the Message window using Cmd-M (Macintosh) or Ctrl-M (Windows). In the Message window, type the name of the handler to test (*helloWorld* without any spaces). Do not precede the name with the word *on*, which is used only to declare a handler, not to run it.

```
helloWorld
```

 Always press the RETURN key (Macintosh) or the ENTER key (Windows) at the end of the line to initiate the command. Example code shown flush left should be typed into the Message window, as opposed to handler definitions that are entered in the Script window.

Congratulations, you are now a Lingo programmer! After accepting your diploma, please step to the right. If your script didn't work, make sure you typed everything correctly and that you entered the script in a *movie* Script window (not a score script, castmember script, field, or text cast member). Choose Control▶Recompile All Scripts. If it still fails, hang your head in shame, or see Chapters 3 and 4.

Calling All Scripts

Typing helloWorld in the Message window *calls* (locates and runs) the handler of the same name. Reopen the script, and change both the name of the handler in the script and the name you type in the Message window to something new. If the names don't match, what happens? Did you remember to recompile the script by closing its window? Set the *Using Message Window Recompiles Scripts* option under Preferences▶General to ensure that the latest version of a handler is executed. See "*Compiling Scripts*" later in this chapter.

Note above that "Hello World" is automatically incorporated by the *alert* command into the alert dialog. You can change the displayed text by specifying any *string* (series of characters) in place of "Hello World" (don't forget the quotes). The specified string is said to be an *argument* to the *alert* command, and it is used to customize the dialog. See "*Commands and Functions*" and "*Parameters and Arguments*" later in this chapter for complete details on using arguments with built-in Lingo commands and custom handlers.

Previously we created an arbitrarily named custom handler and called it from the Message window by using its name.

 You can add more handlers after the end of the *helloWorld* handler in the movie script used above, or you can press the "+" button in the Script window to create a second movie script. (You can have a virtually unlimited number of movie scripts).

Naturally, the user will not be typing anything in the Message window. When the user clicks the mouse button or presses a key Director tries to run handlers named *on mouseDown, on mouseUp, on keyDown,* and so on. In practice, you'll create *event handlers* with these reserved names to respond to user events. If you name the handlers incorrectly, they will never be executed. See the *"Events"* section in Chapter 2, and Chapter 9 for more details.

Nested Handler Calls

Just as we can call a handler from the Message window, one handler can call another simply by using its name. As each handler completes its work, control returns to the calling handler. You can picture a hierarchy of *nested* handler calls as an outline that periodically is indented further, then returns to the previous level. Suppose we define several handlers (some of which call other handlers) in a movie script as shown in Example 1-2.

The *put* command prints a message in the Message window and is used throughout the book to peek inside Lingo. The *&&* and *&* operators are used to assemble long strings (see Chapter 7, *Strings*). Lingo lines starting with two hyphens ("--") are comments for the reader's benefit (see *"Comments,"* later in this chapter).

Example 1-2: Nested Handler Calls

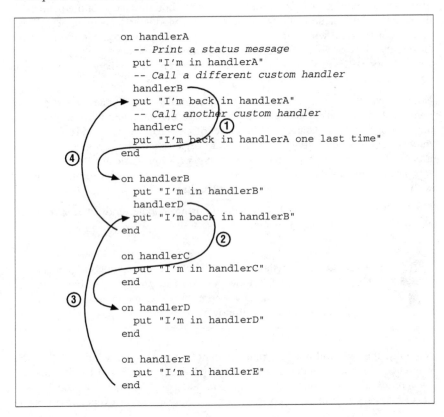

We can then test it from the Message window.

```
handlerA
-- "I'm in handlerA"
-- "I'm in handlerB"
-- "I'm in handlerD"
-- "I'm back in handlerB"
-- "I'm back in handlerA"
-- "I'm in handlerC"
-- "I'm back in handlerA one last time"
```

The series of Lingo handlers that are currently "pending" is known as the *call stack*. The call stack is always shown in the upper left pane of the Debugger window (see Figure 3-1).

Note that *handlerA* calls *handlerB*, which then calls *handlerD*. Control then passes back through *handlerB* and back to *handlerA*. Finally, *handlerA* calls *handlerC*, and control is then returned to *handlerA*. Conceptually, this can be pictured as:

```
handlerA
  handlerB
    handlerD
  handlerC
```

Note that the order of execution *within* a handler is determined by order of the Lingo commands, but the order in which the four handlers are typed into the movie script is irrelevant. Execution begins at our so-called *entry point* (in this case *handlerA*, which was called from the Message window), and Lingo takes detours into each called handler before it returns control to the calling handler. Note that *handlerE* is never called and therefore never executed, even though it has been defined in the same script with our other handlers.

Recursion

Each time a handler is called, a *copy* of it is created temporarily. The copy comes into existence when the handler is called and disappears when the handler completes. You can call a handler hundreds of times, and each occurrence will be independent of the other occurrences. A handler that calls itself, as shown in Example 1-3, is called a *recursive function*, and this technique is called *recursion*.

If we call our recursive function from the Message window, Director will run out of memory. (Save your work before testing this as it may crash your machine.)

Example 1-3: A Recursive Function

```
on recurseTest
  recurseTest
```

Example 1-3: A Recursive Function (continued)

```
    put "End of recurseTest reached"
end recurseTest
```

If you are using recursion, it is probably an accident. As a general rule, you should avoid it. It is like a reflection repeated infinitely between two mirrors; in the extreme case it will crash Director. See Example 6-9, *"Recursively Sorting Sublists* in Chapter 6, *Lists*, Example 8-16, *"Recursive Factorial Function"* in Chapter 8, *Math (and Gambling)*, and Example 14-5, *"Extracting Files in Subfolders"* in Chapter 14, *External Files*, for proper uses of recursion.

Even if we call *recurseTest* only once, it calls itself repeatedly so that Director keeps going "down" an extra level and never comes back up for air. Director will run out of memory before the *put "End of recurseTest reached"* command is ever reached. Note that each time *recurseTest* is called, it spawns another copy of itself. Conceptually, this can be pictured as follows:

```
recurseTest
  recurseTest
    recurseTest
      recurseTest
        ( ad infinitum until Director runs out of memory)
```

Note that it is perfectly acceptable for one handler to call another repeatedly, as is often done using a *repeat* loop (see *"Repeat Loops"* later in this chapter).

Example 1-4: Calling a Function Non-recursively

```
on testIt
  repeat with i = 1 to 100
    someHandler
  end repeat
end

on someHandler
  put "I am inside someHandler"
end
```

Typing testIt in the Message window will print out *"I am inside someHandler"* 100 times with no ill effects because each time *someHandler* completes, control is returned to the top level (in this case, the *testIt* handler).

Entering and Compiling Scripts

There is no magic to entering Lingo scripts. Scripts are typed in script cast members (or attached to non-script cast members) via the Script window. Script cast members appear in the Cast window along with your other assets (bitmaps, fields, and so on). The Script and Message windows include buttons to access pop-up menus of Lingo commands (both alphabetical and by category). You can use these to insert commands into your scripts or to remind you of the correct syntax. Refer to Chapter 2 of this book and to Chapter 2, *Script Basics*, of Macromedia's *Learning Lingo* manual for details on creating scripts and entering your Lingo.

Where Commands Go

All your Lingo code goes between a handler's *on handlerName* and *end* statements.

The exceptions to the rule are:

- Each handler should be separate from other handlers. Handler declarations are not "nested" the way that *if...then* statements can be. Do not start a new handler before *end*ing the first one, as described under "*Common Handler Declaration Errors*" later in this chapter.

- Comments can be placed both inside and outside handlers.

- Property variables must be declared outside any handler.

- Global variables can be declared both inside and outside handlers. Global variables declared within a handler apply only to that handler. Global variables declared outside a handler apply to all handlers in the script following the declaration.

Each Lingo command occupies its own line (although there are some multiline Lingo statements, discussed under "*Multiline Code Structures*" later in this chapter). Each line of Lingo is separated using a carriage return—that is, using the Return key (Macintosh) or Enter key (Windows) on the main keyboard, not the one on the keypad.

You can enter long lines of Lingo code in your script without line breaks; Director will wrap them automatically. To improve readability (as with many examples in this book), long lines of Lingo code can be continued onto the next line using the Lingo continuation character ¬, as shown in the example that follows. This special character is created using Option-Return (Macintosh) or Alt-Enter (Windows).

```
-- Here is a long line of Lingo broken onto two lines
set the member of sprite (the currentSpriteNum) = ¬
    member "Hilighted Button"
```

You can break long lines of Lingo onto more than two lines using an ¬ character at the end of each line (except the last) of the long command. Do not break the long lines (that is, do not use the ¬ character) within quoted strings (see Chapter 7, *Strings*). Do not put anything, even a space, on the same line after a continuation character.

Director ignores leading spaces and automatically indents your Lingo code according to its own rules. For example, all lines within a handler between the *on* and *end* statements are indented at least two spaces. Use the same font and type size throughout the script to make the code more legible and indentation problems obvious. Colorized or formatted text can slow the Script window's response, especially for longer scripts. A single script cast member is limited to 32,000 characters, but you can use as many script cast members as required.

Use the `Tab` key to automatically indent your Lingo code. If the indentation is wrong, you may have omitted necessary keywords or used them in the wrong order. Refer to *"Lingo's Skeletal Structure"* later in this chapter.

The Lingo code you enter is simply text (although you should enter it in a script cast member, not in a text or field cast member). Before it can be run, Director must *compile* your Lingo code into a machine-readable format. (This is analogous to a player piano, which cannot read sheet music but can play a song if is transcribed onto a paper roll.)

When Director compiles a script, it checks that the syntax conforms to the accepted rules and does its best to *parse* (understand) the structure of your Lingo. Compilation is analogous to spellchecking and grammar checking in a word processor. It merely checks that your Lingo code has a recognizable structure and acceptable keywords. It does *not* attempt to actually run your Lingo code.

It would be counter-productive for Director to attempt to compile your scripts as you type them. Use `Control▶Recompile All Scripts` to compile your scripts when you finish typing (see *"Compiling Scripts"* in Chapter 2).

If Director's compiler fails, it displays a script error (a syntax error) that identifies the offending portion of the Lingo, but it may merely reflect a problem that lies elsewhere. You would then correct the Lingo and recompile. If successful, it creates a hidden compiled version of your Lingo script that runs more quickly than it would if Director had to reinterpret your human-readable script every time it runs.

If compilation succeeds, your code is not necessarily error-free and may still cause a so-called *runtime error* when Director attempts to run it. (In this context *runtime* refers to when the script is *executed*, as opposed to when it is *compiled*. This should not be confused with *authoring time* (in Director) vs. *runtime* (in a Projector). Refer to Chapter 3 for more details.

Handler Scope

Handlers are stored in script cast members (excepting those attached directly to other member types); the multiple types of script cast members are explained in great detail in Chapter 2. The script cast member's type (*movie script, score script,* or *parent script*) affects the *scope* of all the handlers declared within it (that is, which other scripts can "see" these handlers and from where they are accessible). We were able to test the example handlers above from the Message window because they were entered in *movie* scripts. (A *movie script* is a script cast member whose type is set to *Movie* in the script cast member's info window). Handlers in movie scripts can be "seen" from the Message window or any other script in the same Director movie (even from scripts in other linked castLibs) because they have *universal* scope.

Had we entered the example handlers in *score* scripts, attempting to use them from the Message window would result in a *"Handler not defined"* error because the scope of score scripts is more limited.

If two handlers in the *same* script cast member have the same name, Director will complain. Neither should you use two handlers with the same name in two *different* movie scripts because the first handler found will intercept all function calls using that name, and the second handler will always be ignored.

Place any handlers that you use in multiple Director movies or multiple Director projects into movie scripts in an external cast library that you can link into your project. Use unique names, perhaps starting with a prefix such as *"lib,"* that are unlikely to conflict with other handlers in a given movie.

Avoid naming your handlers the same as existing Lingo commands (see Table 18-1). A custom handler (stored in a movie script) that has the same name as a built-in Lingo command will intercept (and override) any calls to that Lingo command. If accidental, such an error can be extraordinarily hard to debug.

Contrary to movie scripts, it is very common to use handlers of the same name in *score scripts*. (Again, these are explained in detail in Chapter 2.) The important point is that the handlers in score scripts have a different scope (accessibility) than handlers in movie scripts. For example, most sprite scripts (one type of score script) will contain *on mouseUp* handlers, and most frame scripts (another type of score script) will contain *on exitFrame* handlers. The same handler name can be used in multiple score scripts because they do not have universal scope as do handlers in movie scripts. Director automatically calls only those handlers that are attached to the current frame or the sprite on which the user clicked. Other *on mouseUp* and *on exitFrame* handlers located in other score scripts won't interfere. Refer to Chapter 9 for more details. Likewise, Lingo calls an *on keyDown* handler only if it is attached to the field sprite that has keyboard focus (see Chapter 10).

Example 1-5 demonstrates the different scope of a handler depending on the script type in which it exists.

If the following two handlers coexist in the same *score* script cast member, *handlerA* can call *handlerB* (or vice-versa).

Example 1-5: Handler Scope

```
on handlerA
  handlerB
end

on handlerB
  put "I am doing something, so please stop hovering."
end
```

If the two handlers existed in two separate *score* scripts, however, they would not "see" each other and therefore could not call each other. On the other hand, if *handlerA* was in a *score* script, but *handlerB* was in a *movie* script, *handlerA* could call *handlerB*, but *not* vice-versa. Furthermore, if *handlerB* is in a movie script, it can be called from other handlers in other scripts of any type. Therefore, you should place one copy of your general-purpose utility handlers in a movie script rather than replicating it in multiple score scripts.

 Handlers in movie scripts can be called from anywhere at any time and are usually custom handlers named arbitrarily by the programmer. Handlers in score scripts are generally named to respond to predefined events (such as *mouseUp*) and are called by Director in response to those events.

This example offers a simplified picture of the universe. In actuality, any handler in any script can be called from anywhere if you refer to the script explicitly. You usually refer only to the handler name and let Director decide in which script to find the handler. This is covered in Chapter 2, along with details on the way that handlers in multiple scripts are sometimes called in succession.

See "*Special Treatment of the First Argument Passed*" later in this chapter for details on how the first argument to a function affects which scripts are searched for a matching handler.

Commands and Functions

A *command* tells Director to do something, such as play a sound, but usually does not return any result. Built-in Lingo keywords are referred to as *commands*, but you can create custom handlers that are used just like the built-in commands, essentially extending Director's command set. (The word *command* is also used loosely in many contexts, including to indicate a menu choice.)

The general format of a command is:

```
commandName arg1, arg2, arg3, ...
```

where the arguments (*arg1*, *arg2*, *arg3*, ...) are inputs used by the command, and may be optional or mandatory, and vary in number and type depending on the command. For example, the **alert** command shown previously expected a single string argument. The **puppetSprite** command expects two arguments (an integer and a Boolean value), as in:

```
puppetSprite 17, TRUE
```

A command that returns a result is called a *function* (the terms, though, are often used interchangeably). The result may be a number, a string, or any other data type. The general format of a function is

```
set variableName = functionName (arg1, arg2, arg3, ...)
```

or

```
put functionName (arg1, arg2, arg3, ...) into variableName
```

where again the arguments (*arg1*, *arg2*, *arg3*, ...) may be optional or mandatory and may vary in number and type depending on the function.

For example, the *power()* function requires two arguments and raises the first argument to the power specified by the second argument. You wouldn't ordinarily compute a value and discard the result; you would either print it out in the Message window or store it in a *variable* (a container for data). Below, the result of the calculation is stored in a variable that is arbitrarily named *myValue* (see "*Variable Storage Classes and Data Types*" later in this chapter for details on variables).

```
set myValue = power (10, 2)
```

If you don't store the result in a variable, the function still returns a result that can be used in other expressions (see Chapter 5, *Data Types and Expressions*). This prints the result in the Message window instead of storing it in a variable:

```
put power (10, 2)
-- 100.0000
```

This uses the result of the calculation to decide whether to print a message:

```
if power (10, 2) > 50 then put "That's a big number."
```

In some cases, Director issues a "*Command not defined*" error if you use a function by itself rather than as part of a larger expression:

```
power (10, 2)    -- This causes an error
```

Either use *put power (10, 2)* to print the result of the function call in the Message window or assign the result to a variable, as shown earlier.

If a function does not require any arguments, you must still include the parentheses to obtain the result, such as:

```
put browserName ()
-- "Mac HD:Netscape Navigator Folder:Netscape Navigator"
```

See "*Return Values and Exiting Handlers*" later in this chapter for details on returning values from custom handlers.

Lingo allows *nested* function calls, in which the result of one function is used as an argument to another function, such as:

```
if (random(max(x, y)) > 5) then ...
```

In such a case, the result of *max(x, y)* is used as an argument to the *random()* function. The preceding code is just shorthand notation for:

```
set myValue = max(x, y)
if (random(myValue) > 5) then ...
```

Return Values and Exiting Handlers

This section is next in the logical progression of the chapter, but it will not make sense unless you understand concepts explained later. You can skim it now and revisit it after reading the rest of the chapter. As alluded to earlier, a handler often performs a calculation and returns the result to the calling routine. A handler or Lingo command that returns a value is called a *function*. Most functions require some inputs on which to operate (see "*Parameters and Arguments*" for details). For example, the built-in Lingo function *max()* returns the maximum value from the list of items you send it:

```
put max (6, 9, 12)
-- 12
```

You might write your own custom function that returns TRUE or FALSE based on whether the input is a valid digit between 0 and 9, as shown in Example 1-6.

Example 1-6: Returning a Value from a Function

```
on isDigit someChar
  if "0123456789" contains string (someChar) then
    return TRUE
  else
    return FALSE
  end if
end isDigit
```

In this case, the result (1) signifies the Boolean value TRUE:

```
put isDigit (5)
-- 1
```

 The parentheses surrounding the arguments are mandatory when calling a function that returns a value. Even if the function does not require any parameters, you must still include the parentheses to obtain a result.

If the parentheses are omitted, Lingo would treat *isDigit* as if it were a variable name (see "*Variables and Properties*" later in this chapter) rather than a function name. In the following case, *isDigit* is mistaken for a VOID (valueless) variable, and the *put* statement prints the values VOID and 5 instead of the desired result of the function call.

```
put isDigit 5
VOID 5
```

Note the use of parentheses following rollOver():

```
put rollOver()      -- rollOver() is treated as a function call
-- 7
put rollOver        -- rollOver is treated as a variable name
-- VOID
```

Leaving the Current Handler

Ordinarily a handler terminates when the last statement in it is reached (the *end* statement). Control then returns to whatever called the handler (either another handler or Director itself). In that case, no value is returned to the calling handler, and any calculated result would be lost unless it were stored in a global or property variable. The *return* and *result* commands obtain return values from a handler. The *abort* and *exit* commands terminate a handler prematurely. (They differ from *next repeat* and *exit repeat*, which affect program flow but do not exit the handler). The *quit*, *halt*, *restart*, *shutDown*, *go*, *play*, *play done*, and *pass* commands may also affect the order of Lingo execution.

return

The *return* command exits the current handler and returns control to the calling routine, along with an optional value of any data type. Any statements following the *return* are not executed, which makes *return* convenient for exiting a handler once a particular condition is met or task is completed.

Example 1-7 returns as soon as it finds a sound cast member in the primary castLib. It returns zero (0) if no sound cast member is found. The other details are not important at this point.

Example 1-7: Returning Prematurely from a Function

```
on findFirstSound
  -- Loop through the cast
  repeat with n = 1 to the number of members
    -- Look for a sound castmember
    if the type of member n = #sound then
      -- Return the number of the sound
      -- and we're out of here!
      return n
    end if
  end repeat

  -- If no sound was found, return 0
  return 0
end findFirstSound
```

Test it in the Message window:

```
put findFirstSound()
-- 72
```

The above technique is best used with small handlers. Avoid using multiple *return* statements to exit a large handler from many different points. It makes the code harder to understand and maintain. Storing the eventual return value in a variable and returning it at the end of the handler is often clearer.

You can use *return* without a value, in which case it is identical to *exit*, and the caller receives VOID as the returned value. Note that the *return* command is distinguished by context from the RETURN constant (which indicates the carriage return character).

the result

The result retrieves the result of the last function call, even if it was never stored in a variable when it was returned by the last function call.

```
set x = isDigit (5)
put x
-- 1
isDigit (5)
put the result
-- 1
```

Some commands, such as *preLoad* and *preLoadMember,* do not return a value, but set *the result.*

```
preLoadMember 1, 5
put the result
-- 5
```

abort

Abort aborts the *call stack* (that is, the current Lingo handler *and any handlers that called it*) without executing any of the remaining Lingo statements in any of those handlers. By contrast, *exit* exits only the *current* handler. *Abort* is useful when you want to stop the current action in response to some drastic change. For example, if the user presses the Escape key, you may abort what you are doing:

```
on getUserInfo
  -- Abort if the user hits ESCAPE (ASCII code 27)
  if the key = numToChar (27) then
    abort
  end if
end getUserInfo
```

Abort does not quit Director (see *halt* or *quit*), nor does it abort asynchronous operations in progress (see *cancelIdleLoad, netAbort*). *Abort* aborts only Lingo execution; it does not affect the Score's playback head (see the *pause* command).

exit

Exit (not to be confused with *exit repeat*) causes Lingo to exit the current handler. It exits "up" only one level to the calling handler, as opposed to aborting the entire call stack (see *"Nested Function Calls"* earlier in this chapter). Exit is often used to exit the current handler if some condition is not met:

```
on playVideo
  if not (the quickTimePresent) then
    alert "You can't play video without QuickTime."
    exit
  end if
  -- Remaining statements are run only
  -- if QuickTime is installed.
end playVideo
```

When using *exit*, no return value is sent. Use *return* instead to return a value to the calling handler.

---

quit, halt, restart, *and* shutDown

>   *Quit* and *halt* immediately quit a Projector and are generally used only in a
>   script attached to a Quit button or at the end of a presentation. During devel-
>   opment, *halt* stops the movie without quitting Director. See Chapter 8,
>   *Projectors and the Run-time Environment,* in *Director in a Nutshell* for details
>   on these and other commands, including *restart* and *shutDown.*

go

>   The playback head moves semi-independently remaining of Lingo commands.
>   If you use the *go* command to move the playback head, commands in the
>   handler are still executed *before* jumping to the new frame.

```
on exitFrame
  go frame 50
  put "This will be printed before jumping to frame 50"
end
```

play *and* play done

>   The *play* command works differently than the *go* command. Commands
>   following the *play* command are executed, but not until a *play done*
>   command returns control back to the original script. Commands following
>   *play done* are never reached. Test this using a frame script of the form:

```
on exitFrame
  play frame 50
  put "This will be printed second, not first"
end
```

>   In frame 50, use this frame script to complete the test:

```
on exitFrame
  put "This will be printed first"
  play done
  put "This line won't ever be reached or printed"
end
```

pass

>   The *pass* command aborts the call stack (see the *abort* command). Commands
>   following the *pass* command are never executed. Control immediately jumps
>   to the next script that handles the event being passed (see Chapter 2). For
>   example:

```
on mouseUp
  pass
  put "This line won't ever be reached or printed"
end
```

Dynamic Script Creation

This section is next in the logical progression of the chapter but is fairly
advanced—and irrelevant for most users. You can skim it or even ignore it alto-
gether without significant regret. You can create new Lingo dynamically at runtime
(that is, while Director or even a Projector is running). Using the *do* command or
by setting *the scriptText of member* property, you can actually create new Lingo
from within Lingo! You can dynamically evaluate a string as if it is a Lingo statement using the *value()* function. Most programming languages don't allow this,

and you will rarely use this feature. The following examples are for illustration only and do not necessarily depict likely uses.

Do Statements

The *do* command can compile and execute a string on the fly as if it were a Lingo statement. Although it should not be used haphazardly, it can perform some interesting tricks. Most notably, you can use it to execute an arbitrary command stored in a text file or a field cast member. You can create a pseudo-Message window for debugging Projectors by *do*'ing the text entered in a field cast member:

```
do "beep"
do the text of field "someFieldCastMember"
```

You cannot use *do* to declare global variables without a trick. The following will not work:

```
do "global gSomeGlobal"
do "set gSomeGlobal = 5"
```

To declare a global with a *do* statement, use:

```
do "global gSomeGlobal" & RETURN & "set gSomeGlobal = 5"
```

To make use of a global within a *do* statement, declare the global inside the current handler. So-called "global globals" declared outside the currrent handler are not recognized during a *do* statement. The following example is illustrative only and would never be required in reality:

```
on setGlobal
  global gSomeGlobal
  do "set gSomeGlobal = 7"
end
```

Value Statements

The *value()* function can be used to convert a string into an integer or a float, as is useful when converting string data from a file or user input into a number.

```
set userEntry = value (field "Age in Years")
```

Value() can also evaluate a string or symbol as if it is a variable name:

```
set someVar = "Oh happy days!"
put value ("someVar")
-- "Oh happy days!"
put value (string(#someVar))
-- "Oh happy days!"
```

Setting the ScriptText at Runtime

The *scriptText of member* property contains the Lingo code from a script cast member. The human-readable form of *the scriptText* is stripped when creating Projectors and protecting DIR files (creating DXR files), leaving only the hidden internal compiled version. Even from a Projector, you can create a script dynamically, as shown in Example 1-8.

Example 1-8: Creating Scripts at Runtime

```
-- Set up a string variable containing the text:
on createscript
  set dynaScript = "on newHandler" & RETURN ¬
                   "global gMyGlobal" & RETURN ¬
                   "set gMyGlobal to 52" & RETURN & "end"
-- Create a new movie script cast member, and fill it in.
  set newMovieScriptCastMember = new(#script)
  set the scriptType of newMovieScriptCastMember = #movie
  set the scriptText of newMovieScriptCastMember = dynaScript
end
-- Now you can run it
createscript
newHandler
-- If desired, you can then delete the cast member
erase newMovieScriptCastMember
```

Variables and Properties

You'll often read Lingo properties to obtain information about the user or the run-time environment and set properties to affect the run-time environment. You'll use variables as containers to store and manipulate any type of data, including Lingo properties. Later we'll see how you can define your own properties using so-called *property variables*, which are a particular type of variable but are unrelated to Director's built-in properties.

Built-In Lingo Properties and Constants

Lingo defines dozens of *properties* (not to be confused with programmer-defined property variables, discussed later), which are always preceded by the keyword *the*.

 If you omit the word *the*, Lingo thinks you are referring to a programmer-defined variable, not a Lingo property.

A property may pertain to the overall system, the current movie or MIAW, a cast member, or a sprite. Lingo properties are universally accessible (they can be used from any script at any time), and they may be *static* (fixed) or may change over time or based on user actions. For example, *the platform* property doesn't change unless you switch computers, but *the mouseH* and *the mouseV* properties change whenever the cursor moves.

The general format for setting a Lingo property is:

```
set the property {of object} = value
```

or

```
put value into the property {of object}
```

where *value* is replaced with a meaningful value, *property* is a property name and *object* is usually a sprite, member, or window reference. The following examples set *the locH of sprite* sprite property, *the regPoint of member* member property, and *the soundEnabled* system property. Note that all three properties start with *the*, although no *object* is specified for *the soundEnabled* property because it is a system property, not a property of a sprite or a cast member.

```
set the locH of sprite 1 = 17
set the regPoint of member 1 = point(0,0)
set the soundEnabled = TRUE
```

The general format for reading a Lingo property is:

```
set variableName = the property {of object}
```

such as:

```
set spritePosition = the locH of sprite 1
set memberDepth = the depth of member 1
set mousePosition = the mouseH
```

Some Lingo keywords are *constants* (fixed values) that don't use the word *the*, such as PI, TAB, and SPACE. See Table 5-6.

Common Errors When Using Properties and Constants

The following are common errors when using properties. Refer also to "*Common Errors When Using Variables*" later in this chapter.

Forgetting the word the:
    The following sets stage white by setting *the stageColor* property to zero:

```
set the stageColor = 0
```
However the following defines a local variable, *stageColor*, and assigns it the value zero, which is probably not the desired goal.

```
set stageColor = 0
```
Using a property without the preceding *the* will cause a "*Variable used before assigned a value*" error, such as:

```
if mouseV > 50 then put "The mouseV is greater than 50"
```
(This won't fail in the Message window, but it will fail from within a script).

Confusing a local variable with a property of the same name:
    Here, *mouseH* is a local variable, whereas *the mouseH* is a Lingo property. As the mouse continues to move, the property *the mouseH* will change, but the variable *mouseH* won't change without your explicit instruction.

```
set mouseH = the mouseH
```
Use variable names that are different from Lingo property names to avoid confusion, such as:

```
set lastMouseH = the mouseH
```

Confusing a variable with a Lingo constant of the same name:

Some keywords are reserved *constants* (see Table 5-6) that never change in value, even if you inadvertently try to assign a new value to them. For example, you cannot change the value of *pi*.

```
set pi = 54.36
put pi
-- 3.1416
```

Some properties can not be set:

Many properties can be both set and read, but some can be only read. The *"Cannot set this property"* error may result if you attempt to set a property that is read-only, such as *the mouseH*. Other properties may appear to be settable, but setting them may have no effect. For example, setting *the colorDepth* under Windows, or to an invalid value on the Macintosh, will leave the monitor depth unchanged, although no error results.

Using a "stale" value of a property that has changed:

Many Lingo properties change based on conditions beyond the programmer's control. For example, *the shiftDown* property changes whenever the user presses or releases the Shift key, and it may even change during the execution of, say, your *on keyDown* handler. If necessary, store the current value of a property in a variable (see details that follow), such as:

```
set shiftKeyState = the shiftDown
```

Version

There is a single Lingo global variable (global variables are explained later) named *version* that returns Director's version number (as a string) and can not be set nor cleared with *clearGlobals*. Do not use the name "version" as a variable name.

Use *version* as follows:

```
on testVersion
  global version
   put "The current version is" && version
end testVersion

testVersion
-- "The current version is 6.5"
```

Director also supports the property *the productVersion*, which doesn't require a *global* declaration (although the two methods return different values in Shockwave).

```
put the productVersion
-- "6.5"
```

Using Variables

A *variable* is a *container* for any type of data (such as an integer or a string) that usually stores values that may change or are not known until runtime. You are the master of your own variables. You can create as many as you need and give them whatever names you like. For example, you might store the user's name and his high score in separate variables named *userName* and *highScore*.

 Variables are *not* the algebraic "unknowns" that gave you nightmares in school. They are just convenient placeholders that allow your scripts to be flexible. Variables, unlike built-in Lingo properties, change only at your behest.

Once you've stored a value in a variable (see the next section) you can obtain that value simply by referring to the variable by name. See "*Data Types and Variable Types*," "*Type Assignment and Conversion*," and "*Constants and Symbols*" in Chapter 5 for more details on variables.

Assigning a Value to a Variable, Property, or Field

You store data in a variable, property, or field by *assigning* a value to it in one of the following ways:

```
set item = value
set item to value
put value into item
```

where *item* is a variable name, property (such as *the colorDepth*), or a field reference (such as *field "myField"*).

I *strongly* recommend the first form (*set item = value*) because it clearly delineates the variable or property on the left side of the expression from the value being assigned to it on the right side of the expression. For example:

```
set x = 5
set x = char 1 to 5 of "hello there"
set the soundEnabled = TRUE
set the loc of sprite 5 = point (50, 200)
```

I mention the other forms so that you will understand examples that make use of them, although I find these equivalent expressions harder to decipher:

```
put 5 into x
set x to char 1 to 5 of "hello there"
put TRUE into the soundEnabled
set the loc of sprite 5 to point (50, 200)
```

You *must* use the *put...into* form when replacing part of a string:

```
set x = "helloWorld"
put "H" into char 1 of x
```

These *won't* work:

```
set char 1 of x = "H"
set field 4 = "Some String"
```

But these *will* work:

```
set the text of field 4 = "Some String"
```

```
put "Some String" into field 4
```

Common Misconceptions About Variables

Some Lingo keywords used to assign variables are also used in other ways. Don't confuse *put...into* (which sets a value) with *put* by itself (which prints the value in the Message window).

```
put 5 into x  -- assigns the value 5 to the variable x
put x         -- prints the value of x in the message window
-- 5
```

The keyword *to* is also used in chunk expressions, such as *char 1 to 5 of someString*. In the example below, the first *to* is used to perform the assignment, but the second *to* is used to indicate a range of characters.

```
set x to char 1 to 5 of "hello there"
```

The equals sign (=) is used for both *assignment* and *comparison*. Don't confuse the two uses. In C, the single equals sign is used only for assignment, and the *double* equals sign (==) is used for comparison (see the online Chapter 20, *Lingo for C Programmers*, downloadable from *http://www.zeusprod.com/nutshell/chapters/lingoforc.html*).

```
set x = 5  -- assigns the value 5 to the variable X
if (x = 5) then put "Yeah"  -- Compares x to the value 5
```

The equals sign assigns a value to an item; it does *not* indicate an algebraic equality. In algebra, the following would be meaningless because something can never equal one more than itself:

```
x = x + 1
```

On the other hand, the following is perfectly legitimate and is used frequently in programming.

```
set x = x + 1
```

How is this possible? The right side of the expression always uses the current (old) value for an item. The left side sets the *new* value for an item. The above example means "Take the current value of the variable *x* and add one, and then store the result back into *x* again." So:

```
set x = 4
set x = x + 1
put x
-- 5
```

An assignment statement is not an algebraic equation to be solved. Only one item can appear on the left side of the following assignment statement:

```
set x = 5 - y
```

This is not valid:

```
set x + y = 5
```

Although the two statements above may appear algebraically equivalent, they are not programmatically equivalent. The first one says "Subtract the value of *y* from 5, and then store the result into the variable *x*." The second one, however, is trying to say "Set *x* and *y* so that they add up to 5." This confuses a computer because it wouldn't know whether to set *x* to 4 and *y* to 1, or *x* to 3 and *y* to 2, or one of the infinite number of alternatives.

Variable Types

A variable's *storage class* (local, parameter, global, or property) determines its initial value, its *scope* (by whom it can be accessed), and whether it *persists* (retains its value) over time. Don't confuse a variable's storage class, often called its *type*, with the data type of its *contents*. A variable's *data type* (integer, string, list, etc.) depends solely on the value assigned to it and is independent of its storage class. See Chapter 5.

There are four main storage classes (although *parameters* are generally treated as *local* variables), each of which is created in a different way.

Local Variables

Local variables (or *temporary variables*) are fleeting; they come into existence when they are first assigned a value, and they disappear at the end of the current handler. Use local variables for temporary needs that are confined to the current handler. To create a local variable, pick an arbitrary name, and assign a value to it. Variables such as *i*, *j*, and *k* are commonly used for loops or indices. Variables such as *x* and *y* are commonly used for coordinates.

In this example, *i* and *y* are local variables (everything else is a reserved Lingo keyword).

Example 1-9: Using Local Variables

```
on mouseUp
  set y = the locV of sprite the currentSpriteNum
  repeat with i = 1 to 100
    set the locV of sprite the currentSpriteNum = y + i
    updateStage
  end repeat
  put i
  put y
  showLocals
end
```

Local variables are "private" to the handler in which they are used. The *showLocals* command must be used from *within* the handler for which you wish to display local variables. Likewise, you cannot use *put* from the message window to display a local variable.

Local variables are independent of other variables in other handlers that may have the same name. Because they cannot be used until they are assigned a value, local variables have no default value. Using one before assigning it a value results in a "*Variable used before assigned a value*" error. In this example, *x* is an uninitialized local variable and will cause an error.

```
on mouseUp
  if x = 5 then
    go frame 15
  end if
end
```

See "*Special Treatment of the First Argument Passed*" later in this chapter for an explanation of why using an undeclared local variable as the first argument to a function does *not* generate an error.

Parameters

Parameters are local variables that automatically receive the value(s) of incoming arguments used in the call to the handler (see "*Parameters and Arguments*" and "*Generalizing Functions*" later in this chapter). Parameters are *declared* (named) on the same line as the handler name.

Example 1-10: Using Parameters

```
on someFunction param1, param2, param3
  -- The && operator assembles the string for output
  put "The three input parameters are" && [LC]
       param1 && param2 && param3
end

someFunction 1, "b",  7.5
-- "The three input parameters are 1 b 7.5
```

Parameters can assume different values each time a handler is called. A different copy of the parameters is created each time the handler is called and disappears when the handler ends. Changes to parameters within a handler generally have no effect outside that handler, but modifying a Lingo list passed as a parameter will modify the original list in the calling routine as well. See Chapter 6, *Lists* for important additional details. Don't use the name of a global variable as the name for a parameter or other local variables. See "*Common Errors When Using Variables*" later in this chapter

Global Variables

Global variables (or simply *globals*) are declared using the *global* keyword, and they persist throughout all movies until your Projector quits. They come into existence when a handler that declares them as *global* first runs and can be accessed by any handler that also declares them as *global*. Global variables can be displayed in the Message window using *showGlobals* (the built-in global variable *version* always appears in the list of globals).

```
showGlobals
-- Global Variables --
version = "6.0.2"
```

Whenever you test or set a variable in the Message window it is treated as a global variable.

```
set anyVariable = 5
```

```
showGlobals
-- Global Variables --
version = "6.5"
anyVariable = 5
```

Use *clearGlobals* to reset all global variables to VOID, except for the *version* global, which cannot be cleared. *ClearGlobals* also clears *the actorList* of the current movie in D6.

```
clearGlobals
showGlobals
-- Global Variables --
version = "6.5"
```

Globals can be shared by MIAWs and the main movie. Any change to the value of a global variable is reflected *everywhere* it is used. For clarity, name your globals starting with a "g." Global variables default to VOID (they have no value until one is assigned), but they retain their value even when playback stops or a new movie is loaded (unless *clearGlobals* is called). Shockwave clears global variables if the browser issues a *Stop()* command.

Globals are necessary when you want a variable to outlive the handler in which it is used or to send information between two handlers that are not otherwise connected.

In this example, *gOne* and *gTwo* are global variables shared by two handlers.

Example 1-11: Using Global Variables

```
on startMovie
  global gOne, gTwo
  set gOne = "Hello"
  set gTwo = 7
end
```

This handler can be in a different script than *startMovie*:

```
on mouseUp
  global gOne, gTwo
  if gTwo = 7 then put gOne
end
```

Lingo globals are declared, by convention, at the top of a handler immediately under the handler name; declaring globals in the middle of a handler is allowed but discouraged. You can declare more than one global with the *global* keyword by separating the variables with commas, as shown above. You can instead use a new line for each global declaration, such as:

```
global gOne
global gTwo
```

Globals declared *outside* of a handler (so-called "*global*" globals) are treated as if they were declared within all subsequent handlers within the same script.

For example, if the two handlers above are in the *same* script, the *global* declarations could be moved *outside* the handlers themselves and placed at the top of the script:

```
-- These are "global" globals and can be used
-- by all handlers in this script cast member
global gOne, gTwo

on startMovie
   set gOne = "Hello"
   set gTwo = 7
end

on mouseUp
   if gTwo = 7 the put gOne
end
```

Property Variables

Property variables are declared using the *property* keyword and persist as long as the object of which they are a property exists. (See Chapter 12, *Behaviors and Parent Scripts*, if you are not familiar with object-oriented programming, or just ignore this section for now.)

 Property variables are programmer-defined and should not be confused with the built-in Lingo properties, although both are attributes of their respective objects.

Built-in Lingo properties are predefined attributes of built-in objects, such as sprites and cast members. Property variables are programmer-defined variables that are used to add attributes to their own objects (namely scripts).

Property variables are *instantiated* (created) when the parent script or Behavior that declares them is itself *instantiated* (either by Director or by the programmer). For example, when Director encounters a Behavior attached to a sprite in the Score it instantiates that Behavior and its properties. (This is explained in detail in Chapter 12. For now, just assume that when a Behavior is encountered in the Score, Director assigns appropriate values to any property variables that the Behavior declares.)

Properties can then be accessed by any handler within the same script. Each *instance* (use or occurrence) of the parent script or Behavior gets its own copy of the property variables that are *independent* of other copies (despite having the same name), just as all sprites and cast members have independent properties named *width* and *height*.

Property variables are declared at the top of the parent script or Behavior before the first handler. You can declare multiple property variables, separated by commas, using one *property* statement, or you can use separate *property* statements for each property variable. Property variables default to VOID but are usually assigned a value in a parent script's *new()* handler (or in a Behavior's *getPropertyDescriptionList()* handler; see Chapter 12). When a handler inside a parent script or Behavior is called, its private copies of those property values are used, unlike global variables that are shared among all scripts. For clarity, name your properties starting with a "p."

 Property variables *must* be declared *outside of* any handlers in the script, as shown in the example below.

In this example, *pOne* and *pTwo* are property variables shared by the *new()* and *showProps* handlers, which are both presumed to reside in the same parent script cast member named "ParentScript."

Example 1-12: Using Property Variables

```
property pOne, pTwo

on new me, a, b
  set pOne = a
  set pTwo = b
  return me
end new

on showProps me
  put "pOne is" && pOne
  put "pTwo is" && pTwo
end showProps
```

To test it in the Message window, first instantiate the parent script by calling the *new()* handler. When the programmer instantiates a script, he customarily specifies initial values for the properties by specifying them as arguments to the *new()* handler (although some programmers prefer to assign properties as a separate step from instantiating a script). We create one instance using the integer 6 and the string "hello," for the properties *pOne* and *pTwo*. We then create a second instance with different values to be used as *pOne* and *pTwo*.

```
set instance1 = new (script "ParentScript", 6, "hello")
set instance2 = new (script "ParentScript", 9, "goodbye")
```

We pass an *instance* created using *new()* to *showProps* (either *instance1* or *instance2*). That allows *showProps* to determine the correct properties for each

---

instance separately. Note how the results printed by *showProps* depend on which instance variable we pass to it.

```
showProps (instance1)
-- "pOne is 6"
-- "pTwo is hello"
showProps (instance2)
-- "pOne is 9"
-- "pTwo is goodbye"
```

Note that inside the script that declares them, property variables are accessed by using their name, as shown in *showProps* above. Programmer-defined property variables can also be accessed from *outside* a script instance using the script instance and the keyword *the,* such as:

```
put the propertyVariable of scriptInstance
```

Property variables belonging to scripts can also be accessed by referencing the script itself rather than an instance of the script, such as:

```
put the propertyVariable of (script "myScript")
```

Although they can also be accessed using the keyword *the,* remember that property variables are programmer-defined and are not the built-in Lingo properties that also happen to start with the keyword *the.*

Continuing the example above, you can access the properties of *instance1* and *instance2* without using *showProps,* instead using:

```
put the pOne of instance1
-- 6
put the pTwo of instance2
-- "goodbye"
```

Note that simply typing *put pOne* or *put the pOne* in the Message window would fail because you must specify the script instance that owns the property. If no script instance is specified, the property name must be a built-in system property, such as:

```
put the colorDepth
-- 8
```

Refer to Chapter 12, especially if this section left you thoroughly confused.

Common Errors When Using Variables

The following are the most common errors of both new and experienced programmers when using variables.

Using a variable before assigning a value to it:
   Attempting to use a variable that has never been declared or assigned a value causes a *"Variable used before assigned a value"* error, such as:

```
set the locV of sprite 1 = y
```

(This won't fail in the Message window because *y* will be treated as global containing the value VOID, but it will fail from within a script.)

New local variables must first be assigned a value:

```
set y = 5
set the locV of sprite 1 = y
```

Global variables can be declared with the *global* keyword, without necessarily being assigned a value (we presume the global was assigned a meaningful value elsewhere; if not, it defaults to VOID):

```
global gLocForSprite
set the locV of sprite 1 = gLocForSprite
```

In the following statement, Director complains about the undeclared local variable *y*, which we are attempting to use in the expression although it has not been previously assigned a value. Director does *not* complain about the new local variable *x*, to which we are attempting to assign a value. In other words, the right side of the equation can use only existing variables, but the left side of the equation can be either an existing or a new variable.

Not knowing which storage class to use for a variable:

Use property variables for attributes that have a different value for each instance of a parent script or Behavior or that must persist for the life of the object. Use global variables when a value must outlive the handler, object, or movie in which it is used or must be accessible to multiple handlers, objects, or movies. Use local variables for values that are used only for convenience within the current handler and then discarded, such as indices in a repeat loop or interim steps in a mathematical calculation. Use parameters to accept inputs that can make a handler more flexible (see *"Parameters and Arguments"* later in this chapter).

```
set x = y
```

Not knowing when to use a variable:

Most novices use either too many or too few variables. Use variables whenever you want Director to remember something, such as the results of calculations, user input, lists of items, or anything that you need more than once. Programming is like cooking. You may be able to cook dinner in one pot, or you may need two frying pans and a pressure cooker; it depends on the recipe and your personal style. This example:

```
on mouseDown
  if the locH of sprite (the currentSpriteNum) > 50 then
    put the locH of sprite (the currentSpriteNum)
  end if
end
```

could be rewritten as:

```
on mouseDown
  set myLocH = the locH of sprite (the currentSpriteNum)
  if myLocH > 50 then
    put myLocH
  end if
end
```

Both examples are equivalent, but the second one is somewhat easier to read and maintain because the result of the lengthy expression is stored in *myLocH*, which is then used for comparing and displaying the value.

Using a "stale" value stored in a variable, instead of the current value:

When you assign a variable, it records a snapshot in time. You must recalculate values that are expected to change. The following is wrong because *y* never changes after its initial value is assigned:

```
set y = the mouseV
repeat while y > 50
  put "The mouseV is greater than 50"
end repeat
```

Instead, check the current value of *the mouseV* property repeatedly:

```
repeat while the mouseV > 50
    put "The mouseV is greater than 50"
end repeat
```

Forgetting the keyword the when using a Lingo property name:

Why would *mouseV* cause a *"Variable used before assigned a value"* error?

```
repeat while mouseV > 50
    put "The mouseV is greater than 50"
end repeat
```

Compare the above *repeat...while* statement to the previous example.

Using clearGlobals carelessly:

ClearGlobals indiscriminately resets all global variables to VOID. (In D6, it also sets *the actorList* to [].) This will make any Lingo code that relies on global variables or *the actorList* lose whatever it had stored in them. This is usually a very bad thing, and it can be hard to track down if you are working with multiple programmers or large projects. Set individual globals to VOID to clear them separately instead.

Using the same variable name as both a global and local variable:

The most common error is to declare a variable *global* in one handler and forget to declare it *global* elsewhere.

In that case, it is implicitly a separate local variable in the second handler, despite having the same name as a global in the first handler, such as shown in Example 1-13.

Example 1-13: Common Errors with Global Variables

```
on initGlobal
  global gMyValue
  set gMyValue = 27
end initGlobal

on readGlobal
  -- This causes a syntax error
  put gMyValue
end
```

The second routine must also declare *gMyValue* as a global:

```
on readGlobal
  global gMyValue
  put gMyValue
end
```
Test it from the Message window:
```
initGlobal
readGlobal
   -- 27
```
Here the error is reversed. The programmer forgot to declare *gMyValue* as a global in the first handler.

```
on initGlobal
   -- gMyValue is treated as a local variable.
   -- Setting it has no effect outside the handler.
   set gMyValue = 27
end initGlobal

on readGlobal
   global gMyValue
   -- The global, also named gMyValue, defaults to VOID
   put gMyValue
end
```
Test it from the Message window:
```
initGlobal
readGlobal
-- Void
```

Using a global incorrectly as a parameter:

It is acceptable, even common, to pass a global as an argument to a function (see "*Parameters and Arguments*" later in this chapter). In the receiving function, however, you must decide whether you intend to modify the global or merely use the global's value for a local operation.

In Example 1-14, *gUserTries* is a *local* variable within *gameOver()*. The global of the same name in *finishGame* will *not* be incremented.

Example 1-14: Passing Globals Variables as Parameters

```
on finishGame
  global gUserTries
  gameOver (gUserTries)
end finishGame

on gameOver gUserTries
  set gUserTries = gUserTries + 1
end gameOver
```

This can be rewritten in one of two ways. Here, *gUserTries* is declared *global* within *gameOver()*:

```
on gameOver
  global gUserTries
  set gUserTries = gUserTries + 1
end gameOver
```

Alternatively, a local variable can be used and passed back to *finishGame*.

```
on finishGame
  global gUserTries
  set gUserTries = gameOver (gUserTries)
end finishGame

on gameOver inValue
  return (inValue + 1)
end gameOver
```

La Persistencia de la Memoria

Recall that each time a handler is called, any local variables are discarded when the handler finishes. If you want a variable's value to persist over repeated calls to a handler, you must declare it as a global or property variable. (See Chapter 12 for details on property variables that persist for the life of the object that declares them.)

Example 1-15 counts the number of times that *countMe* is called. Don't forget to reset the global as needed, as shown in *testCount*.

Example 1-15: Persistent Variables

```
on countMe
  global gCounter
  set gCounter = gCounter + 1
  put "This handler has been called" && gCounter && "time(s)"
end countMe

on testCount
  global gCounter
  set gCounter = 0
  repeat with i = 1 to 10
    countMe
  end repeat
end

testCount
-- This handler has been called 1 time(s)
-- This handler has been called 2 time(s)
-- etc.
```

Property variables in *score* scripts (that is, Behaviors) also persist over time (but you can not use them with *castmember* scripts):

```
property gCounter
on mouseUp me
  if gCounter > 10 then
    alert "Are you tired of clicking yet"
  else
    set gCounter = gCounter + 1
  end if
end mouseUp
```

One-Time Initialization

You may wish to perform some initialization once and only once. You can use a global variable, as shown in Example 1-16, to track whether the initialization has taken place.

Example 1-16: One-Time Initialization

```
on startMovie
  global gBeenDone, gUserScore
  -- If the global is VOID, we haven't initialized yet
  if voidP(gBeenDone)
    -- Do initialization here
set gUserScore=0
    -- Set the global flag to indicate its been done
    set gBeenDone = TRUE
  end if
end startMovie
```

Variable-Related Lingo

Table 1-1 shows the Lingo commands related to variables, including declaration, assignment, instantiation, and deallocation of various variable types.

Table 1-1: Variable-Related Commands

Keyword	Usage
ancestor	Reserved name for declaring an ancestor property. See Chapter 12.
birth()	Obsolete, previously used to instantiate an object. See *new*.
clearGlobals	Resets all global variables, except *version*, to VOID. Also clears *the actorList* in D6. Don't use this when working with other programmers who rely on global variables or *the actorList*.
global *gName1* {, *gName2*}	Declares one or more global variables.
global version	Declares the reserved global *version*.
list(), [], or [:]	Allocates a list. See Chapter 6.
mNew	Used to instantiate an XObject. See Chapter 13, *Lingo Xtras and XObjects*.
mDispose	Used to deallocate an XObject instance. Chapter 13.
new (*script*, *args*) new (xtra "*XtraName*")	Creates a child object or Xtra instance.
param(*n*)	Indicates the value of the nth parameter received by a handler. See *the paramCount*.
the paramCount	Indicates the number of parameters received by a handler. Use it to check how many arguments were specified in the function call.

Table 1-1: Variable-Related Commands (continued)

Keyword	Usage
property *pName1*{, *pName2*}	Declares one or more property variables.
property ancestor	Declares an ancestor property. See Chapter 12.
put *variable*	Prints a variable's value in the Message window.[1]
put *value* into *variable*	Assigns a value to a variable. I prefer using the *set* command.
set *variable* = *value* set *variable* to *value*	Assigns a value to a variable. See also *put ... into*
showLocals	Prints all local variables in the current handler. Must be used from within a handler, not from the Message window.
showGlobals	Prints all global variables in the Message window.
Stop()	Stops a Shockwave movie from within the browser and clears global variables.
the *property* {of *object*}	Refers to a built-in Lingo property.
the *property* of *instance*	Refers to a programmer-defined property variable of a parent script or Behavior.
the *property* of *list*	Refers to properties within a property list. See Chapter 6.
version	A global variable containing Director's current version. Use *the productVersion* property to determine the version without declaring a global.

[1] Use *put* from within a handler to display the value of any variable (including local variables) within that handler in the Message window. Global variables can be tested using the *put* command in the Message window iitself. Use the *alert* command to display the value of variables in a dialog box, especially from within a Projector where the *put* command has no effect.

Allocation and Scope of Variables

Local variables in Director are allocated *implicitly* (that is, without your explicit instruction) when you assign a value to them. Global and property variables are allocated explicitly using the *global* and *property* keywords. The amount of memory variables require depends on what is stored in them. Local variables are deallocated automatically when a handler terminates. Properties are deallocated when the object of which they are a property is disposed.

The main concern is objects that you never dispose and global variables (which persist indefinitely) that refer to items that require a lot of memory, such as long lists or strings. Global variables are never truly disposed, but you can reduce the memory they use by assigning them to zero or VOID. (Avoid using *clearGlobals* for this purpose, as it resets all global variables indiscriminately and in D6 it also clears *the actorList*.) Objects are disposed by setting all variables that refer to the object to zero or VOID. See Chapters 12 and 13. Table 1-2 shows the scope of individual variables of the different data storage classes.

Table 1-2: Data Storage Class Scope

Manner in Which Variable Is Declared	Variable's Scope
No explicit declaration; variable is implicitly local	Can be used in current handler, but only after it is assigned a value, using *set...=* or *put...into.*
Declared as arguments in the handler definition	Implicitly local, but automatically initialized to value of incoming arguments. Same scope as a local variable. See *"Parameters and Arguments."*
Assigned a value in Message window	Variables assigned in the Message window are implicitly *global.* They must still be declared global within scripts that wish to make use of them.
Explicitly declared as a global inside a handler	Variable is *global* only within handler in which it is declared.
Explicitly declared as a global outside of any handler, at the top of a script	Variable is *global* only within handlers in the same script cast member *after* the point at which it is declared.
Explicitly declared as a property within a handler	Not supported.
Explicitly declared as a property outside of a handler, at the top of a parent script or Behavior	Property variable is accessible within any handler in the parent script or Behavior. Its scope is limited to the current instance of the script. Outside the script, it can be accessed with *the property of scriptInstance.*
Explicitly declared as a property within an ancestor script	Property variable is accessible within the ancestor script or to any object using that script as an ancestor
Do statement	Scope is only the current *do* statement. See *"Do Statements,"* under *"Dynamic Script Creation."*

Lingo's Skeletal Structure

This section covers the bones on which you'll hang the flesh of your Lingo program. A handful of Lingo commands and functions control program structure and execution. Each line of Lingo is executed in order, unless the Lingo itself changes the flow. Lingo detours to execute any handler names it encounters, as shown in detail under *"Nested Handlers"* in the earlier section, *"Handlers and Scripts."* A detour taken to execute another handler is known as a *subroutine call* in most languages. Refer to Chapter 1, *How Director Works* in *Director in a Nutshell* regarding the difference between Lingo's program flow and the movement of the Score's playback head.

Comments

Although Lingo tells Director what to do, the Lingo code is ultimately written and maintained by humans (or programmers, anyway). Lines starting with two hyphens (--) are comments that Director ignores; they do not increase the execution time. Adding comments to someone else's code is a great way to make sure you understand what it does.

I place comments *before* the code they describe, although some people place them afterward, which seems patently absurd to me. Comments should give a preview, not a postmortem.

Always describe the big picture:
>Include comments at the top of your handler to describe its purpose. Describe *what* the handler does and *why*. Describe the data stored in major variables, such as lists, and which global variables the code uses.

Use comments liberally, even when you are the only programmer:
>Your own comments will help you immensely if you have to fix a bug six months later, or they'll help the next poor slob who has to maintain your code when you take a better job.

Write comments that complement, not simply reiterate, the programming code:
>Your comments should explain what the code is doing at the conceptual level, not the syntactical level. A comment such as *"Set x to zero"* is useless. Use informative comments like *"Reset the user's game score."* Assume that the person reading your comments understands Lingo's basic operation. Don't document how Lingo itself works; document what *your* code accomplishes.

"Comment out" temporary changes or tests:

gComments can exist on separate lines or at the end of a line following other Lingo commands. Anything following a comment character will be ignored until the next carriage return. Lingo does not have a way to create multiline comments, as in C, but you can use the continuation character or use more double-hyphens on subsequent lines.

Example 1-17: Comments

```
-- This is a Lingo comment on its own line

set x = 1 -- This is a Lingo comment at the end of a line

-- Here's a " commented out" command that is ignored
-- set x = 1

-- To create a multiline comment in Lingo,
-- begin each line with its own comment delimiter

-- This is a multiline comment by virtue of the ¬,
continuation character at the end of the previous line

-- Beware! The last line is part of the comment
-- by virtue of the continuation character ¬
set x = 1
```

This example demonstrates appropriate comments.

```
on resetHighScores
  -- This handler clears the high score chart
  global gHighScoreList

  -- Reset the list holding the top scores
  -- and the winners' names
  deleteAll gHighScoreList

  -- Clear the on-screen high score winners chart
  set the text of field "HighScore" = EMPTY

  -- Reset the sprites displaying the highest score
  repeat with i = 12 to 20
    set the member of sprite i = member "BigZero"
  end repeat
end
```

To comment or uncomment your code:

Manually add or delete two hyphens (--) at the beginning of one or more lines of code.

Use the *Comment* and *Uncomment* buttons in the Script window's button bar (see Figure 3-3) to comment or uncomment the currently highlighted line(s).

Use Cmd-Shift-> and Cmd-Shift-< (Mac) or Ctrl-Shift-> and Ctrl-Shift-< (Windows) to comment or uncomment the currently highlighted line(s). (These are available under Director 4's Text menu.) Use the Comment and Uncomment options under the context-sensitive pop-up menu in the Script Window, Ctrl-click (Mac) or right click (Windows).

 A good rule of thumb is one comment for every three lines of Lingo code. Use self-explanatory variable, symbol, and handler names to improve your code's readability.

You can use the Lingo command *nothing* as a placeholder when you don't want to execute any commands. Unfortunately, unlike comments *nothing* takes time for Lingo to "execute."

Multi-line Code Structures

Lingo commands generally occupy a single line (that is, they end when a carriage return is encountered), but Table 1-3 shows Lingo statements that occupy more than one line. Each multi-line command begins with its own special keyword and is terminated by some variation of the *end* keyword. Director automatically indents the statements within the body of a multi-line command two additional spaces. If the indentation is wrong, something is wrong with your Lingo. The Lingo continuation character ¬ should only be used to break long lines, not to "join" the multiple lines that are part of a multi-line structure itself.

The multi-line code fragments shown as examples must be incorporated into a handler for testing; they will not work from the Message window.

Table 1-3: Multi-line Code Structures

Structure	Usage
¬ Created with `Option-Return` (Mac) or `Alt-Enter` (Windows)	Continues Lingo onto next line.

`on handlerName`
`{parameter1,parameter2,…}`
`statements`
`end {handlerName}`[1]
	Handler declaration.

`if expression then`
`    statements`
`else if expression then`
`    statements`
`else`
`    statements`
`end if`
	Executes Lingo conditionally depending if expression is TRUE or FALSE. See "*If...Then Statements*" later in this chapter and see Chapter 5, *Data Types and Expressions*.

`case (expression) of`
`value1:`
`    statements`
`value2, value3:`
`    statements`
`otherwise:`
`    statements`
`end case`
	Executes Lingo when an expression matches one of the specified values (see "*Case Statement*" later in this chapter)

`beginRecording`
`    statements`
`endRecording`[2]
	Score recording.[3]

`tell`
`    statements`
`end tell`
	Window messaging.[4]

`repeat while expression`
`statements`
`end repeat`
	Repeats until expression becomes `FALSE`.

`repeat with item in list`
`statements`
`end repeat`
	Cycles once through all the items in a list.

Table 1-3: Multi-line Code Structures (continued)

Structure	Usage
repeat with *index* = *start* to *end* statements end repeat	Repeats for a range of values increasing by 1.
repeat with *index* = *last* down to *first* statements end repeat	Repeats for a range of values decreasing by 1.

[1] The *handlerName* following the *end* keyword is optional. Include it especially when concluding long handlers whose entirety is not visible in the Script window.
[2] Note that *endRecording* is one word whereas the other *end* commands are two words.
[3] See Chapter 3, *The Score and Animation*, in *Director in a Nutshell*.
[4] See Chapter 6, *The Stage and Movies-in-a-Window*, in *Director in a Nutshell*.

Common Handler Declaration Errors

All handlers start with the keyword *on*, followed by the handler name, and end with the keyword *end*. A script can contain multiple handlers, one after the other. Always end one handler before beginning the next one. Let Director's auto-indentation be your guide.

Example 1-18: Handler Declarations

This is wrong:
```
on mouseUp
    statements

on mouseDown
    statements
end
```
This is right:
```
on mouseUp
    statements
end mouseUp

on mouseDown
    statements
end mouseDown
```

Note the optional use of the handler name after the *end* keyword. This is useful for making sure that you always have a matching *end handlerName* statement for each *on handlerName* statement. A handler declaration can also include parameters (not shown). Refer to "*Parameters and Arguments*" later in this chapter.

Common Multi-Line Structure Errors

Always terminate nested multiline structures from the inside out, as with nested parentheses.

Note the incorrect indentation in Example 1-19 caused by the *end if* incorrectly preceding the *end repeat*, and note how the multi-line structures incorrectly cross, rather than nest.

Example 1-19: Nested Multi-Line Structure Errors

```
Wrong    on mouseUp
           if the clickOn = 3 then
             repeat with x = 1 to 7
                 puppetSprite x, TRUE
           end if
           end repeat
         end
```

Note the corrected indentation, and see how the multi-line structures nest neatly, rather than cross.:

```
Right    on mouseUp
           if the clickOn = 3 then
             repeat with x = 1 to 7
                 puppetSprite x, TRUE
             end repeat
           end if
         end
```

Don't use a continuation character ¬ improperly at the end of a line. Director automatically knows that the multiline command continues on the next line.

The following is *wrong*. You should not use the ¬ character in this case:

```
repeat with x = 1 to 7 ¬
  puppetSprite x, TRUE
end repeat
```

Here is an example of *correctly* using an ¬ character within the *body* of a multi-line code structure to break a long line of Lingo.

```
repeat with x = 1 to 7
  set the member of sprite x = ¬
  member "Pinky and the Brain" of castLib "World Domination"
end repeat
```

Conditional Execution

You can have Director execute different Lingo code in response to various conditions. Any non-zero expression (including negative numbers) is considered TRUE, and only an expression that evaluates to zero is considered FALSE. Refer to Chapter 5 for details on evaluating comparisons, including compound expressions. (These example multi-line code fragments must be placed in a handler for testing.)

If...Then...Else...End If Decisions

The *if* statement will execute different Lingo code based on the value of the specified expression. This allows you to, say, use a single Director movie on both Macintosh and Windows but branch to different code depending on the playback platform, as determined by *the platform* property, such as:

```
if (the platform starts "Windows") then
   -- Do Windows-specific stuff here
else
   -- Do Macintosh-specific stuff here
end if
```

The *if* statement has many possible forms, but I recommend only these. Items shown in curly braces are optional. Note the correct indentation:

Single-Clause If...Then...End If

```
if expression  then
   statement1
   statement2
end if
```

Multiple-Clause If...Then...Else If...Else...End If

The *else if* and *else* clauses are optional:

```
if expression  then
   statement1
{else if expression  then
   statement2}
{else
   defaultAction}
end if
```

For example:

```
if x = 1 then
   go frame "Slide1"
else if x = 2 then
   go frame "Slide2"
else if x = 3 then
   go frame "Slide3"
else
   go frame "End"
end if
```

One-Line and Two-Line If Statements

The following forms are theoretically valid, but they often misbehave in Projectors and within nested *if* statements, so I don't recommend them:

```
if expression  then statement1
```

or

```
if expression  then statement1
else statement2
```

The Classic Three-Line *If Statement*

The one-line and two-line forms of the *if* statement make it hard to tell if the indenting is correct even after Director auto-formats your Lingo.

> Where I use the one-line form of *if...then* in the examples throughout the book, I do so only for brevity. The Lingo compiler occasionally makes errors when evaluating one-line and two-line *if* statements.

Use the following three-line form even for simple *if* statements, *especially* when nesting *if* statements.

```
if (expression) then
    statement
end if
```

By always using an *end if* statement, and by always including a carriage return after the *then* keyword, Director won't get confused and neither will you. The auto-indenting will work reliably and it also makes the code easier to read and debug. See Chapter 3.

Nested *Ifs*

You can nest *if* statements to create the desired logic. It is crucial that you use the three-line *if...end if* construct, rather than the one-line or two-line form. An *end if* always pairs up with the most recent *if* from the inside out. Let Lingo's auto-indentation be your guide.

```
if expression1 then
    if expression2 then
        action1
    else
        action2
    end if
else
    defaultAction
end if
```

Example 1-20 is a typical usage of a nested *if* statement:

Example 1-20: Nested If Statements

```
if field "name" <> EMPTY then
    -- These five lines of code are a nested "if"
    if length(field "name") > 10 then
        alert "Enter only the first ten letters of your name"
    else -- This "else" pairs with the second "if"
        alert "Welcome to my nightmare" && field "name"
    end if --This "end if" pairs with the second "if"

else -- This "else" pairs with the first "if"
    alert "Please enter your name in the field"
end if --This "end if" pairs with  the first "if"
```

Common Errors When Using If Statements

Although conceptually simple, the *if* statement consistently confuses new Lingo programmers. Avoid the common pitfalls shown in the following examples.

Omitting the End If or the Then

There must be one *end if* for each *if* statement. Watch for this, especially with nested *ifs*, such as is shown in Example 1-21.

Example 1-21: Common If Statement Errors

```
if x > 5 then
  if x < 7
    statements
  end if
-- You are is missing an " end if" here
```

If you omit the *then* keyword, you'll also have problems:

```
if x > 5     -- the keyword " then" is missing
  statements
end if
```

Failure to Use Else If

Use one *if...else if...end if* statement instead of a series of *if* statements.

The following is inefficient because if *x* equals 5, it will never equal 6, and vice versa:

```
if x = 5 then
  -- Do something
end if
if x = 6 then
   -- Do something different
end if
```

This is more efficient (see also "*Case Statements*" later in this chapter):

```
if x = 5 then
  -- Do something
else if x = 6 then
   -- Do something different
end if
```

Improper Comparison Expressions

The incorrect order of comparison can lead to the wrong code being executed. Some code may never be executed, or code may be executed unintentionally.

In this example, *both if* statements will be executed if *x* equals 5. This may be what you want, but it is more likely a logic error:

```
if x > 0 then
  statements
```

```
end if
  if x > 4 then
      statements
  end if
```

In this erroneous example, the second branch will *never* be executed because the first branch is taken in every case where the second condition would be TRUE:

```
if x > 0 then
  statements
else if x > 4 then
    alternative statements (never reached)
end if
```

In this corrected example, the second branch will be executed *only* if *x* is less than 4 but greater than 0:

```
if x > 4 then
  statements
else if x > 0 then
    alternative statements
end if
```

Nesting If Statement Unnecessarily or Incorrectly

Nested if statements seem to give people fits. Don't use a nested *if* statement when an *if...then...else if...end if* statement will suffice.

The innermost conditional clauses in this example are never executed.

Example 1-22: Nesting If Statements Properly

```
if x = 3 then
  alert "Executed option 3"
  -- This is never executed; if x is 3, it's not 4
  if x = 4 then
    alert "Executed option 4"
    -- This is never executed; if x is 4, it's not 5
    if x = 5 then
      alert "Executed option 5"
    end if
  end if
end if
```

The correct construct is:

```
  if x = 3 then
      alert "Executed option 3"
  else if x = 4 then
      alert "Executed option 4"
else if x = 5 then
  alert "Executed option 5"
      end if
```

Excess End If Statements

Use an *end if* only for each *if,* not for each *else if* (sometimes Director won't complain, but the results won't be what you wanted). Example 1-23 is *wrong.*

Example 1-23: Using End If Improperly

```
if x = 3 then
  alert "Executed option 3"
else if x = 4 then
  alert "Executed option 4"
else if x = 5 then
  alert "Executed option 5"
end if
end if   -- This is not needed
end if   -- This is not needed
```

Extraneous *end if*s can change your logic unintentionally. Contrast the following with the earlier nested *if* example. It will always execute the last *alert* command because it follows the last *end if:*

```
if field "name" <> EMPTY then
  -- These five lines of code are a nested "if".
  if length(field "name") > 10 then
    alert "Enter only the first ten letters"
  else
    alert welcome & field "name"
  end if   -- This terminate the inner "if" statement
end if -- This terminate the outer "if" statement
-- This will always be executed
alert "Please enter your name"
```

Missing End If Statements

Each *if* statement must have a matching *end if.* Erroneous structures at the end of a preceding handler will trickle into the next handler and corrupt the indentation. Note the incorrect indentation in the *mouseDown* handler caused by the missing *end if* in the preceding *mouseUp* handler:

```
on mouseUp
  if the clickOn = 3 then
    if rollover(7) then
      put "Yahoo!"
    end if
    put "whatever"
    -- This is missing an "end if"
end

on mouseDown
  put "Hello"   -- Note incorrect indentation
  end
```

Note the corrected indentation of *put "Hello"* in the *mouseDown* handler:

```
on mouseUp
    if the clickOn = 3 then
        if rollover(7) then
            put "Yahoo!"
        end if
        put "whatever"
    end if    -- That's better!
end

on mouseDown
    put "Hello"
end
```

Inefficient Use of If Clauses:

Look for ways to reduce the number of *if* clauses. Here we've modified the example shown under *"Multiple-Clause If...Then...Else If...Else...End If."* We've reduced the number of clauses by using the value of *x* to construct the name of the destination marker ("Slide1," "Slide2," or "Slide3").

```
if x >= 1 and x <= 3 then
    go frame ("Slide" & x)
else
    go frame "End"
end if
```

Case Statements

The *case* statement conditionally executes Lingo statements based on the value of an item. It is often easier to implement than multiple *if...then* statements, but long *case* statements can be slower than the corresponding *if...then* constructs. Director executes the statement(s) following the first **value** that matches the *case* clause. The colon after *otherwise* is optional, and multiple statements can be included after each value to be matched. Once a match is found and its statements executed, subsequent values and their statements are ignored, and execution continues after the *end case* statement.

```
case (item)of
    value1:
        statement
    value2:
        statement
        statement
    value3, value4:
        statement
    otherwise:
        statement
end case
```

Example 1-24 shows a *case* statement and the equivalent *if* statement.

Example 1-24: Case Statements

```
on keyDown
  case (the key) of
    RETURN: go frame "done"
    TAB, BACKSPACE: beep
    otherwise: pass
  end case
end keyDown
```

The *case* statement is equivalent to the following *if ... then* statement:

```
on keyDown
  if (the key = RETURN) then
    go frame "done"
  else if (the key = TAB) or (the key = BACKSPACE) then
    beep
  else
    pass
  end if
end keyDown
```

To use a comparative expression to branch within a *case* statement, use TRUE in the *case* clause, and enclose the comparative expression in parentheses, such as:

```
on keyDown
  case (TRUE) of
    (the keyCode >= 123 and the keyCode <= 126):
      -- The user pressed an arrow key
    statements
    (the keyCode = 122):
      -- The user pressed F1
    statements
    (the keyCode = 118):
      -- The user pressed F4
    statements
    otherwise:
      alert "Please press an arrow key, F1 or F4"
  end case
end keyDown
```

Repeat Loops

Repeat loops repeat any statements within the body of the loop. They are used to cycle through a series of items, such as elements in a list, or to repeat an operation a specific number of times (they are equivalent to so-called *for...next* loops used in some languages). When the *end repeat* command is reached, execution begins again at the top of the *repeat* loop until some condition causes the loop to terminate. Execution continues at the statement following the *end repeat* command. Use the Debugging window, described in Chapter 3, to examine the exact flow of Lingo as Director executes the steps in the *repeat* loop.

Most repeat loops are very fast, even for hundreds or thousands of iterations, but Director can't do anything else while you are executing a repeat loop, especially in Shockwave.

 Don't use repeat loops that monopolize Director's attention for more than a few seconds.

In Shockwave, you can't check whether an operation completed with *netDone()* from within a repeat loop because Director doesn't perform network operations during a repeat loop. Likewise, Director doesn't update all system properties or update the Stage automatically during a repeat loop.

The repeat loop has four forms (3 forms of *repeat with* plus *repeat while*), as shown earlier in Table 1-3. The example multi-line code fragments must be placed in a handler for testing.

The *repeat while* command repeats as long as an expression is TRUE. If the expression never becomes FALSE, it will be an infinite loop.

Example 1-25: Repeat Loops

```
repeat while (the stillDown = TRUE)
  put "The mouse is still down"
end repeat
```

The *repeat with* commands loop through a range of values. Although not necessarily apparent, the three forms of the *repeat with* loop all use an *index variable* (counter) that changes automatically each time the loop is executed.

In this example, the index variable (*i*) starts at the initial value (in this case 1) and increments each time through the loop until it hits the upper bound (in this case 100). If the initial value is greater than the upper limit, the statement(s) within the loop are never executed.

```
repeat with i = 1 to 100
    put "The next number is" && i
end repeat
```

The following is the equivalent *repeat while* loop to the above *repeat with* loop. You can see that *repeat with* loops are more convenient.

```
set i = 1
repeat while i <= 100
  put "The next number is" && i
  set i = i + 1
end repeat
```

The *repeat with...down to* command repeats for a decreasing range of values. In this case, the index variable (*i*) is decremented (not incremented) each time through the loop.

```
repeat with i = 100 down to 1
```

```
    put string(i) && "Bottles of beer on the wall..."
  end repeat
```

The *repeat with...in* command cycles once through all the items in a list. (Refer to Chapter 6 or ignore this example for now.) Each time through the loop, *i* is automatically set to the next item in the list. Use the following to loop through an irregular set of numbers:

```
  set myList = [12, 17, 52, 43]
  repeat with i in myList
    put "The next item in the list is" && i
  end repeat
```

The variable *i* is *not* an integer in the previous example; it is actually the contents of the next item in the list. The previous example can be simulated with a standard *repeat with* loop, as follows:

```
  set myList = [12, 17, 52, 43]
  repeat with j = 1 to count (myList)
    set i = getAt (myList , j)
    put "Item number:" && j
    put "The next item in the list is" && i
  end repeat
```

In the last example, note that the index variable *j* is an integer and can be used to print a list element's position within the list. You must manually intialize and increment an index variable to obtain a similar counter if using a *repeat with...in* loop, such as:

```
  set myList = [12, 17, 52, 43]
  set j = 1
  repeat with i in myList
    put "Item number:" && j
    put "The next item in the list is" && i
    set j = j + 1
  end repeat
```

Altering Loop Execution

Use *next repeat* to skip the current iteration of a *repeat* loop and to continue with the next iteration.

```
  repeat with x = 1 to the number of members
    if the memberType of member x = 0 then
      next repeat
    end if
    put "Item" && x && "is type" && the memberType of member x
  end repeat
```

Use *exit repeat* to exit the current repeat loop immediately. Program execution continues with the statement following the *end repeat* statement. *Exit repeat* exits only the current (innermost) repeat loop, and it will not exit nested *repeat* loops. Use *exit*, or *abort*, or a flag to exit multiple loops, as shown in Example 1-26.

(Again, use the Debugging window to examine the exact flow of Lingo as Director executes the following code.)

Example 1-26: Nested Repeat Loops

```
on findIt
  global gFoundIt
  set gFoundIt = FALSE
  -- Search for a #shape cost member
  repeat with y = 1 to the number of castLibs
    repeat with x = 1 to the number of members of castLib y
      set thisItem = the memberType of member x of castLib y
      if thisItem = #shape then
        set gFoundIt = member x of castLib y
        exit repeat -- exit the innermost loop
      end if
    end repeat
    -- exit the outermost loop too
    if gFoundIt then
      exit repeat
    end if
  end repeat

  -- Execution continues here after loop
  if gFoundIt then
    put "Found shape cast member at" && gFoundIt
  else
    put "Shape cast member not found."
  end if
end
```

Manually Controlling the Loop's Counter

Lingo does *not* precalculate the number of iterations it will perform for a *repeat... with* loop. Rather, it reevaluates the expression each time through the loop. In the following example, we manually increment the index variable (*i*) to step by two rather than one. Note that we add only 1 to *i*, not 2, because Lingo will automatically increment *i* once each time the loop is executed.

Example 1-27: Customized Repeat Loops

```
on printEvenNumbers
  repeat with i = 0 to 100
    put i
    set i = i + 1
  end repeat
end printEvenNumbers
```

Avoid manually setting the index variable within a *repeat* loop unless you need to change the number of loop iterations. Setting it incorrectly can lead to an infinite loop.

After a loop completes, the index normally is one greater than the ending value:

```
on testRepeat
  repeat with i = 1 to 100
    put i
  end repeat
  put "The ending value for i is" && i
end testRepeat

testRepeat
-- 1
-- 2
-- <etc.>
-- 99
-- 100
-- "The ending value for i is 101"
```

Infinite Loops

An *infinite loop* is a *repeat* loop that will never be exited because the conditional expression never turns FALSE. (Apple's street address in Cupertino, California, is One Infinite Loop). An infinite loop will appear to hang the computer, and you must abort the Projector or halt the movie to stop it.

The most simple infinite loop is shown in Example 1-28.

Example 1-28: Infinite Loops

```
repeat while TRUE
  -- do something
end repeat
```

Unless you add an *exit repeat*, Lingo will never exit such a *repeat* loop:

```
startTimer
repeat while TRUE
  if the timer > 60 then
    exit repeat
  else
    -- do something
  end if
end repeat
```

But this would be better written as:

```
startTimer
repeat while the timer <= 60
  -- do something
end repeat
```

It is easy enough to create an infinite loop accidentally. The following will loop forever, assuming the loop takes less than 60 ticks to execute, because *startTimer* is *within* the *repeat* loop and keeps resetting the timer.

```
startTimer
repeat while the timer <= 60
  startTimer
  -- do something
end repeat
```

The following would lead to an infinite loop as well. The variable *x* is unintentionally set to 5; the programmer did not realize that *x* is also being used as the loop's index variable.

```
repeat with x = 1 to 10
  put "x" && x
  set x = 5
end repeat
```

A loop will also be infinite if some condition you expect to become FALSE remains TRUE forever. Suppose you are waiting for a sound to start:

```
puppetSound "mySound"
repeat while not soundBusy(1)
  nothing
end repeat
```

If the sound never starts (in this case, you need to add *updateStage* after the *puppetSound* command), Director will loop forever because *soundBusy(1)* will never become TRUE, so *not soundBusy(1)* will always remain FALSE.

 Use the Debugger to diagnose infinite loops and similar problems. See Chapter 3.

Parameters and Arguments

Imagine you own a calculator with buttons that each perform a single complete operation—one button adds 5 plus 7, and another button adds 5 plus 8, and so on. It might be convenient for those limited operations, but the calculator could rapidly become unwieldy. (Similarly, Chinese pictographs are inconvenient for computer usage compared to an alphabet from which you can construct any word.) In reality, each button on a calculator actually represents either an *operand*, such as the number 5, or an *operation*, such as addition, allowing for many possible combinations with relatively few keys.

At the beginning of this chapter we used the *alert* command to display the string "Hello World" in a dialog box. The *alert* command accepts any text string as an *argument*. An argument is analogous to the operands used in the example of a calculator above, and the *alert* command is analogous to the addition button that performs some operation using the argument(s). The words *parameters* and *argu-*

ments are often used interchangeably to indicate inputs that are passed to a function on which it can operate. Strictly speaking, an *argument* is the item specified as part of the function call, and a *parameter* is the same item once it is received inside the function.

Just as the *alert* command can accept *any* string for display, we should strive to make our custom handlers flexible by using variables to represent values that can change. In contrast, using a fixed number, such as 5, or a fixed string, such as "Bruce," in your program is called *hardcoding* a value.

 Instead of *hardcoding* specific values into a handler, *generalize* the function so that it can operate on whatever *arguments* are passed into it.

For example, a handler that finds a file should be flexible enough to find *any* file we ask it to find, rather than always looking for a particular hardcoded filename. Beginning programmers often create two or more copies of the same handler with only minor variations to accomplish nearly identical tasks. Instead, you should create a *generalized* (that is, flexible) version of the handler that accepts arguments (or *parameters*) to accommodate the differences. This is shown in detail in Example 1-31 and 1-32. Let's start with a discussion of how arguments are passed to a function.

Passing Arguments

A simple function performs an operation on the argument(s) passed into it. For example, let's define an *avg()* function that averages two numbers.

Example 1-29: A Handler That Accepts Parameters

```
on avg a, b
  return (a+b) / 2.0
end
```

The names *avg*, *a*, and *b* are chosen *arbitrarily*. Note that there is a space between the handler name (*avg*) and the first parameter (*a*) but that subsequent parameters (such as *b*) are separated by a comma from the previous parameter. The *return* statement sends the answer back to whoever called the function. Without the *return* statement, the answer *avg* calculates would never be known! (Forgetting to return a result is a very common error. If the result from a custom function returns VOID, you probably forgot the *return* statement).

Type the handler in Example 1-29 into a movie script, and test it from the Message window. The *put* command prints the result returned by *avg()*.

```
put avg (5,8)
-- 6.5000
```

The integers 5 and 8 are *arguments* that are operated upon by *avg()*. The arguments are separated by commas. The parentheses are required to obtain the value

---

returned by *avg()*, but parentheses are optional when calling a command that does not return a value, such as *alert*.

The first argument (5) is automatically assigned to the first parameter (*a*), and the second argument (8) is assigned to the second parameter (*b*). In this case, the order of the parameters does not affect the result, but in most cases the order of the parameters is crucial. For example, division is not reflexive: 5 divided by 8 would not be the same as 8 divided by 5.

If the number of arguments does not match the number of parameters, Director won't complain. It is up to you to ensure that the correct number of arguments is specified.

Modify the *avg()* handler to create *newAvg* as follows:

```
on newAvg a, b
    put "The first parameter, a, equals" && a
    put "The second parameter, b, equals" && b
    set answer = (a+b)/ 2.0
    put "The answer is" && answer
end
```

We've added a local variable, arbitrarily named **answer**, which is convenient for holding the value that is printed and then returned to the calling program. Whereas *a* and *b* are *implicitly* assigned to the arguments in the function call, *answer* is explicitly assigned a value using *set...=*.

There is *no* difference (as far as the *newAvg* handler can tell) if we pass integer *variables* as arguments to *newAvg* instead of the integer *literals* 5 and 8. Type each of these lines in the Message window, pressing RETURN after each:

```
set x = 5
set y = 8
put x
newAvg(x, y)
-- "The first parameter, a, equals 5"
-- "The second parameter, b, equals 8"
-- "The answer is 6.500"
```

We don't need to use the *put* command because *newAvg* displays the result itself using *put*, rather than returning an answer.

The parameters within *newAvg*, namely *a* and *b*, are still equated to 5 and 8, respectively. The *values* of the arguments *x* and *y*, not *x* and *y* themselves, are passed to *newAvg*. This is called *passing arguments by value*, rather than *by reference*.

Refer to *"Parameter Passing,"* in Chapter 4 for more details on parameters passed by reference and to Chapter 6 for how this affects Lingo lists.

Generalizing Functions

NewAvg is a generalized handler that can average any two numbers passed into it (we'll see later how to make it accept any number of arguments to average).

Generalized Sprite Handlers

To perform an operation on a sprite you must refer to the sprite by its channel number (or an expression that evaluates to a channel number). For a sprite in channel 1, you might use:

```
on mouseUp
  set the foreColor of sprite 1 = random (255)
end
```

A beginner might create another script to attach to a different sprite in channel 2 as follows:

```
on mouseUp
  set the foreColor of sprite 2 = random (255)
end
```

Not only is this wasteful, but these scripts will fail miserably if you move the sprites to a new channel. Thankfully, Lingo provides several system properties that can be used to generalize a handler. When a script is attached to a sprite, *the currentSpriteNum* property always indicates the sprite's channel number. Therefore, we can replace the two separate scripts with a single sprite script that can be attached to any sprite in any channel and that will always work.

Example 1-30: A Simple Generalized Behavior

```
on mouseUp
  set the foreColor of sprite (the currentSpriteNum) = random (255)
end
```

Refer to Chapter 9 for details on *the currentSpriteNum, the spriteNum of me*, and *the clickOn* properties and how they can be used to generalize handlers for use with any sprite.

Generalizing a Function with Parameters

The following is a more sophisticated example of a generalized function, but the principle is the same (feel free to skip this section if it is confusing). Let's suppose you want to check if the file "FOO.TXT" exists.

You might write the code shown in Example 1-31 (see Chapter 14 for an explanation of this Lingo and a more robust example).

Example 1-31: A HardCoded Function

```
on doesFooExist
  -- Use the FileIO Xtra to try to open the file FOO.TXT
  set fileObj = new (xtra "FileIO")
  if objectP(fileObj) then
    openFile (fileObj, "FOO.TXT", 1)
```

Example 1-31: A HardCoded Function (continued)

```
  set result = status (fileObj)
  -- A result of 0 indicates success
  if result = 0 then
    alert "FOO.TXT exists!"
  else
    -- Print the error message in the Message window
    put error (fileObj, result)
    alert "FOO.TXT can't be found"
  end if
  -- Clean up after ourselves
  closeFile (fileObj)
  set fileObj = 0
  end if
end doesFooExist
```

Now suppose you want to check if a different file exists. Most beginners would duplicate this long block of code, then change the filename in the *openFile()* function call from "FOO.TXT" to their new filename.

Never duplicate near-identical long blocks of code. Your code becomes harder to debug—and much harder to change if you do find a bug. *Always* generalize the code into a utility function that you can add to your "tool belt" for future use.

Below we've created a generalized function. Note that it accepts a file name as a parameter. *The name that you specify gets substituted automatically for the file-Name parameter and is used in the openFile command.* Note also that it *returns* either **TRUE** (1) or **FALSE** (0) to indicate whether the file was found. If it couldn't be found, you may want to return the error code that was obtained from the FileIO Xtra's *status()* call. (It is good practice to simply return some result or status and let the caller decide whether to post an alert message or do something else.) Beyond that, it is essentially the same handler as shown in Example 1-31. Try to make your utility code as non-intrusive as possible, and clean up after yourself. Note that we opened the file in read-only mode to avoid failing if the file was already open. We also closed the file when done to clean up after ourselves. Example 1-32 is primarily for illustration. The FileIO Xtra will search in the current folder if *the searchCurrentFolder* is **TRUE** (the default). It will also search the list of paths, if any, in *the searchpaths.* It may not work correctly with long filenames under Windows. Thus Example 1-32 is not completely robust.

Example 1-32: A Generalized FileExists Function

```
on fileExists fileName
  -- Use the FileIO Xtra to open the specified file
  set fileObj = new (xtra "FileIO")
  if objectP(fileObj) then
    -- Open file with mode = 1 " read-only"
    openFile (fileObj, fileName, 1)
```

Example 1-32: A Generalized FileExists Function (continued)

```
    set result = status (fileObj)
    -- A status of 0 indicates success
    if result = 0 then
      set found = TRUE
    else
      -- Display the error for debugging
      put error (fileObj, result)
      set found = FALSE
    end if
    closeFile (fileObj)
    set fileObj = 0
    -- Return TRUE or FALSE to indicate if the file exists
    return found
  end if
end fileExists
```

Now we can easily determine if *any* file exists, such as:

```
    put fileExists ("FOO.TXT")
    -- 1
    put fileExists ("FOOPLE.TXT")
    -- 0
```

Or use it as follows:

```
    if fileExists ("FOO.TXT") then
      -- Do whatever I want to with the file...
      -- such as open and read it
    else
      alert "The file can't be found"
    end if
```

Using a Generalized Function

Let's revisit the simple *newAvg* handler. Add the following handler to your movie script that already contains the *newAvg* handler shown earlier.

Example 1-33: Using Generalized Functions

```
on testAvg
  newAvg (5, 3)
  newAvg (8, 2)
  newAvg (4, 4)
  newAvg (7, 1)
end
```

Choose Control▶Recompile Script, and then test *testAvg* from the Message window.

testAvg

You should see the output of the *newAvg* function repeated four times.

Now, type this in the Message window:

```
newAvg (5)
```

What happens and why? What is the value of the second parameter within the *newAvg* handler? It defaults to VOID, as do all unspecified parameters, because only one argument was specified in the function call. What happens if we forget to specify the *fileName* when calling our *fileExists()* function created earlier?

Let's create a simple *divide* function (in reality you'd just use "/" to divide):

```
on divide a, b
  return float(a) / b
end
```

```
put divide (5,5)
-- 1.0000
```

What happens if we forget to specify the parameter used as the divisor?

```
put divide (7)    -- This causes an error
```

Special Treatment of the First Argument Passed

We saw earlier that an error occurs when a local variable is used before it is assigned a value. Enter the code shown in Example 1-34 in a movie script, and recompile the script.

Example 1-34: Special Treatment of First Argument to a Function Call

```
on testFirstArg
  dummyHandler(x)
end testFirstArg
```

Isn't *x* an unassigned local variable? Shouldn't it generate a *"Variable used before assigned a value"* error message? Before answering that, let's alter *testFirstArg* and recompile the script:

```
on testFirstArg
  dummyHandler(x, y)
end testFirstArg
```

The variable *y* is also an unassigned local variable. Why does it generate an error message, if *x* did not? The answer lies in the unique way that Lingo treats the first argument to any function call.

 Even though it is an error, Lingo does not complain if the first argument to a function call is an undeclared local variable (in this case *x*).

Multiple scripts may contain handlers of the same name. When you call a function, Lingo must decide which script to look in first. If the first argument to the function call is a special entity called a *script instance* (see Chapter 2), Director runs the handler in that particular script rather than performing its usual search to find the right script automatically. Lingo allows *anything* as the first argument to a function call because it does not verify script instances or handler names during compilation. (At runtime it will most likely cause an error, though).

> If the first argument passed to a custom function call *is* a script instance, Lingo searches *only* that script instance for the specified handler. Therefore, you can not pass a script instance as the first parameter to a handler in a movie script because Lingo won't look in the movie script!

Suppose you want to call a movie script's handler from a Behavior, and suppose you want to pass in the Behavior's *script instance* as an argument. Assume that this is the Behavior script.

Example 1-35: Passing a Script Instance as an Argument

```
on mouseUp me
  displayInfo (me)
end
```

This is the movie script:

```
on displayInfo someScriptIntanceOrObject
  put the spriteNum of someScriptIntanceOrObject
end
```

What will happen? Director will issue a "*Handler not defined*" error because it will look for the *displayInfo* handler *only* in the Behavior script (but it won't find it). You can move the *displayInfo* handler into the Behavior script, in which case it will be available only to instances of that Behavior, or you can rewrite the example as shown in the code that follows. Note that we add a dummy VOID argument as a placeholder for the first argument to the function call, which allows our script instance to become the *second* argument. Because the second argument is not afforded any special treatment, Lingo searches the usual hierarchy and finds the *displayInfo* handler in the movie script!

Rewrite the *displayInfo* function call as:

```
on mouseUp me
  displayInfo (VOID, me)
end
```

In the *displayInfo* handler declaration in the movie script we must add a dummy parameter to "catch" the first dummy argument:

```
on displayInfo dummyParam, someScriptIntanceOrObject
  -- Use a dummy argument as the first parameter
  -- to allow an object to be passed as second argument.
  put the spriteNum of someScriptIntanceOrObject
end
```

A script instance or *child object* (which can be thought of as the same thing) is often *intentionally* passed as the first argument to force Lingo to look in the correct script for the correct handler or property variables. See the example of property variables in the earlier "*Variable Types*" section and Chapters 12 and 13.

Optional Arguments and Varying Argument Types

Lingo's built-in commands typically complain if you pass the wrong number or unexpected type of arguments, but some accept arguments of different data types and/or a variable number of arguments ("*variable*" is used here to mean "*varying*," not a Lingo *variable*). For example, the second argument to *setaProp()* is either a property name or a property value, depending on whether the first argument is a property list or linear list. Likewise, the *puppetSound* command accepts either one or two arguments, and some arguments to the *puppetTransition* command are optional.

You can also design your custom handlers to allow a variable number of parameters or arguments of varying data types. This makes it easier to create generalized functions rather than multiple, highly similar versions. If you are creating a library of functions for yourself or others, it also makes those functions more flexible and easier to use by the calling routine.

Your function will typically require one or more mandatory arguments that should be placed at the beginning of the parameter list. Optional arguments should be placed after the required parameters. If the caller specifies fewer arguments than the number of parameters you are expecting, later parameters will be VOID.

The *playSound* example that follows accepts the name or number of a sound to play and an optional sound channel number. If no channel is specified, it plays the sound in channel 1. Note the use of *voidP()* to check whether the caller has specified the requested parameters.

Example 1-36: Function Accepting Varying Arguments

```
on playSound soundID, chan
  if voidP(soundID) then
    alert "A sound must be specified"
    exit
  end if
  -- Use channel 1 if the caller does not specify a channel
  -- Or specifies an invalid channel
  if voidP(chan) then
    set chan = 1
  else if not integerP(chan) or ¬
    (integer (chan) < 1  or integer (chan) > 8) then
    put "Channel should be an integer from 1 to 8"
    set chan = 1
  end if
  -- Play the sound
  puppetSound chan, the number of member soundID
  updateStage
end

-- This plays "woof" in channel 1 (the default)
playSound ("woof")
```

Example 1-36: Function Accepting Varying Arguments (continued)

```
-- This plays "bark" in channel 3
playSound ("bark", 3)
```

Note that we also check whether the channel number passed in is an integer and whether it is a valid sound channel number. Our example also accepts either a sound cast member's number or its name, just like as built-in *puppetSound* command. We could enhance the error checking to make sure the specified cast member is a sound.

Refer to Example 5-3 in Chapter 5, *Coordinates, Alignment and Registration Points*, in *Director in a Nutshell*. It accepts parameters in numerous formats and includes substantial error checking.

You can extend the *playSound* example to create a handler that accepts additional optional arguments, but note that the caller cannot pass a value for an optional argument unless all preceding arguments have been specified. For example, if we wanted to add a flag to *playSound* indicating whether to wait for the sound to play, we could add another optional parameter called *waitFlag*.

Example 1-37: Placeholder Arguments

```
on playSound soundID, chan, waitFlag
  -- Beginning of handler is the same code as example above
  -- but is omitted here for brevity
  puppetSound chan, the number of member soundID
  updateStage
  -- This will wait if waitFlag is non-zero. It will
  -- not wait if waitFlag is omitted, and therefore VOID
  if waitFlag then
   repeat while soundBusy (chan)
     nothing
   end repeat
  end if
end
```

 Arguments and parameters are always matched up by *position*. The first argument in the function is assigned to the first parameter in the handler definition, and so on.

In this example, if the caller specifies only two arguments, the second argument will be used as the second parameter (*chan*). If the caller wants to specify *waitFlag* (the third parameter), he or she must specify three arguments, including a placeholder for *chan*.

```
-- The second argument is assumed to be the second
-- parameter and is mistakenly
-- interpreted as a channel number
playSound ("bark", TRUE)
-- Instead, use 1 as a placeholder for the chan parameter
playSound ("bark", 1, TRUE)
```

Variable-Length Parameter Lists

In the previous example, some arguments are optional, but the maximum number of arguments is known. You can also create handlers that accept an unknown (ostensibly unlimited) number of arguments. The *paramCount* property and *param()* function decipher an unknown number of arguments passed into a handler. *The paramCount* indicates the total number of parameters received and *param(n)* returns the nth parameter.

Example 1-38: Variable Number of Parameters

```
on countParams
   put "Total Params:" && the paramCount
   repeat with n = 1 to the paramCount
      -- This statement prints out each parameter's
   -- number and its value by building a fancy string
      put "Param" && n & ":" && param(n)
   end repeat
end countParams


countParams ("Hello", "there", 5)
-- "Total Params: 3"
-- "Param 1: Hello"
-- "Param 2: there"
-- "Param 3: 5"
```

Note that no parameters are declared in the handler definition of *on count-Params*. It will accept any number of parameters, as would be appropriate if we wanted to, say, average any number of values. If we expected a fixed number of parameters, we could instead declare some parameters (in this case *a*, *b*, and *c*) when we define our handler, such as:

```
on newCountParams a, b, c
   put "Total Params:" && the paramCount
   put "Param a:" && a
   put "Param b:" && b
   put "Param c:" && c
   put "Param 1:" && param(1)
   put "Param 2:" && param(2)
   put "Param 3:" && param(3)
end newCountParams

newCountParams ("Hello", "there", 5)
-- "Total Params: 3"
-- "Param a: Hello"
-- "Param b: there"
-- "Param c: 5"
-- "Param 1: Hello"
-- "Param 2: there"
-- "Param 3: 5"
```

We can access the first parameter as either *a* or *param(1)*. Likewise, we can access the second parameter as either *b* or *param(2)*, and so on. That is, *param(1)* is always the first parameter, not merely the first *unnamed* parameter.

Note that named parameters are easier to work with when you know how many to expect, but *param()* and *the paramCount* are more flexible. Use any combination of the two. Refer to Example 8-6 and 8-7 which use *the paramCount* and *param()* to take the sum or average of an indeterminate number of arguments.

Parameter Error Checking

The *playSound* example discussed previously ignores extraneous arguments (that is, if more arguments are specified than the number of parameters expected), as do many Lingo commands. You can always check *the paramCount* to warn the caller if too many or too few arguments are specified, such as:

```
if the paramCount > 3 then alert "No more than 3 please"
```

or

```
if the paramCount <> 4 then alert "Expected 4 params"
```

You can also check the type of each argument, as described in detail in Chapter 5:

```
if not integerP(param(1)) then
  alert "First parameter must be an integer"
  exit
  end if
```

The *verifyParams()* function shown in Example 1-39 checks whether the parameter(s) passed into a handler are of the expected data type(s). The details are fairly complex, but you don't need to understand them at this point.

 You can often use a handler as a *"black box."* You don't need to know what happens inside the box; you need to know only what *inputs* it requires and what *outputs* it provides.

Likewise, you may provide handlers to others without supplying details on how they work. You need not understand all the magic as long as you trust the wizard behind the curtain. This book and its companion, *Director in a Nutshell*, try to dispel some of the mystery about how Director and Lingo work.

The *verifyParams()* function shown in Example 1-39 accepts a property list containing parameters and their expected data types (it checks only for integers, floats, and strings). See Chapter 6 if you don't understand lists, or just skip the details for now. *VerifyParams()* returns TRUE if the number and type of parameters are correct and FALSE otherwise. You can extend *verifyParams()* to handle more data types or to post an alert dialog instead of printing errors to the Message window.

Example 1-39: Verifying Parameters

```
on verifyParams  verifyList, numInput
  -- Check the number of parameters vs. the number expected
  set numExpected = count (verifyList)
  if numInput < numExpected then
    put "Too few parameters. Expected" && numExpected
```

Example 1-39: Verifying Parameters (continued)

```
      return FALSE
   else if numInput > numExpected then
     put "Too many parameters. Expected" && numExpected
     return FALSE
   end if
 -- Check each item in the list and its data type
   repeat with x = 1 to count (verifyList)
     set nextItem = getAt (verifyList, x)
     case (getPropAt(verifyList, x)) of
       #integer:
         if not integerP (nextItem) then
           put "Expected integer for parameter" && x
           return FALSE
         end if
       #float:
         if not floatP (nextItem) then
           put "Expected float for parameter" && x
           return FALSE
         end if
       #string:
         if not stringP (nextItem) then
           put "Expected string for parameter" && x
           return FALSE
         end if
       otherwise:
           put "Unsupported type for parameter" && x
           return FALSE
     end case
   end repeat
   return TRUE
end verifyParams
```

You can use *verifyParams()* to check if your routine is called with the correct number and type of arguments. This is useful for debugging your own code or for trapping errors if you distribute your code for others to use. *VerifyParams()* expects a property list containing each parameter and its expected data type. The following verifies whether *a* is an integer, *b* is a string, and *c* is a float. It also checks whether exactly three parameters have been received.

```
on myHandler a, b, c
  -- Make sure that we received the expect parameters
  if not (verifyParams([#integer:a, #string:b, #float:c],[LC]
       the paramCount)) then
    alert "Something was wrong"
    exit
  end if
  -- Otherwise everything is okay and we can proceed.
  statements
end myHandler
```

Test it from the Message window:

```
myHandler (12.5, "a", 5.7)
-- "Expected integer for parameter 1"
```

```
myHandler (12, 6, 5.7)
-- "Expected string for parameter 2"

myHandler (5, "a")
-- "Too few parameters. Expected 3"
```

Reader Exercise: Modify *Verify Params()* to return an error string.

See also Example 8-4, *"Clipping a Value to a Valid Range,"* in Chapter 8.

Congratulations!

Whew! You now have a foundation on which to build a greater understanding of Lingo. Even the most complex programs are built with simple components—variables, handlers, keywords, *repeat* loops, and *if* statements—so don't be intimidated. With patience, you can (de)construct very complicated programs. Refer to Table 18-1, for a list of all Lingo keywords so that you can distinguish them from variables and custom handler names. Look at examples of other people's Lingo code. Try to recognize the various pieces of the Lingo puzzle. (Remember diagramming sentences in English class, where you picked out the verbs, subjects, adjectives, and prepositional phrases?) Which items are variables? Which are keywords? Which are parameters? Which items are arbitrarily chosen by the programmer, and which are dictated by Lingo's grammar or syntax?

This single chapter has covered material from both beginner and intermediate programming courses that might be spread out over many months. We also touched on some very advanced concepts that will serve you well as you read the rest of this book. Don't be discouraged if you didn't understand a lot of it, or if you skipped the more intimidating parts. Re-visit this chapter frequently, and you'll find new treasures each time. It may seem hard to believe now, but when you look back on this chapter a year from now, most of the things that confused you will seem quite simple.

Most of this chapter applies to other programming languages you may encounter. If Lingo is your first programming language, rest assured that picking up additional languages becomes much easier. In Chapter 4 we compare Lingo to C/C++ so that you can see both the nitty-gritty details of Lingo and how other languages may differ.

Even though this "book work" may seem tedious, it will allow you to breathe new life into all your Director projects once you are out in the field. (Don't forget to save your test Director movie periodically).

I leave this chapter with a reminder that I can point you in the right direction and even provide a map of the terrain and a steady compass, but you are ultimately your own navigator for the journey that lies ahead.

This exchange took place in the Director support forum:

Q: *What is* TRUE?

A: How about trying, *put* TRUE?

Where else but Lingo can you find out what is TRUE with a mere nine keystrokes?

CHAPTER 2

Events, Messages, and Scripts

Events and Messages

This chapter covers the foundation on which every Director project is built—interactivity. How does Director respond to user events? How can you control the flow of both Lingo and the Score? How does Director know which Lingo to execute? If you are new to Lingo, I explain everything in great detail below.

Users familiar with D5 should note these important changes in D6:

- Score scripts are now *instantiated* and "know" who they are (they receive the *me* parameter indicating their script instance and, indirectly, their sprite number).

- Sprites can have multiple scripts (Behaviors) attached, all of which can receive the same events. A sprite might have multiple *mouseUp* and *mouseDown* handlers in different attached Behaviors.

- Behaviors are instantiated scripts that can have *custom properties* applied each time they are used in the Score. Multiple Behaviors can be "piled on" a sprite, allowing you to modularize your Behaviors. (One Behavior might have just a *mouseUp* handler, and one might have just a *mouseDown* handler). These factors can *dramatically* reduce the total number of scripts required.

- A single frame script can span multiple frames in the script channel, just as sprites now span multiple frames.

- Many new events are broadcast in parallel to multiple sprites and the frame script (including *beginSprite*, *endSprite* and *prepareFrame*).

- The new *mouseWithin, mouseEnter,* and *mouseLeave* events make it much easier to handler rollovers on a per-sprite basis, rather than checking for rollovers in a frame script. The traditional mouse event hierarchy remains in place.

- The new *beginSprite* and *endSprite* events make it easy to create self-reliant sprite scripts and frame scripts that initialize and clean up after themselves.

- The new *prepareMovie* and *prepareFrame* events allow you to perform initialization *before* the current frame is drawn on stage.

You Look Like a Programmer to Me

Let's begin with a tangible example upon which we can build a true understanding of how Director handles events via Lingo scripts. Figure 2-1 shows the portions of the Score that are relevant to Lingo scripting. Turn *on* the *Script Preview* and turn *off* the *Director 5 Style Score Display* option under File ➤Preferences➤Score and turn on the *Sprite Toolbar* using View➤Sprite Toolbar to make your Score look like Figure 2-1. Refer to Chapter 3, *The Score and Animation,* in *Director in a Nutshell* for many more details on using the Score effectively.

For a quick overview of placing scripts in Director, refer the *Scripts* topic in the online Help and to Chapter 2, *Script Basics,* of Macromedia's *Learning Lingo* manual.

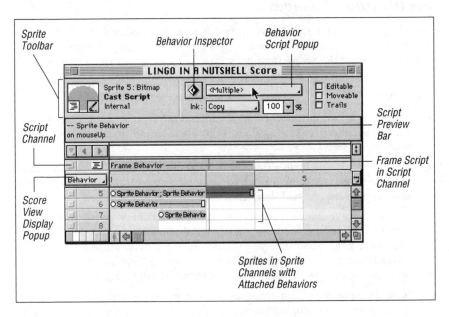

Figure 2-1: Scripts in the Score

The two most common Lingo operations are controlling the playback head and creating clickable buttons. We'll cover these in detail later in this chapter, but you should get your feet wet immediately. We'll make Director wait in a particular frame using a *frame script* in the Script channel, and we'll make a sprite clickable by attaching a *sprite script* to it.

Example 2-1: Basic Frame and Sprite Scripts

1. Open your test movie (which you should have begun in Chapter 1, *How Lingo Thinks*) and open the Score window. The position of the playback head is indicated by the red rectangle with a vertical line running through it.

2. Create a bitmap cast member and drag it to the Score or Stage to create a sprite in channel 1. Tween the sprite's position so that it animates across the Stage when the playback head moves. (If you don't know how to animate a sprite refer to Chapter 3, *Working with Cast Members,* and Chapter 4, *Working with Sprites,* in Macromedia's *Using Director* manual or see Help►Learning Director.)

3. Rewind and play the movie, and watch the playback head move in the Score. It may loop back to frame 1 when it hits the last frame if you've turned on looping (see Control►Loop Playback). Stop the movie.

4. Choose a frame at which to pause the animation by double-clicking that frame's cell in the script channel (this opens a Script window). We could use the Tempo channel instead, but the point is to learn Lingo.

5. Enter the following script (you'll need to type only the middle line, as the first and last should be provided), and close the Script window.

```
on exitFrame
  go to the frame
end
```

6. Rewind and play the movie. The playback head should hold on the frame in which you've added the script, but note that the movie is still playing (not paused). Now stop the movie.

7. Highlight the sprite in channel 1, and click the Script Preview bar or Choose Modify►Sprite►Script to open up another Script window.

8. Enter the following script (you'll need to type only the middle line, as the first and last should be provided), and close the Script window.

```
on mouseUp
  alert "You are so good looking!"
end
```

9. Again rewind and play the movie. Click outside the sprite somewhere on the Stage. What happens? Now click on the sprite.

You should experiment with both the frame script (the one with the *exitFrame* handler attached to the script channel) and the sprite script (the one with the *mouseUp* handler attached to the sprite). To edit an existing script, highlight either the sprite or script channel cell, and click the Script Preview bar. After changing and closing a script, rewind and play the movie.

Change the *mouseUp* handler in the sprite script to the following, and retest it:

```
on mouseUp
  go frame1
end
```

What happens if you put an *alert()* command inside the *exitFrame* handler? What happens if you add the following *mouseDown* handler whitin the same sprite script after the *mouseUp* handler?

```
on mouseDown
  put "I reached the mouseDown handler"
  beep
end
```

Add your own *mouseDown* and *mouseUp* handlers to the frame script that differ from those in the sprite script. What happens if you click outside the sprite before the playback head arrives in the frame with the frame script? (Be sure to open the Message window and click both inside and outside the sprite.)

Finally, add the following handler to the end of the sprite script:

```
on beginSprite
  alert "I reached the beginSprite handler in frame" ¬
    the frame && "for sprite" && the currentSpriteNum
end
```

Experiment until you have a firm grasp of when the different handlers in the different scripts are being called or until you are totally confused. Then start with a new movie, and try it all again. Add, change, and remove handlers one at a time to see how they affect playback. For now you should use only one script for the sprite and one script for the frame. Each script can have multiple handlers, such as:

```
on mouseDown
  put "I detected a mouseDown"
end

on mouseUp
  put "I detected a mouseUp"
end
```

You should have seen these outcomes:

- The *mouseDown* and *mouseUp* handlers in the *sprite script* run only when you click on the sprite, not when you click outside it.

- The handlers in a *frame script* apply only when the playback head is in the frame with that frame script (that is, a frame script in frame 10 has no effect if the playback head is in another frame). You can use the same frame script over a range of frames in the script channel, just as you would use a sprite over a range of frames in a sprite channel.

- The *mouseDown* and *mouseUp* handlers attached to a sprite (if present) take precedence over those in the frame script when you click on the sprite. If you click *outside* the sprite, the frame script receives the *mouseDown* and *mouseUp* messages, but the sprite does not.

- A sprite receives the *beginSprite* message once and only once when the playback head enters the sprite span for the first time.

An *Event Tester* movie is available at the download site cited in the *Preface*.

Where the Hell Are My Scripts?

The number of ways to create, locate, attach, and access scripts is mind-boggling. Many users can't even find scripts once they've been created. Your preference settings can make scripts more difficult to find and edit. Force yourself to experiment with a few simple scripts until you truly understand the following. Later in the chapter I detail all the interface options that pertain to scripts, but this will give you a good head start:

Scripts in the Script Window

All scripts of every type (movie, score, parent, and cast scripts) are accessible via the Script window (Cmd-0 [Macintosh] or Ctrl-0 [Windows] with a *zero*, not an "o"). Page through all scripts using the arrow buttons at the top of the Script window. The window's title bar indicates a script's cast member number and type.

Scripts in the Cast Window

Cast scripts appear in the Script window but do not have their own slot in the Cast window, as do other scripts. Use the *Script* button in the Cast window to open cast scripts (which are attached to cast members). Set the *Show Cast Member Script Icons* option under File➤Preferences➤Cast to add an extra icon in the Cast window thumbnail of cast members with cast scripts attached.

Score scripts, movie scripts, and parent scripts appear in their own cast member slots in the Cast window. To find Script cast members search for cast members of type *Behavior and Script* using Edit➤Find➤Cast Member or Cmd-; (Macintosh) or Ctrl-; (Windows).

Scripts in the Score Window

To see the scripts attached to items in the Score use View➤Display ➤Behavior or set the Score View Display popup (See Figure 2-1) to *Behavior*. Highlight a script cast member in the Cast window, then use Cmd-H (Macintosh) or Ctrl-H (Windows) to find where it is used in the Score.

Note the frame scripts attached to the Script Channel (see Figure 2-1).

Scripts in the Sprite Toolbar and Sprite Inspector

Only score scripts (not movie scripts, parent scripts, or cast scripts) appear in the Behavior script popup in the Sprite Toolbar (in the Score window) or the Standalone Sprite Inspector (see Table 2-2, *Script-Related Interface Commands*). Existing score scripts can be applied by highlighting the sprite(s) or frame(s) in the script channel and selecting a score script from the script popup. Score scripts can also be dragged from the Cast window and dropped into the Score.

The script popup shows the currently attached script, but it isn't equipped to handle multiple scripts attached to a single sprite (the popup's display changes to <Multiple> in that case). You can also the script popup's *New Script* option to add a new score script or use its *Clear Script* option to detach all scripts from highlighted sprites or frames.

Scripts in the Behavior Inspector

The Behavior Inspector (opened with the "*" key on the numeric keypad) is the best place to view *multiple* score scripts attached to a sprite. See Figure 12-1, *Behavior Inspector window*. When you double-click a script cast member in the Cast window Director will *either* open the script itself for editing in the Script window or open the Behavior Inspector (based on your `File➤Preferences➤Editors➤Behaviors` preference setting). Regardless of this preference, you can open the Behavior Inspector using the *Behavior Inspector* button in the Sprite Toolbar (see Figure 2-1) or Sprite Inspector. You can access a script's text from *within* the Behavior Inspector via its *Script* button (see Figure 12-1).

If you've inherited a Director project or are trying to understand an example movie, begin by stepping through each frame of the Score. Notice the Behaviors attached to sprites and to the Script channel. Then cycle through all the scripts in the Script window, paying special attention to movie scripts (hopefully the programmer has documented their code). Cycle through the bitmaps in the Paint window to get a feel for the artwork, and note any cast members with associated cast scripts. Set breakpoints in any scripts you find confusing (see Chapter 3). This will open the Debugger when the script is reached so that you can examine it more closely. Bear in mind that some scripts and cast members may not be used. A typical Director movie contains a lot of dead wood, and is ill-suited for imitation. Stick with demonstration movies designed as such by skilled programmers.

We'll see more about using scripts to create an interactive presentation later in the chapter, but first I'll explain what Director does behind the scenes.

Script Templates

Director anticipates the type of handler you'll want to add depending on the type of script you create. For example, if you create a new score script while highlighting a sprite, it will assume you want a *sprite* script and automatically include the template for an *on mouseUp* handler. But if you create a new score script by double-clicking in the script channel, Director will instead assume you want a *frame* script and automatically include the template for an *on exitFrame* handler. Don't be misled by the templates. You can replace or supplement them with any handler you prefer. Keep in mind that both sprite scripts and frame scripts are score scripts. It is only by virtue of where they are attached to the Score that the distinction is made. See Table 2-1, *The Phantom Script Bug*, for additional details on default handlers in each type of script.

An Inexcusable Bug in Script Creation

Director's script templates work well most of the time. The trouble comes in when you close a new Score script without adding any text to it. Director will create a reference to a phantom script cast member that is prone to later disappearance.

Understanding how to reproduce the "phantom script" bug should help you avoid accidentally corrupting your Score's script references.

Example 2-2: The Phantom Script Bug

1. Double-click in a frame in the script channel. Director will open a new Script window, complete with an *on exitFrame* template, and add a reference in the script channel to the new script cast member.
2. Immediately close the Script window without typing anything into it. Note that there is still a reference in the script channel to this script.
3. Double-click the same cell in the script channel. It opens the same Script window, but note that now the *on exitFrame* template has disappeared. The script is now empty. As such, Director is prone to delete it the next time it is opened.
4. Note the Script window's cast member number, then close the Script window again.
5. Set the `File➤Preferences➤Cast➤Media Type Icons` option to *All Types*.
6. Open the Cast window, and find the script cast member created previously. It should have a script icon in the corner of its thumbnail.
7. Highlight the cast member, and hit the *Cast Member Script* button in the Cast window or choose `Modify➤Cast Member➤Script`. The Script window opens and still contains an empty score script.
8. Position the Script window and Cast window so that you can see the script cast member's thumbnail in the Cast window while the Script window is active.
9. Watch the script cast member's thumbnail in the Cast window carefully while you close the Script window. The script cast member's thumbnail will disappear, indicating that the cast member slot is now vacant.
10. Highlight the vacated cast member slot in the Cast window.
11. Open the Paint window using `Cmd-5` (Macintosh) or `Ctrl-5` (Windows) and create a simple bitmap. Close the Paint window. The bitmap cast member now occupies the slot vacated by the empty script.
12. If you have stuck with me this far and are thinking "Who cares?" look back in the Score. The script channel still contains a reference to the original script cast member's slot even though it is now occupied by a bitmap!

In other words, we have just introduced a corruption into the Score. The script channel should refer only to score scripts, never to assets such as bitmaps! If you later add a cast script to the bitmap cast member, Director treats the *cast* script as a *frame* script! You can create similar corruption by creating and immediately closing a sprite script and then reusing its slot for something else.

Another possibility is that the phantom script's slot is re-used when you create a different script elsewhere in the Score. In that case, the new script will be unintentionally referenced from the old frame or sprite with an incorrect script reference.

Director 5 behaves the same as Director 6, but Director 4 would remove the reference in the Score if you aborted the script entry as described. Notice also that flipping past such a phantom script in the Script window as you page through your scripts will cause it to disappear. Always manually remove any phantom references in the Score unintentionally created by virtue of having closed a brand new script window. Use the Behavior Inspector or the script popup in the Sprite Inspector to remove the erroneous reference from the Score. Refer to Example 3-12 in *Director in a Nutshell* for a utility that analyzes the Score for this type of corruption.

Using the *move member* command does *not* update references in the Score for the moved asset. It too can lead to the a Score that references cast members of the wrong type.

Events Versus System Properties

Director generates dozens of different events that allow Lingo to respond to mouse clicks and more. When an *event* occurs, Director sends a *message* to an *event handler* in an appropriate script. (In practice, the terms *event* and *message* are used interchangeably). An *event handler* is any Lingo handler that responds to (*traps*) any of the built-in Director events shown in Table 2-6, *The SpriteNum of me Property* through Table 2-8, *Mouse and Keyboard Events*.

Director also allows you to check the state of system properties, such as whether the mouse is being depressed, at any time. The distinction between event handlers and system properties is critical.

Events handlers are called *once* each time an event, such as a mouse click, occurs. Event handlers must have the same name as the message/event they wish to trap, preceded by the keyword *on*. An *on mouseUp* handler would trap *mouseUp* events. System properties describe the *current* state of the computer, mouse, or keyboard and can be checked manually at any time.

For example, the event handler *on mouseDown* is called *once* when the user first presses the mouse. The system property *the mouseDown* evaluates to TRUE if the mouse is *currently* being pressed. Refer to Chapter 9, *Mouse Events*, and Chapter 10, *Keyboard Events*, for details on mouse and keyboard events and related properties.

Order of Event Execution

Director generates events whenever the playback head is moving. The screen is redrawn after the *prepareFrame* event (new in D6), but before the *enterFrame* event. Use *prepareFrame* to initialize sprite properties before the sprites in a frame are drawn.

Director processes events and updates the Stage only when the playback head is moving. If your tempo is very slow, such as one frame per second, button response may appear sluggish. Likewise, Director does not process events at all while your Lingo handler is running. Keep handlers short, and especially avoid lengthy *repeat* loops to allow Director time to process events.

 Events are sent and received *sequentially* (one at a time), not simultaneously (all at once). You must understand the order in which they are sent and to whom, in order to know where to place your scripts.

Events, Scripts

The Lingo Messaging Hierarchy

Director passes each event to various scripts to give them an opportunity to respond to that event. When Director encounters an event handler that matches the event (that is, a handler named *on eventName*), that handler will be executed. Each event is sent to only the appropriate scripts. For example, mouse clicks are passed to the scripts attached to the sprite on which the user clicked, not to other sprites elsewhere on the Stage. Key clicks are passed to scripts attached to the field sprite with keyboard focus, not to other field sprites nor to non-field sprites for which keyboard events are meaningless.

The path that an event takes though various Lingo scripts is called the *Lingo messaging hierarchy.*

If no handler is found in a given script, the event is passed onto the next script.

Most events are passed along the hierarchy until Director finds a handler that responds to that event, which usually *consumes* the event.

Events that don't get trapped are ignored. For example, if your scripts contain only *mouseUp* handlers, any *mouseDown* events will be ignored. (An explicit function call to a custom handler, however, will generate an error if the handler is not found.)

Handlers that trap events can explicitly pass those events along the hierarchy or specifically prevent them from being passed any further using *pass, dontPassEvent,* and *stopEvent.* We'll return to the messaging hierarchy in the *"Trapping Events with Scripts"* and *"Message Processing Order"* sections after examining the different types of scripts in more detail.

Lingo Script Types

Where should Lingo scripts be placed? The answer depends on the event you wish to trap (respond to) and when you want to trap it.

No Scripts Required

Macromedia advertises Director 6's Behaviors as "scriptless authoring." You *can* use Behaviors without understanding the specifics of what they do, but they are still scripts, even if someone else wrote them. At a minimum, you must understand how to attach scripts in the Score and how Director processes events. Behaviors are score scripts, but *configurable* Behaviors are very different from the simple score scripts you may have used in Director 5. Refer to Chapter 12.

In some cases, Director handles the desired task without scripting. The Tempo channel can be used to wait a specific length of time, to wait for a mouse click or key press, or to wait for a sound or video to play. Editable text fields handle keyboard input automatically when the *editable of member* or *editable of sprite* property is set. Refer to Chapter 10 in this book and Chapter 12, *Text and Fields*, in *Director in a Nutshell* for details.

A Dizzying Array of Scripts

Director's terminology is very confusing regarding the various types of scripts. Although the *scriptType of member* property returns only three different values (*#movie*, *#score*, and *#parent*) there are actually six types of scripts. (Movie scripts, parent scripts, three subspecies of score scripts (frame scripts, score scripts, and Behaviors), plus cast scripts, which don't have their own *scriptType*).

 There can be a virtually unlimited number of scripts of each type in a Director movie. Each script can contain one or more handlers, but the total length of a single script cannot exceed 32,000 characters. Create libraries of scripts in external castLibs that can be shared among multiple movies.

Cast Scripts

A *cast member* script (or simply *cast script*) is one way to make a bitmap sprite clickable. It is associated with a *cast member* in the Cast window but takes effect automatically for any *sprite* created from that cast member. (Recall that a sprite is an instance of a cast member that has been placed in the Score or on the Stage. Refer to Chapter 1, *How Director Works*, in *Director in a Nutshell*.) Cast scripts ordinarily respond to mouse events, such as *mouseUp*.

Cast scripts are entered in the Script window like other scripts, but they are affixed permanently to an asset cast member (bitmap, field, video, and so on). They are *not* given their own separate cast members as are other scripts; they don't have a *scriptType of member* property, and their *type of member* property depends on the asset to which they are attached, such as *#bitmap*.

Some Linguists prefer cast scripts because they are easy to find (they are always attached to the cast member that uses them) and are associated only with any sprites created from a cast member. (Cast scripts are never applied via the Score window as are Score scripts.)

I *never* use cast scripts; I use *sprite scripts* instead (see "Sprite Scripts"). I don't like to permanently tie a sprite's actions to the bitmap cast member it uses. A cast script is exclusive to the cast member to which it is attached and can not be shared by sprites that use a different cast member. Furthermore, if you change a sprite's *member of sprite* property, the cast script of the sprite's old member disappears when that member is replaced. Thus, you would need to duplicate the same cast script for the normal, rollover, and depressed states of a button, which is downright wasteful. Furthermore, if you replace bitmap cast members, you may inadvertently lose cast scripts attached to those bitmaps.

Finally, a sprite can have both sprite scripts and cast scripts attached to it, which tends to be confusing (handlers in sprite scripts override handlers in cast scripts).

 Cast scripts are *not* instantiated, can not have properties, and do *not* receive the new *beginSprite, endSprite,* and *new* events that are sent to sprite scripts (see Table 2-9, *Frame-Related Events,* and Table 2-11, *Miscellaneous Events*).

Score Scripts

Score scripts are any scripts that are attached to sprite channels or the script channel in the Score (they have a *scriptType of member* property of *#score*). Frame scripts, sprite scripts, and Behaviors are all variants of score scripts and are all entered via the Script window into their own script cast members. Director makes no distinction between the various flavors of Score scripts in the Cast window, Behavior Inspector, or the Sprite Inspector's script popup. You must keep track of whether a score script is supposed to be used as a sprite script or a frame script. It is even possible, though less common, that the same score script would be used as both a frame script and a score script.

 Score scripts (that is, Behaviors) are treated differently in D6 than in D5. They are *instantiated,* can have properties, and can receive many new events. See *"Script Instances"* later in this chapter.

Behaviors

Macromedia now uses *Behavior* as a general term for all score scripts, and your old sprite scripts and frame scripts now appear in the Behavior Inspector, as do all score scripts. Macromedia's manual say that Behaviors are identical to score scripts (which is how Director treats them), but Behaviors usually have configurable properties whereas traditional score scripts did not. Behaviors are attached like any other score scripts to the script channel or sprite channel(s). Macromedia provides some predefined Behaviors under Xtras▶Behavior Library. Refer to Chapter 12 for details on the differences between simple score scripts and true "Behaviors" that take advantage of new features in Director 6.

Even if you never write or use configurable Behaviors, plain vanilla sprite scripts have new capabilities in Director 6. Multiple sprite scripts can be attached to a single sprite, and all sprite scripts receive a slew of new messages, including *beginSprite* and *mouseEnter.* See Table 2-11.

Sprite Scripts

Sprite scripts are attached to sprites via the Score window and typically contain handlers that respond to mouse events such as *mouseUp*. (See Table 2-7 through Table 2-11.) Sprite script handlers override any handlers of the same name in a cast script. A single sprite script can be attached to multiple sprites over many frames of the movie. I strongly suggest that you use sprite scripts to the exclusion of cast scripts. In addition to the drawbacks of cast scripts mentioned previously, it is very easy to remove a sprite script from a sprite without actually deleting it from the Cast window. If you change your mind, you can easily reapply the sprite script using the script popup in the Sprite Toolbar. With a cast script, you need to delete your Lingo, comment it out, or resort to Lingo tricks to disable it temporarily.

Frame Scripts

Frame scripts are attached to the Score's Script channel and ordinarily contain *on exitFrame* handlers. (See Table 2-7 through Table 2-11.) You can attach only one script to each frame, but that script can contain multiple handlers and can call additional handlers residing in movie scripts. Because sprite scripts in D6 receive several events previously sent only to frame scripts, a sprite script with, say, an *exitFrame* handler can act as a surrogate frame script.

Movie Scripts

Movie scripts (which have a *scriptType of member* property equal to *#movie*) may contain the following handlers, which all serve very different purposes:

- Handlers to trap events that are passed only to movie scripts, most notably *prepareMovie*, *startMovie* and *stopMovie*.

- Standard event handlers that you'd find in other types of scripts, such as *mouseUp* and *keyDown* (but they are reached only if the events are not intercepted earlier by sprite scripts, cast scripts, or frame scripts).

- *Primary event handlers* for *mouseUp, mouseDown, keyUp, keyDown,* and *timeOut* events that are called before the events are sent to other types of scripts.

- Custom handlers that are called from other scripts (recall that handlers in movie scripts are accessible from any other script).

Movie scripts are entered into separate script cast members via the Script window, but they are *never* attached to the Score. They do *not* appear in the script popup in the Sprite Toolbar or Sprite Inspector, nor in the Behavior Inspector. Searching for cast members that are *not* used in the Score (via the Edit➤Find➤Cast Member➤Usage) will *not* list movie scripts, even though they are, in fact, *not* used in the Score. This prevents you from accidentally deleting them as unneeded. Refer to Chapter 1 for practice working with movie scripts.

Parent Scripts

Parent scripts, like movie scripts, are entered into separate script cast members via the Script window but are not attached to the Score. You can create a parent script only by manually changing its type to *Parent* in the script cast member info window (or setting its *scriptType of member* property to *#parent*).

Parent scripts are used to dynamically create child objects and are the spiritual kin of customizable Behaviors. Both are written in an object-oriented style, although only the latter are attached to elements in the Score. Refer to Chapter 12.

Parent scripts do *not* appear in the script popup in the Sprite Toolbar or Sprite Inspector, nor in the Behavior Inspector. Searching for cast members that are *not* used in the Score (via the Edit➤Find➤Cast Member➤Usage) *will* list parent scripts. Even though they are *not* used in the Score, they may be used via Lingo, so be careful to avoid deleting them accidentally.

Creating and Manipulating Scripts

Table 2-1 shows the myriad ways to create each type of Script, all of which are edited in the Script window (Window➤Script).

 In D6.0.1 and later, use the "+" button in the Script window to create a new blank script of the *same* type as the current script, except that a new *movie* script is created if the current script is a cast script.

Prior versions of Director always created a new *movie* script when you clicked the "+" button in the Script window. You can always change a script's type in its cast member info dialog box. Open multiple script windows by holding down the Option key (Macintosh) or Alt key (Windows) when clicking the "+" button.

You can duplicate any type of script to create another script of the same type. Duplicating a cast script *duplicates the entire cast member,* including its script.

Table 2-1: Creating Various Script Types

Script Type (Default Handler)	To Create or Edit
Cast Scripts (on mouseUp)	Select cast member, then: Click *Cast Member Script* button in Cast window or media editing window (Paint, Video, Text, Field). Click *Script* button in Cast Member Info window. Choose Modify➤Cast Member➤Script. Cmd-' (Mac) or Ctrl-' (Windows). Pop-up➤Cast Member Script (click on sprite in Score).[1]

Table 2-1: Creating Various Script Types (continued)

Script Type (Default Handler)	To Create or Edit
Sprite Scripts (on mouseUp)	Select sprite(s), then: Start typing. Click Script Preview Bar. Choose *New* from *Script* popup in Sprite Inspector or Sprite Toolbar. Choose Modify➤Sprite➤Script. Cmd-Shift-' (Mac) or Ctrl-Shift-' (Windows). Pop-up➤Script (click on sprite in Score).[1]
Frame Scripts (on exitFrame)	Select cell(s) in script channel, then: Start typing. Double-click in script channel. Click Script Preview Bar. Choose *New* from *Script* popup in Sprite Inspector or Sprite Toolbar. Choose Modify➤Frame➤Script. Pop-up➤Frame Script (click in Score effects channels).[1]
Behaviors (None)	Choose *New* from *Script* popup in Sprite Inspector or Sprite Toolbar. Choose *New Behavior* from the *Behavior* pop-up in the Behavior Inspector. See Chapter 12 and Table 2-2, *Script-Related Interface Commands*.
Movie Scripts (None)	Cmd-Shift-U (Mac) or Ctrl-Shift-U (Windows) opens lowest numbered movie script or creates a new one. Highlight empty cast member slot and press Cmd-0 (Mac) or Ctrl-0 (Windows). *new(#script)* creates a new movie script and returns its member number.
Parent Scripts (None)	Set script's type to *Parent* in Script Cast Member Info window or set *the scriptType of member* to #parent.
Primary Event Handlers (N/A)	Primary event handlers are handlers, not separate script cast members. Define them within movie scripts.

[1] A context-sensitive menu can be accessed using Ctrl-click (Mac) or right mouse click (Windows) in the specified window or specified area of the specified window.

Table 2-2 lists the many interface options that affect Lingo scripts. Refer to Chapter 3, *Lingo Coding and Debugging Tips*, for details on the commands under the `Control` menu related to debugging. Refer to Figure 12-1, for details on the Behavior Inspector window.

Table 2-2: Script-Related Interface Commands

Operation	Command
Open Script window	`Window`➤`Script`. Cmd-O (Mac) or `Ctrl-O` (Windows). Double-click script cast member.[1]
Create new scripts	Choose *New Script* from *Script* pop-up menu in Sprite Toolbar or Sprite Inspector. See Table 2-1.
Choose whether to edit script in Behavior Inspector or Script window by default[1]	`File`➤`Preferences`➤`Editors`➤`Behaviors`.
Change script's type to #movie, #score or #parent.	Script *Type* popup in cast member info window (see *the scriptType of member* property).
Open Message window	`Window`➤`Message`. Cmd-M (Mac) or `Ctrl-M` (Windows).
Show/Hide the toolbar in the Message window	`View`➤`Message Toolbar`.[2]
Show/Hide the toolbar in the Script window.	`View`➤`Script Toolbar`.[2]
Pop-up menu of most (but not all) Lingo commands	*Alphabetical* and *Categorized Lingo* buttons in Message window or Script window toolbars.
Show/Hide Sprite Inspector	`Window`➤`Inspectors`➤`Sprite`. "/" key on numeric keypad. Cmd-Opt-S (Mac) or `Ctrl-Alt-S` (Windows).
Show/Hide the Sprite toolbar in the Score window	`View`➤`Sprite Toolbar`.[2]
Apply existing Behaviors (sprite scripts of frame scripts) to sprite channels and the script channel	Select script from *Script* pop-up menu in Sprite Toolbar or Sprite Inspector. Drag Behaviors from Cast window to sprites in Score or on the Stage. Drag Behaviors from Cast window to script channel in Score.
Detach (clear) Behaviors from sprite channels and the script channel	Choose *Clear Script* from *Script* pop-up menu in Sprite Toolbar or Sprite Inspector. Detach individual Behaviors in Behavior Inspector by highlighting script and pressing delete.
Delete a movie script	Delete portions of the script in the Script window, or delete the entire movie script cast member.

Table 2-2: Script-Related Interface Commands (continued)

Operation	Command
Delete a cast script	Select and delete all the text (including white space) in the cast script window.
Change Score's display to show Behaviors and scripts attached to sprites	View➤Display. View➤Display➤Behavior. *Display* pop-up menu in Score.
Show/Hide Script Preview Bar	File➤Preferences➤Score➤Script Preview. Pop-up➤Script Preview[3] (at top of Score window). In Director 5 use the small a button at the far right edge of Score window.
Show/Hide Behavior Inspector	Window➤Inspectors➤Behavior. "*" key on numeric keypad. Cmd-Opt-; (Mac) or Ctrl-Alt-; (Windows). *Behavior Inspector* button in Sprite Toolbar or Sprite Inspector. Pop-up➤Behaviors[1] (click on sprite in Score or on Stage). Double-click script cast member.[1] Click green *Behavior* button shown using View➤Sprite Overlay➤Show Info.
Modify properties of a Behavior	Apply a Behavior as shown above. Click *Parameters* button in Behavior Inspector. Double-click Behavior in Behavior Inspector.
Open cast library of predefined Behaviors	Xtras➤Behavior Library.
Search for text in Script window	Edit➤Find➤Text. Cmd-F (Mac) or Ctrl-F (Windows).
Find where script selected in Cast window is used in Score	Edit➤Find➤Selection. Cmd-H (Mac) or Ctrl-H (Windows).
Locate handler matching highlighted word (locates handlers only in movie scripts)	Click *Go To Handler* button in Message window. Opt-click (Mac) or Alt-click (Windows) on handler name in Script or Message window.
Find a handler by name	Edit➤Find➤Handler. Cmd-Shift-; (Mac) or Ctrl-Shift-; (Windows). Pop-up➤Find Handler[3] (in Message window).
Find all movie script, score script, and parent script cast members, but not cast members with cast scripts attached[4]	Edit➤Find➤Cast Member➤Type➤*Behavior and Script*. Cmd-; (Mac) or Ctrl-; (Windows).

Table 2-2: Script-Related Interface Commands (continued)

Operation	Command
Recompile all scripts (see "*Compiling Scripts*")	`Control`➤`Recompile All Scripts`. `Cmd-Shift-Opt-C` **(Mac)**, `Alt-C-C` or `Ctrl-Shift-Alt-C` **(Windows)**.
Recompile scripts when you use the Message window	`File`➤`Preferences`➤`General`➤*Message Window Recompiles Scripts.*
Show icons for cast members with cast scripts in Cast window	`File`➤`Preferences`➤`Cast`➤*Show Cast Member Script Icons.*
Show icons for script cast members in Cast window	`File`➤`Preferences`➤`Cast`➤`Media Type Icons`➤*All Types.*
Disable all Lingo scripts	`Control`➤`Disable Scripts`.
Disable script channel's Lingo scripts	*Mute* button for script channel in Score window.
Use a movie file from an earlier version of Director	`Modify`➤`Movie`➤`Properties`➤*Allow Outdated Lingo* (settable only when upgrading from Director 4 movies).

[1] Double-clicking a script cast member opens either the Behavior Inspector or the Script window based on the `File`➤`Preferences`➤`Editors`➤`Behavior` setting.
[2] The Sprite Toolbar, Script Toolbar, and Message Toolbar can be toggled with `Cmd-Shift-H` (Mac) or `Ctrl-Shift-H` (Windows) when the appropriate window is active (Sprite Toolbar appears in Script window).
[3] A context-sensitive menu can be accessed using `Ctrl-click` (Mac) or right mouse click (Windows) in the specified window or specified area of the specified window.
[4] See Example 2-3 to find cast members with cast scripts attached.

Finding Cast Members

Using `Edit`➤`Find`➤`Cast`➤`Type`➤*Behavior and Script* finds all movie scripts, score scripts, and parent scripts but lumps them together and doesn't find cast members that have cast scripts attached.

Example 2-3 locates the cast members of the specified type: #movie, #score, #parent, or #cast. (Note that *#cast* is a symbol I've made up and not a built-in script type.)

Example 2-3: Locating Individual Script Types

```
on findScripts lookFor
  repeat with y = 1 to the number of castLibs
    repeat with x = 1 to the number of members of castLib y
      case (the type of member x) of
        #empty:
          nothing
        #script:
          if (the scriptType of member x) = lookFor then
            put "Member" && x && "is a" && lookFor && "script"
          end if
        otherwise:
          if lookFor = #cast then
```

Events, Scripts

Example 2-3: Locating Individual Script Types (continued)

```
            if the scriptText of member x <> EMPTY then
                put "Member" && x && "has a cast script"
            end if
        end if
    end case
  end repeat
 end repeat
end findScripts
```

You can find scripts of a particular type, like this:

```
findScripts #movie
findScripts #score
findScripts #parent
findScripts #cast
```

Compiling Scripts

There are four ways to recompile the *current* Lingo script:

- Close the Script window via the close box, or by pressing `Enter` on the keypad.
- Change a script's cast member's script type in its Info dialog box.
- Duplicate a Script, using `Edit`➤`Duplicate` (`Cmd-D` (Mac)or `Ctrl-D` (Windows)).
- Set a breakpoint by clicking in the Script window's left margin (unreliable).

There are three ways to recompile *only* the scripts that have changed since the last compilation:

- Use the Message window (assuming the *Message Window Recompiles Scripts* option is checked under `File`➤`Preferences`➤`General`).
- Play the movie (the period (.) on the keypad is the easiest shortcut).
- Save a movie, using *Save, Save As, Save and Compact*, or *Save All*.

There are three ways to force recompilation of *all* scripts, a process that may be time-consuming on large projects:

- Choose `Control`➤`Recompile All Scripts`.
- Use `Cmd-Shift-Opt-C` (Mac) or `Ctrl-Shift-Alt-C` or `Alt-C-C` (Windows).
- Use the *lightning bolt* button in Script window.

The following will *not* recompile scripts (convenient when you wish to ignore a syntax error):

- Typing text into a script or reformatting it with the `Tab` key.
- Closing the Script window if you previously canceled a compilation warning for the current script.
- Using the arrow buttons in the Script window to go to another script.
- Creating a new script in the Script window using the "+" button.

- Using the Message window if the *Message Window Recompiles Scripts* option under `File`►`Preferences`►`General` is inactive.

 Sometimes Director loses track of which scripts need to be recompiled. The compiled (*tokenized*) code that Director executes may *not* match the text you see in the Script window. This bug can make it very hard to figure out why your scripts are misbehaving.

Forcing Director to recompile all scripts will usually resynchronize the tokenized version of the script and fix the problem. Try recompiling all scripts several times, resaving your movie, and then restarting Director. If a Director file is permanently corrupted, copy the scripts and Score into a new movie. You may need to copy the text of each script (not the entire script cast member, but only the text within it) into new scripts in a new movie to repair severe corruption.

Primary Event Handlers

Director sends *mouseDown, mouseUp, timeOut, keyUp* and *keyDown,* and *alert* events to so-called *primary event handlers,* which get first crack at those events before they're sent elsewhere. (See also Chapters 3, 9, and 10 and Chapter 11, *Timers and Dates,* for details.

 Use *primary event handlers* to trap events before they are sent to 'tvsprites or to handle events on a movie-wide basis.

The primary event handlers are set via the system properties shown in Table 2-3.

Table 2-3: Primary Event Handlers

Primary Event Handler	Called When the Following Occur
the alertHook	Script errors and *alert* commands. See Chapter 3.
the keyDownScript	*KeyDown* events. See Chapter 10.
the keyUpScript	*KeyUp* events. See Chapter 10.
the mouseDownScript	*MouseDown* events, but not *rightMouseDown* events. See Chapter 9.
the mouseUpScript	*MouseUp* events, but not *rightMouseUp* events. See Chapter 9.
the timeOutScript	The *timeoutLapsed* exceeds the *timeoutLength*. See Chapter 11.

Define primary event handlers by setting the appropriate system property to a one-line Lingo command or handler name enclosed in quotes (except for *the alert-*

Hook described later). If you use a handler name, naturally you should define a matching handler in a *movie* script that will be called when the event occurs.

The following code calls the custom *checkKeyCommand* handler when a key is pressed, and the custom *myTimeoutHandler* handler when a timeout occurs.

Example 2-4: Primary Event Handlers

```
set the keyDownScript = "checkKeyCommand()"
set the timeOutScript = "myTimeoutHandler()"
```

Then in a movie script, you must define the handlers themselves:

```
on checkKeyCommand
  alert "The user pressed" && the key
end

on myTimeoutHandler
  alert "You took too long"
end
```

 Use a unique name for your primary event handlers. Do *not* assign the primary event handler properties to the name of the event itself, such as *mouseDown* or *mouseUp*.

The following is probably *wrong* because it would require you to create an *on mouseDown* handler in a movie script. Such a handler would then be called *both* as the primary event handler and again as a catch-all if the *mouseDown* event is not trapped elsewhere.

```
set the mouseDownScript = "mouseDown()"
```

Likewise, setting *the timeoutScript* to "*timeOut*" would cause an *on timeOut* handler in your movie script to probably be called *twice* instead of once.

You can disable all events of a particular type by setting the appropriate primary event handler to the Lingo command *dontPassEvent*, such as:

```
set the mouseDownScript = "dontPassEvent"
set the mouseUpScript   = "dontPassEvent"
```

To cancel a primary event handler (that is, to no longer intercept those events), assign it to the EMPTY string.

```
set the mouseDownScript = EMPTY
set the keyUpScript = ""
```

Primary event handlers can be reassigned on the fly. Note that there are no primary event handlers for the *rightMouseUp* and *rightMouseDown* events.

Primary event handlers are unique to each movie and are reset to EMPTY when the authoring environment is halted. Set them as needed in each movie's *prepareMovie* handler (or the *startMovie* handler in D5).

Intercepting Errors and Messages

The AlertHook

The alertHook is a new feature in Director 6, similar to a primary event handler, used to intercept any error messages. Instead of posting an alert box when an error occurs or when you call Lingo's *alert* command, Director will call your *alert-Hook* handler. Refer to Chapter 3 for more details.

Intercepting Built-In Lingo

Any built-in Lingo command can be replaced by a custom handler of the same name. For example, if you want the *put* command to display an alert box instead of writing to the Message window, you can define an *on put* handler in a movie script.

Example 2-5: Intercepting Built-In Lingo Commands

```
on put msgText
  alert msgText
end
```

In most cases, such scripts should be used only for debugging purposes.

 If you create a handler that inadvertently has the same name as a Lingo command, your handler will prevent the real Lingo command from executing. See Table 18-1, *Lingo Command and Keyword Summary*, for a list of Lingo keywords to avoid using as handler names.

For example, if you have an *on startTimer* handler, using the Lingo command *startTimer* will call your handler rather than actually resetting *the timer* property.

You can't augment or customize a Lingo command by creating a custom handler that then calls the Lingo command you've replaced. The following *on put* handler that itself calls *put* is a very bad idea. Save your work before attempting to test it.

```
on put msgText
  put "This is my custom handler"
  put msgText
end
```

The above code will cause an infinite loop and most likely crash Director. (See *"Recursion"* in Chapter 1). See Example 3-4, *Overriding Built-in Lingo Functions* for related coding suggestions.

Handler Scope

Table 2-4 summarizes the *scope* of handlers stored in each type of script. A handler's scope determines from where it is accessible (that is, where it can be "seen"). See *"Special Treatment of the First Argument Passed"* in Chapter 1 and

"Custom Messages and Simulated Events" later in this chapter for details on explicitly sending messages to a particular script.

Table 2-4: Handler Scope

Handlers in	Can Be Called From
Cast script, sprite script, or sprite Behavior	Any other handler within the same script or by Director when the user interacts with the sprite with which it is associated.
Frame script or frame Behavior	Any other handler within the same script or by Director when the playback head is in the frame with which it is associated.
Parent script	Any handler within the same script or by any outside script passing in a valid *script instance* (child object ID). See Chapter 12.
Ancestor script	Any handler within the same script or by any child object declaring it as its ancestor. Chapter 12.
Movie script	Any handler anywhere in the same movie, or by Director if no other scripts intercept the event, or from the Message window.
Movie script in external cast	Any handler in any movie that links to that cast library. It can only be called from the Message window if the external castLib is *linked* to the currently open movie.[1]
Xtras	Can be called from any script, although it sometimes requires a valid instance of the Xtra be created first. See Chapter 13, *Lingo Xtras and XObjects*.
Built-in Lingo commands and functions	Any handler anywhere in any movie, or from the Message window. Some so-called built-in commands actually require Xtras. See Chapter 13.

[1] If you've opened a castLib using File➤Open➤Cast or using the Xtras menu, you can't call its scripts from the Message window unless you first link the castLib to the current movie using Modify➤Movie➤Casts or using Lingo's *filename of castlib* property.

Script-Related Lingo

Table 2-5 lists the script-related Lingo commands. Refer to Table 1-1 in Chapter 1 for details on Lingo specifically related to variables. See *"Dynamic Script Creation"* in the same chapter for details on creating Lingo on the fly at runtime. Refer to Chapter 3 for details on the *put, trace,* and *traceLogFile* commands. Refer to Table 2-14 for details on the *call, callAncestor, sendSprite,* and *sendAllSprites* commands.

Table 2-5: Script-Related Lingo

Command	Usage
the actorList	List of objects to receive *stepFrame* messages. See Chapter 6, *Lists*, and Chapter 12.
ancestor	Set the ancestor script of a Behavior or Parent script. See Chapter 12.
do *string*	Compiles and executes a string as if it were a Lingo command.

Table 2-5: Script-Related Lingo (continued)

Command	Usage
new()	Instantiates a parent script such as `set myChild = new (script "SomeParent")`
the frameScript	Determines the member number of the script in the script channel of the current frame.
put *variable*	Displays a variable's value in the Message window.
script "*ScriptName*"	Identifies a script; used within the *new()* function.
the script of member *whichMember*	Returns the script name of the specified member.[1]
the script of menuItem *n*	Determines action taken when a menu item is chosen from a custom menu. See Chapter 14, *Graphical User Interface Components,* in *Director in a Nutshell.*
the scriptsEnabled of member *movieMember*	Determines whether scripts are active for a #movie cast member.
the scriptInstanceList of sprite *whichSprite*	A list of script instances attached to a sprite.[2] See Chapter 12.
the scriptNum of sprite *whichSprite*	Determines the member number of the first sprite script attached to a sprite. Returns 0 if no scripts are attached or if only a cast script is used.[2]
the scriptText of member	Determines the text of the script of a script cast member, or the cast script attached to other cast members. Always returns EMPTY in a Projector.
the scriptType of member *whichMember*	Tests or sets the type of a script cast member (#score, #movie, or #parent). Corresponds to *Type* option in Script Cast Member Info dialog box.
the trace	Displays executing Lingo in Message window.
the traceLogFile	Records Message window output to text file.
the type of member *whichMember*	Returns #script for standalone script cast members, but returns asset type(such as #bitmap) of other cast members even if they have cast scripts attached.
value()	Evaluates a string, as if it were a Lingo expression.

[1] *The script of member* property is undocumented and unsupported. It works for script cast members, and for non-script cast members that have an attached cast script. It causes errors for non-script cast members lacking a cast script.
[2] See *"Script Instances"* later in this chapter.

Script Instances

In Director 6, Behavior scripts (that is, score scripts used as frame scripts and sprite scripts) are *instanced* or *instantiated,* meaning that Director creates a copy of the script each time it is encountered. Each instance can have its own properties. Because sprites can have multiple Behaviors attached, D6 has a new *scriptInstanceList of sprite* property that includes all the script instances for a given sprite. You can check *the scriptInstanceList of sprite* only during the sprite's lifetime while the movie is playing (when the movie is stopped *the scriptInstanceList* is an empty list). The *scriptInstanceList* returns a list of *script instances, not* a list of script cast member numbers. It does not include the cast script, if any, because cast scripts are never instanced.

The older *scriptNum of sprite* property returns only the first sprite script's member number, and it does not indicate if multiple scripts are attached. There is supported Lingo to get a list of all score script cast members attached to a sprite, nor can you set them during a Score Recording session. (See the unsupported UI Helper Xtra's getBehaviorMemRef() and getBehaviorInitial.zeus() methods described in Chapter 17, *Changed, Undocumented, and Misdocumented Lingo.*) You can use the Behavior Inspector to see the multiple attached scripts. At runtime you can use *the scriptInstanceList* to send messages to any instance, and you can even add to *the scriptInstanceList* dynamically.

To Me or Not To Me

Lingo uses the *me* parameter to identify the object receiving an event. *Me* is the script instance of the current script, and it is passed as the first parameter to the handler being called, as follows:

```
on mouseUp me
  put "My script instance is" && me
end
```

The *me* parameter is sent to sprite scripts and frame scripts receiving an event (because they are instantiated), but not to cast scripts or movie scripts. For example:

- When a *cuePassed* event is generated, the *on cuePassed* event handler receives *me* as the first parameter to frame scripts and sprite scripts, but not to movie scripts and cast scripts
- Behaviors receive *me* when used as a sprite script or frame script, where *me* is a script instance reference.
- Parent scripts receive *me* for all method calls, where *me* is the child object. Refer to Chapter 12.

In most cases, you use *me* to access properties of an object. When used with parent scripts and child objects, *me* is used as follows:

```
put the propertyName of me
```

When used with Behaviors, the only property associated with the script instance (*me*) by default is *the spriteNum,* which indicates the sprite's channel, and can be used to access other sprite properties.

Example 2-6: Using the Me Script Instance Variable

```
on beginSprite me
  set the foreColor of sprite (the spriteNum of me) = random (255)
end
```

The value of *me*, as sent to a sprite script, must by definition be one of the items in *the scriptInstanceList*. You can determine the "stacking order" of a Behavior (that is, whether it is the first sprite script attached to a sprite).

Example 2-7: Determining the Stacking Order of a Behavior

```
on beginSprite me
  -- Determine whether we are the first attached Behavior
  set myInstanceNum = getPos (the scriptInstanceList of ¬
    sprite the spriteNum of me, me)
  set totalCount = count(the scriptInstanceList of ¬
    sprite the spriteNum of me)
  put "The behavior is number" && myInstanceNum && ¬
    "of" && totalCount && "attached to this sprite"
end
```

The scriptInstanceList is empty when a sprite's *new()* handler is called, but it is *populated* (filled) with *all* attached sprite instances by the time the its *first begin-Sprite()* handler is called. Thus, the above handler can count all the instances, even if it is the first instance itself.

The scriptInstanceList is a *sprite* property, so it does not apply to frame scripts. There can be only one frame script attached to a frame, and its script instance is indicated by *me*.

Determining the Current Sprite's Number

In Chapter 1, we discussed generalizing a handler to make it flexible rather than hardcoding fixed sprite numbers. *The spriteNum of me* and *the currentSpriteNum* both indicate the sprite channel number (from 1 to 120) to which the script is currently attached.

These properties were added in Director 6 because sprites receive many new events (*beginSprite, endSprite, mouseEnter, mouseLeave, mouseWithin*, and so on) that do *not* require mouse clicks (limiting the usefulness of the older *the clickOn* property).

Here *the currentSpriteNum* is used to determine a sprite's own location. If it is later sent a *resetMe* message, the sprite's original location will be restored.

Example 2-8: Determining a Sprite's Number from Within an Attached Behavior

```
property pOrigLoc

on beginSprite me
  -- Store my sprite's original position
  set pOrigLoc = the loc of sprite (the currentSpriteNum)
end

on resetMe me
  -- Reset me position to its original location
  set the loc of sprite (the currentSpriteNum) = pOrigLoc
end
```

In Director 6, mouse handlers in sprite scripts receive *me*, which indicates the current *script instance* (occurrence of the script).

 Don't forget to declare *me* as the first parameter to your handler. It is required when using *the spriteNum of me*. See *"Special Treatment of the First Argument Passed"* in Chapter 1 for details on how to pass *me* to other handlers *outside* the Behavior.

Example 2-9: The SpriteNum of me Property

```
on mouseUp me
  put "My sprite is" && the spriteNum of me
end
```

One alternative is to explicitly declare the property *spriteNum* at the top of your Behavior and access the property as *spriteNum*, rather than *the spriteNum of me*.

```
property spriteNum
on mouseUp me
  put "My sprite is" && spriteNum
end
```

In cast scripts *the currentSpriteNum* returns the same sprite number as it does for sprite scripts, but it returns 0 from within both frame scripts and movie scripts.

Within frame scripts *the spriteNum of me* returns -5. In movie scripts and cast scripts you can't use it because the scripts are not instantiated (*me* is void).

Refer to *"Determining Which Sprite Was Clicked"* and *"Determining Which Sprite Was Rolled Over"* in Chapter 9 for details on using *the clickOn* property and *rollOver()* function from frame scripts and movie scripts.

Trapping Events with Scripts

Each Director event is usually sent to the scripts in the following order, but there are a lot of exceptions, as noted below:

1. Primary event handler(s)
2. Sprite Behavior(s) and cast script(s)
3. Frame script of current frame
4. Movie scripts

 Director 6 added many new events that are *broadcast* to both sprite scripts and the frame script in the current frame. Sprite scripts can prevent events from reaching cast scripts, and frame scripts can prevent events from reaching movie scripts.

Score events (such as *exitFrame*) are *broadcast* to all sprites and the frame script. Sprite events (such a *beginSprite*) are sent to whatever sprite span(s) or frame script span begins or ends in a frame. Mouse events (such as *mouseUp*) are generally sent to only one sprite at a time and only passed the frame scripts if not trapped by a sprite.

Let's examine what happens in detail at each of these levels:

Primary Event Handler

If a primary event handler is defined, it receives the event first. By default, it passes the message onto other scripts rather than consuming it.

Sprite Behaviors (Sprite Scripts) and Cast Scripts

Many sprites have no scripts attached, and some have multiple scripts attached. Even sprites with scripts may ignore most events, trapping only those of interest. Refer to Chapter 9 for many more details on how sprites trap mouse events. For this discussion, you need only understand that mouse events are sent only to the first sprite that traps them.

If the *member of sprite* property is changed, the *cast script* (if any) changes along with it. *Sprite scripts* are unaffected by changing *the member of sprite* property, which is why I prefer them over cast scripts.

Sprites handle events in the following order:

Behaviors receive the events in the order in which they are attached to the sprite. (See Example 2-8, *Determining a Sprite's Number from Within an Attached Behavior*).

Cast script receives events *after* sprite scripts.

If the sprite ignores an event, it is passed onto any sprites underneath it that appear in lower-numbered sprite channels in the Score.

If you move playback head during a *mouseDown* handler (with a *go frame* command), the *mouseUp* event will occur in the destination frame, perhaps over a different sprite.

Frame Script

A frame script (that is, a Behavior) attached to the current frame's script channel receives frame-related events (*exitFrame*, etc.) in all cases and also any mouse-related events (*mouseUp*, etc.) that are not trapped by any sprites. See *"Leaving the Current Handler"* in Chapter 1 for important details on how the *go frame* and *play frame* commands affect the order of execution when jumping between various frames.

Movie Scripts

Movie scripts receive certain movie-based events (*prepareMovie, startMovie, stopMovie,* etc.) and also any mouse events not trapped by sprite scripts, cast scripts, or frame scripts and frame events not trapped by frame scripts. You can have a virtually unlimited number of movie scripts residing in different castLibs. Movie scripts are checked for the handler of interest, starting with the lowest-numbered movie script cast member in the lowest-numbered cast library, until the event is trapped.

Never use the same handler name in more than one *movie* script. Only the first one will ever be called.

You can check whether a handler of the same name already exists in a movie script, by Option–clicking (Macintosh) or Alt-clicking (Windows) the name of your handler in the Script window or Message window. This does not search score scripts or cast scripts, nor does it reveal if there are multiple handlers of the given name. Use Edit➤Find➤Text or Edit➤Find➤Handler to perform a more thorough search.

Movie and Window Events

The events in Table 2-6 are generated automatically when a Projector starts up, when a movie starts or stops, or when MIAWs change state. These events are sent only to movie scripts. Refer to Chapter 6, *The Stage and Movies-in-a-Window,* in *Director in a Nutshell* for details on window events. See Table 2-7 and Table 2-11 for mouse-related, frame-related, and sprite-related events, some of which are sent to movie scripts.

The *prepareMovie, startMovie,* and *stopMovie* handlers for each movie in a multimovie project are often called more than once.

The aforementioned movie event handlers are called when using *go movie* or *play movie* to start a new movie, or *quit* (but not *halt*). They are even called if you go to the current movie using

```
go movie the movieName
```

Use a global variable to track whether initialization has been performed already and prevent reinitialization every time the movie starts, as shown in Example 1-16, *One-Time Initialization.*

Table 2-6: Messages Sent to Movies and MIAWs

Message	Sent When	Stage	MIAW	Shock-wave
startUp[1]	To external LINGO.INI file only when the Projector starts.			
prepareMovie[2]	Sent to new movie when starting, *before* first frame is drawn.	•	•	•[3]
startMovie	Sent to new movie when starting, *after* first frame is drawn.	•	•	•[3]
stopMovie	Sent when a movie ends or stops.	•		•[4]
closeWindow[5] openWindow	MIAW's window (or Stage window) opens or closes.	•	•[5]	
activateWindow[6] deactivateWindow[5,6] moveWindow resizeWindow zoomWindow	MIAW's window becomes the active window, loses focus, or is moved, resized, or zoomed.		•	

[1] There is no *shutDown* event. Provide a *Quit* button that runs any clean-up routine before exiting the Projector. See Chapter 10 for details on preventing the user from aborting the Projector via keyboard shortcuts.
[2] *PrepareMovie* is new in Director 6. The *updateStage* and *go* commands are disabled when called from an *on prepareMovie* handler (and also from *prepareFrame, beginSprite, endSprite,* and *stepFrame* handlers).
[3] *PrepareMovie* and *startMovie* are sent when a Shockwave movie starts or the Browser sends the *Play()* command from JavaScript.
[4] *StopMovie* is sent when a Shockwave movie stops, the user leaves the HTML page, or the Browser sends the *Stop()* command from JavaScript.
[5] The *closeWindow* event is sent to a MIAW if the *close window* command is used or the user clicks the window's close box. It is not sent when the *forget window* command is used. The *deactivateWindow* event is sent when the *forget window* command is used, but only if the window is open and visible at the time.
[6] The *activateWindow* and *deactivateWindow* events are not sent under Windows when a MIAW loses or gains focus due to another application. These events are generated by and for Director-owned windows only.

Movie Event Order

Example 2-10 shows the events generated when the main movie launches (and eventually dismisses) a MIAW. It also shows the events generated when using the *play movie* command to play a new movie on the Stage and using *play done* to return to the original movie (the same events are generated when using *go movie*). Only the movie-related events are shown. See *"Event Processing Order"* later in this chapter for more details on other Director events.

Note in Example 2-10 that when a MIAW is launched, the Stage does not receive *prepareMovie, startMovie,* or *stopMovie* events, but the MIAW receives *prepareMovie* and *startMovie* events. The Stage and the MIAW alternately process events while they both run. When the MIAW is dismissed, the Stage is not notified. (Check *the windowList* to determine if there are open MIAWs.)

When a new movie replaces the original movie on the Stage, and vice versa, both movies receive appropriate *stopMovie, prepareMovie,* and *startMovie* events. The movies do not run simultaneously.

In Example 2-10, the entity processing the event (STAGE, MIAW, NEWMOVIE) is shown at each step.

Example 2-10: Sequence of Movie-Related Events

The startUp event sent only if you have an external LINGO.INI file.
LINGO.INI *startUp*
STAGE *prepareMovie*
STAGE *startMovie*
Now click a Sprite button that opens a MIAW. The main movie is still running.
STAGE *mouseUp-->open window "MIAW"*
    MIAW *openWindow*
    MIAW *prepareMovie*
    MIAW *startMovie*
    MIAW *activateWindow*
Both the MIAW and the Stage process interspersed enterFrame, idle, and exitFrame events in succession.
STAGE *idle*
STAGE *exitFrame*
STAGE *prepareFrame*
STAGE *enterFrame*
    MIAW *idle*
STAGE *idle*
    MIAW *idle*
STAGE *idle*
    MIAW *idle*
    MIAW *exitFrame*
    MIAW *prepareFrame*
    MIAW *enterFrame*
The MIAW may receive resizeWindow, moveWindow, zoomWindow, and closeWindow events based on the user's actions.
    MIAW resizeWindow
Using forget window only calls deactivateWindow if the window was open and visible. Click a sprite button that forgets the MIAW.
STAGE *mouseUp-->forget window "MIAW"*
    MIAW *deactivateWindow*
The MIAW is closed. Now let's play another movie on stage.
STAGE *mouseUp-->play movie "NEW MOVIE"*
STAGE *stopMovie*
The original movie has stopped.
    NEW MOVIE *prepareMovie*
    NEW MOVIE *startMovie*
  NEW MOVIE receives miscellaneous events while it plays
Let's return to the original movie.
    NEW MOVIE *mouseUp-->play done*
    NEW MOVIE *stopMovie*
The original movie will now be restarted.
STAGE *prepareMovie*
STAGE *startMovie*

Example 2-10: Sequence of Movie-Related Events (continued)

Quitting or stopping the main movie calls stopMovie.
STAGE *mouseUp-->quit*
STAGE *stopMovie*

Mouse, Keyboard, and TimeOut Events

Whenever the user clicks or moves the mouse or presses a key, Director generates an event. It also generates *timeOut* events if the period of user inaction
exceeds *the timeoutLapsed* property (see Chapter 11).

Mouse and keyboard events are processed between the *enterFrame* and *exit-
Frame* events. If a mouse event causes the playback head to leave the current
frame, the *exitFrame* handler in the frame script will not be called, but the
endSprite handler will be called (assuming that the jump is to a frame outside the
span of the current frame script). Likewise, the sprite's *endSprite* handler will be
called if the jump puts the playback head outside the sprite's span. Therefore, it is
best to perform any cleanup in the *endSprite* handler attached to either the sprite
or the script channel.

Mouse and keyboard events travel through the scripts as shown from left to right
in Table 2-7. The table also indicates whether an event is passed by default or
consumed by the specified script (although this can be overridden). A script
consumes an event only if it has an appropriate event handler defined. If not
consumed, the event passes onto the next script to the right in the table. Refer to
the *"Mouse-Opaque Sprites"* and *"Cursor-Opaque Sprites"* sections of Chapter 9 and
to Chapter 10 for important details of how Director handles mouse clicks and rollovers when sprites overlap, plus a list of mouse and keyboard system properties.

See Table 2-8 through Table 2-11 for frame-related and sprite-related events, many
of which are trapped by sprites in addition to those events shown below.

Table 2-7: Mouse and Keyboard Events

Event/Message	Primary Event Handler	Sprite Script	Cast Script	Frame Script	Movie Script
mouseDown mouseUp[1]	Pass	Consume	Consume	Consume	Consume
rightMouseDown rightMouseUp		Consume	Consume	Consume	Consume
mouseEnter[2] mouseLeave[2] mouseUpOutside[2] mouseWithin[2]		Consume	Consume		
buttonClicked[2]		Consume	Consume		

Table 2-7: Mouse and Keyboard Events (continued)

Event/Message	Primary Event Handler	Sprite Script	Cast Script	Frame Script	Movie Script
keyDown[3] keyUp[3]	Pass	Consume	Consume	Consume	Consume
timeOut	Pass			Consume	Consume

[1] Editable text fields only trap *mouseUp* events when they do not have focus. Once a field gains focus, *mouseUp* events are passed straight to the frame script (this is a bug).
[2] These events are new in Director 6. See Chapter 9.
[3] *KeyUp* and *KeyDown* events are sent only to the scripts of *editable* field sprites and possibly frame and movie scripts. If these events are trapped, use the *pass* command to send the keystrokes to the field sprite on stage.

Frame and Sprite Events in the Score

Director generates frame-related events as the playback head progresses through the Score and generates additional sprite events whenever a sprite span (or a frame script span in the script channel) begins or ends. The events are shown in Table 2-8 and Table 2-9 in the order in which they are typically generated.

All frame-related events are sent repeatedly while looping in a frame. The *prepareFrame, enterFrame,* and *exitFrame* handlers are broadcast to all sprites in Director 6. Even if handled by one or more sprites, the messages are still sent to the frame script and possibly the movie script.

The Director 6 CD includes a utility that removes any frame-related handlers attached to *sprites* from Director 5 movies being upgraded to D6. See *"Unexpected Handler Evaluation"* in the D6 *ReadMe* file and see *Director 6 CD/Goodies/Movies/ Cleaner/Clean.DIR* for the utility itself.

Table 2-8: Frame-Related Events

Message	Sent When
stepFrame	Broadcast to all members of *the actorList* when the playback head is about to leave a frame or loop in a frame.
prepareFrame[1]	Broadcast to frame script and all sprite scripts *before* next frame is drawn.
stepMovie	*StepMovie* has been obsolete since D4 and is no longer recognized. Use *enterFrame* instead.
(frame redraw)	Director does not issue an event when the frame is drawn, but it is drawn after the *prepareFrame* event and before the *enterFrame* event.
enterFrame[1]	Broadcast to frame script and all sprite scripts *after* frame is drawn, including any palette or transition effect, but before Tempo channel settings such as *Wait for Sound* are obeyed.

Table 2-8: Frame-Related Events (continued)

Message	Sent When
idle	At least one *idle* event is sent per frame, and possibly many more, while the time allocated to a frame (as determined by the tempo) has not yet elapsed. See *the idleHandlerPeriod*.
exitFrame[1]	Broadcast to frame script and all sprite scripts *after* any Tempo channel delays are obeyed.

[1] Broadcast separately to all sprites, plus the frame script in the script channel. PrepareFrame is new in D6. EnterFrame and exitFrame are sent to sprites for the first time in D6.

Table 2-9 shows sprite-related events. These are triggered by a sprite beginning or ending in the Score or sprites with cue points being played. Refer to the earlier section, *"Mouse and Keyboard Events,"* for more events that are also sent to sprites but are triggered by user actions.

Table 2-9: Sprite-Related Events

Message	Sent When
new	Sent to any new sprite spans (or to a new frame script span) starting in the next frame *before beginSprite* and before the frame is drawn. *Not* sent when looping back to the beginning of a sprite or frame script span (only sent when first entered).
beginSprite	Sent immediately after the *new* event to the same entities, as shown above. Sent *before* the sprite is actually drawn on stage.
endSprite	Sent to any ending sprite spans (or to an ending frame script span). *Not* sent when the end of a span is reached if the playback head loops back to any part of the span, but it *is* sent when leaving a sprite at any point along its span to go to another frame outside the span.
cuePassed	Sent when a cue point in a digital video, audio, or Shockwave audio sprite is reached. See Chapter 15, *Sound and Cue Points*, in *Director in a Nutshell*.

Miscellaneous Events

The miscellaneous events shown in Table 2-10 occur at unpredictable times. See *"The AlertHook"* earlier in this chapter and Chapter 3 for details on *the alertHook*. property. See Chapter 11, *Shockwave and the Internet*, in *Director in a Nutshell* for details on the *streamStatus* and *EvalScript* events, and the *externalEvent* command.

Table 2-10: Miscellaneous Events

Message	Sent When
alertHook	If *the alertHook* property is set, the *alertHook* event is sent when an error that would otherwise bring up an alert dialog occurs or if the *alert* command is called.
streamStatus	Sent at indeterminate intervals during streaming playback of Internet content if *the tellStreamStatus* is TRUE.

Table 2-10: Miscellaneous Events (continued)

Message	Sent When
EvalScript	Evaluates a message sent *from* a browser to a Shockwave movie.
externalEvent	The *externalEvent* command sends a message from a Shockwave movie *to* the browser. See *"Custom Messages and Simulated Events"* later in this chapter.

Where Events Are Sent

Table 2-11 shows the events discussed in Table 2-8 through Table 2-10, plus the *getBehaviorDescription, getPropertyDescriptionList,* and *runPropertyDialog* events discussed in Chapter 12. See Table 2-6, which lists events generated when movies or windows open and close. Also see Table 2-7, which lists events generated by user actions (mouse or keyboard events) or inaction (timeout events).

Table 2-11: Events Generated by Frames and Sprites

Event/Message Type	Sprite Script	Cast Script	Frame Script	Movie Script
prepareFrame[1,2]	•	•	•	•
enterFrame exitFrame	•[1]	•[1]	•	•
stepFrame[2]	Maybe[3]	Maybe[3]	Maybe[3]	Maybe[3]
new[1]	•		•	
beginSprite[1,2] endSprite[1,2]	•		•	
idle			•	•
getBehaviorDescription[1] getPropertyDescriptionList[1] runPropertyDialog[1]	•[4]		•[4]	
cuePassed[1]	•	•	•	•
alertHook[1]	Maybe[5]	Maybe[5]	Maybe[5]	Maybe[5]
streamStatus[1]				Maybe[6]
EvalScript[1]				•
externalEvent[1,7]				

[1] New in Director 6.
[2] The *updateStage* and *go* commands are disabled when called from *stepFrame, prepareFrame, beginSprite,* and *endSprite* handlers (and *prepareMovie* handlers, too). Place *updateStage* and *go* commands in *exitFrame* handlers instead.
[3] Sent only if item is in *the actorList.* See *"The ActorList"* later in this chapter.
[4] The *getBehaviorDescription, getPropertyDescriptionList,* and *runPropertyDialog* events are completely unlike standard Director events. They *are* sent when the movie is *not* playing, but they are *not* sent when the movie *is* playing.

5 The *alertHook* property can point to a script of any type, but the message is not passed among scripts. The value returned by the handler determines whether the message is consumed or generates an alert dialog box.
6 The *on streamStatus* event handler is called only if *tellStreamStatus* is TRUE.
7 The *externalEvent* command is used to *send* an event from any type of script to the browser.

Message Processing Order

Director generates many events continually. (This is one reason it is hard to follow the output of the *trace* command in the Message window—there's too much of it.) Some events are sent every frame, whereas others are sent only at startup or when encountering a new sprite in the Score.

Figure 2-2 shows the Score for my *Event Test* movie that is used in Example 2-11. (This movie is available from the download site cited in the *Preface.*)

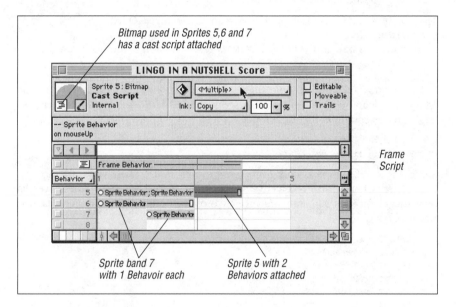

Figure 2-2: Event Test Movie

In Figure 2-2, note the frames in which each sprite begins or end. The frame script and the sprite in channel 5 both span all three frames of the Score (and sprite 5 has two Behaviors attached). The sprite in channel 6 begins in frame 1, ends in frame 2, and has one Behavior attached. The sprite in channel 7 begins and ends in frame 2 and also has one Behavior attached. All sprites also have cast scripts attached to their cast members.

Example 2-11 shows the event sequence generated by the three-frame movie shown in Figure 2-2. You will often ignore the majority of events, but Director sends events in a non-intuitive order that you should understand. Remember that the Stage is drawn between the *prepareFrame* and *enterFrame* events, as indicated in Example 2-11.

The number and order of *idle* events depend on *the frameTempo* (set to 30 fps in this example) and *the idleHandlerPeriod* (defaults to 0). In the example there is only one *idle* event per frame. (That is 30 *idles* per second, so keep your idle handlers slim!) If *the frameTempo* is set to 1 fps and *the idleHandlerPeriod* is set to 20 ticks (one-third of a second), there would be three *idle* events per frame (that is, three *idles* per second). In that case, the *idle* events would occur before the *exitFrame* events, rather than after them.

In Example 2-11 all events have been manually *pass'*ed so that they are received by all entities that can trap them. All items of interest have been added to *the actorList* so that they receive *stepFrame* messages. The current frame number (*the frame*) is shown in parentheses at the end of each line.

Example 2-11: Message Processing Order

The *startUp* event is sent only if you have an external LINGO.INI file:
LINGO.INI: *startUp*
PrepareMovie is new in D6. Note that *startMovie* is no longer the first event:
MOVIE script: *prepareMovie* (1)

Frame scripts can span multiple frames and receive *new* and *beginSprite* events when their span begins or ends in the script channel (*unrelated* to sprite channels beginning or ending in the same frame):

    FRAME script: *new* (1)
    FRAME script: *beginSprite* (1)

Sprites now receive *new* and *beginSprite* events in D6. Behaviors are not yet instantiated when sprites receive *new* events, but each script attached receives its own *new* event (that is, sprite 5 receives two of each event—one for each attached Behavior):

    SPRITE 5: *new* (1)
    SPRITE 5: *new* (1)
    BEHAVIOR 1 of SPRITE 5: *beginSprite* (1)
    BEHAVIOR 2 of SPRITE 5: *beginSprite* (1)
    SPRITE 6: *new* (1)
    BEHAVIOR 1 of SPRITE 6: *beginSprite* (1)

Items in *the actorList* receive *stepFrame* messages:

    MOVIE script: *stepFrame* (1)
    FRAME script: *stepFrame* (1)
    BEHAVIOR 1 of SPRITE 5: *stepFrame* (1)
    BEHAVIOR 2 of SPRITE 5: *stepFrame* (1)
    BEHAVIOR 1 of SPRITE 6: *stepFrame* (1)

PrepareFrame is new in D6 and is broadcast to all sprites and the frame script. It occurs *before* each frame is drawn:

    BEHAVIOR 1 of SPRITE 5: *prepareFrame* (1)
    BEHAVIOR 2 of SPRITE 5: *prepareFrame* (1)
    CAST script of SPRITE 5: *prepareFrame* (1)
    BEHAVIOR 1 of SPRITE 6: *prepareFrame* (1)
    CAST script of SPRITE 6: *prepareFrame* (1)
    FRAME script: *prepareFrame* (1)
    MOVIE script: *prepareFrame* (1)

Frame 1 is drawn here. *StartMovie* was the first event in D5. In D6, use *prepare-Movie* for initialization instead:

```
MOVIE script: startMovie (1)
```

The *enterFrame* event is now sent to sprites, as well as frames, in D6:

```
BEHAVIOR 1   of SPRITE 5: enterFrame (1)
BEHAVIOR 2   of SPRITE 5: enterFrame (1)
CAST script of SPRITE 5: enterFrame (1)
BEHAVIOR 1   of SPRITE 6: enterFrame (1)
CAST script of SPRITE 6: enterFrame (1)
FRAME script: enterFrame (1)
MOVIE script: enterFrame (1)
```

The frequency and position of idle events depends on the frame rate and *the idleHandlerPeriod*. There is at least on idle per frame, perhaps more.

```
FRAME script: idle (1)
MOVIE script: idle (1)
```

The *exitFrame* event is now sent to sprites, as well as frames, in D6:

```
BEHAVIOR 1   of SPRITE 5: exitFrame (1)
BEHAVIOR 2   of SPRITE 5: exitFrame (1)
CAST script of SPRITE 5: exitFrame (1)
BEHAVIOR 1   of SPRITE 6: exitFrame (1)
CAST script of SPRITE 6: exitFrame (1)

FRAME script: exitFrame (1)
MOVIE script: exitFrame (1)
```

Frame 1 is still visible on the Stage, but *the frame* property returns 2 as Director begins to process events for frame 2:

```
MOVIE script: stepFrame (2)
FRAME script: stepFrame (2)
<stepFrame events sent to other actorList items as above (2)>
```

Sprite 7 begins in this frame and receives *new* and *beginSprite* events, plus the *prepareFrame* event along with other sprites:

```
SPRITE 7: new (2)
BEHAVIOR 1 of SPRITE 7: beginSprite (2)

BEHAVIOR 1   of SPRITE 5: prepareFrame (2)
BEHAVIOR 2   of SPRITE 5: prepareFrame (2)
CAST script of SPRITE 5: prepareFrame (2)
BEHAVIOR 1   of SPRITE 6: prepareFrame (2)
CAST script of SPRITE 6: prepareFrame (2)
BEHAVIOR 1   of SPRITE 7: prepareFrame (2)
FRAME script: prepareFrame (2)
MOVIE script: prepareFrame (2)
```

Frame 2 is drawn on the Stage. Transition and palette changes in frame 2 take effect as the frame is drawn. No events are sent while the frame is drawn.

```
<enterFrame and idle events sent as above (2)>
```

All items receive *exitFrame* events, including those sprites that are about to end:

```
BEHAVIOR 1  of SPRITE 5:  exitFrame (2)
BEHAVIOR 2  of SPRITE 5:  exitFrame (2)
CAST script of SPRITE 5:  exitFrame (2)
BEHAVIOR 1  of SPRITE 6:  exitFrame (2)
CAST script of SPRITE 6:  exitFrame (2)
BEHAVIOR 1  of SPRITE 7:  exitFrame (2)
FRAME script:  exitFrame (2)
MOVIE script:  exitFrame (2)
```

The *endSprite* event is sent to sprites 6 and 7, which end in this frame, but it is not sent to the frame script, which still has not ended:

```
BEHAVIOR 1 of SPRITE 6:  endSprite (2)
BEHAVIOR 1 of SPRITE 7:  endSprite (2)
```

Frame 2 is still visible on the Stage, but *the frame* property returns 3 as we begin to process events for the next frame:

<stepFrame and prepareFrame events sent as above (3)>

Frame 3 is drawn on the Stage. Transition and palette changes in frame 3 take effect as the frame is drawn. No events are sent while the frame is drawn:

<enterFrame, idle and exitFrame events sent as above (3)>

We're are now in the clean-up phase. In the last frame of a non-looped one-frame movie (that doesn't use *go the frame*), an extra *prepareFrame* event (not shown) is sent as if to prepare the next frame (*the frame* property still returns 3). In the last frame of all non-looped movies, another *enterFrame* event (shown here) is sent too.

```
BEHAVIOR 1  of SPRITE 5:  enterFrame (3)
BEHAVIOR 2  of SPRITE 5:  enterFrame (3)
CAST script of SPRITE 5:  enterFrame (3)
FRAME script:  enterFrame (3)
MOVIE script:  enterFrame (3)
```

Note that the *stopMovie* event is sent *before endSprite* events in the last frame:

```
MOVIE script:  stopMovie (3)

FRAME script:  endSprite (3)
BEHAVIOR 1 of SPRITE 5:  endSprite (3)
BEHAVIOR 2 of SPRITE 5:  endSprite (3)
```

Initialization and Clean-up

In Director 5, it was difficult to set a sprite's properties before the Stage was drawn. You had to use *go frame n* to move the playback head, then puppet and update sprites before leaving the current handler or issuing an *updateStage* command. Likewise, you had to manually unpuppet all sprites that had been puppeted, making clean up difficult.

Director 6's new events allow sprites and frames to be *self-manag-ing*. They can initialize and clean up after themselves.

Director 6's new *beginSprite* event allows you to initialize properties when a frame script span or sprite span is first entered, and *endSprite* allows you to clean up when you leave. These events are sent even to sprites that were not clicked. Avoid reading or setting sprite properties in the *prepareMovie* handler before the Score data has been read. Use *beginSprite* to change sprite properties before the first frame is drawn instead.

Table 2-12 shows the best place to initialize or clean up various Lingo entities.

Table 2-12: Initialization and Clean-up

Entity	Initialization	Clean-up
Projector	*on startUp* in LINGO.INI file.	Custom *quitButton* handler attached to a quit button.[1]
Stage Movie	*on prepareMovie* [2] (use *on startMovie* in D5).	*on stopMovie.*
MIAW	*on openWindow.*	*on closeWindow* and *on deactivateWindow* (*stopMovie* events are not sent to MIAWs).
Frame script span[2]	*on beginSprite*[2] (don't use *prepareFrame*, which gets called repeatedly).	*on endSprite*[2] (don't use *exitFrame*, which gets called repeatedly).
Every Frame	*on prepareFrame*[2] (use *on enterFrame* in D5).	*on endSprite*[2] (use *on mouseUp*[3] in D5).
Sprite span[2]	*on beginSprite*[2] (in D5 you must initialize sprites before jumping to the frame in which they appear).	*on endSprite*[2] (use *on mouseUp*[3] in D5).
Cast script	Manual initialization.[4]	Manual initialization.[4]

[1] There is no *shutDown* event in Director. You must prevent the user from exiting via the keyboard in order to gain control of the exit sequence. In a single-movie project, you can use the *on stopMovie* handler for clean-up, but it is called whenever the movie stops.
[2] New in Director 6.
[3] The *on exitFrame* handler is not reliable for clean-up because it is not called when a user event sends the playback head to another frame. You must manually perform clean-up in, say, a *mouseUp* handler or jump to a frame where clean-up is performed.
[4] Cast scripts are not instanced or notified when a sprite begins. Avoid cast scripts entirely by using sprite scripts instead.

Manually Passing and Stopping Messages

A given script either ignores an event or traps (handles) it. Most events are consumed if a script has an event handler that traps them but are passed onto other scripts in the hierarchy if no such handler is found. (Some events are broad-cast to multiple entities even when trapped by other scripts, and the primary event handlers pass on all events by default). The default behavior can be overridden using the *pass, dontPassEvent,* and *stopEvent* commands.

 The *pass* command aborts the call stack immediately; Lingo statements following it are ignored.

pass

The *pass* command passes an event to the next level of the messaging hierarchy when it would otherwise be consumed. Use this in a sprite script to pass on the *mouseUp* event to the frame script too:

```
on mouseUp me
    -- Do usual mouseDown handling here
  pass
end mouseUp
```

dontPassEvent

The *dontPassEvent* command prevents an event from being passed to the next level of the messaging hierarchy. Use it to consume events in primary event handlers, which pass along events by default. When used in a sprite Behavior, *dontPassEvent* prevents the event from being passed to the frame script or movie script, but it does *not* prevent the event from being passed to other Behaviors attached to the same sprite (see *stopEvent*).

stopEvent

The *stopEvent* command (new in D6) prevents further Behaviors attached to the same sprite from receiving the event, unlike *dontPassEvent*.

Table 2-13 describes the default message passing behavior of each script type. In all cases, it can be overridden using the commands above. Note that some events (such as *prepareFrame, enterFrame,* and *exitFrame*) are broadcast and don't rely on being passed from, say, a sprite to a frame script.

Table 2-13: Script Message Passing Behavior

Script Type	Usage Notes
Primary event handlers	Events are passed by default,[1] but can be stopped using *dontPassEvent* or *stopEvent*. Primary event handlers are assigned using properties (such as *the mouseUpScript*).
Sprite script	Events are passed to all Behaviors (sprite scripts) attached to a sprite. Mouse, keyboard, and frame events are passed to the cast script only if not handled by one of the Behaviors, but *beginSprite* and *endSprite* events are not. Events can be explicitly passed to cast scripts with *pass*.
Cast script	Mouse and keyboard events are consumed, if handled; otherwise they are passed onto the frame script. Frame events and *beginSprite* and *endSprite* events are broadcast separately to frame scripts. Events can be explicitly passed to frame scripts with *pass*.

Table 2-13: Script Message Passing Behavior (continued)

Script Type	Usage Notes
Frame script	Events are consumed, if handled; otherwise they are passed onto the movie script. Events can be explicitly passed to movie scripts with *pass*.
Movie scripts	Most events reach movie scripts only if they are ignored by other scripts (or a primary event handler is defined). Movie events (such as prepareMovie) come straight to the movie script. Events are passed to any movie script, starting with the lowest-numbered movie script in the lowest-number cast. The first handler that traps the event consumes it. The *pass* command will *not* pass the event from one movie script to another (but you can use custom messages to fake this).
Behaviors	Behaviors process events as either frame scripts or sprite scripts do, depending on how they are used.
Parent Scripts	Parent scripts usually receive only those messages sent explicitly to them (or *stepFrame* messages if they are added to *the actorList*). If no handler exists in the parent script, events are passed to ancestor script (if any).

1 The entries for *the mouseDownScript* and *the mouseUpScript* in Macromedia's *Lingo Dictionary* are incorrect; *pass* is not needed in primary event handlers because they pass on events by default.

The ActorList

The *stepFrame* message is sent only to items in the *actorList*. Therefore, *the actor-List* provides a convenient way to notify a list of objects each time the playback head moves. Prior to D6, in which sprites receive frame events, it could be used to animate a group of sprites. In Director 6, it can still be used to notify parent scripts and child objects (which don't receive events by default) when the playback head moves.

Any instance added to *the actorList* continues to receive *stepFrame* messages even when the underlying scripts have changed or been deleted. This also prevents the instance from being released, perhaps leading to a memory leak. Refer to Chapter 12 for details on making a sprite automatically add itself to (and delete itself from) *the actorList*. Use the following, perhaps in your *on stopMovie* handler, to clear *the actorList*:

```
deleteAll (the actorList)
```

 Avoid modifying *the actorList* from within a *stepFrame* handler. It will crash some versions of Director.

Simulating Events and Messages

Lingo can send messages explicitly to a script or object (that is, script instance), as outlined in Table 2-14.

Table 2-14: Custom Events and Manual Messages

Command	Usage
call	Sends a message to one or more scripts or script instances. The message does not enter the usual hierarchy and is sent only to the specified destination script(s) or instance(s).
callAncestor	Sends a message to the parent script of an object.
send	Unsupported equivalent of *call*.
sendAncestor	Unsupported equivalent of *callAncestor*.
sendSprite	Sends a message to a sprite in the current frame. The message does not enter the usual hierarchy and is passed only to the sprite script(s) and cast script for one sprite. sendSprite (*spriteNum*, *#message* {, *args...*})
sendAllSprites	Sends a message to all sprites in the current frame. The message does not enter the usual hierarchy and is passed only to the sprite script(s) and cast scripts of all sprites. sendAllSprites (*#message* {, *args...*})
Xtra instance	Custom messages are sent to an Xtra instance as follows: set myInstance = new (Xtra "MyXtra") myInstance (#message {, *args...*})
Parent Scripts	Custom messages are sent to a child object as follows: set myChild = new (script "Parent Trap") myChild (#message {, *args...*})

Custom Messages and Simulated Events

You can pass your own messages to any sprite, script, or script instance using *sendSprite, sendAllSprites, call,* or *callAncestor.* In the following examples, *args...* represents one or more optional arguments. Don't include the curly braces or the ellipses.

A `scriptInstance` can be a script reference, such as:

```
script whichScriptMember
script "SomeScriptName"
script scriptNumber
```

Or it can be an object, such as:

```
set newScriptInstance = new (script "SomeBehavior")
```

To send a message to (that is, to call a specific handler in) the scripts attached to one or more *sprites*, use:

```
sendSprite (spriteNumber, #message {, args...})
sendAllSprites (#message {, args...})
```

To send a message to (that is, to call a specific handler in) a specific *script* or `scriptInstance`, use:

```
call (#message, script whichScriptMember {, args...})
call (#message, scriptInstance {, args...})
```

You can even specify a *list* of scripts or script instances to receive the message:

```
call (#message, [script 1, script 2, ...]  {, args...})
call (#message, [instanceA, instanceB, ...] {, args...})
```

Use *sendSprite()* or *sendAllSprites()*, not *call()*, to send a message to a *sprite*. The following two statements are equivalent:

```
sendSprite (spriteNumber, #mouseUp)
call (#mouseUp, the scriptInstanceList of sprite spriteNumber)
```

This is *wrong*:

```
call (#mouseUp, sprite 1)   -- Wrong!
```

To send a message to an instance's parent script, use:

```
callAncestor (#message, scriptInstance {, args...})
```

If using Director 4.0.4 or Director 5.0, use these undocumented commands that do the same thing as *call()* and *callAncestor()*:

```
send (#message, script scriptMember)
sendAncestor (#message, scriptInstance {, args...})
message (script whichScriptMember {, args...})
message (scriptInstance {, args...})
```

 You can test handlers in *score* or *cast* scripts (not just movie scripts) from the Message window by specifying the script castmember as the first parameter.

For example, a *mouseUp* message can be sent to a button named "myButton":

```
mouseUp (script "myButton")
```

Use Lingo's *do* command to generate a string to be executed on the fly. Use *do* to execute a command that is unknown. Here we execute whatever text string is received from the browser in Shockwave.

```
on externalEvent someString
  do someString
end
```

These examples assume that *myChildObj1* and *myChildObj2* are script instances and that *moveIt* is a custom handler in the appropriate script.

```
call (#moveIt, script "SomeParentScript", 10)
call (#moveIt, [myChildObj1, myChildObj2], 10)
moveIt (script "MyParentScript", 10)
myChildObj1(moveIt)
callAncestor (#moveIt, myChildObj1, 10)
callAncestor (#moveIt, [myChildObj1, myChildObj2], 10)
send (#mouseUp, script "TargetScript")
```

Custom Message Errors and Return Values

When sending a custom message, the return value and any possible errors vary with the command used, the message sent, and the number of objects to which the message is sent.

If a message is sent to *multiple* script instances using *sendSprite*, *sendAllSprites*, or using a *list* of script instances with *call*, the return value is the value returned (which may be VOID) by the *last* script responding to the message. If no scripts respond, then the return value is *<Null>*. In all cases, the Lingo property *the result* is *not* set and evaluates to VOID.

When Director issues events, they are simply ignored if no scripts trap them, but if you send the message to a *single* script instance using *call* or *callAncestor*, and that script instance does not recognize the event, a *"Handler not defined"* script error is displayed.

 Messages sent manually with *sendSprite* and *sendAllSprites* are sent only to sprites. They are *not* passed through the usual messaging hierarchy to unspecified sprites, frame scripts, movie scripts, or the primary event handlers.

Sending an event such as *#closeWindow* does not actually close a window. It merely runs the *on closeWindow* handler. To close a window, use the *close window* command.

Refer to Chapters 9 and 10 for details on simulating and flushing mouse and keyboard events with Xtras.

CHAPTER 3

Lingo Coding and Debugging Tips

Lingo Coding Tips

Programming is often an iterative process. You need not write perfect code that does everything the first time you run it. Start simple, and test each step along the way. Before you know it, you will be building real Lingo programs.

Many of the tips and techniques discussed throughout this book won't mean anything to you until you've programmed for a while. (Refer to "*Entering and Compiling Scripts*" in Chapter 1, *How Lingo Thinks*). Revisit the earlier chapters after completing a project. What would you do differently the next time? Try to practice the following Lingo techniques:

Plan Ahead

Plan your design and layout of the presentation and the Lingo you'll need. A formal design helps both beginners and experienced Linguists spot problems and opportunities.

Be organized. If your Lingo code starts messy and scattered, it will only get worse. Well-structured code gets easier, not harder, to debug toward the end of a project.

Develop and maintain a library of utility Lingo routines (this book is a good start). Store them in externally linked casts for easy inclusion in other projects.

Don't confuse analysis with implementation. The mechanics of Lingo are sometimes easier than figuring out *what* Lingo you need to write. See "*Envisioning Your Lingo*" later in this chapter.

Structure your Score and Cast so that it makes your Lingo easier to write as described in Chapter 1, *How Director Works*, in *Director in a Nutshell*.

Use comments effectively as described in the "*Comments*" section of Chapter 1.

Develop a programming style, and use it consistently. For example, I always use sprite scripts and never use cost scripts.

Avoid the errors cited in the *"Common Errors When Using Properties and Constants," "Common Errors When Using Variables," "Common Handler Declaration Errors,"* and *"Common Errors When Using If Statements"* sections in Chapter 1.

Use Scripts and Handlers Effectively

Use the correct type of script for your handlers, as described in Chapter 2, *Events, Messages, and Scripts.* Avoid cast scripts. Use sprite scripts.

Take advantage of Behaviors; see Chapter 12, *Behaviors and Parent Scripts.*

Understand how and when different Lingo is executed. See Chapters 1 and 2, Chapter 9, *Mouse Events,* Chapter 10, *Keyboard Events,* and Chapter 11, *Timers and Dates.*

Standardize on either mousedown or mouseup handlers. Use exit Frame instead of enter Frame.

Use Lingo Variables and Director's Tools Effectively

Use the multi-line form of *if* statements, as shown under *"If Statements"* in Chapter 1. This works more reliably and makes it easier to tell whether an *if statement's* dependent clause is being executed in the Debugger.

Avoid using dozens of global variables. Use Lingo lists rather than individual variables to hold related items (see Chapter 6, *Lists*). A single Behavior or Parent script can have dozens of properties, which can be accessed via a single instance variable (see Chapter 12). A single global list can replace dozens of separate global variables or hold dozens of child instance variables.

Lingo lists are much faster than strings variables or fields when searching and sorting a list of strings. If necessary, correct strigns to lists. See Example 6-29.

Familiarize yourself with all the Lingo keywords in Chapter 18, *Lingo Keyword and Command Summary.*

Use the Lingo pop-up menus in the Message window and Script window to remind yourself of the correct syntax for many Lingo commands. This is especially helpful to avoid mistyping commands such as *on getPropertyDescriptionList* (which is under "G" not "O" in the Lingo menu).

Use the Message, Watcher, and Debugger windows as described later in this chapter.

Lingo does not automatically optimize your code.

Minimize the number of comparisions and minimize the number of statements within a repeat loop by setting fixed values outside the loop.

Use Descriptive Names in your Lingo code

Name your local, global, and property variables, and your handler names descriptively.

Adopt naming conventions to make it easy to distinguish between variable types. For example, begin global variables' names with a "g," property variables' names with a "p," and so on.

Use mixed case to make your variables and handler names easier to read such as *gUserScore* or *sumItemsInList*. (These names are case-insensitive. Refer to Appendix C, *Case-Sensitivity, Sort Order, Diacritical Marks, and Space-Sensitivity*.)

Use symbols instead of integer codes as described in the "*Symbols*" section of Chapter 5, *Data Types and Expressions*. (See Example 5-2, "*Replacing Integer Codes with Symbols*.")

Declare globals at the top of handler or the top of your script. It is hard to find globals declared midway through a script.

Avoid Hardcoding; Build in Flexibility

A cast member's number will change if it is moved in the Cast. Although the Score refers to members by number, those references are updated automatically when a cast member moves. In your Lingo, refer to cast members by name instead of by number. Name your cast members uniquely so that Lingo always finds the right one.

A frame's number will change if you add, delete, or move frames in the Score. Use either a relative marker number (see the *marker()* function) or a marker name (see the *label()* function) to refer to a frame.

Use Lingo properties to dynamically determine the current sprite's number, as shown in Example 9-2, "*What's My Sprite Number?*" in Chapter 9. That way, the same script can be attached to a sprite in any channel, and sprites can be relocated to other channels, and it will still work. If necessary, use global variables to refer to sprite channel numbers.

Use convenience functions (see Figure 2-2) for common tasks, such as playing sounds.

Generalize your Lingo handlers as shown in "*Generalizing Functions*" in Chapter 1.

Save Time During Testing and Debugging

You can write small utilities that, say, print out all the information about a sprite. Such utilities are vital additions to your Lingo tool belt.

Rather than waiting forever to test a *timeOut* condition, simulate a *timeOut* event by setting *the timeoutLapsed* to *the timeoutLength*.

Use keyboard shortcuts or global variables to skip long introductions during debugging (see Example 3-7).

If your project involves a game or exercise that requires a long time to play, save the state of the game to a text file (see Chapter 14, *External Files*). Leave the feature in for users if applicable.

Coding Debugging and Troubleshooting Resources

This chapter is about the *process* of Lingo coding and debugging. It can not possibly address all the specific examples or bugs that probably interest you, nor can it troubleshoot your particular problem. Many excellent Director examples are available on the sites listed in the *Preface*. Refer to the following for specific information about bugs, coding, and debugging.

UpdateStage Quirk List—a list of many bugs in Director 5 and 6
   http://www.updatestage.com/

Director On-line Bug Database —under construction and growing
   http://www.director-online.com (Search under Resources)

General Debugging Hints
   http://www.zeusprod.com/technote/debug.html

Troubleshooting Applications
   http://www.zeusprod.com/technote/debugapp.html

Search Macromedia's site using these TechNote numbers as the search key:
   TechNote 3508: *Troubleshooting and Developing Your Logic*

   TechNote 3130: *Tips for Troubleshooting GPFs with Director for Windows*

   Tech Note 3129 (or 3130RM): *Debugging and Bugproofing Director Movies*

 Director has its share of bugs. Participating in an online mailing list or newsgroup is the best way to stay abreast of them and get answers to your vexing questions.

Coding Techniques

Wrapper Functions

If you have trouble remembering the name or function of a particular Lingo command, create a *wrapper script* that uses a name more meaningful to you. This wrapper script is easier to understand than the ambiguously named *getOne()* Lingo list command.

Example 3-1: Wrapper Scripts

```
on getPropByValue myList, value
  -- Return theProperty Name based on the value
  return getOne (myList, value)
end

put getPropByValue ([#a:5, #b:7], 7)
-- #b
```

The extra subroutine call takes a small but finite amount of time to execute. If performance is an issue, you can reinstate the original list function names before completing your project.

If you are "wrapping" a function that returns a value, your wrapper script should return the value to the original caller.

This is *wrong*:

```
on getPropByValue myList, value
  -- Oops, we forgot to send the return value back
```

```
     getOne (myList, value)
  end
```

```
-- We get a VOID value because no value was returned by the wrapper script:
put getPropByValue ([#a:5, #b:7], 7)
-- VOID
```

Convenience Functions

A *convenience function* is one that calls another function but fills in one or more parameters with default values. For example, suppose we want to play voice-overs in sound channel 1 and ambient music in channel 2. We could hardcode the channel for each sound, or we could use global variables to represent the sound channels, but two convenience functions are easier and cleaner.

Example 3-2: Convenience Functions

```
on playVO someSound
  -- play voice-overs in channel 1
  sound playFile 1, someSound
end
```

```
on playAmbient someSound
  -- play ambient sounds in channel 2
  sound playFile 2, soundSound
end
```

We can then use these from other scripts:

```
   playVo ("intro.aif")
   playAmbient ("mood.aif")
```

Suppose the voice-overs are in a subfolder call "VO," the ambient sounds are in a subfolder named "AMBIENT," and all sound files end in ".AIF." We can extend our convenience functions to build the path automatically.

Example 3-3: Ultra-Convenience Functions

```
on improvedPlayVO someSound
  -- play voice-overs in channel 1
  set the pathSeparator = the last char of the pathName
  sound playFile 1, the pathName & "VO" & ¬
    pathSeparator & someSound & ".AIF"
end
```

```
on improvedPlayAmbient someSound
  -- play ambient sounds in channel 2
  set the pathSeparator = the last char of the pathName
  sound playFile 2, the pathName & "AMBIENT" & ¬
    pathSeparator & someSound  & ".AIF"
end
```

We can then use the sound files name without the .AIF extension or the folder name, such as:

```
improvedPlayVO ("intro")
improvedPlayAmbient("mood")
```

We can easily add more features or debugging statements to our convenience functions. We might check that *someSound* is a valid string and that the sound file exists at the specified path. We might add options to wait for playing sounds to finish or to terminate sounds in other channels.

Redirection or Override Functions

You can override built-in Lingo functions by defining a Lingo handler of the same name in a movie script. This will display all *put* statements in *alert* dialog boxes instead of in the Message window:

Example 3-4: Overriding Built-in Lingo Functions

```
on put msgText
  alert msgText
end
```

Instead of using *put* statements in your Lingo code, call a custom *output()* handler that will then call the *put* statement if feasible.

```
on mouseUp me
   output "Mouse was clicked on sprite" && the spriteNum of me
end
```

This displays messages in the browser status line when run from Shockwave, or in a field cast member when run from a Projector. You could modify it to even write to a file for debugging purposes.

```
on output msgTxt
   -- In authoring mode, print to the message window
   case(runMode) of
     "Author": put msgText
     "Plugin": netStatus msgText
     "Projector": put msgTxt & RETURN after field "output
Display"
   end case
end output
```

Consolidate Common Code Blocks into a Single Centralized Function

You'll often need to perform the same operation multiple times throughout your project. Create one function that does it for you. If you need to make a correction or addition, you need to do it in only one place, as with the convenience functions in Example 3-3.

The handler shown in Example 3-5 returns TRUE if the project is running under Windows.

Example 3-5: Centralized Code

```
on onWindows
  if the platform contains "Windows" then
   return TRUE
  else
    return FALSE
  end if
end
```

Use it as follows (don't forget the parentheses) whenever you must determine the platform:

```
if onWindows() then
   -- Do Windows-specific things here
  else
   -- Do Macintosh-specific things here
  end if
```

Optional Debugging

Use a global variable, such as *gDebug*, to execute statements for testing purposes only, as shown in Example 3-6.

Example 3-6: Optional Debugging Code

```
on mouseUp me
  global gDebug
  if gDebug then
     alert "Mouse Up reached in sprite" && the spriteNum of me
  end if
end
```

Turn the debugging statement on an off selectively using:

```
set gDebug = TRUE
set gDebug = FALSE
```

Shortcuts During Testing

Don't make yourself sit through the same introductory animation 1000 times. Use the Option key (Mac) or Alt key (Windows) to skip to the main menu.

Example 3-7: Testing Shortcuts

```
on mouseUp
  global gDebug
  if the optionDown and gDebug then
    go frame "mainMenu"
  end if
end
```

Alternative Code and Easter Eggs

You can also use the Option key (Macintotsh) or Alt key (Windows) to provide alternate functionality during testing—or to create *Easter Eggs* (hidden surprises) for users.

Example 3-8: Debugging Shortcuts

```
on prepareMovie
  global gDebug
  if the optionDown and gDebug then
    -- Make timeouts happen quickly (every five seconds)
    set the timeoutLength = 300
  end if
end
```

Example 3-9: Easter Eggs

```
on mouseDown
  if the optionDown and the doubleClick then
    -- Jump to a secret hidden screen when the user
    -- Option-double-clicks (Mac) or Alt-double-clicks (Windows) on this sprite
    go frame "Easter Egg"
  end if
end
```

Error Checking

Always perform error checking to *avoid* potential problems. If you detect an error, you can post more meaningful messages than Director's default errors. You might also be able to ignore the problem (such as by using an appropriate default value).

Checking the User Configuration

At the beginning of your Director presentation you should check whether the user's system is configured to meet your guidelines. You can check the platform, memory, monitor resolution, monitor color depth, QuickTime version, and more. Refer to Chapter 8, *Projectors and the Runtime Environment,* in *Director in a Nutshell.* Refer to Chapter 13, *Lingo Xtras and XObjects,* to check whether Lingo Xtras are installed and refer to Chapter 19, *The Lingo Symbol Table,* to determine whether Sprite Asset Xtras are installed.

Checking Whether Lingo Commands Succeeded

Most Lingo commands succeed all the time. Some commands, however, may not succeed or may succeed only partially. Always check whether the result is what you expected. For example, attempting to instantiate an Xtra will fail (if the Xtra is not installed) or will return a valid object reference to indicate success.

Example 3-10: Checking the Return Value

```
set myFileObject = new (xtra "FileIO")
if not objectP(myFileObject) then
  alert "An error occurred. FileIO may not be installed"
else
  -- Perform FileIO Operations here
end if
```

Refer to Chapters 13 and 14 for details.

Checking Whether the Programmer Made a Mistake

Programmers often neglect to head off potential problems in the way they or someone else uses their Lingo code. For example, in Chapter 6, I may write a handler that assumes that a valid list is being used. Technically, it is a good idea to check whether an item is a Lingo list before trying to use a list-related function:

Example 3-11: Checking for a List Parameter

```
on doSomething inList
  if not listP(inList) then
    alert "I need a list, man!"
    exit
  else
    statement(s)
  end if
end
```

Note that you never expect these errors to occur, but it makes it much easier to detect and debug problems should the programmer (that is, you) use incorrect parameters when calling your routine.

Checking User Input

When accepting user input, it is wise to check whether the user entered a valid response. See Chapter 10 for details on preventing certain keystrokes by the user. You should ensure that the user enters all required fields and doesn't exceed the allowed length for any text entry.

Likewise, if the user is allowed to drag a sprite around the screen you should constrain the sprite within appropriate boundaries using *the constraint of sprite* property.

Range Checking

You should perform range checking whenever accepting numeric values. For example, if you write a handler to draw a circle, you may wish to prevent the circle from having a radius outside certain limits. Use *min()* and *max()* to restrict the range of allowable inputs, as shown in Example 8-4," under *"Checking and Clipping Values Within a Range"* in Chapter 8, *Math (and Gambling)*.

Also prevent overflow errors as shown in Example 8-15, *"Preventing Overflow Conditions While Calculating Factorials,"* in Chapter 8.

Status Checking

You should check the status of slow operations before assuming they have completed. For example, *netDone()* tells whether a network operation has completed. Use status checking to avoid erroneous information. For example, you should check *the state of member* of an SWA cast member before checking its other attributes (which return meaningless values until the SWA starts).

Bullet-Proofing

In extreme cases involving user input, error checking and range checking may constitute more than half your Lingo code. Prudent error checking doesn't require you to go overboard. Excessive error checking can make your code very difficult to follow and can slow performance. That said, most new programmers perform too little error checking rather than too much.

Assuming Default Values

It is often a good idea to assume default values if incorrect ones are received by your function. Here we play a sound in channel 1 if no sound channel is specified. You might change it to use channel 3 or the first unused sound channel instead to avoid conflicts with sound channels 1 and 2 in the Score.

Example 3-12: Assuming Default Values

```
on playSoundWithDefault someSound, soundChan
  if not integerP(soundChan) then
    set soundChan = 1
  end if
  -- Play the sound from our Sounds folder
  set the pathSeparator = the last char of the pathName
  sound playFile soundChan, the pathName & "SOUNDS" & ¬
    pathSeparator & someSound & ".aif"
end
```

Refer to Example 1-36 under *"Optional Arguments and Varying Argument Types"* in Chapter 1 for more details.

Envisioning Your Lingo

Most beginners obsess over the *syntax* of Lingo in part because they have no idea what Lingo they should be writing.

Translating your needs into specific Lingo is a learned skill that will come with practice.

It is not always easy to translate from the real world to the mathematical and logical world of Lingo. You must envision both the result *and* the individual steps to get you there. *You* must give your variables meaning, just as we give words meaning in our native language. As Sheila Tobias writes[*] regarding solving math word problems:

"For a period of indeterminate length, one flounders. How can one flounder constructively?"

Coding, Debugging

Director Doesn't Know Anything

How do you know what you need to tell Director to do?

See Table 18-1 for a list of Lingo commands. If there is a command to perform a specific operation, such as play a sound, then Director knows how to do that. If not, you need to break the problem down into steps Director understands.

Try to recognize the *steps* that you go through every day to perform common tasks. Practice codifying the steps for each task as you would instruct a robot to perform the same task.

Director is pretty dumb. You need to be very explicit about the steps to follows. Director executes proper and improper orders alike without question as long as it understands your syntax (see Chapter 1).

Translating Reality to Lingo

We use abstract representations all the time. For example, when reading a map, we know that it is not on a 1:1 scale and that the road is black asphalt even though the map shows it as a red line. How do you create an abstract representation of, say, a user quiz in Lingo?

You need to do three things:

Define the information of interest.
Determine what to do with that information.

---

[*] Sheila Tobias, Chapter 5, "*Word-Problem Solving: The Heart of the Matter* ," in *Overcoming Math Anxiety* (New York: W.W. Norton & Company), 1993 ISBN 0-393-03577-8.

Determine when to act upon it.

To store a piece of information, create a Lingo variable to hold it. (See Chapter 1). A variable is like the noun in a sentence. It is the *thing* that you will be working with. In a quiz, the thing you need to record is the test score, so create a variable to hold it. If you need to store a series of related things, such as a user's score on several quizzes, consider using a Lingo list (see Chapter 6). If you need the data for an extended period of time, you'll need to store it in a persistent variable (a global or property variable) rather than a local variable.

To perform some action or calculation, create a Lingo handler. A handler is like the *verb* in a sentence. For example, you might create a handler to sum all the elements in the list of test scores or to average such a list. (See Chapters 6 and 8 for examples.)

Once you've created variables that hold the data and handlers to manipulate it in some way, you need to tell Director when to perform the steps and in what order. You'll ordinarily perform some action in response to a user event. For example, you might grade the user's quiz when he or she clicks a *Grade Me* button, or you might grade it when he or she has answered the last question. The first solution requires the user to explicitly initiate the action and is appropriate for lengthy quizzes in which the user has a chance to review and change answers. The latter is appropriate only for brief quizzes in which the user cannot review previous answers.

Each time the user enters a correct response you would add points to the variable holding their score. How do you know if the user entered a correct response? That depends on the quiz. If the user is entering text, you might compare his response to the correct answer when the user presses RETURN. Here we increment the global variable *gScore* if the text field contains the word "Einstein."

Example 3-13: Tracking the User's Score

```
on keyDown me
  global gScore
  if the key = RETURN then
    if the text of member (the member of sprite ¬
      the spriteNum of me) contains "Einstein" then
      set gScore = gScore + 1
      alert "Correct!"
    else
      alert "Wrong!"
    end if
  else
    pass
  end if
end
```

In the case of a multiple choice quiz, you can attach the "scoring logic" to the button for the correct answer (wrong answers might subtract from the score):

```
on mouseUp
  global gScore
  set gScore = gScore + 1
```

```
    alert "Congrats"
    go frame "Next Problem"
end
```

 Use cast member names and marker names to take some action in Director in response to user input.

For example, if the user selects the word lion" from a menu you might change a placeholder sprite to a cast member named "lion" (by setting *the member of sprite* property), play a sound called "lion" (using *puppetSound "lion"*), or jump to a frame named "lion" (using *go to frame "lion"*).

Feedback

Everything you've mastered in life has been learned via feedback.

 Most people never learn to program because they get no direct feedback from experienced programmers. See the *"Common Errors"* sections in each chapter, or ask for help on the mailing lists and newsgroups cited in the *Preface*.

Beginners need to learn how to do things the right way, which comes from imitating other people's techniques. How do you learn how *not* to do things the wrong way? Don't hesitate to ask questions on one of the Director-related mailing lists (listed in the *Preface*). Take the time to examine and define your problem. Even if you don't get a good answer from someone, trying to explain the problem to others will help you to clarify it and thus help you solve it.

The Four Questions

There is a huge difference between these four questions:

"Why *doesn't* my program accomplish XYZ?"
"*How* can I accomplish XYZ?"
"*Why* does my program do what it does?"
'*What* does my program actually *do*, if not XYZ?"

Most beginners want an answer to the first question. Most experienced Linguists will offer answers to the second question. This book, especially Chapters 1 and 2, answers the third question. The Lingo Debugger will answer the fourth question.

Zen and the Art of Debugging

Debugging is the single most important skill in programming, if not in life. Debugging, like most worthwhile pursuits, is a learned art, but I've rarely seen it taught.

This section is aimed at those who have never debugged, at least not successfully, and probably don't know how to use the Lingo Debugger.

The title of the well-known book, *Zen and the Art of Motorcycle Maintenance*, was taken from a book on Zen archery. A Zen archer holds his bow awkwardly over his head so that it is clearly impossible to "sight" the target. Instead, he attempts to "become one" with the target; he seeks not to act, but only to confirm what already *is*. He does not aim and shoot, but rather recognizes that the arrow has already been released, has already flown toward its target, and has already made a bull's-eye. If you watched the 1998 Winter Olympics from Nagano you could pick out the athletes that *knew* they would win before the competition began. Almost invariably they were right. The competition itself was merely a confirmation of that which they had already envisioned from an early age. And so it is with programming and debugging.

 To debug is to recognize that the problem has already been solved; you simply unearth the solution as one would unearth a diamond. *Before* it is possible to debug a problem, you must convince yourself *that it is possible* to debug the problem.

There are many paradoxes in programming and debugging. You must be confident that you can solve a problem yet admit that you probably made a mistake somewhere. You must fight the urge to lay blame on yourself or on Director, but at the same time be unbiased in assessing who or what is the culprit. Debugging is at the very core of what it means to be conscious: to have control over one's present and future, and to recognize that you had control over your past whether you exercised it or not.

 To debug is to follow whatever path wherever it may lead and yet to control the ultimate destination. Don't confuse bugs with *de*bugging. Bugs suck. Debugging is fun.

As you might have guessed I am passionate about debugging. It gets me excited! It should get you excited, too! It is invigorating to learn, to solve, to succeed. So keep your eye on the prize—in this case, a working multimedia project.

How to Think Like a Programmer

Debugging is a skill that comes naturally to some people, but it can be learned by all. Whether you are a programmer, psychiatrist, doctor, plumber, car mechanic, or parent you use debugging techniques unconsciously many times each day. Once you're conscious about debugging, you can apply its benefits to all aspects of your professional and personal life.

Debugging is not for defeatists. When you sit down to debug, think about those activities that come easily to you, that invigorate you, that give you confidence. Type this in the Message window, and press RETURN:

```
alert "You are a Lingo god (Your Name Goes Here)"
```

What the Hell is Debugging Anyway?

The banishing of bugs is just the *result* of debugging. Debugging itself is a *process* whose principals apply to any situation.

 Debugging is the *systematic challenging of our assumptions.*

To debug is to verify or expose as incorrect that which we had previously assumed to be true. You must recognize your assumptions before you can challenge them. Eventually this will illuminate the misconception that led to the error. Debugging usually includes a lot of testing to find bugs and verify their exact nature and the steps that lead to them.

 Do not assume that the information available on Director from various sources, even Macromedia, is completely true. Much of it is outdated, only partially true, or just plain wrong.

Debugging Is the Systematic Challenging of Assumptions

Every time I've heard the story of the Wright brothers, it is emphasized that they were bicyclists. Perhaps incorrectly, I always inferred that it was exceedingly unlikely that two bicycle mechanics would invent the first viable airplane (all historical disputes aside). But the Wright brothers were no dummies; they built the world's first wind tunnel and tested tiny model airfoils in it. This saved them months of construction and failures that had plagued other wing designers.

 Systematic trial and error, not to be confused with dumb luck, is a potent debugging technique. Take notes on the exact nature of your tests and the results.

Be Systematic

You already know how to be systematic. If I asked you to guess a number between 1 and 100 and told you whether it was higher or lower than your guess, what would your first guess be? Surely, you would guess 50 because whatever the answer it *cuts the problem in half.* Perform tests that narrow down the problem regardless of the outcome of the test.

Challenge Your Own Assumptions

At Kitty Hawk, North Carolina, there are three stone markers marking the length of the first three flights of the Wright Flyer. Each successive flight is longer than the last, and flights of 20 miles soon followed. Others had built gliders, but the Wright Brothers realized that sustained flight required the ability to steer the plane in gusty winds. The Wright Flyer's wings could be bent at the tips by a series of wires (this mechanism was the precursor to modern wing flaps). By challenging the assumption that the wing's lift characteristics were the limiting factor, they were able to design a steerable wing that allowed the pilot to keep the plane aloft.

Make a conscious effort to recognize the assumptions you are making when you run into a problem. If a sound file won't play, are you assuming that it is a valid sound file in the correct location? Test the sound file outside of Director, verify its location and the Lingo used to point to that location, and so on.

Debugging Tips

When you encounter a problem try the following:

- Use the Debugger to examine your Lingo code. There is little point in guessing when you have a potent diagnostic tool available.

- Establish what *is* working to rule out possible sources of error and to focus your attention on likely suspects. If no sounds play, you might suspect a hardware or configuration problem.

- Establish the cause and effect. Determine whether the problem is repeatable and the exact steps to reproduce it.

- Define acceptable criteria for success. If a problem is hardware- or configuration-related, you may choose simply not to support that configuration.

- Check the easiest things first even if they are less likely to be the source of the problem, but eventually you must check the difficult things too.

- Check carefully for spelling mistakes. Delete and retype a line of code if it is causing you problems. Use the correct number and order of parameters. (It is easy to mix up the parameters in the *offset()* command, for example). Use the Lingo pop-up menus in the Message window and Script window to remind yourself of the correct syntax for most Lingo commands.

- Don't overlook the obvious. Before checking your Lingo printing code with a fine-toothed comb, check that the printer is plugged in and the power switch is on. If sounds don't play, check the speaker connections and the volume.

- Try the operation outside of Director, if possible. Try a test print from another application, or play your problematic video in MoviePlayer. If it works elsewhere, your Lingo or possibly a Director conflict are to blame.

- You can't debug two unknowns at once. Change only one thing at a time.

- Programming and debugging are iterative processes. You will often make incremental progress rather than write perfect code the first time. There is no harm in experimenting, but undo any changes that did not fix the problem before you try something new. Don't simply layer change upon change without understanding what each change accomplishes. Most beginners use too much Lingo, whereas less is called for.

- Isolate the problem by creating a simple test movie. This will act as your "control" or "reference sample" (to borrow laboratory terminology). If it doesn't reflect the problem, the problem is perhaps related to other factors within your project. Eliminate MIAWs, external castLibs, Xtras, or anything that may be clouding the issue. Restart your computer with minimal extensions.

- Don't obsess over one bug to the exclusion of other items. A good night's sleep is sometimes the best debugger. (Some programmers debug in their dreams!)

- Check that you are using the correct type of script. Choose `Control[>]Recompile All Scripts` to make sure you are running the latest version of your scripts.

How might you debug the situation where a lamp plugged into an outlet won't turn on? Is the problem the wall switch, the lamp, the lamp's switch, the light bulb, the outlet, the fuse, or the house's wiring? Perhaps there is a power outage. How are the debugging techniques you'd use applicable to Lingo debugging?

Suppose that 10 percent of new light bulbs are faulty. If *two* new light bulbs both fail in your lamp, there is only a 1 percent chance that *both* light bulbs are faulty. The problem most likely lies elsewhere.

 "Swapping" components is a valuable debugging tool. Retreat to a known working configuration, then establish what is *different* between the working version and the buggy one.

Test with a different data file, a different computer, a different browser, or even a different version of Director to reveal the faulty component. Refer to Appendix C, *Checklists*, in *Director in a Nutshell* for a sample bug report form. See also *http://www.zeusprod.com/nutshell/bugform.html*.

The Lingo Debugger

A good programmer can often correct simple errors by simply inspecting the code, just as a good speller doesn't need a dictionary or a spellchecker. But experienced programmers constantly use the Lingo Debugger whereas beginners don't even seem to know it exists. Refer to Chapter 4, *Troubleshooting*, in Macromedia's *Learning Lingo* manual for a brief overview.

The Debugger is a diagnostic tool. It does not debug your program for you any more than an X-ray cures disease. The Debugger can show you what Lingo commands are being executed and the values held in various variables. See also the Watcher window inFigure 3-4.

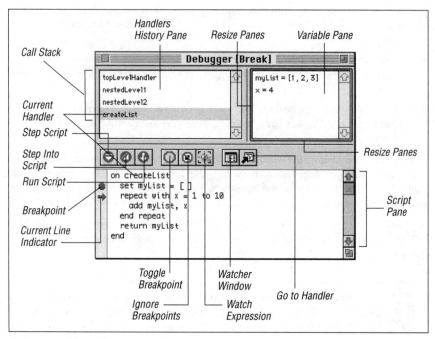

Figure 3-1: The Debugger Window

Script Errors

When Director compiles a script—see "*Entering and Compiling Scripts*" in Chapter 1 and "*Compiling Scripts*" Chapter 2—it checks that your Lingo code has a recognizable structure and acceptable keywords. It does *not* attempt to actually run your Lingo code. Recompile to help find typographical errors.

A so-called *compile-time* or *syntax error* causes a dialog box to appear, indicating what Director *suspects* is wrong.

 Script errors are your friends. Read the error message carefully; Director will tell you which line confused it.

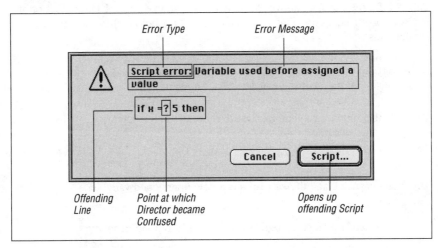

Figure 3-2: A Script Error Dialog

Unfortunately, when you close the Script window (which recompiles the script) and the script error dialog appears (see Figure 3-2), the *Script* button will not always take you to the exact line causing the problem. Usually you can guess which line was the problem, unless you have an extremely long script or a long line of Lingo code (such as a big list or quoted string).

If you are unsure which line in the script is the problem, choose the *Cancel* button, then run the movie using the **Enter** key on the numeric keypad. Director will recompile the script and post the error dialog a *second* time. This time, choosing the *Script* button opens the Script window with the cursor at the *exact* location of the error.

One common compile-time error is *"Script Error: Variable used before assigned a value."* Director *thinks* that you are trying to use a local variable that you've not previously set equal to something, but it could be another problem.

If you forgot to assign a value to a variable, do so before using it in another expression. You may have also misspelled the variable name, forgot to declare it as a global, forget to declare an incoming parameter, used a Lingo property without the keyword *the*, or used a function name without the required parentheses.

This will generate an error because Lingo has never heard of *b* before it was used on the right side of an expression.

Example 3-14: Fixing a "Variable Used Before Assigned a Value" Error

```
on test
  set a = b
end
```

This will fix the problem above. Note that new variables must be used first on the left side of an equation (that is, assigned a value) before they can be used for anything else.

```
on test
  set b = 7   -- Assign a value to a new variable b
  set a = b   -- Assign a value to a new variable a
end
```

This will also fix the problem; because *b* is declared as a parameter:

```
on test b
  set a = b   -- Assign parameter b to a new variable a
end
```

This fails because Lingo thinks *ticks* is a new unassigned variable:

```
set a = ticks
```

This works because Lingo recognizes *the ticks* as a built-in property:

```
set a = the ticks
```

See "*Common Errors When Using Properties and Constants,*" "*Local Variables,*" and "*Common Errors When Using Variables*" in Chapter 1.

The Script window's auto-indent feature should alert you to mismatched multiline code blocks such as *if...then...else...end if* statements. To make sense of the auto-indenting, use the Text Inspector, Command-T (Mac) or Ctrl-T (Windows), to choose a uniform font and point size for all the text in your Script window. I like the 9-point Monaco font on the Mac and Terminal font on Windows. Match Software (*http://www.matchfonts.com*) offers a font featuring fixed widths, exaggerated distinctions between similar characters, and clearer delineation of punctuation characters to help avoid the syntax errors common when using traditional fonts.

If Director can't understand your syntax you might get an "*Expected THEN*" or "*Expected END IF*" or similar error when you compile the script. Refer to Appendix E, *Error Messages and Error Codes*, for details on solving each error.

If compilation succeeds, your code is not necessarily error-free and may still cause a so-called *run-time error* when Director attempts to execute it.

One common run-time error is "*Script Error: Handler not defined.*" Director *thinks* that you are calling a custom handler that doesn't exist, but it could be something else.

If you choose the *Debug* button from the run-time error dialog, Director will open the Debugger, but the error will have already occurred. You can examine the variables in the handler, as described in "*Examining Problems in the Debugger and Watcher Windows.*"

You may have also mistyped the handler name in either the function call or the handler definition, misspelled a Lingo command, or used an invalid parameter as the first argument to a function call. For example, calling the *count(someVar)* function where *someVar* is not a valid list will cause an error. See "*Special Treatment of the First Argument Passed*" in Chapter 1 and "*Invalid List Declarations*" and *"Lingo List Commands"* in Chapter 6 for details. See Appendix E for details on all error messages.

Breakpoints

Unlike most of Director's tools, the Debugger is useful only when Director and Lingo are actually running. When the movie stops, the Debugger window is empty and inactive. You will rarely open the Debugger window manually. Instead, Director will automatically open the Debugger when it encounters a *breakpoint.*

 A *breakpoint* tells Director to open the Debugger and allow you to examine the state of the Lingo at that point. The program is still "running," but it waits at the breakpoint for you before executing the next step.

The easiest way to set a breakpoint at a particular line in a Lingo script is to click in the left margin of the script in the Script window. A red dot should appear to indicate the breakpoint (see Figure 3-3). When you run the application, the Debugger will open when Director hits the breakpoint. (You can't set a breakpoint on commented lines or on the first and last lines of your handler definition.) Director tries to recompile the script when you set a breakpoint. If you are having trouble setting one, close the Script window, then recompile and reopen the Script window. Try setting the breakpoint again.

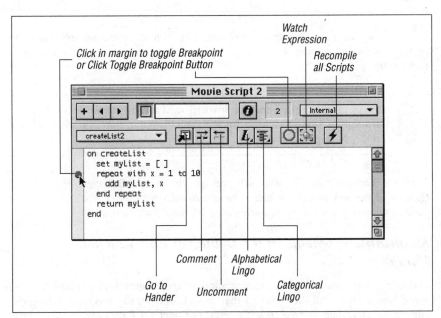

Figure 3-3: Setting a breakpoint in the Script window

A breakpoint works only if Director actually attempts to execute the line of Lingo for which you've set a breakpoint. If the breakpoint is never reached, it has no effect.

Set the breakpoints before Director reaches your Lingo. For example, a breakpoint in a *mouseDown* handler, will be reached when you click on the sprite to which the handler is attached. See Chapter 2 to figure out which Lingo will be executed and where your breakpoint will be reached. See *"Debugging"* in Chapter 4, *Lingo Internals*, for information on how the Lingo Debugger differs from debuggers in other languages, such as C.

There is no way to cause an immediate break into whatever Lingo code may be executing at the moment. Director will break into Lingo only at points where you have previously set a breakpoint, although you can add and remove breakpoints while the program is running.

You can create a conditional breakpoint by setting a breakpoint on a line within an *if...then* statement.

Example 3-15: A Conditional Breakpoint

```
on someHandler msg
  if condition then
    nothing   -- Set a breakpoint on this line
  end if
end
```

You can set as many breakpoints as you like before or during execution by clicking in the left margin of the Script window. Director will stop at each one it encounters.

 Director stops *before* the line marked with the breakpoint executes. If a line of Lingo assigns a value to a variable, it won't be assigned until you step *past* it.

During execution you can also set breakpoints in the Debugger window by clicking in the left margin or using the *Set Breakpoint* button. See Table 3-4 for additional breakpoint commands accessible via the `Control` menu.

Examining Problems in the Debugger and Watcher Windows

The upper left pane of the Debugger window (see Figure 3-1) displays the *call stack*, which shows all the handlers that were called on the way to reaching the current handler. (See *"Nested Handler Calls"* in Chapter 1 for an explanation of the call stack.) In the simplest case of, say, a *mouseDown* handler attached to a sprite, only the current handler is shown in the call stack pane. You can click on any handler name in the call stack, and Director will show you the line in the earlier routine that led to the current breakpoint.

The upper right pane shows the local and global variables in use by the current handler. Often, simply seeing the current value of a variable is enough to make you realize the problem. Be on the lookout especially for values that are VOID that you forgot to initialize.

Director is unique in that you can edit scripts even while Director is running.

 You can't edit the script *in* the Debugger window, but you can open the original script using the Debugger's *Script Go to Handler* button. Editing a script that is running will usually confuse the debugger. It will warn you to recompile the scripts.

You can highlight any expression in the Debugger window and click the *Watch Expression* button The expression appears in the Watcher window, which updates every time the expression changes.

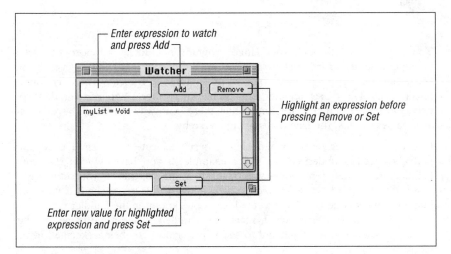

Figure 3-4: The Watcher window

Use the Watcher's *Add* button (see Figure 3-4) or the *Watch Expression* button in the Message window to add any expression or Lingo properties such as *the mouseH* to the watched list. What happens as you move the mouse around?

To set a variable's value, highlight its entry in the Watcher window and type only the new value (not an equation) into the *Set* field and click the *Set* button.

Stepping Through Your Lingo Code

You can use the three green arrows in the Debugger window (see Figure 3-1) to step slowly through your Lingo code. The *Step Script* arrow executes one Lingo command. If you instead have more than one function on a line such as:

```
set x = random (count([myList]))
```

the Debugger won't step to the next line immediately. The first *"Step Script"* command executes the nested *count()* function. Use *Step Script* again to execute the *random()* function and advance to the next line of Lingo.

The *Step Into Script* arrow steps into any custom Lingo handler on the line. You can't step into built-in Lingo commands, and in such cases, the *Step Into Script* arrow will act like the *Step Script* arrow. Try out the *Step Into Script* arrow with Example 1-2 under *"Nested Handler Calls"* in Chapter 1.

The *Run Script* arrow makes Lingo run until the next breakpoint is reached. If no more breakpoints are set, Director simply continues running.

 Closing the Debugger window is the same as clicking on the *Run Script* arrow. Use Cmd-. (Mac) or Ctrl-. (Windows) instead to stop Director.

You can not step through your Lingo program indefinitely. Suppose you set a breakpoint in an *on mouseDown* handler. At the end of that handler, even if you single-step through your Lingo code, control returns to Director. The only way to regain control is to set another breakpoint in another Lingo handler that you expect to be reached at a later time. Thus, there is no way to follow a given event as it passes through the Lingo messaging hierarchy.

One common error occurs when Lingo doesn't execute the desired code, and perhaps executes undesired code. For example, if you have two *on startMovie* handlers in two different movie scripts, the first one will run. If you set a breakpoint in the second *on startMovie* handler, it will never be reached. If you can't figure out what code is being executed, set a breakpoint in the handler you *expect* to execute. If it is never reached, search for handlers of the same name in other scripts, or use *the trace* command to see which scripts *are* being executed in the Message window.

Once you confirm *which* Lingo is being accidentally called, you can set a breakpoint in the appropriate handler. The Debugger will open the next time it is called. Look at the call stack to figure out what led to that code being reached.

Table 3-1: Checking Code and Variables

To Do This	Use This
See if your code is ever being reached	Set a breakpoint in the code. If the breakpoint is reached, the Debugger will open. During authoring, you can also use *put* statements to print a message when the handler is reached. From a Projector (or when authoring) use an *alert* statement.
Check why your code is not being reached	Back up to a known point that *is* reached. If code within a *case* or an *if...then* statement is not reached, check the expression(s) being evaluated and the logic.
Check what code is being executed	Use *set the trace = TRUE* or the *Trace* button in the Message window to view the Lingo being executed in the Message window. Start at a known point and step through the Debugger line by line. Set breakpoints in locations you expect to reach, or even those you don't expect to reach.
Check the value of a global	Use *showGlobals*, the Watcher window, the Message window, a *put* or *alert* statement, or look in the (upper right) variables pane in the Debugger.
Check the value of a local variable	Use *showLocals*, *put* or *alert* from within a handler, or set a breakpoint in that routine and use the Watcher or Debugger window's (upper right) variables pane
Check the value of any expression	Use either the Message window (except for local variables) or the Watcher window.

The Message Window

Setting breakpoints is convenient, but it can be very tedious for the Debugger to constantly appear when the handler of interest is called repeatedly.

 Use the Debugger to examine Lingo code very closely. Use *put* statements to display "running results" in the Message window without interrupting execution and use the Watcher window to monitor an expression or variable's value.

As shown throughout the earlier chapters, the Message window is a console where you can see the output of various commands and enter commands of your own. The output of the *put, trace, traceLoad, showGlobals, showLocals, showXlib, netStatus*, and *externalEvent* commands appears in the Message window during authoring.

Message window output can be saved to a file using *the traceLog-File*. Output from the *alert* command does not appear in the Message window. If you need a record of the contents of the alert dialogs, see the *on alertHook* below.

The Mighty Put

The output of any other function or the value of any global variable or Lingo property can be displayed in the Message window using the *put* command.

Example 3-16: Using Put From the Message Window and Scripts

```
put the loc of sprite 1
put gDebug
put cacheDocVerify()
put "The value of x is" && x
```

You can also use the *set* command to create or change the value of globals (but not local variables) in the Message window:

```
set gDebug = TRUE
```

For local variables, you will need to use *put* and *set* statements from within the script (or use the Watcher window at the appropriate time):

```
on myScript
  set x = 5
  put "The value of x is" && x
end
```

The Trace, TraceLoad, TraceLogFile

Set *the trace* to TRUE (or use the *Trace* button in the Message window) to log all Lingo being executed to the Message window. As the output can be verbose, you may turn it on selectively from within your scripts using the code shown in Example 3-17.

Example 3-17: Using Trace, TraceLoad, and TraceLogFile

```
on myHandler
  set the trace = TRUE
  -- Code of interest you want to trace
  set the trace = FALSE
end
```

Use *the traceLoad* to analyze loading and unloading of cast members.

```
set the traceLoad = 1   -- brief output
set the traceLoad = 2   -- verbose output
set the traceLoad = 0   -- shut off traceLoad output
```

Use *the traceLogFile* to record subsequent output to the Message window to a log file.

```
set the traceLogFile = the pathName & "output.txt"
put "This will be sent to the output file"
```

The traceLogFile doesn't work in a Projector and doesn't copy existing text from the Message window (you can do that by hand). *The traceLogFile* doesn't generate any text itself. Use *the trace* or *put* commands to send output to both the Message window and *the traceLogFile.* Cancel it using:

```
set the traceLogFile = EMPTY
```

 Cut and paste the text from the Message window into a field cast member to use Director's search functions to find an item of interest. Use *the traceLogFile* for output that exceeds the capacity of the Message window (and hence disappears).

Coding, Debugging

Alert

Use the *alert* command as shown in Table 5-5 to display any string in a dialog box. (See the MUI *Alert()* function in Chapter 15, *The MUI Dialog Xtra,* to create fancier alert dialogs. MUI Alert dialogs are unaffected by the discussion that follows regarding *the alertHook,* and are not supported under Windows 3.1.)

The built-in Lingo *alert* command typically posts a dialog box immediately, which can be prevented using an *on alert* handler in any movie script.

Example 3-18: Simple Override of Default Alert Dialog

```
on alert  alertText
  put "Please be quiet" &&  alertText
end
```

The AlertHook and On AlertHook

The previous technique is necessary only in Director 5 and earlier. D6 allows you to trap alert messages *and system error messages* with a custom handler and optionally prevent Director from displaying alert messages to the user. First, create an *on alertHook* handler, then assign *the alertHook* property to point to the *script cast member* containing that handler. The *on alertHook* handler can reside in any type of script, not just a movie script. Don't try to set *the alertHook* property to the name of a handler, as is done with the primary event handler properties (see Chapter 2).

Example 3-19: The AlertHook

This is wrong:
```
set the alertHook = "alertHook()"
```
This is right:
```
set the alertHook = script "Error Trap"
```

Terry Schusslaer reports that *the alertHook* can also be assigned to a script instance (i.e., child object) or even a list of script instances. Thus an entire list of objects could be notified when an error occurs.

The *on alertHook* handler intercepts *both alert* commands and error dialogs generated by Director. The *on alertHook* handler receives parameters that provide information about the nature of the error:

```
on alertHook me, err, msg
    return alertCode
end
```

me

Represents the instance of the script itself

err

Describes one of four possible error types:

"Script runtime error": Generated by *alert* command, or, say, an "*Index out of range*" error

"Script syntax error": Generated by incorrect script being compiled or run

"File error": Generic file error

"File read error": Error reading a file

There is no simple way to distinguish between a true Director run-time error and an innocent alert message created using the *alert* command. The err parameter is the same in both cases. You can add a distinguishing characteristic, such as an initial space, to your alert strings, or disable *the alertHook* before using *alert*, or use the MUI *Alert()* method.

msg

Describes the text of the error message that would ordinarily be displayed in the error dialog, such as "*Handler not defined.*"

alertCode

The alertCode returned by *on alertHook* determines what happens *after* the handler completes. If *the alertHook* is assigned to a *list* of script instances, the returned alertCode from the *last* script instance is the one used (as when using *call*).

Table 3-2: AlertHook Return Codes

Code	Authoring Mode	Projector (Runtime)
-1	Suppress all dialogs. Halt movie if fatal error.	Suppress all dialogs. Quit without warning if error occurs.
0	Same as default: Present *Debug/Script/Cancel* dialog. Halt movie if fatal error.	Same as default: Present *Stop/Continue* dialog for non-fatal errors.
1	Suppress all dialogs. Halt movie, open debugger if fatal error.	Suppress all dialogs. Ignore error and continue if possible.

Table 3-2: AlertHook Return Codes (continued)

Code	Authoring Mode	Projector (Runtime)
2	Suppress all dialogs. Halt movie, open Script window if fatal error.	Suppress all dialogs. Quit without warning if error occurs.

If *on alertHook* returns codes -1, 1, or 2, no error dialogs are ever posted (see exceptions later in this chapter).

 If the code returned by *on alertHook* is -1 Director won't show any dialog when you have a syntax error or run-time error during authoring. Director will simply stop. This can be very confusing when testing from the Message window or trying to recompile scripts.

If *on alertHook* returns 0, the typical alert dialog is posted in the usual way. You can explicitly post a custom dialog when using other return codes by calling *alert* from within your *on alertHook* handler. (This does *not* call *on alertHook* again and does *not* cause an infinite loop or recursion).

Example 3-20: Using On AlertHook

```
on prepareMovie
  -- Look for on alertHook handler in script " Error Trap"
  set the alertHook = script "Error Trap"
end

on stopMovie
  -- Let Director handle alerts normally (no custom trap)
  set the alertHook = 0
end
```

If *the alertHook* points to a script without an *on alertHook* handler, it has no effect. In a script cast member named "Error Trap" add the script:

```
on alertHook me, err, msg
  put "The Error is:" && err
  put "The Message is:" && msg
  -- You are allowed to call alert from within on alertHook!
  alert "I like this message better"
  -- Open debugger for fatal errors. Ignore other alerts
  return 1
end
```

Use the following to automatically open the Script window during authoring whenever there is any error, without requiring you to respond to an error dialog!

```
on alertHook me, err, msg
  if the runMode = "Author" then
    case (err) of
```

```
      "Script runtime error":
        -- Open debugger
        return 1
      "Script syntax error":
        -- Open Script Window
        return 2
      otherwise:
        return 0
    end case
  else
    -- For projectors, use standard Alert dialogs.
    return 0
  end if
end
```

You can trap specific errors by examining the *msg* parameter received by *on alert-Hook*. This example presents an error containing the word "somestring" from displaying a dialog.

```
on alertHook me, err, msg
  "somestring"
  if msg contains "somestring" from displaying a dialog then
    return 1
  else
    -- Display alert dialog for other errors
    return 0
  end if
end
```

Debugging Projectors and Shockwave

The Debugger is not available in Projectors or Shockwave, which makes it harder to debug Projector-specific errors (under Windows 3.1 especially) and Shockwave-specific errors. These techniques can also be used to debug MIAWs.

To debug a Projector:

- Test your Windows 3.1 (16-bit) Projector first on a Windows 95 machine where it is easier to switch back to authoring to perform tests or corrections.

- Use the LINGO.INI file (as described in Chapter 8, *Projectors and the Runtime Environment,* in *Director in a Nutshell* and in Appendix D, *The DIREC-TOR.INI and LINGO.INI Files*) to set global variables that can affect your Projector at runtime.

- Use a *stub* projector as described in Chapter 8 in *Director in a Nutshell* and in the Zeus TechNote at *http://www.zeusprod.com/technote/stub.html*. Stub Projectors allow you to quickly retest changes made in the authoring mode without rebuilding your Projector.

To debug Shockwave:

- Use the *netStatus* command to display variables, strings, and Lingo properties.

- Create a local test HTML page that loads your Shockwave movie without requiring it to be uploaded to a server. (Use Netscape, not MIE, for local testing.)

- Test in various browsers with different versions of the plug-ins.

To debug both Shockwave and Projectors:

- Do as much debugging as possible during authoring.

- Add error-checking code as shown previously to deal with potential errors intelligently.

- Use *alert* commands to display variables, strings, and Lingo properties.

- Use *the runMode* to execute or avoid code as needed for that specific environment. For example:

```
if the runMode <> "Plugin" then
  -- Place commands that don't work in Shockwave here.
end if
```

- Create a pseudo-Message window by sending output to a field sprite placed on stage (see *output* function under Example 3-4). Use another field to enter "commands" and execute them using the *do* command.

A Simple Sample Debugging Session

You should become adept at using the Debugger, and there is no substitute for practice. Start with a fresh Director movie that doesn't have any scripts. Use:

```
set the alertHook = 0
```

to cancel any *alertHook* in effect to make sure that error dialogs *are* displayed.

Suppose we want to create a handler that returns a list of numbers from 1 to 10.

Type the following into a movie script cast member exactly as shown. (There are supposed to be errors; this is a de*bugging* example.)

Example 3-21: A Simple Sample Debugging Session

Example 3-21a: Initial attempt to create handler
```
on createList
  repeat x = 1 to 10
    add myList, x
end
```
Before closing the script window type createList in the Message window and press Return. You should get a *"Handler not defined: createList"* error. Why? Because we haven't compiled the script, so Director doesn't know about our new handler yet.

Close the Script window to compile the script. Oops, we get an *"Expected WHILE or WITH"* error. What is wrong? Click the *Script* button in the error dialog to reedit the script. We've mistyped the *repeat* command and need to add the word *with*. Correct it as follows.

Example 3-21b: Improved repeat loop including "with"
```
on createList
  repeat with x = 1 to 10 -- Correct this line
    add myList, x
end
```
Close the script again; this time we get an *"Expected END REPEAT"* error. We forgot the *end repeat* for our *repeat* loop.

Example 3-21: A Simple Sample Debugging Session (continued)

Example 3-21c: Improved repeat loop including "end repeat"
```
on createList
  repeat with x = 1 to 10
    add myList, x
  end repeat -- Add this line
end
```

Press the **Tab** key to reformat the script. Close the script one more time. Ah ha, success! The Script window closes without incident, and we assume that all is well. Finally we can test it from the Message window:

```
createList
```

What? We get another *"Handler not defined:add myList,x"* error! I thought we just compiled the script and Director should now be able to find our *createList* handler (assuming we entered it in a movie script and not a score script). Look carefully. This is a *new* error message complaining about the line *"add myList, x,"* not the old error complaining about *createList.* Is it claiming that the *add* command is not defined? (That seems puzzling.) Well, at least it is getting to our script! How do we know that?

Use the *Script* button in the error dialog to open the Script window and set a breakpoint by clicking in the margin of the script next to the line:

```
repeat with x = 1 to 10
```

Run *createList* again from the Message window, and the Debugger window should open. There should be a green horizontal arrow atop the red breakpoint, indicating the current line of Lingo to be executed, as shown in Figure 3-5.

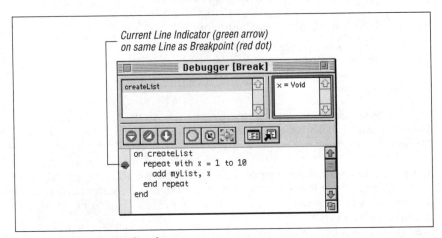

Figure 3-5: Reaching a breakpoint

Look in the Variables pane of the Debugger window. It says *x = Void.* Perhaps that is the problem. Shouldn't it be a number from 1 to 10? Recall that breakpoints occur *before* the line they're on is executed. Click the *Step Script* button once (it's

---

the leftmost of the three green arrow buttons). Director advances to the next line of Lingo, and the value of *x* is now 1, as shown in the Variables pane. All is well.

Click the *Step Script* button again. Holy debug, Batman! Another error! (Actually it is the same error we saw before; we just took longer to reach it this time.) Click the *Debug* button in the error dialog to get back to the Debugger.

Director is still choking on the line "*add myList, x.*" We check the Macromedia *Lingo Dictionary*, online help, or Chapter 6 of this book and see that we have the right syntax for the *add* command (the first parameter is supposed to be a list, and the second parameter is the item to add to the list). Surely the *add* command exists, and we didn't misspell its name, so why do we get a "*Handler not defined*" error?

In the Debugger window, click on the word *myList* and click the *Watch Expression* button (the Script and Message windows have similar buttons). The Watcher window comes up and tells us that *myList* is *Void*. Consulting Appendix E's list of error messages we see that "*Handler not defined*" errors will appear when using a Lingo list function, such as *add*, where the first parameter is not a list. Sure enough, *myList* is not a list.

You can't edit the script that appears in the Debugger window, so open the Script window using the *Go to Handler* button in the Debugger window.

Let's define *myList* at the beginning of our handler as shown in Example 3-21d.

Example 3-21d: Attempt to initialize myList

```
on createList
  myList = []   -- Add this line
  repeat with x = 1 to 10
    add myList, x
  end repeat
end
```

Close the window to recompile the script, and unfortunately you'll get a "*Misplaced operator*" error. This is apparently one step up and two steps back! Again consulting Appendix E (we'll learn these errors soon) we see that we forgot the word *set* when assigning a value using the equals sign. Fix the script as shown in Example 3-21e, and close the window to recompile.

Example 3-21e: Corrected initialization of myList

```
on createList
  set myList = []  -- Correct this line
  repeat with x = 1 to 10
    add myList, x
  end repeat
end
```

Making sure that the breakpoint is still in place, we test *createList* from the Message window again. The Debugger comes up, and we now see *myList* defined in the upper right Variables pane. Click the *Step Script* button a few times, and watch the list grow! Isn't that cool! Are you excited about debugging yet?

By stepping through the script we can also see how Director returns to the top of the *repeat* loop and increments *x* each time it hits the *end repeat* command. This is fun, but it would get tedious for a longer loop, so click on the *Run Script* green arrow button (the rightmost of the three) to continue execution.

The script disappears from the Debugger window. Note that the breakpoint at the top of the *repeat* loop is obeyed only when the loop is first entered. Open the Script window again, and set a breakpoint on the line *add myList, x*.

Run *createList* from the Message window; again, the Debugger should appear. Even if you use the *Run Script* button in the Debugger, notice that a breakpoint *within* a repeat loop interrupts Lingo execution every time through the *repeat* loop. Toggle the breakpoint(s) off (by clicking on them), and use the *Run Script* button to continue Lingo execution.

Life is good! But wait, we've completely forgotten that our original goal was to obtain the list from *createList*. In the Message window we now type:

```
put createList
-- Void
```

That's no good! Director thinks we are referring to a *variable* named *createList* following the *put* command, unless we use parentheses, such as:

```
put createList()
```

The Debugger opens if there are any breakpoints in *createList*, but when the script completes the Message window still shows the wrong result:

```
-- Void
```

Why isn't the *createList* handler returning the correct list? We reinspect our *create-List* handler and verify that `myList` is a list of integers, and not *Void*. Debugging always looks darkest just before the dawn. Inspiration hits (or we reread the earlier chapters or ask people for help online) and we realize that we forgot to return the list from the handler! Correct *createList* to read as follows.

: Example 3-21f: A completed handler

```
on createList
  set myList = []
  repeat with x = 1 to 10
    add myList, x
  end repeat
  return myList  --Add this line
end
```

One more time with feeling:

```
put createList()
-- [1, 2, 3, 4, 5, 6, 7, 8, 9, 10]
```

Yahoo! That may have seemed like lot of work, but soon enough you will be able to write and debug such a handler in less than a minute. Remember the principles you used to step through scripts, examine variables, and so on. They will serve you well.

Lingo Debugging Commands

Table 3-3 shows Lingo commands convenient for debugging.

Table 3-3: Debugging-related Lingo Commands

Command	Usage
alert	Display a message or variable's value in a dialog. See Table 5-5.
Alert(MUI)	Display a message or variable value in a multi-button dialog. See Chapter 15.
the alertHook	Intercept *alert* and error messages before they cause a dialog to appear. See *on alertHook*.
error (FileIO)	Interpret an error code returned by the FileIO Xtra. (The FileIO XObject used the *mError* method instead). See Chapter 14 and Table E-3.
externalEvent	Strings sent to the Browser using *externalEvent* from within Shockwave are displayed in the Message window during authoring.
getError()	Return an error code related to an SWA cast member. Requires SWA Streaming Xtra. See Table E-4.
getErrorString()	Return an error string related to an SWA cast member. Requires SWA Streaming Xtra. See Table E-4.
ilk()	Check a variable's type. See Table 5-4.
listP()	Check if a variable is a list. See Table 6-6.
MoaErrorToString (MUI Xtra)	*MoaErrorToString()* interprets MOA error codes returned by some Lingo commands. See Table E-7.
netError()	Check the result of a network operation. See Table E-6.
netStatus()	Display message in Browser status line (Shockwave) or Message window (authoring).
objectP()	Check if an item is an object, such as a script instance returned by instantiating an Xtra or Parent Script, or a list.
on alertHook	Handle *alert* and error messages. See *the alertHook*.
put	Print a message or variable's value in the Message window. (authoring only)
put...into	Set the value of a variable, property, or field. See *set*!
the result	Return the result of the previous function call.
set...= / set...to	Set the value of a variable or property. Global variables and Lingo properties can be set in the Message window. Local variables can be set in the Watcher window.
showGlobals	Show global variables in the Message window.
showLocals	Show local variables in the Message window (must be called from within a handler to see its local variables).

Table 3-3: Debugging-related Lingo Commands (continued)

Command	Usage
showXlib	Show a list of open Lingo Xtras and XObjects in the Message window.
status (FileIO)	Check the status of the previous FileIO operation. See Chapter 14 and Appendix E.
the trace	Set *the trace* to TRUE to display each line of Lingo in the Message window as it executes.
the traceLoad	Set *the traceLoad* to 1 or 2 to display brief or verbose information about the cast members being loaded from disk into RAM. See Chapter 9, *Memory and Performance*, in *Director in a Nutshell*.
the traceLogFile	Send the Message window output of *the trace* command and *put* statements to a log file.

Table 3-4 summarizes the shortcuts and GUI buttons relating to debugging and breakpoints.

Table 3-4: Debugging Options in the Interface

Menu	Mac	Windows	See Also
Window➤Message	Cmd-M	Ctrl-M	View➤Message Toolbar
Window➤Debugger	Cmd-`	Ctrl-`	Breakpoints
Window➤Watcher	Cmd-Shift-`	Ctrl-Shift-`	*Watch Expression* button in Debugger, Script, and Message windows
Window➤Script	Cmd-0	Ctrl-0	*Go to Handler* button in Debugger window
Control➤Disable Scripts	N/A	N/A	Script channel mute button in Score and *the scriptsEnabled of member* property
Control➤Toggle Breakpoint	Cmd-Shift-Opt-K[1]	F9	*Toggle Breakpoint* button in Debugger window, or click in margin of script
Control➤Watch Expression	Cmd-Shift-Opt-W	Shift-F9	*Watch Expression* button in Debugger, Script, and Message windows
Control➤Remove All Breakpoints	None	Alt-C-A	N/A
Control➤Ignore Breakpoints	Cmd-Shift-Opt-I	Alt-F9	*Ignore Breakpoints* button in Debugger window

Table 3-4: Debugging Options in the Interface (continued)

Menu	Mac	Windows	See Also
Control➤Step Script	Cmd-Shift-Opt- ↓	F8	*Step Script* button in Debugger
Control➤Step Into Script	Cmd-Shift-Opt- →	F10	*Step Into Script* button in Debugger
Control➤Run-Script	Cmd-Shift-Opt-↑	F5	*Run Script* button in Debugger, or close Debugger window
Control➤Recompile All Scripts	Cmd-Shift-Opt-C	Shift-F8 or Alt-C-C	*File➤General➤Prefere nces ➤Using Message window recompiles scripts*
set the trace = TRUE	N/A	N/A	*Trace* button in Message window

[1] The keyboard shortcut for toggling breakpoints on the Macintosh doesn't work.

This chapter has outlined Director's debugging tools, but I"ve also tried to convey the mindset necessary for debugging. Refer frequently to the debugging tips and checklists as you hone your investigative skills. Above all, never allow yourself to be intimidated by a bug. They can smell fear.

Coding, Debugging

CHAPTER 4

Lingo Internals

This chapter covers Lingo's internal operation, with an emphasis on comparing it to C and C++. You should be familiar with Chapter 1, *How Lingo Thinks*, before proceeding. You should also understand Director's paradigm as explained in Chapter 1, *How Director Thinks*, in *Director in a Nutshell*. Refer to Chapter 10, *Using Xtras*, in *Director in a Nutshell* and Chapter 13, *Lingo Xtras and XObjects*, in this book for details on extending Director (especially if you are a skilled C programmer). If you are unfamiliar with C, portions of this chapter will make no sense to you. Either ignore it, or read the books on C cited at the end of Chapter 13.

Lingo Internals

There wasn't room in this book for a full comparison of Lingo and C. Luckily, an extensive comparison can be found in the downloadable Chapter 20, *Lingo for C Programmers*, at *http://www.zeusprod.com/nutshell/chapters/lingovsc.html*. Even if you are not a C programmer, comparing Lingo to another language illuminates numerous issues, and it is highly recommended reading.

Memory, Pointers, and Memory Access

Director's memory usage is dominated by multimedia content, primarily graphics, rich text, and nonstreaming audio. In Lingo, you don't explicitly allocate RAM, as with *malloc* or *alloc* in C. There is no low-level access to RAM or to Director's off-screen buffer, except via Xtras. Nor are there *address* or *indirection* operators, as in C, that would give access to a variable's memory space. In Lingo, items are disposed of by setting them equal to 0, except for XObject instances, which are freed with *mDispose*. When an item in memory is no longer referenced by any variables, Director will deallocate and recapture the memory (using *reference count-based garbage collection*), but on an ambiguous schedule. (Refer to Chapter 9, *Memory and Performance*, in *Director in a Nutshell* for details on allocating and

freeing memory, loading and unloading assets, and Director's memory requirements.)

Compilation, Interpretation, and Performance

Lingo is not *compiled*, but rather *tokenized* into *byte-code*. The byte-code is the
same on both the Macintosh and Windows platforms, and it is translated at
runtime by the Projector into machine-specific instructions. This is convenient for
cross-platform development, but it does not offer the speed of assembler. Because
Lingo is not compiled, there are no separate compiler or compiler directives.

Director's `Modify►Movie►Properties►`*Allow Outdated Lingo* option controls
how Director interprets the Lingo of movies created in previous versions of
Director. It is available only when upgrading movies from prior versions. Your
concern is not necessarily the new Lingo features, but rather the changes in the
behavior of existing functions that might break legacy code. Such a change from
version to version would be exceedingly rare in a language such as C, but it is
common in Director. In Director 6, the major alteration from prior versions
involves sprite message passing (see Chapter 2, *Events, Messages, and Scripts*).
Refer to Appendix B, *Changes in D6 Through D6.5*, and to Table 17-2 for details
on other changes in D6.

Lingo executes egregiously slowly compared to C. You must be
much more conscious of both media requirements and program execution times, even for simple things like loops. There is no compiler
optimization. You must manually optimize your code, such as by
moving assignment statements outside of *repeat* loops.

The performance of your Lingo code may be dwarfed by the time required to load
media assets or download Shockwave data.

Dynamic Compilation

Throughout this book I use the term *compile* as it's used by Macromedia to indicate the tokenizing of a script. When you recompile a script, Director checks only
the syntax and for uninitialized local variables. It does not perform any type
checking, nor does it validate the number of parameters to a function call. There is
no Lingo equivalent to C's *lint* utility, which warns about global variables that are
also declared as locals, unused local variables, and similar potential errors.

Director automatically compiles any uncompiled scripts when you play your
movie. There is no lengthy recompilation of scripts that haven't changed.

There is no linking of object modules and libraries into an executable, so Director will not warn you if you refer to a nonexistent
function.

An error will not occur until runtime if a function cannot be found. In Director, *linking* means to attach an external cast library to a Director movie; it has no relation to linking object modules into an executable, as in C. (To create an executable, see File▶Create Projector and see Chapter 8, *Projectors and the Run-time Enviroment, in Director in a Nutshell.*)

Lingo gives you the convenience of, but is somewhat faster than, an interpreted language. The same Lingo can be run on multiple platforms, because it is not stored in a machine-specific format such as assembler. Unfortunately, you pay for the development benefits with the slow runtime performance.

See *"Compiling Scripts"* in Chapter 2 for details on compiling scripts and on addressing problems with corrupted scripts.

Lingo's dynamic compilation allows you to rapidly change and test your Lingo. Lingo can even be modified or created at runtime, by setting *the scriptText of member* property or using the *do* or *value* command. Even the base class of an object can be changed dynamically. (See Chapter 12, *Behaviors and Parent Scripts.*)

Director does not support header files, macro definitions, or inline macros, as C does. Subroutine calls take several orders of magnitude longer in Lingo than in C, so you should use in-line code when performance is crucial.

Language Definition

C's command set is exceedingly simple, and its syntax and structure are uniform, efficient, and elegant. By comparison, Lingo is verbose, lumbering, and wildly inconsistent. Whereas C provides very low-level access, Lingo provides high-level commands to play sounds or download bitmaps. Whereas C's command set is limited to a few dozen keywords, Lingo has more than 500 commands and properties specific to media, GUIs, and event processing. Lingo incorporates many of the support functions ordinarily found in C libraries such as *stdio.*

Lingo handlers are declared using the *on* keyword, but there is no parameter type checking or return value type checking associated with a function declaration or separate function prototype, as in C. Lingo uses the keyword *the* to identify properties, such as *the clickOn,* and *the mouseH.*

Lingo does not support bit-wise operations or complex numbers. They require an Xtra or other custom code.

Parameters and Variables

In Lingo, most data types, including strings, are passed by value, except lists (and other objects), which are passed by reference. Therefore, changing the contents of a list within a handler will change the list in the calling routine. See Chapter 6, *Lists.* Lingo doesn't support indirection, so non-list data types can be passed back to the calling routine using *return* or a *global* declaration only. In Lingo, you can also pass multiple parameters in a list or object, which can then be modified.

In Lingo, the parentheses surrounding the arguments to a function are mandatory only when that function returns a value. Unlike C, the parentheses are optional when the calling routine is not receiving a return value.

In Lingo, if the calling routine omits an argument to a function, the corresponding parameter inside the function is set to VOID. In C, an error would be generated by the precompiler, or the omitted argument would result in the corresponding parameter holding a meaningless value.

Lingo, as with C, allows nested function calls, such as:

```
set x = random (max(y, z))
```

Unlike C, in Lingo, you can *not* perform a variable assignment within a nested function call. (Recall that Lingo assignment requires the keyword *set*). These attempts would cause syntax errors in Lingo:

```
if (x = max(y, z) > 7) then....
if (set x = max(y, z) > 7) then....
```

Refer also to the *"Parameters and Arguments"* section of Chapter 1. Lingo variable and function names are case-insensitive and can be exceedingly long (about 250 characters). In C, variable and function names are strictly case-sensitive.

Declarations, Type Checking, and Conversion

In comparison to C, Lingo's data typing is loose to the point of being obscene. Lingo never explicitly declares a variable's data type, nor a function's return type, as opposed to C, which is strongly typed. A Lingo variable's data type is implicitly defined by the type of data assigned to it, and it can be changed by simply assigning a new datum to it.

Data Type Checking and Conversion

Lingo does not verify the number or type of arguments to a function call, nor does it support function prototyping, as in C. In C, because every variable's type is fixed, it is assumed that you know a datum's type. Because Lingo is so loosely typed, it provides functions—most notably *ilk()*, *integerP()*, *floatP()*, *stringP()*, *voidP()*, and *objectP()*—to determine a datum's type. Refer to Table 5-4, *"Ilk Return Values"* in Chapter 5, *Data Types and Expressions*. Refer to the *"Parameters and Arguments"* section of Chapter 1 for techniques for manually verifying parameters passed to a function.

Lingo casually converts between various data types with sometimes puzzling results, as opposed to C-style coercion and conversion, which is usually explicit. Refer to "Type Conversion" in Chapter 5.

Lists, Arrays, and Structures

Lingo lists encompass both C arrays and structures. Unlike C arrays, Lingo lists are allocated automatically and can change size arbitrarily. There is no dimension statement or *malloc* statement in Lingo, and a single list can contain data of differing types *simultaneously*. A two-dimensional array is implemented as a list of lists in Lingo, but its elements cannot be referenced as a one-dimensional array, as is often done in C. Unlike most Lingo data types, lists are passed by reference, not value. See Chapter 6, *Lists*, for more details. See the downloadable Chapter 20 for a complete comparison of data types in Lingo and C.

Strings

String are a distinct data type in Lingo, not an array of characters as in C. When working with Lingo strings, you need not allocate a specific number of bytes, nor should you worry about null-termination. A Lingo string with no characters has zero-length, as reported by the *length()* function. Lingo strings are allocated automatically and dynamically. Whereas a Lingo field is limited to 32,000 characters (31.25 K), a string variable can be much larger (up to 2 MB). Unfortunately, because Lingo strings are passed on the stack by value (which is very inefficient), attempting to call the *length()* function with such a large string can overflow Director's stack.

Passing strings on the stack by value is one reason Lingo's text processing is egregiously slow.

You cannot directly modify a string argument to a Lingo function. Instead, you must modify a copy of the string and pass it back as a return value. Refer to Chapter 7, *Strings*, for many more details on string manipulation in Lingo, especially concatenation. See Chapter 14, *External Files*, for details on reading and writing strings using external files. See Chapter 12, *Text and Fields*, in *Director in a Nutshell* for details on displaying strings on stage.

Event and Error Trapping

Director implements a so-called event loop in which it continually waits for events. In Lingo, you need only create handlers, such as *on mouseUp*, that respond to these events, such as *mouseUp* (see Chapter 2). There is no need to subscribe to any particular events, as events are dispatched to the appropriate scripts automatically.

Lingo does not have robust error trapping or true interrupts. Errors typically generate an alert dialog box. You can perform your own error checking to prevent this. See "*The alertHook*" section in Chapter 3, *Lingo Coding and Debugging Tips*.

Debugging

Director has a Debugger (see Chapter 3), but it is not as robust as traditional debugging tools. For one thing, you can change the code at runtime, in which case the Debugger will warn you that scripts need to be recompiled! If you close the Debugger window, Director immediately regains control. You must stop the Director movie itself to halt Lingo execution and recompile your scripts.

In C programming, the application programmer is at the *top* of the hierarchy. If you set a breakpoint in the C debugger, you can step through your program indefinitely. Even if you call library routines to perform lower-level functions, control always boomerangs back to you.

By contrast, in Director the Lingo programmer is sandwiched between the library of Lingo commands (on the bottom) and Director's main event loop (on the top). (And the Debugger can debug only *Lingo* code. It has no access to the C code of Xtras or of Director itself, nor direct access to the Lingo of MIAWs.) Because Director's event loop is *above* your Lingo code, it periodically regains control, and there is nothing you can do to stop it. Suppose you set a breakpoint in an *on mouseDown* handler. At the end of that handler, even if you single-step through your Lingo code, control returns to Director's event processing loop. The only way to regain control is to set another breakpoint in another Lingo handler that you expect to be reached at a later time. Thus, there is no way to follow a given event as it passes through the Lingo messaging hierarchy.

Likewise, there is no way to cause an immediate break into whatever Lingo code may be executing at the moment. Director will break into Lingo only where you have *previously* set a break point. If you understand the material covered in detail in Chapters 1 and 2, you will be able to figure out where to set your breakpoints.

The Director movie stops when you press Cmd-. (Mac) or Ctrl-. (Windows) to interrupt execution, but you aren't afforded the opportunity to enter the Debugger. In fact, there is a good chance that Director's C code, and not the Lingo interpreter, is running at any given time, so there is no way that Director can pass control to the Lingo Debugger at the arbitrary time at which the user halts Director's execution.

File I/O, Character Streams, and Printing

All Lingo file input and output is done using the FileIO Xtra, which comes with Director. Refer to Chapter 14.

Lingo does not support pipes or redirection. Editable fields automatically accept keystrokes, but you can use an *on keyDown* handler to trap keyboard input explicitly. Refer to Chapter 10, *Keyboard Events*.

Instead of C's formatted *printf* statement, use the *put* command to print items in the Message window, which behaves as *stdout*. You can redirect the output from the Message window to a log file using *the traceLogFile* property.

Lingo Object-Oriented Programming Versus C++

Lingo provides an object-oriented model, described in Chapter 12, *Behaviors and Parent Scripts*. Refer also to Chapter 12, *Parent Scripts and Child Objects*, of Macromedia's *Learning Director* manual. Director allows you to mix and match OOP and procedural programming. Table 4-1 compares the terminology for Lingo and C++.

Table 4-1: Lingo versus C++ Terminology

C++ Term	Lingo Term
Class	Parent script
Base class or super class	Ancestor script

Table 4-1: Lingo versus C++ Terminology (continued)

C++ Term	Lingo Term
Instance	Child object or child instance
Inherited or derived class (descendant)	A child object with an ancestor
Handler or procedure	Method
Instance variable or member variable	Property variable
Constructor	*new* method
Deconstructor	None; set variable referencing object to 0
`this`	*me*

Class Hierarchy and Inheritance

Lingo's class hierarchies are much looser than C++'s. In C++, a class's *base class* is defined in the *constructor*, before the class is even compiled. In Lingo, a child object's *ancestor* property is set at runtime; it can even change dynamically. A single child object can inherit only from a single ancestor script (multiple inheritance is not supported). For a child object to inherit additional methods from additional ancestors, its direct ancestor must declare its own ancestor. Note that in Lingo, the term *parent* refers not to a *parent class* or *base class*, but merely to the *parent script* (that is, class definition) of which the *child object* is an instance. In the simplest case, a single parent script is instantiated to create one or more copies of itself (so-called child objects). Thus, a child object is not necessarily a descendent of some base class, and its parent script is not necessarily an *inherited* or *derived class*.

The following features of C++ have no equivalent in Lingo:

- Abstract class
- Multiple inheritance
- Templates

Encapsulation

It is impossible to *encapsulate* a child object fully. Lingo objects can be manipulated by some list functions, and they are passed by reference, as are Lingo lists. The Lingo *count()* and *getAt()* functions can extract a child object's property variables. These properties can also be read or set by code external to the object using:

```
set the property of childObject = value
```

There is no equivalent to C++'s `static`, `public`, `private`, and `friend` handlers. Methods within a child object are private by default, but any message can be sent to a child object using the *call()* function. Its ancestor can be called using *callAncestor()*. A child can refer to its ancestor's properties (after declaring its ancestor) using:

```
set the property of the ancestor of me = value
```

Refer to Chapter 12 for a thorough discussion of objects in Director.

The downloadable Chapter 20 (cited earlier) covers many more details that dead-tree publishing constraints did not allow here. It is an invaluable Lingo syntax primer for C programmers, and a glimpse into the world of C for Linguists. It is an in-depth comparison of Lingo and C, including numerous useful tables comparing data types and commands in the two languages.

PART II

Lingo Data Types and Expressions

CHAPTER 5

Data Types and Expressions

This chapter covers data types, expression evaluation, and operators. Refer to Chapter 1, *How Lingo Thinks*, for a discussion of variables, and to Chapter 8, *Math (and Gambling)*, for details on numeric data types. Refer to Chapter 7, *Strings*, for details on string manipulation and to Chapter 6, *Lists*, for many details on lists. See also Chapter 19, *The Lingo Symbol Table*, for a detailed discussion of symbols.

Data Types and Variable Types

In addition to Lingo keywords, Lingo uses *constants*, *variables*, *symbols*, and *literals*, which can contain various data types such as integers, floats, and strings.

Constants
> Constants are common values, such as PI, FALSE, and TRUE, that are predefined in Lingo for convenience.

Literals
> Literals are fixed values specified by the programmer, such as 6 (an integer literal), and "flubber" (a string literal).

Symbols
> Symbols are a convenient way to represent strings or integers. Lingo includes some symbols, such as *#digitalVideo*, and the programmer can define others.

Variables
> Variables contain data that can change. A variable, such as myHighScore, may equal 5 at one point but later be updated so that it equals 7.

Lingo data types, summarized in Table 5-1, include those common to most languages, as well as *objects* and other complex types that are unique to Lingo. Note that there is no double-precision float type or short integer type. Lists are roughly equivalent to arrays and structures. Refer to Chapters 1 and 6 for a discussion of variables and lists, and refer to Chapter 4, *Lingo Internals*, and the downloadable Chapter 20, *Lingo for C Programmers*, for a comparison of Lingo and C data types.

Table 5-1: Data Types

Data Type	Usage and Range
Boolean	A TRUE or FALSE value (equal to 1 or 0, respectively)
constant	Predefined string, integer, or float, such as TAB, TRUE, or PI.
integer	Whole number, which may be negative, 0, or positive. Lingo does not support octal or hexadecimal integers. See the bonus downloadable examples (http://www.zeusprod.com/nutshell/examples.html) for a utility to convert between different number bases.
float	Decimal (floating-point number), which may be negative, 0.0, or positive.
instance	An "occurrence" or "clone" of a parent script, Behavior, or Xtra. Each instance is independent of other instances and can have custom values for any properties it declares. (In D3.1.3, property variables were called *instance* variables.)
list	Array containing values of any data type, including integers, floats, strings, symbols, and even other lists. See Chapter 6.
literal	Fixed string, integer, or float, such as "hubbaloo", 7, or 6.9.
me	An object reference passed to Behaviors representing the current script instance.
media	Data type used by *the media of member* property.
member	A reference of the form (*member memberNum* of castLib *castLibNum*). Refer to the Chapter 4, *CastLibs, Cast Members and Sprites*, in *Director in a Nutshell*.
object	Complex structure returned when a parent script or Xtra is instantiated. Refer to Chapter 12, *Behaviors and Parent Scripts*, and Chapter 13, *Lingo Xtras and XObjects*.
picture	Data type used by *the picture of member* property.
point	A list of two integer elements (*x, y*) that define a point. See Chapter 6.
property	A symbolic value used to tag an item in a list, a Lingo property (such as *the colorDepth*), or a property variable, as described in Table 5-2.
rect	A list of four integer elements (*left, top, right, bottom*) or two points that define a rectangle. See Chapter 6.
script	A reference to a script, such as a parent script, used with the *new* command. Also a type of object.
sound	A reference to a sound.
string	Series of zero or more characters enclosed in quotes. The constant EMPTY equals "" (a zero-length string).
symbol	A name preceded by a "#" used in place of strings or integers. See Chapter 19.

Table 5-1: Data Types (continued)

Data Type	Usage and Range
void	A void value contains no data whatsoever. Global variables are VOID before being assigned a value. VOID is not the same as EMPTY or zero and is represented by the constant VOID (new in D6).
xtra	An object representing an Xtra. See Chapter 13, *Lingo Xtras and XObjects*.

Table 5-2 lists each variable "class." A variable can hold any type of data. See the *"Variables and Properties"* section of Chapter 1 for details on the several classes of variables and how they differ.

Table 5-2: Variable Types

Variable Class	Notes
global	A global variable is declared with the *global* keyword and is accessible from any handler in which it is declared as a global, or from all handlers within a script if it is declared at the top of the script.
local	A local variable need not be declared explicitly, although it must be assigned a value (such as, *set x = 5*) before being used in an expression.
property	A property is declared with the *property* keyword within a parent script or Behavior, but can be accessed from other scripts indirectly. The term "property" also refers to Lingo properties and property lists, but the keyword *property* is only used with property variables. See Chapters 6 and 12.

Type Assignment and Conversion

In Lingo you need not declare a variable's data type before using it. Its type is implicitly determined by the kind of data you store in it using the *set* command. You can also use *put...into* to assign a variable or *put...after* to append data to a string variable. You can print out the value of a variable in the Message window using the *put* command.

```
set x = 5          -- x is now an integer
set x = "foo"      -- x is now a string
put "bar" after  x  -- This appends a string after x
put x              -- This displays the value of x
```

Note that the assignment operator, "=", is *not* strictly the algebraic operator "equals." The expression on the right-hand side is calculated, then assigned to the variable on the left. Therefore the expression:

```
set x = x + 1
```

is perfectly valid and commonly used to increment a variable (Lingo does not have increment or decrement operators, as does C). See Chapter 1, *How Lingo Thinks*, for details.

Note that Lingo also uses the "=" operator for comparisons, unlike C, which uses the separate "=="operator for comparisons.

In most languages, a variable must contain the same type of data throughout its life, but in Lingo, a variable's type can be changed at any time. Lingo converts between data types as necessary, without warning.

Operands in an expression or comparison must be of the same type, and Lingo will implicitly convert operands as necessary. If you concatenate an integer with a string, Lingo will automatically convert the integer to a string. In comparisons, it will convert the second operand to the type of the first (in most cases) before performing the comparison. For example, in the expression:

```
if "1" = 1 then put "Tell me it's true, baby!"
```

Director *implicitly* converts the integer 1 to the string "1" before performing the comparison.

You can *explicitly* check or convert a datum's type using the functions shown in Table 5-3.

There are several reasons to explicitly convert a datum's type:

Converting text entry to other data types
All fields (including user input) and data read from external files are treated as string data. Even if the user enters a number, you must use the *value()*, *integer()*, or *float()* function to convert it from a string to a numeric data type.

Ensuring accuracy of math calculations
To perform a calculation with floating-point accuracy, at least one operand must be a float. Use the *float()* function if necessary.

Ensuring valid comparisons
To ensure that operands are converted to the expected data types before the comparisons are made, use one of Lingo's type conversion functions, such as *integer()* or *string()*. See Table 5-3.

To freeze a list's current state
Use the *string()* function to convert a list to a string, which gives a snapshot of the list at a given time.

To provide the required arguments to a function
Many commands require parameters of a certain type. For example, the *alert* command will not display an integer it is first converted with *string()*. See Table 5-5.

Type Checking

There are several reasons to perform type checking:

To determine an unknown value's type
You may need to decide whether user input is of the correct type. For example:

```
if not integerP(value(field "Age")) then
  alert "Please enter a valid age"
end if
```

To check parameters' types

You can check whether the parameters passed to a function are of the correct type, or whether they were passed at all:

```
on addThem a, b
   if not (ilk(a) = #integer or ilk(a) = #float) then
      alert "The first item must be a number"
      return VOID
   else if not (ilk(b) = #integer or ilk(b) = #float) then
      alert "The second item must be a number"
      return VOID
   else
      return (a + b)
   end if
end addThem
```

To check whether a value has been initialized

Use *voidP()* to decide whether a global variable has already been initialized, and to avoid initializing it twice. See Example 1-16.

To perform error checking

Many functions return different types of values depending on whether the operation was successful. Always check the return value when instantiating an Xtra to make sure it is an object. If not, it may be an integer error code (see Examples 12-7 and 19-3).

```
set myFileInstance = new (Xtra "FileIO")
if not objectP(myFileInstance) then
   alert "Couldn't instantiate FileIO"
end if
```

Refer to the lengthy Example 1-39, *"Verifying Parameters,"* under *"Parameter Error Checking"* at the end of Chapter 1.

Table 5-3: Type Checking and Conversion

Lingo Function	Usage
#*symbolName*	Symbol operator (#) defines a symbol, such as #*mySymbol*
charToNum()	Converts ASCII character to ASCII code. See *numToChar()* and Appendix A, *ASCII Codes and Key Codes.*
factory()	Returns TRUE if operand is an open XLibrary, such as *factory ("SerialPort").*
float()	Converts data to floating-point value (*the floatPrecision* affects the number of digits displayed).
floatP()	Returns TRUE if operand is a floating-point value.
ilk(*datum*)	Returns *datum*'s type (see Table 5-4).
ilk(*datum, type*)	Returns TRUE if *datum* is of the specified *type* (#rect, #point, #linearList, #list, #propList, etc.). See Table 5-4.
integer()	Converts data to integer value.[1]

Table 5-3: Type Checking and Conversion (continued)

Lingo Function	Usage
integerP()	Returns TRUE if operand is an integer value.
listP()	Returns TRUE if operand is a linear list, property list, rect, or point. See Chapter 6.
numToChar()	Converts ASCII code to ASCII character. See *charToNum* and Appendix A.
new()	Creates an instance (that is, child object) from a parent script or Xtra, or a new cast member of a specified type.
objectP()	Returns TRUE if operand is an object, including a list, script, sound, Xtra, or instance of an Xtra or parent script. See ilk (datom, #object) in Table 16-1.
pictureP()	Returns TRUE if operand is a picture. See *the picture of member*.
set... = set... to	Assigns a value to a variable, which implicitly sets the variable's type (also sets Lingo properties).
string()	Converts data to a string.
stringP()	Returns TRUE if operand is a string.
symbol()[2]	Converts an item to a symbol.
symbolP()	Returns TRUE if operand is a symbol.
#*symbolName* + 0	Determines a symbol's position in Lingo's symbol table. See Chapter 19.
value()	Converts a string to a number.
voidP()	Returns TRUE if operand is VOID.

[1] *Integer()* will not convert a string containing a decimal point or "+". Use *value()* first.
[2] The *symbol()* function is new in D6. Use *value ("#" & stringVar)* to convert an item to a symbol in earlier versions of Director.

Table 5-4 lists the value returned by the various forms of the *ilk()* function. You can also use the form *the ilk of,* instead of *ilk().* The *ilk of member* property always returns *#member*. In most cases, you can also use *ilk (item, #symbol)* to obtain a Boolean result. Beware: In some cases, the result does not jibe with the *ilk(item)* call; for example:

```
set childObject = new (script "Parent Script")
put ilk (childObject)
-- #instance
put ilk (childObject, #instance)
-- 0   -- FALSE!
put ilk (childObject, #object)
-- 1   -- TRUE!
```

Refer also to Chapter 6 for details on using *ilk()* with lists, and to *ilk()* in Table 16-1.

Table 5-4: Ilk Return Values

ilk Function	Result	See Also
ilk(actor())	#actor	Undocumented Lingo
ilk (7.5)	#float	floatP()
ilk (*me*) ilk (getAt (the scriptInstanceList of sprite *n*, 1))	#instance	beginSprite()
ilk (new (xtra "*XtraName*")) ilk (new (script "*parentScript*"))	#instance	objectP()
ilk (3)	#integer	integerP()
ilk (list(1,2,3,4))	#list	listP()
ilk (the media of member 1)	#media	the media of member
ilk (the score)	#media	the score
put ilk (member *whichMember* of castLib *whichCast*) put ilk (the member of sprite *whichSprite*)	#member	the member of sprite
put ilk(factory ("SerialPort"))	#object	objectP()
put ilk (member *olemember*)	#ole	
ilk (the picture of member *bitmapMember*)	#picture	pictureP()
ilk (point (*x, y*))	#point	ilk (*list*, #point)
ilk ([#a:1]	#propList	ilk (*list*, #propList)
ilk (rect(*l, t, r, b*))	#rect	ilk (*list*, #rect)
ilk (sound *soundMember*)	#sound	the type of member
ilk (sprite *whichSprite*)	#sprite	the type of sprite
ilk ("abc")	#string	stringP()
ilk (field *fieldMember*)	#string	stringP
ilk (#foo)	#symbol	symbolP()
ilk (*VOID*)	#void	voidP()
ilk (the stage)	#window	open window
ilk (xtra "FileIO")	#xtra	new()
put new (xtra "FileIO")	-- <Xtra child "FileIO" 1 21341fa>	factory(), mMessageList(), objectP

Table 5-4: Ilk Return Values (continued)

ilk Function	Result	See Also
put new (script "Parent Test")	-- <offspring "Parent Test" 1 21340b0>	objectP()

Using *ilk()* with a case statement may be preferable to using the individual functions that check whether an operand is of a particular type.

If using *ilk()* with list operands, don't forget that *listP()* checks for all types of lists, whereas *ilk()* distinguishes the multiple types:

```
case ilk(datum) of
    #integer, #float: -- whatever
    #list, #propList, #rect, #point: -- whatever
    otherwise: -- whatever
end case
```

Or use this:

```
if integerP (datum) or floatP(datum) then
    -- whatever
else if listP(datum)
    -- whatever
else
    -- whatever
end if
```

Type Conversion Caveats

Unexpected results can occur when you do not understand Lingo's type conversion mechanism. For example, whenever you perform a math calculation with integer operands, the result is an integer. Therefore the following expression yields the integer 1, not 1.6666. Refer to Chapter 8.

```
put 5/3
-- 1
```

The *integer()* function will not properly convert strings containing a "+" sign, "-" sign, or a decimal point. Convert such strings with the *value()* function first.

```
put integer ("4")
-- 4
put integer ("+4.5")
-- Void  -- Wrong!
put integer (value("+4.5"))
-- 5
put integer("-4")
-- -4
put integer("4-5")
-- 4  -- Wrong!
put integer(value("4-5"))
-- -1
```

Users of earlier versions of Director often mistakenly use the following to increment the cast member of a sprite.

```
set the member of sprite 5 = (the member of sprite 5) + 1
```

Director cannot reconcile the integer and member data types, resulting in the right side evaluating to 0, which makes the sprite disappear! You can see this evaluated in the Message window using:

```
put member 4 + 1
-- 0
```

The proper approach is to increment *the memberNum,* which is an integer, such as:

```
set the memberNum of sprite 5 = ¬
    the memberNum of sprite 5 + 1
```

Refer to Chapter 4 in *Director in a Nutshell* for more details.

Refer to Chapters 6 and 8 for details on how Lingo handles expressions containing both lists and numbers, such as:

```
put [1, 4, 6] * 7.2
-- [7.2000, 28.8000, 43.2000]
```

Table 5-5 will give you a good practical understanding of the different data types and implicit and explicit type conversion. Try typing these commands in the Message window to see what happens. Do you understand why some fail and others succeed? Use the *put* command instead of the *alert* command, and observe whether the results differ. See "*String Operators*" later in this chapter and Chapter 7 for more details on *concatenating* (joining) strings with the *&* and *&&* operators.

Table 5-5: Data Type Conversion Practice

Command	Comments
alert "You are a Lingo God"	Believe it!
alert "Yoo" & "Hoo!"	& concatenates the two strings into one string.
alert "Yoo" && "Hoo!"	&& concatenates the two strings and adds a space between them.
alert "Yoo", "Hoo!"	The second string ("Hoo") is ignored because *alert* expects only one parameter.
alert 6	6 is an integer, so this fails.
alert "6"	"6" in quotes is a string.
alert string(6)	*String()* converts any data type to a string.
alert	*Alert* expects one parameter, so this fails.
alert ""	Two double quotes in a row is the empty string.
alert EMPTY	EMPTY is predefined as "" by Lingo.

Table 5-5: Data Type Conversion Practice (continued)

Command	Comments
alert "EMPTY"	"EMPTY" in quotes is not the same as the reserved Lingo word EMPTY.
alert "myString"	Is "*myString*" a variable or a literal?
alert myString	*myString* is assumed to be a variable because it is not in quotes. Its initial value is VOID when used in the Message window.
set myString = "You're Cool!" alert myString	After assigning a value to *myString*, what happens?
alert x	*x* is assumed to be a variable. What does it contain?
set x = 7 alert x	After assigning a value to *x*, what happens?
alert string (x)	*String()* forces the conversion to a string.
alert "The value of X is" && x	*x* is implicitly converted to a string because it is concatenated with a string.
alert ["a", "b", "c"]	Is a list of strings the same as a string? No! So this fails!
alert string (["a", "b", "c"])	What does the *string()* function do?

Constants

Lingo defines numerous constants and symbols (see Table 5-6) that make it easier to write and interpret a Lingo script. Constants are just shorthand for commonly used integers, characters, and floating-point numbers.

Table 5-6: Lingo Constants

Constant	Value	ASCII Code
BACKSPACE	Backspace key or Delete key	8 (Ctrl-H)
e[1]	Natural log base; float value 2. 71828182845905	N/A
EMPTY	Null character, ""	0
ENTER	Enter key on keypad	3 (Ctrl-C)
FALSE	Integer 0 (zero)	N/A
LF[1]	Linefeed	10 (Ctrl-J)
PI[2]	Float value 3.14159265358979	N/A
QUOTE	Quote character """	34
RETURN	Return key on main keyboard,.	13 (Ctrl-M)
SPACE[2]	Space bar (" ")	32

Table 5-6: Lingo Constants (continued)

Constant	Value	ASCII Code
TAB	Tab key	9 (Ctrl-I)
TRUE	Integer 1 (one)	N/A
VOID²	Nonexistent or <void>	N/A

¹ *e* and LF are *not* built-in constants, but you may wish to define them as shown in Example 5-1. See Chapter 8.
² The constants PI, SPACE, and VOID, are new in Director 6. Define them for use in earlier versions of Director as shown later in this chapter.

Example 5-1: Simulating Constants Using Globals

```
on defineGlobalConstants
  global LF, e
  global PI, SPACE, VOID
  global version

  set LF = numToChar(10)   -- Line Feed
  set e  = exp (1)         -- natural logarithm

  -- These are already defined in D6. Define them manually for earlier versions
  if integer (char 1 of version) < 6 then
    set PI = pi()
    set SPACE = " "
    -- All unassigned global variables default
    -- to VOID, so this isn't necessary assuming
    -- you never assigned a value to VOID.
    set VOID = value("<void>")
  end if
end defineGlobalConstants
```

Symbols

Lingo symbols are used to represent special items that would otherwise be difficult to remember or interpret. For example, *the type of member* property returns symbols such as *#bitmap* and *#sound* that are easy to understand.

A Lingo symbol is defined by using the # character proceding a symbol name:

#symbolName

A symbol gives you the descriptive benefit of strings, with the speed and efficiency of integers. Use alphanumeric characters for your symbol names (without any spaces). Director may get confused if you create symbols with integers or floating-point numbers as their names. It will convert them to numbers instead of symbols, defeating the purpose.

These should be *avoided*:

```
set x = #69    -- Avoid symbols that are integers
put ilk (x)
```

```
-- #integer
set y = #7.4     -- Avoid floating point numbers too
put ilk (y)
-- #float
set z = #buckle my shoe  -- No Spaces allowed!
```

These are fine:

```
set x = #attribute69
set y = #node7_4
set y = #buckle_my_shoe
```

Lingo defines many symbols that are used by many of its commands and functions. For example, *#integer* is a predefined Lingo symbol:

```
put ilk(5)
#integer
```

You can understand the benefit of symbols when you see the cryptic integer codes for ink types (see *the ink of sprite*) and transition types (see *the frameTransition* and *puppetTransition.*). If Macromedia had used symbols instead of integer codes, you wouldn't have to use:

```
set the ink of sprite whichSprite = 8
```

You could instead use something like:

```
set the ink of sprite whichSprite = #matte
```

Unfortunately, *the ink of sprite* property doesn't recognize symbols, although many Lingo commands do. Refer to Chapter 16, *Enumerated Values*, for a complete listing of all the different integer codes, symbols, and strings used for various Lingo commands.

Also, unfortunately, there is no easy way to assign a specific integer or other value to a symbol. In other words, a symbol *is* itself; it is not a variable that can hold other types of data. (Symbols can be converted to strings using the *string()* function. Refer also to the *symbol()* and *symbolP()* functions in Table 5-3.)

```
put string (#buckle_my_shoe)
-- "buckle_my_shoe"
```

Lingo property lists often use symbols as their property names (although other data types can be used as well). Refer to "Property Lists" in Chapter 6, or skip this example for now.

For example, this is a property list using several new symbols:

```
set myPropList = [#apples: 5, #bananas: 7, #papayas: 3]
```

Symbols are convenient for referring to items in the property list, such as:

```
put myPropList
-- [#apples: 5, #bananas: 7, #papayas: 3]
put the apples of myPropList
-- 5
set the bananas of myPropList = 2
put myPropList
-- [#apples: 5, #bananas: 2, #papayas: 3]
```

Likewise, you could create a global property list of the integer codes for each type of ink, such as shown in Example 5-2.

Example 5-2: Replacing Integer Codes with Symbols

```
on startMovie
  global gInkList
  set gInkList=[#Copy: 0, #Transparent: 1, #Reverse: 2,  ¬
    #Ghost: 3, #NotCopy: 4, #NotTransparent: 5,           ¬
    #NotReverse: 6, #NotGhost: 7, #Matte: 8, #Mask: 9,    ¬
    #Blend: 32, #AddPin: 33, #Add: 34, #SubtractPin: 35,  ¬
    #BackgroundTransparent: 36, #Lightest: 37,            ¬
    #Subtract: 38, #Darkest: 39, #: 40]
end
```

And then use it like this:

```
on mouseUp
  global gInkList
  set the ink of sprite (the currentSpriteNum) = ¬
    the matte of gInkList
end mouseUp
```

See Chapter 19 for many more details on built-in Lingo symbols and their limitations. Despite the *Lingo Dictionary's* claim to the contrary, symbols are sensitive to diacritical marks. See Appendix C, *Case-Sensitivity, Sort Order, Diacritical Marks, and Space-Sensitivity.*

Operators

Lingo can perform calculations and evaluate expressions using a variety of operators. Arithmetic operators are explained in Chapter 8. Operators with a higher precedence are performed first. Use parentheses to override the default evaluation order. See "Precedence Caveats" below.

Comparison Operators

Lingo supports the usual complement of comparison operators, as shown in Table 5-7. Use these in conditional expressions, such as *repeat while...* and *if... then*, to compare various data types or whether a Boolean property is TRUE or FALSE.

The <, <=, >, and >= operators perform *case-sensitive* string comparisons whereas the =, <>, *contains*, and *starts* operators are *case-insensitive*. See Appendix C.

Table 5-7: Comparison Operators

Operator	Comparison	Precedence
<	less than	1
<=	less than or equal to[1]	1
<>	not equal to[1]	1
=	equal to[2]	1
>	greater than	1
>=	greater than or equal to[1]	1
contains	*string1* contains *string2*	N/A
starts	*string1* starts *string2*	N/A
intersects	*sprite1* intersects *sprite2*	N/A
within	*sprite1* within *sprite2*	N/A

[1] Note that "><," "=<," and "=>" are *not* acceptable alternatives to "<>," ">=," and "<=."
[2] When used within an *if* or *repeat while..*, statement the equals sign ("=") compares whether two values are equal. It does not assign a value, as it does when used with the *set* command.

Comparison Caveats

Implicit Type Conversion

Lingo allows comparison between different data types, but it will convert one operand to the type of the other before performing the comparison. Therefore, this statement evaluates to TRUE, even though you might expect otherwise:

```
if "2" = 2 then put "They're equal"
```

String Comparison

String comparison may be case-sensitive depending on the comparison operator used (see the earlier note). All string comparison is sensitive to diacritical marks, such as accents, despite the Macromedia documentation's claims to the contrary. Refer to Chapter 7 and Appendix C for more details on string operators and case-sensitivity.

Lists

Lists are compared on an element-by-element basis, not "by reference." Two variables pointing to two different lists are considered equal if the lists contain identical elements.

Boolean Properties and Logical Operators

A *Boolean* property can only be TRUE or FALSE. For example, *the shiftDown* is a Boolean property indicating whether the Shift key is currently being pressed. Director uses the constants TRUE and FALSE to conveniently represent 1 (which indicates TRUE) and 0 (which indicates FALSE).

Logical operators evaluate *Boolean expressions*, which evaluate to either 1 (TRUE) or 0 (FALSE), as shown in Table 5-8.

Table 5-8: Boolean Operators

Operator	Boolean Result	Precedence
a and *b*	TRUE if both *a* and *b* are TRUE	4
a or *b*	TRUE if either *a* or *b* is TRUE	4
not (*x*)	Logical negation; TRUE only if *x* is 0, otherwise FALSE	5
TRUE	TRUE equals 1 (one)	N/A
FALSE	FALSE equals 0 (zero)	N/A

Lingo evaluation of logical expressions is very inefficient. Lingo will evaluate the second half of an *and* or *or* statement, even if the first half is enough to determine whether the overall expression is TRUE or FALSE.

In the following expression, if `myList` is not a list, the expression *count(myList)* will cause a "*Handler not defined*" error (you can't use *count()* on something that is not a list).

Example 5-3: Avoiding Evaluation of the Second Clause in a Compound Expression

```
if listP(myList) and count(myList) > 5 then
  -- whatever
end if
```

If the second expression in a compound statement will *possibly* cause an error, you should use nested *if* statements to ensure that the second expression is not evaluated unless necessary. (This will also speed up your code especially if you are performing many comparisons inside a *repeat* loop.)

```
if listP(myList)
  if count(myList) > 5 then
    -- whatever
  end if
end if
```

Lingo does not provide an *exclusive or (XOR)* logical operator, but I do.

Example 5-4: XOR Logical Function

```
on xor a, b
  if a and b then
    return FALSE
  else if a or b
```

Example 5-4: XOR Logical Function (continued)

```
      return TRUE
   else
      return FALSE
   end if
end
```

 The *not* keyword will toggle a Boolean property on and off, such as
set the visible of sprite x = not (the visible of sprite x).

Implicit Comparison to Zero

There is no need to explicitly check for non-zero comparisons. Any nonzero integer expression is treated as being true, though not necessarily equal to the constant *TRUE* (1).

Example 5-5: Implicit and Explicit Comparisons

```
if (the clickOn) then put "They clicked a sprite of interest"
```

This is equivalent to:

```
if (the clickOn) <> 0 then put "They clicked a sprite of interest"
```

Here are some other expressions of interest:

```
if (-5) then put "It is true"
-- "It is true"
put TRUE
-- 1
put FALSE
-- 0
put not (-5)
-- 0
put not (FALSE)
-- 1
```

For other data types, you must make an explicit comparison, such as:

```
if (floatVar <> 0) then put "Float comparison is TRUE"
if (stringVar <> EMPTY) then put "String has something in it"
if voidP(x) then put "The value of x is VOID"
```

Forever TRUE

You can use **TRUE** to create an indefinite *repeat* loop, assuming you provide a mechanism to exit the loop based on some condition, such as:

```
   repeat while TRUE
      if the mouseDown then exit repeat
   end repeat
```

Be aware that some system properties, such as *the stillDown*, don't update within a repeat loop.

Compound Expressions

Any expression in an *if* or *repeat...while* statement may be a compound statement joined by the logical operators *or* or *and*. Refer to "*Logical Operators*" earlier in this chapter for caveats when evaluating compound expressions, involving lists separated by a logical operator.

Common Errors in Compound Expressions

Most errors in compound expression evaluation are caused by misunderstanding the precedence of the various operators. Always use parentheses around what you want to be evaluated first, then test your logic by evaluating the expression from the inside out.

In this example, the programmer wants to check if the user pressed the *TAB* or *BACKSPACE* key. Here is a typical error when trying to compare an item to two or more possible values.

Example 5-6: Subtle Errors in Compound Comparisons

```
if the key = TAB or BACKSPACE then
  beep
end if
```

But the above is equivalent to:

```
if (the key = TAB) or (BACKSPACE <> 0) then
  beep
end if
```

Because *BACKSPACE* is never equal to 0, the compound expression will always be *TRUE*, and Lingo will *always* execute the *beep* statement.

This is also wrong:

```
if the key = (TAB or BACKSPACE) then
  beep
end if
```

because the above is equivalent to:

```
if the key = 1 then
  beep
end if
```

Because the expression *(TAB or BACKSPACE)* is evaluated first (due to the parentheses) and that expression always returns 1 (that is, *TRUE*), the *beep* will execute only if *the key = 1* (which happens to be the *Ctrl-A* character).

The two halves of a compound statement must stand on their own.

The correct construction is:

```
if (the key = TAB) or (the key = BACKSPACE) then
  beep
end if
```

Refer also to the *case* statement in Chapter 1, which is easier to use than *if...then* statements when trying to compare one variable or property against multiple possible values.

String Operators

Lingo provides two different concatenation operators to assemble strings—"&" and "*&&*"—as shown in Table 5-9. See Table 5-7 for other operators that work with strings. Refer to Chapter 7 for more details and examples, and see "Precedence Caveats" below.

Table 5-9: String Operators

Operator	String operation	Precedence
&	Concatenates two strings	2
&&	Concatenates two strings, but adds a space between them	2
" (double quote)	Delimits beginning or end of a string	1

Precedence Caveats

In some cases you must use parentheses to override the default order in which an expression is evaluated.

String Precedence

You must use parentheses with commands that have a higher precedence than the string concatenation symbol.

This will fail:

```
open window the pathname & "myMovie"
```

It is interpreted incorrectly as:

```
(open window the pathname) & "myMovie"
```

Use this instead:

```
open window (the pathname & "myMovie")
```

Cast Member and Sprite Reference Precedence

This calculates *the memberNum of sprite 5* and then adds 1:

```
put the memberNum of sprite 5 + 1
```

It is interpreted as:

```
put (the memberNum of sprite 5) + 1
```

Use parentheses to refer to a different sprite number, in this case sprite 6:

```
put the memberNum of sprite (5 + 1)
```

Boolean Precedence

The Boolean operator *not* has a higher precedence (5) than the precedence of the equals sign (1).

The following expression will never work:

```
if not the colorDepth = 8 then...
```

It is interpreted as:

```
if (not(the colorDepth)) = 8 then...
```

Because *the colorDepth* is always non-zero, the expression *not (the colorDepth)* is always zero.

So the above condition is always FALSE because it is interpreted as:

```
if 0 = 8 then...
```

The correct construction is:

```
if (the colorDepth <> 8) then...
```

or

```
if not (the colorDepth = 8) then...
```

Until you've mastered data types and expressions, use the Message and Watcher windows to evaluate expressions, and use the Debugger window to examine the path that Lingo follows through your *if...then* structures. Refer to Chapter 3, *Lingo Coding and Debugging Tips*, and when in doubt, use extra parentheses. Even if they are not needed by Lingo, they will make your code more readable by grouping the elements in an expression conceptually.

CHAPTER 6

Lists

List Basics

There are two major types of Lingo lists—*linear lists* and *property lists*. Refer to Chapter 5, *Coordinates, Alignment, and Registration Points*, in *Director in a Nutshell* for an additional details on *rects* and *points*, which are list-style structures sharing characteristics of both linear and property lists.

Lists (called *arrays* in most languages) are convenient for storing and retrieving related data. A list consists of zero or more elements, which can be of any data type, enclosed in square brackets. Elements are separated by commas.

Simplify global variable management by using a single global list with multiple properties instead of individual global variables.

You do *not* need to allocate a specific amount of memory or number of elements for a list. Director handles the housekeeping as elements are added or deleted. Elements are often referred to by their *index* (that is, their position in the list).

The index of the first element's in a list is 1, not 0 as in some other languages. Do not use 0 or negative numbers as indices.

Linear Lists

A linear list is a simple comma-delimited list of elements, defined using the *list()* function or by enclosing items within square brackets. Each element can be of any data type. Use *list()* without any elements, or empty brackets, [ ], to create a zero-element linear list. Here are some example linear lists:

```
set emptyList = [ ]
set myList1 = [1, 2, 3]
set myList2 = list (1, 7, #fumble, "Apples", 6.5, "Money")
```

Don't include brackets within the *list()* function unless you intend to create a list *within* a list.

```
put list([1,2,3])
-- [[1, 2, 3]]
```

Property Lists

Each element in a property list consists of a *property name:property value* pair (or simply a *property:value* pair), separated by a colon, such as #myProp:7. The value can be of any data type. The property name is usually a Lingo-style symbol (see "*Symbols*" in Chapter 5, *Data Types and Expressions*) but can be of any data type.

In fact, any alphanumeric characters used as a property name (except quoted strings) are converted to symbols.

Avoid using a float value as the property name because Director may not properly retrieve such elements, especially under Windows. Define a property list by enclosing one or more *property:value* pairs, separated by commas, within square brackets. Use a single colon within two brackets, [:], to create a zero-element property list. If your keyboard lacks square brackets, see Example 6-1. Here are some example property lists:

```
set emptyPropList = [:]
set myPropList1 = [#a:1, #b:2, #c:3]
set myPropList2 = [#name:"apples", #quantity:5]
```

Note that the property names *fruit* and *calories* are assumed to be symbols, not variables.

```
set myPropList3 = [fruit:"bananas", calories:12]
put myPropList3
-- [#fruit: "bananas", #calories: 12]
```

Property:value pairs are always added to or deleted from property lists as a unit. The *deleteAll()* command leaves a property list equal to [:] (empty, but still a property list).

Rects and Points

Rects and points are covered in detail in Chapter 5 in *Director in a Nutshell*. Rects and points are list-like structures that can be manipulated using many of Lingo's list functions. With some functions, rects and points behave like property lists; with other functions, they behave like linear lists. Rects and points are not affected usefully by commands that add or delete elements, and they should be used only with commands that get and set the value of existing elements. If you insist on playing Dr. Frankenstein, you can use *deleteAt()* to create a *franken*-rect with only three elements, but *count()* will always return 4 for rects and 2 for points. See the "*Rect and Point Operations*" section later in this chapter.

Creating Lists

Table 6-1 shows the commands for defining lists.

A "vanilla" list contains *either* linear elements or *property:value* pairs, not both. A property list, however, can be a sub-element within a linear list, and vice versa.

Rects and points are defined with parentheses, not square brackets. Linear lists and property lists can both contain rects and points. A rect can consist of two points.

If your keyboard lacks square brackets, you can still create *linear* lists with the *list()* function. See Example 6-1 to create *property* lists.

The following utility creates an empty property list that can be populated with elements using other list commands.

Example 6-1: Creating Property Lists on Keyboards Without Square Brackets

```
on createPropList
    -- Left bracket is ASCII 91. Right bracket is ASCII 93
    return value(numToChar (91) & ":" & numToChar (93))
end createPropList
```
First, create the list and then add elements using *addProp*:
```
set myPropList = createPropList()
addProp (myPropList, #propA, 5)
put myPropList
-- [#propA: 5]
```

See also Example 6-27, "*Creating a Property List from Two Linear Lists.*"

Table 6-1: Commands to Define Lists

Command	Usage	Creates	Linear Lists	Property Lists	Points/ Rects
[ ]	Defines a linear list	Linear list	Yes	N/A	N/A
list(*elements*)	Defines a linear list	Linear list	Yes	Error	N/A
[:]	Defines a property list	Property list	N/A	Yes	N/A
point(*x, y*)	Defines a point	Point	N/A	N/A	Point
rect(*l, t, r, b*)	Defines a rect	Rect	N/A	N/A	Rect
duplicate(*list*)	Creates independent copy of a list, *sorted* if original was sorted	Same type as original list	Yes	Yes	Yes
value(string(*list*))	Creates independent *unsorted* copy of a list[1]	Same type as original list	Yes	Yes	Yes

[1] The list won't be considered "sorted" by Lingo, but the *value(string())* function does not change the order of the existing elements. See "Sorting, Adding, and Changing List Elements" later in this chapter.

Invalid List Declarations

The following are all *invalid* uses of lists.

The following causes a "Handler not defined" error because `myList` is not a property list, as required by *addProp()*:

```
set myList = [1,2,3]
addProp myList, #a, 1
```

The following causes an "Operator expected" error because *list()* can't create property lists:

```
put list (#a:5, #b:4)
```

The following causes a *"Property list did not start with a property name"* error because the third element includes a property name, but the first two did not:

```
set myList = [1,2,#a:4]
```

The following causes a *"Property or value missing"* error because the last element includes a property name but no property value:

```
set myList = [#lowell:1, #paul:2, #kenny:3, #sam]
```

The following causes an *"Operator expected"* error, even though the last element includes a colon, because it still lacks a property value:

```
set myList = [#lowell:1, #paul:2, #kenny:3, #sam:]
```

Valid List Declarations

The following are all acceptable ways of initializing lists.

Linear list with various data types:

```
set myList = [#a, void, 7.5, 2, "foo"]
```

Linear list containing property list as the second element:

```
set myList = [1, [#a:1, #b:5, #c:3], 6, "foo"]
```

Property list containing property lists and linear lists as values:

```
set myList =  [#someList: [#a:1, #b:5], #otherList: [1,2,4]]
```

Property list containing a rect and a point as values:

```
set myList =  [#myRect: rect(2,4,8,7), #myPoint: point(1,3)]
```

If you specify a value but omit the property name for a property list element, Lingo inserts a property name equal to the element's index. The following is not recommended, but it will work, as long as the value missing a property name is not a symbol.

```
set myList = [#a:1, "asd", #c:3, 5, 7.5, void]
put myList
-- [#a: 1, 2: "asd", #c: 3, 4: 5, 5: 7.5000, 6: Void]
```

If you add a variable to a list, the variable's *current* value is added to the list. If the variable's value changes, the list remains unchanged.

```
set x = 5
set myList = [x]
```

```
set x = 7
put x
-- 7
put myList
-- [5]
```

If you use a non-list variable as a value in a list, the list will include the variable's current contents. Even if the variable changes, the list will not. If you try to use a variable name as a property name it will be converted to a symbol:

```
set myVar = #someSymbol
set myList = [myVar:1]
put myList
-- [#myVar: 1]
```

Use the following to convert the symbolic property name (*#myVar*) in the previous example back to the value of the variable *myVar*.

```
put value(string(getPropAt (myList, 1)))
-- #someSymbol
```

This technique can be used to create a list of variable names, rather than a list of the values of the variables. In most cases, you are better off simply using a list rather than trying to track variables within a list.

Assigning, Passing, and Duplicating Lists

Lists can be assigned to any local, global, or property variable. (A property variable (which is defined using the *property* keyword) should not be confused with a Lingo property (such as *the clickLoc*), a property list, or a property *of* a list. Refer to "*Child Object Properties*" later in this chapter and to Chapter 1, *How Lingo Thinks*, and Chapter 12, *Behaviors and Parent Scripts*.)

A list variable *points* to the *beginning* of the list in memory; it does *not* contain a copy of the entire list. Lists are passed by *reference*, not by value, allowing for efficient passing of large lists between handlers.

 If you assign one list variable to another variable, or pass a list variable as an argument to a handler, both entities point to the same list. If either list changes, both change because they point to the same data in memory.

In Example 6-2, deleting the elements in *listA* removes them from *listB*.

Example 6-2: Two Variables Pointing to a Single List

```
set listA = [1,2,3]
set listB = listA
put listB
-- [1, 2, 3]
deleteAll (listA)
put listB
-- []
```

(The *deleteAll* command used here has worked since Director 4, but it was undocumented until Director 6.)

Use either the *duplicate(list)* or *value(string(list))* function to make an independent copy of a list. (Using *value()* alone has no effect, and the lists remain linked.)

In Example 6-3, note that changes to `listA` no longer affect `listB`.

Example 6-3: Dissociating Two Lists

```
set listA = [1,2,3]
set listB = duplicate (listA)
deleteAll (listA)
put listA
-- []
put listB
-- [1, 2, 3]
```

If you pass a list into a handler and modify that list within the handler, the original list in the calling routine is modified as well.

Example 6-4: Modifying Lists Passed to a Handler

```
on listPass
  set myList = [3,2,1]
  put "MyList started as" && myList
  adjustList (myList)
  put "MyList ended up as" && myList
end listPass

on adjustList someList
  sort someList
end adjustList
```

Note that *myList* is altered by *adjustList()*:

```
listPass
-- "MyList started as [3, 2, 1]"
-- "MyList ended up as [1, 2, 3]"
```

Don't modify the original list passed into a handler unless that is the specific intent, as with the *deleteRange()* handler in Example 6-15. Instead, work on a *copy* of the list, and return the altered version via a *return* statement.

In Example 6-5, I've modified *adjustList()* to create a separate list that it returns to the caller, and I've also modified *listPass()* to receive the returned list.

Example 6-5: Using a List in a Handler Without Modifying the Original List

```
on listPass2
  set myList = [3,2,1]
```

Example 6-5: Using a List in a Handler Without Modifying the Original List

```
    put "MyList started as" && myList
    set workList = adjustList2 (myList)
    put "MyList ended up as" && myList
    put "WorkList ended up as" && workList
end listPass2

on adjustList2 someList
    set workList = duplicate(someList)
    sort workList
    return workList
end adjustList2
```

Note that *myList* is *not* affected by the changes made within *adjustList2()*.

```
listPass2
-- "MyList started as [3, 2, 1]"
-- "MyList ended up as [3, 2, 1]"
-- "WorkList ended up as [1, 2, 3]"
```

Using Lists to Return Multiple Values from a Handler

This section assumes that you have read and understood *"Parameters and Arguments"* in Chapter 1, *How Lingo Thinks*. Arguments of most data types are passed to handlers by *value*. If you want to modify a single variable, it is easy to set it to the return value of a function, such as:

```
    set  x = power (10, 2)
```

But, suppose you wanted to swap the value of two integer variables. You'd need to modify them *both*, but a function can return only *one* value. This won't work:

```
    set x = 1
    set y = 2
    swapInts (x, y)
```

You can *not* write a *swapInts()* function that modifies two variables because it is the *value* of the variables, and not the variables themselves, that are passed to *swapInts()*. In C, you could manually pass the *address* of the variables (that is, pass them *by reference*) if you wanted to swap two variables. In Lingo you have to use a third variable to swap them manually (and you can not use a function to do it), such as:

```
    set temp = x
    set x = y
    set y = temp
```

Arguments that are *lists* or *objects*, however, are passed by reference. The called function receives the list itself, not just a copy of its contents. Therefore, you can pass in, and return, a series of arguments as elements within a list.

Example 6-6: Using Lists to Return Multiple Values from a Handler

```
on mouseUp
    set myList = [#low: the mouseH, #high: the left of sprite 5]
    if the low of myList > the high of myList then
        swapHighLow (myList)
```

Example 6-6: Using Lists to Return Multiple Values from a Handler (continued)

```
    end if
    put "myList has been swapped:" && myList
end

on swapHighLow inList
  set temp = the low of inList
  set the low  of inList = the high of inList
  set the high of inList = temp
end
```

Example 6-6 is merely for illustration. In practice you would simply sort the list.

Cleaning Up After Lists

Director deallocates the memory used for a list when no variables still point to it. To deallocate a list and free memory, assign all variables that pointed to the list to 0.

```
    set myList = 0
```

 Clear all global lists (and other objects) in MIAWs to allow them to be removed from memory.

Multidimensional Arrays

Linear lists are one-dimensional. Property lists are essentially lists of 2 by *n* elements. You can create multidimensional arrays using lists *within* lists. Irv Kalb discusses his multidimensional array object in the *Lingo User's Journal (September 1995 Volume 1, Number 3) (http://www.penworks.com)*.

This linear list of three property lists might represent a high score chart or student test scores.

Example 6-7: Creating and Reading Multidimensional Lists

```
on printHighScores
    set highScores = [ ¬
      [#name: "Jane", #score: 85, #level: 8], ¬
      [#name: "Dick", #score: 75, #level: 7], ¬
      [#name: "Spot", #score: 95, #level: 9]]
  repeat with x in highScores
    put the name of x && "scored" && the score of x
  end repeat
end

printHighScores
-- "Jane scored 85"
-- "Dick scored 75"
-- "Spot scored 95"
```

In the previous example, you could instead use a double repeat loop, extracting the data using indices instead of property names. Note the use of the nested *getAt()* statements in the following example:

```
repeat with i = 1 to count (highScores)
  repeat with j = 1 to count (getAt(highScores, i))
    put getAt(getAt (highScores, i), j)
  end repeat
end repeat
```

C programmers will notice that Lingo's syntax for accessing list elements is horribly verbose.

Lists as a Database

Lists operations are much faster than text string manipulation (see Chapter 7, *Strings*). Sort your lists for faster access. Lists are capable of maintaining a database of several thousand elements. You can use lists to store and manipulate data at runtime, and you can use the FileIO Xtra to read the data from or write the data to an external text file for permanent storage. Refer to Chapter 14, *External Files*, for details.

For more extensive database capabilities, consider a third-party Xtra, such as those listed in 10, Using Xtras, in Director in a Nutshell (also available at http://www.zeusprod.com/nutshell/links.html)

Keep in mind that Director's Cast is a multimedia database. You can use lists or database Xtras to store castmember names but use the Cast itself to store the media. For example, you could create a huge database of songs, cross-referenced by artist, title, and genre, and then play them from the cast using *puppetSound* (or from external files using *sound playFile*).

Lingo List Commands

The names of Lingo's list-related commands suck. You'll probably leave the *O'Reilly* bookmark (included at the back of this book) planted firmly in this chapter. See *"Making Sense of List Commands"* later in this chapter for hints on finding the right list command, or create *wrapper scripts* that use names that are easier to remember but simply call a single Lingo function, such as:

```
on getPropByValue myList, value
  -- Return the value obtained from getOne
  return getOne (myList, value)
end
```

Refer to Chapter 3, *Lingo Coding and Debugging Tips*, for details on wrapper scripts.

Some list commands work with both linear lists and property lists, but others work exclusively with one or the other. The same list command may behave differently or accept different arguments when used with different list types. There are multiple commands that have the same effect on certain list types.

Using the wrong type of list, or a non-list, as the first argument to a list function will cause the (highly misleading) *"Handler not defined"* error. See Examples 3-21c through 3-21f.

Use *listP()* or *ilk()* to check if your variable is the correct type of list. (See Example 5-3, *"Avoiding Evaluation of the Second Clause in a Compound Expression,"* under *"Boolean Properties and Logical Operators"* in Chapter 5 for important details.) If necessary, initialize the list inside the current handler, or declare it as a global variable if it is defined elsewhere.

Many list functions do not return a meaningful value. Instead, they modify the list used as the first argument. You cannot use the following syntax because *add()* does not return a list:

```
set myList = add([], 7)
```

Use this instead:

```
set myList = []
add (myList, 7)
```

Making Sense of List Commands

List commands often use one attribute of an element—its position (*index*), property name (*property*), or property value (*value*)—to determine some other attribute. For example, you can read the property at a certain position or the value associated with a certain property.

These tips may help you make sense of the list commands:

- The first argument to any list command must *always* be a valid list. (If not, you'll be greeted with a *"Handler not defined"* error.)

- If a value is required, it is *always* the *last* argument in the parameter list (that is, specified after the position or property name).

- The "At" commands—*addAt()*, *setAt()*, *getAt()*, *deleteAt()*—all use an element's *position* in the list as the second argument.

- Specifying an index less than 1 or greater than the number of elements in the list will cause an *"Index out of range"* error with most, but not all, functions. *AddAt()* and *setAt()* accept indices beyond the end of the current list, adding elements as needed. Check the *count()* of a list to ensure that your index is in range. Some property list functions fail if you specify a nonexistent property name, but *setaProp()* will append the specified property, if necessary.

- Most "Prop" commands—*addProp()*, *setProp()*, *getProp()*, *getPropAt()*—work with property lists but not linear lists.

- The "aProp" commands—*getaProp()*, *setaProp()*, *deleteProp()* (there is no *deleteaProp*)—are intended for property lists but emulate *getAt()*, *setAt()*, and *deleteAt()* when used with linear lists.

- Only the commands that *create* lists (shown in Table 6-1) *return* a list as the result of the function call. Commands that *modify* lists do not return a new list, but rather modify the list passed as the first argument "in place."

- The "Get" and "Find" commands—*getProp()*, *getAt()*, *getLast()*, *getOne()*, *get-Pos()*, *getProp()*, *getPropAt()*, *findPos()*, *findPosNear()*—always return a *single* datum, such as a position, property, or value. You must use two separate commands to retrieve, say, both an element's property and its value.

- Some commands return error codes, whereas others issue alert dialogs if the parameters are invalid.

Sorting, Adding, and Changing List Elements

Lingo can optionally sort a list using the *sort* command. Sorting affects the order in which subsequent elements are added, and it affects the speed of commands that access the list by value (but not by position). The *add, findPos(), findPosNear()*, and *getOne()* commands work faster with sorted lists. (The *findPosNear()* function is intended for sorted lists and does not work fully with unsorted lists.) A list remains sorted unless some command cancels its "sort-edness". I refer to such a list as *unsorted* because Lingo no longer considers it truly sorted although existing elements remain ordered. A list's sort-edness affects the speed with which its elements accessed and how *future* elements are added.

Sort Order

A sort is always performed in *ascending* order.

Linear lists are sorted by *value*.

Example 6-8: Sort Order of Linear and Property Lists

```
set myList = [1, 7, #fumble, "Apples", 6.5, "Money"]
sort myList
put myList
-- [1, 6.5000, 7, "Apples", #fumble, "Money"]
```
Property lists are sorted by *property name*.
```
set myList = [#r:1, #q:7, #g:#fumble, #b:"Apples", ¬
    #a:6.5, #c:"Money"]
sort myList
put myList
-- [#a: 6.5000, #b: "Apples", #c: "Money", #g: #fumble, ¬
    #q: 7, #r: 1]
```

When sorting elements of different types, note that numbers are sorted before strings and symbols. Symbols are treated like strings and are sorted alphabetically, comingled with strings (although the string "a" will be placed before the symbol #a). Refer to Appendix C, *Case-Sensitivity, Sort Order, Diacritical Marks, and Space-Sensitivity*, for details on the exact sort order of strings with varied case, strings and symbols with diacritical marks, and non-alphanumeric characters (which differ on the Macintosh and Windows).

Recursive Sorting

If you sort a list that in turn contains *other* lists, *only* the primary list is sorted. Example 6-9 recursively sorts all sublists (to any number of levels) within a list using recursion.

Example 6-9: Recursively Sorting Sublists

```
on recursiveSort inputList
  -- Sort whatever list is passed in. This will be the
  -- top-level list at first, but will be a sublist if
  -- this is called recursively.
  sort inputList
  repeat with thisElement in inputList
    -- If this element is itself a list, keep sorting
    if listP(thisElement) then
      recursiveSort(thisElement)
    end if
  end repeat
end recursiveSort
```

Example 6-9 modifies the original list passed into the handler. It is left as an exercise to the reader to write a nondestructive version that returns a sorted listed without modifying the original list used as the input. (Bear in mind that you can't simply duplicate the list each time the routine is called because it is called recursively and you must work on the same list following the initial call.)

See Example 8-8, "*Recursively Counting Elements in a List,*" in Chapter 8, *Math (and Gambling)* for another example of recursion.

Reverse Sorting and Reverse Ordering

For a descending sort, you can either access a sorted list backwards or create a list that is sorted in reverse order.

This *reverseSort()* handler uses the *reverseList()* handler defined in Example 6-11 to return an inverted, independent copy of the original sorted list. The reverse sort is a one-time operation; new elements will not be automatically sorted.

Example 6-10: Reverse Sort

```
on reverseSort inList
  if listP(inList) then
    set newList = duplicate (inList)
    sort newList
    return reverseList (newList)
  else
    alert "Did not receive a valid list"
    return VOID
  end if
end reverseSort
```

You can use this *reverseList()* handler to reverse unsorted lists as well.

Example 6-11: Reversing Unsorted Lists

```
on reverseList inList
  if not listP(inList) then
    alert "Did not receive a valid list"
    return VOID
  end if
  set listCount = count(inList)
  if ilk (inList) = #propList then
  --reverse a property list
    set newList = [:]
    repeat with x = listCount down to 1
      addProp newList, getPropAt (inList, x), [LC]
        getAt (inList, x)
    end repeat
  else
  --reverse a linear list
    set newList = [ ]
    repeat with x = listCount down to 1
      add newList, getAt (inList, x)
    end repeat
  end if
  return newList
end reverseList
```

Sorting and List Performance

Sorting a list takes negligible time unless the list is very long. Elements are *retrieved* more quickly from sorted lists, but *adding* elements to a sorted list is marginally slower. For short lists you won't notice any performance difference, but if you are accessing a large list many times, you should sort the list. If you are adding many elements, it is preferable to sort the list once after all (or most) elements are added.

Creating a list is much slower than accessing its elements, so you should initialize a list only once. Building a list incrementally is *much* slower than declaring an entire list at once. If the list is fixed, declare it using one of the functions in Table 6-1, rather than adding elements manually. Avoid repeatedly initializing a list while looping in a frame. Initialize it once in the previous frame, and access it via a global declaration instead.

Windows machines are generally faster than comparable Macintoshes for list creation and access, but it is unlikely you will notice the difference unless using very large lists.

Table 6-2 shows some speed comparisons for various operations. All operations were performed 10,000 times on a simple linear or property list containing 2750 elements. Note that *getAt()* operates at the same speed for sorted and unsorted lists because it accesses elements by their position only. *GetAt()* is marginally faster than *getaProp()*, even for sorted lists. These tests accentuate very minor absolute differences, so you might not notice any speed differences for small lists or fewer operations.

Table 6-2: Sorted List versus Unsorted List Speed Comparison

CPU/Speed	getaProp() Unsorted	getaProp() Sorted	getAt() Sorted or Unsorted
Mac 68040 (33 MHz)	2390 ticks	99 ticks	74 ticks
PPC 601 (66 MHz)	1056 ticks	38 ticks	28 ticks
PPC 604e (225 MHz)	250 ticks	10 ticks	6 ticks
Pentium (166 MHz)	528 ticks	28 ticks	22 ticks

Adding Elements to Sorted and Unsorted Lists

Once a list is sorted, Lingo inserts new elements in sorted order, when using *add()*, *addProp()*, *setProp()*, and *setaProp()*. A list created by *duplicate(list)* is sorted if the original list was sorted. A list created using *value(string(list))* is not sorted by default.

The *append()* and *addAt()* commands cancel a list's "sort-edness," but existing elements remain in their previous order. Subsequent elements added with any command, including *add()*, are *not* inserted in sorted order unless the list is resorted.

Although undocumented, *add()* can be used with the same syntax as *addAt()*—namely *add(list, position, value)*—which unsorts the list, as would *addAt()*.

There is no *addPropAt()* command. Properties are added to the end of unsorted property lists or sorted by property name in sorted property lists.

When using *addAt()* or *add()*, if you specify a position beyond the end of the list, Lingo fills in the intervening items with zeroes.

Example 6-12 creates a 10-element list full of zeroes.

Example 6-12: Populating a List with Zeroes

```
set myList = [ ]
addAt(myList, 10, 0)
put myList
-- [0, 0, 0, 0, 0, 0, 0, 0, 0, 0]
```

List Commands That Add and Modify Elements

Table 6-3 shows commands that add, change, and sort elements. None of these commands return a meaningful value, but rather modify the list passed as the first argument. Only the *setAt()* and *set the property of list* commands work with rects and points because the number and position of elements in a rect or point are fixed.

Table 6-3: Commands That Add, Change, and Sort Elements

Command	Usage	Linear Lists	Prop Lists	Points/ Rects
add(*list, val*)	Inserts value in sorted order or appends value[1]	Yes	Error[2]	Ignored
addAt(*list, index, val*) add(*list, index, val*)	Inserts value *before* element at specified position[3]	Yes	Error[2]	Ignored
addProp(*list, prop, val*)	Inserts *property:value* pair in sorted order or appends pair[1]	Error[2]	Yes	Error[2]
append(*list, val*)	Appends value to list[3]	Yes	Error[2]	Ignored
setaProp(*propList, prop, val*)[4] setaProp(*list, index, val*)[5]	Replaces or inserts[1] value by property name or position	Yes, by index[5]	Yes, by prop name[4]	Yes, by prop name[4]
setAt(*list, index, val*)[6]	Replaces item by position[3]	Yes	Yes	Yes
setProp(*list, prop, value*)	Replaces value by property name	Error[2]	Yes[7]	Error[8]
set the *property* of *list*[9]	Sets property's value by its property name	Error	Yes	Yes
sort(*list*)	Sorts linear list by value or property list by property	Yes	Yes	Ignored

[1] Inserts item at end of unsorted list or in sorted order for sorted lists.
[2] Causes *"Handler not defined"* error.
[3] Ignores the sort order and cancels sort-edness of list. Inserts item at specified location or appends to list.
[4] For property lists, the second argument to *setProp* is assumed to be a property name, not an index, even if it is an integer. The property will be added if it does not exist, as with *addProp()*. For rects and points, the second argument to *setProp* must be one of the valid rect or point properties, and not an integer (see Table 6-9). *SetaProp* also accepts a child object instance instead of a list as the first parameter.
[5] For linear lists, *setaProp* is identical to *setAt* and requires an integer index as the second argument. Specifying anything else causes an *"Integer Expected"* error.
[6] For linear lists, if the index is beyond the limit of the list, *setAt()* will append to the list. For property lists, the index must be within the limits of the list. Use the index 1 or 2 for points or an index from 1 to 4 for rects.
[7] For property lists, *setProp* causes a *"Handler not defined"* error if the property does not exist. Use *setaProp()* instead.
[8] *setProp* always fails for rects and points. Use *setaProp* instead.
[9] *Set the property of list* causes a "Property not found" error if the property does not exist. For property lists, use *setaProp()* instead. For rects and points, use only the valid rect and point properties.

Deleting Elements

Table 6-4 shows the commands that delete elements from a list. Deleting an element from a property list deletes its *property:value* pair. These commands should not be used with, and are generally ignored by, rects and points (using *deleteOne()* can corrupt a rect or point).

The *deleteOne()* function is case-sensitive when locating a string value to delete. It is *not* case-sensitive when accessing elements by symbol names instead of strings. Also see *getOne()*, *getPos()*, and Example 6-13.

Note the changing contents of `myList` in the examples below. In each succeeding example, `myList` contains the value from the previous command. *DeleteOne()* returns 1 if successful or 0 otherwise.

Example 6-13: Case-Sensitive Deletion of String Values

Define a list with strings of varied case.

```
set myList = [#a:"banana", #b:"BaNaNa"]
put myList
-- [#a: "banana", #b: "BaNaNa"]
```

Try to delete an item by matching the string "*BANANA*" in the list.

```
put deleteOne (myList,"BANANA")
-- 0
```

The list doesn't change because "*BANANA*" (all capital letters) doesn't match any items, so none were deleted.

```
put myList
-- [#a: "banana", #b: "BaNaNa"]
```

This deletes property #b (not property #a) because the match is case-sensitive:

```
put deleteOne (myList,"BaNaNa")
-- 1
put myList
-- [#a: "banana"]
```

This deletes property #a because the match is again case-sensitive:

```
put deleteOne (myList,"banana")
-- 1
put myList
-- [:]
```

Note that the final list is an empty *property* list, not an empty *linear* list.

Example 6-14 demonstrates that symbols are case-insensitive when used with list functions.

Example 6-14: Case-Insensitive Deletion of Symbolic Values

Define a list with symbols (instead of strings) of varied case.
```
set myList = [#a:#banana, #b:#BaNaNa]
```

Note that Director immediately converts symbols with the same name to the same case:

```
put myList
-- [#a: #banana, #b: #banana]
```

Below, property #a is deleted because it is the first property with a symbol value matching *#BaNaNa* (regardless of case).

```
put deleteOne (myList,#BANANA)
-- 1
put myList
-- [#b: #banana]
```

Likewise, any case-insensitive match is sufficient to delete property #b:

```
put deleteOne (myList,#BANana)
-- 1
put myList
-- [:]
```

Table 6-4: Commands That Delete List Elements

Command	Usage	Return Value	Linear Lists	Prop Lists
deleteAll(*list*)[1]	Deletes all elements from a list, leaving list type unchanged	0	Yes	Yes
deleteAt(*list*, *index*)	Deletes element by position	0	Yes[2]	Yes[2]
deleteOne(*list*, *val*)	Deletes first element with specified value	0: failure 1: success	Yes	Yes
deleteProp(*list*, *prop*)	Delete first element with specified property name	0: failure[3] 1: success	Yes[2,3]	Yes

[1] The *deleteAll* command is convenient for deleting all elements without knowing (or changing) a list's type. It has worked since Director 4 (although it was undocumented until Director 6). See also the custom *deleteRange()* handler in Example 6-15.
[2] Invalid indices cause an "*Index out of Range*" error. Check the range first.
[3] Using *deleteProp()* with a linear list requires an integer instead of a property, in which case it emulates *deleteAt()*; *deleteProp()* is intended for property lists and always returns 0 for linear lists.

You can check whether *deleteOne()* and *deleteProp()* returned TRUE (1) to determine whether the operation succeeded. Bear in mind that *deleteProp()* always returns 0 for linear lists.

 When you delete an item in a list, all subsequent items move up one place (their indices change). Delete items in reverse order from the list to avoid any problems.

The *deleteAt()* command deletes only one element at a time and *deleteAll()* deletes them all. The *deleteRange()* handler below deletes a range of elements. It first ensures that **deleteFrom** is less than **deleteTo**, then it deletes elements from the highest index down to the lowest. (Reader quiz: What happens if you delete from the lowest to highest index instead?)

Example 6-15: Deleting a Range of Elements

```
on deleteRange inList, deleteFrom, deleteTo
  -- Ensure that deleteFrom is less than deleteTo
  if deleteFrom > deleteTo then
    set temp = deleteFrom
    set deleteFrom = deleteTo
    set deleteTo = temp
  end if
  -- Prevents errors from invalid index ranges
  set deleteFrom = max (1, deleteFrom)
  set deleteTo = min (count (inList), deleteTo)
  -- Delete backwards in list
  repeat with x = deleteTo down to deleteFrom
      deleteAt (inList, x)
  end repeat
  return inList
end deleteRange

put deleteRange ([#a, #b, #c, #d, #e, #f], 2, 4)
-- [#a, #e, #f]
```

There is no built-in *deleteLast()* function. Use:

```
deleteAt (inList, count (inList))
```

Getting Info About, and Elements from, Lists

Table 6-5 shows commands that provide information about, or extract elements from, a list.

 GetOne(), *getPos()*, and *findPos()* are *case-sensitive* when searching by strings values! They are *not* case-sensitive when accessing elements by symbol names instead of strings.

Note the case of each string and the result of each query in Example 6-16..

Example 6-16: Case-Sensitive Searching of String Values

```
set myList = ["banana", "Banana"]
put getPos (myList ,"banana")
-- 1
put getPos (myList ,"Banana")
-- 2
put getPos (myList ,"BANANA")
-- 0
```

Again, note the case of each string and the result of each query:

```
set myList = [#a:"banana", #b:"Banana"]
put getOne (myList,"banana")
-- #a
put getOne (myList,"Banana")
-- #b
put getOne (myList,"BANANA")
-- 0
```

As in Example 6-14, getOne(), getPos(), and findPos() are case-insensitive when searching for symbols.

Table 6-5: Commands That Read from Lists

Command	Usage	Returns	Linear Lists	Prop Lists	Points/ Rects
count(*list*)	Counts items in list	item count	Yes	Yes	Yes
ilk(*list*), listP(*list*), or ilk(*list*, #type)	Determines list's type	See Table 6-6	Yes	Yes	Yes
findPos(*list*, *prop*)[1]	Finds the position of the first occurrence of property	position, or VOID if not found	No	Yes	No
findPosNear (*list*, *prop*)[2]	Finds position (from 1 to count()+1) at which specified property name belongs in list	position at which property belongs	No	Yes	No
getaProp (*list*, *prop*)[3] getaProp(*list*, *index*)[4]	Gets value by property name (for propLists, rects, and points) or position (for linear lists)	value, or VOID if property not found[5]	Yes, by index[4,6]	Yes, by prop name[3]	Yes, by prop name[5]
getAt(*list*, *index*)	Gets value by position	value[6]	Yes	Yes	Yes
getLast(*list*)	Gets value of last element	value, or VOID if list is empty	Yes	Yes	Yes
getOne(*list*, *val*)[7]	Gets first property or position that matches value	prop, or position, or 0 if not found	Yes[7]	Yes[8]	Yes[7]
getPos(*list*, *val*)	Gets first position that matches value	position, or 0 if not found	Yes[7]	Yes	Yes[7]
getProp(*list*, *prop*)	Gets value of property	value	Error[9]	Yes[10]	Error[11]

Table 6-5: Commands That Read from Lists (continued)

Command	Usage	Returns	Linear Lists	Prop Lists	Points/ Rects
getPropAt(*list*, *index*)	Gets property name by position	property name	Error[9]	Yes[6].	Yes[6]
min(*list*), max(*list*)	Determines minimum or maximum value in list[12]	min or max value	Yes	Yes	Yes
the property of *list*	Gets the value of a property	value	Error	Yes[13]	Yes[13]

[1] *FindPos()* is intended for property lists and expects a property as an argument. It does not return useful information for linear lists, nor for rects and points, even when used with valid rect and point properties. Use *getaProp()* for rects and points instead.

[2] *FindPosNear()* is intended for *sorted* property lists. It returns the position of an exact match or the position at which the specified property would be inserted were it added to the list. The return value is between 1 and *count(list)*+1. For unsorted lists, it returns the position of an exact match; otherwise it returns *count(list)*+1. For non-property lists, it does not return meaningful information.

[3] For property lists, the second argument to *getaProp()* is assumed to be a property name, not an index, even if it is an integer. For rects and points, the second argument to *getaProp()* must be one of the valid rect or point properties (see Table 6-7). Use of an integer position causes a *"Symbol expected"* error.

[4] For linear lists, *getaProp()* is identical to *getAt()* and requires an integer index as the second argument. Specifying anything else causes an *"Integer Expected"* error.

[5] If the property is not found within a rect or a point, *getaProp()* causes a "Property not found" error. If the property is not found within a property list, *getaProp()* returns VOID, which is indistinguishable from a property with a value of VOID.
VOID may be returned as an error code:
```
put getaProp ([#a:1, #b:3, #c:void], #d)
-- Void
```

VOID may also be returned as a property's value:
```
put getaProp ([#a:1, #b:3, #c:void], #c)
-- Void
```
[6] Invalid indices cause an *"Index out of Range"* error. Check range first.

[7] For linear lists, rects, and points, *getOne()* and *getPos()* are identical and return the position at which the first occurrence of the value is found or 0 (zero) if it is not found.

[8] For property lists, *getOne()* returns the name of the first property with the specified value. If not found, it returns 0 (zero), which is indistinguishable from a property named 0, so you shouldn't use 0 as a property name.
Zero may be returned as an error code:
```
put getOne ([#a:1, #b:3], 7)
-- 0
```

Zero may also be returned as the matching property's name:
```
put getOne ([#a:1, 0:3], 3)
-- 0
```
[9] Causes a "Handler not defined" error.

[10] For property lists, *getProp()* causes a "Handler not defined" error if the property does not exist. Use *getaProp()* instead.

[11] *getProp()* always fails for rects and points. Use *getaProp()* instead.

[12] *min()* and *max()* work with all list element types, including strings. (They are case-sensitive; see Appendix C.)

[13] Using the property of *list* causes a *"Property not found"* error if the property does not exist. For property lists, use *getaProp()* instead. For rects and points, use only valid rect and point properties.

Performing Math with Lists

You can use standard math operators (+, -, *, /, and mod) to alter the contents of a single list as shown in Example 6-17.

Example 6-17: Math Operations Performed on Entire Lists

```
put [1,2,4] * -6
-- [-6, -12, -24]
put [1,2,4] - 7
-- [-6, -5, -3]
put -[1,2,4]
-- [-1, -2, -4]
put [1,2,4] / 2.0
-- [0.5000, 1.0000, 2.0000]
put [1,2,4] mod 2
-- [1, 0, 0]
```

You can also perform calculations using two lists as shown in Example 6-17.

The resulting list is the length of the shorter of the two lists.

Example 6-18: Math Operations Performed with Two Lists

```
put [1,2,4] + [7,8,9,10]
-- [8, 10, 13]
put [1,2,4] - [7,9]
-- [-6, -7]
put [1,2,4,12,15] * [4,5,6,12]
-- [4, 10, 24, 144]
put [10,20,40] / [4,5,6]
-- [2, 4, 6]
put [10,20,40] mod [4,5,6]
-- [2, 0, 4]
```

See also Example 8-6, "*Summing a List of Values*" and other examples in Chapter 8.

Lists in Expressions

Lingo treats lists within expressions in a somewhat arbitrary, if not capricious, manner. Testing is the only way to determine how Lingo will interpret a given expression, usually falling into one of these categories:

The list is treated as a single entity.

Note that the entire list is converted to a string:

```
put string (myList)
-- "[1, 3, 4]"
```

The logical expression is not applied to each element. The list itself is a non-zero entity, so the logical *not* of the list is FALSE.

```
put not ([0,2,3])
-- 0
```

The entire list, not just the first element, is compared to the other operand when using = or <>, such as:

```
put ([4,5,6]) <> 4
-- 1
put ([4,5,6]) = 4
-- 0
```

Contrast this with the inequality operators below.

Lists are compared on an element-by-element basis. Two variables pointing to two different lists are considered equal if the lists contain identical elements.

```
set x = [1, 2, 3]
set y = [1, 2, 3]
put x = y
-- 1
```

The first element of the list is used in the expression.

In the following example, the comparison is made between the first element of the list and the right side of the expression:

```
put ([4,5,6]) > 3
-- 1
put ([4,5,6]) > 5
-- 0
```

Contrast this behavior with that of = and <>. Comparisons involving two items, with <, >, and =, can *all* be FALSE because of Lingo's differing rules for evaluating inequalities and equalities.

The operation is invalid or otherwise ignored.

Attempting to use a list in a Boolean expression causes an *"Integer expected"* error:

```
if (myList) then put "foo"
```

Both of these comparisons are FALSE, so nothing is printed:

```
if myList = FALSE then put "It's FALSE"
if myList = TRUE then put "It's TRUE"
```

To check the existence of a list, use *listP()*. One of the following two statements will cause a message to print:

```
if listP(myList) = FALSE then put "It's FALSE"
if listP(myList) = TRUE then put "It's TRUE"
```

The *float()* function is ignored when used with lists:

```
put float ([1,2,3])
-- [1, 2, 3]
```

A list is a complex data structure that cannot be integer-ized:

```
put integer ([9,8,7])
-- Void
```

The results returned from various Lingo functions are not always consistent. Note that a list is an object according to *objectP()* but not according to *ilk()*:

```
put objectP([1,2,3])
-- 1
```

```
put ilk([1,2,3], #object)
-- 0
```

Non-list Variables in Compound Expressions

In the following expression, if *myList* is not a list, the expression *count(myList)* will cause a "*Handler not defined*" error (you can't use *count()* on something that is not a list).

```
if listP(myList) and count(myList) > 5 then
  -- whatever
end if
```

Use the construct shown in Example 6-19 instead:

Example 6-19: Preventing Non-list Arguments from Being Passed to List Commands

```
if listP(myList) then
  if count(myList) > 5 then
    -- whatever
  end if
end if
```

See Example 5-3, "*Avoiding Evaluation of the Second Clause in a Compound Expression*," under "*Boolean Properties and Logical Operators*" in Chapter 5 for details on logical expression evaluation.

Commands by List Type

The following section details the commands that perform common operations on each type of list. Refer to prior tables for functions common to all lists, such as *min()*, *max()*, and *count()*.

Determining a List's Type

You may need to determine a list's type to decide which commands to use with it. You can use *listP()* to determine whether a datum is any of the four possible types of lists, and you can use *ilk()* for more detailed information about a list's type. You can use *listP()* in *if...then* statements and *ilk()* in *case* statements (see Chapter 5 for a comparison between *ilk()* and *listP()*). Two forms of the *ilk()* command are used with lists:

ilk(variableName)

> This form of *ilk()* returns a *symbol* indicating the data type of the item, such as #list, #propList, #rect, or #point for the four list types. Note that linear lists return #list, not #linearList. There are dozens of possible return values when using *ilk()* with other data types, such as #integer and #float. See Table 5-4.

ilk(variableName, #dataType)

> This form of *ilk()* returns a *Boolean* indicating whether the item is of the specified data type. Note that ilk(*list*, #list) returns TRUE for all types of lists and is equivalent to listP(*list*). Use ilk(*list*, #linearList) to check

only whether a list is a *linear* list. There are many symbols against which you can check an item's data type, as shown in Table 16-1.

With the exception of #list and #linearList, note that these two forms of *ilk()* are equivalent when used with lists:

```
if ilk(list) = #dataType then ...
```

or:

```
if ilk(list, #dataType) = TRUE then...
```

For example, to check if a list is a property list, use either:

```
if ilk(list) = #propList then ...
```

or:

```
if ilk(list, #propList) = TRUE then...
```

Table 6-6 shows the return values of the *ilk()* function. The second column shows the symbolic values returned by the *ilk(list)* form, and the remaining columns show the Boolean values returned by the *ilk(list, #dataType)* form.

Table 6-6: Ilk() Return Values

Data Type	ilk()	#list[1]	#linearList	#propList	#point	#rect
linear list	#list	TRUE	TRUE	FALSE	FALSE	FALSE
property list	#propList	TRUE	FALSE	TRUE	FALSE	FALSE
point	#point	TRUE	FALSE	FALSE	TRUE	FALSE
rect	#rect	TRUE	FALSE	FALSE	FALSE	TRUE
Nonlist	other	FALSE	FALSE	FALSE	FALSE	FALSE

[1] Same results a list().

Linear List Operations

Table 6-7 details operations for linear lists. You can also use *count()*, *min()*, *max()*, and *duplicate()* in the standard ways. Sorted linear lists are sorted by value.

Table 6-7: Linear List Operations

To Do This	Use This	Notes
Initialize a linear list	[ ], list(), duplicate(), value(string())	The list must be initialized before using any other list functions.
Determine if list is a linear list	if ilk (list, #linearList) or if ilk(list) = #list	Note different symbol names for the two forms of ilk(). ilk(list) never returns #linearList. See Table 6-6.

Table 6-7: Linear List Operations (continued)

To Do This	Use This	Notes
Add a value in sorted order	*add(list, val)*	Adds item to end of unsorted list or in order for sorted list.
Add a value at a specific position	*addAt(list, index, val)*, or *add(list, index, val)*[1]	Pads missing elements with zeroes. Unsorts sorted lists.
Add a value to the end of the list	*append(list, val)*, or *add(list, val)*	*Append* unsorts a previously sorted list. *Add* only appends to unsorted lists.
Replace an element by position	*setAt(list, index, val)*, or *setaProp(list, index, val)*	Element is added if it doesn't already exist. Pads missing elements with zero.
Delete elements by position or value.	*deleteAll(list)*, *deleteAt(list, index)*, or *deleteOne(list, val)*[2]	Deleting elements changes indices of subsequent elements.
Get the value at a specific position or last position	*getAt(list, index)*, or *getaProp(list, index)*, or *getLast(list)*	*getAt()* and *getaProp()* are identical for linear lists.
Find the position of a specific value	*getOne(list, val)*[2] or *getPos(list, val)*[2]	Returns position of first match or zero if no match
Sort items by value	*sort(list)*	Commands that append data unsort the list.

[1] Undocumented variation of add() function.
[2] Case-sensitive

Property List Operations

Table 6-8 details operations for property lists. You can also use *count()*, *min()*, *max()*, and *duplicate()* in the standard ways. There is no *addPropAt()* command. Properties are added to the end of unsorted property lists or sorted by property name in sorted property lists.

Table 6-8: Property List Operations

To Do This	Use This	Notes
Initialize a property list	[:], duplicate(), value(string())	The list must be initialized before using any other list functions.
Determine if list is a property list	ilk (list, #propList) or ilk(list) = #propList	Correct symbol is *#propList*, not *#propertyList*. See Table 6-6.
Add a *property:value* pair	addProp(*list, prop, val*) or setaProp(*list, prop, val*)	*addProp()* adds item to end of unsorted list or in order for sorted list. *setaProp()* adds the property if it does not already exist.

Table 6-8: Property List Operations (continued)

To Do This	Use This	Notes
Replace a property's value by its property name	setaProp(*list, prop, val*) or setProp(*list, prop, val*)	*setaProp()* adds the property if it does not already exist. *setProp()* causes error if property does not exist.
Replace a property's value by position	setAt(*list, index, val*)	*setAt()* causes error if index is out of range. It does not add elements when used with property lists.
Delete elements by position or value	deleteAll(*list*), deleteAt(*list, index*), deleteOne(*list, val*)[1]	An element's *property:value* pair is always deleted as a unit.
Get the value of a specific property	getaProp(*list, prop*), or getProp(*list, prop*), or put the *prop* of *list*	If property is missing, *getaProp()* returns VOID, whereas *getProp()* and put the *prop* of *list* cause errors.
Get the name of the property at a specific position	getPropAt(*list, index*),	Index must be within range.
Get the value at a specific position or last position.	getAt(*list, index*) or getLast(*list*)	Index must be within range.
Get the first property name with a specific value	getOne(*list, val*)[1]	*getOne()* is case-sensitive! Returns property name or zero if not found.
Find the position of the nearest property name matching input	findPosNear(*list, prop*)[1]	Works best with sorted lists. See footnote 2 to Table 6-4 for return values.
Find the position of a specific property	findPos(*list, prop*)[1]	Returns index number or VOID.
Find the position of a specific value	getPos(*list, val*)[1]	Returns index number of first match or zero if not found.
Sort items by property name	sort(*list*)	Commands that append data, unsort the list.
Sort items by value	Can't be done automatically for property lists	Use a linear list, or sort it manually instead.

[1] Case-sensitive

Rect and Point Operations

Lingo's list commands interact with rects and points in bizarre ways. Some commands treat rects and points as linear lists, and others treat them as property lists.

A point can be thought of as a list of the form point(*x, y*) = [#locH:*x*, #locV:*y*].

A rect can be thought of as a list of the form rect(*l*, *t*, *r*, *b*) = [#left:*l*, #top:*t*, #right:*r*, #bottom:*b*]. A rect can also be specified as rect(point(*l*, *t*), point(*r*, *b*), but it is immediately converted to the rect(*l*, *t*, *r*, *b*) form.

The embedded properties of points and rects can be shown with this utility that reads the property names from any list.

Example 6-20: Extracting Unknown Properties from a List

```
on readProps listObj
  set objectType = ilk (listObj)
  put "This #" & objectType && "has" && [LC]
          count (listObj) && "properties"
  repeat with x = 1 to count (listObj)
    set thisProp = getPropAt (listObj, x)
    set thisValue = getaProp (listObj, thisProp)
    put "#" & thisProp & ":" && thisValue
  end repeat
end readProps


readProps(the clickLoc)
-- "This #point has 2 properties"
-- "#locH: 114"
-- "#locV: 83"


readProps(the rect of the stage)
-- "This #rect has 4 properties"
-- "#left: 0"
-- "#top: 0"
-- "#right: 160"
-- "#bottom: 120"
```

 The *readProps()* utility in Example 6-20 can read properties from a *child object* or *Behavior instance*, too. See Chapter 12.

The names *#locH* and *#locV* (for points), and *#left*, *#top*, *#right*, *#bottom* (for rects) are generally the *only* valid property names for use with list commands requiring a property name. You can use them as:

```
set the locH of myPoint = 17
set the top of myRect = 52
```

Rects also support *reading* two additional properties; height and width

```
put the width of myRect
set someVar = the height of myRect
```

Table 6-9 details the list operations for rects and points. You can also use *count()*, *min()*, *max()*, and *duplicate()* in the standard ways. Note that rects and points are generally not affected in a useful way by commands that add or delete elements, but they do work with commands that get and set the value of elements.

Table 6-9: Rect and Point Operations

To Do This	Use This	Notes
Define a rect	*rect(1, t, r, b)*, or *rect(point(1, r), point(t, b))*	Rects always have four elements and cannot be defined with *list()*, [ ], or [:].
Define a point	*point(x, y)*,	Points always have two elements and cannot be defined with *list()*, [ ], or [:].
Determine if list is a rect	*ilk(rect)* = #rect or *ilk (rect, #rect)* = TRUE	*ilk (rect, #list)* returns TRUE.
Determine if list is a point	*ilk(point)* = #point, or *ilk (point, #point)* = TRUE	*ilk (point, #list)* returns TRUE.
Add a value	Can't be done. Rects and points ignore the *add()*, *addAt()*, and *append()* commands and *addProp()*causes an error.	Points always have two elements, and rects always have four.
Replace a value by property name	*setaProp(rectOrPoint, prop, val)*, or set the *prop* of *rectOrPoint*	Don't use *setProp()*. It causes errors in all cases, even when using "standard" rect and point properties.
Replace a value by position	*setAt(list, index, val)*	Use an index within range. (1-2 for points, 1-4 for rects).
Delete elements	Can't be done. *deleteAll()*, *deleteAt()*, and *deleteProp()* are ignored.	*deleteOne()* corrupts the point or rect structure.
Get the value of a specific property (#left, #top, #right, #bottom, #locH, or #locV)[1]	*getaProp(rectOrPoint, prop)* or put the *prop* of *rectOrPoint*[1]	Don't use *getProp()*. It causes errors in all cases, even when using "standard" rect and point properties.
Get the value at a specific position, or last position	*getAt(rectOrPoint, index)* or *getLast(rectOrPoint)*	Index must be within range.
Find the position of a specific property	The order of properties for rects and points is fixed.	Rects are always in the order (#left, #top, #right, #bottom). Points are always in the order (#locH, #locV).
Find the position of a specific value	*getPos(rectOrPoint, val)*, or *getOne(rectOrPoint, val)*	Returns index number of first match or zero if no match.
Sort items by value or property name	Can't be done for points and rects.	Points and rects ignore the *sort()* command.

[1] You can also use *put the width of rect*, and *put the height of rect*, but you cannot set these properties.

Lists

Looping with Lists

There are two ways to extract each element in a list (see *"Repeat Loops"* in Chapter 1 for an overview of Lingo repeat loops). The following work for both linear lists and property lists.

You can loop for the number of elements returned by *count()*, using an integer index to extract data from the list. This gives you complete control, especially if the number of elements in the list is changing. The index variable (*i*) can also be used for other purposes, such as printing out an element's number.

Example 6-21: Printing Each Element's Position in a List

```
on showList someList
  set numElements = count (someList)
  repeat with i = 1 to numElements
    put "Element number" && i && "is" && getAt(someList, i)
  end repeat
end showList
```

Note that we counted the number of elements only *once*, rather than every time through the loop. If adding or deleting elements within the loop, you must instead recalculate the number of elements each time.

You can also use the *repeat with...in* syntax, which automatically extracts each value from the list.

Example 6-22: Printing Each Element's Value Only

```
on showList2 someList
  repeat with listValue in someList
    put "The value is" && listValue
  end repeat
end showList2
```

Note in Example 6-22 that *listValue* is the *value* of the current element, not an *index* (as was *i*). See *"Repeat Loops"* in Chapter 1 for important additional tips for working with the *repeat with...in* command.

List Utilities

Randomized Lists

The following handler creates a nonrepeating random list of *n* numbers (Refer to Chapter 8 for details on the *random()* function.) The trick is to place the numbers 1 through *n* into random locations throughout the list as it is built.

Example 6-23: Creating a List of Random Numbers

```
on randomNumberList n
  -- Initialize an empty list
  set myList = [ ]
  -- Create a list with the requested number of elements
```

Example 6-23: Creating a List of Random Numbers (continued)

```
repeat with x = 1 to n
  -- Insert the next number in a random place in the list
    addAt (myList, random(x), x)
  end repeat
  return myList
end randomNumberList

put randomNumberList (10)
-- [8, 10, 7, 5, 1, 3, 9, 4, 2, 6]
```

The following *incorrect* routine (which you'll often see used) will likely result in some numbers being repeated in the list. It incorrectly adds random numbers that may already exist in the list because the *random()* function may generate the same number multiple times. See *"How Random Is Random?"* in Chapter 8 for details.

Example 6-24: Incorrect (Nonrandom) List Creation

```
on incorrectRandom n
  -- Initialize an empty list
  set myList = [ ]
  -- Create a list with the requested number of elements
  repeat with x = 1 to n
  -- Add a random number to the list
    add (myList, random(n))
  end repeat
  return myList
end incorrectRandom

put incorrectRandom  (10)
-- [9, 1, 6, 4, 4, 10, 2, 3, 9, 4]
```

This handler returns a randomized version of any linear list or property list, leaving the original list intact. Note that this randomizes an *existing* list, which differs from creating a random list, as shown above.

Example 6-25: Randomizing an Existing List

```
on randomizeList inList
  -- Exit if a valid list is not passed in
  if not listP(inList) then
    return void
  end if

  -- Initialize any empty list of the correct type
  if ilk (inList, #propList) then
    set outList = [:]
    set propList = TRUE
  else
    set outList = [ ]
    set propList = FALSE
  end if
```

Example 6-25: Randomizing an Existing List (continued)

```
-- Work with a separate copy of the list
set work = duplicate (inList)
-- Loop while there are still elements in the list
repeat while count(work)
  -- Select an element at random
  set next = random (count(work))
  if propList then
  -- Add the property element to the output list
    addProp (outList, getPropAt(work, next), ¬
                      getAt (work, next))
  else
    -- Add the linear element to the output list
    add (outList, getAt (work, next))
  end if
  -- Delete the element just selected
  -- so that it can't be used again
  deleteAt (work, next)
end repeat

return outList
end randomizeList
```

Nonrepeating Random Numbers in a Range

Suppose you want to simulate a game of Bingo. You'll need to generate a nonrepeating list of items that are chosen at random from the pool of remaining "game pieces."

One approach is to create a *randomized* list and then step through it *sequentially*. You can retraverse the list to repeat the "random" pattern.

An alternate technique is to create a *sequential* list, but *randomly* choose an item which you then *delete* from the list. (We'll use this technique in Chapter 8 to simulate a deck of cards.) The latter approach requires us to rebuild the list when it is emptied.

Suppose you want to create a randomized slide show. You may want to rerandomize the list of slides each time through *and* prevent the same slide from being shown twice in a row (if the last item from the previous round is the first item chosen in the next round). The following handler returns a *nonrepeating* random number from 1 to n. Every number from 1 to n is used once before any number is used twice, and the same number is never returned twice in a row. The key is to store the last number in a global variable and perform a lookup using *getPos()* to delete it from the newly regenerated list.

Example 6-26: A Nonrepeating Random Number Generator

```
on getUniqueRandomNumber n
  global gList, gLastNumber

  if voidP(gList) then set gList = randomNumberList(n)
```

Example 6-26: A Nonrepeating Random Number Generator (continued)

```
if count (gList) = 0 then
  -- Recreate the list
  set gList =  randomNumberList(n)
  -- Locate and delete the last number from the new list
  set pickIt = getPos (gList, gLastNumber)
  deleteAt (gList, pickIt)
end if

-- Pick a random number and delete it from the list
set pickIt = random (count(gList))
set gLastNumber = getAt (gList, pickIt)
deleteAt (gList, pickIt)
return gLastNumber
end getUniqueRandomNumber
```

Converting List Types

Example 6-27 creates a linear list from a property list by stripping off the property names. It also works with rects and points.

Example 6-27: Converting a Property List to a Linear List

```
on convertToLinearList inList
  set outList = [ ]
  repeat with x in inList
    add outList, x
  end repeat
  return outList
end convertToLinearList

put convertToLinearList ([#fee: 3, #fie: 5, #fo: 6, #fum: 2])
-- [3, 5, 6, 2]
```

Example 6-28 builds a property list from two linear lists. The first list contains property names, and the second list contains values. The two lists must be of equal length.

Example 6-28: Creating a Property List from Two Linear Lists

```
on linearListToPropList symbolList, valueList
  set outList = [:]

  if not listP (symbolList) or not listP (valueList) then
    alert "This handler requires two lists"
    return VOID
  else
    set elements = count(valueList)
    set symbolCount = count (symbolList)
    if elements <> symbolCount then
      alert "Both lists must have the same length"
      return VOID
    end if
```

Lists

Example 6-28: Creating a Property List from Two Linear Lists (continued)

```
  end if

  repeat with n = 1 to elements
    addProp outList, getAt(symbolList, n), getAt(inList, n)
  end repeat
  return outList
end linearListToPropList

linearListToPropList ([#fee, #fie, #fo, #fum], [3,5,6,2])
put the result
-- [#fee: 3, #fie: 5, #fo: 6, #fum: 2]
```

This example could be modified to use the *createPropList()* handler from Example 6-1. That would allow people lacking square brackets on their keyboards to create property lists from two linear lists defined with the *list()* function.

Congratulations, you are now a *ListMeister* as well as a Lingo God!

Other Lingo Commands That Use Lists

Many Lingo commands and properties return or require linear lists, property lists, rects, and points. Refer to Chapter 5 in *Director in a Nutshell* for a detailed list of commands using rects and points.

Linear Lists

The following Lingo commands use true Lingo linear lists (not property lists). These can be manipulated like any other Lingo list, although many can be only read, not set.

> *the alertHook[1] (can assign to a list of script instances)*
> *the actorList (list of objects)*
> *the castMemberList of member[1] (list of members for Custom Cursor Xtra)*
> *the cuePointNames of member[1] (list of strings)*
> *the cuePointTimes of member[1] (list of integers)*
> *the cursor of sprite (list of one or two 1-bit cast members)*
> *cursor (list of one or two 1-bit cast members)*
> *the deskTopRectList (list of rects)*
> *the scoreSelection (list of lists that has changed format in D6)*
> *the searchPath (list of strings)*
> *the searchPaths (list of strings)*
> *the selection of castLib (list of lists)*
> *the windowList (list of windows)*
> *the scriptInstanceList of sprite[1] (list of script instances)*

---

1 New in D6

Property Lists

The following Lingo functions use true Lingo property lists (not linear lists). These lists can be manipulated like any other Lingo list.

These two handlers both return property lists that describe the parameters used in a Behavior. The author of a Behavior must define these lists in these handlers. Director asks for them when needed (see Chapter 12).

> on *getPropertyDescriptionList* (returns list use to create dialog)
> on *runPropertyDialog* (returns list of custom values for properties)

The UI Helper Xtra included with D6.5 provides a *getBehaviorInitializers()* function that returns the property list passed to on *runPropertyDialog*.

The MUI Dialog Xtra is a veritable orgy of property lists and nested lists. Refer to Chapter 15, *The MUI Dialog Xtra*, and to the downloadable Chapter 21, *Custom MUI Dialogs*, for details on these commands that use property lists:

> *Alert()*
> *GetItemPropList()*
> *GetWidgetList()*
> *GetWindowPropList()*
> *Initialize()*
> *ItemUpdate()*

Pseudo-Lists

There are several Lingo commands that don't use Lingo lists but use *pseudo-lists* that you might confuse with, or wish to convert to, true Lingo lists.

Child Objects Properties

Although child objects are not identical to property lists, they can also contain properties that can be manipulated like a property list using the *count()*, *getAt()*, *getPropAt()*, and *setaProp()* commands. Refer to Chapter 12 for details. The properties of a child object can be extracted using the *readProps()* handler in Example 6-20.

Text Lists and Pick Lists

These commands don't use true Lingo lists but rather use text strings that are list-like:

> *item of, word of, line of, char of chunk expressions* (see Chapter 7)
> *the labelList* (see Example 6-29)
> *mMessageList* (see Chapter 13)
> *xFactoryList* (see Chapter 13)

For example, *the labelList* returns a text string with each marker label name on a separate line. Such strings can not be used with the list commands but can be parsed as described under "*Text Parsing*" in Chapter 7. It is, however, fairly trivial to convert a text string delimited by carriage returns (as is *the labelList*) to a true Lingo list.

Example 6-29: Converting a Text String to a Lingo List

```
on convertLinesToList textList
  set realList = []
  -- Convert a list from a text string
  -- to a true Lingo list
  repeat with x = 1 to the number of lines in textList
    add (realList, line x of textList)
  end repeat
  return realList
end convertLinesToList
```

The output below will depend on your *labelList*:

```
put convertLinesToList (the labelList)
-- ["menu1", "menu2", "New Marker"]
```

The generalized handler above can extract lines of text from *any* string:

```
put convertLinesToList ("Oh" & RETURN & "Atlanta")
-- ["Oh", "Atlanta"]
```

Refer to the example under *"Text Parsing"* in Chapter 7 that parses all types of strings, not just those with multiple lines delimited by carriage returns.

Don't confuse Lingo lists with text lists from which the user can choose an item. There is no way for the user to "see" a Lingo list unless its contents are copied to a field cast member. Use field cast members themselves for user interaction.

Refer to Chapter 12, *Text and Fields*, in *Director in a Nutshell*.

Variable-Length Parameter Lists

Lingo handlers can accept any number of parameters. The Lingo commands *param()* and *the paramCount* are list-like functions that decipher the parameters passed into a handler. *The paramCount* represents the total number of parameters, and *param(n)* returns the *n*th parameter, analogous to the *count()* and *getAt()* list functions. Refer to *"Parameters and Arguments"* in Chapter 1 for a detailed discussion of using *the paramCount* and *param()* to decipher variable-length parameter lists.

Likewise, the *externalParamCount()*, *externalParamName()*, and *externalParamValue()* functions are used to access a "list" of the parameters specified in the HTML tag used to embed a Shockwave movie in an HTML page. Refer to Chapter 11, *Shockwave and the Internet*, in *Director in a Nutshell* for details.

CHAPTER 7

Strings

In this chapter we explore string manipulation commands and techniques. Chapter 10, *Keyboard Events*, covers detecting and analyzing keyboard input. See also Chapter 12, *Text and Fields*, in *Director in a Nutshell*, which covers the different types of cast members that can display text in Director, fonts and character mapping, scrolling text, and field-related Lingo including hypertext functions.

Strings and Chunk Expressions

A *string* is a collection of characters that can include non-visible characters such as spaces and carriage returns. A *chunk expression* is Macromedia's term for a string or a *substring* (a portion of a string). To *concatenate* two strings is to join them together to form a single string. The different chunk types are summarized in Table 7-1, and the Lingo commands that manipulate strings are shown in Table 7-2.

Chunk Expressions

A chunk expression usually takes the form:

```
chunk firstChunk {to lastChunk}
```

where `chunk` is either `char`, `word`, `item`, or `line`, and `firstChunk` and `lastChunk` are integers.

If `firstChunk` is less than 1, the result is the entire string! If `lastChunk` is less than `firstChunk`, the result is EMPTY (unless `lastChunk` is 0, in which case `firstChunk` is returned).

The following quirk occurs on both platforms in D6.0.2 and prior versions. Instead of returning an EMPTY string, if the starting chunk is 0 or negative, the chunk expression returns the entire string:

```
put char 0 of "Macromedia"
-- "Macromedia"
put char -1 to 3 of "Macromedia"
-- "Macromedia"
```

Let's create a test string that contains the strings "Macromedia,Inc." and "Rules" separated by a RETURN character. In the examples below, the RETURN character manifests itself as a new line, causing the output to continue on the next line.

Example 7-1: Chunk Expressions

```
set testString = "Macromedia,Inc." & RETURN & "Rules"

put testString
-- "Macromedia,Inc.
Rules"

put char 10 to 20 of testString
-- "a,Inc.
Rule"

put word 1 of testString
-- "Macromedia,Inc."

put item 2 of testString
-- "Inc.
Rules"

put line 1 of testString
-- "Macromedia,Inc."
```

Chars

A *char* is any byte (single character) and includes SPACE and RETURN characters in its character count. Note that RETURN is the 16th character in the test string in the example above.

Words

A *word* is any sequence of characters separated by whitespace (a SPACE, TAB, or RETURN, but *not* a comma). Note that in the example above, Lingo returned the first word of the string without the trailing RETURN character. Note also that "Macromedia,Inc." was considered a single word because there are no spaces in it. If there were a space, the results would have differed. Note that the first word includes the comma:

```
put word 1 of "Macromedia, Inc."
-- "Macromedia,"
```

Note that any intervening spaces are *not* considered part of the word:

```
put word 2 of "Macromedia, Inc."
-- "Inc."
```

An *item* is any sequence of characters delimited by *the itemDelimiter*, which defaults to a comma. Note that the RETURN is *not* an item delimiter, so *item 2 of testString* includes everything after the comma, even the RETURN character and the text on the next line. In the following, note that the returned string includes a leading spaces but not the comma:

```
put item 2 of "Macromedia, Inc."
-- " Inc."
```

Lines

A *line* is any sequence of characters separated by a RETURN character. The returned string does not include the RETURN character itself, so taking *line 1 of chunkExpression* is a good way to strip off trailing RETURN characters.

String Containers

Anything that holds a string can be used in a chunk expression.

String Literals

Any set of characters enclosed in quotes is considered a string.

```
put item 2 of "Macromedia, Inc."
-- " Inc."
```

String Variables

Any variable containing characters is also a string.

```
set myName = "Bruce"
put the numbers of chars in myName
-- 5
```

Fields

A cast member itself is not a string, but the *contents* of a field cast member is a string. The expression *field "myField"* is roughly equivalent to *the text of member "myField"* except that the latter extracts a *copy* of the text in the field. So, to affect a field, you would use the field itself, not a copy of the text within it. Create a field cast member named "*myField*" to test Example 7-2.

Example 7-2: Assigning Text to a Field Cast Member

These are all valid:

```
put "Bruce" into field "myField"
put "Hello " before member "myField"
put "Goodbye" after member "myField"
put length (field "myField")
delete char 1 to 5 of field "myField"
```

These are incorrect:

```
put "hello" before the text of field "myField"
put length(member "myField")
```

Symbols

Symbols are not strings, but they give the descriptive benefit of strings, plus the speed and storage efficiency of integers. Refer to Chapter 6, *Lists*, and

Chapter 19, *The Lingo Symbol Table*, for details. A symbol can be converted into a string as follows:

```
put string (#left)
-- "left"
```

Table 7-1 summarizes the chunk expression function. Note that the substrings returned by each function omit the separator(s) but include all other characters.

Table 7-1: Chunk Expressions

Chunk	Separator (omitted from return string)	Returned String May Include
char	N/A	Everything
word	SPACE, TAB, or RETURN	Commas
item	*the itemDelimiter* (defaults to comma)	Everything except *the itemDelimiter*
line	RETURN	SPACE, TAB, and commas

String Comparisons

You'll often want to compare two strings, perhaps to see if the user entered a correct response. But Lingo string comparisons are not as simple as you might think.

 The <, <=, >, and >= operators perform *case-sensitive* string comparisons that differ cross-platform. The = and <> operators and the *offset, contains,* and *starts* functions are *case-insensitive. All* string comparisons are *sensitive* to diacritical marks, such as accents, despite the documentation's claims to the contrary.

Strings can be equal only if they have the same length. Use the *starts* function to compare the beginning of strings of unequal length. Refer to Appendix C, *Case-Sensitivity, Sort Order, Diacritical Marks, and Space-Sensitivity,* for many important details, plus utilities to perform case-insensitive comparisons and convert between cases.

Lingo String Commands

Table 7-2 summarizes the Lingo string commands. Note that items in curly braces are optional.

Table 7-2: Lingo String Commands

Command	Usage
string1 & *string2*	Concatenates two strings.

Table 7-2: Lingo String Commands (continued)

Command	Usage
string1 && *string2*	Concatenates two strings and adds a space between them.
string1 = *string2*	Returns TRUE if *string1* equals *string2* (case-*insensitive*).
string1 <> *string2*	Returns TRUE if *string1* does not equal *string2* (case-*insensitive*).
string1 < *string2*	Returns TRUE if *string1* is less than *string2* (case-*sensitive*).
string1 <= *string2*	Returns TRUE if *string1* is less than or equal to *string2* (case-*sensitive*).
string1 > *string2*	Returns TRUE if *string1* is greater than *string2* (case-*sensitive*).
string1 >= *string2*	Returns TRUE if *string1* is greater than or equal to *string2* (case-*sensitive*).
char *firstChar* {to *lastChar*} of *chunkExpression*	Refers to one or more characters in a chunk expression.
chars (*chunkExpression*, *firstChar*, *lastChar*)	Extracts a range of characters from a chunk expression.
charToNum(*character*)	Converts a character to its ASCII code. See *numToChar()* and the ASCII table in Appendix A, *ASCII Codes and Key Codes*.
contains	*string1* contains *string2* returns TRUE if *string2* is contained within *string1* (case-*insensitive*).
delete *chunkExpression*[1]	Deletes the specified substring, such as *delete line 1 to 5 of field "myField"*.
EMPTY	The EMPTY string, equivalent to a pair of double quotes with nothing in it (""), not even a space.
ENTER	Indicates the Enter key on the numeric keypad (not the main keyboard), which is ASCII code 3. Refer to Chapter 10 and Appendix A.
hilite *chunkExpression* of *chunkExpression*	Highlights any chunk of a field, such as *hilite word 5 of field "myField"*. See *selStart* and *selEnd*. (This command is unrelated to *the hilite of member* checkbox and radio button property.)
field	Refers to a field cast member and, by implication, its contents. See *"String Containers"* earlier in this chapter.
ilk(*datum*, #string)	Returns TRUE if *datum* is a string.
item *firstItem* {to *lastItem*} of *chunkExpression*	Refers to one or more items in a chunk expression.
the itemDelimiter[2]	Specifies the delimiter used to separate items when parsing a string . See *"Text Parsing"* later in this chapter.
the last *chunk* of *chunkExpression*	Refers to the last char, item, line, or word in a chunk expression.

Table 7-2: Lingo String Commands (continued)

Command	Usage
length(*chunkExpression*)	Calculates the length of a chunk expression.
the length of *chunkExpression*	Calculates the length of a chunk expression.
line *firstLine* {to *lastLine*} of *chunkExpression*	Refers to one or more lines in a chunk expression.
the lineCount of member *whichMember*	Indicates the number of lines of the field, where wrapped lines count as more than one. Contrast with *the number of lines*.
the number of chars in *chunkExpression*	Returns the number of characters in a chunk expression.
the numbers of items in *chunkExpression*[2]	Returns the number of items in a chunk expression. See *the itemDelimiter*.
the number of lines in *chunkExpression*	Returns the number of lines in a chunk expression, as indicated by RETURN characters, not wrapped text.
the number of words in *chunkExpression*	Returns the number of words in a chunk expression.
numToChar(*asciiCode*)	Converts an ASCII code to a character. See *charToNum()* and the ASCII table in Appendix A.
offset (*findString*, *lookInString*)	Returns the starting location of the first occurrence of *findString* in *lookInString* (*case-insensitive*). If not found, it returns zero.
put *chunk* after *chunkExpression*	Appends text to a string or field, such as: *put "foo" after char 5 of field "myField"*.
put *chunk* before *chunkExpression*	Adds text at the beginning of a string or field, such as: *put "foo" before char 5 of field "myField"*.
put *chunk* into *chunkExpression*	Replaces text in a string or field, such as: *put "foo" into char 5 of field "myField"*.
QUOTE	Indicates the double-quote character ("), ASCII code 34. Used to add quotes within a string. *See "String Concatenation"* later in this chapter.
RETURN	Indicates a carriage return character (Ctrl-M), ASCII code 13, created with Return key (Mac) or Enter key (Windows) on the *main* keyboard, not the numeric keypad. Used also to separate lines and words in a chunk expression.[3]
the selection[4]	Returns a string containing the highlighted portion of the current editable field. See *the selStart* and *selEnd*.
the selEnd[4]	Determines the last character selected in the currently editable field. See *hilite* and *the selection*.

Table 7-2: Lingo String Commands (continued)

Command	Usage
the selStart[4]	Determines the first character selected in the currently editable field. See *hilite* and *the selection*.
SPACE	Indicates the SPACE character (" "), ASCII code 32. Used to separate words in a chunk expression.
starts	*string1* starts *string2* returns TRUE if *string1* begins with *string2* (case-insensitive).
#string	Symbol returned by *ilk()* function for strings.
string()	Converts data to a string.
stringP()	Returns TRUE if operand is a string.
symbol()	Converts data to a symbol.
TAB	Indicates the TAB character (Ctrl-I), ASCII code 9. Used to separate words in a chunk expression. Refer also to *the autoTab of member* property.
value(*string*)	Converts a string to another data type, such as a float, integer, or list. See Chapter 5, *Data Types and Expressions*.
word firstWord {to *lastWord*} of *chunkExpression*	Refers to one or more words in a chunk expression.

[1] Using *delete* with a decreasing integer, such as *delete char 10 to 1 of field whichField*, crashed D6.0 but was fixed in D6.0.1.
[2] *The number of items* did not work properly in D6.0 when using lowercase "c" as *the itemDelimiter*, but it was fixed in D6.0.1.
[3] ASCII code 13 is used as a line separator in Director on both Macintosh and Windows, although most Windows applications use the combination of ASCII 10 (CR) and ASCII 13 (LF) for standard text file line separation. See Chapter 14, *External Files*.
[4] *The selStart* and *the selEnd* properties determine the currently selected text of the field currently with keyboard focus. They are specified as *the selStart* and *the selEnd* (without the keywords *of member* or *of sprite*) and can be both tested and set. Setting them to the same value creates a blinking insertion point. Set *the selEnd before* setting *the selStart* for reliable results. See Example 10-5 and Example 10-6 in Chapter 10.

Refer to Table 5-3, *"Type Checking and Conversion"* in Chapter 5 for more information about converting strings to other data types. Refer also to Table 5-5, *"Data Type Conversion Practice."*

String Sizes and String Functions

Lingo can perform many different string operations, such as searches and comparisons.

 String operations are comparatively slow, especially with large strings. Very large strings severely degrade performance of string commands and may cause crashes.

Fields are limited to 32,000 characters, but strings held in memory can be much larger (up to about 2 MB). Furthermore, access to strings held in memory is somewhat faster than the same string held in a field cast member.

Use the *length()* function (not *the size of member*) to determine the length of the text in a field or in any string. Director 6.0 failed when taking the *value()* of a string greater than 32 KB in length, but this was fixed in Director 6.0.1.

Here are some more example string commands; create a field cast member named "*myField*" before you begin, and examine it at each step.

Example 7-3: String Function Practice

```
set the text of member "myField" = "Hello Sailor!"
put the last word of field "myField"
-- "Sailor!"

delete char 1 to 3 of field "myField"
set the foreColor of char 1 to 3 of field "myField" = 125

put "yippee" before field "myField"
put "yopee" after field "myField"
put the length of field "myField"
-- 21

put field "myField"
-- "yippeelo Sailor!yopee"
```

String Concatenation

Lingo uses the *&* and *&&* operators to concatenate strings. The only difference is that *&&* adds an extra space in the output string. You can concatenate as many strings as you like into one big string, as shown in Example 7-4.

Example 7-4: String Concatenation Practice

```
set x = 5
put "The value of x is:" && x
-- "The value of x is: 5"

-- Use & and not && to build file paths without spaces
set myDocPath = the pathName & "EXAMPLE.PDF"
put myDocPath
-- "MacHD:Music:Bands:Feat:EXAMPLE.PDF"

put "The value of x in parentheses: (" & x & ")"
-- "The value of x in parentheses: (5)"

set name = "Dolly"
put "Hello" & name
-- "HelloDolly"
```

Example 7-4: String Concatenation Practice (continued)

```
put "Hello" && name
-- "Hello Dolly"

on showMovie
   put "This example shows the movie path in quotes," && ¬
      QUOTE & the pathName & the movieName & QUOTE & ¬
      ", in the middle of a long line"
end showMovie

showMovie
-- "This example shows the movie path in quotes,
 "C:\Book\Test.DIR", in the middle of a long line"
put "This string includes "& RETURN &" a line break"
-- This string includes
a line break
```

Note the following:

- Don't forget the *&* and *&&* operators. This is wrong: *put "X equals" x.*

- Double quotes (") must always appear in matching pairs.

- Lingo treats single quote marks or fancy opening and closing curly quote marks like any other character within the string.

- Literal strings always go *within* a pair of quote marks.

- Spacing *outside* the double quotes is ignored.

- The & and && operators, variables, Lingo properties, and the QUOTE constant go *outside* the double quotes.

- The Lingo continuation character ¬ must be *outside* the double quotes.

- Use &, not &&, when concatenating items to construct a file path.

 Use concatenation to create strings that exceed 256 characters.

You must use parentheses with certain commands that have a higher precedence than the concatenation symbol. This will fail:

```
open window the pathname & "myMovie"
```

Use this instead:

```
open window (the pathname & "myMovie")
```

See Example 14-1 and Example 14-3, which use for examples of using string concatenation to build platform-specific file paths from a combination of Lingo properties, variables, and string literals.

Text Parsing

We saw in Example 7-1 that the *char*, *word*, and *line* functions could be used to extract a substring from a larger string. But the most powerful Lingo string parsing command is the *item* function when used in conjunction with *the itemDelimiter* property. *The itemDelimiter* determines what character Lingo uses to distinguish one item from the next. It defaults to a comma (,) but can be set to any character. If you set it to a RETURN character, the *item* function would be the same as the *line* function. If you set it to a SPACE, the *item* function would be similar to the *word* function but would not treat RETURN or TAB characters as word separators. Let's revisit Example 7.1, using the same test string.

Example 7-5: ItemDelimiter Practice

```
set testString = "Macromedia,Inc." & RETURN & "Rules"
```

Let's start with *the itemDelimiter* equal to a comma (the default):

```
set the itemDelimiter =","
put item 1 of testString
-- "Macromedia"
put item 2 of testString
-- "Inc.
Rules"
```

Let's see what happens if we change *the itemDelimiter* to a SPACE:

```
set the itemDelimiter = SPACE
put item 1 of testString
-- "Macromedia,Inc.
Rules"
put item 2 of testString
-- ""
```

In this example, because there is no SPACE in the test string, the first item is the same as the whole string, and the second item is EMPTY (there is no second item).

If we change *the itemDelimiter* to a RETURN character, the *item* function behaves like the *line* function.

```
set the itemDelimiter = RETURN
put item 1 of testString
-- "Macromedia,Inc."
put item 2 of testString
-- "Rules"
```

You can set *the itemDelimiter* to any valid character.

 Be sure to set *the itemDelimiter* to something that reliably distinguishes item breaks from the data itself, and reset it to the original value when you're done.

The following example returns the drive letter or name from the current path. It takes advantage of the fact that a colon (:) is used to separate both the Windows drive letter and the Macintosh drive name from the remainder of their respective paths. It is polite to set *the itemDelimiter* back to the value it started with, just in case someone is relying on it to be the default comma or some other value.

Example 7-6: Determining the Drive ID using the ItemDelimiter

```
on getDrive inputPath
  -- Save the old itemDelimiter
  set oldDelimiter = the itemDelimiter
  -- Drive ID is set off by a colon on both platforms
  set the itemDelimiter = ":"
  set drive = item 1 of inputPath
  -- Restore the old itemDelimiter
  set the itemDelimiter = oldDelimiter
  return drive
end getDrive

put getDrive(the applicationPath)    -- Mac
-- "MacHD"
put getDrive(the applicationPath)    -- Windows
-- "C"
```

Refer to Chapter 14 for details on parsing text from an external file and more details on parsing file paths to determine folder and file names.

Parsing or searching through large amounts of text, such as from an external file, can be slow. The *TextCruncher* Xtra by Yair Sageev (*http://www.itp.tsoa.nyu.edu/ ~student/yair/texcruncher/HTML/YairTextCruncher.html*) provides fast cross-platform text processing, including parsing and search and replace.

Accepting and Evaluating User Input

To allow a user to enter text at run-time, you must use a field sprite and set its *editable of sprite* property to TRUE (or use the *Editable* checkbox in the Cast Member Property dialog, or in the Sprite Toolbar/Inspector). See Chapter 12, in *Director in a Nutshell* for details on working with field cast members.

Example 7-7 checks whether the user entered a valid name (one contained in *nameList*) when he or she presses RETURN. Attach this script to an editable field sprite. Refer to Chapter 10 for details on detecting keyboard input.

Example 7-7: Evaluating User Input

```
on keyDown me
  -- Set up list of acceptable inputs
  set nameList = ["Bruce", "Bruce Epstein", "BAE"]

  -- When the user hits the RETURN key...
  if the key = RETURN then
    -- Get the contents of the field
    set thisField = the member of sprite the spriteNum of me
    set thisName = the text of thisField
```

Strings

Example 7-7: Evaluating User Input (continued)

```
      -- Check if the name is in the list of names
      -- (this search is case-sensitive)
      if getPos (nameList, thisName) then
        alert "Hello" && thisName & "!"
      else
        alert "Do I know you" && thisName & "?"
      end if
    else
      -- Any other key than RETURN gets sent to field sprite
      pass
    end if
end keyDown
```

Searching and Replacing Text

The *SearchAndReplace()* example shown in Macromedia's *Lingo Dictionary* and the online Help under the *offset()* function is wrong. It returns an incorrect string if the original string begins with the characters to be replaced. For example, note that this duplicates the initial "M" incorrectly:

```
put SearchAndReplace ("Micromedia", "Mi", "Ma")
-- "MMacromedia"
```

Here is a corrected version. It performs a check to make sure that it doesn't copy the initial character improperly.

Example 7-8: Corrected Search-and-Replace Routine

```
on SearchAndReplaceCorrected input, oldString, newString
  set output to ""
  repeat while input contains oldString
    set position to max (1, offset(oldString, input))
    if position > 1 then
      put char 1 to position -1 of input after output
    end if
    put newString after output
    delete char 1 to (position + length(oldString)-1) of input
  end repeat
  put input after output
  return output
end SearchAndReplaceCorrected

put SearchAndReplaceCorrected ("Micromedia", "Mi", "Ma")
-- "Macromedia"
```

If you write your own search-and-replace routine, be sure that you traverse the input string only once. This will avoid an infinite loop if the replacement string contains the same characters as those being replaced.

The TextCruncher Xtra also provides fast search-and-replace functions.

CHAPTER 8

Math (and Gambling)

Dust off your dunce cap. This chapter covers mathematical, geometric, and trigonometric operations for both the mathematically adept and the numerically challenged. If you are one of the latter, at least you'll enjoy the section on gambling at the end of the chapter. Refer to Chapter 5, *Data Types and Expressions*, for details on data type conversion, expression evaluation, logical operators, and comparison operators. See Chapter 6, *Lists*, for an introduction to rects and points and mathematical operations with lists. Refer to Chapter 5, *Coordinates, Alignment, and Registration Points*, in *Director in a Nutshell* for more details on rects, points, coordinate systems, and alignment of sprites on the Stage.

The cross-platform *MathXtras* from Maxwell Technologies (*http://www.maxwell.com/MathXtras*) provide these math-related functions: customizable on-screen calculator, scrolling odometer-style counter, equation editor, graphing functions, spreadsheet tables, and even sliders and speedometers.

Arithmetic Operators

Director supports the usual complement of arithmetic operators, as shown in Table 8-1. Operations with a higher precedence are performed first. Operations with the same precedence are performed left to right. The order of evaluation can be overridden with parentheses. Refer also to Table 5-7 and 5-8, which detail the precedence of comparison and Boolean operators. If one or both operands in an expression are floats, the result is a float. If both operands are integers, the result is an integer.

Division in Lingo does not work the way you learned it in school! Lingo performs *integer*, *modulo*, and *float* division.

Table 8-1: Arithmetic Operators

Operator	Usage	Precedence
( )	overrides default precedence[1]	5
-	unary negation operator[2]	5
*	multiplication	4
/	division	4
mod	modulo division	4
-	subtraction[2]	3
+	addition	3
=	assignment[3]	1

[1] Nested parentheses are evaluated from the innermost pair outward. Parentheses are also used when calling Lingo functions. See Chapter 1, *How Lingo Thinks*.
[2] The precedence of the minus sign depends on whether it is used as a unary or binary operator. If placed before a single operand, it has precedence 5; if placed between two operands it has precedence 3.
[3] The equals sign is used to assign variables using the *set* command and also in comparisons. See "*Comparison Operators*" in Chapter 5.

Some functions, such as *power()*, always returns a float regardless of the operands' type. Refer to Chapter 5 in this book and to Chapter 4, *CastLibs, Cast Members and Sprites*, in *Director in a Nutshell* for details on using mathematical operators with cast member references.

You can use string operands with all the operators shown in Table 8-1, but only the "=" operator (used to assign or compare two strings) returns a meaningful result. For example, if you attempt to "add" the strings "a" + "b" you get a large integer. For best results, convert strings using *value()*, *integer()*, or *float()* first.

You can add, subtract, multiply, and divide two or more lists:

```
put [1, 2, 3] + [4, 5, 6]
-- [5, 7, 9]
```

You can perform mathematical operations on entire lists.

```
put [1, 2 , 3] * 2
-- [2, 4, 6]
```

Lists operate on other lists one element at a time. Standalone numbers operate on the entire list.

The following adds the first two lists element-by-element, then adds 1 to each element, then adds the last list element-by-element as well. The first element in the result (14) is equal to 1 + 4 + 1 + 8, and the second element in the result (17) is equal to 2 + 5 + 1 + 9, and so on.

```
put [1,2,3] + [4,5,6] + 1 + [8,9,10]
-- [14, 17, 20]
```

Refer to Examples 6-17 and 6-18 for details on performing math with Lists.

See "*Comparison Operators*" in Chapter 5 for details on the <, >, <=, >=, and = comparison operators that can be used with both numbers and strings.

Integer and Modulo Division

Integer division is convenient for determining the number of "wholes" when converting between different units. Modulo division is convenient for determining what's left over.

Integer Versus Floating-Point Division

Division is performed using the "/" character. *Integer division* (in which the remainder is dropped) is performed if *both* operands are integers. Therefore, 5/3 evaluates to 1, not 1.667. To perform floating-point division, ensure that at least one operand is a floating-point number *before* the division is performed. Create a float constant by including a decimal point; convert a variable to a float using the *float()* function.:

Example 8-1: Integer Versus Floating-Point Division

```
put 3/5          -- The remainder is dropped
-- 0
put 5/3          -- The remainder is dropped
-- 1
put float(5/3)   -- You've converted the result to a float!
-- 1.0000
set x = 5
put float(x)/3   -- Convert one operand to a float first
-- 1.6667
put 5.0/3        -- Use a float as an operand
-- 1.6667
put -5/3.0       -- The result may be negative
-- -1.6667
```

Division by Zero

Attempting to divide by zero causes a "*Cannot divide by zero*" error. This is most often caused by a variable containing the wrong value, such as an uninitialized global variable or an incorrect parameter passed to a function. Check the value of all operands in the Debugger if you encounter this problem (see Chapter 3, *Lingo Coding and Debugging Tips*). Don't forget that an integer division may be truncated to zero.

This causes a division by zero error:

```
set x = 3/5    -- Integer division is performed
put 7/x        -- Causes an error because x is 0!
```

Use something like this instead:

```
set x = float(3)/5    -- Force float division to be performed
put 7/x
-- 11.6667
```

Modulo Division

Modulo division calculates the integer remainder of a division. If the first number is an even multiple of the second, the result is 0. If not, the result is the integer remainder.

Example 8-2: Modulo Division Practice

```
put 10 mod 7    -- The remainder is 3
-- 3
put 10 mod 5    -- 10 is evenly divisible by 5
-- 0
```

Unlike ordinary division, in which division by zero is not allowed, if the modulus is 0 the result is always 0:

```
put 10 mod 0    -- The result is 0
-- 0
```

The result always take the sign of the first operand, regardless of the sign of the modulus:

```
put -5 mod 3
-- -2
put 5 mod -3
-- 2
put -5 mod -3
-- -2
```

Modulo division works only with integer operands. If either operand is a floating-point number, the result is meaningless.

Compare these two routines. One converts minutes to fractional hours, the other to HH:MM format.

Example 8-3: Converting Time Units Using Integer, Modulo, and Floating-Point Division

```
on minutesToHours numMinutes
  return numMinutes / 60.0
end

on minutesToHHMM numMinutes
  -- Eliminate any decimal portion
  set numMinutes = integer(numMinutes)
  -- Use integer division to get the number of "whole" hours
```

Example 8-3: Converting Time Units Using Integer, Modulo, and Floating-Point Division (continued)

```
set hours = numMinutes / 60
-- Modulo division gives the number of left-over minutes
set minutes = numMinutes mod 60
-- Format it in typical HH:MM style
return string(hours) & ":" & string(minutes)
end

put minutesToHours (90)
-- 1.5000
put minutesToHHMM (90)
-- "1:30"
```

Refer to Examples 11-4, 11-5 and 11-6 in Chapter 11, *Timers and Dates*, for more time conversion utilities.

Math Functions

Director supports the usual complement of math functions, as shown in Table 8-2. Refer to Table 8-3 and Table 8-4 for exponentiation and trigonometric functions.

Table 8-2: Math Functions

Lingo Keyword	Usage and Range
abs()	Calculates the absolute value of a number. Returns float or integer. Used to calculate unsigned values, such as distances.
add()	The *add* command pertains only to lists and is *not* a mathematical function. See the "+" operator.
charToNum()[1]	Converts ASCII character to ASCII code. See *numToChar()*.
FALSE	Constant equivalent to zero (0). See TRUE.
float()	Converts string or integer to floating-point value. See the *floatPrecision*.
floatP()	Returns TRUE if operand is a floating-point value.
the floatPrecision[2]	Determines the number of decimal places used to display floats (default is 4). Does not affect calculation accuracy.
INF or -INF[2]	Indicates an *overflow* condition caused by a number larger than maximum allowed float or an undefined value.
integer()	Rounds floats to the *nearest* integer. *integer(-.5)* is rounded to -1, not zero. Use *value()* to convert strings first.
integerP()	Returns TRUE if operand is an integer.
max()	Returns maximum number from a list or comma-delimited series. Also works with strings.
the maxInteger[2]	Returns the maximum supported integer (2147483647), which equals $2^{31}-1$.

Table 8-2: Math Functions (continued)

Lingo Keyword	Usage and Range
min()	Returns minimum number from a list or comma-delimited series. Also works with strings.
mod	Modulo division operator.
NAN[2]	Indicates an invalid number (Not a Number).
numToChar()[1]	Converts ASCII code to ASCII character. See *charToNum()*.
pi() *or* PI[3]	Constant equivalent to the mathematical constant pi π to 14 decimal places (that is, 3. 14159265358979). See *the floatPrecision*.
put	Prints a value in the Message window
put...into	Assigns a value to a variable, or puts a string into a field. See *set*.
random*(n)*	Returns a pseudo-random integer between 1 and *n*, *where n >= 1*. See *"Random Numbers"* later in this chapter.
the randomSeed	Seed used to generate random numbers. Can be tested or set. See "Random Numbers" later in this chapter.
set...= or set...to	Assigns a value to a property or variable.
string()	Converts any value to a string.
TRUE	Constant equivalent to one (1). See FALSE.
value()	Converts a string to a float or integer.
VOID	Constant equivalent to VOID (no value).
voidP()	Returns TRUE if operand is VOID. Useful for checking for uninitialized global or other VOID values.

[1] See Chapter 7, *Strings*, Chapter 10, *Keyboard Events*, and Appendix C, *Case-Sensitivity, Sort Order, Diacritical Marks, and Space-Sensitivity*, for details on *numToChar()* and using *charToNum()* to perform case-sensitive string comparisons.
[2] See *"Rounding and Precision"* and *"Numbers Out of Range"* later in this chapter.
[3] There was a bug with PI in Director 6 that was fixed in D6.0.1. See *"Geometry and Trigonometry"* later in this chapter.

Minimum and Maximum

The *min()* and *max()* functions return the minimum or maximum value from either a series of items or a single list. They behave unreliably when you mix both simple items and lists or provide two or more lists.

```
put max([5,6,7])
-- 7
put min(12, 25, 32)
-- 12
```

Don't do this:

```
put min([1, 4, 5], 12)
```

Use *min()* and *max()* to restrict the range of allowable inputs, as shown in Example 8-4.

The *min()* and *max()* functions will also work with strings, or even with mixed lists of both strings and numbers. Beware because string comparisons differ cross-platform. Refer to Appendix C for details.

Checking and Clipping Values Within a Range

The following handlers can be used to check whether a value is within a desired range or to clip it to the desired range. These are useful when requesting data entry. Also refer to the *constrainH()* and *constrainV()* functions, and *the constraint of sprite* property. See also Example 1-39, *"Verifying Parameters,"* in the *"Parameter Error Checking"* section of Chapter 1.

Example 8-4: Clipping a Value to a Valid Range

```
on clipValue checkVal, minVal, maxVal
    -- Make sure that checkVal is between minVal and maxVal
    set temp = checkVal
    -- Note the use of min() and max(). This is correct!
    set temp = max (temp, minVal) -- use max() to ensure minimum value
    set temp = min (temp, maxVal) -- use min() to ensure maximum value
    return temp
end clipValue

put clipValue (45, 1, 100)
-- 45
put clipValue (150, 1, 100)
-- 100
set userVal = clipValue (value (field "userEntry"), 1, 100)
```

Example 8-5: Checking If Values Are Within Range

```
on validRange inVal, minVal, maxVal
    if (inVal < minVal) or (inVal > maxVal) then
        return FALSE
    else
        return TRUE
    end if
end validRange
Use the validRange() handler such as;
if not validRange(value (field "userEntry"), 1, 100) then
    alert "Please enter a valid number between 1 and 100"
end if
```

Sum

Example 8-6 calculates the sum of a series of numbers. You can pass it individual numbers, lists of numbers, or both.

Refer to *"Variable-Length Parameter Lists"* in Chapter 1 for details on *the paramCount* and *param()* commands used later in this chapter.

Example 8-6: Summing a List of Values

```
on sum
    -- Reset sum to zero (this is used to hold our answer)
```

Example 8-6: Summing a List of Values (continued)

```
  set retSum = 0
  -- Deal with an indeterminate number of parameters
  repeat with n = 1 to the paramCount
    -- If a list is found, count its elements separately
    if listP(param(n)) then
      repeat with x in param(n)
        -- Add from the list (and recurse if necessary)
        set retSum = retSum + sum(x)
      end repeat
    else if integerP(param(n)) or floatP(param(n)) then
      -- Add non-list parameters individually
      set retSum = retSum + param(n)
    end if
  end repeat
  -- Here's the answer. Fetch! Good dog.
  return retSum
end sum
```

```
put sum (1,3,4,8)
-- 16
put sum([12, 13, 16] + [5,6, 7])
-- 59
```

Compare this to the result from the addition of two lists:

```
  put [12, 13, 16] + [5,6, 7]
  -- [17, 19, 23]
```

Reader Exercise: Use Example 8-6 as a basis to create custom min() and max() functions that properly accept multiple lists as inputs.

Average

Example 8-7 calculates the average of series of numbers or lists of numbers. It works very similarly to, and makes use of, the *sum()* function from Example 8-6. It also requires the *recursiveCount()* function from Example 8-8 which counts all the elements in a list including all sublists.

Example 8-7: Averaging a List of Values

```
-- Use the sum() and recursiveCount() functions
-- to calculate the average of all items in a list.
on average
  set total = 0
  set itemCount = 0
  repeat with n = 1 to the paramCount
    set total = total + sum (param(n))
    set itemCount = itemCount + recursiveCount (param(n))
  end repeat
  return float(total)/ itemCount
end average
```

Example 8-8: Recursively Counting Elements in a List

```
-- Count all elements in a list, including sublists
on recursiveCount inList
  if listP(inList) then
    repeat with x in inList
      set itemCount = itemCount + recursiveCount(x)
    end repeat
  else
    set itemCount = itemCount + 1
  end if
  return itemCount
end recursiveCount

put average  (1,3,4,8)
-- 4.0000
put average  ([12, 13, 16], [5,6])
-- 10.4000
put average  ([12, 13, 16, [1, 2, 3]], [5,6])
-- 7.2500
```

Exponents, Roots, and Logarithms

Director supports the exponentiation functions shown in Table 8-3.

Table 8-3: Exponentiation Functions

Function	Calculates	Return Data Type
log(x)	Natural logarithm of x, where x > 0	Always a float.
power (base, x)	Exponent, $base^x$	Always a float.
sqrt(x) the sqrt of x	Square root of a x., where x > 0	Returns same type as x.
exp(x)	Exponent e^x where e is the natural logarithm base (2.7183)	Always a float.
nEx	Exponential notation, $n * 10^x$	Always a float.

Using math functions such as *power()* or *log()* with bogus or extremely large or small values can crash Windows systems.

The default LINGO.INI file invokes the float-to-string conversion code, which prevents future crashes in other math functions. See Appendix D, *The DIRECTOR. INI and LINGO.INI Files*, for details.

Logarithms

Taking the *log()* of 0 or a negative number results in a meaningless value, as described under *"Numbers Out of Range."*

The natural logarithm base, *e*, can be calculated as:

```
set e = exp (1)
```

In mathematics, the natural logarithm is usually written as *ln()*, and the base-10 log is usually written as *log()*. But, the Lingo *log()* function performs the *natural* logarithm. Example 8-9 calculates the base-10 logarithm.

Example 8-9: Calculating the Log Base 10

```
on log10 x
  return (log(x) / log(10))
end

put log10(100)
-- 2.0000
```

Exponents

The *sqrt()* function always returns the positive square root of a number, never the negative square root. Taking the square root of a negative number returns 0, so use *abs()* first.

```
put  sqrt (-9)
-- 0
put  sqrt (abs(-9))
-- 3
```

The operand must be a floating-point number to prevent the result from being rounded.

```
set x = 8
put sqrt (x)
--3
put sqrt (float(x))
--2.8284
```

Use *power()* with a fractional exponent to take the cube root. Make sure that the exponent is a float, as shown in Example 8-10:

Example 8-10: Calculating Powers

```
put power (27, .3333)    -- The result is not exact
-- 2.9997
put power (27, 1/3)      -- 1/3 = 0 (integer division). wrong!
-- 1.0000
put power (27, 1.0/3)    -- This is correct
-- 3.0000
```

Use *power()* with a negative exponent to calculate fractions, or even a fractional exponent:

```
put  power (10,-3)
-- 0.0010
put  power (10,5.2)
-- 158489.3192
```

Exponential notation uses an e or E, not to be confused with the natural logarithm base e defined in the previous example. Note that there must not be any
spaces in these expressions.

Example 8-11: Exponential Notation

```
put 1e5              -- equivalent to 1 * power (10, 5)
-- 100000.0000
put 5E-3             -- equivalent to  5 * power (10, -3)
-- 0.0050
put 2.5E+4           -- equivalent to  2.5 * power (10, 4)
-- 25000.0000
```

Numbers greater than or equal to 1e100 are returned in exponential notation:

```
put 3.5 * power (10, 112)
--   3.500000000e+112
```

Geometry and Trigonometry

See Examples 5-3 and 5-4 in Chapter 5 of *Director in a Nutshell* (or in the downloadable examples) for utilities that calculate the area of a rectangle and the
distance between two points. Director supports the usual complement of trigonometric functions—sine, cosine, tangent, and arc tangent—as shown in Table 8-4.
Lingo trig functions accept an angle, *theta*, expressed in radians. There are 2π
radians per 360 degrees, or π radians per 180 degrees.

Example 8-12: Converting Between Radians and Degrees

```
on degreesToRadians degrees
  return (pi * degrees/ 180.0)
end degreesToRadians

on radiansToDegrees radians
  return integer(radians * 180.0 / pi)
end radiansToDegrees
```

When used as a parameter to a function call in Director 6.0, the constant *pi* erroneously equals VOID. Either use *pi()* with parentheses or,
preferably, upgrade to Director 6.0.1 or later.

Table 8-4: Trigonometric Functions

Trig Function	Range for Operand	Result Range
atan(x)	$-\infty <= x <= \infty$	$-pi/2 <= atan(x) <= pi/2$

Table 8-4: Trigonometric Functions (continued)

Trig Function	Range for Operand	Result Range
cos(*theta*)	0 <= *theta* <= 2*pi	-1 <= cos(*theta*) <= 1
sin(*theta*)	0 <= *theta* <= 2*pi	-1 <= sin(*theta*) <= 1
tan(*theta*)	-pi/2 <= *theta* <= pi/2	-∞ <= tan <= ∞

Refer to the downloadable examples (*http://www.zeusprod.com/nutshell/examples. html*) for derivations of the arcsine and arccosine, hyperbolic trig functions and a Behavior that moves a sprite along a sine wave path. (That example also shows how to build a list of data points to feed a trig function with, say, 50 points from 0 to 2π.

Area of a Circle

This function calculates the area of a circle with the specified radius.

Example 8-13: Calculating the Area of a Circle

```
on circleArea radius
  return (pi() * power(radius, 2))
end circleArea

put circleArea (5)
-- 78.5398
```

Moving a Sprite in a Circle or Along an Ellipse

Trig functions can be used to determine the path along a circle or similar path. This Behavior script moves a sprite along an elliptical path as the playback head moves. Set the same *X* and *Y* radii to create a circle. Similar Behaviors can be written for parabolic, hyperbolic, and Bezier paths. Refer to Chapter 12, *Behaviors and Parent Scripts*.

Example 8-14: Elliptical Motion Behavior

```
-- Elliptical Sprite Path Behavior
property pCenterX, pCenterY, pAxisX, pAxisY
property pSteps, pStepSize, pTheta

on beginSprite me
  set pStepSize = (2 * pi) / pSteps
  set pTheta = 0
end beginSprite

on exitFrame me
  set x = pAxisX * sin(pTheta) + pCenterX
  set y = pAxisY * cos(pTheta) + pCenterY
  set the loc of sprite (the spriteNum of me) = point (x, y)
  set pTheta = pTheta + pStepSize
```

Example 8-14: Elliptical Motion Behavior (continued)

```
end exitFrame

on getPropertyDescriptionList
  return [  ¬
  #pCenterX: [#comment: "Center X", #format: #integer, ¬
       #default: (the stageRight - the stageLeft)/2 ],  ¬
  #pCenterY: [#comment: "Center Y", #format: #integer, ¬
       #default: (the stageBottom - the stageTop)/2 ],  ¬
  #pAxisX: [#comment: "Radius X", #format: #integer, ¬
       #default: (the stageRight - the stageLeft)/4 ],  ¬
  #pAxisY: [#comment: "Radius Y", #format: #integer, ¬
       #default: (the stageBottom - the stageTop)/4 ],  ¬
  #pSteps: [#comment: "Steps Per Rotations", ¬
        #format: #integer, #default: 60 ]]
end

on getBehaviorDescription
  return "Makes a sprite move in an elliptical path."
end getBehaviorDescription
```

Number Systems and Formats

Never include commas, dollar signs, or formatting symbols when specifying numbers. Only the digits 0-9 and the characters +, -, and the decimal point are valid numeric symbols (exponential notation also uses the letter "E" or "e").

Rounding and Precision

The manner in which integers and floats are stored and manipulated by computers limits their maximum range and precision.

Display Precision

Director performs all floating-point calculations to 15 significant digits. Floating-point values are never *permanently* rounded, but are merely *displayed* rounded to the number of decimal places specified by *the floatPrecision*. Refer to "*Float Truncation*" later in this chapter for tips on avoiding errors due to the quirks of floating-point math.

```
set the floatPrecision = 4
put pi
-- 3.1416
set the floatPrecision = 15
put pi
-- 3.141592653589790
put 5.12345678901234567
-- 5.123456789012350
```

Numbers Out of Range

The maximum floating-point number is approximately +/-1.797693135e+308. Larger numbers return INF (on Macintosh) or -INF (under Windows) to indicate infinity.

Math

```
put 2e+308  -- Number is greater than max float
-- INF
put log (0)
-- INF
```

Attempting an invalid calculation may return a meaningless value.

```
put log(-1)
-- NAN                    -- Macintosh
put log(-1)
-- 0.0000000000e+0    -- Windows
```

The maxInteger returns the maximum positive integer (2147483647, which equals 2^{31}-1). The minimum integer is -2147483648 (Macintosh) or -2147483647 (Windows). *Adding* to *the maxInteger* or *subtracting* from the minimum integer is undefined. It will result in meaningless values—often large numbers of the opposite sign.

```
put the maxInteger
-- 2147483647
put the maxInteger + 5
-- -2147483644
```

Using *integer()* on floats larger than *the maxInteger* is undefined. On the Macintosh this returns *the maxInteger*, but on Windows it returns 0 or another arbitrary value.

```
put integer(1e100)
-- 2147483647               -- Macintosh
put integer(power(2,50))
-- 0                        -- Windows
```

Example 8-15 calculates factorials (which exceed *the maxInteger* for inputs greater than 12 and exceed the maximum allowable float for inputs greater than 170). The *factorial()* function returns an integer, unless *the maxInteger* would be exceeded, in which case it returns a float. (If the maximum allowed float is exceeded, it returns "INF," or infinity.) Note that it checks for a possible *overflow* condition (exceeding *the maxInteger*) *before* actually performing the calculation. What happens if you take out this check and never switch to floating-point math? (Hint: The function still returns an answer. Is it correct?)

Example 8-15: Preventing Overflow Conditions While Calculating Factorials

```
on factorial x
    -- The maxFloat is not defined by Lingo, so we define it.
    set maxFloat = 1.797693135e+308
    -- Factorials are only valid for positive integers
    -- If the input is 0, the result is 1.
    if x < 0 or not integerP(x) then
        alert "Input must be a positive integer"
        return VOID
    end if

    set calcFact = 1
    repeat with y = x down to 1
        -- Prevent possible integer overflow
```

Example 8-15: Preventing Overflow Conditions While Calculating Factorials

```
    if (the maxInteger / float(y)) < calcFact then
      if not floatP (calcFact) then
        -- Use floating-point number to avoid overflow
        set calcFact = float (calcFact)
      end if
    end if

    -- Quit if we've overflowed the maxFloat as well
    set calcFact = calcFact * y
    if calcFact > maxFloat then
      put "Floating point overflow"
      -- There is no sense continuing
      exit repeat
    end if

  end repeat
  return calcFact
end
```

For the recursion fans in the crowd, here is a recursive version (without all the error checking). It always returns a float (or "INF" for inputs greater than 170).

Example 8-16: Recursive Factorial Function

```
on recursiveFactorial x
  if x < 0 then
    return VOID
  end if
  if x = 0 then
    return 1.0
  else
    return (x * recursiveFactorial (x-1))
  end if
end recursiveFactorial
```

Integer Rounding

The *integer()* function always rounds floats, including negative numbers, to the nearest integer.

Integer() will properly convert strings containing a "+" sign, "-" sign, or decimal point. Use *value()* to convert the string to a number first, as shown in Example 8-17. See also *"Type Conversion Caveats"* in Chapter 5.

Example 8-17: Integer Rounding

```
put integer ("+4.5")
-- Void
put integer (value("+4.5"))
-- 5
put integer (-.5)
-- 1
```

Integer Truncation

Example 8-18 truncates a float to an integer.

Example 8-18: Integer Truncation

```
on truncateToInt input
  if input = 0 then
    return 0
  else if input > 0 then
    return integer(input - .5)
  else
    return integer(input + .5)
  end if
end truncateToInt
```

Here you can see the difference between the rounded and truncated values.

```
put integer(7.69)
-- 8
put truncateToInt (7.69)
-- 7
put truncateToInt (-.5)
-- 0
```

Float Rounding

Example 8-19 rounds a floating-point number to the specified number of decimal places. Be sure to set *the floatPrecision* such that you can see the results.

Example 8-19: Float Rounding

```
on roundFloat floatNum, decPlaces
  if voidP(decPlaces) then set decPlaces = the floatPrecision
  set factor = power (10, decPlaces)
  set temp = integer(factor * floatNum)
  set result = float(temp) / factor
  return result
end roundFloat
```

Or you can use this technique that rounds to the number of places specified in *the floatPrecision*:

```
set roundedFloat = value(string(origFloat))
```

Float Truncation

Example 8-20 truncates a float to the specified number of decimal places.

Example 8-20: Float Truncation

```
on truncateFloatVal floatVal, decPlaces
  if voidP(decPlaces) then set decPlaces = the floatPrecision
  set text = string (floatVal)
  set decimal = offset (".", text)
  if decimal = 0 then
```

Example 8-20: Float Truncation (continued)

```
    return floatVal
  else
    set newText = (char 1 to (decimal + decPlaces) of text)
    return float(newText)
  end if
end truncateFloatVal
```

Note the difference between the original, rounded, and truncated values.

```
set the floatPrecision = 5
put roundFloat (6.9925, 3)
-- 6.99300
put truncateFloatVal (6.9925, 3)
-- 6.99200
```

If your floating-point comparisons are not evaluating as expected, it may be due to a rounding error. Round or truncate the floats before the comparison, or compare whether two numbers differ by less than a small amount.

If there is a small discrepancy in two floating-point numbers, they will not be equal when compared. If the following fails to achieve the expected result:

```
if floatVal1 = floatVal2 then...
```

Try this instead:

```
if abs(floatVal1 - floatVal2) < .000001 then...
```

Unit Conversion

Example 8-21 converts between common temperature scales. Similar routines can be written to convert the units for distance, mass, and so on. Refer also to Example 8-3, 11-4, 11-5, and 11-6.

Example 8-21: Temperature Conversion

```
on celsiusToFahrenheit c
  return ((c * 9) / 5.0) + 32
end celsiusToFahrenheit

on FahrenheitToCelsius f
  return ((f-32) * 5) / 9.0
end FahrenheitToCelsius

put celsiusToFahrenheit(0)
-- 32.0000
put FahrenheitToCelsius(212)
-- 100.0000
```

Converting Between Number Systems

Director doesn't have any support for binary, octal, or hexadecimal numbers (although Director 3.1.3 used a modified octal notation to refer to cast member slots in the Cast window). Refer to the downloadable examples for a utility that converts from any number system, such as decimal (base 10), to a system with a different base, such as hexadecimal (base 16). The downloadable examples include a utility that prints out binary and hexadecimal number tables, and a utility that translates between Roman numerals and Arabic numbers that is too cool for words.

Random Numbers

You'll need random numbers to simulate games of chance or to provide random variation in, say, the order of pictures in a slide show.

How Random Is Random?

The *random(n)* function will generate a pseudo-random integer between 1 and *n*, inclusive. The sequence of numbers generated by repeated calls to *random()* is based on *the randomSeed* and therefore not truly random. *The randomSeed* is initialized using the system clock when Director is first launched. Although *the randomSeed* remains unchanged (unless you set it explicitly), the OS maintains an internal random number seed that changes each time you call *random()*. Setting *the randomSeed* to a particular number will always result in the same sequence of pseudo-random numbers (although the sequence is different on Macintosh and Windows platforms). The following will make the *random(n)* function regenerate the previous sequence of random values again (assuming you use the same value for *n* each time):

```
set the randomSeed = the randomSeed
```

You can use *the ticks*, which is likely to be unique, as a new *randomSeed*.

 Each value returned by *random()* is independent of previous values returned by previous calls, like flipping a coin.

Random Numbers of Different Ranges

Using *random(n)*, where *n* is less than 1, results in meaningless values. To generate numbers in other ranges, add or subtract a fixed number from the result returned by *random()*.

Example 8-22: Generating Random Numbers in Various Ranges

To generate random numbers between 0 and 10, use:
```
set newNumber = random(11) - 1
```
To generate random numbers between -100 and 100, use:
```
set newNumber = random(201) - 101
```

Example 8-22: Generating Random Numbers in Various Ranges (continued)

To generate random numbers between 50 and 100, use:
```
set newNumber = random(51) + 49
```
To generate random decimals between 0 and 1, use:
```
set newNumber = (random(101) - 1)/100.0
```
To generate floating-point numbers, add a random integer to the decimal:
```
set newNumber = random(n) + (random(101) - 1)/100.0
```

The Online Casino

You look like a gambler to me. Let's get started on the video casino that the Internet is so sorely lacking. (These examples are for entertainment only. Only a sociopath like my friend Gardner would actually use Director to take real money from people with a gambling addiction. Do something more productive with your time, please.)

Simulating Dice Rolls and Coin Flips

A pair of dice can be simulated as shown in Example 8-23.

Example 8-23: Simulating a Pair of Dice
```
on diceRoll
  return random(6)+ random(6)
end diceRoll
```

Or if you prefer:
```
    on diceRollList
       return [#die1: random(6), #die2: random(6)]
    end diceRollList
```

Reader quiz: Is the following correct in all cases or will it sometimes return an invalid result?
```
    on diceRoll
       return random(12)
    end diceRoll
```

A coin flip can be simulated as shown in Example 8-24.

Example 8-24: Simulating a Coin Flip
```
on coinFlip
  if random(2) = 1 then
    return #heads
  else
    return #tails
  end if
end coinFlip
```

Or if you prefer:
```
    on coinFlip
       return getAt ([#heads, #tails], random(2))
```

Math

```
     end coinFlip
```

Let's test our coin flip and see how balanced it is.

```
on testCoinFlip numFlips
   set flipResults = [#heads:0, #tails:0]
   repeat with x = 1 to numFlips
     -- Store the coin flip for use in the next statement
     set thisFlip = coinFlip()
     --This increments the #heads or # tails property in the list. See Chapter 6.
     setProp flipResults, thisFlip, ¬
          (getProp (flipResults, thisFlip) + 1)
   end repeat
   put flipResults
 end
```

Note that we stored the value of *coinFlip()* before using it in the *setProp()* and *getProp()* commands. The following would flip the coin twice, perhaps with differing results:

```
setProp flipResults, coinFlip(), ¬
     (getProp (flipResults, coinFlip()) + 1)
```

Simulating a Deck of Cards

You can use the techniques shown for dice rolls and coin flips whenever a random event is independent of previous results. This is *not* the case with decks of cards, where we must keep track of the cards already chosen. The easiest approach is to delete each card as it is chosen randomly from the list of remaining cards. When all cards have been used we start with a new deck. If you are not familiar with Lingo lists, refer to Chapter 6.

Example 8-25: One-Eyed Jacks Are Wild

```
on newDeck
  global gCardList
  put "Getting a new deck of 52 cards..."
  -- Create a list of all the cards in a 52-card deck
  set gCardList = ["1H", "2H", "3H",  "4H", "5H", "6H", ¬
      "7H", "8H", "9H", "10H", "JH", "QH", "KH",          ¬
      "1C", "2C", "3C",  "4C", "5C", "6C",                ¬
      "7C", "8C", "9C", "10C", "JC", "QC", "KC",          ¬
      "1S", "2S", "3S",  "4S", "5S", "6S",                ¬
      "7S", "8S", "9S", "10S", "JS", "QS", "KS",          ¬
      "1D", "2D", "3D",  "4D", "5D", "6D",                ¬
      "7D", "8D", "9D", "10D", "JD", "QD", "KD"]
end newDeck

on drawCard
  global gCardList
  -- Create list if it has not been initialized
  if not listP(gCardList)  then newDeck()
  -- Re-create list if all the cards have been chosen
  if count (gCardList) = 0 then newDeck()
```

Example 8-25: One-Eyed Jacks Are Wild (continued)

```
-- Randomly pick one of the remaining cards in deck
set pickIt = random (count(gCardList))
set thisCard = getAt (gCardList, pickIt)

-- Delete the chosen card, so it can't be picked again
deleteAt (gCardList, pickIt)
return thisCard
end drawCard
```

This test handler lists each card in the Message window and changes sprite 1 to show the graphic cast member that presumably has been created with the matching name, such as "JD" for the jack of diamonds:

```
on testCards
  repeat with x = 1 to 52
    set nextCard = drawCard()
    put "Card drawn..." & nextCard
    set the member of sprite 1 = member nextCard
  end repeat
end testCards
```

In the above example, we didn't *shuffle* the deck but rather choose the next card at random from an ordered list (more like a magic trick than a poker game). You can instead create a truly random list and then pull items from that list in sequential order. The following handler shuffles our deck of cards: It relies on the custom *randomizeList()* function shown in Example 6-24 in Chapter 6.

Example 8-26: Randomizing an Existing List

```
on shuffleDeck
  global gCardList
  newDeck()
  set gCardList = randomizeList (gCardList)
end shuffleDeck
```

Write a simple handler that reads from *gCardList* sequentially instead of randomly. Do the cards look shuffled?

How would you create a blackjack "shoe" of multiple decks? How would you create a crooked card game?

See the downloadable examples for a handler that simulates a simple slot machine.

Math

PART III

Lingo Events

CHAPTER 9

Mouse Events

Mouse Events

Let's explore Director's sometimes counter-intuitive handling of mouse-related events. (See Chapter 2, *Events, Messages, and Scripts,* for details on Director's overall event handling and script creation.) This chapter is about understanding mouse event processing, not about creating buttons per se. Refer to Chapter 14, *Graphical User Interface Components,* in *Director in a Nutshell* for details on custom cursors and on creating well-behaved buttons and using the new Custom Button Editor Xtra. See also Example 4-6. "Manipulating Sprite Properties to Add Interactivity to a Button" in Chapter 4, *CastLibs, Cast Members, and Sprites,* in *Director in a Nutshell.*

Whenever the mouse button is pressed or released, Director generates *mouseUp, mouseDown, rightMouseUp,* or *rightMouseDown* events. Attach scripts with matching *event handlers* to turn the sprite into a clickable button.

Note that for simple linear presentations, the Tempo channel can be used to wait in a frame for a mouse click (or key press) before advancing the playback head. In prior versions of Director, the Tempo channel would ignore mouse events while waiting for time to elapse or for a sound or digital video to play. This limitation has been removed in Director 6 (although the Tempo channel doesn't work in Shockwave).

 The new *mouseEnter, mouseLeave,* and *mouseWithin* events are sent when the cursor enters or leaves a sprite with a corresponding handler attached (no mouse click is required). Leave *the idleHandlerPeriod* at its default setting (0) when using these events.

Suppose you have two overlapping sprites in channels 1 and 2, as shown in Figure 9-1. The *top-most* sprite in the higher channel (channel 2) with be in the foreground, and the sprite in the lower channel (channel 1) will be *obscured* (covered partially by the sprite in channel 2). (If I say that sprite 1 is *below* sprite 2, I am referring to their appearance on the Stage, not their relative positions in the Score window sprite channels.)

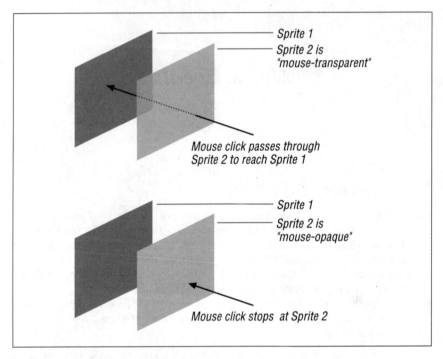

Figure 9-1: Two overlapping sprites

Create two rectangular bitmap sprites in the Paint window and overlap them partially on Stage, as shown in Figure 9-1. Attach the following sprite script to the sprite in channel 1 (not channel 2).

Example 9-1: Basic Mouse Events

```
on mouseUp
  put "MouseUp detected by sprite" && the clickOn
end
```

Set the movie to loop using the Control Panel, then rewind and play the movie. If you click on the top-most sprite in channel 2 (which has no script) in the region where it overlaps sprite 1, you should see the following in the Message window:

```
-- "MouseUp detected by sprite 1"
```

Note that the event registers for sprite 1, not sprite 2, because Director generally ignores sprites that don't have scripts attached. As far as Director is concerned, the top-most sprite is *mouse-transparent* (mouse clicks pass right through it).

Now attach the following *mouseDown* script to the sprite in channel 2.

```
on mouseDown
    put "MouseDown detected by sprite" && the clickOn
end
```

Rewind and play the movie and click on the top-most sprite again. Notice that the *mouseDown* handler in sprite 2 not only intercepted the *mouseDown* event, it *also* prevented the *mouseUp* event from reaching the obscured sprite behind it in channel 1.

Sprites intercept events that occur within their boundary. Use the *matte* ink to respond only to events within the irregular outline of the sprite. When other inks are used, the sprite responds to mouse events within its entire bounding rectangle.

Mouse-Opaque Sprites

It is important to understand mouse event handling clearly because it is at the heart of every Director project—and many programmer bugs. Macromedia uses the term *mouse-opaque* in the D6.0 *ReadMe* file to describe sprites that intercept mouse click events as described previously.

A sprite that has an *on mouseUp, on mouseDown, on rightMouseUp,* or *on rightMouseDown* handler attached becomes *mouse-opaque* and prevents *all four* of those mouse events from passing through to any sprites beneath it.

You can think of a mouse-opaque sprite as a sponge that absorbs mouse clicks or as an umbrella that prevents mouse events from landing on any sprites below. A *mouse-transparent* sprite can be thought of as a piece of clear glass that casts no shadow. It neither detects the events nor prevents them from reaching other sprites. In Director 5, *any* script attached to a sprite turned the sprite mouse-opaque (that is, would prevent underlying sprites from receiving mouse events). In Director 6, this was changed so that only those four handlers named previously cause a sprite to become mouse-opaque. This allows sprites to react to new messages, such as *beginSprite*, without necessarily being mouse-opaque. To force a sprite to be mouse-opaque in Director 6, you can attach a dummy script that has *only* a comment in it (and no handlers declared), such as:

```
-- This dummy script makes the sprite mouse-opaque
```

This makes the sprite mouse-opaque without actually trapping one of the four special mouse click events. See text that follows for details on *the clickOn*, which works only for sprites that have a script attached.

 Mouse-opaque sprites prevent the four mouse click messages only from being sent to *other sprites*. They don't prevent untrapped mouse events from passing to frame scripts or movie scripts, nor do they prevent other scripts attached to the *same* sprite from receiving events.

For example, even if a sprite has a *mouseDown* handler attached, it prevents only *mouseDown* events from, say, reaching the frame script. Any *mouseUp* events would still reach the frame script (if the latter had a *mouseUp* handler). See Chapter 2 for details on how events are usually passed through the script hierarchy.

If a *mouseUp, mouseDown, rightMouseUp,* or *rightMouseDown* handler passes an event with the *pass* command, the event is not forwarded to other sprites. It passes first to the sprite's cast script (if any) and then on to the frame script and possibly the movie script. You must manually broadcast the mouse click message using *sendSprite* or *sendAllSprites* for it to reach multiple sprites.

This discussion of mouse-opaque sprites pertains only to mouse *click* events. Other types of mouse cursor events are discussed next.

Cursor-Opaque Sprites

The mouse-opacity of a sprite has no effect on how the new *mouseEnter, mouseLeave,* and *mouseWithin* events are handled. I've coined the name *cursor-opaque sprites* to describe Director's special handling of these new events based on the cursor position (not mouse clicks). Again, suppose you have two overlapping sprites (see Figure 2-1), and the bottom (partially obscured) sprite has *mouseEnter, mouseLeave,* and *mouseWithin* handlers attached. If the top-most sprite does not have one of these three handlers attached, too, it is *cursor-transparent* and is completely ignored by Director in regard to cursor-related events. Thus, if the cursor enters the top-most sprite but is still within the *obscured* sprite's boundaries, the obscured sprite continues to receive *mouseWithin* messages. *MouseEnter* or *mouseLeave* messages are *not* generated as the cursor enters or leaves the overlapping area of the two sprites. It is as if the top-most sprite didn't even exist.

Now if you add a *mouseEnter, mouseLeave,* or *mouseWithin* handler to the top-most sprite, it will become *cursor-opaque* and be "seen" by Director cursor events. Rolling into the overlap area will now send *mouseWithin* events to the top-most sprite, not the bottom sprite. Paradoxically, even though the top-most sprite now prevents *mouseWithin* events from reaching the obscured sprite, rolling between the two overlapped sprites now generates *mouseEnter* and *mouseLeave* events for *both* sprites. The second cursor-opaque sprite acts as a "foil" (in the dramatic sense) for the first sprite.

A cursor-opaque sprite receives a *mouseLeave* event when it becomes invisible or is moved off-stage.

Custom Buttons created with the Button Editor Xtra ignored *mouseEnter*, *mouseWithin*, and *mouseLeave* events in D6.0, but this problem was fixed in D6.0.1.

Checking for Mouse Events

The sections below explore the question, "Who am I?". Use them to write generalized Behaviors that work regardless of the sprite to which they are attached.

Director automatically dispatches events to the correct sprite. You need not attempt to determine which sprites were clicked from a frame script. Instead, attach appropriate mouse event handlers directly to the sprites of interest.

Frame scripts that manually check which sprite was clicked are considered extremely poor style in Director. The following approach should be avoided:

```
on exitFrame
  if the clickOn = 1 then
    -- Do action for sprite 1
  else if the clickOn = 2 then
    -- Do action for sprite 2
  end if
end
```

Instead, attach, say, *on mouseUp* handlers to each sprite of interest, as in:

```
on mouseUp me
  -- Perform some action for this sprite
end
```

See the tip under *"Determining Which Sprite Was Rolled Over"* regarding the analogous issue with rollover-related events.

Determining the Current Sprite's Number

In Chapter 1, *How Lingo Thinks,* we discussed generalizing a handler to make it more flexible. To reiterate, you should avoid "hardcoding" sprite channel numbers, such as:

```
on mouseUp
  set the foreColor of sprite 2 = random (255)
end
```

If possible, you should instead use a system property to determine the sprite's channel number automatically, so that the script will work for any sprite to which it is attached, even if you move the sprite to another channel.

In the "*To Me or Not To Me*" section of Chapter 2, we saw how *the currentSpriteNum* and *the spriteNum of me* always indicate the sprite channel number to which the script is currently attached.

Example 9-2: What's My Sprite Number?

```
on mouseUp
  -- Set the current sprite's foreColor to a random color
  set the foreColor of sprite (the currentSpriteNum) = ¬
    random (255)
end
```

To use *the spriteNum of me* property, you must declare *me* as a parameter following the handler name as shown:

```
on mouseUp me
  -- Declare "me" (see above) when using "the spriteNum of me"
  set the foreColor of sprite (the spriteNum of me) = ¬
    random (255)
end
```

Determining Which Sprite Was Clicked

Use *the clickOn* property or *clickOn()* function to determine the last sprite that the user clicked.

 The clickOn. property and *clickOn()* function ignore sprites without scripts.

If you click a scriptless sprite, *the clickOn* will register for the first sprite beneath it that has a script attached. If no sprites under the mouse click have scripts, *the clickOn* returns 0, as it does if you click on the Stage.

From within the *mouseUp* or *mouseDown* handler of the sprite that was clicked, *the clickOn* would be the same as *the currentSpriteNum*. In prior versions of Director you will often see Lingo code such as:

```
on mouseUp
  set the foreColor of sprite (the clickOn) = random (255)
end
```

The spriteNum of me and *the currentSpriteNum* were added in Director 6 because sprites receive many new events that do *not* require mouse clicks. They are useful from within *beginSprite, endSprite, mouseEnter, mouseLeave,* and *mouseWithin* handlers, as well as *mouseUp* and *mouseDown* handlers. The *SpriteNum* of me is useful only from within script scripts (where it returns the current sprite's number); from within cast scripts (which don't receive the *me* instance) use the *CurrentSpriteNum* instead. From within frame scripts and movie scripts *the current SpriteNum* and *the SpriteNum of me* are not meaningful.

However, *the clickOn* returns the last sprite clicked even when checked from a frame script, movie script, or different sprite script. (*The clickOn* and *clickOn()* do not update within a handler. The value returned is that obtained from before the handler was called.)

The clickLoc property (or *clickLoc()* function) returns the point where the mouse was last clicked, relative to the upper left corner of the Stage. The mouse may have moved since it was clicked, so check *the clickLoc* rather than *the mouseH* or *the mouseV*. (*The clickLoc* does not update within a handler. The value returned is that obtained from before the handler was called.)

Determining Which Sprite Was Rolled Over

Director 6 vastly simplifies rollover detection. Simply attach *mouseEnter* and *mouseLeave* handlers that highlight and unhighlight the button of interest (say, by swapping and restoring its *member of sprite* property). In prior versions of Director, you must use the *rollover()* function from within a frame script or movie script.

The rollover property and *rollover()* function (without any argument) return the number of the sprite being rolled over (or 0 when rolling over the Stage). The *rollover(n)* function (where *n* is a sprite number) returns a *Boolean* value indicating whether the cursor is over the specified sprite. Theoretically, if *the rollover* equals *n*, then *rollover(n)* should return TRUE, but the different forms of the *rollover* command disagree when the cursor is over the Stage. So *rollover(0)* is always FALSE, even though it should theoretically return TRUE when *the rollover* or *rollover()* returns 0.

Furthermore, the different forms of the *rollover* command may disagree when testing the rollover for overlapping or invisible sprites. *The rollover* returns the number of the top-most *visible* sprite. *Rollover(n)* will return TRUE even if sprite *n* is invisible or not the top-most sprite. But *the rollover* and *rollover()* forms of the command ignore invisible sprites. Either refrain from testing *rollover(n)* on invisible sprites, or move the sprite off-stage instead.

The mouseMember property returns *the member of sprite* property of the top-most visible sprite over which the mouse resides. You can check it against the *rollover(n)* value, such as:

```
on exitFrame
  if rollover(5) and [LC]
    (the mouseMember = the member of sprite 5) then
    put "We are apparently rolling over sprite 5"
  end if
end
```

This code is reliable only if the same cast member is not used for multiple overlapping sprites.

In Director 6, you rarely need to use *the rollover* property or *rollover()* function. Instead use *mouseEnter, mouseWithin,* and *mouseLeave* handlers attached to the sprites of interest to handle rollover conditions, or the Custom Button Xtra to handle button rollover states automatically.

Invisible Sprites

In Director 5, only mouse-related events were sent to sprites. In Director 6, sprites receive other new events unrelated to the mouse. In Director 5, setting *the visible of sprite* property to FALSE hid the sprite and disabled all of its handlers (which were all mouse-related). This was equivalent to muting the sprite's channel in the Score window. In Director 6, *the visible of sprite* property affects only mouse-related events for that sprite. The *beginSprite, endSprite, prepareFrame, enterFrame,* and *exitFrame* handlers can be disabled only by muting the sprite's channel in the Score window. (Muting disables all events for that sprite channel, but setting *the visible of sprite* affects only its visibility and mouse-related events).

Standard Mouse Events

In the simplest case, Director generates a *mouseDown* event when the user *depresses* the mouse button and a *mouseUp* event when the user *releases* the mouse button. A given script may contain handlers that trap all, some, or no mouse events.

 You should generally trap either *mouseUp or mouseDown* events (see text that follows for caveats when trapping both events).

The *mouseDown* and *mouseUp* messages may be sent to *different* sprites possibly in different frames if the *mouseDown* handler moves the playback head. Trapping both messages can lead to two different sprites unintentionally responding to a single mouse click sequence. During the time between the two events, other messages, such as *mouseEnter,* may be generated. Table 9-1 lists mouse events in the order in which they are generated, *assuming the simplest case in which a user clicks a sprite.* In reality, multiple *mouseEnter, mouseWithin,* and *mouseLeave* events can be generated after the *mouseDown* event and before the *mouseUp* event. As the user moves the cursor among various sprites, many mouse rollover events may be generated without any mouse click events being sent.

The frequency of *mouseEnter, mouseLeave,* and *mouseWithin* events depends on *the idleHandlerPeriod.* Rollover events are unusably sluggish if *the idleHandlerPeriod.* is not set to 0.

The events shown in column 1 of Table 9-1 should not be confused with the properties in Table 9-5.

Table 9-1: Mouse Click and Roll Events

Event	Generated When or If:	Left	Right
mouseEnter[1]	Cursor enters a sprite's outline[2]	•	•
mouseWithin[1]	Cursor is within a sprite's outline[2] (sent *repeatedly*)	•	•
mouseDown	Left mouse button depressed	•	
rightMouseDown	Right mouse button depressed		•
mouseLeave[1]	Cursor leaves a sprite's outline[2]	•	•
mouseUpOutside[1,3]	Either mouse button released outside a sprite[2] after being depressed inside a sprite	•	•
mouseUp	Left mouse button released	•	
rightMouseUp[3]	Right mouse button released		•
buttonClicked[1,4]	Mouse is released (not pressed) over a Custom Button sprite	•	

[1] New in Director 6.0.
[2] See the *"Cursor-Opaque Sprites"* section earlier in this chapter. The *mouseEnter, mouseWithin,* and *mouseLeave* events obey the matte outline of bitmap sprites using the matte ink, but not for QuickDraw shape sprites. For other inks, the outline is the sprite's bounding box.
[3] There is no on *rightMouseUpOutside* event.
[4] The *buttonClicked* message is sent only if the *enabled of member* or *enabled of sprite* property of the custom button is TRUE. See Chapter 14 in *Director in a Nutshell*.

Table 9-2 shows how each mouse event is passed through the Lingo messaging hierarchy. A given event may be handled by a primary event handler, sprite script(s), cast script, frame script, or movie script. Refer also to the Table 2-7 in Chapter 2.

See the discussion of mouse-opaque and cursor-opaque events at the beginning of this chapter. Untrapped mouse click events are passed onto frame or movie scripts.

Mouse Events

Use *rollover()*, which is a *function*, not an *event*, to check for rollovers from within frame and movie scripts

Table 9-2: Mouse Event Passing

Event/Message Type	Message Passing
mouseDown	mouseDownScript→Sprite scripts and/or cast scripts of mouse-opaque sprites →Frame script→Movie scripts.
mouseUp[1]	mouseUpScript→Sprite scripts and/or cast scripts of mouse-opaque sprites →Frame script→Movie scripts.
mouseEnter mouseLeave mouseWithin	Sprite scripts and/or cast scripts of cursor-opaque sprites. (See "*Cursor-Opaque Sprites*" earlier in this chapter.) These events are never passed to frame or movie scripts.
mouseUpOutside	Sprite scripts and/or cast scripts of sprite that received original *mouseDown* or *rightMouseDown* event. See "*MouseUpOutside Events*" later in this chapter.
rightMouseDown[2] *rightMouseUp*[1,2]	Sprite scripts and/or cast scripts of mouse-opaque sprites →Frame script→Movie scripts.
buttonClicked	Sent by Custom Buttons to sprite scripts and/or cast script of clicked sprite only. Not sent to obscured sprites or passed to Frame script or Movie script.

[1] The *mouseUp* and *rightMouseUp* outside events are sent directly to the frame script, bypassing the sprite and cast scripts, if they follow a *mouseUpOutside* event and *the buttonStyle* property is TRUE.
[2] There are no primary event handlers for the *rightMouseUp* and *rightMouseDown* events.

MouseUpOutside **Events and** *the ButtonStyle*

Director 6 generates a new event, *mouseUpOutside*, if the user depresses the mouse button over a mouse-opaque sprite and then subsequently releases the mouse button over a different sprite or no sprite. It is not generated if the user clicks first on the Stage or a non-clickable sprite.

There is no *rightMouseUpOutside* event. *MouseUpOutside* is generated whether the original mouse click was a *mouseDown* or *rightMouseDown* event. *MouseUpOutside* events are sent, if appropriate, before and in addition to (not instead of) *mouseUp* or *rightMouseUp* events. The system property *the buttonStyle* determines whether Director sends a *mouseUp* (or *rightMouseUp*) event following a *mouseUpOutside* event.

The *mouseUpOutside* event is sent only to the original sprite over which the *mouseDown* or *rightMouseDown* occurred. The second sprite, over which the cursor is released, receives the *mouseUp* or *rightMouseUp* event instead (only if *the buttonStyle* is FALSE, the default).

If *the buttonStyle* is FALSE (the default) a button will highlight as the mouse rolls over it, even if the mouse button was pressed over another sprite initially. (A bitmap sprite will only highlight if its *Hilight When Clicked* option is set in its Cast Member Properties dialog box. This option is unrelated to *the hilite of member* property. Mouse-opaque shape sprites always highlight when clicked.) When the mouse button is released, the sprite under the mouse will receive a *mouseUp* (or *rightMouseUp*) event. This is called *list style* in the *Lingo Dictionary* and is appropriate for buttons that make up a list of choices.

If *the buttonStyle* is TRUE (so called *dialog style*) only the initial button receiving the *mouseDown* will highlight. When the mouse button is released, the sprite under the mouse will *not* receive a *mouseUp* (or *rightMouseUp*) event, unless it was the original sprite. In this case, the *mouseUp* (or *rightMouseUp*) event is sent directly to the frame script (and possibly the movie script), bypassing any sprite scripts or cast scripts attached to the sprite over which the mouse was released.

Double-Clicks

The Boolean system property *the doubleClick* indicates whether the two last mouse clicks occurred within the time interval set in the Macintosh or Windows Mouse Control Panel. *The doubleClick* depends on the interval between the two *mouseDown* or *rightMouseDown* events, not the two *mouseUp* or *rightMouseUp* events. The Mac Finder is slightly different in that it requires that both the two *mouseDown* and two *mouseUp* events all occur in the prescribed interval. Under Windows, even if the two clicks involve the two different mouse buttons (right and left), they would still constitute a double-click. *The doubleClick* is automatically reset to FALSE when the elapsed interval between clicks exceeds the operating system's double-click setting.

There is no way to read or change the user-defined double-click interval from Lingo, but you can create your own double-click handler to simulate this. Likewise, you must manually detect triple-clicks, if so desired.

 Consumer titles should avoid requiring the user to double-click the mouse. Especially in children's games, you should ignore rapid-fire events.

For example, if a single button is used to start and stop a song in a children's game, many children will click the button rapidly twice. This would start and then immediately stop the song. If the double-click interval is very short, checking *the doubleClick* property will not prevent spurious mouse clicks.

 The doubleClick is a system property that can be checked, not an event that can be trapped. The first mouse event is always sent separately from the second mouse event that sets *the doubleClick*.

In Example 9-3, the *mouseUp* handler will be called *twice* if the user double-clicks—once with *the doubleClick* equal to FALSE and again with it equal to TRUE. Thus, the *singleClickAction* will be called first, before the user has double-clicked.

Example 9-3: Responding to Both Single- and Double-Clicks

```
on mouseUp
  if the doubleClick then
    doubleClickAction
  else
    singleClickAction
  end if
end
```

Solve the problem using the following handler described in detail in Macromedia's *Lingo Dictionary* or online *Help* under the *doubleClick* keyword entry. (Note that this example tramples any existing timers that use *the timer* property. See Chapter 11, *Timers and Dates*, for ways to avoid this.)

Example 9-4: Preventing a Double-Click from Executing the Single-Click Action

```
on mouseUp
  if the doubleClick then
    exit
  else
    startTimer
    repeat while the timer < 20
      -- Simulate check for double-click before
      -- deciding whether to perform singleClickAction
      if the mouseDown then
        doubleClickAction
        exit
      end if
    end repeat
    singleClickAction
  end if
end
```

Eating Rapid-Fire Clicks

The system property *the lastClick* is reset to 0 at the time of each click. Therefore, it reflects the time since the *current* click. It is not useful for preventing double-clicks unless you store the previous value in a variable and do some extra math, as follows. Example 9-5 prevents clicks closer than 60 ticks (1 second) apart from being allowed.

Example 9-5: Preventing Rapid-Fire Clicks

```
property pLastMouseClick

on mouseDown me
  if voidP(pLastMouseClick) then
    set pLastMouseClick = the ticks - 61
  end if
```

Example 9-5: Preventing Rapid-Fire Clicks (continued)

```
if (the ticks - pLastMouseClick) < 60 then
    exit
else
    set pLastMouseClick = the ticks
end if
-- Perform work here.
end
```

Use this to disable double-clicks entirely:

```
set the mouseUpScript = "if the doubleClick then stopEvent"
```

Multi-button Mice

Most projects use only the left mouse button under Windows and the single Macintosh mouse button, but Director supports two of the three Windows mouse buttons and can emulate a two-button mouse on the Macintosh.

> In the authoring mode, Director uses the right mouse button under Windows and `Control-click` on the Macintosh for context-sensitive menus. Refer to Chapter 2, *Being More Productive,* in *Director in a Nutshell* for details on these shortcuts.

Note that the following commands ignore the right mouse button:

    on mouseUp
    on mouseDown
    the mouseUpScript
    the mouseDownScript

Conversely, the following *do* respond to, affect, or reflect the state of the right mouse button:

    on mouseUpOutside
    on rightMouseUp
    on rightMouseDown
    the clickOn
    the doubleClick
    the emulateMultiButtonMouse
    the lastClick
    the lastEvent
    the mouseDown
    the mouseUp
    the rightMouseDown
    the rightMouseUp
    the stillDown

The following are not affected by the left mouse button:

    on rightMouseUp
    on rightMouseDown

the rightMouseDown
the rightMouseUp

Windows Right Mouse Button

Director for Windows supports the left and right mouse buttons. The middle button, if any, is always ignored. The Windows 95 Mouse Control Panel allows the user to configure the mouse for a right-handed user (*left* mouse button is the primary button) or a left-handed user (*right* mouse button is the primary button). For simplicity, Director uses the primary mouse button in the default case and refers to the secondary button as the "right" button. For a left-handed mouse setup, Director treats the physically rightmost button as the *primary* button, and events such as *rightMouseUp* and *rightMouseDown* would correspond to the user's physical left mouse button. In short, Director for Windows remaps the buttons properly, so you don't have to worry about the user configuration. For simplicity, I refer to the secondary mouse button as the "right" mouse button. Penworks (*http:// www.penworks.com*) publishes a free utility, *SwapEm*, which dynamically reverses the right and left mouse buttons via Lingo.

Table 9-3 shows the events generated by each of the Windows mouse buttons and the simulated Macintosh mouse buttons. It also shows the properties that each action sets. Note that *mouseUpOutside* events may be generated for either mouse button. See "*Mouse Event Idiosynchrasies*" for possible errors when using multi-button mice.

Table 9-3: Mouse Button Events

User Action	Message Sent	Also Sets Properties
left mouse button click	mouseDown	the mouseDown the stillDown the clickOn the clickLoc the lastEvent the lastClick the doubleClick (if applicable)
left mouse button release	mouseUp	the mouseUp
left mouse released outside	mouseUpOutside	the mouseUp
right mouse button click	rightMouseDown	the rightMouseDown the mouseDown the stillDown the clickOn the clickLocthe lastEvent the lastClick the doubleClick (if applicable)

Table 9-3: Mouse Button Events (continued)

User Action	Message Sent	Also Sets Properties
right mouse button release	rightMouseUp	the rightMouseUp the mouseUp
right mouse released outside	mouseUpOutside	the mouseUp
middle mouse button click	*<none>*[1]	N/A
middle mouse button release	*<none>*[1]	N/A

[1] Some of the third-party Xtras cited at the end of this chapter can read the middle mouse button under Windows.

Note that your standard *mouseUp* and *mouseDown* handlers will never be triggered if the user clicks the right mouse button. You can remind him to click the left mouse button by placing a handler such as this in a movie script:

```
on rightMouseDown
   alert "Please use the left mouse button instead."
end
```

In practice, using the *alert* command can interfere with custom palettes. Refer to Chapter 13, *Graphics, Color, and Palettes,* and to Chapter 14 in *Director in a Nutshell.*

The system property *emulateMultiButtonMouse* and the state of the Control key are always ignored in regard to mouse events under Windows.

Macintosh Right Mouse Button

Macintosh mice typically have only one button. If the system property *emulate-MultiButtonMouse* is TRUE (the default is FALSE), Director generates *rightMouseUp* and *rightMouseDown* events when you Control-click, as shown in Table 9-4. Note that the event type (right versus left) is determined when the mouse button is first pressed, regardless of whether the state of the Control key changes before the mouse button is released. That is, there is never a *rightMouseUp* event without a preceding *rightMouseDown* event, nor a *mouseUp* event without a preceding *mouseDown* event. Note that *mouseUpOutside* events may be generated in either case.

Table 9-4: Macintosh Mouse Button Mapping

User Action	emulateMulti-ButtonMouse	Control Key	Message Sent
mouse click	FALSE	N/A	mouseDown
mouse release	FALSE	N/A	mouseUp
mouse click	TRUE	Up	mouseDown
mouse release	TRUE	Up	mouseUp

Table 9-4: Macintosh Mouse Button Mapping (continued)

User Action	emulateMulti-ButtonMouse	Control Key	Message Sent
mouse click	TRUE	Down	rightMouseDown
mouse release	TRUE	Down	rightMouseUp
mouse release outside original sprite	N/A	N/A	mouseUpOutside

Mouse Properties

Numerous system properties provide information about the current mouse button state, the last mouse click event, and the current mouse position. Most of these events can be tested but not set. Table 9-5 summarizes all the system properties related to the mouse button state, and Table 9-6 summarizes the system properties related to the position of the mouse cursor.

Table 9-5: Mouse Button State System Properties

Property Name	Usage	Left Button	Right Button
the buttonStyle	Determines whether *mouseUp* and *rightMouseUp* event are sent to other sprites or only to the frame following a *mouseUpOutside* event.	•	•
the clickLoc	Point on stage where mouse was last clicked. See Chapter 5, *Coordinates, Alignment, and Registration Points*, in *Director in a Nutshell*.	•	•
the clickOn	Sprite number of last mouse-opaque sprite clicked, or 0 (zero) to indicate the Stage.[1]	•	•
the currentSpriteNum	Sprite number of the sprite to which the current Lingo handler is attached.[1]	•	•
the doubleClick	Boolean indicating whether last mouse event constituted a double-click.	•	•
the emulateMultiButtonMouse	Boolean indicating whether to treat Control-clicks as right mouse clicks on Macintosh.		•
the lastClick	Time (in ticks) since last mouse click. See Chapter 11.	•	•
the lastEvent	Time (in ticks) since last mouse click, mouse roll, or key press. See Chapter 11.	•	•
the mouseDown	Boolean indicating whether *either* mouse button (left or right) is depressed.	•	•
the mouseDownScript	Primary event handler for *mouseDown* events. Not called for *rightMouseDown* events.[2]	•	

Table 9-5: Mouse Button State System Properties (continued)

Property Name	Usage	Left Button	Right Button
the mouseUp	Boolean indicating whether *both* mouse buttons (left or right) are up.	•	•
the mouseUpScript	Primary event handler for mouseUp events. Not called for *rightMouseUp* events.[2]	•	
the rightMouseDown	Boolean indicating whether the right mouse button is depressed.		•
the rightMouseUp	Boolean indicating whether the right mouse button is up.		•
the spriteNum of me	Sprite number of the sprite receiving the message.[1]		•
the stillDown	Boolean indicating whether the mouse button is still depressed following a *mouseDown* or *right-MouseDown* event. Returns FALSE if mouse has been released in the interim.	•	•

[1] See *"Which Sprite Was Clicked On or Rolled Over?"* earlier in the chapter.
[2] Note there are no *rightMouseUpScript* or *rightMouseDownScript* properties.

The properties in Table 9-6 change when the cursor moves, regardless of the state of the mouse button(s).

Table 9-6: Mouse Location/Movement System Properties

Property Name	Usage
cursor *whichCursor*	Changes cursor when cursor is over the Stage. See Chapter 14 in *Director in a Nutshell.*
the cursor of sprite *whichSprite*	Changes cursor when cursor is over a particular sprite. See Chapter 14 in *Director in a Nutshell.*
the lastEvent	Time (in ticks) since last mouse click, mouse roll, or key press.
the lastRoll	Time (in ticks) since last mouse movement.
the immediate of sprite *whichSprite*	Obsolete; required in Director 3.1.3 to detect mouseDown events.
the mouseCast[1]	Obsolete; use *the mouseMember* instead.
the mouseMember[1]	Cast member over which cursor is located (even sprite's without scripts).
the mouseChar[2]	Character position under cursor in field sprite.
the mouseH	Cursor's horizontal position relative to left edge of the Stage.

Mouse Events

Table 9-6: Mouse Location/Movement System Properties (continued)

Property Name	Usage
the mouseItem[2]	Item number under cursor in field sprite. See *the itemDelimiter*.
the mouseLine[2]	Line number under cursor in field sprite.
the mouseV	Cursor's vertical position relative to top of Stage.
the mouseWord[2]	Word number under cursor in field sprite.
the preLoadEventAbort	Determines whether a mouse event aborts preloading.
rollover (*n*)	Boolean function, returning TRUE if cursor is over sprite number *n*., even if it is invisible, has no scripts, or is obscured by other sprites.[1]
the rollover rollover()	Indicates the top-most mouse-opaque sprite under the cursor.[1]
the timeoutMouse	Determines whether mouse clicks reset *the timeoutLapsed* property to 0. See Chapter 11.

[1] See *"Which Sprite Was Clicked On or Rolled Over?"* earlier in the chapter.
[2] Refer to Chapter 12, *Text and Fields*, in *Director in a Nutshell* for details on using the *mouseChar, mouseItem, mouseLine,* and *mouseWord* properties.

Mouse Tasks

Table 9-7 shows the handler(s) and scripts(s) used to accomplish common tasks related to the mouse. The trick is to place the correct type of handler in the correct type of script, so that it will be called when the event of interest occurs. For the purposes of this table, I've made up the following short-hand notations:

- *"Mouse click handlers"* include *on mouseDown, on mouseUp, on right- MouseUp, on rightMouseDown,* and *on mouseUpOutside.*

- *"Mouse rollover handlers"* include *on mouseEnter, on mouseLeave,* and *on mouseWithin* (new in D6). In D5 use *the rollover()* function or *the rollover* property instead).

- *"Frame handlers"* include *on exitFrame, on enterFrame, on idle,* and *on pre- pareFrame.*

Note that the effect of these handlers depends on the script in which they are placed.

Table 9-7: Common Mouse Tasks

To Detect This Event or System Property:	Use This Type of Handler, Property or Function:	In This Type of Script:
Mouse clicks on all sprites using a particular cast member	Mouse click handler	Cast member script

Table 9-7: Common Mouse Tasks (continued)

To Detect This Event or System Property:	Use This Type of Handler, Property or Function:	In This Type of Script:
Mouse clicks on a sprite	Mouse click handler	Sprite script
Mouse clicks ignored by all sprites in a frame	Mouse click handler	Frame script
Mouse clicks throughout the entire movie otherwise ignored by other scripts	Mouse click handler	Movie script
All left mouse clicks *before* they are passed to individual sprites	*the mouseDownScript* or *the mouseUpScript*	Movie script
Rollovers on all sprites using a partic-ular cast member	Mouse rollover handler	Cast member script
Rollovers for an individual sprite	Mouse rollover handler	Sprite script
Rollovers for all sprites within a frame	rollover(n) *or the rollover* within a frame handler	Frame script
Mouse rollovers throughout the entire movie.	rollover(n) *or the rollover* within a frame handler	Movie script
Location of last mouse click	*the clickLoc* property in a mouse click handler	Any script
Current cursor position	*the mouseH* and *the mouseV* properties in any handler	Any script
The last sprite clicked	*the clickOn* property in any handler	Any script
A sprite's channel number	*the spriteNum of me* or *the currentSpriteNum* properties in a mouse click handler or mouse roll-over handler	Sprite or Cast member script
Wait in a frame until the user clicks the mouse	*the mouseDown* property in an *exitFrame* handler or the Tempo Channel *Wait for Mouse Click* option	Frame script (or Tempo channel)

Creating Draggable Sprites

There are a number of ways to allow the user to drag a sprite around the Stage. You can set *the moveableSprite of sprite* property, or you can use the *Moveable* checkbox in the Sprite Inspector or Sprite Toolbar.

You can also use the following script to make a sprite moveable. (In Director 5, you must manually *puppet* the sprite to move it in this manner. Director 6's auto-puppeting feature handles this for you.) Note that it accounts for the potential offset between the click location and the *regPoint* of the sprite's cast member to prevent the sprite from jumping when it is first clicked. This is also a good example of using point-based math. Refer to Chapter 5 in *Director in a Nutshell* and Chapter 6 of this book.

Example 9-6: Dragging a Sprite

```
on mouseDown me
  set mySprite = the spriteNum of me
  set offset = the loc of sprite mySprite - the clickLoc
  repeat while the stillDown
    set the loc of sprite mySprite = ¬
        point (the mouseH, the mouseV) + offset
    updateStage
  end repeat
end mouseDown
```

Mouse Traps

There are a number of ways to prevent mouse events from being processed. See *"Mouse-Opaque Sprites"* at the beginning of this chapter for important details. See item 3 below for a way to prevent rollover events from being recognized.

1. Use *the lastClick* to prevent rapid-fire mouse clicks from being acknowledged (see Example 9-5).

2. Send the user to a frame in which no sprites have mouse handlers attached, so that mouse events are ignored.

3. Use an unstroked, unfilled QuickDraw rectangle (a shape sprite with a zero-width border) in the top-most animation channel with a dummy *mouseUp* and *mouseEnter* handlers. You can alter its *visible of sprite* or *loc of sprite* properties to turn it on or off.

4. You can disable or enable mouse events by calling the handler in Example 9-7 with a Boolean flag, such as *mouseTrap(TRUE)* or *mouseTrap(FALSE)*. Note that this only enables/disables events generated by the left mouse button, not the right mouse button.

Example 9-7: Build a Better Mouse Trap

```
on mouseTrap flag
  if (flag = TRUE) then
    -- Disable mouse events
    set the mouseDownScript = "stopEvent"
    set the mouseUpScript   = "stopEvent"
  else
    -- Allow mouse events
    set the mouseDownScript = EMPTY
    set the mouseUpScript   = EMPTY
  end if
end mouseTrap
```

The *Buddy API* Xtra (*http://www.mods.com.au/budapi*) claims to be able to disable mouse events under Windows. (I have not personally verified this claim.)

Simulating Mouse Events

Lingo does not provide a way to send a mouse event to Director's event queue or to change the cursor's position (*the clickLoc, the mouseH,* and *the mouseV* are all read-only).

The *DirectOS* Xtra (*http://www.directxtras.com/do_doc.htm*) claims to be able to set the cursor position and generate a mouse click for any one of three buttons under Windows. (I have not personally verified these claims.)

The *Buddy API* Xtra (*http://www.mods.com.au/budapi*) claims to be able to set the cursor position under Windows and also restrict the cursor to certain subsections of the screen. (I have not personally verified these claims.) A Macintosh version of the Xtra should be available by the time you read this, but it may not include all the functionality of the Windows version.

Both the DirectOS and Buddy API Xtras provide many other OS-level functions. See also Chapter 10, *Keyboard Events,* and Chapter 14, *External Files.*

The *SetMouse* Xtra (*http://www.gmatter.com/donationware.html* or *http://www. scirius.com*) sets the position of the cursor (cross-platform).

You can manually send mouse messages using *sendSprite, sendAllSprites,* and *call,* such as:

```
sendSprite (spriteNumber, #mouseDown {, args...})
sendAllSprites (#mouseUp {, args...})
```

You can also call a mouse handler in a specific script, using:

```
call (#mouseDown, script n {, args...})
```

You can send a message to a script instance, using:

```
call (#mouseDown, scriptInstance {, args...})
```

If using Director 4.0.4 or Director 5.0, use the form:

```
mouseDown (script n {, args...})
```

as described in the *Lingo Issues* ReadMe file that came with the 4.0.4 update.

 Mouse messages sent via *call* are sent only to the specified entity. They are *not* passed to additional scripts through the usual messaging hierarchy.

Custom Mouse Events

Some Sprite Xtras may generate their own mouse-related events that are more useful than Director's default events. For example, the Custom Button Xtra's sprites generate *buttonClicked* events, but only if the Custom Button is enabled. *MouseUp* and *mouseDown* events are generated even for disabled custom buttons, which is often undesirable. Likewise, version 3.10 (and later) of the Pop-up menu Xtra generates a *menuItemSelected* event when the user selects a valid item from a pop-up menu sprite.

Flushing Mouse Events

Lingo does not provide a mechanism for flushing pending mouse or keyboard events from Director's event queue. We saw earlier how to prevent double-clicks or create a "mouse trap" to absorb all mouse events.

The *FlushEvents* Xtra (*http://fargo.itp.tsoa.nyu.edu/~gsmith/Xtras*) is available for the Macintosh only (and I haven't tried it personally). The Buddy API Xtra will disable mouse events, although it doesn't specifically flush existing events. In most cases, there should be no need to flush mouse events. You should instead structure your Lingo to allow Director to process mouse events continuously, and simply ignore them.

Mouse Event Idiosyncrasies

Mouse events are very reliable when you structure your Lingo correctly, but there are quirks. Consult this list of idiosyncrasies and work-arounds prior to tearing your Lingo apart and your hair out. Also see the quirk list at *http://www.update-stage.com*.

MIAWs

Sprites on the main Stage may receive rollover events even when they are obscured by a MIAW placed over the Stage. This is especially an issue with roll-overs that play sounds. The user will be confused when sounds are triggered for no apparent reason. Avoid using MIAWs on top of sprites with rollover Behaviors or trying to use a cursor-opaque sprite as the background of the MIAW or in the foreground of the main movie (see the earlier section, "*Cursor-Opaque Sprites,*" and the following section, *Shockwave*).

MIAWs will continue to trap mouse events over their *rect of window* area even if the MIAW is closed. You must use *forget window*, or move the window off-screen to prevent it from trapping mouse events. See Chapter 6, *The Stage and MIAWs*, in *Director in a Nutshell*.

Shockwave

Unfortunately, Shockwave does not work identically with every version of every browser on all platforms. This is often beyond Macromedia's control.

Allegedly, MIE 4 on the Macintosh doesn't pass *mouseUp* events to Shockwave movies. Search the 1998 DIRECT-L archives (cited in the *Preface*) for keywords such as "*MIE*" to find one workaround posted by Andrew White.

Shockwave movies also allegedly respond to rollover events even when the browser window is not in the foreground (see the similar problem with MIAWs in the previous section).

Mouse click response in Netscape 4 on the Macintosh may be sluggish through no fault of Macromedia's. Again, search Macromedia's web site or the DIRECT-L archives for details and possible work-arounds.

It has also been reported that Shockwave under Windows may not recognize mouse clicks when the mouse buttons have been configured for left-handed users in the *Mouse* control panel.

Editable Text Fields

The *mouseUp* event is sent to an editable field sprite only if the field does *not* have focus. Once it gains focus, an editable field sprite responds to *mouseDown* events but not *mouseUp* events. The *mouseUp* events are sent straight to the frame script (bypassing the cast script or the scripts of any obscured sprites). If the editable field sprite loses focus, it will again accept a single *mouseUp* event.

Right Mouse Button under Window

Under Windows, Director gets confused when multiple buttons are pressed simultaneously. *The stillDown* turns FALSE even if you hold down the original mouse button while clicking another mouse button.

While the right mouse button is held down, any left mouse button clicks generate *rightMouseDown* and *rightMouseUp* events, rather than the usual left mouse events (*mouseDown, mouseUp* and *the mouseDownScript* and *the mouseUpScript*).

If the left and right mouse buttons are released simultaneously, subsequent left mouse clicks *continue* to generate right mouse events. The error is not corrected until the actual right mouse button is clicked separately. The same bug occurs in D5.0.1, D6.0.2, and D6.5 and presumably other versions. One solution is to duplicate mirror all *mouseDown* and *mouseUp* handlers with *rightMouseDown* and *rightMouseUp* handlers. An Xtra that disables individual mouse buttons may provide a complete solution.

Menu Bars

In version 4.0.3 and earlier of Director, mouse clicks in the top 20 pixels of the screen would be ignored because that area was reserved for the menu bar, even if no menu was in use. Mouse events could be sent manually using the techniques described above from a *mouseDown* handler in a frame script.

Custom Buttons

Custom Buttons did not receive *mouseEnter, mouseWithin,* and *mouseLeave* events in D6.0. Update to Director 6.0.2 or later. Even so, these events become extremely sluggish if *the idleHandlerPeriod* is not 0.

Rollovers

Don't use *rollover(n)* where *n* is a sprite that is not present in the current Score frame. Director will use the bounding rect of the last sprite to use that sprite channel to check for rollovers. Use *mouseEnter* and *mouseLeave* events instead, or move the sprites in question off stage in a prior frame.

Mouse events are the core of Director, even more so with new mouse events in D6. Revisit this chapter whenever Director is not executing the Lingo you expect it to. Improper mouse handling is a common culprit.

CHAPTER 10

Keyboard Events

Keyboard Events

Whenever a standard (non-modifier) key is pressed or released, Director generates a *keyDown* or *keyUp* event. Only script attached to editable field sprites, frame scripts, and movie scripts receive keyboard events. All field sprites, even non-editable ones, can receive the standard sprite events (*mouseUp, mouseDown, mouseEnter, mouseLeave,* and so on) Refer to Chapter 7, *Strings,* for details on manipulating strings and text. See especially Example 7-7. Refer to Chapter 12, *Text and Fields,* in *Director in a Nutshell* for more details on working with fields.

Keyboard characters are sent automatically to an editable field sprite with keyboard focus, *unless* the *keyDown* event is intercepted by an *onkeyDown* handler in a sprite or castmember script first (or explicitly stopped in *the keyDownScript* primary event handler).

The key being pressed "rides along" with the *keyDown* event. If an editable field sprite receives the *keyDown* event, the last key pressed will be added to the field. Non-editable fields, editable fields without keyboard focus, and non-field sprites do not receive *keyDown* and *keyUp* events. Rich text sprites can not be edited at run time. You must use field sprites for dynamic text.

Your *keyDown* handler will be called even when special characters, such as the arrow keys, are pressed. Simply *pass* these onto the field sprite.

Fields will automatically recognize the arrow keys and Delete key to perform rudimentary editing (see *"Editing Keys"* later in this chapter).

The Tempo channel can be used to wait for a key press (or mouse click) before advancing the playback head.

Author-Time versus Runtime Keyboarding

Director uses numerous keyboard shortcuts during authoring. Test your keyboard event handling from a Projector. For example, the `Enter` key on the numeric keypad is valid at runtime, but during authoring, it stops the movie. The following types of keys can be tested accurately only from a projector:

- Numeric Keypad Keys
- `F1`, `F2`, `F3`, and `F4` function keys on Macintosh
- Key combinations using `Command` on the Macintosh, or `Control` or `Alt` under Windows, such as for menu shortcuts
- Arrow Keys
- `Page Up`, `Page Down`, `Home`, and `End` Keys

Note that any open Director windows may interfere with keyboard input. When the Paint window has focus, many non-modifier keys switch between various paint tools (See Chapter 13, *Graphics, Color, and Palettes,* covering the Paint window in *Director in a Nutshell.*) To the extent that you do test keyboard events from within the authoring environment, close any windows, especially the Message window.

The Message window accepts keyboard focus and will interfere with *the selStart, selEnd,* and *selection* properties.

Standard Keyboard Events

Director generates separate keyDown and keyUp messages when a non-modifier key is pressed and released. Modifier keys (such as Shift and Control) don't generate events by themselves, but rather set system properties such as the shiftDown and the controlDown.

Pressing a non-modifier key also sets the system property *the key Pressed,* representing the current key pressed. Even after a key is released, the system properties *the key* and *the keyCode* contain information about it. A given script may contain handlers that trap both, one, or neither keyboard event (*keyUp* and *keyDown*). If a sprite traps only the *keyDown* event, the *keyUp* event will be passed onto the frame script. The *keyDown* message is sent repeatedly while the key is being held down, as long as the playback head is moving.

Table 10-1 shows how each key event is passed through the Lingo messaging hierarchy. A given event may be handled by a primary event handler, sprite script(s), cast script, frame script, or movie script. Primary event handlers pass keyboard events by default. Refer also to Example 2-4 and Tables 2-3 and 2-7 in Chapter 2, *Events, Messages, and Scripts*.

Table 10-1: Keyboard Event Passing

Event/Message Type	Message Passing
on keyDown[1]	keyDownScript →Sprite scripts and/or cast script of editable field sprite with keyboard focus[2] →Frame script →Movie scripts.
on keyUp[1]	keyUpScript →Sprite scripts and/or cast script of editable field sprite with keyboard focus →Frame script →Movie scripts.
TAB	Refer to *the autoTab of member* property.
Quit Keys	Sent to OS, unless *the exitLock* is TRUE. See Tables 10-4 and 10-5.
Menu Keys[3]	Used with menu bar, if applicable.
OS Keys	Generally not trappable. See Tables 10-4 and 10-5.

[1] A conflict in Director 6 for Windows may prevent Director from receiving keyboard events when RSX is installed.
[2] If the *keyDown* message is *not* intercepted by a sprite or cast script, the typed character is sent to the field itself. Otherwise, it is sent only if the *keyDown* handler includes the *pass* command.
[3] The Command key on the Macintosh, and the Control and Alt keys under Windows may be intercepted by any installed menus with keyboard shortcuts. See the "Menus" section in Chapter 14, *Graphical User Interface Components*, in *Director in a Nutshell*.

Multiple and Repeat Keys

When you hold down a non-modifier key, Director will repeatedly send out the corresponding character. It also repeatedly sends the *keyDown* message. On the Macintosh, *the cpuHogTicks*, not the *Keyboard* control panel, determines the frequency of auto-repeating *keyDown* events. Setting *the cpuHogTicks* to 0 generates repeated *keyDown* events most often, but it can interfere with other processes.

If the user presses multiple keys, each one will generate a *keyDown* message when it is pressed and a *keyUp* message when it is released. Therefore, you may receive multiple separate *keyDown* events before receiving any *keyUp* events.

Modifier keys don't generate separate *keyDown* or *keyUp* events, but releasing a modifier key will stop Director from repeatedly sending *keyDown* events even if other keys remain pressed. For example, if you hold down the Shift key and the "A" key, Director will continually send *keyDown* events. If you then release the Shift key, Director will stop generating *keyDown* events even if the "A" key is still depressed. It will then generate the *keyUp* event when the "A" key is released.

 Lingo's system properties *the key, the keyPressed,* and *the keyCode* always indicate the *last* key *pressed*. Their values from within a *keyUp* handler may not necessarily reflect the last key *released*.

Director stores only the most recent keystroke. You can accumulate keystrokes in a field or accumulate them manually in a variable string or list.

This script will accumulate any keystrokes it traps. Assign it to *the keyDownScript* to track all keystrokes.

Example 10-1: Accumulating and Counting Keystrokes

```
on accumulateKeys
  global gKeyList
  if voidP(gKeyList) then set gKeyList = []
  add (gKeyList, the key)
end accumulateKeys

on startMovie
  set the keyDownScript = "accumulateKeys()"
end startMovie
```

Instead of accumulating the actual keystrokes, you could simply count them:

```
on countKeys
  global gKeyCount
  set gKeyCount = gKeyCount + 1
end countKeys

on startMovie
  set the keyDownScript = "countKeys()"
end startMovie
```

Keyboard Properties

Table 10-2 summarizes system properties regarding the current keyboard state and the last key typed. Note that there is no property to indicate whether a non-modifier key is currently being pressed (although you would ordinarily receive repeated *keyDown* events during this time). That is, there is no *the keyDown* property. Refer to the Xtras cited under "Keyboard Xtras" later in this chapter to detect whether a non-modifier key is currently being pressed.

Table 10-2: Keyboard System Properties and Constants

Property Name	Usage
BACKSPACE	Constant indicating the *Backspace* key at the upper right of the main keyboard (marked "delete" or with an arrow on most keyboards).
the boxType of member	Limits the size of keyboard input fields (possible values are #adjust, #limit, #fixed, and #scroll). See Chapter 12 in *Director in a Nutshell*.
charToNum (the key)	The ASCII value[1] of the last key pressed.
the commandDown	Boolean indicating whether the Command key (Mac) or the Control key (Windows) is being pressed.

Table 10-2: Keyboard System Properties and Constants (continued)

Property Name	Usage
the controlDown	Boolean indicating whether the `Control` key (either platform) is being pressed.
the emulateMultiButton-Mouse	Boolean indicating whether to treat `Control`-clicks on the Macintosh as equivalent to right mouse clicks on Windows. See Chapter 9, *Mouse Events*.
ENTER	Constant indicating the `Enter` key on the numeric keypad only.
RETURN	Constant indicating the `Return` key on the main keyboard (usually marked *"Enter"* on PC keyboards).
the exitLock	Boolean indicating whether to prevent the user from quitting the Projector with various keyboard shortcuts. Default is `FALSE` (allows user to quit).[2]
the key	The ASCII character[1] of the last key pressed. Does not update in a repeat loop or *keyDown* handler.
the keyCode	The numeric code[1] to the last key pressed, not its ASCII value. Unaffected by modifier keys.
the keyDownScript	Sets primary event handler for *keyDown* events.
the keyPressed	The ASCII character[1] of the last key pressed. Updates in a repeat loop. New in D6.
the keyUpScript	Sets primary event handler for *keyUp* events.
the lastEvent	Time, in ticks, since last key press, mouse click, or any cursor movement.
the lastKey	Time, in ticks, since last key press.
the optionDown	Boolean indicating whether the `Option` key (Macintosh) or `Alt` key (Windows) is being pressed.
the preLoadEventAbort	Determines whether a key event aborts preloading of cast members (see Chapter 9, *Performance and Memory,* in *Director in a Nutshell*).
the shiftDown	Boolean indicating whether either of the two `Shift` keys is being pressed. Not affected by the state of the `Caps Lock` key. See the *CapsLock* Xtra (*http://www.gmatter.com/donationware.html*).
the timeoutKeyDown	Boolean indicating whether keyboard events reset *the timeoutLapsed* property to 0 (default is `TRUE`). See Chapter 11, *Timers and Dates*.

[1] Refer to Appendix A, *ASCII Codes and Key Codes,* for a list of key codes and ASCII values.
[2] See *"Preventing the User from Quitting"* later in this chapter.

Determining Which Key Was Pressed

The best method for deciphering keystrokes depends on the type of key for which you are looking.

Use *the key* property to distinguish printable characters, such as alphanumerics. Use *the keyCode* to distinguish non-printable keys such as the arrow keys. Use *charToNum(the key)* to determine a key's ASCII value.

The key

The key returns the character string of the last key pressed, or even a non-printable character, such as `Ctrl-M`. Multiple keys may set the same value for *the key*. For example, the character "7" may be generated from the "7" key on either the standard keyboard or the numeric keypad.

The keyPressed

The keyPressed returns the same character as *the key*, but its value updates during a repeat loop. *The keyPressed* is *not* a Boolean value indicating whether a key is pressed.

ASCII—charToNum(character)

To determine the ASCII value of a character, use:

```
Set asciiVal=chartoNum(the key)
```

This is especially useful for distinguishing between uppercase and lowercase letters. Refer to Appendix C, *Case-Sensitivity, Sort Order, Diacritical Marks, and Space-Sensitivity*. It is also convenient when working with comparing the ASCII values of numeric digits (see Appendix A).

numToChar(integer)

NumToChar() converts a number from 0 to 255 into the corresponding character from the ASCII table. Use it to add non-printable characters to an output string, such as:

```
set linefeed = numtochar (10)
```

Note that ASCII values above 127 vary for different fonts. Refer to the character mapping feature of the `FONTMAP.TXT` file as covered in Chapter 12, in *Director in a Nutshell*. Use the Macintosh *Key Caps* desk accessory or the Windows *Character Map* utility (under the Windows 95 Start Menu under `Programs▶Accessories`) to view various characters in different fonts. Under Windows. you can create ASCII characters by holding down the `Alt` key while typing in their ASCII code on the numeric keypad with *Num Lock* on (that is, `Alt+6+5` will create a capital "A").

The keyCode

The keyCode returns a fixed number based on the key's position on the keyboard. It is unaffected by modifier keys and is unique for each key. Whereas *the key* properties returned by the "7" from the standard keyboard and from the numeric keypad are identical, their *keyCode* properties are different. Use *the keyCode* to detect keys for which there are no Lingo equivalents, such as the arrow keys, or whose ASCII values are not standardized. All keyboards on all platforms seem to send the same key codes for each key.

Refer to Appendix A for a complete list of key codes and ASCII codes.

Detecting the Key's Case

The key differentiates between uppercase and lowercase characters, such as "q" and "Q," but Lingo ignores strings' case when compared using the *equals* sign (=) or the *not equals* sign (<>). The following is therefore somewhat redundant:

```
if the controlDown and (the key = "Q" or the key = "q") then
    statement(s)
end if
```

There is no point in checking the state of the Shift key to distinguish between uppercase and lowercase characters, or other keys that have different shifted states. To distinguish between uppercase and lowercase letters, check their ASCII values using *charToNum()*. See Appendix C for complete details, especially Examples C-3 and C-5, which perform case-sensitive comparision and convert text to uppercase. See "*Shift Key*" later in this chapter.

Modifier Keys

Modifier keys are keys that do not generate their own *keyDown* events but rather affect the character generated by other keys. In many cases, they indicate special commands, such as with custom menus (see the "*Menus*" section Chapter 14 of *Director in a Nutshell.*). The modifier keys are different between Macintosh and Windows. Table 10-3 shows the system properties and constants that correspond to various keys.

Table 10-3: Cross-Platform Key Equivalents and Properties

Key	Macintosh	Windows
Alt Key	N/A	the optionDown
Command Key	the commandDown	N/A
Control Key	the controlDown	the controlDown, or the commandDown
Option Key	the optionDown	N/A
Shift Key	the shiftDown	the shiftDown
Caps Lock	Can't tell without Xtra	Can't tell without Xtra
BACKSPACE	delete	backspace
ENTER[1]	Enter key on numeric keypad	Enter key on numeric keypad

Table 10-3: Cross-Platform Key Equivalents and Properties (continued)

Key	Macintosh	Windows
RETURN[1]	Return key on main Macintosh keyboard	Enter key on main PC keyboard

[1] ENTER refers only to the Enter key on the numeric keypad. The key labeled "*Enter*" on the main portion of PC keyboards generates a RETURN character. The Enter key on the numeric keypad will stop the movie during authoring, so you can trap it only from a Projector.

 The modifier key properties update if the state of the relevant key changes, even during a handler's execution. To ensure that you are checking the *initial* state of a modifier key, store the appropriate Lingo property in a variable.

You can then check the variable throughout the handler without fear of its changing. Note below that we store the value of *the shiftDown*, but not the value of *the key*. The latter does not change during a Lingo handler.

Example 10-2: toring the State of Modifier Keys

```
on keyDown
  set shiftKeyDown = the shiftDown
  if shiftKeyDown and the key = "A" then
    statement
  else if shiftKeyDown and the key = "B" then
    statement
  end if
end
```

In reality, example 10-2 is too short to necessitate storing *the shiftDown*. But suppose you want to detect whether the Control key was pressed when the Projector was first started, and if so, skip the introduction of your presentation. You should store *the controlDown* into a global variable (in your *prepareMovie* handler) that you can use long after the Control key is released.

Shift *Key*

Whereas the Shift key capitalizes alphabetic keys, Lingo string comparisons using "=" and "<>" are *case-insensitive*. (See Appendix C for details.) You may want to treat the shifted and unshifted versions of some non-alphabetic keys as the same thing. For example, if the "+" key increases the volume, you may want to check for the unshifted version of the same key ("=" on most keyboards) also. You can also use *the keyCode* to identify a physical key regardless of the Shift key's state.

Caps Lock

Lingo does not recognize the Caps Lock key separately, although using it will capitalize alphabetical characters. See the *CapsLock* Xtra (*http://www. gmatter.com/donationware.html*) to detect its state.

Alt *Key (Windows)*

>The *optionDown* reflects the state of the Alt key, but Alt key combinations are generally trapped by Windows before reaching Director. (There is no *the altDown* property.) By definition, if you are trying to simulate keys that are trapped by Windows, they will be trapped by Windows! Alt key combinations such as Alt-] are sent to Director, but Alt-A through Alt-Z are not. The Alt key will also access custom menus defined with the installMenu command. The Xtras cited under "Keyboard Xtras" below can trap or disable the Alt key in limited cases.

Option *Key (Macintosh)*

>The Option key is used for alternate actions, usually in combination with the Command key.

>Use the optionDown to provide alternate functionality for debugging purposes., as in Examples 3-7, 3-8, and 3-9.

Command *Key (Macintosh)*

>The Command key accesses menu shortcuts on the Macintosh. Certain key combinations are trapped by Director itself during authoring or by the OS during Projector playback and won't reach your handler. Refer to *the exitLock* and *the commandDown.*

Control *Key*

>The Control key, along with *the emulateMultiButtonMouse* property, is used to simulate a multibutton mouse on the Macintosh. Certain key combinations are trapped by Director itself during authoring, or by the OS during Projector playback, and won't reach your handler. Refer to *the exitLock.*

Use *the commandDown.* instead of *the controlDown* property when you want the Control key to perform an operation under Windows and the Command key to perform the analogous operation on the Macintosh (as is the convention).

Special Key Combinations

Many keyboard combinations are intercepted by the OS instead of being sent to your *keyDown* and *keyUp* handlers. These key combinations perform some special OS operation, such as a screen grab, quitting the Projector, or switching to another program. The *exitLock* property disables most of the quit keys, but some key combinations can not be prevented without an Xtra.

Browsers may also intercept certain key combinations, preventing them from reaching your Shockwave movie.

Table 10-4 shows Windows-specific key combinations. To trap the function keys on either platform, use *the keyCode* as described later in this chapter.

Table 10-4: Special Windows Key Combinations

Key Combination	Default Action	How to Prevent It
Escape	Quits Projector.	*the exitLock* = TRUE
Alt-F4	Quits Projector.	*the exitLock* = TRUE
Ctrl-Q	Quits Projector.	*the exitLock* = TRUE
Ctrl-. (period)[1]	Quits Projector.	*the exitLock* = TRUE
Ctrl-W	Does *not* quit Projector, despite claims in documentation.	N/A
Alt Key	Combinations including Alt and an alphabetic key ("A" through "Z") are intercepted by the Windows and not passed to Director.	Not preventable
Alt-Tab	Switches between running Windows tasks.	Buddy API Xtra or DirectOS Xtra[2]
Ctrl-Alt-Del	Brings up task list, with option of restarting computer.	Buddy API Xtra or DirectOS Xtra[2]
Ctrl Key	Executes menu shortcut.	Define shortcuts with *installMenu* command
Ctrl-Print Screen	Screen grab.	Not preventable without Xtra
Windows95 Key	Windows 95 Start Menu.	DirectOS Xtra[2]

[1] The Ctrl-. (period) combination works with the period on both the main keyboard and the numeric keypad.
[2] See "Keyboard Xtras" *later in this chapter.* Some functions may not work under Windows NT.

Table 10-5 shows Macintosh-specific key combinations.

Table 10-5: Special Macintosh Key Combinations

Key Combination	Default Action	How to Prevent It
Escape	No effect.	N/A
Command-Q	Quits Projector.	*the exitLock* = TRUE
Command-. (period)[1]	Quits Projector.	*the exitLock* = TRUE
Command-W	Does *not* quit Projector, despite claims in documentation.	N/A

Table 10-5: Special Macintosh Key Combinations (continued)

Key Combination	Default Action	How to Prevent It
Command-Option-Esc	Gives user option of *Force Quitting* Projector.	Requires third-party Xtra
Restart Key, or Restart Button, or Ctrl-Option-Restart	Gives user option of restarting computer.	Requires third-party Xtra
Command Key	Executes menu shortcut.	Define shortcuts with *installMenu* command
Command-Shift-3	Screen grab.	OSutil Xtra[2]

[1] The Command-, (period). combination works with the period on both the main keyboard and the numeric keypad.

[2] OSutil's *OSSetScreenDump* method can disable basic Macintosh screen captures. See "Keyboard Xtras" *later in this chapter.*

Controlling the Quit Sequence

You may wish to perform some cleanup or post a confirmation or goodbye message when the user quits the projector. To trap special keyboard combinations before they abort the Projector, you'll need to set *the exitLock* to TRUE.

Provide an exit button or key combination that quits the Projector or the user will be stuck! Disabling the quit keyboard combinations is impolite for boring presentations.

Example 10-3: Preventing the User from Aborting

```
on prepareMovie --use an on startMovie handler in D5
  set the exitLock = TRUE
end
```

Trapping Quit Keys Manually

If you've set *the exitLock* to TRUE, you can then trap the quit keys manually in a movie script. Example 10-4 traps the Escape key, Command-Q, or Command-. (period) on the Macintosh and Alt-F4, Control-Q, or Control-. (period) under Windows. *ConfirmQuit* is a custom routine left as an exercise to the reader. See Chapter 15, *The MUI Dialog Xtra*, or Chapter 14, *Graphical User Interface Components*, in *Director in a Nutshell* for details on creating custom dialog boxes to present the user with multiple choices.

Example 10-4: Trapping the Quit Keys

```
on keyDown
  -- Trap the Escape key by checking for ASCII 27
  -- Also trap Alt-F4 under Windows.
  if charToNum(the key) = 27 or ¬
    (the platform starts "Windows" and the optionDown ¬
```

Example 10-4: Trapping the Quit Keys (continued)

```
      and the keyCode = 118) then
    stopEvent
    if confirmQuit() then
      quit
    end if
    exit
  end if

  if the commandDown then
    -- Prevent Cmd/Ctrl-Q andCmd/ Ctrl-. from aborting
    if (the key = "Q" or the key = ".") then
      stopEvent
      if confirmQuit() then
        quit
      end if
    else
      pass
    end if
  else
    pass
  end if
end keyDown
```

Keyboard Focus

Only editable field sprites are eligible to receive keyboard focus. An editable field receives focus if the user clicks on the field or "tabs" to it. A field will also receive focus if it is the only editable field in the current Score frame. Rich text fields are never editable at runtime. Refer to Chapter 12 in *Director in a Nutshell* for details.

 You can pass keyboard focus to a particular field sprite by setting its *editable of sprite* property to TRUE (even if it is TRUE already). Remove keyboard focus by setting *both* its *editable of sprite* and *editable of member* properties to FALSE. Test your Lingo scripts with the Message window closed (it may steal the focus if it is open).

If multiple field sprites are editable, there is no easy way to determine which field currently has focus. You can record a field sprite's number in a global variable whenever it receives a *keyDown* or *mouseDown* event, but no events are sent explicitly when a field sprite gains or loses focus nor is there a system property that indicates the field with keyboard focus.

Creating Editable Fields

The *editable of member* and *editable of sprite* properties determine whether the user can edit the field cast member associated with a field sprite at runtime. Prior to D5 field cast members were callled #text cast members.) The member property corresponds to the *Editable* checkbox in the Field Cast Member Properties dialog.

The sprite property corresponds to the *Editable* checkbox in the Sprite Toolbar or Sprite Inspector. (In Director 5, the *Editable* checkbox is to the left of the sprite channels in the Score window.)

A field is user-editable if *either* its *editable of sprite* or *editable of member* property is TRUE. Non-field sprites are never editable, even if their *editable of sprite* property is TRUE.

Auto-Tabbing

Director allows you to tab between editable fields by setting *the autoTab of member* property to TRUE or setting the *Tab to Next Field* checkbox in the Field Cast member Info Dialog box.

AutoTab determines whether the Tab key is intercepted by an editable field or whether it passes focus to the next editable field sprite. The sprites' channel numbers, not their on-stage positions, determine the tabbing order. *AutoTab* does not determine whether a field sprite can *receive* focus. That is determined by whether the field is editable.

You must manually trap the Return key and arrow keys to use them to navigate between editable fields. See Example 10-10.

Highlighted Text and the Insertion Point

Use the *hilite* command or *the selStart* and *the selEnd* properties to highlight a portion of a field, and *the selection, the selStart,* and *the selEnd* properties to determine the currently highlighted characters. The Message window interferes with *the selStart, selEnd,* and *selection* properties. Activate your test scripts by attaching them to buttons rather than testing them from the Message window.

You must set *the selEnd before* setting *the selStart* to get them to update reliably.

The selStart and *the selEnd* represent positions *after* characters. If *the selStart* and *the selEnd* are both 1, the insertion point is between characters 1 and 2. Set them both to 0 to insert keystrokes before the first character.

Example 10-5: Setting the Insertion Point

```
on setInsertionPoint fieldSprite, cursorPosition
  -- Force focus onto this sprite
  set the editable of sprite fieldSprite = TRUE
  -- Set the selEnd first for reliability
  set the selEnd   = cursorPosition
  set the selStart = cursorPosition
```

Example 10-5: Setting the Insertion Point (continued)

```
    return cursorPosition
end setInsertionPoint
```

This forces focus onto a sprite and positions the cursor at the end of its field:

```
    on beginSprite me
      set mySprite = the spriteNum of me
      setInsertionPoint (mySprite, ¬
            length(field (the member of sprite mySprite)))
    end beginSprite
```

Setting *the selEnd* and *the selStart* to different values highlights the text between them (or you can use the *hilite* command).

Example 10-6: Setting the Highlight in a Field

```
on hilightText fieldSprite, startChar, endChar
  set the editable of sprite fieldSprite = TRUE
  -- Set the selEnd first for reliability
  set the selEnd    = endChar
  set the selStart = startChar-1
  return the selection
end hilightText
```

This highlights characters 1 to 3 of the current sprite (assumed to be a field):

```
    hilightText (the currentSpriteNum, 1, 3)
```

Filtering Keyboard Input

In the default case, any characters typed by the user will appear in an editable field. You can intercept keyboard input, *before* it appears in the field, with a *keyDown* handler attached to the field sprite. Movie-wide key events can also be trapped with *the keyDownScript*. Refer to the previous examples.

 Keyboard events not trapped by a field's sprite or cast script are passed to the frame script or movie scripts. If you attach a *keyDown* handler to a sprite, you must include the *pass* command for the field cast member to actually receive the keyboard character(s).

It is possible to attach multiple *keyDown* handlers to a single sprite. Table 10-6 shows what happens when *keyDown* events are passed or consumed explicitly or implicitly. See Table 10-1 for the event passing order.

Table 10-6: KeyDown Event Passing

Command Used in First Behavior	Passed to Other Behaviors?	Passed to Editable Field?
pass	Yes	Only if all Behaviors issue pass

Table 10-6: KeyDown Event Passing (continued)

Command Used in First Behavior	Passed to Other Behaviors?	Passed to Editable Field?
<None specified> or *dont-PassEvent*	Yes	No, but later Behaviors can manually append character to field
stopEvent	No	No

Don't forget to trap undesirable keys when requesting user input. Example 10-7 shows how to filter out certain keys and perform some action when the Return or Enter key is pressed. This *keyDown* handler attached to a field sprite prevents the user from entering any spaces.

Example 10-7: Disallowing Characters

```
on keyDown me
  if the key = RETURN or the key = ENTER then
    -- Process the user entry
    set contents = the text of member ¬
      (the member of sprite (the spriteNum of me))
    alert "You entered" && contents
  else if the key = SPACE then
    -- Beep if they enter a SPACE
    beep
  else
    -- This sends the key event onto the editable field
    pass
  end if
end keyDown
```

 You generally will not want to allow the user to include the Return character in a field. Trap the Return key unless allowing multiline inputs.

The previous example traps the Return character explicitly. Example 10-8 rejects the Return character because it allows only the digits 0 through 9 to be passed through. It assumes that there is a separate *submit* button that reads the field's contents.

Example 10-8: Allowing Only Specific Characters

```
on keyDown
  if ("0123456789" contains the key) then
    pass
  else
    stopEvent
  end if
end keyDown
```

Reader Exercise: Modify Example 10-8 to allow other characters used to enter numbers, such as "=," "-", and ".".

To limit the length of a field, you can set *the boxType of member* to either #fixed or #limit. Refer to Chapter 12 in *Director in a Nutshell*. That's usually easier than trying to track the length of the field manually. If you try to stop user input after a certain number of characters, you must allow for the possibility that the user is pressing the Delete key or that highlighted characters will be deleted by the next key pressed. It is easier to check the final length of the string once the user has "submitted" it, rather than testing it at every keystroke.

Simulating a Password Entry Field

Because an *onkeyDown* handler in a score script or castscript intercepts keys before they are passed to the field, you can modify them before they are displayed. You could capitalize all letters, for example. Example 10-9 simulates a password entry field using asterisks. Note that the field is updated manually, and that the original key is *not* passed with *pass* (unless it is one of the standard editing keys). Manually passing characters to a field requires us to manually simulate some of the things that Director does automatically if we just pass the characters (we want to send asterisks instead). Note the tricks we use to figure out whether to insert the characters or replace highlighted text and how we reset the cursor insertion point.

Example 10-9: Password Entry Field

```
property pPassword
property pMyMember

on beginSprite me
  set pMyMember = the member of sprite (the spriteNum of me)
  -- Clear the password field
  set pPassword = EMPTY
  put EMPTY into member pMyMember
end

on keyDown me
  -- Mask the field with asterisks.  Change this to
  -- "set maskCar = the key" to see password entry
  set maskChar = "*"

  if the key = RETURN or the key = ENTER then
    -- Check the password when they hit RETURN or ENTER
    -- Perhaps check name against a master list or file.
    if verifyPassword (pPassword) = TRUE then
      go frame "Top Secret"
    else
      alert "Access Denied"
    end if
  else if isEditingKey() then
    -- Allow the editing keys (arrows, delete) to pass
    pass
  else
```

Example 10-9: Password Entry Field (continued)

```
   -- Determine what portion of the field to replace
   set insertPoint = max(1, the selStart + 1)
   set endPoint    = max(1, the selEnd)
   -- We're inserting at the cursor location
   if insertPoint = endPoint then
      -- Add the key to the secret password
      put the key before char insertPoint of pPassword
      -- But display the masking character (asterisks)
      put maskChar before char insertPoint [LC]
         of member pMyMember
   else
      -- Replace highlighted characters similar to above
      put the key into char insertPoint to endPoint [LC]
         of pPassword
      put maskChar into char insertPoint to endPoint [LC]
         of member pMyMember
   end if
   -- Update the cursor insertion point manually
   -- Set the selEnd first for reliability
   set the selEnd   = insertPoint
   set the selStart = insertPoint
   end if
end keyDown

-- Check for common editing keys that we'll allow through (See Example 10-10.)
on isEditingKey
   case (the key) of
      BACKSPACE, TAB:  return TRUE
   end case

   case (the keyCode) of
      -- This checks for delete key and the arrow keys
      51, 117, 123, 124, 125, 126:
         return TRUE
      otherwise:
         return FALSE
   end case
end isEditingKey

-- Write your own verification routine
on verifyPassword password
 If password = "platypus" then
 else return TRUE
 end if return FALSE
end
```

Editing Keys

By default, editable fields support only the Delete (Backspace) key and the arrow keys for editing. The left and right arrow keys move the cursor one character, and the up and down arrow keys jump to the beginning and end of the field. The Tab key jumps between fields (assuming *the autoTab of member* property is TRUE.).

You must manually implement cut, copy, paste. You may want to make the up and down arrow keys move between fields. Use the Return key to jump to the next field of a multifield input screen, or submit a single field entry.

Table 10-7 shows *the keyCodes* of common editing keys you can use to control keyboard navigation between multiple editable fields.

Table 10-7: Editing Keys

Key	ASCII	the keyCode
RETURN	13	36
Left Arrow	28	123
Right Arrow	29	124
Up Arrow	30	126
Down Arrow	31	125
Help (or insert)	5	114
Home	1	115
Page Up	11	116
Page Down	12	121
End	4	119
BACKSPACE	8	51
Del (keypad)	127	117
ENTER	3	76

You can allow the user to navigate between editable fields (see *"Keyboard Focus"* earlier in this chapter) using the up and down arrows, and the Return, Home, and End keys, as follows. (Use *the autoTab of member* property or *AutoTab* checkbox to jump between fields without Lingo scripting.)

Example 10-10: Special Handling of Editing Keys

```
on keyDown
  case (the keyCode) of
     125:  -- Down arrow
           -- Perhaps send focus onto the next field
           -- by setting its editable of sprite property
           126: -- Up arrow
           -- Perhaps send focus onto the previous field
           115:  -- Home key
           -- Send keyboard focus to first field
           119:  -- End key
           -- Switch keyboard focus to last field
     otherwise:
```

Example 10-10: Special Handling of Editing Keys (continued)

```
        if the key = RETURN then
            -- Process field or jump to next field
        else
            pass
        end if
    end case
end
```

Numeric Keypad Input

Director ignores input from the numeric keypad by default. To allow numeric keypad input, you must evaluate *the keyCode* generated by each key, and if it corresponds to a key from the numeric keypad, append the appropriate character to the field.

Table 10-8 shows the keys you may want to trap for interpreting numeric keypad input. Note that *the keyCode* numbers skip a beat between the "7" and the "8" on the keypad. In Director 5, the "7" and "8" keys on the keypad erroneously returned the same code

---

 Whenever dealing with numbers, don't confuse the characters "0" through "9," whose ASCII values range from 48 to 57, with the ASCII values 0 through 9, which are all unprintable control characters. See Appendix A.

Example 10-11 reads numbers from the keypad (note the workaround to handle the fact that the *keyCodes* skip number 90).

Example 10-11: Trapping the Numeric Keypad Keys

```
on keyDown me
  -- This handles the keypad chars 0 through 7
  if (the keyCode >= 82) and (the keyCode <= 89) then
    set thisChar = numToChar (the keyCode-34)
  -- This handles the keypad chars 8 and 9
  else if (the keyCode >= 91) and (the keyCode <= 92) then
    set thisChar = numToChar (the keyCode-35)
  else
    -- Let all other keys pass through
    set thisChar = the key
  end if
  put thisChar after member ¬
      (the member of sprite (the spriteNum of me))
end
```

Table 10-8: Numeric Keypad Codes

Key	ASCII	keyCode
. (period)	46	65
Enter	3	76
+	43	69
-	45	78
*	42	67
/	47	75
=	61	81
num lock/clear	27	71

Key	ASCII	keyCode
0	48	82
1	49	83
2	50	84
3	51	85
4	52	86
5	53	87
6	54	88
7	55	89
8	56	91
9	57	92

Function Keys

To trap the function keys, use the key codes shown in Table 10-9. Like other key codes, these are the same on the Macintosh and Windows.

Table 10-9: Function Keys

Function Key	ASCII	keyCode
F1	16	122
F2	16	120
F3	16	99
F4	16	118
F5	16	96
F6	16	97
F7	16	98
F8	16	100
F9	16	101
F10	16	109
F11	16	103
F12	16	111
F13	16	105

Table 10-9: Function Keys (continued)

Function Key	ASCII	keyCode
F14	16	107
F15	16	113

Keyboard Tasks

Table 10-10 shows the handler(s) and scripts(s) used to accomplish common tasks related to the keyboard. The trick is to place the correct type of handler in the correct type of script, so that it will be called when the event of interest occurs.

Table 10-10: Common Keyboard Tasks

To Detect	Use This Type of Handler or Property	In This Type of Script
Keyboard input for all sprites using a particular cast member	*on keyDown*	Castmember script
Keyboard input for a sprite	*on keyDown*	Sprite script
Keyboard input ignored by all sprites in a frame	*on keyDown*	Frame script
Keyboard input throughout the entire movie otherwise ignored by other scripts	*on keyDown*	Movie script
All keyboard input *before* it is passed to individual sprites or frames.	set *the keyDownScript*	Place primary event handler in movie script
Keyboard input from numeric keypad	*on keyDown*	Sprite or cast member script
Key being pressed at any time	set *the keyDownScript*	Place primary event handler in movie script
Key being released at any time	set *the keyUpScript*	Place primary event handler in movie script
Modifier keys	Check the *commandDown, controlDown, optionDown,* or *shift-Down* property	Any
The last key pressed	Check the *key, keyPressed, keyCode* property	Any
Whether a specific key is pressed	Use third-party Xtras described under "keyboard xtras" later in this chapter	Any

See "Keyboard Focus" earlier in the chapter to force keyboard focus on a sprite. There is no easy way to detect which sprite has keyboard focus.

Key Trap

There are a number of ways to prevent key events from being processed. You can simply send the user to a frame in which no sprites have key handlers attached.

You can disable or enable key events by calling the following handler with a Boolean flag, such as *keyTrap(TRUE)* or *keyTrap(FALSE)*.

Example 10-12: Key Trap

```
on keyTrap flag
  if (flag = TRUE) then
    -- Disable key events
    set the keyDownScript = "stopEvent"
    set the keyUpScript   = "stopEvent"
  else
    -- Allow key events
    set the keyDownScript = EMPTY
    set the keyUpScript   = EMPTY
  end if
end keyTrap
```

Simulating Keyboard Events

Lingo does not provide a mechanism for setting *the key, the keyCode,* or *the keyPressed* or for directly sending a keyboard event to Director's event queue. (See the "keyboard Xtras" later in this chapter.)

You can manually send keyboard messages using *sendSprite, sendAllSprites,* and *call,* such as:

```
sendSprite (spriteNumber, #keyDown {, args...})
sendAllSprites (#keyUp {, args...})
```

You can also call a *keyDown* handler in a specific script, using:

```
call (#keyDown, script n {, args...})
```

You can send a message to a script instance, using:

```
call (#keyDown, scriptInstance {, args...})
```

If using Director 4.0.4 or Director 5.0, you can use the forms:

```
keyDown (script n {, args...})
send (#keyDown, scriptInstance {, args...})
```

 Keyboard messages sent manually are sent only to the specified entity. They are *not* passed to additional scripts through the usual messaging hierarchy.

Keyboard Xtras

Xtras provide a number of keyboard-related functions not possible via Lingo alone.

Flushing Keyboard Events

Lingo does not provide a mechanism for flushing pending mouse or keyboard events from Director's event queue. A number of older (often unsupported) XObjects, such as *"Johnny"* and *"MISC_X"* flushed pending mouse and keyboards events. The *FlushEvents* Xtra (*http://fargo.itp.tsoa.nyu.edu/~gsmith/Xtras)* by Geoff Smith is available for the Macintosh only (and I haven't tried it personally).

The OSutil Xtra (*http://www.ddce.cqu.edu.au/imu/tools/Director/Xtras*) by Paul Farry has an *OSFlushEvents* method that purportedly flushes mouse and keyboard events. I've used this Xtra for other chores with good success, but I have no experience with this method.

The KeyPoll Xtra (see next section) can disable keyboard input but doesn't flush pending events.

Polling for Keys and Multiple Simultaneous Keys

The KeyPoll Xtra (*http://www.gmatter.com/donationware.html*) (developed by Brian Gray, formerly of Macromedia) allows you to do the following on all major platforms:

- Check whether the key with a specific *keyCode* is being pressed.

- Get a list of the *keyCodes* of all keys currently being pressed.

- Disable/enable all keyboard events from reaching the system-level queue.

Allegedly, the Macintosh reports up to two character keys being pressed in addition to any combination of the five modifier keys or the arrow keys. Brian Gray reports that more than two characters keys are sometimes detectable. Details can be found in *Inside Macintosh: Macintosh Toolbox Essentials* at *http://developer. apple.com/*.

The *CapsLock* Xtra (also at *http://www.gmatter.com/donationware.html*) can detect the state of the Caps Lock key.

See also the Buddy API and DirectOS Xtras in the next section.

Sending Key Events and Disabling Keys

The *Buddy API* Xtra (*http://www.mods.com.au/budapi*) claims to be able to check which keys have been pressed (and also simulate key events and disable keyboard input) under Windows using the *baSendKeys, baKeyIsDown, baKeyBeenPressed, baDisableKeys,* and *baDisableSwitching* methods. (I have not personally verified these claims, but I have heard uniformly positive comments about Buddy API in general and their tech support was responsive.) A Macintosh version of Buddy API should be available by the time you read this.

The *DirectOS* Xtra (*http://www.directxtras.com/do_doc.htm*) claims to be able check which keys have been pressed (and also disable certain key combinations) under Windows. (I have no personal experience with this Xtra).

Both the DirectOS and Buddy API Xtra provide many other OS-level functions. See also Chapter 9 and Chapter 14, *External Files*.

See also the other Xtras listed earlier.

Keyboard Event Idiosyncrasies

Authoring Caveats

During authoring, Director may intercept certain keyboard events. Refer to the discussion at the beginning of this chapter. When trying to edit or highlight text in editable field sprites, Director's Message window is a frequent trouble-maker. Close all Director windows, or test from a Projector if necessary.

Kiosks Without Keyboards

If you are creating a kiosk without a keyboard, you can use a simulated graphic touch-screen to allow for user input. Simply have each sprite's *mouseUp* handler append the appropriate character to the input field.

RSX Conflict

RSX is a sound driver from Intel that has some conflicts with Director for Windows. RSX can prevent Director for Windows (D6.0, D6.0.1, and D6.0.2) Projectors played full-screen from receiving keyboard events. Macromedia has apparently acknowledged the problem, but no fix has been released as of May 1998. If possible, ask your users to disable RSX.

Keyboard Events to Frame and Movie Scripts

There have been reports that frame scripts and movie scripts may not receive keyboard events unless at least one editable field sprite is present in the current frame. Place one off-stage, if necessary. I have not seen this behavior myself, and it is not clear that it is a separate issue from the RSX conflict.

MIAWs

A movie-in-a-window whose window has focus will intercept keyboard events even if it does not have any editable text fields. You can click on the Stage to ensure that it has focus so that the main movie receives keyboard events properly.

In a movie script of the MIAW, use the code shown in Example 10-13 to send keyboards events to the Stage.

Example 10-13: Passing Key Events from MIAWs

```
on keyDown
  tell the stage
    do (the keyDownScript)
```

Example 10-13: Passing Key Events from MIAWs (continued)

```
  end tell
end keyDown
```

In the main movie, you can define *the keyDownScript* to execute the handler of your choice. The main movie can check *the key* to determine the last key pressed, or even use *moveToFront the stage* to bring itself to the foreground.

In the main movie you might use:

```
on startMovie
  set the keyDownScript = "customKeyDownHandler"
end

on customKeyDownHandler
  put "The key is" && the key
  -- Do any custom keyboard handling here
end
```

Menu Bars

When using a custom menu, Windows intercepts keyboard combinations using the Alt and Ctrl keys, and the Mac OS intercepts keyboard combinations using the Command key.

MouseUp Events

The *mouseUp* event is only sent to an editable field sprite if the field does *not* have focus. See Chapter 9 for details.

Shockwave

Shockwave movies may not receive keyboard events until receiving focus via a mouse click. Some developers add a "Click here to start" button to solve the problem.

The browser may trap certain keyboard shortcuts, preventing those key combinations from reaching your Lingo scripts. Avoid browser-specific keyboard shortcuts.

KeyCode Tester

You'll want your own keyboard tester to check the return values of idiosyncratic keys not listed in this chapter or Appendix A (such as those with higher ASCII values created using the Option or Alt keys). Attach this script to an editable field sprite. It prints out the results in the Message window.

Example 10-14: Your Own KeyCode Tester

```
on keyDown
  put "key:" && the key
  put "keyCode:" && the keyCode
  pass
end
```

You may need to close the Message window before pressing keys, then open it afterward to see the results. You could get fancy and send *the keyCode* output to another field shown elsewhere on stage. Refer to the *"Keyboard Lingo"* Show Me in the online Help (or Macromedia's Web site), or download the keyboard tester from http://www.zeusprod.com/nutshell/examples.html.

Keyboard Potential

Don't overlook the potential to use your keyboard for good. Try implementing the following:

- Use the keyboard to set the volume (Hint: Use *the soundLevel*).

- Use keyboard shortcuts for custom menu options (see the *"Menus"* section of Chapter 14 in *Director in a Nutshell*).

- You can accept simultaneous input from multiple daisy-chained Macintosh ADB keyboards. Lingo can't tell which keyboard sent the event, so it is fun for collaboration, not gaming.

Keyboard handling in Director is far from elegant, but this chapter has armed you with the knowledge to steer clear of many pitfalls. Refer frequently to the quirk list at *http://www.updatestage.com/* because many keyboard idiosyncrasies encountered are not the fault of your Lingo code.

CHAPTER 11

Timers and Dates

This chapter covers timers, delays, timeouts, dates, times, and time unit conversion. Although I would like to have covered cue points and tempos in this book, I felt that they were intimately tied to the Score and Director's media elements (sound and digital video), which are the purview of *Director in a Nutshell*. Therefore, synchronization and cue points are covered in Chapter 3, *The Score and Animation,* Chapter 15, *Sound and Cue Points,* and Chapter 16, *Digital Video,* of that book.

Timers and Delays

Timers are useful for adding fixed delays to your presentation. They are more reliable than waiting for the playback head to reach a given frame because Director's frame rate varies. Refer to Chapter 1, *How Director Works,* and Chapter 3 in *Director in a Nutshell* for details on how Director's frame-based paradigm compares with time-based media, such as digital video.

 Many, but not all, Director commands measure time in *ticks*. There are 60 ticks per second. See "Lingo!" by Tab Julius (published by New Riders) for a detailed discussion of timer resolutions on various platforms. The resolution of Director timers is not very accurate (it is accurate only to about 4 ticks under Windows 3.1). Use a Quick-Time sprite with a long silent soundtrack and *the movieTime* property for highly accurate timing.

Timers

Each movie and MIAW has a single stopwatch-style timer (*the timer*), but Director has a perpetual timer from which you can construct additional timers.

Don't call *startTimer* in a utility handler to be used by other programmers. It resets *the timer*, which will interfere with any code that relies on it.

Table 11-1: Lingo Timers

Lingo Command	Usage
the ticks	Time in ticks (1/60th of a second) since the machine was started, not since Projector started.
startTimer	Resets *the timer, the lastEvent, the lastKey, the lastClick,* and *the lastRoll* properties to 0.
the timer	Resettable timer, in ticks. See *startTimer*.

StartTimer and *the timer* work together—use *startTimer* to begin timing, then check *the timer*. Note that *the timer* runs indefinitely (until restarted by *startTimer*) and never generates any timeout events regardless of the time elapsed. *The timer* runs even if *startTimer* has never been called, in which case it reflects the amount of time the Projector has been running. A custom timer allows you to delay with greater accuracy than the Tempo channel settings, and it does not prevent interactivity, as the the *delay* command does.

 Avoid calling *startTimer* in utility handlers because it may break code relying on *the timer*. Don't call repeatedly, such as in an *enterFrame* handler, while waiting for *the timer* to reach a certain limit.

Reset the timer in an *on beginSprite* handler attached to the frame script. It *won't* be called repeatedly while the playback head loops.

Example 11-1: A Custom Timer

```
on beginSprite
  startTimer
end

on exitFrame
  -- This waits for 5 seconds
  if the timer < 60 * 5 then
    go the frame
  end if
end
```

Waits

Waiting for a Fixed Time

When the *delay* command is called within the body of a Lingo script, the delay doesn't begin until the current handler ends, and commands after the *delay* command are executed *before* the delay occurs.

Example 11-2: Delay Command versus Custom Wait Function

```
on exitFrame
  put "Hello"
  delay 2 * 60
  put "This command is executed before the delay
end
```

Refer to Chapter 3, *The Score and Animation,* in *Director in a Nutshell* for details and more examples.

Avoid the *delay* command by implementing your own custom handler. Note that we generate an artificial starting time without using *startTimer.* This avoids breaking any code that depends on *the timer.*

```
on wait numTicks
  set startTime = the ticks
  repeat while the ticks < startTime + numTicks
    nothing
  end repeat
end
```

 Always check your timer with a comparison operator (> or <) rather than an equal sign (=) so that the comparison need not be evaluated at an exact time to be TRUE.

Waiting for Media

There are several ways to wait for sounds and digital video (in addition to using Cue Points or the Tempo channel). These examples demonstrate the syntax of timing-related commands but are not ideal because the tight *repeat* loops lock out interactivity. See Chapters 15 and 16 in *Director in a Nutshell* for improved ways to wait for media.

Wait for sounds to start or end using the *soundBusy()* function:

Example 11-3: Waiting for Media

```
on waitForSound channel
  repeat while soundBusy(channel)
    nothing
  end repeat
end
```

Wait for a particular point in a sound by checking *the currentTime of sound* function:

```
on waitForSoundTime   channel, soundTime
   repeat while (the currentTime of sprite channel < soundTime
      nothing
   end repeat
end
```

Wait for a particular point in an SWA cast member using *the currentTime of sprite* function:

```
on waitForSWAtime channel, SWATime
   repeat while (the currentTime of sprite channel < SWATime)
      nothing
   end repeat
end
```

You can wait for a digital video in several ways, including checking *the movieTime of sprite* and *the movieRate of sprite* properties.

```
on waitForVideo channel
   repeat while the movieTime of sprite channel < ¬
         the duration of member (the member of sprite channel)
      updateStage
   end repeat
end
```

Table 11-2 lists the commands that are used to time various types of media. Refer again to Chapters 15 and 16 in *Director in a Nutshell* for details on Cue Points. See also Table 11-4.

Table 11-2: Media Timing

Media Type	Lingo of Interest
sound	soundBusy(), currentTime of sound, cuePointTimes of member
SWA	currentTime of sprite, duration of member, cuePointTimes of member, state of member
digital video	movieTime of sprite, movieRate of sprite, duration of member, currentTime of sprite, cuePointTimes of member, frameRate of member, digitalVideoTimeScale

TimeOuts

Director generates *timeOut* events when the user doesn't do anything for a specified length of time. This may indicate that the user has left or is very confused. *TimeOut* events can be trapped with an *on timeOut* handler or a *timeOutScript* primary event handler. Table 11-3 shows the time-out related Lingo.

Table 11-3: Time-out Properties

Command	Usage
the lastClick[1]	Time in ticks since last *mouseDown* or *rightMouseDown* event. See *the timeoutMouse*.

Table 11-3: Time-out Properties (continued)

Command	Usage
the lastEvent[1]	Time in ticks since last *mouseDown*, mouse roll, or *keyDown* event regardless of the settings of *the timeoutMouse* and *the timeoutKeyDown*.
the lastKey[1]	Time in ticks since last *keyDown* event. See *the timeoutKeyDown*.
the lastRoll[1]	Time in ticks since mouse was last moved. Never resets *the timeoutLapsed*.
on timeOut	Handler that traps *timeOut* events when placed in frame script or movie script. See Table 2-7.
the timeoutKeyDown	Boolean indicating whether key clicks reset *the timeoutLapsed* to 0. Default is TRUE.
the timeoutLapsed	Time in ticks since the last activity (depends on properties below).
the timeoutLength[2]	The time period of inactivity, in ticks, required to generate a *timeout* event. Default is 10,800 ticks (3 minutes).
the timeoutMouse[2]	Boolean indicating whether mouse clicks reset *the timeoutLapsed* to 0. Default is TRUE.
the timeoutPlay[2]	Boolean indicating whether branching to a movie resets *the timeoutLapsed* to 0. Default is FALSE.
the timeoutScript[2]	Defines primary *timeOut* event handler. Default is EMPTY. See Table 2-3.

[1] Reset by *StartTimer*.
[2] Reset to default values when Director stops during development, but not reset when branching to a new movie.

A *timeOut* event is generated when *the timeoutLapsed* surpasses *the timeout-Length*. *The timeoutLapsed* is not a Boolean property, and it does *not* indicate whether a timeout has actually occurred. Instead it represents the pending elapsed time since the last activity. Each Movie-in-a-Window has independent versions of the timeout-related properties, such as the *timeoutLength*, *timeoutLapsed*, and *timeoutScript*.

Six operations reset *the timeoutLapsed* to 0, which postpones the *timeOut* event, if applicable:

- The mouse being clicked, if *the timeoutMouse* is TRUE.
- A key being pressed, if *the timeoutKeyDown* is TRUE.
- Playing a movie (using *go movie* or *play movie*), if *the timeoutPlay* is TRUE.
- *The timeoutLapsed* reaching the value of *the timeoutLength*. This also generates a *timeOut* event and resets *the timeoutLapsed* whether the event is handled or not
- A *timeOut* event handler being exited.
- Manually setting *the timeoutLapsed* property to 0.

Changing *the timeoutLength* property does *not* reset *the timeoutLapsed* to 0, but you can manually do so to postpone a time out. Moving the mouse does not reset the *timeoutLapsed*.

Testing TimeOuts During Development

Using the mouse or keyboard in the Message window will reset *the timeoutLapsed* (unless you first set *the timeoutMouse* and *the timeoutKeyDown* to FALSE, which must be done after the movie starts playing, not before).

> *The timeoutLapsed* can be manually set to 0, or any other value, despite the Macromedia documentation's claim to the contrary. You can advance *the timeoutLapsed* manually to hasten a time out, or even set it to a negative number to arbitrarily lengthen the time until the next timeout.

Trapping TimeOut Events

Trapping a *timeOut* event is a four-step process:

1. Create a *timeOut* handler in a movie script or frame script, which will perform the desired actions when a time out occurs.

    a. If your handler is named *on timeOut*, you need not set *the timeoutScript*.

    b. Set *the timeoutScript* primary event handler, only if you want to call a handler other than, or in addition to, the *on timeOut* handler. Use the *timeoutScript* to change timeout handlers on the fly

2. Optionally set *the timeoutLength*., whose default is 10,800 ticks (3 minutes).

3. Optionally change *the timeoutKeyDown, the timeoutMouse,* or *the timeout-Play* properties to control which events reset *the timeoutLapsed.*

Optionally set *the timeoutLapsed* to 0 to begin the time-out period afresh. (See previous text for a list of things that reset *the timeoutLapsed*.)

The *lastClick, lastEvent, lastRoll,* and *lastKey* system properties can be checked at any time to indicate when those particular events occurred, but they have no effect on *timeOut* events.

> *The timeoutScript* is *not* reset when branching to another movie. A *timeout* event will generate a script error if the handler defined by *the timeoutScript* can not be found in the new movie. Place any universal *timeOut* handler in a movie script in an external shared cast, or clear *the timeoutScript* in the movie's *stopMovie* handler (or reassign it in the *prepareMovie* handler of the destination movie).

Handling Timeouts

Macromedia's *Lingo Dictionary* states that an *on timeOut* handler must be placed in a movie script, which is not entirely true. When a timeout occurs, the *timeOut* event is sent to the primary event handler (specified by *the timeoutScript*), then to any *on timeOut* handler in the frame script, and finally to any *on timeOut* handler in a movie script.

Upon entering the *on timeOut* handler or the handler defined by *the timeout-Script, the timeoutLapsed* is reset to 0, and it is *again* reset when leaving the handler. Even though *the timeoutLapsed* property increments while the *timeOut* handler is running, no additional *timeout* events are generated or recognized during that period.

Setting *the timeoutLength* to 0 is a bad idea because it will cause *timeOut* events to be generated repeatedly. Assuming your movie does not include any *on timeOut* handlers in a movie script, you can enable and disable *timeOut* events by setting *the timeoutScript* to some command or to EMPTY. If you use an *on timeOut* handler in a movie script, you can set *the timeoutLength* to *the maxInteger* to prevent timeouts during lengthy animations.

Mouse roll events never reset *the timeoutLapsed* or prevent *timeOut* events. For greatest accuracy, check *the lastRoll* property within a frame script or *idle* handler to determine whether the user has moved the mouse. If so, you may want to manually reset *the time-outLapsed* to 0 (zero).

Time Units

Table 11-4 lists the time units of all time-related Lingo commands. See "*Converting Time Units*" later in this chapter. See Table 16-1 for possible values for some of the entries in Table 16-1. Refer to Chapters 15 and 16 in *Director in a Nutshell* for details on the commands that pertain to media elements. Note that *the duration of member* property has different units for SWA, digital video, and transition cast members.

Director often measures time in *ticks*. One tick equals 1/60th of a second.

Table 11-4: Time Units

Lingo Command	Media Type	Time Units
the bitRate of member	SWA	Bits per second; 0 if SWA is not playing.
the chunkSize of member	Transition	Pixels per chunk in each step of the transition (1 to 128).
the cpuHogTicks	N/A	Ticks (default 20). Higher numbers hog more time for Director (Mac only).
the cuePointTimes of member	Video, Sound, SWA	Milliseconds.

Table 11-4: Time Units (continued)

Lingo Command	Media Type	Time Units
the currentTime of sprite	Video, SWA	Milliseconds.
the currentTime of sound	SWA, Sound	Milliseconds.
DIRECTOR.INI	Sound	Sound buffer length settings are in milliseconds. See Appendix D, *The DIRECTOR.INI and LINGO.INI Files.*
the date (long | short | abbreviated)	N/A	Day, month, and year. See *"Date Formats"* later in this chapter.
delay	N/A	Ticks.
the digitalVideoTimeScale	Video	Units per second[1] (defaults to 60 units per second, that is, ticks). If set to 0, *the timeScale of member* is used.
the doubleClick	N/A	Boolean property; double-click interval is set in *Mouse* control panel. See Chapter 9, *Mouse Events.*
the duration of member	Video	1/*digitalVideoTimeScale* (default is ticks[1]).
the duration of member	SWA	Seconds (0 until SWA starts playing).
the duration of member	Transition	Milliseconds.
the frameRate of member	Video	Frames per second.[2] See Table 16-1.
framesToHMS()	N/A	Frames to "$sHH:MM:SS.FFD$".[3]
the frameTempo	N/A	Frames per second.
HMStoFrames	H/A	"$sHH:MM:SS.FFD$"[3] to frames.
the idleHandlerPeriod	N/A	Ticks (default 0). Higher numbers slow all idle processing including *mouseEnter, mouseLeave,* and *mouseWithin* events!
the idleLoadPeriod	N/A	Ticks (default 0). Higher numbers slow idle loading but speed other idle processing.
the lastClick	N/A	Ticks (see *the timeoutMouse*).
the lastEvent	N/A	Ticks.
the lastKey	N/A	Ticks (see *the timeoutKeyDown*).
the lastRoll	N/A	Ticks.
the movieRate of sprite	Video	*n* x "intrinsic frame rate". See Chapter 16 in *Director in a Nutshell.*
the movieTime of sprite	Video	1/*digitalVideoTimeScale* (default is ticks[1]).
netLastModDate()	N/A	"Thu Jan 30, 1997 12:00:00 AM GMT".
the netThrottleTicks	N/A	Ticks.

Table 11-4: Time Units (continued)

Lingo Command	Media Type	Time Units
the percentPlayed of member	SWA	Percent of bytes played (should be comparable to percent of time).
the percentStreamed of member	SWA	Percent of bytes streamed.
the preLoadTime of member	SWA	Seconds.
puppetPalette *whichPalette* {, *speed, nFrames*}	Palette	*Speed* in 1/4 seconds (0 to 120). Higher numbers are slower.
puppetTempo *framesPerSecond*	N/A	Frames per second.
puppetTransition *whichTrans* {, *time, chunkSize, changeArea*}	Transition	*Time* in 1/4 seconds (0 to 120). *chunkSize* (1 to 128). Higher *times* are slower; higher *chunkSizes* are faster.
the sampleRate of member	SWA	Samples per second (Hertz).
the size of member	All	Bytes.
sound fadeIn *whichChannel* {, *speed*}	Sound	Ticks (default is 15 * 60 / tempo).
sound fadeOut *whichChannel* {, *speed*}	Sound	Ticks (default is 15 * 60 / tempo).
the state of member	SWA	Code indicates whether SWA is playing. See Table 16-1.
the startTime of sprite	Video	1/*digitalVideoTimeScale* (default is ticks[1]).
the stopTime of sprite	Video	1/*digitalVideoTimeScale* (default is ticks[1]).
on streamStatus	N/A	See *bytesSoFar, bytesTotal* arguments.
Tempo channel *Wait* settings	N/A	Seconds.
the ticks	N/A	Ticks (1/60th of a second).
the time (long | short | abbreviated)	N/A	"*HH:MM:SS tt*" where *tt* is "AM" or "PM" (see "*Time Formats*").
the timeoutLapsed	N/A	Ticks.
the timeoutLength	N/A	Ticks, default is 10,800 ticks (3 minutes).
the timer	N/A	Ticks.
the timeScale of member	Video	Units per second. Defaults varies. See "*Time Scales*" later in this chapter.
trackNextKeyTime	Video	1/*digitalVideoTimeScale* (default is ticks[1]).
trackNextSampleTime	Video	1/*digitalVideoTimeScale* (default is ticks[1]).

Timers & Dates

Table 11-4: Time Units (continued)

Lingo Command	Media Type	Time Units
trackPreviousKeyTime	Video	1/*digitalVideoTimeScale* (default is ticks[1]).
trackPreviousSampleTime	Video	1/*digitalVideoTimeScale* (default is ticks[1]).
trackStartTime (member or sprite)	Video	1/*digitalVideoTimeScale* (default is ticks[1]).
trackStopTime (member or sprite)	Video	1/*digitalVideoTimeScale* (default is ticks[1]).
zoomBox `startSprite, endSprite, delayTicks`	N/A	delayTicks = delay in ticks between each step of zooming rectangles. Default is 1.

[1] *The digitalVideoTimeScale* property affects the units used for timing digital videos, such as *the movieTime of sprite* and *the duration of member* properties. Those properties are not always measured in ticks, as claimed in Macromedia's manual. See "Time Scales."

[2] See Chapter 16 in *Director in a Nutshell* for more details on the special meanings of negative *frameRate of member* settings.

[3] See "Converting Time Units" later in this chapter for using *framesToHMS()* and *HMStoFrames()*

Time Scales

The digitalVideoTimeScale system property determines the time scale used to track digital video cast members, as measured in units per second. If *the digitalVideoTimeScale* = 60 (the default), the time scale is 1/60th of a second (that is, measured in ticks). Set *the digitalVideoTimeScale* to 0 to use the time scale of the currently playing digital video. *The digitalVideoTimeScale* property will then return 0 (zero), but Director will actually use *the timeScale of member* property as the basis for timing each digital video.

The timeScale of member property is intrinsic to the video format and cannot be changed. For QuickTime movies *the timeScale of member* is 600 (1/600th of a second) on the Macintosh and 30 (1/30th of a second) under Windows. For Video for Windows (AVI files) it is 60 (1/60th of a second).

The *duration of member* and *the movieTime of sprite* are measured in units of "1/ the digitalVideoTimeScale." If *the digitalVideoTimeScale* is, say, 600, those properties are measured in 1/600th of a second, not ticks (1/60th of a second).

Converting Time Units

You will often need to convert between different time units when working with various Lingo commands.

Use floats for your calculations to prevent truncation by integer division. See Chapter 8, *Math (and Gambling)*, for details.

Example 11-4 shows some convenient conversion utilities. See Example 11-6 for a generalized conversion utility.

Example 11-4: Time Unit Conversion Utilities

```
on ticksToSeconds numTicks
  return (numTicks/60.0)
end
```

Example 11-4: Time Unit Conversion Utilities (continued)

```
on secondsToTicks numSeconds
  return (numSeconds * 60)
end

on millisecondsToTicks  numMilliseconds
  return (1000 * numMilliseconds/60.0)
end

on ticksToMilliseconds numTicks
  return (60 * numTicks/1000.0)
end
```

The following could be used when comparing values that use *the digitalVideo-TimeScale* to ones measured in milliseconds. These assume that *the digitalVideoTimeScale* has not been set to 0, in which case *the timeScale of member* property should be used instead, as in Example 11-5.

```
if getLast (the cuePointTimes of member "mySound") > ¬
    DVTSToMillseconds (the duration of member "myVideo) then
  put "Last cue point is after the end of the video."
end if

on DVTSToMillseconds  numInDVTS
  return (the digitalVideoTimeScale * numInDVTS/1000.0)
end

on millisecondsToDVTS  numMilliseconds
  return (1000 * numMilliseconds /¬
          float(the digitalVideoTimeScale))
end
```

Refer to *Example 8-3* in Chapter 8 for utilities that convert minutes to hours.

Frames Per Second to Time

The *framesToHMS()* and *HMStoFrames()* functions convert between frames per seconds and hours, minutes, and seconds. They are designed especially for converting units when using NTSC video whose frame rate is not exactly 30 fps (it is 29.97 fps). But they can be used to convert any units into HH:MM:SS format. Refer to Table 16-1 for details on the format of the arguments and return values of these commands.

This converts the duration of member into *sHH:MM:SS.FFD* format.

Example 11-5: Converting Between Frames to HH:MM:SS

```
on getDVtime dvMember
  if the digitalVideoTimeScale <> 0 then
    set frameRate = the digitalVideoTimeScale
  else
    set frameRate = the timeScale of member dvMember
  end if
```

Example 11-5: Converting Between Frames to HH:MM:SS (continued)

```
    set duration = the duration of member dvMember
    return framesToHMS (duration, frameRate, FALSE, TRUE)
end getDVtime
```

```
put getDVtime ("myVideo")
-- " 00:00:12.80 "
```

Refer to "*Text Parsing*" in Chapter 7, *Strings*, for details on how you might parse the hours, minutes, and seconds from the returned string.

You can estimate the time of your Score (assuming a constant frame rate) as shown in Example 11-6.

Example 11-6: Score Duration and Arbitrary Conversion

```
put framesToHMS (the lastFrame, the frameTempo, FALSE, TRUE)
-- " 00:00:35.70 "
```

You can convert between any two arbitrary units as follows:

```
on convertUnits convertIt, fromUnits, toUnits
    -- Set calculation precision's (significant digits).
    set precision = the floatPrecision ¬
            + length(string(convertIt))
    set temp = framesToHMS (convertIt*precision, ¬
            fromUnits , FALSE, TRUE)
    set answer = HMSToFrames  (temp, toUnits, FALSE, TRUE)
    return  answer / float((60 units per second)precision)
end convertUnits
```

This example converts 400 ticks (60 units per second) to an equivalent number of milliseconds (1000 units per second):

```
put convertUnits (400, 60, 1000)
-- 6667.5000
```

Reader exercise: Rewrite the *convertUnits()* example to accept symbolic values such as #milliseconds, #ticks, #seconds, and #hours for the *fromUnits* and *toUnits* parameters. See the end of the chapter for one possible solution

Date and Time Functions

You might want to know the date and time to create a Projector that expires after a certain date (see Example 11-7) or to provide a different introduction depending on the day of the week. The *date* and *time* are always returned as strings, but their format will vary with the user's configuration and language. Use the *value()* function to convert a portion of the string to an integer.

Date Properties

Both Macintosh and Windows support separate short date and long date formats, which are used by Director's *the short date* and *the long date* properties. Table 11-5 shows the basic date formats. Under Windows 3.1, the date format is

---

set in the *International* control panel and stored in the SYSTEM.INI file. Under Windows 95, it is configured using the *Date* tab of the *Regional Settings* control panel (not the *Date/Time* control panel). On the Macintosh, it is configured using the *Date Formats* option in the *Date & Time* control panel.

Table 11-5: Date Formats

Date Command	Format Depends on	Typical U.S. Example
the date the short date	OS's short date setting, such as MM/DD/YY	12/05/97
the abbr date the abbrev date the abbreviated date	OS's long date setting with abbreviated month name and weekday	Fri, Dec 05, 1997
the long date	OS's long date setting	Friday, December 05, 1997

Date Formats and Y2K

The user may have changed the style of the date formats including the order of the fields within each format. Moreover, the default format varies for different countries and languages.

 You should not rely on a specific date format when parsing the system date.

To accurately determine the day, month, and year, you must account for the user's chosen format, country, and language. You can't rely on a specific field order, nor a specific date delimiter. See *http://www.zeusprod.com/chapters/datetime.html* for details. The unsupported UI Helper Xtra included with D6.5 includes a *getDate()* function that returns the current year, month, and day in a list.

```
put getDate
-- [98, 5, 28]
```

 With the year 2000 ("*Y2K*") upon us, you should handle the turn of the century gracefully. Below I assume that a two-digit year greater than 50 is in the range 1951 and 1999 and years below 51 are in the range 2000 through 2050.

Example 11-7 can be used to create a Projector that expires on a given date. It requires the UI Helper Xtra. The downloadable examples (*http://www.zeusprod.com/nutshell/examples.html*) include a Lingo-only solution that attempts to determine the user's system date, but an Xtra that returns the system date in a known format is the only foolproof solution.

Example 11-7: Projector Expiration and Y2K

```
on startMovie
  set expire = FALSE
  set year  = getAt(getDate(), 1)
  if year > 50 then
    set year = year + 1900
  else
    set year = year + 2000
  end if
  set month = getAt(getDate(),2)
  set day   = getAt(getDate(),3)
  -- Set the Expiration date.
  set expireYear = 1998
  set expireMonth = 6
  set expireDay = 9
  -- Comparing dates is non-trivial!
  if year > expireYear then
    set expire = TRUE
  else if year = expireYear then
    if month > expireMonth then
      set expire = TRUE
    else if month = expireMonth and day >= expireDay then
      set expire = TRUE
    end if
  end if
  if expire = TRUE then
    alert "Sorry, this program expired June 9, 1998."
    halt
  end if
end
```

The UI Helper Xtra is not supported under Windows 3.1 and doesn't return the century. Penworks DateMaster Xtra (*http://www.penworks.com*) returns the date (inculding the century) in a known format, converts between Julian and Gregorian dates, checks for valid dates and leap years, and returns the weekday.

See also the DateTime Xtra (*http://www.scirius.com*) or the *OSutil* Xtra's (*http:// www.ddce.cqu.edu.au/imu/tools/Director/Xtras*) *OSConstDate* method. The *Buddy API* Xtra (*http://www.mods.com.au/budapi*) will return the date of a Windows file.

Time Formats

Directors *the time* property returns the current hours and minutes, and *the long time* property includes seconds as well. Table 11-6 shows the basic time formats. Director for Windows ignores the time format setting under the *Time* tab of Windows 95's *Regional Settings* control panel; it always uses a standard format for the time. Director for Macintosh obeys the time format specified via the *Time Formats* option in the *Date & Time* control panel.

Table 11-6: Time Formats

Time Command	Format	Example
the time[1,2,3] the abbr time the abbrev time the abbreviated time the short time	*HH:MM tt*	06:09 PM
the long time[4]	*HH:MM:SS tt*	06:09:59 AM

[1] *HH* = one- or two-digit hours from 01 to 12, or 00 to 24, depending on user preferences.
[2] *MM* = two-digit minutes (00 to 59).
[3] *tt* = AM or PM, or EMPTY, depending on user preferences.
[4] *SS* = two-digits seconds (00 to 59).

Parsing the Time

The user can change the time formats, and the default format varies for different countries and languages. See *http://www.zeusprod.com/chapters/datetime.html* for details. The downloadable example files include a Lingo-only solution that attempts to determine the user's system time, but an Xtra that returns the system time in a known format is the only foolproof solution. (Refer to the date Xtras cited previously; some of them also return the system time in a known format.)

Timing Utilities

Timers can be used to track user response times, analyze performance, or limit the time spent on an activity, as discussed below. See Chapter 9, *Perfomance and Memory*, in *Director in a Nutshell* for optimization tips.

Gauging Performance

Use the type of loop shown in Example 11-8 to gauge Lingo's performance when trying to optimize your code. For an accurate test, perform the operation enough times, such as 1000, to last a few seconds.

Example 11-8: Timing Performance

```
on testSpeed
  startTimer
  repeat with x = 1 to 1000
    -- Test performance of something in here....
    set dummy = 5
  end repeat
  put "The test took" && the timer && "ticks"
end
```

Don't include *put* statements within your timing loop as they are very slow and will distort your results. If necessary, store results in a variable and print them out later.

Stop Watch Timer Object

Example 11-9 is a stop watch object and a test script showing its usage. See Chapter 12 for details on object-oriented Scripting.

Here is the *Stop Watch Object* Parent Script:

```
property pLastElapsedTime, pRunning, pRunningTime

on new me
  resetStopWatch (me)
  set pRunning = FALSE
  return me
end new

on resetStopWatch me
  set pLastElapsedTime = 0
  set pRunningTime = the ticks
end resetStopWatch

on startStopWatch me
  if not pRunning then
    -- If not already running, record the start time
    set pRunningTime = the ticks
    set pRunning = TRUE
  end if
end startStopWatch

on stopStopWatch me
  if pRunning then
    -- If not already stopped, increment the elapsed time
    set pLastElapsedTime = (the ticks - pRunningTime) ¬
        + pLastElapsedTime
    set pRunning = FALSE
  end if
end stopStopWatch

on reportElapsedTime me
  if pRunning then
    set tickTime = pLastElapsedTime + ¬
        (the ticks - pRunningTime)
  else
    set tickTime = pLastElapsedTime
  end if
  -- Report is in seconds
  return (tickTime/60.0)
end reportElapsedTime

on isWatchRunning me
  return pRunning
```

```
      end isWatchRunning
```

Example 11-9: Stop Watch Timer

```
-- Test the StopWatch child object
on testStopWatch
  set watch1 = new (script "Stop Watch Object")
  startStopWatch (watch1)
  put "isWatchRunning" && isWatchRunning(watch1)
  stopStopWatch (watch1)
  put "Elapsed Seconds:" && reportElapsedTime (watch1)
end testStopWatch
```

And You Thought I Forgot

Here is one possible solution to the reader quiz in Example 11-6. What happens in the example below if the user passes in integer values instead of symbols? What happens if the symbols are invalid?

Example 11-10: Symbolic Version of Conversion Utility

```
on convertSymbolicUnits convertIt, fromUnits, toUnits
  -- Each property is converted to units per second
  set timeList = [#milliseconds:1000, #ticks:60, ¬
                  #seconds:1, #minutes:1.0/60, #hours:1.0/(60*60)]
  -- Get the numeric equivalent of the symbol
  if symbolP(fromUnits) then
    set fromUnits = getProp (timeList, fromUnits)
  end if
  if symbolP(toUnits) then
    set toUnits = getProp (timeList, toUnits)
  end if
  -- Set the calculation precision (significant digits)
  Set precision = the floatPrecision + length(string(convertIt))
  set temp = framesToHMS (convertIt*precision, ¬
          fromUnits, FALSE, TRUE)
  set answer = HMStoFrames (temp, toUnits, FALSE, TRUE)
  return  answer / float(precision)
end convertSymbolicUnits

put convertSymbolicUnits (400, #ticks, #seconds)
-- 6.7500
```

Asynchronous Operations

This chapter has been primarily concerned with issues of timing and synchronization. When using Shockwave or preloading media, an operation may not complete immediately. You must initiate the operation and then check periodically whether it has completed, using, say, *netDone()* or *mediaReady()*. Refer to Chapter 9, *Memory and Performance*, and Chapter 11, *Shockwave and the Internet,* in *Director in a Nutshell* for more information on asynchronous operations such as idle loading, preloading, and downloading.

PART IV

Applied Lingo

CHAPTER 12

Behaviors and Parent Scripts

The term *Behavior* is used loosely to describe several different types of Lingo scripts. For now, think of Behaviors as score scripts that are easy to customize, even by novices. Macromedia provides a slew of Behaviors under Xtras ➤Behavior Library. Refer to the *Behaviors* Show Me demo movie in the online Help to learn the basics of applying existing Behaviors. See Chapter 5, *Creating Interactivity,* in Macromedia's *Using Director* manual for an overview of the available Behaviors. Macromedia also provides numerous *widgets* (premade UI components) and buttons that use Behaviors to create sprites with complex functionality. See Xtras➤Widget Wizard➤Widget Wizard and Xtras➤Widget Wizard➤Button Library. Refer to Chapter 14, *Graphical User Interface Components,* in *Director in a Nutshell* for a detailed example of using premade widgets and Behaviors.

The *Lingo Behavior Database* is a collection of Behaviors maintained by Renfield Kuroda at *http://www.behaviors.com/lbd/*.

Search the Macromedia site for Technote 08140 for possible ways to distribute protected Behaviors. Refer to the downloadable examples (*http://www.zeusprod. com/nutshell/examples.html*) for a detailed Behavior that simulates the Tempo channel for use in Shockwave (which doesn't obey the Tempo settings).

What Is a Behavior?

The simplest (non-configurable) Behaviors are exactly like Director 5-style score scripts attached to either a sprite or the script channel. To add a "beep-when-clicked" Behavior to a sprite, you can use the simple script.

Example 12-1: A Ludicrously Simple Behavior

```
on mouseDown
  beep
end
```

Even such plain vanilla Director 5-style score scripts appear in the Behavior Inspector. For the remainder of this chapter the terms *score script* and *Behavior* will be used interchangeably.

 Director 6 allows each sprite to have multiple Behaviors attached. Although only one Behavior can be attached to each frame in the script channel, you can attach an *on exitFrame* handler to a *sprite* channel to emulate multiple frame scripts.

Support for multiple scripts per sprite allows you to *modularize* your scripts into smaller pieces and attach more scripts as needed. For example, suppose two sprites have the same *mouseEnter* response but different *mouseDown* responses. You could attach the same *on mouseEnter* Behavior to both sprites and then add separate *on mouseDown* Behaviors to each. If their *mouseDown* responses are similar (perhaps differing only in the sound to be played on *mouseDown*), a single customizable Behavior could be written to handle *mouseDown* events for both sprites.

A Behavior can be thought of as a score script with easily customizable attributes, such as which sound to play when an event occurs. They can also be thought of as Parent scripts attached to sprites. Behaviors are instantiated when the playback head enters the sprite span to which they are attached. The custom properties for each instance are stored with the Score data and read back at runtime.

A Behavior's properties persist for the life of the sprite, and Behaviors can access any property of any other Behavior attached to the same sprite using:

```
the property of sprite (the spriteNum of me)
```

Creating Simple Behaviors

The Behavior Inspector can be used as a simple Behavior *Constructor*. Refer again to Chapter 5 in Macromedia's *Using Director* and the *Behaviors* Show Me demo movie.

Example 12-2: Writing Simple Scripts Via the Behavior Inspector

To watch Director construct the script as you select *Events* and *Actions* to add:

1. Open the Behavior Inspector using the "*" key on the numeric keypad or Window▶Inspectors▶Behavior.

2. Click the *Edit Pane Expander* (see Figure 12-1) to expand the editing pane.

3. Select *New Behavior* from the *Behavior* popup, and name the Behavior.

Example 12-2: Writing Simple Scripts Via the Behavior Inspector (continued)

4. Open the Script window using the *Script* button at the top of the Inspector.

5. Use the *Events* popup and *Actions* popup to build your script.

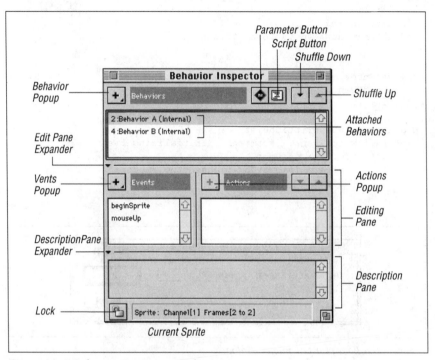

Figure 12-1: Behavior Inspector window

The Behavior Inspector doesn't create true *"Behaviorized"* scripts with all the fancy attributes of Behaviors. It just helps novices to create basic score scripts without typing in the Script window. A true Director 6-savvy Behavior usually has user-defined properties and a minimal help string to explain its use.

 Roy Pardi offers a *Behavior Writer Xtra* to ease *some* of the mechanics of writing your own Behaviors. See *http://www.tiac.net/users/rpardi/behaviorwriter/*.

Let's create a Behaviorized version of the beeping button script shown earlier. When the Behavior—shown in Example 12-3 is attached to a sprite Director uses the property list returned by *ongetPropertyDescriptionList()* to create a dialog (see Figure 12-2) that lets the user customize the Behavior. From the dialog, the developer can choose which type of mouse event triggers the beep.

Example 12-3: A simplified beeping Behavior

```
property whichEvent
on mouseUp me
   if whichEvent = #mouseUp     then beep
end

on mouseDown me
   if whichEvent = #mouseDown   then beep
end

on mouseEnter me
   if whichEvent = #mouseEnter then beep
end

on getPropertyDescriptionList
   return [#whichEvent: [#comment: "Initializing Event:", ¬
           #format:  #symbol, ¬
           #range:   [#mouseUp, #mouseDown, #mouseEnter], ¬
           #default: #MouseUp]]
end
```

Parameters for "Beep! Beep!"

Initializing Event: mouseUp ▼   OK   Cancel

Figure 12-2: Behavior parameter dialog

Even this simplified Behavior is much more complicated than a standard sprite script, and it still just creates a beep! (Macromedia's Behavior Library includes an even more complicated *Sound Beep* Behavior).

In this case, the dialog includes a pop-up menu with three possible values for the *whichEvent* property (*#mouseUp*, *#mouseDown*, and *#mouseEnter*), as defined in the *#range* attribute of the *#whichEvent* property. At runtime, the Behavior beeps if the mouse event (such as *mouseDown*) matches the trigger event chosen for *whichEvent*.

This may seem a poor candidate for a Behavior because it complicates a very simple script. Behaviors, however, allow a novice to add *customized* behaviors without Lingo scripting.

 Behaviors are sometimes hard to create and ugly to read, but easy to use.

Using the Behavior Inspector

Apply existing Behaviors by dragging them from the Cast window to a sprite or the script channel, or by using the *Behavior Script* popup in the Sprite Toolbar or Sprite Inspector. A Behavior's *scriptType of member* property must be *#score*, not *#movie* or *#parent*, or it will not appear in Behavior Inspector. If you open the Behavior Library, its scripts show up in the Behavior popup, too.

Open the Behavior Inspector using the "*" key on the numeric keypad or Window ▶Inspectors▶Behavior.

If View▶Sprite Overlay▶Show Info is active, you can open the Behavior Inspector using the little green icon that appears next to the selected sprite on the Stage.

Behaviors, Parent Scripts

You can add your own Behavior Libraries to the ones under the Xtras menu, as described in Chapter 4, *CastLibs, Cast Members, and Sprites,* in *Director in a Nutshell* (add "*Library*" to the cast name and drop it in the Xtras folder).

If you are a novice using other people's Behaviors, set File▶Preferences ▶Editors▶Behaviors to edit scripts in the Behavior Inspector, the Script window. *See "Where the Hell Are My Scripts?"* and Table 2-2 in Chapter 2, *Events, Messages, and Scripts.*

Inside the Behavior Inspector

The Behavior Inspector is very malleable. Use the *Edit Pane Expander* and *Description Pane Expander* buttons (see Figure 12-1) to customize it to your liking.

The *Lock Selection* button prevents the Behavior list from changing if the Score selection changes.

The repertoire of *Actions* for automatic script construction is very limited, but it gives you a basic feel for Lingo scripting. The *Wait until Click or Key Press* Action creates incorrect Lingo code (*puppetTempo -8*), and should not be used.

When a Behavior is applied to a sprite or frame, you will be prompted to customize its properties, if applicable.

To change its properties *after* a Behavior has been attached to the Score, use the *Parameter* button in the Behavior Inspector.

To use the *Parameter* Button:

*   Highlight a sprite or frame with a Behavior attached, then highlight the desired Behavior in the Behavior Inspector.

- At least one property must be declared with the *property* keyword at the top of a Behavior script, or the *Parameters* button will be inactive.

- A Behavior must declare an *on getPropertyDescriptionList* handler, or the *Parameters* button will have no effect.

Behavior Inspector Pitfalls

Selecting the frame script channel and then creating a new Behavior using the Behavior Inspector will create a script in the cast, but it will not appear in the Score until dragged there. (If you highlight a sprite and create a Behavior, it will be attached automatically.)

You can add Behaviors to multiple selected sprites. If multiple sprites are selected, deleting a Behavior via the Behavior inspector deletes it from only the *first* sprite selected. Choose *Clear Script* from the script popup in the Sprite Toolbar or Sprite Inspector to clear all scripts from multiple sprites.

Behaviors and their properties persist only for the life of the sprite to which they are attached. Use global variables or parent scripts for more persistent data.

Objects of Mystery

Now that some of the mystery has been dispelled about Behaviors, let's discuss their cousins, parent scripts. I'll show you why, when, and how to use *Object-Oriented Programming* (OOP). Once you are introduced to the concepts, I'll then cover the terminology in more detail (refer also to the *Glossary*). Finally, I'll cover some practical examples. When you finish this chapter you'll realize that the "Great and Powerful Oz" is just some guy behind a curtain. So take a deep breath, repeat after me ("Parent scripts, child objects and Behaviors, oh my!"), and soon you'll be more at home with OOP than Dorothy was in Kansas.

For a comparison of object-oriented Lingo with C++, refer to Table 4-1 in Chapter 4, *Lingo Internals,* and see the downloadable Chapter 20, *Lingo for C Programmers.* Read Chapter 12, *Parent Scripts and Child Objects,* in Macromedia's *Learning Director* manual for another perspective on object-oriented programming. Refer also to the *Simple Child Object* and *Multiple Child Objects* Show Me demo movies in the online Help.

A Procedural Stopwatch

Typical Lingo scripting is *procedural* because you create *procedures* (*functions* or *handlers*) to perform a particular task. For example, the *average()* function might average two numbers.

Example 12-4: A Trivial Procedural Example

```
on average a, b
    return (a+b)/2.0
end
```

If a script calls a procedure, the only communication between them is via the value returned by the function to caller.

A function is like a one-night stand. It has a fleeting existence and typically performs a single operation.

Let's create a stopwatch using a procedural approach. The code in Example 12-5 belongs in a movie script. We must use global variables to communicate between the various functions and to maintain the current state of the timer. (This example is *heavily* simplified and not very robust. See Example 11-9 for a robust object-oriented version of this script.) Note that we used the name *runTimer* instead of *startTimer* to prevent conflicts with the Lingo *StartTimer* command.

Example 12-5: A Procedural Stopwatch

```
global gCurrentTime, gStartTime
-- Reset the timer to 0
on resetTimer
  set gCurrentTime = 0
end resetTimer

-- Start the timer running
on runTimer
  set gStartTime = the ticks
end runTimer

-- Stop the timer (assumes timer was running)
on stopTimer
  set gCurrentTime = (the ticks - gStartTime)
end stopTimer

-- Report the timer's value (assumes timer is stopped)
on reportTimer
  return (gCurrentTime/60.0)
end reportTimer
```

We could use our stopwatch to check how long Lingo takes to print out the numbers: from 1 to 100

```
    -- Test the timer functions
    on testTimer
      resetTimer
      runTimer
      repeat with x = 1 to 100
        put x
      end repeat
      stopTimer
      put reportTimer()
    end testTimer
```

This procedural approach is adequate for a single timer, but we would need to create additional global variables to avoid conflicts between multiple timers.

Object-Oriented Programming

Let's dive right in and create an *object-oriented programming* (OOP) version of our stopwatch. OOP is ideal because we can build a timer *object* (a reusable template), and create multiple *instances* (clones) of it that operate independently. Each instance can maintain its own *properties*, which are semi-private variables, as described in Chapter 1, *How Lingo Thinks*.

 Lingo allows you to mix procedural and object-oriented programming. Some people go overboard and turn everything into an object. Use whatever is best for a given situation.

An *object* (that is, a copy of a script) can contain several *methods* (handlers) to perform its desired actions. For example, a Timer object might behave like a stopwatch with four buttons (*resetTimer*, *runTimer*, *stopTimer*, and *reportTimer*), each implemented by a different method. An object's methods are stored in a template called a *parent script*. You don't ordinarily use the template directly; you use a copy or *instance* of the template in the form of a child object. This allows you to create multiple independent copies.

 You can use parent scripts as semi-private code libraries without the risks of naming conflicts associated with handlers in movie scripts. A handler named *StartTimer* inside an object would *not* conflict with the Lingo *StartTimer* command because they have differing scopes. See "Handler Scope" in Chapter 2.

Although unusual, instead of instantiating a parent script, you can access its handlers as:

```
set variable = someHandler (script "ParentScript", args)
```

You can even access a parent script's properties *without* instantiating it.

The Life and Death of an Object

The terminology required for objected-oriented programming can be summed up in a few sentences. Some of the terminology is redundant or used loosely. (Refer to the *Glossary* for complete definitions of each term used in this chapter.) Click your ruby slippers together as you repeat three times:

 A *parent script* defines the *properties* (attributes) and *methods* (functions) of an *object*. A *child object* is an *instance* (copy or clone) of the parent script and is *instantiated* (created) using the *new()* method. An object is disposed of when no variables refer to it.

Let's look at all this in more detail.

Creating a Parent Script

Example 12-6: Creating a Child Object from a Parent Script

To create a child object from a parent script:

1. Create a script cast member to hold the parent script (it is convenient to name the cast member, too). Use the popup in its cast member info window to set its type to *Parent*, or set its *scriptType of member* to *#parent*.

2. Write the Lingo methods for the *parent script* as shown later. You'll need an *on new* method and other optional methods.

3. In a *separate* script (or the Message window) *instantiate* (create an instance of) the parent script using the *new()* function, and store the instance in some variable.

4. Use the instance (the **child** object) created above to call the other methods in the object. Because you specify the child object when calling other methods, Director knows which instance's properties and methods to use.

Behaviors,
Parent Scripts

A Very Simple Parent Script

Here is a very simple parent script. It defines one property and only one method (*crying*) besides the *on new* method.

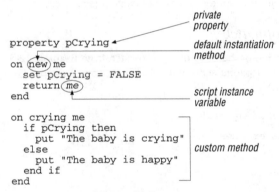

```
property pCrying

on new me
  set pCrying = FALSE
  return me
end

on crying me
  if pCrying then
    put "The baby is crying"
  else
    put "The baby is happy"
  end if
end
```

private property

default instantiation method

script instance variable

custom method

Figure 12-3: Anatomy of a Parent script

If the *on new* handler is omitted, Director uses a default *on new* handler that just returns the child object instance variable (*me*) such as:

```
on new me
   return me
end
```

If the earlier parent script is in a cast member named "Mommy," you can create and manipulate a child object, such as shown in Example 12-7.

Example 12-7: Instantiating and Using a Child Object

```
set baby = new (script "Mommy")
crying(baby)
-- "The baby is happy"
set the pCrying of baby = TRUE
crying(baby)
-- "The baby is crying"
```

You can create as many children as you like, and each can have its own *pCrying*
property.

 If you don't store the returned *child object instance* (in this case, into
the variable *baby*) there is little point in instantiating the object
because you won't be able to refer to it later. In fact, it will be disposed of immediately.

Whereas a single child object instance may be stored in a global variable, related
child object instances are commonly stored in global lists for later use:

```
global gChildList
if not listP(gChildList) then set gChildList = []
addAt (gChildList, new (script "Mommy"))
```

Using a single global list reduces the number of variables needed. Furthermore
each instance can be used to access all the properties of each object.

An Object-Oriented Stopwatch

Here is an object-oriented version of the procedural stopwatch from Example 12-5.
This Lingo should be placed in a parent script named "Timer." (See Example 11-9
for a more robust timer object.)

Example 12-8: An Object-Oriented Stopwatch

```
property pCurrentTime, pStartTime

on new me
  return me
end

-- Reset the timer to 0
on resetTimer me
  set pCurrentTime = 0
end resetTimer

-- Start the timer running
on runTimer me
  set pStartTime = the ticks
end runTimer

-- Stop the timer (assumes timer was running)
```

Example 12-8: An Object-Oriented Stopwatch (continued)

```
on stopTimer me
  set pCurrentTime = (the ticks - pStartTime)
end stopTimer

-- Report the timer's value (assumes timer is stopped)
on reportTimer me
  return (pCurrentTime/60.0)
end reportTimer
```

Note these differences from the procedural version in Example 12-5:

- *Property* variables (beginning with the letter "p" for clarity) are used instead of *global* variables. Properties are declared with the keyword *property*, and can contain a different value for each instance of the object (that is, each timer). If we used globals, multiple timers would trample the values held in the globals.

- We added an *on new* method that will be used to instantiate the object.

- The variable *me* indicates the current instance of the child object. It is returned by *new()* when the child object is created and is typically stored in some variable by the caller. It is then used when calling other methods to identify the child object, so that Director can retrieve its properties rather than the properties of some other instance.

We can test the Timer as shown in Example 12-9. It creates two separate instances of the Timer object. The first one times the overall operation, and the second one times the inner repeat loop.

Example 12-9: Testing a Timer Object

```
-- Test the Timer child object
on testTimerObj
  -- Instantiate two timers
  set timer1 = new (script "Timer")
  set timer2 = new (script "Timer")
  -- Start timer1 running
  resetTimer (timer1)
  runTimer (timer1)

  put "Testing the speed of the repeat loop"
  repeat with y = 1 to 10
    -- Start timer2 running
    resetTimer (timer2)
    runTimer (timer2)

    repeat with x = 1 to 1000
      set dummy = 5
    end repeat
    -- Pause and read timer2
    stopTimer (timer2)
    put "1000 Iterations took" && reportTimer(timer2) && "seconds"
  end repeat
```

Example 12-9: Testing a Timer Object (continued)

```
  -- Pause and read timer1
  stopTimer (timer1)
  put "The whole test took" && reportTimer(timer1) && "seconds"
  -- Dispose of timer objects by setting them to zero
  set timer1 = 0
  set timer2 = 0
end testTimerObj
```

Note that we could instantiate dozens of timers without any conflicts or need for multiple global variables. Each timer maintains its own set of properties.

I Gotta Be Me

Director uses the *me* variable to refer to a child object instance within the parent script itself. See also *"Script Instances"* in Chapter 2.

Enter Example 12-10 this into a parent script called "Eden."

Example 12-10: Paradise Lost? Not as Lost as the Reader!

```
property pGender
property pName
property pKnowledge

on new me, gender, name
  set pGender    = gender
  set pName      = name
  set pKnowledge = FALSE
  return me
end

on eatApple me
  set pKnowledge = TRUE
end

on getKnowledge me
  return pKnowledge
end

on ShowInfo me
  put pName && "is" && pGender
end

on GetName me
  return pName
end

on getGender me
  return pGender
end

on testKnowledge me
  if pKnowledge then
```

Example 12-10: Paradise Lost? Not as Lost as the Reader! (continued)

```
    put pName && "is banished"
  else
    put pName && "is innocent"
  end if
end
```

Test it in the Message window. Note that the arguments to the *new()* function call are used to initialize properties for that particular object.

```
set edenList = []
add edenList, (script "Eden", #male,    "Adam")
add edenList, new (script "Eden", #female, "Eve")
```

When calling *ShowInfo()* we specify an object from our *edenList*:

```
showInfo(getAt(edenList,1))
-- "Adam is male"
showInfo(getAt(edenList,2))
-- "Eve is female"
```

When we call *eatApple()*, we again specify a child object instance. We need not be aware what it does internally.

```
eatApple (getAt(edenList,2))

testKnowledge (getAt(edenList,1))
-- Adam is innocent
testKnowledge (getAt(edenList,2))
-- Eve is banished
```

Notice that we indirectly set and accessed the *pKnowledge* property from outside the parent script without even knowing it! The object handles the details for us! One can access any property of an object from *outside* the object, using:

```
put the property of object
```

 OOP purists will insist that you should never directly access a property of an object from outside the object. You should instead access them only via accessor methods, such as *getName()* and *get-Gender()* in Example 12-10.

An accessor method simply returns the value of a property of the object, allowing us to write:

```
getName (getAt(edenList,1))
-- Adam
```

Thus we have not violated the *encapsulation* of the child object. The *getName()* method can be changed without breaking any outside code. Any code that uses the accessor method will continue to work.

Common Errors with Parent-Child Scripting

There are several common errors you will surely commit.

Omitting return me at the end of your on new handler:
> Without *me*, a child object instance will not be returned, and the caller will get a meaningless value.

Omitting me when declaring other methods, such as on eatApple me:
> Without *me*, you won't be able to set a child object's properties, such as Knowledge from within the method.

Not storing the child object instance returned by the new() call:
> Unless you store the return value, you won't be able to access the object later (in fact, the instance will be disposed of if nothing references it).

Failing to assign values to the properties:
> You can either assign properties in the *new()* method or use a separate *init()* method to allow for reinitialization without reinstantiation.

Trying to access a method within an object without first calling new():
> You generally should instantiate the object using *new()* before calling its other methods. *New()* accepts a *parent script* as the first argument. All other methods accept a *child instance* as the first argument, such as:

```
set childObj = new (script "parentScript")
someMethod (childObj)
```

> If you decline to instantiate the object first, as described in the tip under "Object-Oriented Programming" earlier in this chapter, you are manipulating the properties of the parent script itself, and not of a child object.

Creating a parent script with type #movie:
> Lingo doesn't complain if your parent scripts are of type *#movie*, but the handlers in movie scripts have global scope, which can lead to conflicts or handlers being run unintentionally. If the parent script's type is *#score*, it will inadvertently appear in the script popup in the Sprite Toolbar. (Note that a Behavior's script type should be *#score* for this very reason.)

When to Use Object-Oriented Programming

Parent scripts and child objects have the hallmarks of a long-term relationship. Objects are created manually, tend to shun outsiders, and persist until disposed.

Parent-child scripting is generally a good idea to accomplish the following:

- Create objects that are defined by the current state of their properties, such as timers. An object remembers its own state (i.e., properties) and is therefore much easier to use and maintain without global variables.

- Create objects that persist over time or that require multiple operations. For example, the FileIO Xtra is just an object written in C. It allows you to manipulate external text files (via methods, just like a child object), including the ability to open, read, write, delete, search, and close the file. The object keeps track of the properties, including the file's name and the location and the last position read within the file.

- Create code that is independent of other code. Objects are *encapsulated* (insulated) so that they can be developed separately from other code. Other Lingo primarily interacts with objects via the defined methods. Although this can simplify development and maintenance of some projects, it is not the panacea some people claim it to be.

- Create classes of objects in a hierarchy. Objects can *inherit* behaviors from *ancestors*, allowing you to create a tree of related objects. For example, a family tree of birds and reptiles may share a common ancestor that has an *egg-Laying* method.

 Two objects created from different Behaviors or parent scripts can both have *methods* of the same name that do completely different things.

You can send a single message to multiple objects without knowledge of their internal operation. Each object will respond appropriately, allowing you to deal with differing objects in a uniform way. Refer to "The ActorList" discussed later.

When to Use Behaviors

Behaviors are appropriate when you want a sprite or group of sprites to respond to Director and user events in a certain way. They can be attached to the script channel as well.

 Behaviors are like casual dating. A Behavior can be attached to multiple sprite or frames, and a sprite can have multiple Behaviors attached. A Behavior is automatically associated with the sprite to which it is attached, and its lifespan coincides with that of the sprite span.

You should use Behaviors for multiple items with similar properties, such as bouncing balls or space aliens. Although all instances of the object would be intrinsically similar, they can have significantly different values for each property of the object. For example, a ball's properties may include speed, acceleration, diameter, mass, elasticity, and color. Example 8-14 is a sample Behavior that moves a sprite along an elliptical path. The user can specify the foci and major and minor axes of the ellipse.

Child Object References

When you create or use a child object, Director keeps track of how many *references* there are to that object (how many things use it).

An object reference takes the form:

```
<offspring "parentScriptName" referenceCount IDnumber>
```

If you create an object without storing the return value, the *referenceCount* is just one (the object refers to itself long enough to print in the Message window).

Example 12-11: Child Object References

```
put new (script "parent script")
-- <offspring "parent script" 1 27c252a>
```

Because you made no record of the object, it will be disposed of at Director's whim. When you create an object and store the return value, Director increments the *referenceCount* to 2 because a variable now refers to it as well:

```
set myChild = new (script "parent script")
put myChild
-- <offspring "parent script" 2 27c24f8>
```

Note that a new *IDnumber* was assigned, and this object has no relation to the previously created object.

Now assign a new variable to the existing object:

```
set newVariable = myChild
put myChild
-- <offspring "parent script" 3 27c2548>
```

Note that the *referenceCount* has increased, but the *IDnumber* has stayed the same. When you are done with an object, set any variables that use it to 0. When no variables or lists refer to an object, Director will dispose of it.

```
set myChild = 0
set newVariable = 0
```

There is *no* built-in Lingo to determine the following at runtime:

- A list of objects that currently exist. You need to store the objects as you create them, usually in a list.

- A list of objects derived from a given parent script or the parent script of a given object.

- The number of variables that reference a given object, or what particular variables reference a given object. Short of clearing all global variables, there is no way to clear references to a particular object to ensure that it is released.

 You can create a root ancestor for all parent scripts that logs each child object created. You would also explicitly call a *destroy* method to remove the object from the global list.

The unsupported UIHelper Xtra (included with D6.5's *Save as Java* Xtra) has two methods that read Behavior references and their property settings. These are *unsupported*:

getBehaviorMemRef (spriteNum, nthBehaviorNum)

The function returns the script member number of the *nthBehaviorNum* attached to *spriteNum* in the current frame.

getBehaviorInitializers (spriteNum, nthBehaviorNum)

The function returns the user-specified values for the properties of the *nthBehaviorNum* attached to *spriteNum* in the current frame. These are the settings entered in the *Parameters* dialog created via *getProperty-DescriptionList()*.

You can use an object's *on new* handler to set properties that may help track the information previously discussed. For example, you could set a property called *pParent* that contained the name of the parent script from which the object was being created. You can also use the *string()* function to convert the object reference into a string, then try to parse that for the parent script name and *referenceCount*. But the act of passing in the object reference and trying to parse it increases the *referenceCount*.

 Avoid having an object refer to itself. An object with a property that contains a reference to the object itself will never be released from memory unless you specifically clear the property to "break the chain".

Child Object Properties

Although child objects themselves are not identical to property lists, the properties of a child object can be extracted using the property list functions, such as *count()*, *getAt()*, *getPropAt()*, and *setaProp()*. Refer to Example 12-10 and the *read-Props()* utility in Example 6-19 of Chapter 6, *Lists*, that will extract an object's properties.

Example 12-12: Reading Properties of Child Objects

```
set gAdam = new (script "Eden", #male, "Adam", FALSE)
readProps (gAdam)
-- "This #instance has 3 properties"
-- "#pGender: male"
-- "#pName: Adam"
-- "#pKnowledge: 0"
```

To determine the value of any property associated with any Behavior attached to a sprite, you can use:

```
put the property of sprite whichSprite
```

For example, assuming sprite 3 has the "Eden" script attached from Example 12-10:

```
put the pName of sprite 3
-- "Adam"
```

If more than one attached Behavior contains the same property, the value will be returned for the first Behavior found with the specified property. If you want to get a property of a specific Behavior, you can extract it from *the scriptInstanceList*, which contains a list of attached Behavior script instances.

```
put the pName of getAt (the scriptInstanceList of sprite 3, 2)
-- "Eve"
```

You can use global variables instead of properties to create values that are common across all instances of an object. Of course, the global will be universal throughout the entire movie, as would any global.

Behaviors versus Other Script Types

Now that you understand a bit about objects, let's revisit Behaviors. Ironically, Behaviors are most useful to users at opposite ends of the spectrum. Beginners can use prewritten Behaviors without understanding their inner workings, and experts can create their own powerful Behaviors. I'll assume you are somewhere in between and that most of the Behaviors in the Behavior Library are too simple for your needs, yet you have no idea how to construct your own Behavior or even when you should try.

What Is a Behavior Script?

When I first used Behaviors I thought of them as parent (that is, object-oriented) scripts tied to a sprite or frame. Now that I've used them for a while, I think of them as instantiated score scripts. Table 12-1 shows some important differences among these three types of scripts. For the purposes of this table, the term *score script* refers to simple Director 5 style score scripts (In D6, a score script is a Behavior is a score script.)

Table 12-1: Behaviors, Score Scripts, and Parent Scripts

Type	Instantiated?	Attached to	Script Type	User-configurable Properties?	Easy to Write?	Easy to Use?
Score Script	Yes[1]	Sprite or Frame	#score	No	Easiest	Medium
Behavior	Yes[1]	Sprite or Frame	#score	Usually	Hardest	Easiest
Parent Script	Manually[2]	Nothing	#parent	No	Medium	Hardest

[1] All score scripts are instantiated automatically by Director 6 when the sprite or frame to which they are attached is encountered, even though they might not have any properties.
[2] Parent scripts are manually instantiated by the programmer using *new()*.

Differences Among Behaviors, Sprite Scripts, and Frame Scripts

Behaviors are technically a type of score script. Like all score scripts, they are treated as either frame scripts or sprite script depending on whether they are attached to the script channel or a sprite channel. When designed to be attached

---

to a sprite, they predominantly respond to sprite-related events, such as *mouseUp*. When designed to be attached to a frame, they predominantly respond to frame-related events, such as *exitFrame*.

Differences Between Behaviors and Parent Scripts

Parent scripts and Behaviors are both object-oriented scripts. When a parent script or Behavior is used, Director creates an *instance* of it, which can be thought of as a copy, or clone, with its own set of values for each property (attribute).

Object-oriented means that the script acts as a template for a living, breathing entity with a life of its own. When a parent script is instantiated, a new child object is spawned. The child object owes it creation to the original parent script, yet it operates independently from the parent script and from any other siblings created from the same parent.

A Behavior is like a parent script that is used in the Score; it also has extra code to create a dialog that allows a user to customize properties easily. When a Behavior is encountered in the Score, Director creates a *script instance* that is analogous to a child object.

 Behaviors are attached to either a sprite or a frame in the Score and created and disposed of automatically by Director when a sprite span begins or ends. They are initialized automatically by Director with the Parameters specified during authoring rather than via an *on new* handler.

Child objects of Parent scripts are created and disposed of manually by the programmer and aren't tied to sprites or frames. The association between a Behavior and the frame or sprite to which it is attached is *automatic*.

Use Behaviors to add some functionality to an entity in the Score. Suppose you want to alert the user whenever they are inactive for five minutes. You can either attach an appropriate timeout Behavior to the frame or to the sprite used as a prompt. When the timeout occurs, change the sprite prompt or play an audio warning.

Behaviors require the programmer to do *more* work, but the user to do *less* work. When creating a Behavior, you must specify all the information that Director needs to create a dialog box that prompts the user for the necessary properties.

Anatomy of a Behavior

Behaviors don't *require* anything beyond what is in any other sprite script or frame script. A sprite Behavior may perform any initialization in an *on beginSprite* handler and often traps mouse events using mouse handlers, such as *on mouseUp*. Frame Behaviors also often perform any initialization in an *on beginSprite* handler and do their remaining work in *on exitFrame* handlers. (Don't perform frame initialization in a *prepareFrame* handler because it is called every frame.)

Handlers in Behaviors automatically receive *me* (which contains a reference to the current script instance) as the first argument. Movie scripts and cast scripts are not instantiated, and their handlers don't receive *me*.

Behaviors often include *getPropertyDescriptionList* and *getBehaviorDescription* methods. The optional *runPropertyDialog* method is less common.

 The *getBehaviorDescription, getPropertyDescriptionList,* and *runPropertyDialog* events are completely unlike standard Director events. They are *not* sent when the movie *is* playing, but they *are* sent when it is *not* playing. *RunPropertyDialog* and *getPropertyDescriptionList* can be called frequently when using the Behavior Inspector, and they can wreak havoc if they do not return a proper list. You should not set breakpoints in these handlers, as it is easy to create an infinite loop. They should call only built-in Lingo commands, and not custom handlers, because at compile time such handlers are not yet valid. You have been warned.

Table 12-2: Behavior-Related Event Handlers

Message	Description
on getBehaviorDescription	Called when the Behavior is highlighted in the Behavior Inspector. The return string appears in the bottom pane of the Behavior Inspector.
on getPropertyDescriptionList	Called when the script is compiled, attached to a sprite or frame, or the *Parameters* button is used in the Behavior Inspector. Also called to retrieve default parameters for use by *on runPropertyDialog.*
on runPropertyDialog	Call whenever the *Parameters* dialog would be displayed. The default property values returned by *on getPropertyDescriptionList* are sent to the *on runPropertyDialog* handler, which can modify them to return a custom list of properties.

The GetBehaviorDescription Method

The *on getBehaviorDescription* method should return a text string describing the Behavior. The Help message is displayed in the Description Pane of the Behavior Inspector. It typically describes the parameters the Behavior accepts and specifies whether it is intended as a sprite script or a frame script.

Example 12-13: The GetBehaviorDescription Method

```
on getBehaviorDescription me
  return "This is some help text"
end
```

The GetPropertyDescriptionList Method

Director uses the *on getPropertyDescriptionList* method to create a dialog box to prompt the user for property settings. The method should return a *property* list of only those properties that are *user-settable* for a given Behavior. For *each* property, specify the property's name, followed by attributes that control its appearance in the dialog box. Example 12-14 shows a sample property list with only one user-settable property. (The *#range* attribute is optional and has two possible formats.)

Example 12-14: The GetPropertyDescriptionList Method

```
on getPropertyDescriptionList me
  set propList = [¬
    #propertyName: ¬
    [#comment: "user prompt", ¬
     #format: dataType, ¬
     {#range: [#min:minValue, #max:maxValue] |¬
             [value1, value2, ...valuen],  ¬}
     #default: defaultValue] ¬
    ]
  return propList
end
```

#propertyName
> The name of the property variable that you want to let the user set. It should also be defined at the top of the Behavior script, using:
>
> `property propertyName`

#comment: "userPrompt"
> The text defined by *#comment* will appear in the dialog box presented to the user. Keep the text short and descriptive.

#format: dataType
> The *#format* entry tells Director what data type the user should be allowed to input. The allowed values are shown in Table 12-3.

#default: defaultValue
> The *#default* entry specifies an initial value for *#propertyName* and should be of the type specified by *#format*. The *#default* can be set to a variable's name that will be evaluated at runtime.

#range
> The optional *#range* entry can be *either* a linear list of enumerated values (which will appear as a pop-up menu) or a property list specifying a *#min* and *#max* range.

 The *getPropertyDescriptionList* example in Director's online Help does *not* document the *#range* entry. It is also missing a comma after #fieldNum in the line "addProp description, #field-Num, [#default:1,."

The title of the *Property* dialog is set to the cast member name (or the cast member number if the name is EMPTY). Use a descriptive cast member name to remind yourself what the Behavior does.

Because the Behavior parameters popup uses the MUI Xtra, it is beholden to the same limitations. You can fit only about 15 parameters on a 640-by-480 screen before the dialog fails to appear. See *http://www.updatestage.com/previous/970801.html#item3* for details. A Behavior can have many properties, but the *Parameters* dialog may fail if more than 15 of those properties are specified in the list returned by *on getPropertyDescriptionList*. Implement a custom MUI dialog via the *on runPropertyDialog* handler if necessary (see the downloadable Chapter 21, *Custom MUI Dialogs*).

The #format Code

The *#format* of a property in the property description list determines how the user is prompted and what type of data he or she is allowed to enter. Table 12-3 and Table 12-4 show the *#format* codes that let you select from a pop-up list of items of the specified type, such as bitmap cast members, sound cast members, or marker labels. For example, if you are writing a Behavior that requires a sound, you might let the user pick that sound from a list of sound cast members by using a *#format* of *#sound* for the property of interest.

 Using a *#format* such as *#graphic* that may encompass hundreds of cast members will create a popup with hundreds of entries, taking considerable time and possibly crashing the system.

Table 12-3: #format Codes for Cast Member Types

Message	Sent When
#format	Matching *the type of member* property
#bitmap	#bitmap cast members only
#button	#button cast members only
#digitalVideo	#digitalVideo cast members only (excludes #quickTimeMedia)
#field	#field cast members only (not #richText)
#filmLoop	#filmLoop cast members only
#graphic	#bitmap, #btned, #button, #digitalVideo, #field, #filmLoop, #movie, #ole, #picture, #PopMenu, #richText, #shape, #SWA (any cast member type that can be used in a sprite channel)
#member	all cast member types (those listed above for #graphic, plus #palette, #script, #sound, and #transition)
#movie	#movie cast members only (not movie scripts)

Table 12-3: #format Codes for Cast Member Types (continued)

Message	Sent When
#ole	#ole cast members only
#palette	built-in palettes, plus #palette cast members
#picture	#picture cast members only
#richText	#richText cast members only
#shape	#shape cast members only
#script	#script cast members only
#sound	#sound cast members only (not #SWA)
#transition	built-in transitions, plus #transition cast members

Note that *getPropertyDescriptionList* doesn't recognize *#ActiveX*, *#btned*, *#flash*, *#SWA*, *#quickTimeMedia*, *#text*, or *#xtra* as separate cast member types.

Table 12-4 shows the *#format* options that don't pertain to a cast member types, but rather to "pure" data types (floats, integers, Booleans, symbols, and strings) and other Director entities (cursors, markers, and inks).

Table 12-4: Non-Castmember Behavior #format Codes

#format	User sees	#default	#range
#boolean	Checkbox	TRUE or FALSE	N/A
#cursor	Pop-up menu	Installed cursors[1]	None or enumerated
#float	Entry field, slider, or pop-up menu[2]	0.0 or your choice	#min/#max, none, or linear list
#ink	Pop-up menu	Name of your choice	None or enumerated
#integer	Entry field, slider, or pop-up menu[2]	0 or your choice	#min/#max, none, or linear list
#marker	Pop-up menu	previous, loop, and next	previous, loop, next, plus any custom marker labels
#string	Entry field or pop-up menu[3]	EMPTY or your choice	None or linear list
#symbol	Entry field or pop-up menu[3]	EMPTY or your choice	None or linear list

[1] List of available cursor resources varies between Mac and Windows, but may include Arrow, I-Beam. Crosshair, Crossbar, Watch, Blank, Help, Finger, Hand, Closed Hand, No Drop Hand, Copy Closed Hand, Pencil, Eraser, Select, Bucket, Lasso, Dropper, Air Brush, Zoom In, Zoom Out, Vertical Size, Horizontal Size, and Diagonal Size. List does not include custom 1-bit cast members used as cursors (use #bitmap instead).
[2] If a #min/#max #range is specified the user sees a slider. If a linear list is used for #range, the user sees a popup menu. If no range is specified, the user sees a text entry field.
[3] User sees entry field or popup menu depending on #range as per footnote 2.

Here is an example *getPropertyDescriptionList()* if you were to turn the *Eden* script from Example 12-10 into a Behavior.

Example 12-15: Behaving Yourself in Paradise

```
property  pGender, pName, pKnowledge

on eatApple me
  set pKnowledge = TRUE
end

on getPropertyDescriptionList me
  set propList = [[LC]
    #pGender:[#default: #male,  #format: #symbol, ¬
                #comment: "Gender", #range:[#male, #female]], ¬
    #pName:   [#default: EMPTY,  #format: #string,¬
                #comment: "Person's Name"], ¬
    #pKnowledge: [#comment: "Tree of Knowledge",  ¬
                #default: FALSE, #format: #boolean] ¬
  ]
  return propList
end
```

 The *on getPropertyDescriptionList* is called only at authoring time to store the default properties for a Behavior. Those properties are applied when the script is instantiated at runtime. Don't forget to *return* the property list you've built.

The RunPropertyDialog Method

Despite its name, the *on runPropertyDialog* handler is never called at runtime. It is called only when a Behavior's *Parameter* dialog would otherwise appear during authoring. If present in a Behavior, the *on runPropertyDialog* handler is called to set values for the properties without prompting the user via the *Parameter* dialog. It receives a list of default values of the properties returned from *on getPropertyDescriptionList*. In Example 12-16, *defaultProps* is *[#pGender: #male, #pName: "", #pKnowledge: 0]* before the handler is called, and *[#pGender: #male, #pName: "Seth", #pKnowledge: 0]* afterwards.

Example 12-16: The RunPropertyDialog Method

```
on runPropertyDialog me, defaultProps
  set the pName of defaultProps = "Seth"
  return defaultProps
end
```

The Lingo Dictionary and online Help have incorrect entries for *run-PropertyDialog*.

Behavior and Parent Script Lingo

Table 12-5 covers Lingo pertaining to Behaviors and parent scripts.

The text of scripts is limited to 32,000 characters, so it easy to run out of room when creating complex objects.

You can use the ancestor property to create objects that use multiple scripts, but the management can get annoying. Hopefully, Macromedia will address the 32,000 characters *scriptText of member* limit in Director 7.

Table 12-5: Behaviors and Parent Scripts Lingo

Command	Usage
the actorList	A list of object instances that receive the *stepFrame* message. Use to send messages to child objects each time playback head moves.

ancestor	A property of a child object that points, not to the parent script, but to a "grandparent" script of your choosing.
	`property ancestor`
	`set ancestor = new (script "Ancestor Script")`

birth (script "*Parent Script*")	Obsolete. Use *new()* instead.
call (#*handlerName*, *script* | *scriptInstance* | *objectList* {, *args*})	Sends a custom message to a one or more scripts, script instances, or child objects.
callAncestor (#*handlerName*, *script* | *scriptInstance* | *objectList* {, *args*})	Sends a custom message to the ancestor of one or more script instances or child objects.
the currentSpriteNum	Indicates the current sprite number from within a Behavior attached to a sprite.
getBehaviorInitializers(*spriteNum*, *behaviorNum*)	Returns the list of default property values passed to *on runPropertyDialog*. Requires *UI Helper* Xtra, included with D6.5.
getBehaviorMemRef(*spriteNum*, *behaviorNum*)	Returns an absolute cast member reference of the specified behavior attached to *spriteNum* (or 0). Requires *UI Helper* Xtra, included with D6.5.
me	Identifies the current script instance. Returned by *new()* when the child object is created and used as a parameter to Behavior and object methods.

Table 12-5: Behaviors and Parent Scripts Lingo (continued)

Command	Usage
new()	Used to create a new instance of a parent script or Behavior. `set childObj = new (script "ParentScript" {, args...})`
on getPropertyDescriptionList	Returns a property list defining all the user-settable properties of a Behavior. See Table 12-2.
on getBehaviorDescription	Returns a text string describing the Behavior, displayed in Behavior Inspector as Help text. See Table 12-2.
on new	Handler called when a parent script is instantiated. Must return a script instance (*me*)
on runPropertyDialog	Changes Behavior's properties without user intervention. Suppresses *Parameter* dialog. See Table 12-2.
on stepFrame	Handler to perform some action each time the *stepFrame* message is sent to *the actorList*.
property *propertyVar*	Defines a semi-private variable for a Behavior or parent script.
script *"Parent"* or script *scriptNum*	Used with *new()* to refer to a Parent Script.
the scriptInstanceList of sprite	A list of Behavior instances attached to a given sprite. Available only while Director is running. See *getBehaviorMemRef()*.
the scriptType of member	Script type should be set to #score for Behaviors and #parent for parent scripts.
send (object, #*message*)	Unsupported variant of *call()*.
sendAllSprites (#*message* {, *args*})	Sends a message to all sprites in the current frame.
sendAncestor (*object*, #*message*)	Unsupported variant of *callAncestor()*.
sendSprite (*whichSprite*, #*message* {, *args*})	Sends a message to a particular sprite in the current frame.
the spriteNum of me	Indicates the current sprite number from within a Behavior attached to a sprite.

Handler Evaluation with Behaviors

New Sprite Events Sent to Behaviors Used as Sprite Scripts

See Chapter 2 for a full description of events. In Director 6, Score scripts attached to the sprite channels now receive *new, enterFrame,* and *exitFrame* messages (plus many other new messages). These handlers would not have been called when playing in Director 5. The Director 6 CD includes a cleaner utility in the `Goodies\Movies\Cleaner` folder, and D6.0.2 now warns about these when updating from Director 5 movies. (See the Director 6 *ReadMe* file.)

For backwards compatibility the Shockwave for D6 plug-in does not send *enter-Frame* and *exitFrame* messages to sprites if the movie file being played is of pre-Director 6 vintage. It does send the *new* message to sprites however.

Handler Execution, The ScriptInstanceList, and the SpriteNum of Me

As described in Example 2-11 in Chapter 2, the *new* event is sent to sprites before the *beginSprite* event. If a Behavior defines an *on new* method, it is called before *the scriptInstanceList* is populated with any Behavior instances, and before the property values are assigned. Therefore, you can't manipulate *the scriptInstanceList* or assume that Behavior properties have been defined in an *on new* handler.

If a score script is going to be used as both a sprite Behavior *and* instanced explicitly via the *new()* function, then the *on new* handler should declare and set the *spriteNum of me* property. (It is set automatically when an instance of the script is created for a Behavior, but not if *new()* is called explicitly.)

Refer to the Director 6 *ReadMe* and Director 6.0.1 *Updates* file for more details.

The ActorList

The *stepFrame* message is sent only to items in the *actorList*. In Director 6, sprites receive *prepareFrame, exitFrame,* and *enterFrame* events, but *the actorList* can still be used to notify Parent scripts and child objects (which don't receive events by default) when the playback head moves. Refer to "The ActorList" in Chapter 2 for more details. Note that each item on *the actorList* can have its own *on stepFrame* handler to take appropriate action when the playback head advances.

The following can be used to add and remove items from *the actorList*.

Example 12-17: The ActorList

```
on addToActorList dummy, object
  -- only add objects to the actorList
  if not objectP(object) then
    alert "Not an object" && object
    exit
  end if
  -- Don't add it if it is already on the list
  if getPos (the actorList, object) = 0 then
    add the actorList, object
  end if
end addToActorList

on removeFromActorList dummy, object
  -- Remove the item from the actorList
  set offset = getPos (the actorList, object)
  if offset then
    deleteAt (the actorList, offset)
  end if
end removeFromActorList
```

See Example 1-34 under "Special Treatment of the First Argument Passed" in Chapter 1 for details on why the above uses a dummy parameter instead of passing *object* as the first parameter.

The following uses the utilities in Example 12-17 cause a Behavior instance to automatically add its sprite to (and delete its sprite from) *the actorList*. The sprite will then receive *stepFrame* events.

```
on beginSprite me
  addToActorList (void, the spriteNum of me)
end

on endSprite me
  removeFromActorList (void, the spriteNum of me)
end
```

To clear the actorList entirely, you can use *deleteAll(the actorList)* or simply set it to [].

 The *clearGlobals* command also clears *the actorList* in D6, although it didn't do so in D4 or D5.

Adding Behaviors at Runtime

The scriptInstanceList of sprite property is a Lingo list of instantiated Behaviors. Until the playback head enters the sprite of interest, *the scriptInstanceList* is the EMPTY list ([]). See "Script Instances" in Chapter 2 for details.

You can't set *the scriptInstanceList* during authoring or even a Score Recording session because it is a list of instances, not script numbers. *The scriptNum of sprite* returns only the first attached Behavior, but you can use the *getBehaviorMemRef()* function included with the *UI Helper* Xtra (included with D6.5) to count the number of attached Behaviors and determine their member numbers.

Example 12-18: Getting Attached Behaviors

```
on getBehaviors spriteNum
  set n = 1
  set memList = [ ]
  repeat while (TRUE)
    -- This requires the UI Helper Xtra
    if getBehaviorMemRef (spriteNum, n) = 0 then
      exit repeat
    else
      add memList, member getBehaviorMemRef (spriteNum, n)
      set n = n + 1
    end if
```

Example 12-18: Getting Attached Behaviors (continued)

```
  end repeat
  return memList
end getBehaviors
```

You can add Behaviors to a sprite at runtime by adding a script instances to its *scriptInstanceList* (but only if at least one Behavior was already attached).

Example 12-19: Adding Behaviors At Runtime

```
set newBehavior = new(script"BehaviorScript" {, args})
add (the scriptInstanceList of sprite n, newBehavior)
```

Hopefully this chapter has dispelled the mysterious aura surrounding object-oriented programming and Behaviors. You should have recognized the deep parallels between programmer-defined objects and Director's built-in entities (members, sprites, windows, lists, and so on). All such entities have properties that can be manipulated without intimate knowledge of their internal structure.

Although some zealots create objects for *everything*, then create more objects to manage their objects, I use OOP selectively. Develop your own style. Regardless of your enthusiasm for OOP, you should add it to your arsenal. If you've understood this chapter, you'll also understand that some tasks cry out for OOP. Properly applied, it will make your code easier to write and more maintainable.

CHAPTER 13

Lingo Xtras and XObjects

Xtras

Director supports several distinct types of Xtras. This chapter discusses *Lingo Scripting Xtras* (or simply *Lingo Xtras*), which add new commands to Lingo, such as the ability to read and write external files (provided by the *FileIO* Xtra). Lingo Xtras are a replacement for older XObjects supported in prior versions of Director. A library of Lingo routines can also "extend" Director, but Lingo Xtras are typically written in C.

Other types of Xtras, such as *Sprite Asset* Xtras, and general installation and compatibility issues are discussed in detail in Chapter 10, *Using Xtras*, in *Director in a Nutshell*. See the *Preface* of this book for links to Xtras-related sites. See Chapter 14, *External Files*, and Chapter 15, *The MUI Dialog Xtra*, for details on the *FileIO* and *MUI Dialog* Xtras. See Chapter 14, *Graphical User Interface Components*, in *Director in a Nutshell* for details on the *Custom Button Editor, Custom Cursor*, and *Popup Menu* Xtras.

 To install an Xtra for authoring, put it in the *Xtras* folder where Director is installed. To install it for runtime, place it in an *Xtras* folder where the Projector resides.

If an Xtra is not recognized, see Chapter 10 in *Director in a Nutshell*, or *http://www.zeusprod.com/technote/xtrainst.html* for installation troubleshooting.

ShowXlib

Lingo Xtras don't appear in Director's GUI, although some (most notably Print-OMatic, ScriptOMatic, and Popup Menu) provide Help files under the **Xtras** menu. Most Lingo Xtras can only be "found" in the Message window using the *showXlib* command, shown here for my Macintosh (your display may vary).

Example 13-1: ShowXlib Output for Director for Macintosh

```
showXlib
-- XLibraries:
--    Xtra: ScriptColor
--    Xtra: PrintOMatic_Lite
--    Xtra: NetLingo
--    Xtra: QTVRXtra
--    Xtra: Mui
--    Xtra: fileio
-- "*Standard.xlib"
--    XObject: SerialPort      Id:200
--    XObject: XCMDGlue        Id:2020

put the number of xtras
-- 6
```

The list shows only *Lingo* Xtras that ship with Director, third-party Lingo Xtras that you've installed, and open XObjects. Note that the two XObjects listed at the bottom (which are embedded in Director for Macintosh's Resource fork) are *not* included in Director's count of *the number of Xtras* (nor are non-Lingo Xtras). Use *xFactoryList(EMPTY)* to return a list of open XObjects. In Director for Windows you will see a somewhat different output without the XObjects, and perhaps including the DirMMX Xtra.

The QTVR 1.0 Xtra that ships on the Director 6 CD is a *Lingo* Xtra, not a *Sprite Asset* Xtra. As such, it appears in the list of Xtras shown by *showXlib*, if installed. Likewise, the NetLingo Xtra provides a library of new Lingo commands that appear as "built-in" Lingo (NetLingo commands are built into Shockwave.) Some MIX Xtras, such as the SWA Streaming Xtra, (a MIX Xtra) provide a few functions (in this case *getError()* and *getErrorString()*) but still do *not* appear in the list above. Sprite Xtras (Flash Asset, Custom Cursor, Popup Menu) allow you to get and set properties of a new asset type but don't appear in the *showXlib* list.

Including Xtras with a Projector

Lingo scripting Xtras are never automatically included with a Projector. When using Lingo Xtras with Projectors, you can:

- Place them in an *Xtras* folder at the same level as the Projector.

- Add them manually to the list of files in the Projector using File[➤]Create Projector.

- Include them manually via Modify[➤]Movie[➤]Xtras. They will be included only if the movie is added to the Projector and the *Check Movies for Xtras* option is used when building the Projector.

- Use the *Include Network Xtras* option when building the Projector. This includes the NetLingo Xtra and other non-Lingo net-related Xtras required when linking to content at a URL.

I strongly recommended the first option as there are numerous problems with bundled Xtras. See Chapter 10 in *Director in a Nutshell.* I leave Xtras, movie files and castLibs external, and create a plain vanilla "stub" Projector, as described in Chapter 8, *Projectors and the Run-Time Environment*, in *Director in a Nutshell.* See also *http://www.zeusprod.com/technote/stub.html.*

If your Lingo code uses an Xtra that is not present at runtime, Director will generate a "Handler not defined" script error. If you use any of the NetLingo Xtra's commands (see Example 13-2), include the NetLingo Xtra.

See Chapter 10 in *Director in a Nutshell* for more details on which Xtras you should ship with your Projector.

Lingo Scripting Xtras

Lingo Xtras usually include several (perhaps many) new *methods* (custom Lingo functions).

All Lingo Xtras should support a *mMessageList()* method that displays a list of the other methods supported by the Xtra, and sometimes includes brief documentation.

Example 13-2 lists the methods within the NetLingo Xtra, which appear as built-in Lingo commands.

Example 13-2: The Output from NetLingo's mMessageList()

```
put mMessageList (xtra "NetLingo ")
-- "xtra NetLingo
* netStatus * --
* getNetText  * --
...
* browserName * --
* tellStreamStatus * --
"
```

The NetLingo Xtra's *mMessageList* lists only the method names, but no documentation. (See *"Deciphering the mMessageList."*) You'll often need to consult the separate documentation provided with the Xtra. (In this case, the *NetLingo* methods are described in the Lingo Dictionary, online Help, and Lingo pop-up menus.) Typing the *mMessageList* command is tedious. Add the utility in Example 13-3 to a movie script.

Example 13-3: Relief from mMessageList()

```
on xhelp xtraName
  if voidP(xtraName) then
```

Example 13-3: Relief from mMessageList() (continued)

```
   set xtraName = "FileIO"
  end if
  put mMessageList (xtra xtraName)
end xhelp
```

Xhelp() prints out the Help text for the specified Xtra or for the FileIO Xtra if none is specified.

```
xhelp "mui"
```

Deciphering the mMessageList

Most Lingo Xtra's *mMessageList* method provides more information than does NetLingo's. Here are excerpts from FileIO Xtra's Help text.

Example 13-4: Deciphering FileIO mMessageList()

```
put mMessageList (xtra "FileIO")   -- or use the xhelp utility

-- "xtra fileio -- CH 18apr97
new object me -- create a new child instance
-- FILEIO --
fileName object me -- return fileName string of the open file
...
openFile object me, string fileName, int mode -- opens named file.
valid modes: 0=r/w 1=r 2=w
...
+ version xtraRef -- display fileIO version and build information
in the message window
* getOSDirectory -- returns the full path to the Mac System Folder
or Windows Directory
"
```

FileIO's *mMessageList* is very sketchy. It claims that the *new()* method requires an object, but it actually accepts an Xtra reference and returns an object. See Chapter 14 for complete FileIO documentation.

 The *new()* method is rarely listed in the output shown by *mMessage-List()*. It is implicitly present if the Xtra implements any instance-level methods, and is itself an Xtra level method.

There are three types of Lingo ScriptingXtra methods, as shown in Example 13-4 and as explained in Table 13-1.

Table 13-1: FileIO's Different Types of Methods

Method Type	Indicator[1]	Usage
Global	*	set *systemDir* = getOSDirectory()

Table 13-1: FileIO's Different Types of Methods (continued)

Method Type	Indicator[1]	Usage

Xtra-Level	+	`put version (Xtra "FileIO")`
		`-- "FileIO 1.0.1 May 31 1996"`
		`set myInstance = new (Xtra "FileIO")`

Instance-Level	(none)	`openFile (myInstance, "foo.txt", 1)`

[1] Sometimes the indicator is missing, or a method may be implemented as both an instance-level and Xtra-level method.

Filename() is an instance-level method that requires an object reference (as indicated by *object me*) and returns a string. *OpenFile()* is another instance-level method that requires three parameters—an object reference, a string *fileName*, and an integer *mode*. The *version()* method requires an Xtra reference because it is an Xtra-level method, as indicated by the "+" at the beginning of the line. The *getOSDirectory()* method does not require an object or Xtra reference because it is a global method, as indicated by the "*" at the beginning of the line.

Global-Level Methods

Global-level methods (often indicated by a "*") perform a single operation and do not maintain any "state." They do not require the name of, nor an instance of, the Xtra. All global method names should be unique (this is up to the creator of the Xtra). Use global methods as you would other Lingo commands. For example, all the *NetLingo* commands (such as *gotoNetPage*) that appear to be built into Lingo are actually global-level methods within the NetLingo Xtra (see Example 13-2).

The FileIO Xtra's global-level *getOSDirectory()* method can be called as shown in Table 13-1 (the parentheses are mandatory).

Xtra-Level Methods

Xtra-level methods (often indicated by a "t"), require an Xtra name such as *xtra* "FileIO" within parentheses. The *mMessageList()* method is an Xtra-level method supported by all Lingo Xtras.

```
put mMessageList (Xtra "FileIO")
```

The *version()* method is an Xtra-level method supported by the *FileIO* Xtra.

Xtra-level method names need not be unique because the Xtra name tells Director which Xtra to use.

The *new()* Xtra-level method must be supported by any Xtra that has instance-level methods, as described in the next section. It is used to *instantiate* an Xtra, such as:

```
set myInstance = new (Xtra "FileIO")
```

Instance-Level Methods

Instance-level methods are called using the *instance handle* returned by the *new()* method. Multiple instances of a single Xtra can be used to control, say, multiple files, with each instance referring to a different file.

Using Instance-Level Methods

Using an Xtra with instance-level methods is analogous to using a parent script and child objects (see Chapter 12, *Behaviors and Parent Scripts*). First, instantiate the Xtra using the *new()* method, and then use the returned instance handle (referred to as *object me* in *FileIO's mMessageList*) to call the instance-level method(s).

Use *objectP()* to check whether *new()* returned a valid instance handle (in the case of *FileIO*, the value returned by *new()* is an error code if it is not an object). Example 13-5 is for illustration only. Refer to Chapter 14 for robust examples using *FileIO*.

Example 13-5: Using Instance-Level Methods

```
on testFileIO
  global gFileInstance
  -- 'new' is an Xtra-level method requiring an Xtra name
  set gFileInstance =  new (xtra "FileIO")
  -- Check if a valid instance handle was created.
  if not objectP (gFileInstance) then
    alert "something didn't work"
  else
    -- Use the instance handle (gFileInstance) to call the
    -- instance-level methods (createFile, writeString, etc.)
    createFile (gFileInstance, the pathName & "junk.txt")
    openFile (gFileInstance, the pathName & "junk.txt", 2)
    writeString (gFileInstance, "Yahoo!" & RETURN)
    setFinderInfo (gFileInstance, "TEXT ttxt")
    closeFile (gFileInstance)
    -- Dispose of the instance by setting it to zero
    set gFileInstance = 0
  end if
end testFileIO
```

Programming with Xtras

Director allocates some memory each time an Xtra is instantiated and reclaims the memory when an instance is no longer being used (when there are no variables or lists that reference it). You can use a single instance throughout your project by assigning it to a global variable rather than repeatedly instantiating and disposing the Xtra. (If an Xtra has a memory leak this may minimize its effect.) Table 13-2 shows Lingo commands that pertain to Xtras. Refer to Table 13-3 for Lingo more specific to XObjects.

Table 13-2: Xtra-related Lingo Commands

Commands	Usage
mMessageList (xtra "*XtraName*")	Lists the available methods for an Xtra, such as: `put mMessageList (xtra "FileIO")`
the name of xtra *whichXtra*	Returns the name of an Xtra based on its number.
the netPresent	Returns TRUE if the *NetLingo* and *NetFile* Xtras are installed. Don't use the *netPresent()* function. See Table 17-1.
new (xtra "*XtraName*")	Instantiates an Xtra and returns the instance handle, such as: `set xtraInstance = new (xtra "FileIO")`
the number of xtras	Returns the number of scripting Xtras installed.[1]
objectP (*xtraInstance*)	Returns TRUE if the item is an object, such as an instance handle returned by *new()*. (Other types of objects are listed under *ilk()* in Table 16-1.)
set *xtraInstance* = 0	Disposes of an instance handle.[2]
showXlib	Lists installed Lingo Xtras and XObjects in the Message window.
xtra	See *new()* and *the name of xtra*.
xtras	See *the number of xtras*.
Xtra-specific Global methods	Just use method name, such as this one from *FileIO*: `getOSdirectory()`
Xtra-specific Xtra-level methods	Use Xtra's name, such as: `put version (xtra "FileIO")`

Xtra-specific instance-level methods	Use instance created by *new()*, such as:
	`set xtraInstance = new (xtra "FileIO")`
	`createFile (xtraInstance, "myFile.txt")`

[1] *The number of xtras* and *the name of xtra* properties pertain only to Lingo Scripting Xtras, not to XObjects or other types of Xtras.
[2] The memory used by an instance is freed when no variables reference the instance. Director reclaims the memory from unreferenced instances periodically. Refer to "*Object References*" in Chapter 12.

Detecting Installed Xtras

The *showXlib* command displays Lingo Scripting Xtras in the Message window. From Lingo Example 13-6 returns a list of the installed Lingo Scripting Xtras.

Example 13-6: Listing Installed Lingo Scripting Xtras from Lingo

```
on installedLingoXtras
  set xtraList = []
  repeat with n = 1 to the number of xtras
```

```
   add (xtraList, the name of xtra n)
   end repeat
   return xtraList
end installedLingoXtras

put installedLingoXtras()
-- ["NetLingo", "QTVRXtra", "Mui", "fileio"]
```

The name of an Xtra (case-insensitive) is fixed internally. It is unaffected by the Xtra's external filename. See *showXlib* and *the name of xtra*.

Example 13-7's utility returns 1 (TRUE) if the specified Lingo Scripting Xtra is installed.

Example 13-7. Checking Whether a Specific Lingo Scripting Xtra is Installed

```
on isInstalled xtraName
  repeat with n = 1 to the number of xtras
    if the name of xtra n = xtraName then
       return TRUE
    end if
  end repeat
  return FALSE
end isInstalled

put isInstalled ("FILEIO")
-- 1
```

See *Example 19-3, "Checking If an Asset Xtra Is Installed,"* to check whether a Sprite Asset Xtra is installed.

Xtras versus XObjects, XFCNs, XCMDs, and DLLs

Prior to Director 5, Director could be extended via other types of external code modules, referred to collectively as *XObjects*. XObjects were generally limited to functionality external to Director, such as copying files, checking RAM, and performing serial I/O, although some XObjects read from or drew to the Stage. XObjects were replaced by Lingo Scripting Xtras. Additional new Xtra types add functionality not possible with XObjects (authoring tools, new cast member types, transitions, and import filters). Some XObjects *may* work with Director 5.0 and 6.0, but those that access Director 4.0's Cast or Score or read from its screen buffer, such as the *StageToCast* XObject, will not. You are generally better off using an Xtra if one is available, especially when using 32-bit projectors under Windows 95 or NT.

Xlib

An *Xlib* is a general term for an external file containing one or more Xtras or XObjects.

 16-bit XObjects (DLLs) can be used with 32-bit Projectors under Windows 95, but not Windows NT. Even so, they are prone to errors if Windows 95 relocates them in RAM, unless the DLL locks itself in RAM to prevent this.

XObjects

XObjects refers to both Macintosh and Windows add-ons created with the older XObject Developers Kit from Macromedia. They generally conformed to the standards described under *"Using an XObject."* On the Macintosh they were generally given names ending in "XObj" and had a File Type of 'Xobj'. Windows XObjects use the .DLL extension.

XFCNs and XCMDs

XFCNs and *XCMDs* are Hypercard-compatible code resources that can be used by Director. Director's built-in XCMDglue XObject provides the necessary interface to access XFCNs and XCMDs from Director. (See "Using XFCNs and XCMDs" later in this chapter).

DLLs

A true Windows XObject is a DLL that includes a Lingo *message table* that allows Lingo to access the DLL's internal commands. "Standard" Windows DLLs lacking a message table can be used with Director via *DLLglue* (see http://download.macromedia.com.pub/xobjects/DLLGLU.ZIP). See also Xobglu16.DLL and Xobglu32.DLL which come with D6.

XObjects versus Xtras

Those familiar with XObjects should note several major differences when programming with Xtras, as shown in Table 13-3.

Table 13-3: XObjects versus Xtras

To Do This	Xtras	XObjects
Open and close the XLib	Managed automatically when placed in *Xtras* folder or bundled with Projector.	Use *openXLib* and *closeXLib*, or add XObject to Macintosh Projector's resource fork manually.
Display list of Xtras and XObjects	Show XLib	put XFactoryList(EMPTY)
Display list of supported methods[1]	put *mMessageList* (xtra "*XtraName*").	*XObjName* (mDescribe).
Create an instance	set *instance* = new (xtra "*XtraName*" {, args...}).	set *instance* = *XObjName* (mNew {, args...}).

Table 13-3: XObjects versus Xtras (continued)

To Do This	Xtras	XObjects
Use an instance-level method	*method* (*instance*).	*instance* (*mMethod*).
Dispose of an instance[2]	set *instance* = 0.	*instance* (mDispose).

[1] Note that *mMessageList()* requires the *put* command, and the name of the Xtra must be in quotes. *mDescribe* does not require *put* and uses the name of the XObject without quotes. Use the *internal* name of the Xtra or XObject (as shown via *showXlib* or *xFactoryList*), not its external filename.
[2] An instance of an Xtra is disposed of implicitly when no variables refer to it.

XObject Lingo

Table 13-4 shows the Lingo used with XObjects.

> The *external* name in the Finder (Mac) or File Explorer (Windows) is used only with *openXlib* and *closeXLib*. The *internal* name used with *mNew*, *mDescribe*, and so on, is not necessarily the same as the external name. See *showXlib* and *xFactoryList*.

Macintosh XObjects, XFCNs, and XCMDs can be added manually to a Projector's resource fork using ResEdit. In that case, don't use *openXlib* or *closeXlib*.

Table 13-4: XObject Commands

Commands	Usage
closeXLib {*xLibPath*}	Closes XLibrary specified by *xLibPath*. If *xLibPath* is omitted, it closes all open XLibs opened with openXLib.[1]
factory	Returns an object reference if the XObject exists. ```if objectP(factory ("SerialPort")) then put "Serial Port XObject present" end if```
mDescribe	Displays the list of supported methods. ```XObjName (mDescribe)```
mDispose	Disposes of an XObject instance.[2] ```if objectP(instance) then instance (mDispose)```
mInstanceRespondsTo	Determines if instance recognizes a certain message. ```putinstance(mInstanceRespondsTo, #message)```
mName	Returns the name of the XObject associated with an instance. ```put instance (mName)```

Xtras & XObjects

Table 13-4: XObject Commands (continued)

Commands	Usage
mNew	Creates an instance of an Xobject. `set instance = XObjectName (mNew {, args})`
mPerform	Sends a message to an instance. `instance (mPerform, "message" {, args})`
mRespondsTo	Determines is an XObject responds to a certain message. `XObjectName (mRespondsTo, #message)`
objectP(*XObjectInstance*)	Determines if an item is an instance (use for error checking value returned by *new()*). `if objectP(instance) then put "It's an object".`
openXlib *xLibPath*	Opens XLibrary specified by *xLibPath*.. Not recommended for Xtras.
showXlib	Lists installed Lingo Xtras and XObjects in the message window.[3]
xFactoryList *(XLib |* *EMPTY)*	Returns a list of XObjects within specified *XLib*. (Must already be opened with *openXlib*), or a complete list of open Xobjects if `EMPTY` is specified.
Use an instance-level method	`instance (mMethod).`

[1] *CloseXlib* does not close XLib resources embedded in the Macintosh resource fork. *CloseXlib* will close only those Xtras opened with *openXLib* (not recommended), not those opened automatically by Director when installed in the Xtras folder (as is recommended).

[2] Always check if something is an object before attempting to use *mDispose*, or Director might crash. Use *mDispose* only with XObjects, never with Xtras.

[3] *ShowXlib* under Windows shows the name of the external XLib file, not the *internal* name of older Windows XObjects. Consult the XObject's documentation or use *XFactoryList()* to determine it.

 Many of the XObject commands, such as *mInstanceRespondsTo* and *mDescribe*, no longer seem reliable in D5 and D6. Never open both the FileIO XObject and FileIO Xtra at the same time. Director easily confuses the two, and neither will work if both are used.

Deciphering mDescribe

The output of the *mDescribe* method for XObjects is analogous to the *mMessage-List* output from Xtras. Here is part of the output from the *SerialPort* XObject's *mDescribe* method.

Example 13-8: Deciphering mDescribe

```
put SerialPort (mDescribe)
-- Factory: SerialPort ID:200
-- SerialPort, Tool, Version 1.2, 10nov93
-- © 1989, 1990 MacroMind, Inc.
-- by John Thompson and Jeff Tanner.
```

Example 13-8: Deciphering mDescribe (continued)

```
II    mNew, port --Creates an instance of the XObject.
 X    mDispose --Disposes of the XObject.
 I    mGetPortNum --> the port.
IS    mWriteString, string --Writes out a string of chars.
II    mWriteChar, charNum --Writes a single character.
 S    mReadString --> the contents of the input buffer.
 I    mReadChar --> a single character.
 I    mReadCount --> the number of characters in the input buffer.
 X    mReadFlush --Clears out all the input characters.
III   mConfigChan, driverNum, serConfig
IIII  mHShakeChan, driverNum, CTSenable, CTScharNum
IIII  mSetUp, baudRate, stopBit, parityBit
```

As with *mMessageList*, *mDescribe's* output is unstandardized, cryptic, and unreliable at best. The first letter in the first column generally indicates the return value, and subsequent letters indicate the data type of parameters to be passed in. The instance parameter required is often not shown. Table 13-5 shows how to interpret the code letters from *mDescribe* (but often you must make and educated guess). For example, *mWriteString* accepts an instance and a string as its two parameters. *mReadFlush* accepts only the instance as a parameter and returns no value. *mReadString* accepts only the instance as a parameter and returns a string.

Table 13-5: XObject mDescribe Codes

Code	Meaning
X	No return value
I	An integer or Boolean value, or instance returned by *mNew()*
S	A String
P	A picture, such as *the picture of member "Cake"*
O	An object instance, returned by *mNew()*
V	A variable argument list

Using an XObject

XObjects not included in the Macintosh resource fork must be opened and closed manually. For example, Director 4 for Windows opened the FileIO XObject within the *on startUp* handler in the LINGO.INI file (see Appendix D). In a typical scenario, you might perform the operations shown in Example 13-9.

Example 13-9: Using an XObject

```
global objInstance
on initializeXObject
  -- Open the correct XLib for the platform
  if the platform starts "Windows" then
    openXLib "WinXObj.DLL"
```

Example 13-9: Using an XObject (continued)

```
else
    openXLib "Macintosh XObject"
end if

  -- Try to create an instance
  set gObjInstance = XObjectName (mNew)
  if not objectP(gObjInstance) then
    alert "Error returned:" && gObjInstance
  end if
end initializeXObject

on useXObject
  if objectP(gObjInstance) then
    -- Perform some operation
    gObjInstance (mSomeXObjectMethod)
  end if
end useXObject

on cleanupXObject
  -- Dispose of the instance, if any
  if objectP(gObjInstance ) then
    gObjInstance (mDispose)
  end if
  -- Close the XLib too
  if the platform starts "Windows" then
    closeXLib "WinXObj.DLL"
  else
    closeXLib "Macintosh XObject"
  end if
end cleanupXObject
```

Note that all the above handlers share the *global gObjInstance* declaration. In practice, you would call *initializeXObject()* before you need to use the XObject, then you would call *useXObject()* or use an XObject method directly as many times as necessary, and finally you would call *cleanupXObject()* when you are done using the XObject.

Using an XCMD or XFCN

A Hypercard XCMD or XFCN can be opened or closed like other XLibs, but it is never instantiated. The translation is handled transparently by the XCMDglue XObject built into Director for Macintosh. Simply use the functions as global-level methods, as shown in Example 13-10.

Example 13-10: Using an XFCN or XCMD

```
openXlib "XFCNname"
set someVariable = XFCNcommand(args)
closeXLib "XFCNname"
```

Writing Your Own Xtras

If you want to write your own Xtras, you have two choices:

- Write simple Tool Xtras as MIAWs using Lingo. You will be limited to those features that are accessible via Lingo.

- Write any type of Xtra that you like in C/C++. You will still be limited to some degree by what Macromedia has made available via the MOA XDK, but you can access much more than is available via Lingo, including the graphics buffers and the Score data.

Bad reasons to write Xtras include:

- You don't know how to accomplish something in Lingo, and you haven't tried.

- You want a new feature of little importance that Director doesn't handle.

- You are shipping tomorrow and need a new feature.

- You don't want to pay for an existing Xtra (It is usually *markedly* cheaper to buy an existing Xtra than to develop one.)

Good reasons to write Xtras include:

- You are skilled in C, and you are sure that Lingo won't handle your task.

- Lingo handles the task, but not nearly fast enough.

- You have a lot of spare time on your hands.

- No existing Xtra performs a mission-critical task.

The Director Xtras market is small and competitive. It is non-trivial to develop, market, and distribute a software product. Unless you have some skill in that area, I suggest you stick to custom development, which can be quite lucrative and is much easier.

Even if you are not an Xtra developer, you will find many Director nuggets hidden in the Director 6/Authorware 4 XDK documentation included on the D6 CD in the Macromedia/XDK_d6a4 folder. For starters, try *http://Macromedia/XDK_d6a4/docs/html/mmdg/mmgtg.htm*.

Refer also to Chapter 4, *Lingo Internals*, and the downloadable Chapter 20, *Lingo for C Programmers*.

MOA XDK

The Macromedia Open Architecture (MOA), based on Microsoft's Component Object Model (COM), provides a mechanism for Macromedia and third-party developers to enhance and extend various Macromedia products. There are separate Xtra Development Kits (XDKs) for Director/Authorware, Freehand, and SoundEdit, but Xtras that do not perform application-specific operations may work with multiple Macromedia products. For example, Transition Xtras can be used in both Director and Authorware, and pixel filter Xtras can be used in Freehand, Director, and xRes.

The Director 6/Authorware 4 XDK, also includes many examples and templates. You will need to be proficient in C/C++ before attempting to write a MOA Xtra. Refer to the various books that O'Reilly offers on C and C++ including:

> *Practical C Programming* by Steve Oualline
> *Practical C++ Programming* by Steve Oualline
> *C++: The Core Language* by Gregory Satir and Doug Brown

Macromedia has a very active Xtra Developers Program. It includes a very technical e-mail list devoted to XDK issues with a dedicated (and *dedicated*) Macromedia Engineer to support your efforts. The broader community of Xtra developers is also very knowledgeable and supportive.

Xtras Developer Programs
> *http://www.macromedia.com/support/program/xtrasdev.html*
>
> *http://www.macromedia.com/support/xtras.html*

Supported Compilers

The MOA XDK is supported on both Macintosh and Windows. A good place to start is on the Director 6 CD under *Macromedia\XDK_d6a4\readme.htm*.

Windows Compilers

On Windows, it is strongly recommended that you use Microsoft Visual C/C++ (*http://www.microsoft.com*). Other compilers will allegedly work, but you will need to tweak the header files, and technical support is not provided.

The compiler supported for developing Windows 3.1 (16-bit) Xtras is MSVC++ 1. 52. The compiler supported for developing Windows 95/NT (32-bit) Xtras is MSVC++ 4.2 or higher. VC5 is not yet officially supported, but it works fine.

Macintosh Compilers

On the Macintosh it is strongly recommended that you use Metrowerks CodeWarrior (*http://www.metrowerks.com*). Other compilers may work but are not supported.

Metrowerks makes *very* frequent updates to its compiler, and Macromedia may not support the latest version. If you have a *later* version of Code Warrior, contact Metrowerks for a free copy of the earlier version that Macromedia supports. The current version is CodeWarrior Professional Release 3 (CWP3), but probably not by the time you read this. The older Code Warrior version 10 (CW10) was the supported compiler for the Director 6 XDK, but later versions work well with D6.X.

As evidenced by D6.5, Xtras are the future of Director, a future of great promise. Xtras can stretch Director's technical limits as you stretch your creative bounds.

CHAPTER 14

External Files

External Files

Director works with many different external files. Table 14-1 addresses external applications and the documents that they use.

Table 14-1: External File Operations

To Do This	Refer To	See Also
Run an external application	*open*	See *"External Applications."*[1]
Open an external document, such as a PDF or HTML file	*open...with*	See *"External Applications."*[1]
Choose an external application or document from a dialog	*FileIO* Xtra, *MUI* Xtra, or third-party Xtra[1]	See *"File Dialogs"* later in this chapter.
Open a Web browser or HTML page	*browserName()* *gotoNetPage*	See Chapter 11, *Shockwave and the Internet*, in *Director in a Nutshell*.
Read or write a Windows INI file or the Registry file	Third-party Xtra such as Buddy API[1]	See *"Operating System Files"* later in this chapter.
Read or write text file	*getPref, setPref*, or *FileIO* Xtra	See *"External Text Files"* later in this chapter.
Create an Installer	Third-party installer software or Xtra[1]	See Appendix C, *Checklists*, in *Director in a Nutshell* for third-party installers
Copy, move, or delete files	Download NetThing, FileIO, FileXtra, or third-party Xtras[1]	See *"External Applications"*[1]

[1] See "External Applications" later in the chapter for a list of Xtras that perform many system-level operations.

Lingo Commands for External Files

Table 14-2 lists the Lingo commands that pertain to external files in some way.

Table 14-2: External File-Related Lingo Commands

Lingo Command	Usage
@[1]	Specifies platform-independent relative path, such as "@\myFolder".
the applicationPath[1]	Path to Director during authoring or to Projector at runtime. Excludes application name (see *the movieName*). (Causes error in Shockwave.)
browserName()	Gets or sets the default browser path. See *goToNetPage*. (Disabled in Shockwave.)
closeResFile *resFile*	Close a Macintosh resource file (obsolete).
closeXlib *xLibFile*	Closes an Xtra or XObject opened with *openXlib*. See Chapter 13, *Lingo Xtras and XObjects*.
copyToClipboard member *whichMember*	Copy data to clipboard. (Disabled in Shockwave.)
downloadNetThing (*url*, *localFile*)[2]	Downloads an item (HTML page, Shockwave movie, GIF or JPEG image) to local file or copies one local file to another. Disabled in Shockwave. See *preloadNetThing*.
the fileName of castLib[2]	Gets or sets the *fileName* of an internal or external castLib. Can be used to point to a new external castLib.
the fileName of member[2]	Gets or sets the *fileName* of a linked cast member (sound , bitmap, video). Can be used instead of *importFileInto* to link to media dynamically.
the fileName of window	Gets or sets the *fileName* of a MIAW.
getPref (*prefFile*)[2]	Retrieves text from *prefFile* in preferences folder (see *setPref* and "*Preferences Files*" later in this chapter).
getNthFileNameInFolder (*folder*, *fileNum*)[1]	Reads filenames from specified directory, including invisible files on the Macintosh, but excluding invisible files under Windows. (It "sees" invisible files on a Macintosh server even when accessed from a Windows PC.) Becomes slow when *fileNum* becomes large (especially on Macintosh). Disabled in Shockwave. See "*Parsing File Paths*" later in this chapter.
goToNetPage *url*, *target*	Opens default browser with HTML file (see *browserName*). URL can be local file.
importFileInto *member*, *filePathOrURL*[2]	Imports file, including one at a remote URL into Cast. Avoid importing large files during authoring as they consume RAM.
mci *commandString*	Under Windows, the *mci* command can perform many file- and device-related operations.[3]

Table 14-2: External File-Related Lingo Commands (continued)

Lingo Command	Usage
the movie[1]	Name of the current movie[4] (excludes path). From the *first* movie in a Projector, it returns the name of the Projector instead. Same as *the movieName*.
the movieFileFreeSize	Disk space (in bytes) that would be saved if you use File[➤]Save and Compact
the movieFileSize	Current size of the Director movie file on disk.
the movieName[1]	Name of the current movie[4] (excludes path). From the *first* movie in a Projector, it returns the name of the Projector instead. Same as *the movie*.
the moviePath[1]	Folder of current movie[4] (excludes name of movie). Same as *the pathName*.
the number of xtras	Returns number of open Lingo Scripting Xtras.
open *appFilePath*[1]	Opens an external application. *AppFilePath* should be a complete path, not just a filename.
open *documentPath* with *appFilePath*[1]	Opens an external document with an external application. *AppFilePath* and *documentPath* should be complete paths, not just a filename.
openDA	Opens a Macintosh Desk Accessory (obsolete).
openResFile	Opens a Macintosh Resource file (obsolete).
openXlib *XlibFile*	Opens an XObject. Not recommended for Xtras. See Chapter 13.
the pathName[1]	Folder of the current movie[4] (excludes name of movie). Same as *the moviePath*.
pasteClipBoardInto member *whichMember*	Pastes data from clipboard into a member. Causes error in Shockwave.
preloadNetThing(*url*)[2]	Downloads an item (HTML page, Shockwave movie, GIF or JPEG image) to browser's or Projector's cache[5] folder. See *netDone()* and *downloadNetThing()*.
save castLib *whichCast*, {*filePath*}	Saves the specified castLib to an external file. Use this to export an internal castLib. Doesn't save protected castLibs.
saveMovie {*filePath*}	Saves the current movie to an optional *filePath*. Doesn't save protected movies.
the searchCurrentFolder[1]	Boolean (default is TRUE) indicating whether to look in current folder when resolving filenames, such as when using FileIO or searching for linked media

External Files

Table 14-2: External File-Related Lingo Commands (continued)

Lingo Command	Usage
the searchPath[1]	Lingo list of file paths to search when Director can't find the desired media (default is []). Same as *the searchPaths*.
the searchPaths[1]	Same as *the searchPath*.
setPref *prefFile, text*[2]	Writes text to *prefFile* in preferences folder (see *getPref* and *"Preferences Files"* later in this chapter).
showResFile	Displays contents of Macintosh Resource File (obsolete).
showXlib	Lists open XObjects and Xtras in the Message window. See Chapter 13.
the streamName of member[2]	Returns URL of SWA cast member. Same as *the URL of member*.
sound playFile *soundChannel, filePath*	Plays external AIFF or WAVE file.
the traceLogFile	Specifies a file to which to log Message window output, (sets it to EMPTY to close the file). See Chapter 3, *Lingo Coding and Debugging Tips*.
the URL of member[2]	Returns URL of SWA cast member. Same as *the streamName of member*.
the updateMovieEnabled	If TRUE, movies are saved automatically when branching to another movie. Not recommended in Projector. Default is FALSE. Doesn't save protected movies.
xFactoryList (*xLib* | EMPTY)	Returns a list of XObjects within specified *xLib*. (must already be opened with *openXlib*) or a complete list of open Xobjects if EMPTY is specified.

[1] See "File Paths" later in this chapter.
[2] New or updated to support URLs in Director 6.
[3] See *http://space.tin.it/internet/gchoo/html/tech_index.html* and *http://www.zeusprod.com/technote/mci.html* for a summary of *mci* commands. See also "Windows 3.1 Multimedia," by Roger Jenings (Que) or "Win32 Programmer's Reference," vol. 2. (Microsoft Press).
[4] The *movie, movieName, moviePath,* and *pathName* properties all return EMPTY during authoring until the movie is saved for the first time.
[5] *PreloadNetThing* creates and uses an invisible and temporary cache folder on the system's boot drive even when running from locked volumes such as CD-ROMs.

File Paths

File paths are specified differently on each platform. See Table 14-3.

Macintosh pathnames take the general form:
    hardDriveName:folderName1:folderName2:fileName

Windows pathnames take the general form:
    X:\folder1\folder2\filename.ext

Windows uses "*" as a wildcard to match any string and as a wildcard to match a single character. The *ISO 9660* standard is a disk format commonly used with CD-ROMs, but a full discussion is beyond the scope of this book. The ISO 9660 standard is implemented differently on each platform, and occasionally imposes additional restrictions on filenames and paths (see footnotes 3 and 5 to Table 14-3). The excellent white papers, *Introduction to ISO 9660* and *Compact Disc Terminology* (available from *http://www.cinram.com*, or by calling 1-800-433-DISC), provide details on the ISO 9660 standard and common extensions. See also Appendix C in *Director in a Nutshell* for details on CD-ROM issues.

Table 14-3: Macintosh and Windows Path Specifications

Item	Macintosh	Windows 3.1/DOS	Windows 95/NT
Drive ID[1]	Name (27 chars)	Letter A-Z	Letter A-Z
Drive delimiter	:	:\	:\
Path delimiter	:	\	\
Max fileName length	31 chars	8 chars + 3-letter extension	245-255 chars[2]
Max folder name length	31 chars	8 chars	245-255 chars[2]
Max overall file path length[3]	> 255 chars (virtually unlimited)	67 chars	245-255 chars[2]
File type identified by	Hidden 4-character File Type[4]	3-letter extension	3- or 4-letter extension
Files associated with application by	Hidden 4-character Creator Code[4]	WIN.INI or Windows Registry entry tied to 3-letter extension	WIN.INI or Windows Registry entry tied to 3-or 4-letter extension
Acceptable characters in filenames[5]	Anything except colon(:)[6], even spaces	Only A-Z, 0-9, or _^$~!#%&-{}@-`'(), but not commas, backslashes, spaces, more than one period, or \/:*?"<>		Any character, including spaces, except \/:*?"<>| (but cannot begin with a space)
Case-sensitive[5]	No[7]	No	No

[1] Macintosh drive names don't change unless the user changes them. Windows drive letters vary on each machine; CD-ROMs typically are letter D or later.

[2] The exact limit cited in Microsoft's documentation varies. Abide by the Windows 3.1 limits to be safe under all flavors of Windows. Long Windows pathnames may be reported using a tilde (~). For example, when retrieving the *browserName()* at "*C:\ Program Files\Netscape*" the pathname may be returned as "*C:\Progra~1\Netscape*." Windows translates to the long filename internally.

[3] ISO 9660 paths are limited to a maximum of eight folders deep. The Joliet Standard for Windows CD-ROMs is limited to 64 characters. Director only loads Xtras up to five folders deep within the *Xtras* folder.

[4] Some Macintosh applications, including Director, also recognize files by their equivalent three-letter DOS extension. See Chapter 4, *CastLibs, Cast Members, and Sprites*, in *Director in a Nutshell* for a list of file types that Director recognizes.

[5] At its most restrictive level ISO 9660 filenames allow only capital letters, digits, and the underscore. Hyphens are typically converted to underscores by CD-ROM burning software if the *ISO 9660-compatible* option is checked. UNIX and URLs on UNIX servers are also case-sensitive. See Appendix C, *Case-Sensitivity, Sort Order, Diacritical Marks, and Space-Sensitivity*.

[6] If you try to enter a colon within a Macintosh *Save File* dialog box, it is ignored. When renaming files in the Finder, colons are converted to hyphens.

[7] Only Macintosh files' hidden File Types and Creator codes are case-sensitive.

External Files

Director automatically adjusts the file paths of linked cast members, but not those used in Lingo commands. For maximum compatibility use Windows 3.1-style "eight dot three" filenames. See "Path and File Specifications" at *http://www.zeusprod.com/technote/filepath.html*.

If Director can't find a file, it will bring up the dreaded, "*Where is...?*" dialog box. Simply point to the new location for the asset, and Director will update *the file-Name of member* property accordingly when you save the file (but not within Projectors). *The searchPaths* is a list of paths that Director searches at runtime if it can't find the media at the specified location. (It also searches the current folder if *the searchCurrentFolder* is TRUE, which is the default.) Use the *add, addAt, delete,* and *deleteAt* commands to modify the *searchPaths,* but setting many paths slows disk access considerably.

Avoid the problem by keeping external files in the same folder with the Director movie or Projector and always keep files in the same relative positions during development and runtime. Refer to Example 4-8 "Checking for Linked Cast Members" in Chapter 4, *CastLibs, CastMembers, and Sprites* in *Director in a Nutshell.* "Finding Linked Cast Members" later in this chapter.

Macintosh File Types and Creator Codes

 Macintosh files' hidden File Types and Creator Codes identify a file's format and "parent" application. They are always four characters, *case-sensitive,* and space-sensitive. See "File Types, Creator Codes, and Extensions," at *http://www.zeusprod.com/technote/filetype.html*.

A Macintosh file's File Type and Creator Code can be viewed and changed with *ResEdit, Drop•Info, FileTyper, DeskTop Folder* or a similar utility.

Example 14-1 uses the Finder's *Find File* extension to view a file's File Type or Creator Code.

Example 14-1: Viewing File Type and Creator Codes

1. Choose File[➤]Find (Command-F) from the Finder's menu.
2. Choose "*file type*" or "*creator*" from the leftmost popup in the *Find File* window.
3. Drag and drop a file onto the middle third of the *Find File* window.

Refer to the FileIO Xtra's *setFinderInfo* and *getFinderInfo* methods.

Files and Folders on the Desktop:

Files and folders on the Macintosh desktop are referenced using "Desktop Folder" after the drive name and before the remainder of the path.

A file named "myDocument" on the desktop would be referred to as:
    MyHD:Desktop Folder:myDocument

A document within a folder on the desktop is referenced in a similar manner:
    MyHD:Desktop Folder:MyFolder:myDocument

Each Macintosh drive has its own "Desktop Folder." There is a space between the words "Desktop" and "Folder."

Files on the Windows 95 Desktop are stored in the hidden folder:

    C:\Windows\INF\Desktop\

Common File Problems

If your document can not be found, check for the following errors:

- Files may not be located where you think they are.

- Filenames or folder names or extensions may be misspelled.

- Extraneous spaces appear or spaces may be missing in filenames or folder names. (The FileIO Xtra treats filenames with spaces incorrectly under Windows).

- Invalid characters may be included in the pathname or filename.

- The drive letter, which varies on the PC, may be missing or incorrect.

- The drive name or desktop folder name on the Macintosh may be missing or incorrect.

- One or more folder names may be omitted within the path.

- The maximum filename or pathname length may be exceeded.

- Incorrect, missing, or excess path separators may be used. Use ":\" after the drive letter and backslashes (\) to separate items in the path under Windows. Use colons ":" as the path Separator on the Macintosh.

- A Windows *shortcut* or Mac *alias* may be used but not supported by a particular command, such as the Lingo *open* command.

- Long filenames or file names with spaces may be used under Windows when they are not supported by a particular command. You may need to use a tilde (~) to shorten the pathname. (See footnote 2 to Table 14-3.)

- Hidden files may not be supported. Director movies should not be hidden. *GetNthFileNameInFolder* treats hidden folders differently on the Macintosh and Windows.

- Beware of file operations over networks due to drive letter remapping and privileges or protection issues.

- File may be in use by another application. Always check the error status of any file operations.

- Windows applications, especially Adobe Acrobat, may require that the *working directory* be set to the same folder as the one containing the document to open. (This requires a third-party Xtra.)

- Under Windows 3.1, a limited number of file "handles" are available. Avoid having more than a few files open at once.

- The *Save as Java* feature of Director 6.5 requires that the Director file be located in a path that does not use long filenames (i.e., is "eight-dot-three").

- A command, such as *openFile()* in the FileIO Xtra, may be unexpectedly searching the current folder and *the searchPaths* if the file is not found in the specified folder.

Specifying File Paths in Lingo

You must often build a complete file path to an unknown location. As long as you know the location *relative* to the folder of the current Director movie or Projector you can use Director's properties that provide the current path can be used to construct absolute paths to other files.

The *pathName* represents the current folder, and includes a trailing "\" (Windows) or ":" (Macintosh) path separator. It allows you to specify a path to any file in the same folder as:

```
set somePath = the pathName & "somefile.ext"
```

But what if you need to specify a subfolder? You can use the "@" relative path operator to construct platform-independent paths (this is misdocumented in the *Lingo Dictionary*), but not all commands (such as those in the *FileIO* Xtra) support the "@" operator. The "@" operator is automatically replaced by *the moviePath* and any colons (":"), forward slashes ("/"), or backslashes ("\") are converted to the appropriate path separator for the current platform, such as:

```
go to movie "@/myMedia/myMovie"
```

 The "@" operator resides inside the quotes, whereas *the pathName* and similar properties reside outside the quotes.

I never use the "@" because it is prone to errors. To extract the path, Director ignores everything after the last backslash (Windows) or the last colon (Macintosh). If you specify a path such as: "D:\myMedia/myMovie.dir" Director assumes "D:\" is the path and that the movie name is "myMedia/myMovie." The movie will work on Windows because the complete path is passed to the Windows OS, which allows both forward slashes and backslashes. But it will fail on the Mac. Likewise, a forward or backward slash (which are legal characters) in a Macintosh file can confuse Director's file path parsing when transferred to Windows.

I prefer to create platform-specific paths manually, using the following trick to determine the path separator for a particular platform.

```
set the pathSep = the last char of the pathName
```

Then, if your subfolder is named, say, "DOCS" you can use:

```
set docPath = the pathName & "DOCS" & pathSep & "myFile.txt"
```

To move *up* one folder from the current path, you can either delete the end of the path (Hint: set *the itemDelimiter* and use *delete the last item*) or use this approach.

For Windows, add two dots and backslash. On the Macintosh, add an extra colon.

Example 14-2 assumes you are branching to a movie named "Demo" in the folder above the current movie's folder.

Example 14-2: Moving Down or Up One Folder

```
if the platform contains "Windows" then
  go movie the pathName & "..\DEMO"
else
  go movie the pathName & ":DEMO"
end if
```

There is no need to specify .DIR extension as Director will look for .DIR, .DXR or .DCR files automatically when using *go movie* or *play movie*. (Shockwave usually requires the .DCR extension. Director for Windows will mistakenly attempt to open a folder of the same name, if present, so don't name your folders the same as your Director movies.)

You should ensure that your path includes a trailing file separator before appending a filename.

Example 14-3 adds a trailing backslash or colon to a file path, but only if needed.

Example 14-3: Ensuring a file path separator

```
on ensurePathSep inPath
  set pathSep = the last char of the pathName
  set tempPath = inPath
  -- Make sure that the file separator is present
  -- Add trailing backslash or colon to file path if needed
  if the last char of tempPath <> pathSep then
    put pathSep after tempPath
  end if
  return tempPath
end ensurePathSep
```

For example, to create a file in the system directory you might construct a path such as:

```
set filepath = ensurePathSep (getOSdirectory())& "myfile.txt"
```

Table 14-4 shows how to specify some of the common paths.

Table 14-4: File Paths

To Write to	Save File Path	Notes
Same folder as Projector[1]	`set savePath = the applicationPath`	Path includes trailing separator
Same folder as current movie[1]	`set savePath = the pathName`	Path includes trailing separator

Table 14-4: File Paths (continued)

To Write to	Save File Path	Notes
Director Preferences folder	Use *setPref* or FileIO Xtra	`Setpref` won't work when running from CD-ROM.
Mac System Preferences folder	`set savePath = getOSdirectory() & "Preferences"`	Won't work for foreign language Macs that use a different name. Use OSutil Xtra.
Windows directory[2]	`set savePath = getOSdirectory() & "\"`	Under Windows, you must add a trailing slash to FileIO's *getOSdirectory()* method.
Other system folders of custom folder	Third-party Xtra[3]	Many third-party Xtras create folders at runtime.

[1] You cannot use the current folder to save files if running from a CD-ROM.
[2] `Getosdirectory` requires the FileIO Xtra.
[3] See "External Applications" later in the chapter for a list of Xtras that perform many system-level operations.

Parsing File Paths

The following example returns just the filename from the specified path. It sets *the itemDelimiter* to the file separator used on the current platform—the backslash (\) for Windows and the colon (:) for Macintosh. For example, a Windows path might be `C:\Folder1\Folder2\MyMovie.MOV`, and the equivalent Mac path might be `MacHD:Folder1:Folder2:MyMovie.MOV`. Note that we restore *the itemDelimiter* so as not to alter it.

Example 14-4: Extracting the FileName from a Path

```
on getFileName inputPath
  set oldDelimiter = the itemDelimiter
  set the itemDelimiter =  the last char of the pathName
  set myFile = the last item of inputPath
  set the itemDelimiter = oldDelimiter
  return myFile
end getFileName

put getFileName (the fileName of member 37)
-- "myMovie.mov"
```

See *Example 7-6*, in Chapter 7, *Strings*, for a utility to parse the drive letter or drive name from a file path.

Use *getNthFileNameInFolder* to return a list of files, or use -1 as the file number to extract the last folder in the path.

```
put lastFolder = getNthFileNameInFolder (the pathName, -1)
```

See Example 1-32 for a utility that check if a file exists.

Example 14-5 recursively traverses the directory structure to display the contents of all subfolders of the specified path.

Example 14-5: Extracting Files in Subfolders

```
on listFiles inPath
  put RETURN & "List of folder" && inPath
  set x = 1
  set fileSep = the last char of the applicationPath
    -- Check until there are no more files in the folder
    repeat while getNthFileNameInFolder(inPath, x) <> EMPTY
    -- Check if each item is itself a subfolder
    set thisItem = getNthFileNameInFolder(inPath, x)
    if getNthFileNameInFolder(inPath & thisItem, 1) ¬
      <> EMPTY then
      -- If it is a subfolder, then recurse!
      listFiles (inPath & thisItem & fileSep)
    else
      put thisItem
    end if
    set x = x + 1
  end repeat
end listFiles
```

Refer to Example 8-9, in Chapter 8, *Projectors and the Runtime Environment*, in *Director in a Nutshell*, to detect the CD-ROM drive letter under Windows at runtime (or use one of the Xtras cited later in this chapter).

File Dialog Boxes

You'll often let the user choose either the filename or folder or both for saving and retrieving files. See the *setFilterMask, displayOpen*, and *displaySave* methods of the FileIO Xtra documented later in this chapter to create File Open and File Save dialog boxes.

You can also use the MUI Dialog Xtra (except under Windows 3.1) to create file dialog boxes.

Example 14-6: MUI File Save Dialog

```
testMUI
  set MuiInstance = new (xtra "Mui")
  if not objectP (MuiInstance ) then
    alert "Error. MUI Xtra not installed"
    exit
  end if
  -- Display a File Save Dialog
  set path = FileSave (MuiInstance , "defaultFile", "prompt")
  -- See Macromedia Technote 12372 on detecting Cancel button
  if path = defaultFile then
    put "User hit cancel"
  else
    put "User chose" && path
```

Example 14-6: MUI File Save Dialog (continued)

```
  end if
end
```

This displays a File Open dialog:

```
    set MuiInstance = new (xtra "Mui")
    set path = FileOpen (MuiInstance , "defaultFile")
    if path = defaultFile then
      put "User hit cancel"
    end if
```

This displays a URL dialog:

```
    set MuiInstance = new (xtra "Mui")
    set url = GetURL (MuiInstance , "http://www.zeusprod.com", TRUE )
```

The second parameter is the default URL, and the last parameter is a Boolean indicating whether the dialog is movable. There is no way to tell if the user clicked *Cancel* in the URL dialog, but you can construct your own dialog as described in the downloadable Chapter 21, *Custom MUI Dialogs.*

Note that the previous functions provide only the user interface. It is up to you to actually access the filename or URL returned by these methods.

The *FileIO* Xtra does not let you pick *only* a folder (without a file), nor does it let you specify an initial default folder in which to begin file browsing. Refer to the Xtras at the end of this chapter, which have those capabilities.

Table 14-5: User Selection Files and Folders

To Let User Choose	Use This
FileName, but not folder	Field sprite or custom MUI Dialog box
Folder, but not filename	Third-party Xtra, such as PickFolder[1]
File starting from preferred folder	Third-party Xtra such as FileXtra[1]
Filename and folder to open	FileIO's *displayOpen* method or MUI's *FileOpen* method.
Filename and folder to save	FileIO's *displaySave* method or MUI's *FileSave* method.
Limit the files shown in file browser dialog	FileIO's *setFilterMask* method
A URL to enter	Field sprite or MUI's *GetURL* method.

[1] See "External Applications" later in the chapter for a list of Xtras that perform many system-level operations.

FileIO

The FileIO Xtra is used to read and write text files, but it can not access remote URLs (use NetLingo commands such as getNetText), nor is it designed for binary files (see the BinaryIO Xtra at *http://www.updatestage.com/xtras/*).

Director 4 used the older *FileIO* XObject. Director 5 included both the XObject and the Xtra versions, which conflicted if they were both used.

The older Macintosh *FileIO XObject* was embedded in the resource fork of the Director 4 and 5 authoring package *and* D4 Projectors (but not D5 Projectors). The XObject is discontinued in D6, but it is included in a separate resource file under *Director 6 CD:Macromedia:Discontinued:FileIO XObject:FileIO XObject.rsrc*.

The older Windows *FileIO XObject* (that is, FILEIO.DLL) was opened automatically during authoring in D4 and D5 via an *openXlib* command in the *on startUp* handler in the default LINGO.INI file. To use it from a Windows Projector you had to include FILEIO.DLL with the Projector and either use *openXlib* or the default LINGO.INI file to open it. (See Appendix D, *The DIRECTOR.INI and LINGO.INI Files*, for details on LINGO.INI.) Under Windows, FILEIO.DLL is no longer installed by default, but it can be found on the D6 for Windows CD under *D:\Macromedia\Discontinued\FileIO XObject\Fileio.dll*. It is not compatible with 32-bit Projectors and should not be used any more.

If using Director 5 or 6, you should use version 1.0.3 (or later) of the *FileIO Xtra*. The *FileIO* Xtra is installed by default in the **Xtras/Media Support** folder one level down from Director. Check its version in the Message window.

```
put version (xtra "FileIO")
-- "FileIO for Director 6.0 (1.0.3 Dec 8 1997)"
```

If the *version()* command fails, either the Xtra is not installed or you still have version 1.0 that shipped with D5.0.

If using any of *FileIO's* methods, you must include the Xtra(s) shown in Table 14-6 with your Projector, preferably in an *Xtras* folder one level down from your Projector (I recommend against bundling Xtras into Projectors. See Chapter 10, *Using Xtras*, in *Director in a Nutshell* for details.)

Refer to:

* The example Director movie on the Director 6 CD under *Goodies/Movies/FileIO Behaviors.DIR*.

* TechNote #3192, "FileIO Xtra Examples," on Macromedia's Web site.

* Chapter 5 (written by me) of *Director Power Solutions* from New Riders (ISBN 1-56205-665-4) for details on using *FileIO* to save and retrieve text files including a high score chart.

Table 14-6: FileIO Xtras

Projectors	Xtra Name
Any Macintosh Projector	FileIOXtraFat
16-bit Windows Projectors running under Win 3.1 or Win 95/NT	FILEIO16.X16
32-bit Windows Projectors (Win 95/NT only)	FILEIO.X32

The Director 6 for Macintosh CD includes a *ReadMe* file under Director 6 CD:Macromedia:FileIO v.1.0.2 Release:FileIO Notes. This is not included on the D6 for Windows CD, but a similar *ReadMe* came with the FileIO v1.0.1 update. Or see TechNotes on Macromedia's site

Table 14-7 shows the FileIO Xtra's high-level methods. See Table 14-8 for the instance-level methods.

Table 14-7: FileIO's Global and Xtra-Level Methods

FileIO Xtra	Use
put mMessageList (xtra "FileIO")	Returns brief documentation.
set *instance* = new (xtra "FileIO")	Instantiates the Xtra.
put version (xtra "FileIO")	Return the FileIO Xtra's version.
set *systemPath* = getOSdirectory()[1]	Returns path to Window directory or Macintosh System folder.

[1] The correct name is "*getOSdirectory*," not "*getOSdir*" as claimed in some *FileIO* documentation.

File Operations

Files can be opened in *Read/Write, Read-only,* and *Write-only* mode, which affects the allowable commands. Data is always read and written sequentially from the position in the file indicated by the *getPosition()* method. The file position defaults to 0. Data written to a file either lengthens the file automatically or overwrites existing data following the current file position. To append data, set the position to the end of the file using:

```
setPosition (instance, getLength(instance))
```

There is no way to delete data from a file without deleting the entire file.

The methods in Table 14-8 require a FileIO instance as returned by the new() method shown in Table 14-7.

Table 14-8 shows all the instance-level methods of the FileIO Xtra.

Table 14-8: FileIO's Instance-Level Methods

Method	Notes	File Must Be
closeFile (*instance*)[1]	Close a file that has been previously opened using *openFile()*. Blanks the *fileName()*.	File must be open.
createFile(*instance*, *filePath*)[1]	Create a file. Specify a full *filepath*, or the default folder is *the applicationPath*, not *the pathName*. "@" operator is not supported. You must use *openFile()* after *createFile()*.	File must not be open (or already exist).
delete(*instance*)[1]	Delete the currently opened file.	File must be open.

Table 14-8: FileIO's Instance-Level Methods (continued)

Method	Notes	File Must Be
display-Open(*instance*)[1,2]	Display a platform-specific Open File dialog (includes hidden files). You cannot specify a default filename or folder. Returns the full chosen path or EMPTY if the user canceled the dialog. *DisplayOpen()* gets a pathname but does not open the file. See *setFilterMask, displaySave*.	Doesn't matter.
displaySave(*instance*, *prompt*, *defaultFileName*)[1,2]	Displays a platform-specific Save File dialog with specified prompt and default file. You cannot specify a default folder. Returns the full chosen path or EMPTY if the user canceled the dialog. *DisplaySave()* gets a pathname, but does not create the file. To determine if the user chose to replace an existing file, check if the *status()* returned by *createFile()* is -122 ("File already exists"). See *setFilterMask, displayOpen*.	Doesn't matter.
error (*instance*, *code*)[3]	Translates an integer error code, such as that returned by *status()*, into a string. See Appendix E, *Error Messages and Error Codes*, for list of error codes and error strings.	Doesn't matter.
fileName(*instance*)[3]	Returns the path specified in *openFile()* command (where you should always specify the full path) or EMPTY following a *closeFile()*. It may *not* reflect the actual file opened if *FileIO* searched the current folder or *the searchPaths*. The *create-File()* command may affect it unreliably.	Should be open.
getFinderInfo(*instance*)[3]	Returns the File Type and Creator Code of the current Macintosh file as a string. File does not need to be open. Works with last known open file or sets *status()* to -38 if no file has been opened with *instance*. Returns VOID (under Windows) or defaults to "???? ????" for unknown files and "TEXT ttxt" for .txt files created with FileIO (on the Mac).	Should be open, but mode doesn't matter.
getLength(*instance*)[1]	Gets the length in bytes of the currently open file. Returns VOID if no file is open.	Should be open, but mode doesn't matter.
getPosition(*instance*)[1]	Gets the current (zero-relative) position in bytes within the last open file.	Should be open, but mode doesn't matter.

Table 14-8: FileIO's Instance-Level Methods (continued)

Method	Notes	File Must Be
openFile (*instance*, *filePath*, *mode*)[1]	Use *openFile()* before writing to or reading from a file. (You can open any existing file regardless of previous calls to *displayOpen()*, *displaySave()*, or *createFile()*). Specify a complete path, although the default is *the pathName (not the applicationPath* as for *createFile*) and *mode* is: 0: Read/Write 1: Read-only (no writing) 2: Write-only (no reading) If the file cannot be found at the specified path, FileIO will look in the current folder if *the searchCurrentFolder* is TRUE (the default) and *the searchPaths*. Under Windows, it may work with incorrect spaces in the filename. Opening "readme.txt" (without a space) will find "read me.txt" (with a space). FileIO also finds invisible (hidden) files.	File must be closed and must exist. Previously opened files must be closed with *closeFile()*.
readChar(*instance*)[1]	Reads next character from current file position and advances file position pointer.	Open for Read or Read/Write.
readFile(*instance*)[1]	Reads text from the current file position to the end of the file and advances file position pointer.	Open for Read or Read/Write.
readLine(*instance*)[1]	Reads text from the current position up to and including the next CR/LF and advances file position pointer. Use *line 1 of readLine()* to strip off the CR/LF.	Open for Read or Read/Write.
readToken(*instance*, *skipChar*, *breakChar*)[1]	Reads the next "token" starting at the current position. Set *skipChar* to EMPTY to return all characters,and set *breakChar* to a separating character, such as SPACE. Set both *skipChar* and *breakChar* to "," to parse comma-delimited tokens and strip out any commas.	File must be open for Read or Read/Write.
readWord(*instance*)[1]	Reads next word (as delineated by spaces, not *TAB* or *RETURN*) from current file position and advances file position pointer.	Open for Read or Read/Write.
setFilterMask(*instance*, *mask*)[3]	Affects the files shown in file dialog by *displayOpen* and *displaySave*.	Doesn't matter.
setFinder-Info(*instance*, *typeAndCreator*)[3]	Sets the File Type and Creator Code of the current file as a string. File does not need to be open. Works with last known open file or sets *status()* to -38 if no file has been opened with *instance*. (Has no effect in Windows.)	Should be open, but mode doesn't matter.
setPosition(*instance*, *newPosition*)[1]	Sets the file position of the currently open file. Should be set between 0 and the length returned by *getLength()*. Negative values interfere with reading, and values that are beyond the end of the file may cause crash on next read operation.	Should be open, but mode doesn't matter.

Table 14-8: FileIO's Instance-Level Methods (continued)

Method	Notes	File Must Be
status(*instance*)[3]	Returns the integer code set by the last method called. (0 indicates success.) The *status()*, *error()*, and non-instance-level methods shown in Table 4-6 do not affect the status. *Status()* will not indicate whether a file is open or in what mode it is open. See *error()* or Appendix E to translate the code.	Doesn't matter.
writeChar(*instance*, *char*)[1]	Writes a single character at current file position and advances file position pointer. Writes only first character if longer string is specified.	File must be open for Write or Read/Write.
writeString(*instance*, *string*)[1]	Writes a string to the file at the current file position. Manually include *RETURN* character to add line breaks.	File must be open for Write or Read/Write

[1] Affects the value obtained by *status()*.
[2] Always sets the value obtained by *status()* to 0.
[3] Does not change value obtained by *status()*.

Use a global variable, such as *gFileInstance*, for your Xtra instance and add the following to the Watcher window to track FileIO's progress:

```
fileName(gFileInstance)
status (gFileInstance)
error(gFileInstance, status (gFileInstance))
```

Don't add expressions such as *getPosition(gFileInstance)* to the Watcher window because they'll constantly reset the *error()* status to "OK."

Example 14-7 writes *outputText* to the file specfied by *SaveFilePath*. If no path is specified the user is prompted for a file name.

Example 14-7: Writing to a File

```
on writeToFile outputText, saveFilePath
  -- Use -1 to indicate a failure
  set resultFlag = -1

  set fileXtra = new (xtra "FileIO")
  if not objectP(fileXtra) then
    alert "FileIO Xtra not Installed"
    return resultFlag
  end if

  if voidP (saveFilePath) then
  -- Prompt the user for a Save File if file name not defined
    if the platform contains "Windows" then
      setFilterMask (fileXtra, "All Files,*.*")
    else
      setFilterMask (fileXtra, EMPTY)
    end if
```

External Files

Example 14-7: Writing to a File (continued)

```
    set saveFilePath = displaySave (fileXtra, ¬
      "File To Save", "myData.txt")
    if saveFilePath = EMPTY then
      alert "No save file path has been set"
      return resultFlag
    end if
  end if

-- Attempt to create the file
createFile (fileXtra, saveFilePath)
case (status (fileXtra)) of
  0:  -- Successful file creation
    nothing
  -122:  -- File already exists. -- Delete and recreate it
    -- So that it is not mixed with old data in file
    openFile (fileXtra, saveFilePath, 0)
    delete (fileXtra)
    createFile (fileXtra, saveFilePath)
    if status (fileXtra) <> 0 then
      put "Error:" && error (fileXtra, status (fileXtra))
      return resultFlag
    end if
  otherwise:
    put "Error:" && error (fileXtra, status (fileXtra))
    return resultFlag
end case

  -- Open the file with Read/Write Access
  -- valid modes: 0=read/write, 1=read, 2=write
  openFile (fileXtra, saveFilePath, 0)

  -- Check if it succeeded
if  status (fileXtra) = 0 then
  -- Record the data passed in
  writeString (fileXtra, outputText)
  setFinderInfo (fileXtra, "TEXT ttxt")
  closeFile (fileXtra)
  return 1 -- Success code
else
  put "Error occurred" && error (fileXtra, status (fileXtra))
  return resultFlag
end if
end writeToFile
```

Test it in the Message window. The example assumes that you are passing in a full qualified path. Otherwise it would fail because *createFile* and *openFile* default to different folders:

```
put writeToFile ("here is some text", the pathName & "temp")
-- 1
```

Write to File prompts the user for a path if none is specified:

```
put writeToFile ("here is some text")
```

Example 14-8 reads text from the specified file. If no file path is specified, it prompts the user to select from existing text files.

Example 14-8: Reading from a File

```
-- This routines reads the data back in
on readFromFile readFilePath
  set fileXtra = new (xtra "FileIO")
  if not objectP(fileXtra) then
    return Void
  end if

  if voidP (readFilePath) then
    -- Prompt the user for a text file to read
    if the platform contains "Windows" then
      setFilterMask (fileXtra, "Text Files,*.txt")
    else
      setFilterMask (fileXtra, "TEXTttro")
    end if
    set readFilePath = displayOpen (fileXtra)
    if readFilePath = EMPTY then
      alert "No read file path has been set"
      return resultFlag
    end if
  end if

  -- Open the file with Read Access
  -- valid modes: 0=read/write, 1=read, 2=write
  openFile (fileXtra, readFilePath, 1)
  set resultCode = status (fileXtra)

  -- Check if it succeeded
  if resultCode = 0 then
    set returnData = readFile (fileXtra)
    closeFile (fileXtra)
    return returnData
  else
    put "Error occurred" && error(fileXtra, status(fileXtra))
    return Void
  end if
end readFromFile
```

Test it in the Message window. The example assumes that you are passing in a full qualified path. Otherwise it would fail because *createFile* and *openFile* default to different folders:

```
put readFromFile(the  pathName & "temp")
-- "Here is some text"
```

Read from File() prompts the user for a text file name if none is specified:

```
put readFromFile()
```

FileIO may be confused by file's containing null characters (ASCII 0). It will generally assume that a null character indicates the end of a file or a string to be written.

SetFilterMask

The filter mask set by *setFilterMask()* affects the files shown in the *displayOpen()* and *displaySave()* file dialog boxes.

On Windows, it is a comma-separated string of file types and the associated extensions, of the form:

```
setFilterMask (instance, ¬
        "description, extension {, description, extension}")
```

Example 14-9: SetFilterMask

```
setFilterMask (instance, ¬
     "description, extension {, description, extension}")
setFilterMask (instance, "Text Files,*.TXT") -- Text files
setFilterMask (instance, "All Files,*.*")     -- All files
setFilterMask (instance, "All Files,*.*,Text Files,*.TXT")
```

On the Macintosh, it is a string of up to four case-sensitive four-character File Types (see "Macintosh File Types and Creator Codes" earlier in this chapter).

```
setFilterMask (fileIOinstance, "typeTYPEtypeTYPE")
```

For example:

```
setFilterMask (fileIOinstance, "TEXT")        -- TEXT files
setFilterMask (fileIOinstance, "TEXTPICT")    -- TEXT and PICT files
setFilterMask (fileIOinstance, "MooV")        -- QuickTime files
setFilterMask (fileIOinstance, EMPTY)         -- All Files
```

 Macintosh HTML files use the File Type "TEXT" as do other text files; they don't have a unique File Type. They use TEXT along with other plain text files.

SetFinderInfo and GetFinderInfo

SetFinderInfo and *getFinderInfo* set and read the File Type and Creator Code from a Macintosh file. *SetFinderInfo()* accepts a string of a case-sensitive four-character File Type separated by a space from a case-sensitive four-character Creator Code.

Example 14-10: SetFinderInfo and GetFinderInfo

```
setFinderInfo (instance, "Type Creator")
```
To set the type for text files for *TeachText* or *SimpleText* use:

Example 14-10: SetFinderInfo and GetFinderInfo (continued)

```
setFinderInfo (instance, "TEXT ttxt")
```
For read-only *SimpleText* files use:
```
setFinderInfo (instance, "ttro ttxt")
```
GetFinderInfo() reads the File Type and Creator Codes as a single nine-character string (the two codes separated by a space).
```
set typeCreator = getFinderInfo (instance)
set fileType = char 1 to 4 of typeCreator
set creator  = char 6 to 9 of typeCreator.
```

There are various "Auto-Typer" applets (some come with Macromedia products) that add File Type and Creator Codes to Macintosh files. It is left as an exercise to the reader to write a utility that adds them to Macintosh-compatible files ported from Windows with extensions such as .DIR, .PCT, .MOV, and .AIF.

See Table 16-3, "Supported Import File Formats" under "Importing Media into the Cast" in Chapter 4 of *Director in a Nutshell* for a list of File Type codes for Director-related files. For a large list of codes, see *http://www.angelfire.com/il/szekely/index.html*

Differences Between the FileIO Xtra and XObject

There are many similarities but some major differences between the older FileIO XObject and the FileIO Xtra. With the XObject, an instance is created when the file is opened or created, and the file is closed when the instance is disposed. With the Xtra, an instance can be used with multiple files as long as each is closed before the next one is opened.

The FileIO XObject's *mNew()* method performed all the operations now supported by the FileIO Xtra's *new()*, *openFile()*, *createFile()*, *displayOpen()*, *displaySave()*, *setFilterMask()*, and *setPosition()* methods.

The FileIO XObject supported an "append" mode, which must be simulated with the FileIO Xtra by setting the pointer position to the end of the file, as described previously under "File Operations". The FileIO Xtra also offers native PowerPC and Windows 32-bit support. The *mWriteChar* and *mReadChar* methods of the XObject write and read ASCII codes. The FileIO XObject (that is, FILEIO.DLL) was limited to transferring 64 KB of data in any single read or write operation. That is no longer the case with the 32-bit FileIO Xtra (but is still allegedly the case with the 16-bit FileIO Xtra). Refer to *http://www.zeusprod.com/nutshell/examples.html* an example that buffers file reading and writing in 64 KB segments.

The old FileIO XObject won't work under Windows NT, especially with a 32-bit Projector.

See *http://www.zeusprod.com/nutshell/chapters/fileio.html* for a table comparing each operation between the FileIO XObject and FileIO Xtra.

Preferences File

The *getPref* and *setPref* commands are new in Director 6. They are much easier to use than the *FileIO* Xtra, and they are designed primarily for Shockwave. Shockwave supports Xtras, but you should *not* encourage users to install the *FileIO* Xtra in their Shockwave plug-ins folder because it eviscerates the security features built into the Shockwave plug-in. (*GetPref* and *setPref* can be used from Director or Projectors, but *setPref* won't work from a read-only drive, such as a CD-ROM.)

```
setPref (prefFile, prefText)
set prefText = getPref(prefFile)
```

SetPref writes **prefText** to a **prefFile**, and **getPref** retrieves it. The file must have a .TXT or .HTM extension, and the default is .TXT. You can have multiple preference files, each up to 32 KB in length. Don't specify a folder, as it must reside in the following folders:

From Director or a Projector on the Macintosh the preferences folder is named:

`ApplicationName folder:Prefs:`

It resides one level down from Director or the Projector, such as:

MacHD:Applications:Director 6.0:Director 6.0 folder:Prefs:prefFile.txt
MyDrive:Projector folder:Prefs:prefFile.txt (assuming Projector is in root)

 If the Macintosh Projector name exceeds 24 characters, *setPref* and *getPref* will fail without any notification. Appending the seven characters " *folder*" to create the preferences folder's name will exceed the Mac OS limit of 31 characters per folder name.

From Director or a Projector on Windows the preference folder is named:

`"Prefs"`

It resides one level down from Director or the Projector, such as:

C:\Program Files\Macromedia\Director 6_5\Prefs\prefFile.txt
D:\Prefs\prefFile.txt (assuming Projector is in root)

From Shockwave *setPref* and *getPref* use the Plug-In Support folder where the browser is installed.

For example, on the Macintosh:

Navigator Folder:Plug-ins:NP-PPC-Dir-Shockwave folder:Prefs:prefFile.txt

For example under Windows:

C:\Program Files\Netscape\Program\PLUGINS\NP32DSW\Prefs\prefFile.txt
C:\Program Files\Internet Explorer\Program\NP32DSW\Prefs\prefFile.txt

If for some reason you want to find the Preferences folder used by *setPref* from a Projector, use *the movieName* from the *first* movie in the projector (it yields the Projector's name).

On the Macintosh:

```
set myPrefFolder = the applicationPath & [LC]
  the movieName && "Folder:Prefs:"
```

On Windows:

```
set myPrefFolder = the applicationPath & "Prefs\"
```

Writing Data to a File

You decide how to write out your data to meet your needs. There are many ways to structure your data file. You may separate items by spaces or commas, or you may place each item on its own line. Pick some separator that will not get confused with the rest of your data. You can choose a unique character, such as a tilde, then use *readToken* or *the itemDelimiter* and the *item...of* commands to parse the data.

On the Macintosh, line breaks are written as <CR> (ASCII 13). On the PC, they are written as <CR><LF> (ASCII 13 and 10), which may be important if exporting data to a text database. Although *FileIO* will handle this transparently, you have to add the Lingo constant RETURN wherever you want a line break, such as in the following.

On the Macintosh:

writeString (*FileIOinstance*, "*text*" & RETURN)

On Windows:

writeString (*FileIOinstance*, "*text*" & RETURN & numToChar (10))

Inspect your text file in a word processor to spot potential problems. You'll notice that symbols are stripped of the pound character (#) and that Void values are written out as empty strings. You may not be able to save and retrieve lists that contain Void values or empty sublists (it won't convert them back from strings properly when using the *value()* function). Because objects refer to memory locations, you cannot save and retrieve them to or from a file. Instead, save their *properties* individually and reallocate the object and reassign its properties at runtime (or recreate them from scratch).

You can encrypt your data using third-party Xtras or a simple code of your own design, such as subtracting a fixed number from each character's ASCII value before writing it out. Add a file version string as the first line of your file, or use a custom File Type or extension to increase the chances that the file you're reading is of the correct type.

Parsing Retrieved Data

When data is read from a file, it is always returned as a string. Parse the items using the *readChar, readWord, readLine,* and *readToken* methods in the *FileIO* Xtra, or read all the data using the *readFile* method and parse it with Lingo. See the text parsing commands under "Text Parsing" in Chapter 7.

Use the conversion functions shown in Table 5-3 in Chapter 5, *Data Types and Expressions,* to convert the strings read from the file back into the original data types. You should know exactly how to interpret the data because you should know the order in which you wrote it out in the first place.

Don't forget to re-sort lists that were sorted prior to being stored. Even though the elements may be ordered, Lingo will not treat it as a truly sorted list unless you use the *sort()* command after recreating the List. See Chapter 6, *Lists.*

External Applications

Director does a lot of things well, but Xtras really enhance its ability to deal with external files. These are just some of the Xtras available that will open external applications, copy files, create folders, kill and manage processes, read and write to the Windows Registry and INI files, and much, much more. Consult the links in the *Preface* including *http://www.macromedia.com/software/xtras/director* as it is impossible to list all the Xtras that deal with external files.

Start with the free Xtras: FileIO, which is included with all versions of Director, and FileXtra (*http://www.littleplanet.com/kent/kent.html*), which is freeware and also ships with D6.5.

Zeus Productions (my company)

Sells Xtras that control external applications:

- *http://www.zeusprod.com/products/*
- *zLaunch* (Mac and Windows) launches and waits for external applications in low-memory situations and also covers the desktop.
- *zOpen/zPrint* (Windows) locates the application associated with an external document and uses it to open or print that document.
- *zScript* (Macintosh) adds ability to send and receive AppleEvents to and from Director via AppleScript.

UpdateStage

- Many Xtras that deal with external files, such as *MasterApp* by Glenn Picher and the *Dialogs* Xtra by Scott Kildall (Red Eye Software), previously sold at *http://www.gmatter.com/*, may now instead be found at *http://www.updatestage.com/xtras/*.
- Glenn Picher's *BinaryIO* Xtra (currently in beta for both Macintosh and Windows) reads and writes binary files, including files containing null characters (ASCII 0). See *http://www.updatestage.com/xtras/* or *mailto:gcm@updatestage.com* regarding beta-testing.

The *OSutil* Xtra for Macintosh

Includes many OS-level functions, such as CD Eject, File Copy, and much more (a Windows version may also be available):

> *http://www.ddce.cqu.edu.au/imu/tools/Director/Xtras*It

The Buddy API Xtra for Windows includes many, many OS-level functions of all sorts. (A Macintosh version of Buddy API is in beta.)

> *http://www.mods.com.au/budapi*

The DirectOS Xtra for Windows is similar to Buddy API. Its *SetCurrentDirectory* method sets the default folder, which is useful before using FileIO's *displayOpen()* method.

> *http://www.directxtras.com/do_home.htm*

Refer also to Chapter 9, *Mouse Events*, and Chapter 10, *Keyboard Events*, as the Buddy API and DirectOS Xtras have many uses.

Text parsing and type conversions in Lingo can be very slow, especially when converting strings to lists or vice versa. Refer to Chapter 10, *Using Xtras*, in *Director in a Nutshell* (or *http://www.zeusprod.com/nutshell/links.html*) for a number of Xtras that access external text files and databases.

Printing

Director has a built-in printing command, but for more sophisticated printing, use a third-party Xtra, such as PrintOMatic *(http://welcome.crestedbutte.net/ink/)* or mPrint *(http://www.mediashoppe.com)*, which does not require Lingo.

Table 14-9: Printing

To Do This	Use This
Print a Storyboard from Director during Authoring	`File[▶]Print`
Print from Lingo	Lingo *printFrom*[1] command or PrintOMatic[2] *print* command
Print a cast member	PrintOMatic[2] *print* command
Print external text file	See Example 14-11
Print in landscape mode	PrintOMatic[2]
Print external Acrobat, Word, or other special format using external application	zOpen/zPrint

[1] *PrintFrom* prints the items in the *Score*. It does not print puppeted sprites as they appear on stage.
[2] As of May 1998, the latest version of *PrintOMatic* is sold and supported exclusively by Peter Vanags of Electronic Ink (*http://welcome.crestedbutte.net/ink/*), not g/matter. The lite version that comes with Director 6 does not support all features.

Example 14-11 imports and prints an external text file using *PrintOMatic*'s print command.

Example 14-11: Printing an External Text File

```
set temp = findEmpty(member 1)
importFileInto (member temp, fileToImport)
print the text of member temp
```

The demonstrated method is poor because the text file is imported as a rich text cast member (which is slow and consumes memory). You can either use a third-party Xtra to print an external file using an external application or rewrite Example 14-11 using the FileIO Xtra to read the file's text and store its contents in a field cast member (which is left as an exercise to the reader).

External File Caveats

Working Directory

Some Windows applications, especially Adobe Acrobat require the working directory to be set. 2 Open for Windows (*http://www.zeusprod.com/products/2open.html*) sets the working directory where as Lingo's open command does not. Failure to set the working directory causes an unspecified internal error with Adobe Acrobat.

Drive Errors

Window 3.1 and NT (but not necessarily Windows 95/98) will generate an error when attempting to access a floppy drive while no disk is inserted. Avoid using getNthFileNameInFolder, FileIO, or the SearchPath to access such a drive. Some Xtras may be able to disable these error messages.

CHAPTER 15

The MUI Dialog Xtra

The MUI Xtra is new to Director 6 and can create a variety of custom dialog boxes, including Alert boxes. It is used during authoring by Director and other Xtras. It is installed in the *Xtras/Media Support* subfolder by default, and it must be shipped with your Projector in order to create custom dialogs at runtime.

If using any of the MUI Xtra's methods, you must include the Xtras named "MUI Dialog" (for Macintosh) or "Mui Dialog.x32" (for Windows) with your Projector, preferably in an *Xtras* folder one level down from your Projector. (I recommend against bundling Xtras into Projectors. See Chapter 10, *Using Xtras,* in *Director in a Nutshell* for details.)

The MUI Xtra's main limitation is that it is available only for the Macintosh and 32-bit Projectors under Windows 95/NT. If you are using 16-bit (Windows 3.1) Projectors or Shockwave, you should use one of the alternatives discussed in Chapter 14, *Graphical User Interface Components,* in *Director in a Nutshell.* The MUI Xtra may also conflict with open MIAWs. Close any MIAWs before using the MUI Xtra or any feature of Director that uses MUI, such as the Behavior *Parameters* dialog box. See the following Technote for additional details:

http://www.macromedia.com/support/director/ts/documents/unexpected_error.htm

MUI Alert Dialogs

The MUI Xtra's *Alert()* command creates modal dialogs with up to three buttons. Its text capacity is limited to 255 characters; for longer text blocks you'll need to create a custom dialog (see the downloadable Chapter 21, *Custom MUI Dialogs*). *Alert()* accepts a property list defining the button choices, the text to display, and so on. Example 15-1 creates the dialog shown in Figure 15-1.

Example 15-1: Standard Multibutton MUI Alert Dialog

```
on testMUIalert
    -- Create an instance of the MUI Xtra
```

Example 15-1: Standard Multibutton MUI Alert Dialog (continued)

```
set MUIobject = new (xtra "MUI")
-- The MUI Alert doesn't beep, so let's do so manually.
beep
-- Define the attributes of the dialog in a property list
set alertPropertiesList = ¬
  [#buttons:  #YesNo, ¬
   #default:  2, ¬
   #title:    "Quit", ¬
   #message:  "Are you sure you want to quit?", ¬
   #movable:  TRUE, ¬
   #icon:     #stop]
-- Post the dialog and wait for a user response
set answer = Alert (MUIobject, alertPropertiesList)
-- Dispose of the MUI Object
set MUIobject = 0
-- Check the answer against the possible user choices
put "User chose button" && answer
case (answer) of
  1:   -- User chose first button (in this case 'Yes')
      halt   -- the user chose to quit in this case
  2:   -- User chose second button (in this case 'No')
      go frame 1  -- the user didn't quit, so start over
end case
end testMUIalert
```

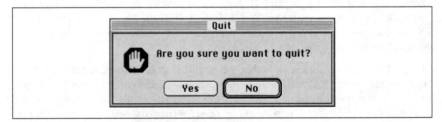

Figure 15-1: Two-Button Alert dialog

Note that *Alert()* returns an integer indicating the number of the button that the user chose. For example, if the alert's buttons are *Yes* and *No*, a return value of 2 specifies that the second button (*No*) was pressed.

Table 15-1 shows each item used to define the Alert dialog. You need only specify the properties for which the default is inadequate, such as *#message* and *#buttons*.

Table 15-1: MUI Alert Properties

Property	Use	Range
#buttons	The buttons that appear in the Alert (in the order in which they are named in each symbol, such as *#AbortRetryIgnore*).	#AbortRetryIgnore, #Ok (default), #OkCancel, #RetryCancel #YesNo, #YesNoCancel.

Table 15-1: MUI Alert Properties (continued)

Property	Use	Range
#default	The ordinal number of the button to use as the default.[1] Specify 0 for no default.	0, 1, 2, or 3 (up to maximum number of buttons). (Default is 1.)
#icon	The type of icon that appears in the alert dialog.[2]	#caution, #error, #note, #question, #stop (default is no icon). See Figure 15-2.
#message	Message string that appears in the alert dialog.	Any string up to 255 characters (default is "<Null>" under Windows, and EMPTY on Mac).
#movable[3]	Indicates whether the dialog is movable.[4]	TRUE or FALSE (default is FALSE on Mac and always TRUE under Windows).
#title	Title string for the Alert dialog.[4]	Any string of up to 255 characters (default is "<Null>").

[1] The default button choice is shown with a thick border and is selected if the user presses RETURN. If #default is omitted, the default is 1. For example, if #buttons is #YesNoCancel, the default choice would be the first button, in this case "Yes."
[2] Omit the #icon property from the list to prevent an icon from being used. Specifying an invalid #icon, such as 0 or an invalid symbol, prevents the dialog from appearing and may cause a crash.
[3] #movable is spelled without an "e" (differs from *the moveableSprite of sprite* property).
[4] The dialog is always movable and always contains a title bar under Windows, regardless of the #movable property. On the Macintosh, the #title is ignored (the Alert box has no title) unless #movable is TRUE. If #movable is TRUE and #title is not specified, the title displays as "<Null>." Use *#title:EMPTY* to blank the title bar.

The *Alert()* dialog automatically displays buttons in English, French, German, or Japanese when running under an OS localized to those languages. For all other languages, the button labels default to English. Create customized buttons in other languages using a custom dialog as described in the downloadable Chapter 21.

Note in Figure 15-2 that the appearance of the icons is platform-specific and that the same graphic is used for multiple *#icon* settings in some cases.

Custom MUI Dialogs

The MUI Xtra can create and control custom dialog boxes (see Figure 15-3) containing buttons, editable fields, labels, sliders, popups, and even bitmaps. (It also creates simple Alert dialogs and File dialogs for saving and opening files or entering URLs, as covered in Chapter 14, *External Files.*)

MUI custom dialog boxes:

- Can contain buttons with custom labels, unlike *Alert()* dialogs
- Can contain numerous user interface elements
- Can include horizontal scrolling editable text fields
- Allow clipboard operations for editable text (doesn't seem to work)
- Can be updated dynamically based on a user's choices
- Use less memory than a MIAW used to simulate a dialog box

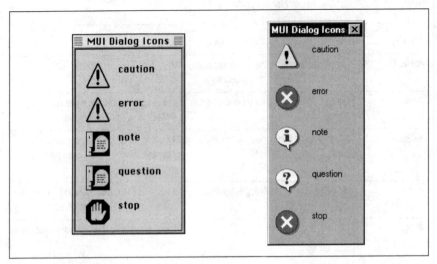

Figure 15-2: Macintosh MUI dialog icons

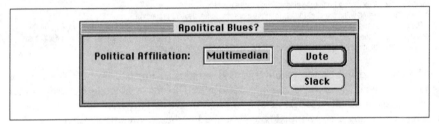

Figure 15-3: Sample Custom MUI Dialog

- Have the same platform-specific appearance as native dialog boxes
- Respond to keyboard commands like native dialog boxes
- Can contain very large text strings (more than 255 characters)

 Due to space limitations, this chapter documents only the MUI Xtra's *Alert()* method. Refer to the bonus online chapter at *http://www.zeus-prod.com/nutshell/chapters/muixtra.html* for details on creating custom dialog boxes with the MUI Xtra.

PART V

Lingo Command Reference

CHAPTER 16

Enumerated Values

Many Lingo commands and functions accept parameters or return values that have a special meaning. For example, *the alignment of member* property can be set to the string *"left," "center,"* or *"right."* Other commands, such as *cacheDocVerify()*, use symbols (in this case, *#always* or *#once*) for their possible values. Still other Lingo commands, such as *the windowType of window,* use integer codes with particular meanings (in this case, the window style). All of these cases are referred to as *enumerated* values.

Table 16-1 shows the meaning of the enumerated values for applicable Lingo commands. This table supplements Table 18-1, "The Lingo Keyword and Command Summary," in which there was not room for the details listed here. Table 16-1 does *not* include Boolean properties (which are either TRUE or FALSE) or functions that accept a continuous range of integer or float values such as *the locH of sprite* property. Refer to Chapter 5, *Coordinates, Alignment, and Registration Points*, in *Director in a Nutshell* for a detailed list of commands that use rects and points.

In Table 16-1, a single symbol may be used with multiple commands. For example, *ilk()*, *the type of member*, *the castType of member*, and *getProperty-DescriptionList's #format* option all use cast member type symbols, such as *#bitmap* and *#digitalVideo*. Likewise, *ilk()* and *getPropertyDescriptionList's #format* option both use additional data type symbols such as *#float* and *#integer*.

Some commands, such as *puppetTransition* and *the transitionType of member,* may use identical enumerated values, but Lingo is often inconsistent. For example, *the framePalette* and *the palette of member* use the integer code -1 to indicate the built-in Macintosh System palette, but *the paletteRef* uses the symbol *#systemMac*, and *puppetPalette* uses the string *"System."*

Example 5-2, "Replacing Integer Codes with Symbols," in Chapter 5, *Data Types and Expressions,* shows how to use a property list to represent the integer codes used for *the ink of sprite* and other Lingo properties. See Table 11-4 for a list of the time units used by various commands.

In Table 16-1, a vertical bar "|" indicates a choice between the specified values. Curly braces {} indicate optional arguments.

Table 16-1: Enumerated Values for Lingo Commands

Command	Enumerated Values
Alert (*MUIinstance, propList*)	*propList* must contain the following properties: #buttons: #Ok | #OkCancel | #AbortRetryIgnore | #YesNoCancel | #YesNo | #RetryCancel #default: 0 | 1 | 2 | 3 (0 indicates no default. 1, 2, or 3 indicates the button from the #buttons option, above). {#icon: #stop | #note | #caution | #question | #error} (Omit for no icon. See Figure 15-2.) #message: "*Message to appear in Dialog*" #movable: TRUE | FALSE #title: "*Dialog title*" Return value from *Alert()* (1, 2, or 3) indicates first, second, or third button from #buttons option. See Chapter 15, *The MUI Dialog Xtra*.

the alertHook and on alert-Hook	*the alertHook* must refer to a script with an *on alertHook* handler, or set it to 0 to disable *alertHook* handling.
	
	`on alertHook me, errorTypeString, errMsgString`
	`  -- whatever`
	`     return -1 | 0 | 1 | 2`
	`end`
	
	Incoming values for *errorTypeString*:
	
	"Script runtime error": Error generated by *alert* command or other runtime error.
	
	"Script syntax error": Error caused by incorrect script being compiled or run.
	
	"File Error": Error caused by file write error.
	
	"File read Error": Error caused by file read error.
	
	The *errMsgString* is the string that would normally be displayed in the alert box.
	
	See Chapter 3, *Lingo Coding and Debugging Tips*.
	
	Your *on alertHook* handler should return a code (see next entry) to control what happens after the error is trapped.

on alertHook (return values)	Code	Authoring Mode	Projector (Runtime)
See Table 3-2 and Examples 3-19 and 3-20	-1	Suppress all dialogs. Halt movie if fatal error.	Suppress all dialogs. Quit without warning if error occurs.
	0	Same as default: Present dialog. Halt movie if fatal error.	Same as default: Present Stop/ Continue dialog for errors
	1	Suppress all dialogs. Halt movie, open debugger if fatal error.	Suppress all dialogs. Ignore error and continue if possible.
	2	Suppress all dialogs. Halt movie, open Script window if fatal error.	Suppress all dialogs. Quit without warning if error occurs.

Table 16-1: Enumerated Values for Lingo Commands (continued)

Command	Enumerated Values
the alignment of member *buttonOrField*	"left" (default) | "right" | "center"
the backColor of member *buttonOrField*	Applies only to color of background in button and field cast members. put *the backColor of member buttonOrField* set *the backColor of member buttonOrField = n* *n* depends on the current monitor color depth. Default is white (or other color set via foreground color chip in Tool Palette). All platforms (Macintosh and Windows): 1-bit, 2-bit, 4-bit, 8-bit: $0 <= n < power(2, the colorDepth)$ Default is 0 (white). 8-bit (256 colors): $0 <= n <= 255$ 0 = white; 255 = black; *n* maps to indices in the current custom palette. Default is 0 (white). Invalid values set to 255. Macintosh only: 16-bit: $0 <= n <= 32767$ 0 = black; 32767 = white; other colors are 15-bit RGB values (5 bits per color). Default is 32767 (white). Higher values are set to (*value mod 32768*). Negative values are "wrapped around" to (*32768-value*). 24-bit or 32-bit, $0 <= n <= 16777215$ 0 = black; 16777215 = white; other colors are 24-bit RGB values (8 bits per color). Default is 16777215 (white). Higher values are set to *value mod 16777216*. Negative values are "wrapped around" to (*16777216- value*). Director automatically remaps the units used to the current bit depth when *the colorDepth* changes. You should check *the colorDepth* before setting any value or possibly create a look-up for each color at different colorDepths, or create reference cast members with the desired colors. Windows 16-bit Projectors (even under Win 95): At depths > 8-bit, *the backColor of member* is treated the same as at 8-bit—an index into the current *custom* palette, not necessarily the Windows system palette. Windows 32-bit Projectors: At depths > 8-bit, *the backColor of member* is treated as an index into the *Windows system* palette, not the current custom palette. See Technotes 00760 and 12118 on Macromedia's site, and see Chapter 13, *Graphics, Color, and Palettes*, in *Director in a Nutshell*.

Table 16-1: Enumerated Values for Lingo Commands (continued)

Command	Enumerated Values
backColor of sprite *shapeOr-Bitmap*	Useful for shape and 1-bit sprites. 0 <= n <= 255. Default is white (0). Values higher than 255 are set to *value mod 256*. Negative values are "wrapped around" to (*256-value*). All platforms: Value is always an index into an 8-bit palette, even in higher (non-palettized) color depths. In 8-bit color, value is index into current active palette. At higher depths, value is index into movie's default palette (see Modify ➤Movie ➤Properties).
the bitRate of member *swaMember*	0 (indicates not playing yet) | 8000 | 16000 | 24000 | 32000 | 48000 | 56000 | 64000 | 80000 | 112000 | 128000 | 160000 See *the state of member* and *sampleRate of member*.
the bitsPerSample of member *swaMember*	0 (indicates not playing yet) Should always be 16 when playing because SWA sounds are always converted to 16-bit sampling. See *the state of member* and *sampleSize of member*.

the blend of sprite	There are only 56 possible blend values from 0 to 100
	
	`repeat with n = 0 to 55`
	`    set the blend of sprite x = n`
	`end repeat`
	
	0,1,3,5,7,9,10,12,14,16,18,20,21,23,25,27,29,30,32,34,36,38,40,41,43,45, 47,49,50,52,54,56,58,60,61,63,65,67,69,70,72,74,76,78,80,81,83,85,87, 89,90,92,94,96,98,100

the boxType of member *fieldMember*	#adjust (default) | #fixed | #limit | #scroll
the buttonStyle	0: buttons receive *mouseUp* events even if *mouseDown* occurred over different button (default). 1: buttons receive *mouseUp* events only if *mouseDown* occurred over same button.
the buttonType of member *buttonMember*	#checkBox | #pushButton | #radioButton (default depends on tool used in Tool Palette).
cacheDocVerify()	cacheDocVerify(#once (default) | #always) or *setting* = cacheDocVerify()

Table 16-1: Enumerated Values for Lingo Commands (continued)

Command	Enumerated Values
call(#*event*, *target* {, *args...*})	Sends any message name, preceded by a pound sign (#), including built-in messages that follow. Specify a custom message as #*customMessage*. #activateWindow | #alertHook | #beginSprite | #closeWindow | #CuePassed | #deactivateWindow | #endSprite | #enterFrame | #exitFrame | #getBehaviorDescription | #getPropertyDescriptionList | #idle | #keyDown | #keyUp | #mouseDown | #mouseEnter | #mouseLeave | #mouseUp | #mouseUpOutSide | #mouseWithin | #moveWindow | #new | #openWindow | #prepareFrame | #prepareMovie | #resizeWindow | #rightMouseDown | #rightMouseUp | #startMovie | #startup | #stepFrame | #stopMovie | #timeout | #zoomWindow See Chapter 2, *Events, Messages, and Scripts*.
callAncestor()	See entry above for *call()*.
the castType of member or castType of cast	This obsolete property returns with same values as *the type of member*, with the exception of field cast members, for which it returns *#text*. (*The type of member* returns *#field* for field cast members.)
the channelCount of member *soundMember*	For non-SWA sound cast members only: 1: mono 2: stereo
the checkBoxAccess	0: User can toggle buttons on and off (default). 1: User can toggle buttons on, but not off. 2: User cannot change toggle setting. Control is via Lingo only.
the checkSize of member	Ranges from 1 to 128 pixels.
the checkBoxType	Checkboxes are: 0: Marked with an "X" (default). 1: Marked with a small solid black square. 2: Filled with solid black.

Table 16-1: Enumerated Values for Lingo Commands (continued)

Command	Enumerated Values
the colorDepth	set the colorDepth = 0 | 1 | 2 | 4 | 8 | 16 | 32 if the colorDepth = 1 | 2 | 4 | 8 | 15 | 16 | 24 | 32 then... Not all Macs or PCs support all color depths. 0: Restores user's *Display* Control Panel setting (only works on some Windows machines, not Macs) 1: 2 colors (black and white) 2: 4 colors 4: 16 colors (Windows VGA palette) 8: 256 colors (palettized mode) 15: Reported by some PCs instead of 16 16: 32,768 colors ("thousands" or "high color") 24: 16,777,216 colors (Windows "true color") 32: 16,777,216 colors (Macintosh "millions") See *the depth of member.*
cpuidGetCPUType (DirMMX Xtra)	Returns code indicating Windows CPU family: 3: 386 4: 486 5: 586 (Pentium) 6: Pentium II
on cuePassed	*on cuePassed {me, } channelID, cuePointNumber, cuePointName* The *me* is a script instance and is passed to frame and sprite scripts, but not movie scripts or cast scripts. *channelID* : for SWA or digital video, the sprite number 1 to 120; for Score sound channels, the symbol #sound1, #sound2; for sounds played via Lnigo, #sound1 though #sound8. *cuePointNumber*: 1 to count(*the cuePointTimes of member*). *cuePointName*: see *the cuePointNames of member.* See Chapter 15, *Sound and Cue Points*, in *Director in a Nutshell.*

Table 16-1: Enumerated Values for Lingo Commands (continued)

Command	Enumerated Values
cursor *whichCursor* the cursor of sprite which- Sprite = *whichCursor*	See "Cursors" in Chapter 14, *Graphical User Interface Components*, in *Director in a Nutshell*. *whichCursor* can be either a reference to 1-bit, 16 x 16 pixel cast members enclosed in a list, such as: [*cursorMember, maskMember*] or one of the following Cursor Resource IDs: -1: Arrow (pointer) 0: None set, reverts to default 1: I-beam 2: Crosshair 3: Crossbar 4: Watch (Mac), hourglass (Windows) 200: Blank (hidden) cursor The following resource IDs may not be supported under Windows in earlier versions of Director: 254: Help Pointer 256: Pencil 257: Square Eraser 258: Selection Crosshair 259: Paint Bucket 260: Open Hand 272: Selection Lasso 280: Pointing Finger 281: Dropper 282: Tempo channel's *Wait for Mouse-click* icon 283: Flashing state of *Wait for Mouse-click* icon 284: Vertical Resize 285: Horizontal Resize 286: Diagonal Resize 290: Closed Hand 291: No Drop Hand 292: Copy Closed Hand 300: V symbol 301: Air Brush 302: Zoom In (magnifying glass with "+") 303: Zoom Out (magnifying glass with "–") 304: Magnifying Glass

Enumerated
Values

Table 16-1: Enumerated Values for Lingo Commands (continued)

Command	Enumerated Values
the depth of member	Note that the values vary slightly from *the colorDepth*. 1: 2 colors (Not necessarily black and white. Can be colorized with background and foreground color chips in Tool Palette) 2: 4 colors 4: 16 colors (Windows EGA palette) 8: 256 colors (palettized mode) 16: 32,768 colors ("thousands" or "high color") 32: 16,777,216 colors ("millions" or "true color")
the digitalVideoTimeScale	Time scale is measured as $1/t$, where t is the current setting. $t = 0$ tells Director to use *the timeScale of member*. See Chapter 11, *Timers and Dates*.
the digitalVideoType of member `videoMember`	#quickTime | #videoForWindows Applies only if *type of member* is *#digitalVideo*.
error (*FileIO Xtra*) and mError(*FileIO XObject*)	See Appendix E, *Error Messages and Error Codes,* for a list of error codes returned by the *FileIO* Xtra and *FileIO* XObject
externalEvent	Can send any external event to Netscape or MIE browser, presumably one you've defined in your HTML for use with LiveConnect or ActiveX. See Chapter 11, *Shockwave and the Internet*, in *Director in a Nutshell*.

Table 16-1: Enumerated Values for Lingo Commands (continued)

Command	Enumerated Values
externalParamName (*paramName*)	There is no limitation on parameter names when using Netscape with an EMBED tag (any parameter name can be specified in quotes). When using MIE, *paramName* must be one of the following. (Within the OBJECT tag used by MIE, these names should be used without the quotes.) "swAudio" "swBackColor" "swBanner" "swColor" "swForeColor" "swFrame" "swList" "swName" "swPassword" "swPreLoadTime" "swSound" "swText" "swURL" "swVolume" "sw1" "sw2" "sw3" "sw4" "sw5" "sw6" "sw7" "sw8" "sw9" See Chapter 11 in *Director in a Nutshell*.
FileIO Xtra and XObject	See Table E-3 in Appendix E for a list of error codes returned by the FileIO Xtra and FileIO XObject
the font of member *fieldMember*	Any valid font name can be used. The default built-in fonts on each platform are: Mac: "Chicago", "Courier", "Geneva", "Helvetica", "Monaco", "New York", "Symbol", "Times", "Palatino" Windows: "Arial", "Courier", "Courier New", "MS Serif", "MS Sans Serif", "Symbol", "System", "Terminal", "Times New Roman" See Chapter 12, *Text and Fields*, in *Director in a Nutshell*.

Table 16-1: Enumerated Values for Lingo Commands (continued)

Command	Enumerated Values
the fontStyle of member *fieldMember*	Mac and Win: "plain", "bold", "italic", "underline", "shadow", "outline", "extend" Mac only: "condense" Multiple attributes are separated by commas within the quotes, such as "bold,italic" or set separately. "Plain" cancels other styles.
the foreColor of member *buttonOrField*	Applies only to color of text in button and field cast members. *put the foreColor of member buttonOrField* *set the foreColor of member buttonOrField = n* *n* depends on the current monitor color depth (not the depth when it was created). Same values as for *backColor of member*, except default is black and can be changed with the *background* color chip in the Tool Palette. 1-bit, 2-bit, 4-bit, 8-bit: default is *power(2, the colorDepth) -1* (black) 8-bit (256 colors): Default is 255 (black) 16-bit: Default is 0 (black) 24-bit or 32-bit: Default is 0 (black)
the foreColor of sprite *shapeOrBitmap*	Use for shapes and 1-bit bitmap sprites. Value is always an index into an 8-bit palette, even in higher (non-palettized) color depths. See *the backColor of Sprite*. 0 <= n <= 255. Default is black (255). Higher values are set to *value mod 256*. Negative values are "wrapped around" to (*256-value*).
the frameLabel	Default marker label in D6 is *"New Marker."* In D5, it was EMPTY. Set *the frameLabel* to 0 to delete the marker. See Table 17-1.
the framePalette	Positive integers indicate custom palette cast members. Negative integers indicate built-in palettes: -1: Mac System -2: Rainbow -3: Grayscale -4: Pastels -5: Vivid -6: NTSC -7: Metallic -8: VGA (4-bit *colorDepth* only) -101: Windows System (Director 4) -102: Windows System (Director 5 and 6)

Table 16-1: Enumerated Values for Lingo Commands (continued)

Command	Enumerated Values
the frameRate of member *videoMember*	1 to 255: Play at fixed frame rate 0: Sync to Soundtrack -1: Play at normal (intrinsic) speed -2: Play as fast as possible
framesToHMS (*frames, tempo, dropFrames, fractionalSeconds*)	*dropFrames* = TRUE | FALSE *fractionalSeconds* = TRUE | FALSE Returns "*sHH:MM:SS:FFD*" *s*: " " if time is positive, or "-" if time is negative *HH*: hours *MM*: minutes *SS*: seconds *FF*: fractional seconds (if *fractionalSeconds* = TRUE) or excess frames (if *fractionalSeconds* = FALSE) *D*: "d" (if *dropFrames* = FALSE) or " " (if *dropFrames* = TRUE) See *HMStoFrames()*
getError() getErrorString()	The integer value returned by *getError()* for SWA cast members corresponds to the string returned by *getErrorString()*. See Table E-4: *GetError()* returns symbolic values for Flash castmembers. See Table E-5.
getFinderInfo (*FileIO Xtra*)	set *typeCreator* = getFinderInfo (*fileIOinstance*) *typeCreator* is a nine-character string (the fifth character is a SPACE): set *fileType* = char 1 to 4 of *typeCreator* set *creator* = char 6 to 9 of *typeCreator*.
GetItemPropList (*MUI Xtra*)	Returns default property list for a MUI widget: [#value: 0, #type: #checkBox, #attributes: [], #title: "title", #tip: "tip", #locH: 20, #locV: 24, #width: 200, #height: 210, #enabled: 1] See the downloadable Chapter 21, *Custom MUI Dialogs*. For widget types for the #value attribute, see *GetWidgetList()*.
getNthFileNameIn-Folder(*folder, fileNum*)	Use -1 as the file number to get the current folder name. put getNthFileNameInFolder (the pathname, -1)

Enumerated Values

Table 16-1: Enumerated Values for Lingo Commands (continued)

Command	Enumerated Values
getPref(*prefFile*)	Reads from text file in default folder. Only valid file extensions are .TXT (default) and .HTM. From Director or Projector, reads from folder one level down from Director or Projector: Macintosh: *ApplicationName* folder:Prefs:*prefFile* Windows: Prefs*prefFile* From Shockwave, reads data from Plug-In Support folder where browser is installed: Macintosh: *Navigator Folder:Plug-ins:NP-PPC-Dir-Shockwave folder:PrefsprefFile* Windows: *C:\Program Files\Netscape\Program\PLUGINS\NP32DSW\Prefs\prefFile* *C:\Program Files\Internet Explorer\Program\NP32DSW\Prefs\prefFile* See Chapter 14, *External Files.*
getPropertyDescriptionList	Must return a property list with the following elements: set propList = [¬ #comment: "prompt", ¬ #default: value , ¬ #format: #bitmap | #boolean | #button | #cursor | #digitalvideo | #field | #filmloop | #float | #frame | #graphic | #ink | #integer | #marker | #member | #movie | #ole | #palette | #picture | #richtext | #script | #shape | #sound | #string | #symbol | #transition | #xtra, ¬ {#range: [#min: value, #max: value] | [enumerated entries]} ¬] See Tables 12-3 and 12-4 and Example 12-4 in Chapter 12, *Behaviors and Parent Scripts.*
GetWidgetList (*MUI Xtra*)	Returns all available MUI widget types: [#dividerV, #dividerH, #bitmap, #checkBox, #radioButton, #PopupList, #edit-Text, #WindowBegin, #WindowEnd, #GroupHBegin, #GroupHEnd, #GroupVBegin, #GroupVEnd, #label, #IntegerSliderH, #FloatSliderH, #defaultPushButton, #cancelPushButton, #pushButton, #toggleButton] See the downloadable Chapter 21, and see *#value* option under *GetItem-PropList().*

Table 16-1: Enumerated Values for Lingo Commands (continued)

Command	Enumerated Values
GetWindowPropList (*MUI Xtra*)	Returns this default window property list: [#type: #normal, #name: "window", #callback: "nothing", #mode: #data, #xPosition: 100, #yPosition: 120, #width: 200, #height: 210, #modal: 1, #tool-Tips: 0, #closeBox: 1, #canZoom: 0] Possible values are: #type: #alert | #normal | #palette #name: "windowName" | "" (EMPTY) #callback: "nothing" | "*callBackHandler*" #mode: #data | #dialogUnit | #pixel #xPosition: integer (-1 means centered) #yPosition: integer (-1 means centered) #width: integer (0 means auto-set) #height: integer (0 means auto-set) #modal: TRUE | FALSE #toolTips: TRUE | FALSE (unsupported) #closeBox: TRUE | FALSE #canZoom: TRUE | FALSE See the downloadable Chapter 21.
gotoNetPage()	gotoNetPage *url* {, *target*} *target* = "_blank" | "_self" | "_parent" | "_top" | "customTargetName"
HMStoFrames (*hms*, *tempo*, *dropFrames*, *fractionalSeconds*)	*hms* = "*sHH:MM:SS:FFD*" See *framesToHMS()*.

the idleLoadMode	Performs idle loading:
	
	  0: Never (default)
	
	  1: During free time between frames
	
	  2: During idle events
	
	  3: As frequently as possible
	
	See Chapter 9, *Performance and Memory*, in *Director in a Nutshell*.

ilk(*datum*)	Possible return values for *ilk (datum)*: #actor | #float | #instance | #integer | #list | #media | #member | #object | #ole | #picture | #point | #propList | #rect | #sound | #sprite | #string | #symbol | #void | #window | #xtra See *Table 5-4*, "Ilk Return Values" in Chapter 5.

Enumerated Values

Table 16-1: Enumerated Values for Lingo Commands (continued)

Command	Enumerated Values
ilk(*datum*, #*type*)	Possible #*types* for Boolean tests: if ilk(*datum*, #*type*) = TRUE then... Same as types for #*ilk*(*datum*), except: Use #*linearList* instead of #*list* (See *Table 6-6* in Chapter 6, *Lists*.) Use #*object* instead of #*instance*, #*window*, or #*actor* (for which *ilk*(*datum*, #*type*) always returns FALSE).
ilk (*datum*, #object)	The following all return 1 (Boolean TRUE): ilk (list(1,2,3), #object) ilk (*me*, #object) ilk (member *anyMember*, #object) ilk (script *scriptMember*, #object) ilk (sound *soundMember*, #object) ilk (sprite *anySprite*, #object) ilk (Xtra "*XtraName*", #object) ilk (*ScriptOrXtraInstance*, #object) ilk (the score) ilk (the stage) ilk (the media of member *anyMember*) ilk (window *windowID*)
Initialize (*MUI Xtra*)	Initialize(*MUIinstance*, ¬ [#windowPropList: *aWindowPropList*, ¬ #windowItemList: *aWindowItemList*]) See the downloadable Chapter 21.

Table 16-1: Enumerated Values for Lingo Commands (continued)

Command	Enumerated Values
the ink of sprite	0: Copy 1: Transparent 2: Reverse 3: Ghost 4: Not Copy 5: Not Transparent 6: Not Reverse 7: Not Ghost 8: Matte 9: Mask 10-31: (Not used) 32: Blend 33: Add Pin 34: Add 35: Subtract Pin 36: Background Transparent 37: Lightest 38: Subtract 39: Darkest See Example 5-2 in Chapter 5 and see Chapter 13 in *Director in a Nutshell*.
the itemDelimiter	, (comma): default or any character you prefer, such as SPACE or RETURN, which are convenient for parsing text. / (forward slash): Convenient for parsing URLs \ (backslash): Convenient for parsing Windows paths : (colon): Convenient for parsing Macintosh paths See Chapter 7, *Strings*.
ItemUpdate (*MUI Xtra*)	See the downloadable Chapter 21 for details.
the machineType	*The machineType* returns 256 for Windows PCs and a CPU-dependent integer codes for Macs (which can be less than or *greater than* 256). For example: 34: Quadra 650 256: IBM-compatible PC (Windows) 513: PowerMac 4400/200 Use *the platform* instead. See *http://www.zeusprod.com/technote/machtype.html*. *The machineType* returned by Shockwave 6.0 was different from the one returned by Director, but this was fixed in SW6.0.1

Table 16-1: Enumerated Values for Lingo Commands (continued)

Command	Enumerated Values

marker("*name*")
marker (*n*)
	marker("name"): first frame number matching that name (or 0 if no match)
	marker (*n*):
	  -*n*: *n*th marker to left of current frame
	  -1: previous marker to left of current frame
	  0: marker in current frame or previous marker to left
	  1: next marker to right of current frame
	  n: *n*th marker to right of current frame

menu:
(as defined for use with *install-
Menu*)
	Menu items character format codes. See "Menus" in Chapter 14 in *Director in a Nutshell*.
	  | (adds script to menu item)
	  / (defines command key shortcut)
	  ((disables (grays out) menu item)
	  (- (adds separator line to menu)
	Macintosh-only:
	  @ (creates Apple menu icon)
	  !✓ (creates checkmark. Exclamation point + `Option-v` (Mac) or `Alt-1-9-5` (Windows))
	  <B (bolds menu item)
	  <I (italicizes menu item)
	  <U (underlines menu item)
	  <O (outlines menu item)
	  <S (shadows menu item)

MixMaxChannels (DIRECTOR.INI)	1 | 2 | 3 | 4 (default) | 5 | 6 | 7 | 8 See Appendix D, *The DIRECTOR.INI and LINGO.INI Files*.
MixMaxFidelity (DIRECTOR.INI)	0: 22.050 kHz, 8-bit, mono 1: 22.050 kHz, 8-bit, stereo 2: 44.100 kHz, 16-bit, stereo 99: Switch formats on-the-fly (default) See Appendix D.
mNew (*FileIO XObject*)	set *fileXObjInst* = FileIO (mNew, *mode*, *fileName*) *mode* : "read" | "?read" | "write" | "?write" | "append" | "?append" See Chapter 14.
MoaErrorToString (*MUI Xtra*)	put MoaErrorToString (*errorCode*) See Table E-7 in Appendix E.
netError()	"OK" or error code indicating download error. See Table E-6 in Appendix E for Error Codes.

Table 16-1: Enumerated Values for Lingo Commands (continued)

Command	Enumerated Values
netMIME()	Common return types include: 　"image\jpeg" 　"image\gif" 　"application/x-director" 　"text/html"
new (#*memberType*)	Possible *memberType*s: #ActiveX[1] | alpha[1] | #bitmap | #btned[1] | #cursor[1] | #digitalvideo | #field | #filmloop | #flash[1] | #movie | #ole (treated as #bitmap on Mac) | #palette | #picture | #popMenu[1] | #QuickTimeMedia[1] | #QD3D_Xtra[1] | #richtext | #script (defaults to movie script) | #shape | #sound | #swa[1] | #transition [1] Requires Xtra Returns error code (-2147219501) when it fails, including for: #text, #pict, #xtra, #actor, #media. See *MoaErrorToString()* and Chapter 19, *The Lingo Symbol Table*.
new (Xtra "*XtraName*")	Returns Xtra instance. See Chapter 10.
new (script "*ScriptName*")	Returns script instance. See Chapter 12.
the numChannels of member *swaMember*	0: (indicates not playing yet) See *the state of member*. 1: mono 2: stereo
on alertHook	See *the alertHook* and Chapter 3.
on getPropertyDescriptionList	See *getPropertyDescriptionList* and Chapter 12.
on runPropertyDialog	on runPropertyDialog me, *initialList* 　return *propList* end Returns list of properties. See Chapter 12.
on streamStatus	See *streamStatus*.
openFile (*FileIO Xtra*)	openFile (*fileIOinstance*, "*fileName*", *mode*) *mode*: 　0: Read/Write 　1: Read-only 　2: Write-only
PALETTE (EMBED tag)	PALETTE = background (default) | foreground background: Browser palette is used foreground: Director palette is used (Not supported by MIE or with OBJECT Tag.)

Enumerated Values

Table 16-1: Enumerated Values for Lingo Commands (continued)

Command	Enumerated Values
the palette of member	See values for *the framePalette*.
the paletteRef of member	Returns (member *whichMember* of castLib *whichCast*) for custom palettes. Returns a symbol for built-in palettes: #systemMac #systemWin #rainbow #grayscale #pastels #vivid #VGA (4-bit colorDepth only) #NTSC #metallic #systemWinDir4
the pattern of member *shapeMember*	Uses pattern chip number in the Tool window's patterns palette: 1 to 64.
the platform	Returns a string indicating the *Projector's* type or the Shockwave plug-in type, not the true platform on which it is running. See Chapter 8, *Projectors and the Runtime Environment,* in *Director in a Nutshell.* Note there are no spaces following the commas in the strings: "Macintosh,68K": Standard Mac Projector (*even if run on a PowerMac*) or FAT Projector run on 68K Mac "Macintosh,PowerPC": Power Macintosh Native or FAT Projector run on PowerPC "Windows,16": 16-bit Projector run under any OS, *including Win 95/NT* "Windows,32": 32-bit Projector run under Win 95 or Win NT "Java *javaVersion, browser, OS*": Java Player *javaVersion*: 1.0 | 1.1 *browser*: IE | Netscape | UnknownBrowser *OS*: Macintosh | Windows | UknownOS such as "Java, 1.1, IE, Windows"
point (*x, y*)	Points are specified as *point (locH, locV).* To access coordinates, use: the locH | locV of *somePoint*
the preLoadMode of castLib *whichCast*	0: When Needed (default) 1: Before Frame One 2: After Frame One
the productName	Reports "Director" from Authoring environment, Projectors, and Shockwave (D5 and later only).

Table 16-1: Enumerated Values for Lingo Commands (continued)

Command	Enumerated Values
the productVersion	(D5 and later only) Possible values are: "5.0" | "5.0.1" | "6.0" | "6.0.1" | "6.0.2" | "6.5" For Shockwave, it differs from *version*: "6.0" | "6.0.1" | "6.5"
proxyServer()	proxyServer #ftp | #http, "*ipAddress*", *portNum* set *portNum* = proxyServer (#ftp | #http, #port) set *IPaddressString* = proxyServer (#ftp | #http) proxyServer #ftp | #http, #stop See File►Preferences►Network.
puppetPalette "*paletteName*"{, *speed*}{, *numFrames*}	Where "*paletteName*" is a string, not a symbol: "system" (*not* "systemMac") "rainbow" "pastels" "grayscale" "vivid" "VGA" (4-bit *colorDepth* only) "NTSC" "metallic" ("systemWin" and "systemWinDir4" are not pre-defined) Also accepts: puppetPalette *memberNumber* puppetPalette "*memberName*" But doesn't accept: puppetPalette member *whichMember*
puppetSound	puppetSound *whichChannel*, "*whichMember*" puppetSound "*whichMember*" puppetSound member "*whichMember*" puppetSound 0 (unpuppets sounds channel 1) puppetSound *whichChannel*, 0 Where *whichChannel* is 0 |1 | 2 | 3 | 4 | 5 | 6 | 7 | 8 Default channel is 1 if none specified. See *MixMaxChannels* for upper sound channel limit on Windows.
puppetTempo *n*	The maximum tempo depends on the version of Director: Director 4.0: 1 to 30 Director 4.0.4: 1 to 60 Director 5: 1 to 120 Director 6: 1 to 500

Enumerated Values

Table 16-1: Enumerated Values for Lingo Commands (continued)

Command	Enumerated Values
puppetTransition	Transition cast members can be specified by member name, member number, or integer code: puppetTransition member "*whichMember*" puppetTransition member *memberNum* puppetTransition *transitionCode* {,*time*} {,*chunkSize* } {, *changeArea*} *time* in 1/4 second increments: 0 to 120 *chunkSize* in pixels: 1 to 128 *changeArea* : TRUE | FALSE See also the *transitionType of member*: Third-party transition Xtras are available. See CleverMedia's (*http://www.clevermedia.com*) *Transition Finder*. Built-in transitions codes are:

Built-in transitions codes:

1: Wipe Right	27: Random Rows
2: Wipe Left	28: Random Columns
3: Wipe Down	29: Cover Down
4: Wipe Up	30: Cover Down Left
5: Center Out Horizontal	31: Cover Down Right
6: Edges In Horizontal	32: Cover Left
7: Center Out Vertical	33: Cover Right
8: Edges In Vertical	34: Cover Up
9: Center Out Square	35: Cover Up Left
10: Edges In Square	36: Cover Up Right
11: Push Left	37: Venetian Blinds
12: Push Right	38: Checkerboard
13: Push Down	39: Strips on Bottom Build Left
14: Push Up	40: Strips on Bottom Build Right
15: Reveal Up	41: Strips on Left build Down
16: Reveal Up Right	42: Strips on Left Build Up
17: Reveal Right	43: Strips on Right Build Down
18: Reveal Down Right	44: Strips on Right Build Up
19: Reveal Down	45: Strips on Top Build Left
20: Reveal Down Left	46: Strips on Top Build Right
21: Reveal Left	47: Zoom Open
22: Reveal Up Left	48: Zoom Close
23: Dissolve Pixels Fast	49: Vertical Blinds
24: Dissolve Boxy Rectangles	50: Dissolve Bits Fast
25: Dissolve Boxy Squares	51: Dissolve Pixels
26: Dissolve Patterns	52: Dissolve Bits

Table 16-1: Enumerated Values for Lingo Commands (continued)

Command	Enumerated Values
the purgePriority of member	Higher number items are purged *first*. 3: Purge Normal (default) 2: Purge Next (purged *after Normal*) 1: Purge Last (purge after *Next*) 0: Never Purge (Unpurgeable. Don't use this.) Streaming data is always unloaded after being played.
putImageIntoCastMember (member *buttonMember*, "*imageString*", member *destMember*)	Values for "*imageString*": "ImageNormal" | "ImagePressed" | "ImageRollover" | "ImageDisabled" | "ImageToggledNormal" | "ImageToggledPressed" | "ImageToggledRollover" | "ImageToggledDisabled" See *setButtonImageFromCastMember( )* and Chapter 14 in *Director in a Nutshell*.
rect (*l*, *t*, *r*, *b*)	Rects are specified as *rect (left, top, right, bottom)*. To access vertices and dimensions, use: the left | top | right | bottom | width | height of rect
the runMode	Works in D5 as well as D6 Director Authoring Environment: "Author" Projectors: "Projector" Shockwave: "Plugin" Java Player: "Java Applet"
runPropertyDialog	see *on runPropertyDialog* and *getPropertyDescriptionList*.
the sampleRate of member *soundMember*	11025 | 22050 | 44100 are common and recomended under Windows, but any number is possible. Macintosh rates (not recommended under Windows): 5563 | 7418 | 11127 | 22254 | 32000 | 44100 | 48000 For SWA members it is the sampling rate of the original source material, such as: 0 (indicates not playing yet) | 11025 | 16000 | 22050 | 44100, but it could be anything. See *the state of member* and *bitRate of member*.
the sampleSize of member *soundMember*	8 | 16 (Pertains to sound cast members. Not applicable to SWA cast members.) See *bitsPerSample of member*.
the scoreColor of sprite *whichSprite*	0 | 1 | 2 | 3 | 4 | 5 (Any value out of range is reset to 5.) *whichSprite* must be > 0. It doesn't accept negative channel numbers for the Effects channels, as does *the scoreSelection*.

Enumerated Values

Table 16-1: Enumerated Values for Lingo Commands (continued)

Command	Enumerated Values

the scoreSelection	*The scoreSelection* is a list of lists:
	
	[[*startChan, endChan, startFrame, endFrame*] {, [*startChan2, endChan2, startFrame2, endFrame2*]}]
	
	Sprite channels use integers 1 through 120. Control channels are identified with negative numbers:
	
	  -5: Tempo Channel
	  -4: Palette Channel
	  -3: Transition Channel
	  -2: Sound Channel 1 (*not* channel 2)
	  -1: Sound Channel 2 (*not* channel 1)
	   0: Frame Script Channel
	
	Format differens in D5 and D6. See Table 17-2.

the scriptType of member	#parent | #score | #movie. Only applies if *type of member* is *#script* and not for cast members with cast scripts attached. (See the *scriptText of member* property and Example 2-3 in Chapter 2.)
send()	See earlier entry for *call* and see Chapter 2.
sendAllSprites()	See earlier entry for *call* and see Chapter 2.
sendAncestor()	See earlier entry for *call* and see Chapter 2.
sendSprite()	See earlier entry for *call* and see Chapter 2.
setButtonImageFromCast- Member (member *buttonMember*, "*imageString*", member *bitmapMember*)	See earlier entry for *putImageIntoCastMember*. See Chapter 14 in *Director in a Nutshell.*

setFilterMask (*FileIO Xtra*)	Macintosh:
	  setFilterMask (*fileIOinstance*, "*fourCharFileType*")
	  setFilterMask (*fileIOinstance*, "TEXT") (case-sensitive)
	  setFilterMask (*fileIOinstance*, EMPTY) (all files)
	Windows:
	  setFilterMask (*fileIOinstance*, "*description, extension*")
	  setFilterMask (*fileIOinstance*, "Text Files,*.txt")
	  setFilterMask (*fileIOinstance*, "All Files,*.*")
	See Chapter 14.

Table 16-1: Enumerated Values for Lingo Commands (continued)

Command	Enumerated Values
setFinderInfo (*FileIO Xtra*)	setFinderInfo (*fileIOinstance,"fourCharFileType fourCharCreatorCode"*) To set text files for TeachText/SimpleText use: setFinderInfo (*fileIOinstance,* "TEXT ttxt") (Note the space between the type and creator code and not that they are both case-sensitive. They are always four characters each.) see *getFinderInfo* and Chapter 14.
setPref (*prefFile, prefText*)	Writes *prefText* to *prefFile* (must have .TXT or .HTM extension) and must reside in folder shown under *getPref()* above.
the shapeType of member *shapeMember*	#line | #oval | #rect | #roundRect Apples only if *type of member* is *#shape*. A *#line* can be either from the lower right to upper left or upper right to lower left, but they both have the same *shapeType*.
sound playFile *whichChannel*	*whichChannel* = 1 | 2 | 3 | 4 | 5 | 6 | 7 | 8
the soundChannel of member *swaMember*	*whichChannel* = 0 | 1 | 2 | 3 | 4 | 5 | 6 | 7 |8 0 means "highest channel available."
the soundLevel	Corresponds to *Sound* Control Panel on the Macintosh. Under Windows, it is determined by the SoundLevel*n* settings in the DIRECTOR.INI file, which adjust the WAV volume. 0: mute (SoundLevel0) 1: softest (SoundLevel1) 2: soft (SoundLevel2) 3: medium soft (SoundLevel3) 4: medium (SoundLevel4) 5: medium loud (SoundLevel5) 6: loud (SoundLevel6) 7: loudest (SoundLevel7) Any negative values cause it to be set to 7 (loudest). See Chapter 15 in *Director in a Nutshell* and Appendix D of this book.

Enumerated Values

Table 16-1: Enumerated Values for Lingo Commands (continued)

Command	Enumerated Values
sprite *whichSprite*	The maximum number for a sprite channel depends on the version of Director: Director 3: 1 to 24 Director 4: 1 to 48 Director 5: 1 to 48 Director 6: 1 to 120 The Java Export Xtra supports up to 500 sprite channels. Some commands, such as *the scoreSelection*, use negative numbers to indicate the control channels in the Score.
the spriteNum of me	Within a sprite script, *the spriteNum of me* returns a number from 1 to 120, but within a frame script, it always returns -5.
the state of member *swaMember*	*The state of member* must be 3, 4, or 5 to check other SWA member properties accurately: 0: Stopped 1: Preloading 2: Preloading completed successfully 3: Playing 4: Paused 5: Done 9: Error 10: Insufficient CPU
status (*FileIO Xtra*)	See Table E-3 in Appendix E for list of error codes obtained by status().
streamStatus	Must use *tellStreamStatus(TRUE)* to activate: on streamStatus *url, state, bytesSoFar, bytesTotal, errorCode* *state:* "Connecting" "Started" "InProgress" "Complete" "Error" *errorCode:* 0 (if *state* is not "Error") Error code if *state* is "Error"
the textFont of cast	Obsolete; see *the font of member*.
the textStyle of cast	Obsolete; see *the fontStyle of member*.

Table 16-1: Enumerated Values for Lingo Commands (continued)

Command	Enumerated Values
the timeScale of member *videoMember*	*The timeScale of member* property is intrinsic to the video format and cannot be changed. For QuickTime movies, *the timeScale of member* is 600 (1/600th of a second) on the Macintosh and 30 (1/30th of a second) under Windows. For Video for Windows (AVI files) it is 60 (1/60th of a second).
the traceLoad	0: Off, no tracing 1: Shows cast member name or number when loaded 2: Shows cast member names, current frame number, current movie or cast, and file seek offset.
trackType(member) or track-Type(sprite)	#video | #sound | #sprite | #text | #music, plus any future types supported by QuickTime.
the transitionType of member	See entry for *puppetTransition*.

the type of member	Built in types:
	#bitmap | #button | #digitalVideo | #empty | #field | #filmloop | #movie | #ole | #palette | #picture | #richtext | #script | #shape | #sound | #transition | #xtra
	(The *type of member* returns *#field* for field cast members and *#richtext* for rich-Text cast members. It does not return *#text* for either of them. See `castType of member`.) See also the *buttonType, boxType, scriptType, shapeType, transitionType,* and *digitalVideoType.*
	The following types require Xtras (this is not a complete list as every asset Xtra has its own type).
	Included with Director 6.x:
	   #btned (*Custom Button Editor* Xtra)
	   #QD3D_Xtra (*QuickDraw 3D*)
	   #SWA (*Shockwave Audio*)
	Included with Director 6.5:
	   #ActiveX (*ActiveX* Xtra, Windows only)
	   #cursor (*Custom Cursor* Xtra)
	   #flash (*Flash Asset* Xtra)
	   #QuickTimeMedia (*QT3 Asset* Xtra. Imports all QuickTime 3-supported media including QTVR)
	Third-party (Demo versions are free):
	   #alpha (*Alphamania*)
	   #popMenu (*PopMenu* Xtra)
	   plus many other third-party Xtra asset types.

Table 16-1: Enumerated Values for Lingo Commands (continued)

Command	Enumerated Values

the type of sprite	This command is obsolete, except during Score Recording, for which you can set it to 16. Director 5 and 6 report 16 as the type for all sprites. Use *put the type of member (the member of sprite whichSprite)* instead.
	Director Version 3.1.3 and earlier reported:
	   0: Inactive
	   1: Bitmap
	   2: Rectangle
	   3: Rounded Rectangle
	   5: Line top left to bottom right
	   6: Line bottom left to top right
	   7: Text
	   8: Button
	   9: Checkbox
	   10: Radio button
	   16: QuickTime and any other unspecified type

version	global version put the version Director: "3.1.3" | "4.0" | "4.0.1" | "4.0.2" | "4.0.3" | "4.0.4" | "5.0" | "5.0.1" | "6.0" | "6.0.1" | "6.0.2" | "6.5" Shockwave: "4.0.4 net", "5.0 net", "5.0.1 net", "6.0 net", "6.0.1 net", "6.5 net" See *the productVersion*.
the volume of member *swaMember* the volume of sound *soundChan*	$0 < volume < 255$ Higher number are louder. Settings out of range are clipped to the allowed range.
the volume of sprite *videoSprite*	$volume <= 0$: Mute $volume > 1$: Higher numbers are louder. Volume can be arbitrarily high, but is often distorted above 255.
WindowOperation (*MUI Xtra*)	WindowOperation (*MUIinstance,* #show | #hide | #center | #zoom | #tipsOn (unsupported) | #tipsOff (unsupported)). See the downloadable Chapter 21.

Table 16-1: Enumerated Values for Lingo Commands (continued)

Command	Enumerated Values
the windowType of window *whichWindow*	The *windowTypes* vary slightly between Mac and Windows. See Chapter 6, *Stage and MIAWs*, in *Director in a Nutshell* for pictures of each of the window types: -1: Default (standard document) 0: Standard document, without zoom box 1: Alert dialog 2: Plain dialog , without title bar 3: Plain dialog with shadow, without title bar 4: Document without resize box 5: Movable modal dialog box (Mac only) 8: Document with zoom box 12: Document with zoom box, without resize box 16: Window with rounded border 48: Floating windoid (Macintosh) 49: Floating windoid (Windows) See Wind-Xtra (*http://www.ncimedia.com/xtras*)
XTRAINFO.TXT file	[#*platform*:"*XtraName*" {, #*platform*:"*XtraName*"}, #type:#*xtraType*] where #*platform*: #name68K: name of Mac 68K version of Xtra #namePPC: name of PowerMac version of Xtra #nameFAT: name of FAT Mac version of Xtra #nameW16: name of Win16 version of Xtra #nameW32: name of Win32 version of Xtra where #*xtraType*: #asset: a sprite or transition Xtra #lingo: a Lingo Xtra #mixin: a default MIX import/export Xtra[1] #mix: an extended MIX import/export Xtra #net: Xtra needed for Web access or URLs[2] #netlib: network WinSock library Xtra #service: Xtra needed to support any MIX Xtras[1] [1] Included in Projectors if "Check Movies for Xtras" is selected. [2] Included in Projectors if "Include Network Xtras" is selected. See Chapter 10, *Using Xtras*, in *Director in a Nutshell*.

Enumerated Values

CHAPTER 17

Changed, Undocumented, and Misdocumented Lingo

This chapter describes underdocumented and undocumented Lingo commands. Refer to the online Help topic "Lingo Elements, New in Director 6," for a list of new Lingo keywords in D6. See Appendix B, *Changes in D6 Through D6.5*, and the Director 6 *ReadMe* file for details on Lingo changes between the D6.0, D6.0.1, D6.0.2, and D6.5 releases.

Underdocumented Utilities and Lingo

Most of the following utilities are officially supported, but they are not covered in the Director manuals, online Help, or Lingo pull-down menus. Many related keywords are included in Chapter 18, *Lingo Keyword and Command Summary*, or in Appendix B.

LINGO.INI and DIRECTOR.INI Files

Both the Macintosh and Windows versions of Director look for a file called LINGO.INI in the same folder as the Projector and run its *on startUp* handler, if any. Refer to Appendix D, *The DIRECTOR.INI and LINGO.INI Files*.

Director for Windows supports many configuration options that are documented only within the comments of the DIRECTOR.INI file. The ones of most interest are:

```
Animation
MixMaxChannels
MixMaxFidelity
SoundLevel0 through SoundLevel7
```

Refer again to Appendix D for details.

Launcher Utility

The Launcher Utility can start either a 16-bit or 32-bit Projector on Windows. Use it to create one clickable icon for all Windows users (analagous to the operation of a

"Fat" Macintosh Projector). See the *Goodies\Launcher* folder on the Director 6 for Windows CD.

Xtras and XObjects

Xtras and XObjects add many commands to Lingo. You generally can obtain the documentation by querying the Xtra or XObject itself using *mMessageList()* or *mDescribe*. Refer to Chapter 13, *Lingo Xtras and XObjects*, and Chapter 10, *Using Xtras*, in *Director in a Nutshell*.

 The latest version of Macromedia's Xtras should be obtained from *http://www.macromedia.com*. Many have been updated along with Director 6.0.2 or D6.5

FileIO *Xtra—Read and Write Text Files*

To see the FileIO Xtra's Help text, type this in the Message window:

```
put mMessageList (xtra "FileIO")
```

The FileIO XObject is discontinued (see *Macromedia/Discontinued/FileIO XObject* on the D6 CD); you should use the FileIO Xtra instead.

For details on the FileIO Xtra and XObject, see Chapter 14, *External Files*.

MUI Dialog *Xtra—Custom Dialog Boxes*

The MUI *Dialog* Xtra creates multibutton dialogs, but it is not supported under Windows 3.1. The documentation regarding the MUI Xtra in the online Help (under "MMUI") is spotty and often wrong.

To see the MUI Xtra's Help text, type this in the Message window:

```
put mMessageList (xtra "MUI")
```

For full documentation on the MUI Xtra's methods, see Chapter 14, Chapter 15, *The MUI Dialog Xtra*, and the downloadable Chapter 21, *Custom MUI Dialogs*.

Custom Button Editor *Xtra—Multi-state Buttons*

The Custom Button Editor Xtra creates multi-state button cast members. It is documented partially in the online Help, but is still considered immature.

For details, see Chapter 14, *Graphical User Interface Components*, in *Director in a Nutshell*.

DirMMX *Xtra*

The DirMMX Xtra is required to take advantage of MMX processors on Windows PCs and has some handy methods for determining a processor's attributes.

Earlier versions of this Xtra conflicted with some Cyrix processors that claim to support MMX, but actually don't. The latest version allegedly fixes the problem.

To see the DirMMX Xtra's Help text, type this in the Message window:

```
put mMessageList (xtra "DirMMX")
```

Refer to Chapter 8, *Projectors and the Runtime Environment*, in *Director in a Nutshell* for complete documentation.

The UI Helper Xtra and FileXtra

The UI Helper Xtra that ships with D6.5 is intended for use only with the *Save as Java* feature. It is completely *unsupported by Macromedia*, but includes two methods to read Behavior references and their property settings:

getBehaviorMemRef (spriteNum, nthBehaviorNum)
> The function returns the script member number of the *nthBehaviorNum* attached to *spriteNum* in the current frame.

getBehaviorInitializers (spriteNum, nthBehaviorNum)
> The function returns the user-specified values for the properties of the *nthBehaviorNum* attached to *spriteNum* in the current frame. These are the settings entered in the *Parameters* dialog created via *getPropertyDescriptionList()*.

The FileXtra, also intended for use only with the *Save as Java* feature and *unsupported by Macromedia*, includes methods to copy files, check drive types, and more. It ships with Director 6.5, and is available separately from *http://www.little-planet.com/kent/kent.html*.

Use the following to see a complete list of these Xtras' methods:

```
put mMessageList (xtra "UiHelper")
put mMessageList (xtra "FileXtra")
```

The ActiveX Xtra and Java Export Xtra

The *ActiveX* Xtra (Windows only) has many functions dealing with ActiveX controls and the *Java Export* Xtra controls Java exporting. Both ship with Director 6.5. Use the following to see a list of their methods:

```
put mMessageList (xtra "ActiveX")
put mMessageList (xtra "JavaConvert")
```

QuickTime-Related Xtras

The Director 6 CD includes the QTVR Xtra installer and the QD3D Xtra installer under the *Macromedia* folder. Both these Xtras provide dozens of commands to control their respective media types, but only the QTVR Xtra shows up in the Message window. The QuickTime 3 Xtra that ships with Director 6.5 is a Sprite Asset Xtra, but supports a single Lingo function, *QuickTimeVersion()*.

Use the following to see a list of the QTVR and QuickTime 3 Xtras' methods:

```
put mMessageList (xtra "QTVRXtra")
put mMessageList (xtra "QuickTimeSupport")
```

Refer to Appendix B, *Changes in D6 Through D6.5*, in this book and to Chapter 16, *Digital Video,* in *Director in a Nutshell* for details.

Flash Asset and Custom Cursor Xtras

The Flash Asset and Custom Cursor Xtras ship with Director 6.5. Refer to Appendix B for a summary of the Lingo properties and commands pertaining to these new cast member types. Refer to Chapter 14 of *Director in a Nutshell* for details on the Custom Cursor Xtra.

Unsupported Xtras

The Director 6 CD includes an unsupported Din Xtra in the *Macromedia\XDK_d6a4\Goodies\Director\SoundXtr\Xtras* folder that provides some functions to deal with streaming audio.

To see the Din Xtra's Help text, type this in the Message window:

```
put mMessageList (xtra "Din")
```

Refer to Chapter 15, *Sound and Cue Points,* in *Director in a Nutshell.*

Serial Port, CommPort, and Other XObjects

Although XObjects are no longer supported, they can be used in some circumstances, especially if no Xtra is available. Refer to Chapter 13.

To see the Serial XObject's Help text, type this in the Message window:

```
put SerialPort (mDescribe)
```

See also *Macromedia\Discontinued\CommPort\CommPort.DLL.*

Undocumented Variations and Misdocumented Lingo

It is frustrating to try to use a Lingo command that doesn't work as advertised, or perhaps at all. The *Lingo Dictionary's* examples are riddled with errors, and I don't attempt to correct them all here. Instead, I address only those statements of "fact" that are incorrect. Table 17-1 lists misdocumented and undocumented Lingo. The syntax for these commands is summarized in Table 18-1. See also Table 16-1 for details on enumerated values. See the topic-centric chapters in both this book and *Director in a Nutshell* for details on each command.

Dozens of Lingo keywords can be used as either properties or functions, such as *rollover()* versus *the rollover.* These undocumented variations are not shown in Table 17-1 but are shown in Table 18-1. Table 18-1 also lists many underdocumented commands that are not listed in the *Lingo Dictionary.* Most of those pertain to Xtras, such as FileIO, MUI, or the Custom Button Editor, or to external files such as LINGO.INI or DIRECTOR.INI (see Appendix D).

Follow along in Macromedia's *Lingo Dictionary* where you can make corrections based on Table 17-1. The undocumented Lingo commands or variations shown in Table 17-1 are presumed reliable, unless flagged as "*unsupported.*"

Table 17-1: Undocumented and Misdocumented Lingo

Command	Use
#*symbol*	Symbols *are* sensitive to diacritical marks. See Appendix C.
=	The equals sign is used for both comparison (with *if*) and for assignment (with *set*).
¬	In the Message window, lines of Lingo are limited to 255 characters, but inside a script they can be much, much, longer.
@	The @ operator represents the *current* folder. The expression "*@/bigFolder*" must be enclosed in quotes and represents a *sub*folder named "bigFolder" within the current folder. See Chapter 14.
add	Accepts optional *position* parameter (same syntax as *addAt*). *add(linearList {, position}, value)*
the alertHook	Can be set to a *list* of script instances. See Chapter 3, *Lingo Coding and Debugging Tips*, and *on alertHook*.
the bottom of rect[1]	Returns the bottom (fourth) coordinate of a rectangle.
buttonClicked[1]	Custom Buttons send the *buttonClicked* event when clicked. See Chapter 9, *Mouse Events*.
char...of	Any chunk expression starting with *char 0* returns the entire string. See Chapter 7, *Strings*. You can use *char...of* with *put...into* to replace a range of characters: `put "media" into char 2 to 4 of "myString"`
clearCache	Clears the cache used for *getNetText* during authoring, despite claims that it works only for Shockwave.
close the stage	Use *close the stage* to hide the Stage as you would a MIAW.
the colorDepth	Windows PCs may report undocumented *colorDepths*, such as 24 instead of 32 and 15 instead of 16. See Table 16-1.
contains	*contains* is sensitive to diacritical marks. See Appendix C.
cuePassed	See *on cuePassed*.
the currentSpriteNum	*The currentSpriteNum* can be tested but not set.
the currentTime	The proper syntax is *the currentTime of sprite* and *the currentTime of member*, not just *the currentTime*.
the cursor of sprite 0	`put the cursor of sprite 0` returns the global cursor previously set using *cursor*.
deleteAll	Works in D4 and D5, although it was undocumented until D6.
deleteProp	Can be used with linear lists (same syntax as *deleteAt()*): *deleteProp(linearList, position)*

Table 17-1: Undocumented and Misdocumented Lingo (continued)

Command	Use
the digitalVideoTimeScale	*The digitalVideoTimeScale* affects the units used for *the duration of member, the movieTime of sprite,* and other digital video timing properties. See "Time Scales" in Chapter 11, *Timers and Dates.*
downloadNetThing()	Can be used to copy local files . See Table 14-2.
the doubleClick	The first two paragraphs under *the doubleClick* entry in the *Lingo Dictionary* describe the second example, not *the doubleClick* itself, which is a system property, not a function.
the duration of member	When used with digital video, *the duration of member* is measured in units that depend on *the digitalVideoTimeScale,* not necessarily ticks. See Table 11-4 in Chapter 11.
the editable of member	A field is editable if *the editable of sprite* property is TRUE, even if *the editable of member* is FALSE.
the editable of sprite	A sprite is editable if its *editable of member* property is TRUE, even if *the editable of sprite* is FALSE. Set *the editable of sprite* to TRUE, even if it is already TRUE, to force focus onto a field sprite.
EvalScript	See *on EvalScript.*
exit tell[1]	Exits a *tell...end tell* construct.
the exitLock	On Windows, the Esc key and Alt-F4 also quit Projectors by default. Ctrl-W and Cmd-W do *not* quit Projectors by default. In the example in the *Lingo Dictionary,* if the user presses the specified keys, there is no point in checking if *the exitLock* is TRUE. If it is FALSE, the Projector will quit before the code is ever reached.
externalEvent	Does not work with all Shockwave plug-in/browser configurations. Works only on PowerPCs and Windows 95/NT, not on 68K Macs or Windows 3.1.
factory()[1]	Returns an object reference if specified XObject is installed: `if objectP(factory("SerialPort")) then...`
the fileSize of member	The *fileSize of member* is listed under "Memory Management" on page 258 in the appendix to the *Lingo Dictionary,* but no such property exists.
findEmpty()	You can specify any castLib, but defaults to castLib 1, not the *activeCastLib.* `findEmpty (member whichMember {of castLib whichCast})`
the floatPrecision	*The floatPrecision* affects only the *display* of floating-point values. All floating-point calculations are always performed at full precision (15 significant digits).
the fontSize of *chunk*	Can set the *fontSize* for a substring using: `set the fontSize of Char 1 to 10 of field "somefield" = n`

Table 17-1: Undocumented and Misdocumented Lingo (continued)

Command	Use
forcePreloadCuePoints()[1]	`forcePreloadCuePoints (member swaMember)` Sent by Director when opening the Tempo dialog to force any current SWA sprites to load their cue points so they can be displayed in the list. You should *not* consider this a supported command. Use at your own risk; it may disappear.
the frameLabel	*The* `frameLabel` can be set at any time in both D5 and D6, not just during a Score Recording session. Setting *the* `frameLabel` to any string (including the EMPTY string) adds a marker at the current frame or renames an existing marker. Setting it to 0 deletes any marker in the current frame. It can also be used to set a comment *after* the marker name (comments appear only in the Marker window or, optionally, when printing). `set the frameLabel = "name" & RETURN & "comment"`
the freeBlock	You may be able to load cast members even if *the freeBlock* is low because Director may be able to purge memory before the next load. See Chapter 9, *Performance and Memory*, in *Director in a Nutshell*.
getNthFileNameInFolder	The correct path to items on the Macintosh desktop is: "*HardDiskName*`:Desktop Folder:etc`" Note space between the words "Desktop" and "Folder," not a colon as shown in the *Lingo Dictionary*.
getPref()	Works in Director and Projectors, and not just Shockwave. See Table 16-1 and Chapter 14.
go movie	Works in Shockwave, but won't provide "Where Is?" dialog if specified movie is not found. If you omit the .DIR, .DCR, or .DXR extension, Windows will be confused by a subfolder named the same as the movie's name without the extension. Shockwave requires the .DCR extension, or it may not be able to locate the file.
the height of rect[1]	Returns the height of a rectangle.
the idleHandlerPeriod	Increasing *the idleHandlerPeriod* (which defaults to 0) adversely impacts all idle processing , including the frequency of *idle*, `mouseEnter, mouseWithin,` and `mouseLeave` events.
the idleReadChunkSize	*The idleReadChunkSize* is a movie-wide property and can *not* be set individually for each member, as implied in the *Lingo Dictionary*.

ilk()	*Ilk()* can test any datum against any symbolic data type, not just Lingo lists. Although they should, these two forms of *ilk()* do not evaluate consistently in all cases:
	
	`if ilk (someItem, #someType) then...`
	`if ilk (someItem) = #someType then...`
	
	See Table 5-4 in Chapter 5, *Data Types and Expressions*.

importFileInto	Can link an external castLib at runtime using: `importFileInto whichMember, "castFile.CST"`

Table 17-1: Undocumented and Misdocumented Lingo (continued)

Command	Use
interface (xtra "XtraName")[1]	Returns the Help text for an Xtra (see *mMessageList*): `put interface (xtra "FileIO")`
the isToggled of sprite	The correct name is *isToggled*, not *isToggle*.
item...of	Any chunk expression starting with *item 0* returns the entire string. See Chapter 7. An item is delimited by the *itemDelimiter*, not necessarily a comma.
the keyDownScript	The event handler designated by *the keyDownScript* passes events by default. The *pass* command is not needed. Use *dontPassEvent* or *stopEvent* to consume it.
the keyUpScript	The event handler designated by *the keyUpScript* passes events by default. The *pass* command is not needed. Use *dontPassEvent* or *stopEvent* to consume it.
the labelString of member	This property pertains only to buttons created with the Custom Button Editor Xtra.
the left of rect[1]	Returns the left (first) coordinate of a rectangle.
the length of *chunk*	Variation that works like *length()* function: `put the length of chunk`
line...of	Any chunk expression starting with *line 0* returns the entire string. See Chapter 7.

the lineHeight of line	Can set *the lineHeight* for an individual line using:
	`set the lineHeight of line whichLine of [LC]`
	`    field "whichField" = new Height`

list()	You can create lists longer than 256 characters in the Script window but not the Message window.
the locH of point[1]	Returns the horizontal (first) coordinate of a point.
the locH of sprite	The example in the *Lingo Dictionary* is very wrong. Compare *the locH* to (*the stageRight - the stageLeft*), not just to *the stageRight*, to determine if the sprite is off the right edge of the Stage. (*The stageRight* property is relative to the left of the monitor; *the locH* is relative to the left of the Stage.) See Chapter 5, *Coordinates, Alignment, and Registration Points*, in *Director in a Nutshell*.
the locV of point[1]	Returns the vertical (second) coordinate of a point.
the locV of sprite	The example in the *Lingo Dictionary* is very wrong. Compare *the locV* to (*the stageBottom - the stageTop*), not just to *the stageBottom*, to determine if the sprite is off the bottom of the Stage. (*The stageBottom* property is relative to the top of the monitor, *the locV* is relative to the top of the Stage.) See Chapter 5 in *Director in a Nutshell*.
log10()[1]	The base-10 logarithm is not defined by Lingo. See Example 8-9 in Chapter 8, *Math (and Gambling)*.
the machineType	Don't use *the machineType* < *256* to check for Macintosh computers. Some Macintoshes have *machineType* > 256. Use *the platform* instead. See Chapter 8 in *Director in a Nutshell*.

Undoc. Lingo

Table 17-1: Undocumented and Misdocumented Lingo (continued)

Command	Use
marker()	Do not use the keyword *the* with *marker()*, despite the examples shown in the *Lingo Dictionary* under *go loop*, *go next*, etc.
the memberType of member	*The memberType of member* is listed in the `Lingo Dictionary`, but it is not a valid property. Use *type of member* instead.
mMessageList()	`mMessageList()` is still the preferred method for displaying an Xtra's other methods (despite the *Lingo Dictionary*'s implication that it is obsolete): `put mMessageList (xtra "FileIO")`
the mostRecentCuePoint	The proper syntax is *the mostRecentCuePoint of sprite* and *the mostRecentCuePoint of sound*, not just *the mostRecentCuePoint*.
the mouseDownScript	The event handler designated by *the mouseDownScript* passes events by default. The *pass* command is not needed. Use *dontPassEvent* or *stopEvent* to consume it.
mouseUpOutside	Ssee *on mouseUpOutside*.
the mouseUpScript	The event handler designated by *the mouseUpScript* passes events by default. The *pass* command is not needed. Use *dontPassEvent* or *stopEvent* to consume it.
move (member)	Returns the new cast member slot to which the cast member was moved. (Warning: Moving cast members with *move()* does *not* update the Score!)
the movie	*The movie* indicates the name of the *Projector* when checked from within the first movie built into a Projector.
the movieName	*The movieName* indicates the name of the *Projector* when checked from within the first movie built into a Projector.
the movieTime of sprite	Measured in units that depend on the *digitalVideoTimeScale*, not necessarily ticks. See Chapter 11.
netLastModDate()	Accepts optional *netID:* `put  netLastModDate(netID)`
netMIME()	Accepts optional *netID:* `put  netMIME(netID)`
netPresent()	The *netPresent()* function is not useful because it is contained within the Xtra for whom's presence it checks . It can only be called if the *NetLingo* Xtra is installed, in which case it always returns TRUE (as it does in Shockwave). If the *NetLingo* Xtra is not installed, it causes an error in Director (but still works in Shockwave). Use *the netPresent* property instead.
the netPresent[1]	The undocumented property *the netPresent* should be used from a Projector or Director instead of *netPresent()*. It returns TRUE if both the *NetLingo* and *NetFile* Xtras are installed and FALSE otherwise. (It returns a large positive integer in Shockwave, for which it is always TRUE.)

Table 17-1: Undocumented and Misdocumented Lingo (continued)

Command	Use
the netThrottleTicks[1]	Lowering *the netThrottleTicks* gives more attention to network operations, causing linked media to download somewhat faster. Increasing *the netThrottleTicks* gives priority to local operations, such as animation. Default is 15. (Completely *unsupported*; works from Director for Macintosh only, not Windows or Shockwave, but you should not rely on it.)
the number of items	An item is delimited by *the itemDelimiter*, not necessarily a comma.
the number of member	The *number of member* reported for movies updated from D4 with a Shared Cast is "kludged" to reflect the same number as it would have in D4. See Chapter 4, *CastLibs, Cast Members, and Sprites*, in *Director in a Nutshell*.
numToChar()	The *ForceUpperCase* example in the *Lingo Dictionary* is very wrong. It corrupts or deletes non-alphabetic characters in the string. See Appendix A, *ASCII Codes and Key Codes*, and Appendix C, *Case-Sensitivity, Sort Order, Diacritical Marks, and Space-Sensitivity*..
offset()	The *SearchAndReplace* example in the *Lingo Dictionary* is wrong. See Example 7-8 in Chapter 7.
on *handlerName*	Handlers in Score scripts generally are not called from outside the script in which they are defined. They are not automatically globally accessible, as are handlers in movie scripts. See Chapter 2, *Events, Messages, and Scripts*.
on alertHook	The *on alertHook* handler can return one of four meaningful values (-1, 0, 1, or 2). See Table 16-1 for correct details.
on cuePassed	The *on cuePassed* handler receives the parameter *me* if it is placed in a sprite script or frame script, but not if placed in a movie script or cast script. See Table 16-1.
on EvalScript	Does not work with all Shockwave plug-in/browser configurations. Works only on PowerPCs and Windows 95/NT, not on 68K Macs and Windows 3.1.
on mouseUpOutside	The example in the *Lingo Dictionary* is very wrong. The *mouseUpOutside* event is not issued unless the mouse button is released outside the sprite. See *mouseWithin* instead. See Chapter 9, *Mouse Events*.
on prepareFrame	The *go, play*, and *updateStage* commands are disabled within the *prepareFrame* handler.
on prepareMovie	The *go, play*, and *updateStage* commands are disabled within the *prepareMovie* handler. Any *quit* commands are delayed until after the playback head moves following *startMovie*.
on runPropertyDialog	The *on runPropertyDialog* handler receives *me* as the first parameter, and the property list returned by *on getPropertyDescriptionList* as the second parameter.
on startUp[1]	Any *on startUp* handler defined in a LINGO.INI file in the same folder as the Projector gets executed when the Projector starts.

Table 17-1: Undocumented and Misdocumented Lingo (continued)

Command	Use
on timeOut	The *on timeOut* handler can be placed in a frame script, too, not just a movie script.
the organizationName[1]	Returns the user's organization name from Director's registration dialog box. Author-time only. Also valid in D5.
the platform	Return string indicates the Projector type or Shockwave plug-in type, *not* the user's current platform. See Table 16-1 and Chapter 8 in *Director in a Nutshell*.
preLoad	*PreLoad* accepts a frame number by default, but it can be used with an explicit member reference as *preLoad (member n)*, which is equivalent to the *preLoadMember n*.
the preLoadRAM	The example shown in the *Lingo Dictionary* is meaningless. See Chapter 9, *Performance and Memory*, and Chapter 16, *Digital Video*, in *Director in a Nutshell*.
printFrom	The *printFrom* command prints what is in the Score, not what is on the Stage. Puppeted sprites are ignored.
the productName[1]	Returns "Director" from Authoring, Projectors, and Shockwave. Also worked in D5.
the productVersion [1]	Returns the same version string as the global variable *version* during authoring and from a Projector, such as "6.0.2" or "6.5". Also worked in D5. In SW it returns "6.0.1," not "6.0.1 net" as does the global *version*.
puppetSound	See Chapter 15, in *Director in a Nutshell* for details on undocumented forms of *puppetSound*.
puppetTempo	Looping in a frame, going backward in the Score, or encountering a new Tempo channel setting all cancel the *puppetTempo*.
the purgePriority of member	The example in the *Lingo Dictionary* is very wrong. Setting its *purgePriority* to 2 causes a cast member to be purged *after* other cast members (with *purgePriority* 3), not *before* them. It means "purge after," not "purge first."
putImageIntoCast-Member	Table 16-1 lists the possible values for the *imageString* parameter used by this command
the ramNeeded	The example in the *Lingo Dictionary* is misleading because *the ramNeeded* includes the RAM used by cast members even if they are loaded. It does not reflect how much *more* RAM is needed to load a frame's assets. See Chapter 9 in *Director in a Nutshell*.
the rect of member	Setting *the rect of member* for field and rich text cast members sets the size of their scrolling box on-stage.
the rect of sprite	Setting *the rect of sprite* for field and rich text cast members sets the size of their scrolling box on-stage.
restart	Restarts Windows despite the *Lingo Dictionary*'s claim to the contrary. See Table 7-2 in Chapter 7, *Cross-Platform and OS Dependencies*, in *Director in a Nutshell*.
the right of rect[1]	Returns the right (third) coordinate of a rectangle.

Table 17-1: Undocumented and Misdocumented Lingo (continued)

Command	Use
rollover()	The *case* statement in Example 2 in the *Lingo Dictionary* is wrong. *Rollover(n)* returns a Boolean value, not the number of the sprite being rolled over.
the rowBytes[1]	Returns (*width of member * depth of member/8*) (where width is rounded up to next even number). *Unsupported*; use at your own risk.
the runMode	*The runMode works in D5, although it was undocumented until D6.*
the safePlayer[1]	This read-only property returns FALSE (0) in Director and TRUE (1) in Shockwave because the latter has security hobbles to disable potentially destructive or invasive Lingo commands. *Unsupported*; use at your own risk.
the script of member	Returns a script reference of the specified cast member. Causes an error for non-script cast members without a cast script attached. See Chapter 2.
the scriptInstanceList of sprite	The *scriptInstanceList* is only settable at runtime (and only for sprites that have a Behavior attached already) and can't be permanently set via Lingo, despite claims in the *Lingo Dictionary*. When the movie is stopped it returns an empty list ([]).
the selEnd	Set *the selEnd before* setting *the selStart* to get them to work reliably. Set them to the same value to set a cursor insertion point. The default is the end of the highlight of the currently selected field, not 0. See Examples 10-5 and 10-6 in Chapter 10, *Keyboard Events*.
the selStart	The default is the beginning of the highlight of the currently selected field, not 0. See *the selEnd*.
send[1]	Sends a message. Same as *call*, except it generates an error if message is not trapped. Works in D4 or later. *Unsupported*.
sendAllSprites	The first argument must be a symbol, such as: `sendAllSprites (#mouseUp)`
sendAncestor[1]	Sends a message. Same as *callAncestor*, except it generates an error if message is not trapped. Works in D4 or later. *Unsupported*.
sendSprite	The second argument must be a symbol such as: `sendSprite (1, #mouseUp)`
the serialNumber[1]	Returns the user's serial number from Director's registration dialog box. Author-time only. Also valid in D5.
setButtonImageFrom-CastMember	Table 16-1 lists the possible values for the *imageString* parameter used by this command.
setPref	Works from Director or a Projector, not just Shockwave. See Table 16-1 and Chapter 14.
shutDown	Restarts Windows rather than simply exiting to Windows 95 desktop or exiting Windows 3.1 as the *Lingo Dictionary* claims.

Undoc. Lingo

Table 17-1: Undocumented and Misdocumented Lingo (continued)

Command	Use
the soundKeepDevice[1]	Controls whether Director releases the sound device control to other drivers, such as QuickTime and RSX. See Chapter 15 in *Director in a Nutshell*.
starts	The *starts* command is sensitive to diacritical marks. See Appendix C.
the startTime of sprite	*The startTime of sprite* does not work unless you set it after the digital video starts playing; even then it doesn't seem reliable. Check *the movieTime of sprite* manually instead.
the stopTime of sprite	*The stopTime of sprite* does not work unless you set it after the digital video starts playing; even then it doesn't seem reliable. Check *the movieTime of sprite* manually instead.
the timeoutLapsed	The `timeoutLapsed` can be set as well as tested, despite claims to the contrary. See Chapter 11.
the timeoutPlay	The *timeoutPlay* has no effect on whether *timeOut* events occur when a movie is playing. Setting it to TRUE resets *the timeoutLapsed* only when using *go movie* or *play movie*, not when simply playing the current movie.
the timer	The *timer* can be set as well as tested, despite claims to the contrary. See Chapter 11.
the top of rect	Returns the top (second) coordinate of a rectangle.
track of member[1]	Returns the type of the first track of a digital video member. Same as *trackType (member, 1)*. Not of any use for multitrack digital video files.
the tracks of member[1]	Returns the number of tracks of a digital video member. Same as *trackCount (member)*.
unload	*Unload* accepts a frame number by default, but it can be used with an explicit member reference as *unload (member n)*, which is equivalent to the *unloadMember (n)*.
the userName[1]	Returns the username from Director's registration dialog box. Author-time only. Also valid in D5.
version	You must declare the global variable *version* before using it in a Lingo script. `global version` `if version starts "6" then...`
the visibility of sprite[1]	Same as *the visible of sprite* property. See Director 6 *ReadMe* regarding visibility.
visible of the stage	Use *set the visible of the stage = FALSE* to hide the Stage.
the volume of sprite	The maximum volume for a QuickTime sprite is greater than 256, although distortion may occur.
the width of rect[1]	Returns the width of a rectangle.

Table 17-1: Undocumented and Misdocumented Lingo (continued)

Command	Use

the windowList	Do *not* clear *the windowList* by setting it to the empty list as shown in the *Lingo Dictionary*. Instead use:
	
	`repeat while count (the windowList)`
	`  forget window 1`
	`end repeat`
	
	See Chapter 6, *The Stage and MIAWs*, in *Director in a Nutshell*.

word...of	Any chunk expression starting with *word 0* returns the entire string. See Chapter 7.

1 This keyword does not appear in the Macromedia *Lingo Dictionary*. Some undocumented keywords can be used safely, but other should be avoided as noted.

Lingo Changes from Director 5

Table 17-2 lists Lingo that behaves differently in D6 than it did in previous versions of Director. Refer to the *Director 6 ReadMe* file for additional details. Refer to the Online Help and Table 18-1 for details on new Lingo commands.

See also the quirk list at *http://www.updatestage.com* and the Bug Database at *http://www.director-online.com*.

Table 17-2: Lingo That Behaves Differently in Director 6

Command	Use
clearGlobals	In D6, *clearGlobals* clears *the actorList* in the current movie in addition to clearing global variables. In D4 and D5 it did not modify *the actorList*.
count()	D6 supports counting the properties of an object, which was previously unsupported. You can also use *getAt()* to extract properties from an object. See Chapter 6, *Lists*.
delay	Commands preceding a *delay* command in an *exitFrame* handler are no longer executed repeatedly, as occurred in D5.
enterFrame	*enterFrame* message is sent to sprites in D6 in addition to frame and movie scripts.
exitFrame	*exitFrame* message is sent to sprites in D6 in addition to frame and movie scripts.
the fullColorPermit	The *fullColorPermit* was supported in Director 3.1.1 and has reemerged in D6.
importFileInto	The name of the imported cast member created by *importFileInto* no longer includes the original file's extension, such as ".AIF" or ".MOV" as it did in D5. Two files with names that differ only by their extension will have the same cast member name upon import.
menu	D6 uses the vertical bar ("|"), instead of the symbol "Å" (created with `Option-x` on the Macintosh or `Alt+0-1-9-7` under Windows) to separate a command from its associated menu item. See Chapter 14 in *Director in a Nutshell*.

Table 17-2: Lingo That Behaves Differently in Director 6 (continued)

Command	Use
the mouseCast the mouse-Member	*The mouseCast* returns a *castNum* (or -1 if the mouse is not over a sprite), but *the mouseMember* returns a *member* reference, not a *memberNum* (or VOID if the mouse is not over a sprite). Both were updated in D6.0.1 to ignore off-stage sprites or off-stage portions of sprites.
new	The *new* message is sent to sprites in D6. The *new* command recurses in D6 if you call *new* from within a parent script's *on new* handler (in D5 it did not recurse). Use *birth*, which does not recurse, instead if birthing objects within your *on new* handler.
on enterFrame	Called for sprite scripts in D6, but not D5.
on exitFrame	Called for sprite scripts in D6, but not D5.
on new	Called for sprite scripts in D6, but not D5.
PI	PI was not defined in D5, but it could be entered by hand (see Example 5-1). It is new in D6, although not mentioned as such in the online Help. It was buggy in D6.0, but was fixed in 6.0.1.
the platform	In D6.5, *the platform* may return "Java *javaVersion, browser, OS*" in addition to "Macintosh,68k", "Macintosh,PowerPC", "Windows,16", and "Windows,32".
the puppet of sprite	*The puppet of sprite* command still behaves the same in D6 as in D5, but there is often no need to use it, as sprite properties are auto-puppeted. See Chapter 4, *CastLibs, Cast Members, and Sprites*, in *Director in a Nutshell*.
the quickTimePresent	*The quickTimePresent* only checks for versions prior to QT3 under Windows. See Chapter 16 in *Director in a Nutshell*.
the rect of member	Allegedly this returned an incorrect value for Xtras in D5 but works in D6. See note in the *Lingo Dictionary*.
the regPoint of member	The registration point of digital video cast members is correctly reported as their center in D6, rather than as their upper left, as in D5. *The regPoint* reported for some Xtras may also have changed.
the runMode	In D6.5, *the runMode* may return "Java Applet" in addition to "Projector", "Author", and "Plugin".
the scoreSelection	*The scoreSelection* returns different values in D6 than it did in D5. A separate sublist is used for each channel of the Score's selection, even if the channels are contiguous. Unlike in D5, you can select discontiguous frames by Cmd-clicking multiple sprites. (Ctrl-click under Windows.)
sound fadeIn	The *sound fadeIn* command in D6 fades from 0 to the current volume setting, not 255 as in D5. See the D6 *ReadMe*.
sound fadeOut	The *sound fadeOut* command in D6 fades from the current volume setting to 0, not from 255 to 0 as in D5. See the D6 *ReadMe*.

Table 17-2: Lingo That Behaves Differently in Director 6 (continued)

Command	Use
SPACE	SPACE was not defined in D5, but it could be simulated using " " (see Example 5-1). SPACE was buggy in D6.0, but was fixed in 6.0.1.
the visible of sprite	*The visible of sprite* disables interactivity on invisible sprites in D6, but not in D5. See the D6 *ReadMe*.

VOID	VOID was not defined in D5, but it could be simulated using *value(<Void>)* (see Example 5-1). VOID was buggy in D6.0, but was fixed in 6.0.1.
	
	D5 and D6 evaluate expressions differently when comparing a VOID value (such as an uninitialized global variable) to 0:
	
	`global voidVar`
	`if (0 = voidVar) then alert "It is TRUE"`
	
	D6 evaluates the above as TRUE, whereas D5 evaluates it as FALSE. Both D5 and D6 evaluate the following as TRUE:
	
	`if (voidVar = 0) then alert "It is TRUE"`

Obsolete Lingo

Refer to the notes in Table 18-1 and to the online Help for a list of obsolete Lingo commands and their preferred replacements. Although they may no longer be officially supported or appear in the *Lingo Dictionary*, they often work fine, sometimes for several versions after being discontinued. Refer to the discussion of the obsolete Lingo at the top of Chapter 18.

Obsolete properties of the form:

    the *property* of cast *whichCastMember,*

should be replaced with the form:

    the *property* of member *whichMember.*

CHAPTER 18

Lingo Keyword and Command Summary

Table 18-1 is an alphabetical list of over 1100 words and phrases that have relevance in Director. That's nearly twice what you'll find in Macromedia's *Lingo Dictionary* or any other single source! Refer to Tables 17-1, and 17-2 in Chapter 17, *Changed, Undocumented, and Misdocumented Lingo*, for details on undocumented and misdocumented Lingo and Lingo that behaves differently in D6 than in earlier versions. Refer to Table 16-1 in Chapter 16, *Enumerated Values,* for details on codes used by each command, such as ink and transition types (and much more). Refer to Chapter 19, *The Lingo Symbol Table,* and the downloadable Chapter 22, *Symbol Table Archaeology,* for the gory details on the Lingo Symbol Table. Refer to Appendix B, *Changes in D6 Through D6.5,* for details on new Lingo in D6.5.

Why a Massive Table?

I think you'll appreciate this thorough list of all Lingo keywords, symbols, commands, properties, and functions. I opted to organize it alphabetically; refer to the appropriate chapters for commands grouped by topic.

Many of the commands summarized in Table 18-1 are covered in detail in other chapters in this book; if not, refer to the companion volume, *Director in a Nutshell.*

Table 18-1 provides a quick syntax reference when you know what command you want. It also helps beginning Linguists (when examining someone else's Lingo code) to distinguish between predefined keywords and variables or handlers that the programmer created. (Some programmers use variables or symbols that have the same name as existing Lingo properties. You should strive to understand Lingo's grammar as explained in Chapter 1, *How Lingo Thinks.*)

The table cross-references all the enumerated types for each command. For example, the word "*bold*," leads to the *fontStyle of member* property; the symbol *#quickTime* leads to *the digitalVideoType of member* property.

Table 18-1 includes:

- All built-in Lingo keywords including all the meaningful entries from Lingo's Symbol Table (see Chapters 19 and 22).

- All commands that are built from multiple keywords, such as *sound playFile.*

- All variants of a keyword. For example, the table lists both the string "*left*" and the Lingo property *the left of sprite.*

- All strings recognized by Lingo, such as "*Author.*"

- Supplemental definitions that are not part of Lingo but are added for your convenience, such as *log10*, CR (carriage return), ESCAPE, LF (line feed).

- Values that are returned by Lingo but never otherwise used, such as INF, NAN, <offspring>, and <Xtra child>.

- Lingo symbols, methods, and strings used by common Xtras and XObjects that come with Director, most notably NetLingo, FileIO, the Custom Button Editor, and DirMMX. The table includes the major items from the MUI Dialog Xtra (see Chapter 15, *The MUI Dialog Xtra,* and the downloadable Chapter 21, *Custom MUI Dialogs*).

- The unsupported Din Xtra that has some interesting methods for controlling streaming audio can be found at *Director 6 CD:Macromedia:XDK for Director 6\Authorware 4:Goodies:Director:SoundXtr:Xtras:Din* or *D:Macromedia\ XDK_d6a4\Goodies\Director\SoundXtr\Xtras\Din.X32.*

- Keywords erroneously described in Macromedia's *Lingo Dictionary* that don't really exist in Lingo.

- Many keywords that are documented only in *ReadMe* files or in the comments of text files, such as DIRECTOR.INI (pertains to Windows only). See Appendix D, *The DIRECTOR.INI and LINGO.INI Files.*

- Undocumented commands that may not appear in one or more of the *Lingo Dictionary*, Lingo pull-down menus, or online Help. See the caveats about undocumented Lingo that follow.

- Undocumented variations or uses of existing commands (see caveats that follow). See Table 17-1 for details on undocumented commands.

With the advent of Xtras, there are an unlimited number of "Lingo" keywords, and I had to cut it off somewhere. I've generally excluded very obscure items, especially if there were too many of them to sneak into the table, such as all the symbols used by the MUI Xtra (but I've included the most important ones or documented them in the other chapters). Naturally, I don't include all the keywords used by third-party Xtras, which could fill a book in their own right. Refer instead to the individual chapters, especially Chapter 13, *Lingo Xtras and XObjects,* and Chapter 10, *Using Xtras,* in *Director in a Nutshell,* where I've tried to point you toward the right Xtra.

Table 18-1 *excludes:*

- Those keywords that are part of Director's built-in Symbol Table but have no known function in Director (see the downloadable Chapter 22).

- Obsolete properties of the form:

  `the property of cast whichCastMember`

  such as *the name of cast 5* that have been obsolete since Director 5 and should be replaced with the form:

  `the property of member whichMember`

- Explicit details on each of the possible values for a property or parameter (see Table 16-1 instead).

- Every possible use of some keywords. Most notably, the Lingo symbols that represent asset types, (*#digitalVideo*, *#bitmap*, etc). can be used with the *new (member)* function, *the type of member* property, and the *#format* parameter within *getPropertyDescriptionList*. Refer again to *Table 16-1.*

- Some methods used by the obsolete *FileIO* XObject. If you need to decipher older code using that XObject, see Chapter 14, *External Files*, and refer to *http://www.zeusprod.com/nutshell/chapters/fileio.html* for a table comparing the methods of the *FileIO* XObject and *FileIO* Xtra.

- Keywords used by third-party Xtras, such as the PrintOMatic and Popup Menu Xtras. Consult the Xtra's documentation instead.

- Keywords used by the new QuickTime 3, ActiveX, Custom Cursor, Flash Asset and Save as Java Xtras (plus the unsupported FileXtra and UI Helper Xtras). As they are not part of the core Lingo language and were added to Director as this book went to press, these are covered in Appendix B, *Changes in D6 Through D6.5.* Many of these are covered in more detail in the companion volume, *Director in a Nutshell*, in Chapter 4, *CastLibs, Cast Members, and Sprites*, Chapter 8, *Projectors and the Run-time Environment*, Chapter 11, *Shockwave and the Internet*, Chapter 14, *Graphical User Interface Components*, and Chapter 16, *Digital Video.*

Conventions Used in the Table

Due to the number of entries, I have favored brevity over clarity in some individual entries. The full syntax variations can be found in the appropriate chapter in either this book or *Director in a Nutshell.*

Typographical Conventions

Refer to the typographical conventions described in the *Preface*. Most notably, optional items are specified with curly braces "{}", and multiple possible values are separated by a vertical bar "|". The following:

```
put the {abbr{ev{iated}} | long | short} date
```

is equivalent to:

```
put the date
put the short date
```

```
put the long date
put the abbr date
put the abbrev date
put the abbreviated date
```

(Note one exception is the vertical bar "|" used to define actions for custom menu options.)

Stylistic Conventions

I have tried to show a realistic example of each keyword's use that I assume you can adapt to your needs. If a generalized example is sufficiently clear I use replaceable parameters, such as *whichMember*, shown in *italics*. It should be obvious from context that they are not reserved words.

In some cases, I have shown multiple possible syntaxes that all accomplish similar goals using a given keyword. Such variations are often undocumented and therefore unsupported. Note that new constants, VOID, SPACE, and PI, did not work in all cases in Director 6.0. This was fixed in Director 6.01, and now *void, the void,* and *void()* are all equivalent, as are *space, the space,* and *space()* and *pi, the pi,* and *pi()*.

Virtually any property that can be set can also be tested, so I generally demonstrate any *settable* properties using an example, such as:

```
set the property of object = value
```

You should assume that such properties can also be *read* using either of these:

```
set myVariable = the property of object
put the property of object
```

I generally demonstrate any functions or properties that return a Boolean value (TRUE or FALSE) using an example of the form:

```
if booleanFunction() then...
if booleanProperty then...
```

In both cases, the remainder of the *if...then...end if* statement is omitted for brevity.

The following terms are used for replaceable items:

member *whichMember*
> A member number or member name. Though not shown, in most cases a full cast menber specfication including a castLib can be used:
>
> ```
> member whichMember of castLib whichCastLib
> ```
> If a command is limited to a specific castmember type member, I use replaceable names such as *VideoMember, SoundMember, SwaMember, fieldMember,* etc.

castLib whichCast
> *whichCast* is a castLib name or number, not a castmember name or number, as the term *cast* was used prior to Director 5.

window *whichWindow*

> A window number or name. Often, *the stage* can be used instead, in which case the keyword *window* should be omitted. See Chapter 6, *The Stage and MIAWs,* in *Director in a Nutshell.*

sprite *whichSprite*

> A sprite number, such as:

```
sprite (the spriteNum of me)
sprite x
sprite 5
```

script *"ParentScript"*

> The name or number of a parent script. If you use a script's number, exclude the quotes.

someItem, someVariable, value, whichMember, videoMember, etc.

> A generic item of the implied type.

property

> A property of the system, of a list, or of an object such as *the backColor of sprite.*

object

> An item that has properties, such as a sprite, member, or child object.

TRUE | FALSE

> A Boolean value, either **TRUE** (1) or **FALSE** (0).

chunkExpression

> Any character string, including a field cast member, or part thereof, such as `char 1 to 10 of field "MyStuff"`. Chunk expressions can also include *item...of, line...of,* and *word...of.* See Chapter 7, *Strings.*

expression

> Any logical expression, such as *x > 5,* that can be evaluated as **TRUE** or **FALSE**. See Chapter 5, *Data Types and Expressions.*

... (ellipses)

> Indicates that subsequent Lingo is omitted, most notably following an *if (expression) then...* statement, but also in chunk expressions such as *item...of.*

Categories and Comments

Each table entry includes the item's general category, whether it works in Shockwave or is new in D6, etc.

New in Director 6

D6 indicates an item that is new in D6. It may have actually been present in earlier versions of Director, but if so, it was undocumented, such as *deleteAll().* Refer to the online Help for a list of new keywords, and see Table 17-2 for a list of commands that existed in previous versions of Director but behave differently in D6. Refer also to *http://www.zeusprod.com/director/d6diff.html* for details on differences from D5 to D6. Entries in Table 18-1 are supported in D5 and D6, and usually D4, unless specifically flagged as *D6.*

Shockwave

SW indicates a command that can be used in Shockwave. Naturally, just about all commands can be used in Shockwave, so I''ve flagged only those that you might not expect to work in Shockwave or that have a different function in Shockwave than in Projectors or during authoring.

URL-enhanced

URL indicates that the command accepts a URL for a file path or movie name. Many existing commands from D5 are URL-enhanced in D6.

Macintosh and Windows Compatibility

Items flagged as **Mac-only** or **Win-only** are platform-specific. These commands are usually ignored on the other platform. For example, Director for Macintosh ignores *mci* commands. If the operation is truly different on the two platforms, I''ve flagged it as "**Differs on Mac/Win.**" See Chapter 7, *Cross-Platform and OS Dependencies*, in *Director in a Nutshell* for details on these commands.

Undocumented Keywords and Supplemental Commands

"Undocumented" is a tricky term. There are many supported entries in Table 18-1 that are documented outside the *Lingo Dictionary*, online Help, or Lingo pull-down menus (such as in *ReadMe* files, Xtras documentation, and the comments of the DIRECTOR.INI file). I''ve marked only the truly undocumented commands as such in the table, but there are dozens of entries that you won't find if you search only the usual suspects.

 Undocumented Lingo should be used at your own risk. It may not work in all configurations, or it may disappear or change in future revisions, and it should not be relied upon. I''ve tried to flag such items as **unsupported** to distinguish them from the merely obscure commands.

Table 18-1 also shows undocumented variations of the syntax, or undocumented uses of a command. Notwithstanding the previous caveats, some of these have been stable for several versions of Director. You can stick with the documented syntax where there is a choice, but even documented Lingo may contain bugs. For example, you should use the undocumented *the netPresent* property instead of the documented *netPresent()* function.

Obsolete Commands

Obsolete indicates a Lingo keyword that is obsolete and is no longer officially supported. Refer also to the online Help, which lists keywords that are newly obsolete in Director 6. Note that many officially obsolete keywords are still quite useful and do not necessarily have a replacement.

Buggy or Erroneously Documented

The *Lingo Dictionary* and its examples are riddled with errors. Although most commands work well when used as I've documented, many will fail if used as most presented by Macromedia and other third-party sources. Factually erroneous statements of measurable impact in Macromedia's documentation are addressed in Table 17-1.

Read-Only Properties and Score Recording

Read-only indicates a property that can be tested but not set, such as *the quick-TimePresent*. Even though a Lingo property cannot be set, there is often some indirect way of changing its value. For example, you cannot set *the number of members* property, but you can add cast members, and that will be reflected in *the number of members*. On the other hand, some properties are truly fixed, barring changing the system configuration, such as *the deskTopRectList* and *the videoForWindowsPresent*. Note that some properties flagged as **Read-Only (SR)** are settable only during a Score Recording session (and otherwise read-only).

Chapter and Topic Cross-Reference

In the third column (labelled "See"). I include a general topic to provide the context for the command and the chapter to find it in.

 L01 through L22 and LA through LE indicate Chapters 1 through 22 and Appendices A through E of *Lingo in a Nutshell*. D01 through D16 indicate Chapters 1 through 16 of *Director in a Nutshell*.

 Many keywords in Table 18-1 must be preceded by the keyword *the*. The *the* is omitted from the leftmost column but is always shown in the example syntax in the second column.

Table 18-1: Lingo Command and Keyword Summary

Keyword	Description or Example	See	Notes
`#symbolName`	`#symbolName`	Data Types (L05)	
`#frameMarker` (within url)	`gotoNetMovie "http://www.zeusprod.com/movie.dcr#myMarker"`	SW (D11)	D6
[] (list operator)	`set myList = [1, 2, 3]` or `set myList = [#a:1, #b:2]`	Lists (L06)	

Table 18-1: Lingo Command and Keyword Summary (continued)

Keyword	Description or Example	See	Notes

¬ (continuation character)	`set x = the width of member ¬`
	`    (the member of sprite ¬`
	`    (the currentSpriteNum))`
	`Option-L` or `Option-Return` (Mac) or
	`Alt-Enter` (Win)
		Lingo (L01)	

\ (backslash)	Windows file path separator:
	`set somePath = the pathName &`
	`"myFolder\myFile.doc"`
		Files (L14)	Win-only

| (menu)	Separates script of menultem such as: `Quit/Q | go to frame "Quit"`	Menu (D14)	
Å (menu)	Separates script of menultem such as: `Quit/Q Å go to frame "Quit"` The character (Å) is created with `Option-x` (Mac) or `Alt+0-1-9-7` (Win).	Menu (D14)	Obsolete
!✓ (menu)	Creates a checkMark on the menu (see *checkMark of menultem*) The checkMark (✓) is created with `Option-v` (Mac) or `Alt+0-1-9-5` (Win). `!✓Some Checkable Option`	Menu (D14)	Mac-only
" (double quote)	`set myString = "Something in quotes"`	Strings (L07), QUOTE	

' (single quote)	Use as string delimiter for externalEvents
	`externalEvent`
	`("MyFunction('param1','param2')")`
		Browser (D11)	SW, D6

& (concatenation)	Concatenates (combines) strings
	`set x = "Some String" &`
	`stringVariable & "More string"`
		Strings (L07)	

&& (concatenation)	Concatenates (combines) strings, with a space between them
	`set x = "SomeString" &&`
	`stringVariable`
		Strings (L07)	

() (precedence)	`set x = (5+4) * 7`
	`open window (the applicationPath &`
	`"miaw1")`
		Math (L08),
		Strings (L07)	

() (function call)	Parentheses are required to obtain a return value from function call. `set currentSetting = cacheDocVerify()`	Lingo (L01)	
((menu)	Disables a menu item in a custom menu: `Save(`	Menu (D14)	

Table 18-1: Lingo Command and Keyword Summary (continued)

Keyword	Description or Example	See	Notes
(- (menu)	Creates a separator line in a custom menu.	Menu (D14)	
* (multiplication)	`set x = 5 * y` `set newList = [1, 2, 3] * 5`	Math (L08), Lists (L06)	
+ (addition)	`set x = 5 + y` `set newList = [1, 2, 3] + 5`	Math (L08), Lists (L06)	
+ (positive)	`set x = +5`	Math (L08), Lists (L06)	
- (subtraction)	`set x = 5 - y` `set newList = [1, 2, 3] - 5`	Math (L08), Lists (L06)	
- (negation)	`set x = -5` `set newList = -[1, 2, 3]`	Math (L08), Lists (L06)	

, (comma)	Separates function arguments and handler parameters:
	`set x = someFunction (arg1, arg2)`
	or
	`on someFunction param1, param2`
	`statements`
	`end someFunction`
		Lingo (L01)	

, (comma)	Separates values in case statements:
	`case (expression) of:`
	`  "A", "B": statement(s)`
	`end case`
		Lingo (L01)	

, (comma)	The default the `itemDelimiter` is a comma:
	`put item 2 of "one, two, three"`
	`-- "two"`
		Strings (L07)	

-- (comment)	`-- This is a comment.`	Lingo (L01)	

@ (relative path operator)	Platform-independent relative path operator:
	`set the fileName of member`
	`whichMember = "@/myFolder/myFile.aif"`
		File (L14)	Table 17-1

@ (menu)	Creates Apple menu when used with *installMenu*: `menu:@`	Menu (D14)	Mac-only

/ (division)	(Performs integer division if operands are integers)
	`set x = y / 5`
	`set x = [10, 9, 8] / 6.5`
		Math (L08),
		Lists (L06)	

/ (menu)	Defines a command key equivalent in a menu: `menu:menuName` `Quit/Q	quit`	Menu (D14)	

Table 18-1: Lingo Command and Keyword Summary (continued)

Keyword	Description or Example	See	Notes
/ (URL path separator)	set *myFile* = "*http://www.zeusprod.com/somefile.html*"	URL (D11)	D6
// (URL scheme separator)	set *myURL* = "*http://www.zeusprod.com/somefile.html*"	URL (D11)	D6
/// (local url)	set *localFile* = "*file:///local/somefile.html*"	URL (D11)	D6
: (property lists)	Separates a *property name:property value* pair in a property list: set *myList* = [#*someProperty*: *someValue*]	Lists (L06)	
: (case)	Ends a dependent clause in a case statement: case (*expression*) of 1: *statement* end case	Lingo (L01)	
: (menu definitions)	Defines a menu: menu: *menuName*	Menu (D14), Fields (D12)	
: (Macintosh file path separator)	set the fileName of member *whichMember* = "MacHD:myFolder:myFile. doc"	Files (L14)	Mac-only
: (URL scheme separator)	"*http://www.zeusprod.com/somefile.html*"	URL (D11)	D6
<*StyleCode* (menu)	Defines Bold (<B), Italic (<I), Outlined (<O), Shadow (<S), Underlined (<U) styles in menus: menu: *menuName* Bold <B | *makeBold()*	Menu (D14)	
< (less-than)	if (*x* < 5) then... if "a" < "b" then...	Expressions (L05), Strings (L07)	(case-sensitive)
<= (less-than-or-equal-to)	if (*x* <= 5) then... if "a" <= "b" then...	Expressions (L05), Strings (L07/LC)	(case-sensitive)
<> (not-equal-to)	if (*x* <> 5) then... if "a" <> "b" then...	Expressions (L05), Strings (L07/LC)	(case-insensitive)
> (greater-than)	if (*x* > 5) then... if "a" > "b" then...	Expressions (L05), Strings (L07/LC)	(case-sensitive)

Table 18-1: Lingo Command and Keyword Summary (continued)

Keyword	Description or Example	See	Notes
>= (greater-than-or-equal-to)	`if (x >= 5) then...` `if "a" >= "b" then...`	Expressions (L05), Strings (L07/LC)	(case-sensitive)
= (comparison)	`if (x = 5) then...` `if "a" = "b" then...`	Expressions (L05), Strings (L07/LC)	(case-insensitive)
= (assignment)	`set x = 5`	Expressions (L05), Strings (L07/LC)	
abbr abbrev abbreviated	`the abbr | abbrev | abbreviated date` `the abbr | abbrev | abbreviated time`	Date & Time (L11)	Read-only
abort	`abort`	Lingo (L01)	
#AbortRetryIgnore	`Alert(MUIinstance, [#buttons:` `#AbortRetryIgnore, ...])`	MUI Xtra (L15)	D6, Table 16-1
abs	`set x = abs(value)`	Math (L08)	
#activateWindow	See *call* and *on activateWindow*	MIAWs (D06)	

activeCastLib	`if the type of member whichMember of`
	`castLib (the activeCastLib) = #empty`
	`then...`
		Cast (D04)	Read-only

activeWindow	`if (the activeWindow = the stage)` `then...`	MIAW (D06)	Read-only

#actor and actor()	`put ilk(actor())`
	`-- #actor`
	`put actor(n)`
	`-- <actor 1 1f7a734>`
		Data Types (L08)	Undocumented

actorList	`add (the actorList, new (parent`
	`"ParentScript"))`
	`deleteAll (the actorList)`
		Events (L02), Lists (L06)	See *stepFrame*

add()	`add (linearList, value)` Accepts optional position parameter, same syntax as *addAt()* *add(list, position, value)*	Lists (L06)	Table 17-1
addAt()	`addAt (linearList, position, value)`	Lists (L06)	
addProp()	`addProp (propertyList, property,` `value)`	Lists (L06)	

Table 18-1: Lingo Command and Keyword Summary (continued)

Keyword	Description or Example	See	Notes
#adjust	set the boxType of member *fieldMember* = #adjust	Fields (D12)	
after	put "MoreText" after field *fieldMember*	Strings (L07), Fields (D12)	
#alert	Dialog window type, see *GetWindowPropList()*	MUI Xtra (D21)	D6
alert	alert "*Some warning*"	GUI (L01/D14)	Table 5-5
Alert (MUI)	Alert(*MUIinstance*, *alertPropertiesList*)	MUI Xtra (L15)	D6
alertHook, on	See *on alertHook* and *alert*	Debug (L03)	D6, Table 16-1
alertHook, the	set the alertHook = script "*Alert Script*" set the alertHook = [*instance1*, *instance2*...]	Debug (L03)	D6
alignment	set the alignment of member *fieldMember* = "left" | "right" | "center"	Fields (D12), Buttons (D14)	

#always	if cacheDocVerify() = #always then...
	cacheDocVerify(#always)
		NetLingo (D11)	D6

ancestor	property ancestor set ancestor = new (script "*Ancestor Script*")	Parent Scripts (L12)	
and	if (x > 7) and (x < 10) then...	Expressions (L05)	
Animation	[Palette] Animation = 0 | 1	DIRECTOR.INI (LD), Palettes (D13)	Win-only
append	append (*linearList*, *value*)	Lists (L06)	
"append" or "?append"	Mode for opening files: set *fileXObjInst* = FileIO (mNew, "append", *fileName*)	FileIO XObject (L14)	Obsolete since D5
applicationPath	set *myFilePath* = the applicationPath & "myDoc.txt"	Files (L14)	D6, fails in SW
#asset	[#nameFAT: "Button Editor", #nameW32: "Buttoned.x32", #type: #asset]	XtraInfo.TXT (D10)	D6
atan()	set x = atan (x) , -pi/2 <= atan(x) <= pi/2	Math (L08)	
"Author"	if the runMode = "Author" then...	Authoring (D08)	D5, D6

Table 18-1: Lingo Command and Keyword Summary (continued)

Keyword	Description or Example	See	Notes
AUTOSTART	`AUTOSTART = true	false`	HTML (D11)	D6, SW
autoTab	`set the autoTab of member fieldMember = TRUE	FALSE`	Fields (D12)	
backColor of member	`set the backColor of member buttonOrField = n` *n*'s range and meaning depend on the monitor color depth	Color(D13), Fields (D12)	Differs Mac/Win, Table 16-1
backColor of sprite	`set the backColor of sprite shapeOrBitmapSprite = n` 0 <= *n* <= 255 for all bits depths greater than 4-bit.	Colors, Palettes, Shapes (D13)	Table 16-1
BACKSPACE	`if (the key = BACKSPACE) then...`	Keyboard (L10)	
background	`PALETTE = background`	HTML (D11)	SW
beep	`beep numberOfTimes`	Sound (D15)	
beepOn	`set the beepOn = TRUE	FALSE`	GUI (D14)	
before	`put "IntroText" before field fieldMember`	Strings (L07), Fields (D12)	

beginRecording	`beginRecording`
	   `statements`
	`endRecording`
		Score Recording (L03)	

#beginSprite	See *call* and *on beginSprite*.	Sprite Events (L02)	D6
behavesLikeToggle of member	`set the behavesLikeToggle of member btnEdMember = TRUE	FALSE`	Button Editor Xtra (D14)	D6
behavesLikeToggle of sprite	`set the behavesLikeToggle of sprite btnEdMember = TRUE	FALSE`	Button Editor Xtra (D14)	D6
birth()	`set childObject = birth (script "Parent Script")` See *on birth*.	Parent Scripts (L12)	Obsolete—see *new*
#bitmap	`if (the type of member whichMember = #bitmap) then...`	Data Types (D04)	
#bitmap	See *getPropertyDescriptionList's* #format option.	Behaviors (L12)	D6
bitRate of member	`put the bitRate of member swaMember`	SWA (D15)	Read-only, Table 16-1
bitsPerSample of member	`put the bitsPerSample of member swaMember`	SWA (D15)	Read-only, Table 16-1

Table 18-1: Lingo Command and Keyword Summary (continued)

Keyword	Description or Example	See	Notes
blend of sprite	`set the blend of sprite whichSprite = percentage`	Graphics, Inks (D13)	
"bold"	`set the fontStyle of member fieldMember = "bold"` see menu item <B command.	Fields (D12), Buttons (D14), Menus (D14)	
#boolean	See *getPropertyDescriptionList's* #format option.	Behaviors (L12)	D6
border of member	`set the border of member fieldMember = nPixels`	Fields (D12)	
bottom of rect	`put the bottom of rect`	Coords (D05)	Read-Only
bottom of sprite	`put the bottom of sprite whichSprite`	Coords (D05)	Read-Only
boxDropShadow of member	`set the boxDropShadow of member fieldMember = nPixels`	Fields (D12)	
boxType of member	`set the boxType of member fieldMember = #adjust	#fixed	#limit	#scroll`	Fields (D12)	Table 16-1

browserName()	`set browserPath = browserName()`
	(Returns EMPTY in Shockwave)
	`browserName newBrowserPath`
		NetLingo (D11)	D6, not for SW

#btned (custom button editor)	`if (the type of member whichMember = #btned) then...`	Button Editor Xtra (D14)	D6
#button (standard buttons)	`if (the type of member whichMember = #button) then...` See *getPropertyDescriptionList's* #format option.	Buttons (D14)	

buttonClicked	`on buttonClicked`
	`    put "custom button was clicked"`
	`end`
		Button Editor Xtra (D14)	D6, Undocu-mented

#buttons	`Alert (MUIinstance, ¬` `[ #buttons : #AbortRetryIgnore, ...]`	MUI Xtra (D14)	D6
buttonStyle	`set the buttonStyle = 0	1`	GUI (D14/L09)	Table 16-1
buttonType of member	`set the buttonType of member buttonMember = #checkBox	#pushButton	#radioButton`	Buttons (D14)	Table 16-1
cacheDocVerify()	`put cacheDocVerify() -- returns VOID in SW` `cacheDocVerify (#always | #once)`	NetLingo (D11)	D6, not for SW
cacheSize()	`put cacheSize() -- defaults to 2000` `cacheSize (newSizeInKiloBytes)`	NetLingo (D11)	D6, not for SW

Table 18-1: Lingo Command and Keyword Summary (continued)

Keyword	Description or Example	See	Notes
call()	call (#*handlerName*, *script* | *scriptInstance* | *objectList* {, *args*})	Events, Parent Scripts (L12)	D6
callAncestor()	callAncestor (#*handlerName*, *script* | *scriptInstance* | *objectList* {, *args*})	Events (L02), Parent Scripts (L12)	D6
cancelIdleLoad	cancelIdleLoad *loadTag*	Memory (D09)	
case	case (*x*) of: *value*: *statements* {otherwise: *statements*} end case	Lingo (L01)	
cast	Used with *the property of cast whichCast*. Use *member* instead.	Casts (D04)	Obsolete
castLib	Used with the fileName | name | number | preLoad-Mode | selection of castLib *whichCastLib*	Casts (D04)	
castLibNum of member	put the castLibNum of member *whichMember*	Casts (D04)	Read-only
castLibNum of sprite	set the castLibNum of sprite *whichSprite* = *newValue*	Casts (D04)	
castLibs	put the number of castLibs	Casts (D04)	Read-only
castmembers	Used with *the number of castmembers*. Use *the number of members* instead.	Casts (D04)	Obsolete
castNum	Used with *the castNum of sprite*. Use *memberNum of sprite* or *member of sprite* instead	Casts (D04)	Obsolete
castType	put the castType of member *whichMember* (Reports *#text* for field castmembers, not *#field* as does *the type of member*.)	Casts (D04)	Obsolete
#caution	Alert(*MUIinstance*, [#icon: #caution, ...])	MUI Xtra (D15)	D6, Table 16-1
center of member	set the center of member *videoMember* = TRUE | FALSE	Video (D16)	
"center"	set the alignment of member *fieldMember* = "center"	Fields (D12)	
centerStage	set the centerStage = TRUE | FALSE	Projectors (D08)	

Table 18-1: Lingo Command and Keyword Summary (continued)

Keyword	Description or Example	See	Notes
changeArea of member	`set the changeArea of member` *transitionMember* `= TRUE	FALSE`	Transitions (D03)	Table 16-1
channelCount of member	`put the channelCount of member` *soundMember*	Sound, not SWA (D15)	Read-only
char...of	`put` *newString* `into char` *fromChar* `{to toChar}` `of` *chunkExpression* `put char` *firstChar* `{to lastChar}` `of` *chunkExpression*	Fields (D12), Strings (L07)	Can't use *set*
char...of, last	`delete the last char of` *chunkExpression* `put the last char of` *chunkExpression*	Fields (D12), Strings (L07)	Can delete, but not set
charPosToLoc	`set` *nearestPoint* `= charPosToLoc` `(member` *fieldMember, nthCharacter*`)`	Fields (D12), Strings (L07)	
chars	`set` *subString* `= chars (string, fromChar, toChar)` `put the number of chars in` *chunkExpression*	Strings (L07)	Read-only
charToNum()	`set` *asciiCode* `=` `charToNum(`*asciiCharacter*`)` `set asciiCode = charToNum("A")`	Keyboard (D10) Strings (L07/LA)	
#checkBox	`set the buttonType of member` *buttonMember* `= #checkBox`	Buttons (D14)	
#checkBox	Also a *MUI* Xtra widget type, see *GetWidgetList()*.	MUI Xtra (L22)	D6
checkBoxAccess	`set the checkBoxAccess = 0 (default)` `| 1	2`	GUI (D14)	
checkBoxType	`set the checkBoxType = 0 (default) |` `1	2`	GUI (D14)	
checkMark	`set the checkMark of menuItem` *whichItem* `of menu` *whichMenu* `= TRUE |` `FALSE`	Menu (D14)	Mac-only
chunkSize	`set the chunkSize of member` *transitionMember* `= n` `(where 1 <= n <= 128)`	Transitions (D03)	
CLASSID	`CLASSID="clsid:166B1BCA-3F9C-11CF-` `8075-444553540000"`	HTML OBJECT (D11)	SW-only
clearCache	`clearCache`	NetLingo (D11)	Table 17-1

Table 18-1: Lingo Command and Keyword Summary (continued)

Keyword	Description or Example	See	Notes
clearFrame	`clearFrame`	Score Recording (L03)	
clearGlobals	`clearGlobals`	Variables (L01)	
clickLoc	`if inside (the clickLoc, the rect of sprite 5) then...` `set clickH = the locH of clickLoc()`	Coords(D05), Mouse (L09)	Read-only
clickOn	`if the clickOn = 0 then beep` `if clickOn() = 5 then...`	Mouse (L09)	Read-only
close *windowID*	`close window windowNameOrNum` `close the stage`	MIAW (D06)	Not for SW
close, sound	`sound close`	Sound (D15)	
closeDA	`closeDA whichDeskAccessory`	External file (L14)	Obsolete, Mac-only
closeFile	`closeFile (fileIOinstance)`	FileIO Xtra (L14)	
closeResFile	`closeResFile whichResFile`	External File (L14)	Obsolete, Mac-only
#closeWindow	See *call* and *on closeWindow*.	MIAW (D06)	Not for SW
closeXlib	closeXlib *xLibFile* (avoid using with Xtras)	XObjects (L13)	

CODEBASE	ActiveX 6.0:
	`CODEBASE="`*http://active.macromedia.com/director/cabs/sw.cab#version=6,0,0,0*`"`
	ActiveX 6.0.1:
	`CODEBASE="`*http://active.macromedia.com/director/cabs/sw.cab#version=6,0,1,6118*`"`
		HTML OBJECT tag (D11)	SW

colorDepth	`set the colorDepth = 0	1	2	4	8	16	32` `if the colorDepth = 1	2	4	8	15	16	24	32 then...` (*colorDepth* reported as 24 instead of 32 under Windows, and possibly 15 instead of 16 on some NT systems)	Color (D13)	Differs on Mac/Win. Table 16-1
colorQD	`if the colorQD then...` (Should always return TRUE in D6)	Color (D13)	Read-only
commandDown	Command key (Mac) or `Ctrl` key (Win) `if the commandDown and the key = "X" then...`	Keyboard (L10)	Differs Mac/Win. Read-only

Table 18-1: Lingo Command and Keyword Summary (continued)

Keyword	Description or Example	See	Notes
#comment	Required element for each property in list return by *getPropertyDescriptionList*	Behaviors (L12)	D6
(comment)	`-- A Lingo comment starts with two hyphens`	Lingo (L01)	
"Complete"	See *state* parameter sent to *on streamStatus* handler	NetLingo, URL (D11)	D6, SW, Table 16-1
"condense"	`set the fontStyle of member` *fieldMember* `= "condense"`	Fields (D12)	Mac
"Connecting"	See *state* parameter sent to *on streamStatus* handler.	NetLingo, URL (D11)	D6, SW, Table 16-1
constrainH()	`if constrainH(`*spriteNum integer*`)` `then...`	Coords (D05)	
constraint	`set the constraint of sprite` *whichSprite* `= spriteNum`	Coords (D05)	
constrainV()	`if constrainV(`*spriteNum, integer*`)` `then`	Coords (D05)	
contains	`if` *string1* `contains` *string2* `then...`	Strings (L01/ L05)	
continue	obsolete (use *go the frame + 1* instead)	Score Navigation (D03)	Obsolete
controlDown	`if the controlDown and the key = "C"` `then...`	Keyboard (L10)	Differs Mac/ Win, Read-only
controller of member	`set the controller of member` *videoMember* `= TRUE	FALSE`	Video (D16)	
copyrightInfo of member	`put the copyrightInfo of member` *swaMember*	SWA (D15)	Read-only
copyToClipBoard	`copyToClipBoard member` *whichMember*	Run-Time (D09)	Avoid in Projectors
cos()	`set` *x* `= cos (`*angleInRadians*`)`	Math (L08)	
count()	`set` *numElements* `= count (`*list*`)`	Lists (L06)	
count()	`set` *numProperties* `= count (script` *whichScript*`)` `set` *numProperties* `= count` `(`*scriptInstance*`)`	Lists (L06), Behaviors (L12)	Table 17-1

Table 18-1: Lingo Command and Keyword Summary (continued)

Keyword	Description or Example	See	Notes
cpuHogTicks	`set the cpuHogTicks = nTicks` (default 20. higher numbers hog CPU for Director)	Performance (D09)	Mac-only
cpuidGetCPUFeatureFlags()	`put cpuidGetCPUFeatureFlags (xtraInstance)`	DirMMX Xtra (D08)	Win-only
cpuidGetCPUModel()	`put cpuidGetCPUModel (xtraInstance)`	DirMMX Xtra (D08)	Win-only
cpuidGetCPUStepping()	`put cpuidGetCPUStepping (xtraInstance)`	DirMMX Xtra (D08)	Win-only
cpuidGetCPUType()	`put cpuidGetCPUType (xtraInstance)`	DirMMX Xtra (D08)	Win-only
cpuidIsGenuineIntel()	`put cpuidIsGenuineIntel (xtraInstance)` Some non-Intel processors may be incompatible with MMX	DirMMX Xtra (D08)	Win-only
CR	`global CR` `set CR = numToChar (13)` `set CR = RETURN`	Keyboard (L10), Files (L14)	Supplemental
createFile()	`createFile (fileIOinstance, "fileName")`	FileIO Xtra (L14)	
crop of member	`set the crop of member videoMember = TRUE	FALSE`	Video (D16)	
cuePassed, on	`on cuePassed {me,} channelID, ¬` `    cuePointNumber, cuePointName` `statements` `end`	Cue Points, SWA, Sound, Video (D15, D16)	D6
cuePointNames	`set thisName = getAt (the cuePointNames of member whichMember, cuePointNumber)`	Cue Points (D15)	D6
cuePointTimes	`set thisTime = getAt (the cuePointTimes of member whichMember, cuePointNumber)`	Cue Points (D15)	Fixed in D6.0.2
currentSpriteNum	`put the scriptInstanceList of sprite (the currentSpriteNum)`	Sprites (L02)	D6
currentTime of sound	`put the currentTime of sound soundChannel`	Sound (D15)	Read-only, D6
currentTime of sprite	`put the currentTime of sprite whichSprite`	SWA, (D15) Video (D16)	Read-only, D6, Buggy
#cursor	See *getPropertyDescriptionList's* #format option.	Behaviors (L12)	D6

Table 18-1: Lingo Command and Keyword Summary (continued)

Keyword	Description or Example	See	Notes
#cursor	Returned as *the type of member* for *Custom Cursor* Xtra cast members	Cursor Xtra (D14)	D6
cursor	`cursor [member bitmapMember, member maskMember]` `cursor cursorResourceID`	GUI (D14)	Differs Mac/Win
cursor of sprite 0	This reads the current value set by *cursor* command `set mainCursor = the cursor of sprite 0`	GUI (D14)	Undocumented, Table 17-1
cursor of sprite	`set the cursor of sprite whichSprite = [member bitmapMember, member maskMember]` `set the cursor of sprite whichSprite = cursorResourceID`	GUI (D14)	Differs Mac/Win
date	`put the {abbr{ev{iated}}	long	short} date`	Date (L11)	Read-only
#deactivateWindow	See *call* and *on deactivateWindow*.	MIAWs (D06)	
#default	`Alert (MUIinstance, ¬` `[#buttons: #YesNo, #default: 1, ...]`	MUI Xtra (L15)	D6
#default	Required element for each property in list return by *getPropertyDescriptionList*	Behaviors (L12)	D6
delay	`delay nTicks` (doesn't delay until current handler terminates)	Timers (L11)	Table 17-2
delete	`delete char	item	word	line start {to end} of chunkExpression`	Strings (L07)	
delete (FileIO)	`delete (fileIOinstance)`	FileIO Xtra (L14)	
deleteAll()	`deleteAll (list)`	Lists (L06)	D6 (undocumented in D4 and D5)
deleteAt()	`deleteAt (list, position)`	Lists (L06)	
deleteFrame	`deleteFrame`	Score Recording (D03)	
deleteOne()	`deleteOne (list, value)`	Lists (L06)	

deleteProp()	`deleteProp (propertyList, property)`
	`deleteProp (linearList, position)`
	(same as *deleteAt*)
		Lists (L06)	

depth of member	`put the depth of member bitmapMember` (See `Modify[▶]Transform Bitmap`)	Colors (D13)	Read-only

Table 18-1: Lingo Command and Keyword Summary (continued)

Keyword	Description or Example	See	Notes
deskTopRectList	`put the deskTopRectList`	Run-Time (D08), Coords, Lists (L06)	Read-only
#digitalVideo	`if (the type of member whichMember = #digitalVideo) then...`	Video (D16)	
#digitalVideo	See *getPropertyDescriptionList's* #format option.	Behaviors (L12)	D6
digitalVideoTimeScale	`set the digitalVideoTimeScale = unitsPerSecond`	Timers (L11), Video (D16)	
digitalVideoType of member	`if the digitalVideoType of member videoMember = #quickTime	#videoForWindows then...`	Video (D16)	Read-only
"Director"	`if the productName = "Director" then...`	Run-Time (D08)	Read-only. Undocumented in D5
displayOpen()	`displayOpen (fileIOinstance)`	FileIO Xtra (L14)	
displaySave()	`displaySave (fileIOinstance,"title", "defaultFileName")`	FileIO Xtra (L14)	
directToStage	`set the directToStage of member videoMember = TRUE	FALSE`	Video (D16)	
do	`do "commandString"` (In Shockwave, *do* can not execute unsupported commands.)	Lingo (L01)	Limited in SW
done	`play done`	Score (L03)	

dontPassEvent	`on mouseDownScriptHandler`
	`    dontPassEvent`
	`end`
	(Does not stop event from being passed to other Behaviors. See *stopEvent*.)
		Events (D02)	Obsolete

doubleClick	`if the doubleClick then...`	Mouse (L09)	Read-only
down	`repeat with x = y down to z...`	Lingo (L01)	
downloadNetThing()	`set netID = downloadNetThing (url, localFile)`	NetLingo (D11)	D6, not for SW, URL
drawRect	`set the drawRect of window whichWindow = rect` `set the drawRect of the stage = rect`	MIAWs (D06), Coords (D05)	
dropShadow	`set the dropShadow of member fieldMember = nPixels`	Fields (D12)	
duplicate()	`set newList = duplicate (list)`	Lists (L06)	

Table 18-1: Lingo Command and Keyword Summary (continued)

Keyword	Description or Example	See	Notes

duplicate (member)	`set newSlot = duplicate (member`
	`fromMember {of castLib originalCast}`
	`{, member newMember of castLib`
	`newCast}`
	Deletes any existing cast member in destination slot.
	Copies to first open castmember slot if none specified.
		Cast (DO4)	Dangerous

duplicateFrame	`duplicateFrame`	Score Recording (DO3)	

duration of member (digital video)	`put the duration of member`
	`videoMember`
	(Measured in *1/the digitalVideoTimeScale*, not ticks)
		Timers (L11), Video (D16)	Read-only. Table 17-1.

duration of member (SWA)	`put the duration of member swaMember` (Measured in seconds)	SWA, not Sound (D15)	Read-only

duration of member (transition)	`set the duration of member`
	`transitionMember= newDuration`
	(Measured in milliseconds)
		Transitions (DO3)	Can be set

editable of member	`set the editable of member` `fieldMember = TRUE	FALSE`	Fields (D12/L10)	
editable of sprite	`set the editable of sprite` `fieldSprite = TRUE	FALSE`	Fields (D12/L10)	
editableText	editableText (see *editable of sprite*)	Fields (D12)	Obsolete
else	See *if...then...else...end if.*	Lingo (L01)	
else if	See *if...then...else if...else...end if.*	Lingo (L01)	
#empty	`if the type of member = #empty then...`	Cast (DO4)	
EMPTY	`if field "someField" = EMPTY then...` `if someString = EMPTY then...`	Fields (D12), Strings (L02)	
emulateMultiBut-tonMouse	`set the emulateMultiButtonMouse =` `TRUE	FALSE`	Mouse (L09)	Mac-only
enabled of member	`set the enabled of member btnEdMember` `= TRUE	FALSE`	Button Editor Xtra (D14)	D6
enabled of menu-Item	`set the enabled of menuItem whichItem` `of menu whichMenu = TRUE	FALSE`	Menus (D14)	
enabled of sprite	`set the enabled of sprite btnEdSprite` `= TRUE	FALSE`	Button Editor Xtra (D14)	D6

end	`on handlerName`
	`    statement(s)`
	`end {handlerName}`
		Scripts (L01/L02)	

Table 18-1: Lingo Command and Keyword Summary (continued)

Keyword	Description or Example	See	Notes

end case	`case (expression) of`
	  `value: statement(s)`
	  `otherwise: statement(s)`
	`end case`
		Lingo (L01)	D5, D6

end if	`if (expression) then`
	  `statement(s)`
	  `else`
	  `statement(s)`
	`end if`
		Lingo (L01)	

end repeat	`repeat with`
	  `statement(s)`
	`end repeat`
		Loops (L01)	

end tell	`tell window whichWindow`
	  `statement(s)`
	`end tell`
		MIAW (D06)	

endRecording	`beginRecording`
	  `statement(s)`
	`endRecording`
		Score Recording (D03)	

#endSprite	See *call* and *on endSprite*.	Sprites, Events (L02)	D6
ENTER	`if (the key = ENTER) then...`	Keyboard (L10)	Can't test during Authoring
#enterFrame	See *call* and *on enterFrame*.	Score, Events (D03, L02)	D6 change, Table 17-2
erase member	`erase member whichMember {of castLib whichCastLib}`	Cast (D04)	Dangerous

ESCAPE	`set ESCAPE = numToChar (27)`
	`if (the key = ESCAPE) then...`
	The Esc key quits Windows Projectors, but not Mac Projectors.
		Keyboard (*exitLock*) (L10)	Supplemental

#error	Used as #icon property with Alert (MUI)	MUI Xtra (L15)	D6, Table 16-1
"Error"	See *state* parameter sent to *on streamStatus* handler.	NetLingo, URL (D11)	D6, SW, Table 16-1
error()	`put error (fileIOinstance, errorCode)`	FileIO Xtra, (L14)	Table E-3
EvalScript()	Netscape: document.*htmlNAMEtag*.EvalScript() MIE: *htmlNAMEtag*.EvalScript() (See *on EvalScript*.)	Browser Scripting, HTML (D11)	D6, SW, PPC Win 95/NT

exit	`on handlerName`
	  `if (expression) then exit`
	`end`
		Lingo (L01)	

Table 18-1: Lingo Command and Keyword Summary (continued)

Keyword	Description or Example	See	Notes
exit repeat	```repeat while TRUE if the mouseDown then exit repeat end repeat```	Lingo (L01)	
exit tell	```on tell if (expression) then exit tell end tell```	MIAWs (D06)	Undocumented. table 17-1.
#exitFrame	See *call* and *on exitFrame*.	Score (D03), Events (L02)	D6 change, Table 17-2
exitLock	```set the exitLock = TRUE	FALSE```	Keyboard (L10)	Differs Mac and Win
exp()	```set someVariable = exp(value)```	Math (L08)	
"extend"	```set the fontStyle of member fieldMember = "extend" -- (see "condense")```	Fields (D12)	Mac-only

externalEvent	Lingo:
	```externalEvent ("JSfunction('param1','param2')")```
	JavaScript:
	```function JSfunction(param1, param2) { //code }```
		NetLingo, Browser Scripting (D11)	D6, SW only, PPC Win 95/NT

externalParam-Count()	```set numBrowserParams = externalParamCount()``` Returns 0 in Director and Projectors	NetLingo, HTML (D11)	SW, D6
externalParam-Name()	```set nthParameterName = externalParamName(n)``` ```set paramExists = externalParamName("paramName")```	NetLingo, HTML (D11)	SW, D6
externalParamValue	```set nthParameterValue = externalParamValue(n)``` ```set paramValue = externalParamValue("paramName")```	NetLingo, HTML (D11)	SW, D6
ExtraMemory	```[Memory] ExtraMemory = kiloBytes```	DIRECTOR.INI (D09/LD)	Win-only
factory ()	Returns TRUE if specified XObject is installed ```if objectP(factory("SerialPort")) then...```	XObjects (L13)	Undocumented
factory	```factory factoryName``` (defined a factory, a precursor to parent scripts and/or lists)	Factories (L13)	Obsolete (D4)
fadeIn	```sound fadeIn soundChannel {, nTicks }```	Sound (D15)	Table 17-2
fadeOut	```sound fadeOut soundChannel {, nTicks }```	Sound (D15)	Table 17-2

Table 18-1: Lingo Command and Keyword Summary (continued)

Keyword	Description or Example	See	Notes
FALSE	`if (expression = FALSE) then...` `set the booleanProperty {of object} = FALSE`	Expressions (L05)	
#field	`if (the type of member whichMember = #field) then...`	Cast (D04)	
#field	See *getPropertyDescriptionList's* #format option.	Behaviors (L12)	D6
field	`put the text of field fieldMember`	Fields (L07/D12)	
FileIO (XObject)	`set fileXObjInst = FileIO (mNew, mode, fileNameOrType) -- use FileIO Xtra instead`	Files (L14)	Obsolete (D5)
"FileIO" (Xtra)	`put mMessageList (xtra "FileIO")`	Files (L14)	
fileName of castLib	`set the fileName of castLib whichCast = "newPath"`	Casts, External Files (D04)	Mac/Win file paths differ
fileName of member	`set the fileName of member whichMember = "newPath"`	Importing, Casts (D04)	Mac/Win file paths differ
fileName of window	`set the fileName of window whichWindow = "filePath"`	MIAWs (D06)	Mac/Win file paths differ
fileName()	`set thisFileName = fileName (fileIOinstance)`	FileIO Xtra (L14)	
FileOpen()	`FileOpen (MUIinstance, fileName)`	MUI Xtra (L14)	D6
FileSave()	`FileSave (MUIinstance, fileName, prompt )`	MUI Xtra (L14)	D6
filled of member	`set the filled of member shapeMember = TRUE	FALSE`	Shapes, Graphics (D13)	
#filmLoop	`if (the type of member whichMember = #filmLoop) then...`	Animation (L03)	
#filmLoop	See *getPropertyDescriptionList's* #format option.	Behaviors (L12)	D6
findEmpty()	`findEmpty (member startMember {of castLib whichCast})` (defaults to castLib 1, not *the activeCastLib*)	Casts (D04)	Table 17-1
findPos()	`set position = findPos (propList, property) -- (returns VOID if not found)` `set position = findPos (linearList, index) -- (returns 0 if index out of range)`	Lists (L06)	
findPosNear()	`findPosNear (list, propertyOrValue) -- (See sort.)`	Lists (L06)	
finishIdleLoad	`finishIdleLoad loadTag`	Memory (D09)	

Table 18-1: Lingo Command and Keyword Summary (continued)

Keyword	Description or Example	See	Notes
#fixed	`set the boxType of member fieldMember = #fixed`	Fields (D12)	
fixStageSize	`set the fixStageSize = TRUE | FALSE`	Run-Tim SW, MIAWs (D06/D08/D11)	Differs in Projectors and SW
#float	`if ilk(number, #float) then...`	Math, Data Types (L08/L05)	
#float	See *getPropertyDescriptionList's* #format option.	Behaviors (L12)	D6
float()	`set floatVariable = float (value)`	Math (L08)	
floatP()	if floatP (*value*) then...	Math (L08)	
floatPrecision	set the floatPrecision = *displayDecimalPlaces*	Math (L08)	
font of member	set the font of member *fieldMember* = "*fontName*" or font of field	Fields, Buttons (D12)	
fontSize	set the fontSize {of *chunkExpression*} of member *fieldMember* = *newSize* put the fontSize of field *fieldMember*	Fields, Buttons (D12)	Table 17-1
fontStyle	set the fontStyle {of *chunkExpression*} of member *fieldMember* = "bold" | "condense" (Mac only) | "plain" | "italic" | "extend" (Mac only) | "underline" | "shadow" | "outline" specified as: set the fontStyle of member *x* = "bold,italic" put the fontStyle of field *fieldMember*	Fields, Buttons (D12)	Table 16-1
forcePreloadCue-Points (member)	`forcePreloadCuePoints (member swaMember)` Forces preloading of an SWA cast member's list of cue points for use in Tempo channel.	SWA, Cue Points (D15)	Unsupported, Table 17-1.
foreColor of member	`set the foreColor of member buttonOrField = n` *n*'s range and meaning depend on the monitor color depth	Color, Buttons, Fields (D12/D13)	Differs Mac/Win, Table 16-1
foreColor of sprite	`set the foreColor of sprite shapeOrBitmapSprite = n` 0 < *n* < 255 for all bits depths greater than 4-bit.	Colors, Palettes, Shapes (D13)	Table 16-1
foreground	`PALETTE=foreground`	HTML EMBED tag (D11)	SW
forget window	`forget window whichWindow`	MIAWs (D06)	Not for SW

Table 18-1: Lingo Command and Keyword Summary (continued)

Keyword	Description or Example	See	Notes

#format	on getPropertyDescriptionList
	  return [#pMyProp: ¬
	    [#format : #float, ¬
	    #comment : "User Prompt", ¬
	    # range: [#min:1.0, # max:10.0],¬
	    #default : member 1]]
	end getPropertyDescriptionList
		Behaviors (L12)	D6, Table 16-1

#frame	See *getPropertyDescriptionList's* #format option.	Behaviors (L12)	D6
the frame	go frame the frame go to the frame if (the frame = *value*) then...	Score (D03)	
frame	go frame *whichFrame* play frame *whichFrame*	Score (D03)	
frameLabel	Adds or renames marker with comment: set the frameLabel = "name" ¬ {& RETURN & "comment"} Deletes marker: set the frameLabel = 0	Score (D03)	Table 17-1
framePalette	set the framePalette = *paletteCode* | *memberNum*	Palettes (D13), Score (D03)	Read-Only (SR)
frameRate of member	set the frameRate of member *videoMember* = *rate*	Video (D16)	Table 16-1.
frameReady()	frameReady({*fromFrame* {, *toFrame*}})	Shockwave, URLs (D11)	SW, D6
frameScript	set the frameScript = *scriptNumber*	Score (D03)	Read-Only (SR)
frameSound1	set the frameSound1 = member *soundMember*	Score (D03)	Read-Only (SR)
frameSound2	put the frameSound2 = member *soundMember*	Score (D03)	Read-Only (SR)
framesToHMS	framesToHMS (*frames*, *tempo*, *dropFrame*, *fractionalSec*)	Timers (L11), Math (L08)	
frameTempo	set the frameTempo = *framesPerSecond*	Score (D01, D03)	Read-Only (SR)
frameTransition	set the frameTransition = *transitionCode*	*memberNum*	Score (D03)	Read-Only (SR)
freeBlock	if the freeBlock < *sizeInBytes* then...	Memory (D09)	Read-Only

Table 18-1: Lingo Command and Keyword Summary (continued)

Keyword	Description or Example	See	Notes
freeBytes	`if the freeBytes < sizeInBytes then...`	Memory (D09)	Read-Only
frontWindow	`put the frontWindow` (see *moveToFront*)	MIAWs (D06)	Read-Only

#ftp	`proxyServer #ftp, "ipAddress",`
	`portNum`
	`set ipAddress = proxyServer (#ftp)`
	`set portNum = proxyServer (#ftp,`
	`#port)`
	`proxyServer #ftp, #stop`
		NetLingo (D11)	D6, not for SW

fullColorPermit	`set the fullColorPermit = TRUE |` `FALSE`	Memory (D09)	D6 (D3) Table 17-2

getaProp()	`set value = getaProp (propList,`
	`property)`
	`set value = getaProp (linearList,`
	`position)`
		Lists (L06)	

getAt()	`set value = getAt (list, position)`	Lists (L06)	

getBehaviorDe-
scription
	`on getBehaviorDescription {me}`
	`    return helpText`
	`end`
		Behaviors (L12)	D6

getChannelCount()	`set numSoundChannels = getChannelCount()` (Returns 8 on Mac. See *MixMaxChannels* for PC)	Din Xtra (D15)	Unsupported
GetCurrentFrame()	Netscape: document.*htmlNAMEtag*.GetCurrent- Frame() MIE: *htmlNAMEtag*.GetCurrentFrame()	Browser (D11) Scripting	D6, SW, PPC Win 95/NT
getError()	`put getError (member swaMember)`	SWA Streaming Xtra (D15)	D6, Table 16-1, Table E-4
getErrorString()	`put getErrorString (member swaMember)`	SWA Streaming Xtra (D15)	D6, Table 16-1, Table E-4

getFinderInfo()	`set typeCreator = getFinderInfo`
	`(fileIOinstance)`
	(See *setFinderInfo* and Table 16-1)
		FileIO Xtra (L14)	Mac-only

getFreeChannel()	`set highestFreeSoundChannel =` `getFreeChannel()`	Din Xtra (D15)	Unsupported
GetItemPropList()	`set defaultProps = GetItemPropList` `(MUIinstance)`	MUI Xtra (L21)	D6
getLast()	`getLast (list)`	Lists (L06)	

Table 18-1: Lingo Command and Keyword Summary (continued)

Keyword	Description or Example	See	Notes
getLatestNetID()	`getLatestNetID()` (The preferred method is to obtain the *netID* as the return value when calling a function such as *downloadNetThing*)	NetLingo Xtra (D11)	Obsolete
getLength()	`set fileLength = getLength` `(fileIOinstance)`	FileIO Xtra (L14)	
getNetText()	`set netID = getNetText (url)` `set netID = getNetText` `(cgiPath?uploadText)` see *netTextResult()*	NetLingo Xtra (D11)	D6, URL
getNthFileNameIn-Folder()	`getNthFileNameInFolder(folderPath,` `fileNumber)` `set folder = getNthFileNameIn-` `Folder(folderPath, -1)`	External Files (L14)	Not for SW
getOne()	`set position = getOne (linearList,` `value)` `set propName = getOne (propertyList,` `value)`	Lists (L06)	
getOSdirectory()	`set macSystemFolder =` `getOSdirectory()` `set windowsDirectory =` `getOSdirectory() & "\"`	FileIO Xtra (L14)	Differs Mac/Win
getPlayStatus()	`set soundPlaying = getPlayStatus` `(soundChan)` Seems to always return TRUE. Use *soundBusy()*.	Din Xtra (D15)	Unsupported, Buggy
getPos()	`set position = getPos (list, value)--` (returns 0 if not found)	Lists (L06)	
getPosition()	`set filePosition = getPosition` `(fileIOinstance)`	FileIO Xtra (L14)	
getPref()	`set prefFileText = getPref (prefFileName)` Valid in Directors and Projectors, but path differs from Shockwave. See Table 16-1.	Browser, Files (D11, L14)	D6, SW, Differs at Run-time
getProp()	`set value = getProp (propertyList,` `property) (error if not found)`	Lists (L06)	
getPropAt()	`set value = getPropAt (propertyList,` `position)`	Lists (L06)	
getPropertyDescrip-tionList, on	`on getPropertyDescriptionList{me}` `    return behaviorPropertyList` `end`	Behaviors (L12)	D6

Table 18-1: Lingo Command and Keyword Summary (continued)

Keyword	Description or Example	See	Notes
getSndLength()	set *soundLength* = getSndLength (*DinInstance*) (in millseconds)	Din Xtra (D15)	Unsupported
getSndPosition()	set *currentTime* = getSndPosition (*DinInstance*) (in milliseconds)	Din Xtra (D15)	Unsupported
GetURL ()	set *url* = GetURL (*MUIinstance*, *sampleURL*, *moveable*) *url* is *sampleURL* if user clicks Cancel button; *moveable* is TRUE | FALSE.	MUI Xtra (L14)	D6, URL
GetWidgetList()	set *supportedWidgetList* = GetWidgetList (*MUIinstance*)	MUI Xtra (L21)	D6
GetWindow-PropList()	set *defaultWindowProps* = GetWindowPropList (*MUIinstance*)	MUI Xtra (L21)	D6
global	global *gVariable1* {, *gVariable2*} {, *gVariable3*}	Variables (L01)	
go frame	go {to} {frame} *whichFrame* {of movie *whichMovie*}	Score (D03)	
go loop	go loop	Score (D03)	
go movie	go {to} {frame *whichFrame* of} movie *whichMovie*	Score (D03)	URL, Differs in SW, Table 17-1
go next	go next	Score (D03)	
go previous	go previous	Score (D03)	
go to	go to {frame} *whichFrame* {of movie *whichMovie*} go to {frame *whichFrame* of} movie *whichMovie*	Score (D03)	URL, Table 17-1
GotoFrame()	Netscape: document.*htmlNAMEtag*.GotoFrame(*n*) MIE: *htmlNAMEtag*.GotoFrame(*n*)	Browser Scripting (D11)	D6, SW, PPC Win 95/NT
GotoMovie()	Netscape: document.*htmlNAMEtag*.GotoMovie(*movie*) MIE: *htmlNAMEtag*.GotoMovie(*movie*)	Browser Scripting (D11)	D6, SW, PPC Win 95/NT
gotoNetMovie()	set *netID* = gotoNetMovie("http://www.zeusprod.com/nutshell/sw/sample.dcr#*someLabel*")	NetLingo Xtra (D11)	D6

Table 18-1: Lingo Command and Keyword Summary (continued)

Keyword	Description or Example	See	Notes
gotoNetPage()	set *netID* = gotoNetPage("http://www. zeusprod.com/nutshell/sw/sample. dcr", "*targetFrameOrWindow*")	NetLingo Xtra (D11)	D6, Table 16-1
#graphic	See *getPropertyDescriptionList's* #format option.	Behaviors (L12)	D6
[Graphics]	[Graphics] WinG = 0 | 1	DIRECTOR.INI (LD)	Win-only
#grayscale	if the paletteRef of member *whichMember* = #grayscale then...	Palettes (DB)	
halt	halt	Lingo (L01)	Differs during authoring
HEIGHT	HEIGHT="*numPixels*"	HTML (D11)	
height of member	put the height of member *whichMember*	Coords (D05)	Read-only
height of rect	put the height of *rect*	Coords, MIAW (D05) (D06)	Read-only
height of sprite	set the height of sprite *whichSprite* = *newHeight*	Coords (D05)	Read-only
help	Used by some third-party Xtras, such as PopMenu: put the help of member *xtraMember*	Xtras (D10)	Unsupported
HighSpoolBufferMs	[Sound] HighSpoolBufferMs = *milliseconds*	DIRECTOR.INI (LD)	Win-only
[High Default Sound] [High Mono Default Sound] [High Mono *SoundCard*] [High Override]	[High {Mono} {Default} {Sound} {Override}] MixBufferMs = *milliseconds* MixBufferBytes = *bytes* MixBufferCount = *n* (2 through 16) MixServiceMode = 0 | 1 | 2 MixIntPeriodMs = *milliseconds* MixIntResolutionMs = *milliseconds*	DIRECTOR.INI (LD)	Win-only
hilite	hilite *chunkExpression* of member *fieldMember*	Fields (L10, D12)	
hilite	set the hilite of member *buttonMember* = TRUE | FALSE	Radio Buttons, Check Boxes (D4)	
HMStoFrames	HMStoFrames (*hms*, *tempo*, *dropFrame*, *fractionalSec*)	Timers. Math (L11) (L08)	

Table 18-1: Lingo Command and Keyword Summary (continued)

Keyword	Description or Example	See	Notes

#http	`proxyServer #http, "ipAddress", portNum`
	`set ipAddress = proxyServer (#http)`
	`set portNum = proxyServer (#http, #port)`
	`proxyServer (#http, #stop)`
		NetLingo (D11)	D6, not for SW

#icon	`Alert(MUIinstance, [#icon: #caution, ...])`	MUI Xtra (L15)	D6
#idle	See *call* and *on idle*.	Events (L02)	
idleHandlerPeriod	`set the idleHandlerPeriod = intervalInTicks` (Default , 0, means "idle as frequently as possible." Higher numbers *lengthen* time between idle events.	Performance (D09)	Table 17-1
idleLoadDone	`if idleLoadDone (loadTag) then...`	Memory (D09)	
idleLoadMode	`set the idleLoadMode = 0	1	2	3`	Memory (D09)	Table 16-1
idleLoadPeriod	`set the idleLoadPeriod = intervalInTicks` (Default, 0, means "idleLoad as frequently as possible." Higher numbers *slow* idle loading.	Memory (D09)	
idleLoadTag	`set the idleLoadTag = loadTag`	Memory (D09)	
idleReadChunkSize	`set the idleReadChunkSize = nBytes`	Memory (D09)	Table 17-1

if	`if (expression) then`
	    `statement(s)`
	`{else if (expression) then`
	    `statement(s)}`
	`{else`
	    `statement(s)}`
	`end if`
		Lingo (L01)	

ilk()	`set itemDataType = ilk (anyItem)` `if ilk (anyItem, #dataType) then...`	Data Types, Lists (L05/L06)	Table 16-1
imageDirect	`set the imageDirect = TRUE	FALSE`	Memory (D09)	Obsolete (D4)
"ImageDisabled"	`putImageIntoCastMember (member buttonMember, "ImageDisabled", member destMember)`	Button Editor Xtra (D14)	D6, Table 16-1
"ImageNormal"	`setButtonImageFromCastMember (member buttonMember, "ImageNormal", member bitmapMember)`	Button Editor Xtra (D14)	D6, Table 16-1

Keywords, Commands

Table 18-1: Lingo Command and Keyword Summary (continued)

Keyword	Description or Example	See	Notes
"ImagePressed"	`putImageIntoCastMember (member buttonMember, "ImagePressed", member destMember)`	Button Editor Xtra (D14)	D6, Table 16-1
"ImageRollover"	`setButtonImageFromCastMember (member buttonMember, "ImageRollover", member bitmapMember)`	Button Editor Xtra (D14)	D6, Table 16-1
"ImageToggledDis-abled"	`putImageIntoCastMember (member buttonMember, "ImageToggledDisabled", member destMember)`	Button Editor Xtra (D14)	D6, Table 16-1
"ImageToggled-Normal"	setButtonImageFromCastMember (member `buttonMember`, "ImageToggledNormal", member `bitmapMember`)	Button Editor Xtra (D14)	D6, Table 16-1
"ImageToggled-Pressed"	putImageIntoCastMember (member `buttonMember`, "ImageToggledPressed", member `destMember`)	Button Editor Xtra (D14)	D6, Table 16-1
"ImageToggledRoll-over"	setButtonImageFromCastMember (member `buttonMember`, "ImageToggledRollover", member `bitmapMember`)	Button Editor Xtra (D14)	D6, Table 16-1
immediate	`set the immediate of sprite whichSprite = TRUE	FALSE--` (use *on mouseDown* instead)	Mouse (L09)	Obsolete (D4)
immediateSprite	immediateSprite (use *on mouseDown* instead)	Mouse (L09)	Obsolete (D4)
importFileInto	`importFileInto member whichMember {of castLib whichCast}, fileNameOrURL`	Import (D04)	URL, avoid at Runtime, limited in SW
in *list*	`repeat with x in list` `end repeat`	Lingo, Lists (L01/L06)	
in *chunk*	`number of {chars	items	lines	words} in chunkExpression` `put the last {char	item	line	word} in chunkExpression`	Strings (L07)	

INF	`set x = 1E400`
	`put x`
	`-- INF`
	`put log(0)`
	`--- -INF`
		Math (L08)	

inflate (rect)	`set newRect = inflate (rect, widthChange, heightChange)`	Coords (D05)	
Initialize()	`Initialize` (*MUInstance, initPropList*)	MUI Xtra (L21)	D6

Table 18-1: Lingo Command and Keyword Summary (continued)

Keyword	Description or Example	See	Notes
initialToggleState of member	`set the initialToggleState of member` *`btnEdMember`* `= TRUE	FALSE`	Button Editor Xtra (D14)	D6
#ink	See *getPropertyDescriptionList*'s #format option.	Behaviors (L12)	D6
ink of sprite	`set the ink of sprite` *`whichSprite`* `=` *`inkCode`* (where *`inkCode`* is 0-9 or 32-39)	Sprites, Colors (D13)	Table 16-1
"InProgress"	See *state* parameter sent to *on streamStatus* handler.	NetLingo, URL (D11)	D6, Table 16-1
insertFrame	`insertFrame`	Score (D05)	
inside()	`if inside (point(`*`x`*`,` *`y`*`), rect(`*`left`*`,` *`top`*`,` *`right`*`,` *`bottom`*`)) then...` `if inside (the clickLoc, the rect of sprite` *`whichSprite`*`, then)`	Coords (D05)	
installMenu	`installMenu {the number of} member` *`fieldMember`* `installMenu` *`memberNumber`*	Menus, GUI (D14)	
#instance	`set` *`fileInst`* `= new (xtra "FileIO")` `if ilk (`*`fileInst`* `) = #instance)` `then...` `put ilk (childObject)` `-- #instance` `put ilk (childObject, #instance)` `-- 0  -- FALSE!`	Data Types (L05)	Table 16-1
instance	`instance` *`instanceVar`* `(obsolete, use` property `instead)`	Variables	Obsolete (D4)
#integer	`if ilk (x, #integer) then...`	Data Types (L05)	
#integer	See *getPropertyDescriptionList*'s #format option.	Behaviors	D6
integer	`set` *`integerVariable`* `= integer (`*`value`*`)` (see *value*)	Math (L08), Data Types (L05)	
integerP()	`if integerP(`*`value`*`) then...`	Math (L08), Data Types (L05)	
interface	`put interface (xtra "FileIO") (use` *`mMessageList`*`)`	Xtras (L13)	Unsupported
intersect()	`if intersect (`*`rect1`*`,` *`rect2`*`) then...`	Coords (D05)	

Table 18-1: Lingo Command and Keyword Summary (continued)

Keyword	Description or Example	See	Notes
intersects	`if sprite sprite1 intersects {sprite} sprite2 then...`	Coords (D05)	

into	`put string into field fieldMember`
	 or
	 `put value into variable`
	 I prefer:
	 `set variable = value`
		Strings (L07)	

isDirMMXloaded()	`if isDirMMXloaded() then...`	DirMMX (D08)	Win-only, Buggy
isPastCuePoint (sound)	`set matchingCuePointsPassed = isPastCuePoint (sound soundChannel, "CuePointName")` `if isPastCuePoint (sound soundChannel,, cuePointNumber) then...`	Cue Points, Sound (D15)	D6
isPastCuePoint (sprite)	`set matchingCuePointsPassed = isPastCuePoint (sprite whichSprite, "CuePointName")` `if isPastCuePoint (sprite whichSprite, cuePointNumber) then...`	Cue Points, SWA, Video (D15)	D6
isToggled of sprite	`set the isToggled of sprite btnEdSprite = TRUE | FALSE` (not "*isToggle*" as listed in *Lingo Dictionary*)	Button Editor Xtra (D14)	D6, Table 17-1
"italic"	`set the fontStyle of member fieldMember = "italic"` See menu item <I command	Fields (D12), Buttons, Menus (D14)	
item...of	`put newValue into item startItem {to endItem} of chunkExpression`	Strings (L07)	Can't use *set*
item...of, last	`delete the last item of chunkExpression` `put the last item of chunkExpression`	Fields, Strings (L07)	Can delete, but not set
itemDelimiter	`set the itemDelimiter = "newDelimiter"` -- (default is comma)	Strings, External Files (L07/L14)	
items	`put the number of items in chunkExpression`	Strings (L07)	Read-only
ItemUpdate()	`ItemUpdate(MUIinstance, itemNum, itemPropList)`	MUI Xtra (L21)	D6
"Java javaVersion, browser, OS"	`if the platform starts "Java" then...`	RunTime (D08)	D6.5, Table 16-1, Table 17-2

Table 18-1: Lingo Command and Keyword Summary (continued)

Keyword	Description or Example	See	Notes
"Java Applet"	`if the runMode = "Java Applet" then...`	RunTime (D08)	D6.5, Table 16-1, Table 17-2
key	`if the key = character then...` `if key() = character then...`	Keyboard (L10)	Read-only
keyCode	`if the keyCode = integer then...` `if keyCode() = integer then...`	Keyboard (L10), ASCII (LA)	Read-only
#keyDown	See *call* and *on keyDown*.	Keyboard (L10)	
keyDown	`when keyDown then` (use *on keyDown* instead)	Keyboard (L10)	Obsolete
keyDownScript	`set the keyDownScript =` `"KeyDownAction"`	Keyboard (L10)	
keyPressed	`if the keyPressed = character then...`	Keyboard (L10)	Read-only
#keyUp	See *call* and *on keyUp*.	Keyboard (L10)	
keyUpScript	`set the keyUpScript = "KeyUpAction"`	Keyboard (L10)	

label	`go label ("labelName")`
	`if label("labelName") = 0 then alert`
	`"Doesn't exist"`
	See *frameLabel* and *marker*.
		Score (D03)	Read-only

labelList	`put the labelList`	Score (D03)	Read-only
labelString of member	`put the labelString of member` `btnEdMember`	Button Editor Xtra (D14)	D6, Read-only
last	`delete the last {char | item | line |` `word} in chunkExpression`	Strings (L07)	Can delete but not set
lastClick	`if the lastClick < ticksInterval` `then...`	Mouse (L09), Timers (L11)	Read-only
lastEvent	`if the lastEvent < ticksInterval` `then...`	Mouse, Keyboard, Timer (L09/L10/L11)	Read-only
lastFrame	`go frame the lastFrame`	Score (D03)	Read-only
lastKey	`if the lastKey < ticksInterval then...`	Keyboard, Timers (L09/L11)	Read-only

Table 18-1: Lingo Command and Keyword Summary (continued)

Keyword	Description or Example	See	Notes
lastRoll	`if the lastRoll < ticksInterval then...`	Mouse Event, Timers (L09/L11)	Read-only
left of rect	`put the left of rect`	Coords (D05)	Read-only
left of sprite	`put the left of sprite whichSprite`	Coords (D05)	Read-only
"left"	`set the alignment of member fieldMember = "left"`	Fields (D12)	
length()	`put length(string)`	Strings, Fields (L07)	
length of	`put the length of string`	Strings, Fields (L07)	Undocumented
LF	`set LF = numToChar (10)`	Files, Text (L14)	Supplement
#limit	`set the boxType of member fieldMember = #limit`	Fields (D12)	
#line	`set the shapeType of member shapeMember = #line`	Shapes (D13)	
line...of	`put newValue into line startLine {to endLine} of chunkExpression`	Strings (L07)	Can't use *set*
line...of, last	`delete the last line of chunkExpression` `put the last line of chunkExpression`	Fields, Strings (L07)	Can delete, but not set
#linearList	`if ilk(list, #linearList) then...`	Lists (L06)	
lineCount	`put the lineCount of member fieldMember`	Fields (D12/L07)	Read-only
#lingo	`[#nameFAT:"FileIOXtraFat",#nameW32:" FILEIO.X32",#nameW16:"FILEIO16. X16",#type:#lingo]`	XtraInfo.TXT (D10)	D6
lineHeight()	`set thisHeight = lineHeight (member fieldMember, lineNum)`	Fields, Buttons (D12)	
lineHeight of member	`set the lineHeight {of line whichLine} of member fieldMember = newHeight`	Fields (D12)	Table 17-1
linePosToLocV	`set vOffset = linePosToLocV (member fieldMember, lineNum)`	Fields, Coords (D12)	
lines	`put the number of lines in chunkExpression`	Strings (L07)	Read-only

Table 18-1: Lingo Command and Keyword Summary (continued)

Keyword	Description or Example	See	Notes
lineSize of member	`set the lineSize of member shapeMember = nPixels`	Shapes (D13)	
lineSize of sprite	`set the lineSize of sprite shapeSprite = nPixels`	Shapes (D13)	
#list	if ilk(*someVariable*, #list) then...	Lists (L06)	
list	list(*element1* {, *element2*..., *elementN*})	Lists (L06)	
listP	if listP(*someVariable*) then...	Lists (L06)	
loaded	if not(the loaded of member *whichMember*) then preLoad member *whichMember*	Memory (D09)	
loc of sprite	set the loc of sprite *whichSprite* = point (*x*, *y*)	Coords (D05)	
locH of point	if (the locH of point(*x*, *y*) > 69) then...	Coords, Lists (D05)	Table 17-1
locH of sprite	set the locH of sprite *whichSprite* = *horizCoord*	Coords (D05)	
locToCharPos	set *charPos* = locToCharPos (member *fieldMember*, point (*x*, *y*))	Coords, Fields (D05/D12)	
locV of point	if (the locV of point(*x*, *y*) > 69) then...	Coords (D05)	Table 17-1
locV of sprite	set the locV of sprite *whichSprite* = *vertCoord*	Coords (D05)	
locVToLinePos	set *lineNum* = locVToLinePos (member *fieldMember*, *pixelsFromTopOfField*)	Coords, Fields (D05/D12)	
LowSpoolBufferMs	[Sound] LowSpoolBufferMs = *milliseconds*	DIRECTOR.INI (LD)	Win-only
log()	set *naturalLog* = log(*value*)	Math (L08)	
log10()	set *logarithm* = log10(*value*)	Math (L08)	Supplemental
long	put the long date put the long time	Date and Time (L11)	Read-only
loop	go loop	Score (D03)	
loop of member	set the loop of member *videoMember* = TRUE | FALSE	Video, Sound (D15/D16)	

Table 18-1: Lingo Command and Keyword Summary (continued)

Keyword	Description or Example	See	Notes

[Low Default Sound]
[Low Mono Default Sound]
[Low Mono Override]
[Low Mono \<SoundCardName\>]
[Low Override]
	`[Low {Mono} {Default} {Sound} {Override}]`
	`MixBufferMs = milliseconds`
	`MixBufferBytes = bytes`
	`MixBufferCount = n (2 through 16)`
	`MixServiceMode = 0 | 1 | 2`
	`MixIntPeriodMs = milliseconds`
	`MixIntResolutionMs = milliseconds`
		DIRECTOR.INI
		(LD/D15)
			Win-only

machineType	`if the machineType = machineCode`
	`then...`
	(use *the platform* instead)
		Runtime (D08)	Read-only,
			differs Mac/Win

"Macintosh,68k"	`if the platform = "Macintosh,68k"` `then...`	Runtime (D08)	Mac-only
"Macin-tosh,PowerPC"	`if the platform = "Macintosh,PowerPC"` `then`	Runtime (D08)	Mac-only
macro	`macro macroName (use on handlerName` `instead)`	Lingo	Obsolete (D4)
map (point)	`set newPoint = map (targetPoint,` `sourceRect, destinationRect)`	Coords (D05)	
map (rect)	`set newRect = map (targetRect,` `sourceRect, destinationRect)`	Coords (D05)	
margin	`set the margin of member fieldMember` `= nPixels`	Fields (D12)	
#marker	See *getPropertyDescriptionList's* #format option.	Behaviors (L12)	D6

marker	`go marker(relativeMarkerNumber)`
	`go marker ("markerName")`
	`if marker("markerName) > 0 then go`
	`"markerName"`
		Score (D03)	

maskMember	`put the maskMember of member`
	`whichMember`
	This property always returns the next cast member after *whichMember*.
		Casts (D04)	Read-only,
			unsupported

mAtFrame	`method mAtFrame (used with`
	`perFrameHook)`
	See *stepFrame* and *the actorList*.
		XObjects (L13)	Obsolete (D6)

Table 18-1: Lingo Command and Keyword Summary (continued)

Keyword	Description or Example	See	Notes
#max	Used with *getPropertyDescriptionList*'s #range:[#min:*minValue*, #max:*maxValue*]	Behaviors (L12)	D6
max()	`max (list)` `max (arg1{, arg2}{, arg3}{, arg4})`	Math, Lists (L06/L08)	

maxInteger	`if x + increment > the maxInteger`
	`then`
	`    set x = float(x) + increment`
	`end if`
		Math (L08)	Read-only

mci	`mci "commandString"`	Devices (L14)	Win-only
mConfigChan	`serialPortInstance (mConfigChan,` `driverNum, serConfig)`	SerialPort XObject (L13)	Mac-only
mDescribe	`XObjectName (mDescribe), such as` `SerialPort (mDescribe)`	XObjects (L13)	
mDispose	`XObjectInstance (mDispose)`	XObjects (L13)	

me	`on new me`
	`    return me`
	`end`
		Parent Scripts
		(L12)	

me	`property someProp`
	`on handlerName me`
	`    set the someProp of me = value`
	`    put the spriteNum of me`
	`end handlerName`
		Behaviors (L12)	

#media	`put ilk (the score)` `-- #media`	Data Types (L05)	
#media	See *getPropertyDescriptionList*'s #format option.	Behaviors (L12)	D6
media	`set the media of member whichMember =` `the media of member sourceMember`	Film Loops + MIAWS	Avoid in Projec- tors
mediaReady	`if not (the mediaReady of member` `whichMember) then go the frame`	Memory (D09/ D11)	Read-only
#member	`if ilk(someItem, #member) then...`	Data Types, Casts (D04/ L05)	
#member	See *getPropertyDescriptionList*'s #format option.	Behaviors (L12)	D6

Table 18-1: Lingo Command and Keyword Summary (continued)

Keyword	Description or Example	See	Notes
member *whichMember* of castLib *whichCastLib*	set the *property* of member *whichMember* {of castLib *whichCastLib*} = *value* set *variable* = the *property* of member *whichMember* {of castLib *whichCastLib*} (*member* replaces the obsolete word *cast*)	Casts (D04)	
member of sprite	set the member of sprite *whichSprite* = member *whichMember* {of castLib *whichCast*}	Sprites (D04)	
memberNum of sprite	set the memberNum of sprite *whichSprite* = the number of member *whichMember*	Sprites (D04)	
members, the number of	put the number of members (replaces *the number of castmembers*)	Casts (D04)	Read-only
memberType of member	Invalid property; do not use. See *type of member.*	Casts (D04)	Erroroneous
"memory"	if getErrorString(member *swaMember*) = "memory" then...	SWA Xtra (LE/ D15)	D6, Table E-4
[Memory]	[Memory] ExtraMemory=*kiloBytes* SwapFileMeg=*megaBytes*	DIRECTOR.INI (LD)	Win-only
memorySize	put the memorySize	Memory (D09)	Read-only
menu	menu: *menuName1* *itemNameA*	*action* *itemNameB*	*action* menu: *menuName2* *itemNameC*	*action* *itemNameD*	*action* (Menu is not a Lingo command. Menu defintion must be entered in field cast member. "|" is to be used literally here; it does not indicate a series of choices. See *installMenu*)	Menus (D14), Fields (D12)	
menuItem	the {name	number	checkMark	enabled	script} of menuItem *whichItem* of menu *whichMenu*	Menus (D14)	
menuItems	put the number of menuItems	Menus (D14)	Read-only
menus	put the number of menus	Menus (D14)	Read-only

Table 18-1: Lingo Command and Keyword Summary (continued)

Keyword	Description or Example	See	Notes
mError	`put FileIO (mError, errorCode)`	FileIO XObject (L14)	Obsolete
#message	`Alert(MUIinstance, [#message: string, ...])`	MUI Xtra (L15)	D6, Table 16-1
#metallic	`if the paletteRef of member whichMember = #metallic then...`	Palettes (D13)	
method	`method methodName (use on handlerName instead)`	Factories	Obsolete (D4)
mGet	`object (mGet, whichElement) (obsolete, use lists and getAt() instead)`	Factories	Obsolete (D4)
mGetHandler	`method within XCMDglue`	XObjects	Obsolete
mGetPortNum	`set portNum = serialPortInstance(mGetPortNum)`	SerialPort XObject	Mac-only
mHShakeChan	`serialPortInstance (mHShakeChan, driverNum, CTSenable, CTScharNum)`	SerialPort XObject	Mac-only
#min	Used with *getPropertyDescriptionList's* #range:[#min:*minValue*, #max:*maxValue*]	Behaviors (L12)	D6
min	`min(list)` `min(arg1{, arg2}{, arg3}{, arg4})`	Math, Lists (L08/L06)	
mInstanceRe-spondsTo	`XObjectInstance (mInstanceRespondsTo, #message) (obsolete, see mMessageList)`	XObjects (L13)	Obsolete
#mix	`[#namePPC:"GIF Import", #nameW32:"GIF Import.x32",#type:#mix]`	XtraInfo.TXT (D10)	D6
MixBufferBytes	`[Low Mono Default Sound] MixBufferBytes = bytes`	DIRECTOR.INI (LD/D15)	Win-only
MixBufferCount	`[Low Mono Default Sound] MixBufferCount = n (2 through 16)`	DIRECTOR.INI (LD/D15)	Win-only
MixBufferMs	`[Low Mono Default Sound] MixBufferMs = milliseconds`	DIRECTOR.INI (LD/D15)	Win-only
#mixin	`[#namePPC:"SWA Streaming PPC Xtra", #nameW32:"SWASTRM.X32", #type:#mixin]`	XtraInfo.TXT (D10)	D6
MixIntPeriodMs	`[Low Mono Default Sound] MixIntPeriodMs = milliseconds`	DIRECTOR.INI (LD/D15)	Win-only
MixIntResolutionMs	[Low Mono Default Sound] MixIntResolutionMs = *milliseconds*	DIRECTOR.INI (LD/D15)	Win-only

Table 18-1: Lingo Command and Keyword Summary (continued)

Keyword	Description or Example	See	Notes
MixMaxChannels	[Sound] MixMaxChannels = 1 | 2 | 3 | 4 | 5 | 6 | 7 | 8	DIRECTOR.INI (LD/D15)	Win-only
MixMaxFidelity	[Sound] MixMaxFidelity = 0 | 1 | 2 | 99	DIRECTOR.INI (LD/D15)	Win-only
MixServiceMode	[Low Mono Default Sound] MixServiceMode = 0 | 1 | 2	DIRECTOR.INI (LD/D15)	Win-only
MixWaveDevice	[Sound] MixWaveDevice = *deviceID*	DIRECTOR.INI (LD/D15)	Win-only
mMessageList (for XObjects)	put *XObjectName* (mMessageList) put SerialPort (mMessageList)	XObjects (L13)	Buggy
mMessageList (for Xtras)	put mMessageList (xtra "*XtraName*") put mMessageList (xtra "FileIO")	Xtras (L13)	
mName	*XObjectName* (mName) (No quotes around name!) *XObjectInstance* (mName)	XObject (L13)	
mNew	set *XObjectInstance* = *XObjectName* (mNew {, args...})	XObjects (L13)	
MoaErrorToString	set *errorString* = MoaErrorToString (*errorCode*) put MoaErrorToString(new (#badAsset)) --"MOA core error: XAsset type unknown"	*MUI* Xtra (L21)	D6, Table E-7
mod	set *remainder* = *x* mod *y*	Math (L08)	
modal of window	set the modal of window *whichWindow* = TRUE | FALSE	MIAWs (D06)	
modified of member	if the modified of member *whichMember* then...	Memory (D09)	Read-only
mostRecentCue-Point of sound	put the mostRecentCuePoint of sound *soundChannel*	Cue Points (D15)	Read-only
mostRecentCue-Point of sprite	put the mostRecentCuePoint of sprite *whichSprite*	Cue Points (D15)	Read-only
mouseCast	put the mouseCast (use *the mouseMember* instead)	Mouse (L09)	Read-only, Obsolete
mouseChar	if the mouseChar > 0 then...	Fields (D12)	Read-only
#mouseDown	See *sendSprite* and *on mouseDown*.	Mouse (L09)	
mouseDown, the	if the mouseDown then...	Mouse (L09)	Read-only

Table 18-1: Lingo Command and Keyword Summary (continued)

Keyword	Description or Example	See	Notes
mouseDownScript	`set the mouseDownScript = "MouseDownAction"`	Mouse (L09)	
#mouseEnter	See *sendSprite* and *on mouseEnter*.	Mouse (L09)	D6
mouseH	`if the mouseH > the width of the stage then alert "Don't go there"`	Mouse (L09)	Read-only
mouseItem	`hilite item (the mouseItem) of member (the member of sprite (the spriteNum of me))`	Fields (D12)	Read-only
#mouseLeave	See *sendSprite* and *on mouseLeave*.	Mouse (L09)	D6
mouseLine	`hilite line (the mouseLine) of member (the member of sprite (the spriteNum of me))`	Fields (D12)	Read-only
mouseMember	`if the mouseMember = member whichMember`	Mouse (L09)	D6, Read-only
#mouseUp	See *sendSprite* and *on mouseUp*.	Mouse (L09)	
mouseUp, the	`if the mouseUp then...`	Mouse (L09)	Read-only
#mouseUpOutside	See *sendSprite* and *on mouseUpOutside*.	Mouse (L09)	D6
mouseUpScript	`set the mouseUpScript = "MouseUpAction"`	Mouse (L09)	
mouseV	`if the mouseV > the height of the stage then put "Don't go there"`	Mouse (L09)	Read-only
#mouseWithin	See *sendSprite* and *on mouseWithin*.	Mouse (L09)	D6
mouseWord	`hilite word (the mouseWord) of member (the member of sprite (the spriteNum of me))`	Fields (D12)	Read-only
#movable	`Alert(MUIinstance, [#movable: TRUE | FALSE, ...])`	MUI Xtra (L14)	D6
move (member)	`set newSlot = move member fromMember {of castLib fromCast } {, member toMember of castLib toCast}` Moves to first open slot in the Cast window if none specified. Does *not* update Score references!	Casts (D04)	Dangerous
moveableSprite	`set the moveableSprite of sprite whichSprite = TRUE	FALSE`	Sprites (D04)	
moveToBack	`moveToBack window whichWindow` `moveToBack the stage`	MIAWs (D06)	Not for SW

Table 18-1: Lingo Command and Keyword Summary (continued)

Keyword	Description or Example	See	Notes
moveToFront	`moveToFront window whichWindow` `moveToFront the stage`	MIAWs (D06)	Not for SW
#moveWindow	See *call* and *on moveWindow*.	MIAWs (D06)	Not for SW
#movie (member type)	`if the type of member whichMember =` `#movie then...`	Casts (D04)	
#movie (member type)	See *getPropertyDescriptionList's* #format option.	Behaviors (L12)	D6

#movie (scriptType)	`if the type of member whichMember = ¬`
	`   #script then`
	`  if the scriptType of ¬`
	`  member scriptMember = #movie then`
	`    statement(s)`
	`  end if`
	`end if`
		Scripts (L02)	

movie, the	`put "This movie's name is" && the` `movie`	Files (L13)	Read-only
movie, the (first movie only)	`put "Projector's name is" && the` `movie`	Runtime (D08)	Undocumented, Table 17-1
movie, go movie, play	`go movie` `play movie`	Score (D03)	URL
movieFileFreeSize	`put the movieFileFreeSize`	Memory (D09)	Read-only
movieFileSize	`put the movieFileSize`	Memory (D09)	Read-only
movieName, the	`put "This movie's name is" && the` `movieName`	Files (L13)	Read-only
movieName, the (first movie only)	`put "Projector's name is" && the` `movieName`	Runtime (D08)	Undocumented, Table 17-1
moviePath	`set docSubFolder = the moviePath &` `"docs"`	Files (L13)	Read-only
movieRate	`set the movieRate of sprite videoSprite = n`	Video (D16)	
movieTime	`set the movieTime of sprite videoSprite = n`	Video (D16)	Table 17-1

mPerform	`XobjectInstance (mPerform, "method" {,`
	`args})` (obsolete, use `XobjectInstance`
	`(method)` instead)
		XObjects (L13)	Obsolete

mPut	`factoryInstance (mPut, item)` (obsolete; use lists and *setAt()* instead)	Factories	Obsolete (D4)

Table 18-1: Lingo Command and Keyword Summary (continued)

Keyword	Description or Example	See	Notes
mRate	set the mRate of sprite *quickTime3Sprite = n*	QuickTime3 Xtra (LB, D16)	D6.5
mReadChar	set *nextChar = serialPortInstance* (mReadChar)	SerialPort XObject (L13)	
mReadCount	set *bufferCharCount =* *serialPortInstance* (mReadCount)	SerialPort XObject (L13)	
mReadFlush	*serialPortInstance* (mReadFlush)	SerialPort XObject (L13)	
mReadString	set *inputString = serialPortInstance* (mReadString)	SerialPort XObject (L13)	
mRespondsTo	if *XObjectName* (mRespondsTo, *#message*) then... if *XObjectInstance* (mRespondsTo, *#message*) then... (obsolete, see *mMessageList*)	XObjects (L13)	Obsolete
mSetHandler	XCMDglue (mSetHandler)	XObjects (L13)	Obsolete (D4)
mSetUp	*serialPortInstance* (mSetUp, *baudRate*, *stopBit*, *parityBit*)	SerialPort XObject (L13)	
mTime	set the mTime of sprite *quickTime3Sprite = n*	QuickTime3 Xtra (LB, D16)	D6.5
multiSound	if not the multiSound then sound playFile 2, *"music"*	Sound (D15)	Read-only
"MUI" (Xtra)	set *MUIinstance* = new (xtra "MUI")	MUI Xtra (L15/ L21)	D6
#music	if trackType(member *videoMember*, *whichTrack*) = #music then... if trackType(sprite *videoSprite*, *whichTrack*) = #music then...	Video (D16)	Read-only
mVerb	XCMDglue (mVerb)	XObjects (L13)	Obsolete (D4)
mVerbDispose	XCMDglue (mVerbDispose)	XObjects (L13)	Obsolete (D4)
mWriteChar	*serialPortInstance* (mWriteChar, *charNum*)	SerialPort XObject (L13)	
mWriteString	*serialPortInstance* (mWriteString, *string*)	SerialPort XObject (L13)	

Keywords,
Commands

Table 18-1: Lingo Command and Keyword Summary (continued)

Keyword	Description or Example	See	Notes
NAME	Required for sending messages to Shockwave movie from browser using JavaScript or VBscript NAME="*MovieName*"	HTML (D11)	D6
name of castLib	set the name of castLib "*myThing*" to "*myThang*"	Casts (D04)	
name of member	set the name of member *whichMember* = "*newName*"	Casts (D04)	
name of menu	put the name of menu *whichMenu*	Menu (D14)	Read-only
name of menuItem	set the name of menuItem *whichItem* of menu *whichMenu* = "*newMenuItemName*"	Menu (D14)	
name of window	put the name of window *whichWindow*	MIAWs (D06)	Not for SW
name of xtra	put the name of xtra *whichXtra*	Xtras (L13)	Read-only
#name68K	[#name68K: "*68KXtra*", #namePPC: "*PPCXtra*", #type:#*xtraType*]	XtraInfo.TXT (D10)	D6, Table 16-1
#nameFAT	[#nameFAT: "*FATXtra*", #type:#*xtraTyp*]	XtraInfo.TXT (D10)	D6, Table 16-1
#namePPC	[#name68K: "*68KXtra*", #namePPC: "*PPCXtra*", #type:#*xtraTyp*]	XtraInfo.TXT (D10)	D6, Table 16-1
#nameW16	[#nameW16: "*Win16.x16*", #nameW32: "*Win32.x32*", #type:#*xtraTyp*]	XtraInfo.TXT (D10)	D6, Table 16-1
#nameW32	[#nameW16: "*Win16.x16*", #nameW32: "*Win32.x32*", #type:#*xtraTyp*]	XtraInfo.TXT (D10)	D6, Table 16-1
NAN	Error code indicating "Not a Number" put log(-1) -- NAN	Math (L08)	Undocumented, Mac-only
#net	[#namePPC:"INetUrl PPC Xtra", #nameW32:"INETURL.X32", #type:#net]	XtraInfo.TXT (D10)	D6
netAbort	netAbort (*netID* | *URL*)	NetLingo (D11)	D6, SW
netDone	if netDone ({*netID*}) then go to frame "It's done"	NetLingo (D11)	D6

netError()	case netError ({*netID*}) of
	  "OK", 0: nothing
	  otherwise: then alert "Net Error"
	end case
		NetLingo (D11, LE)	D6, Table E-6

Table 18-1: Lingo Command and Keyword Summary (continued)

Keyword	Description or Example	See	Notes
netLastModDate()	`set fileModDate = netLastModDate ({netID})` Doesn't work in SW4 and SW5.	NetLingo (D11)	D6, SW
#netLib	`[#namePPC:"NetManage WinSock Lib", #type: #netLib]`	XtraInfo.TXT (D10)	D6

netMIME()	`case netMIME ({netID}) of`
	     `"text/html": gotoNetPage url`
	 `end case`
		NetLingo (D11)	D6

netPresent()	Buggy; use *the netPresent* instead.	Requires NetLingo Xtra (D11/D10)	D6, Buggy, Table 17-1
netPresent, the	`if not the netPresent then alert "Can't access net"`	Does not require NetLingo Xtra (D11/D10)	D6, not for SW, Table 17-1
netStatus	`netStatus "messageString"` Prints in Message window during authoring. Not all browsers supported (ActiveX for MIE 3).	NetLingo, Browser (D11)	D6, SW
netTextResult()	`set lastText = netTextResult ({netID})`	NetLingo (D11)	D6, SW
netThrottleTicks	`set the netThrottleTicks = nTicks`	Internet (D11/D09)	D6, Unsupported, Table 17-1
"network"	`if getErrorString(member swaMember) starts "network" then...`	SWA Xtra (D15)	D6, Table E-4
new (member)	`set newMember = new (#memberType {, {member whichMember} of castLib whichCast})`	Casts, Xtras (D04/D10)	
new (script)	`set scriptInstance = new (script "ParentScript" {, args})`	Parent Scripts (L12)	
new (xtra)	`set xtraInstance = new (xtra "XtraName" {, args})`	Xtras (L13/D10)	

new, on	`on new me`
	     `return me`
	 `end`
		Parent Scripts (L12)	

next	`go next`	Score (D03)	

next repeat	`repeat with x = 1 to 5`
	     `next repeat`
	 `end repeat`
		Lingo (L01)	

Keywords, Commands

Table 18-1: Lingo Command and Keyword Summary (continued)

Keyword	Description or Example	See	Notes
#normal	Dialog window type; see *GetWindowPropList()*.	MUI Xtra (L21)	D6
not	`if not (the soundEnabled) then alert "Turn on the sound"`	Expressions (D05)	
#note	`Alert(MUIinstance, [#icon: #note, ... ])`	MUI Xtra (L15)	D6, Table 16-1

nothing	`case (expression) of`
	`  nonErrorValue: nothing`
	`  otherwise:  put "There was an`
	`error"`
	`end case`
		Lingo (L01)	

\<NoValue>	Returned in D3.1.3 instead of \<Void> or Void	Lingo	Obsolete
#NTSC	`if the paletteRef of member whichMember = #NTSC then...`	Palettes (D13)	
\<Null>	Returned by *sendSprite( )* if the sprite does not have a handler to trap the specified message	Lingo	D6
number of castLib	`put the number of castLib whichCast`	Casts (D04)	Read-only
number of castLibs	`put the number of castLibs`	Casts (D04)	Read-only
number of chars	`put the number of chars in chunkExpression`	Strings (L07)	Read-only
number of items	`put the number of items in chunkExpression`	Strings (L07)	Read-only
number of lines	`put the number of lines in chunkExpression`	Strings (L07)	Read-only
number of member	`put the number of member whichMember`	Casts (D04)	Read-only
number of members	`put the number of members {of castLib whichCast}`	Casts (D04)	Read-only
number of menu-Items	`put the number of menuItems of menu whichMenu`	Menus (D14)	Read-only
number of menus	`put the number of menus`	Menu (D14)	Read-only
number of words	`put the number of words in chunkExpression`	Strings (L07)	Read-only
number of xtras	`put the number of xtras (counts Lingo Xtras only)`	Xtras (D10/L13)	Read-only
numChannels of member	`put the numChannels of member swaMember`	SWA (D15)	D6, Read-only

Table 18-1: Lingo Command and Keyword Summary (continued)

Keyword	Description or Example	See	Notes
numToChar	`set asciiCharacter = numToChar(asciiCode)`	Keyboard (L10), Strings (L07)	Appendix A
#object	`if ilk(item, #object) then...`	Data Types (L05)	Table 16-1

objectP	`set instance = new (Xtra "FileIO")`
	`if not objectP(instance) then`
	`  put "Error occurred"`
	`end if`
		Data Types (L05), Errors (L03)	

of	`the property of object`
	`char | item | line | word n of`
	`chunkExpression`
	`the number of items`
	`case (expression) of...`
		Lingo (L01), Properties (L12), Strings (L07)	

offset (strings)	`set charPosition = offset (findString, lookInString)`	Strings (L07)	Appendix C
offset (rect)	`offset (rect, horizChange, vertChange)`	Coords (D05)	
<offspring>	`put new (script "Parent Test")` `-- <offspring "Parent Test" 1 21340b0>`	Object Type (L12)	
"OK"	`if getErrorString(member swaMember) = "OK" then... (actually returns EMPTY, not "OK")`	SWA Xtra (D15)	D6, Table 16-1
#Ok	`Alert(MUIinstance, [#buttons: #Ok, ...])`	MUI Xtra (L15)	D6, Table 16-1
#OkCancel	`Alert(MUIinstance, [#buttons: #OkCancel, ...])`	MUI Xtra (L15)	D6, Table 16-1
#ole	`if the type of member whichMember = #ole then...`	Member Types (D04)	Win-only

on	`on handlerName {, param1} {, param2...}`
	`  statement(s)`
	`end {handlerName}`
		Events (L02)	

on activateWindow	`on activateWindow`
	`  statement(s)`
	`end`
		MIAWs (D06)	Not for Stage

on alertHook	`on alertHook me, errTypeStr, errMsg`
	`  return -1 | 1 | 1 | 2`
	`end`
		Debugging, Error Trapping (L03)	D6, Table 16-1

Table 18-1: Lingo Command and Keyword Summary (continued)

Keyword	Description or Example	See	Notes
on beginSprite	on beginSprite {me} statement(s) end	Events, Sprites (L02)	D6
on birth	on birth me return me end	Parent Scripts (L12)	Obsolete- see *on new*
on buttonClicked	on buttonClicked put "custom button was clicked" end	Button Editor Xtra (L09/D14)	D6, Undocu-mented
on closeWindow	on closeWindow statement(s) end	MIAWs (D06)	
on cuePassed	on cuePassed {me,} channelID, [LC] cuePointNumber, cuePointName statement(s) end	Cue Points, Sound Video (D15/D16)	D6
on deacti-vateWindow	on deactivateWindow statement(s) end	MIAWs (D06)	
on endSprite	on endSprite {me} statement(s) end	Events, Sprites (L02)	D6
on enterFrame	on enterFrame {me} statement(s) end	Events, Sprites (L02)	D6, Table 17-2.
on EvalScript	on EvalScript -- Respond to browser message here end	Browser (D11)	D6, SW, PPC and Win 95/NT only
on exitFrame	on exitFrame {me} statement(s) end	Events, Sprites (L02)	D6, Table 17-2.
on getBehaviorDe-scription	on getBehaviorDescription {me} return helpText end	Behaviors (L12)	D6
on getPropertyDe-scriptionList	on getPropertyDescriptionList {me} return behaviorPropertyList end	Behaviors (L12)	D6
on idle	on idle {me} statement(s) end	Performance, Memory (D09)	

Table 18-1: Lingo Command and Keyword Summary (continued)

Keyword	Description or Example	See	Notes

on keyDown	`on keyDown {me}`
	`    statement(s)`
	`end`
		Keyboard, Fields (L10)	

on keyUp	`on keyUp {me}`
	`    statement(s)`
	`end`
		Keyboard, Fields (L10)	

on mouseDown	`on mouseDown {me}`
	`    statement(s)`
	`end`
		Mouse (L09)	

on mouseEnter	`on mouseEnter {me}`
	`    statement(s)`
	`end`
		Mouse (L09)	D6

on mouseLeave	`on mouseLeave {me}`
	`    statement(s)`
	`end`
		Mouse (L09)	D6

on mouseUp	`on mouseUp {me}`
	`    statement(s)`
	`end`
		Mouse (L09)	

on mouseUpOut-side	`on mouseUpOutside {me}`
	`    statement(s)`
	`end`
		Mouse (L09)	D6

on mouseWithin	`on mouseWithin {me}`
	`    statement(s)`
	`end`
		Mouse (L09)	D6

on moveWindow	`on moveWindow`
	`    statement(s)`
	`end`
		MIAWs (D06)	

on new	`on new me`
	`    return me`
	`end`
		Parent Scripts, Behaviors (L12)	D6, Table 17-2

on openWindow	`on openWindow`
	`    statement(s)`
	`end`
		MIAWs (D06)	

on prepareFrame	`on prepareFrame {me}`
	`    statement(s)`
	`end`
		Score Events (L02/D03)	D6

on prepareMovie	`on prepareMovie`
	`    statement(s)`
	`end`
		Movie Events, MIAWs (L02/D06)	D6, SW

Table 18-1: Lingo Command and Keyword Summary (continued)

Keyword	Description or Example	See	Notes

on resizeWindow	`on resizeWindow`
	`    statement(s)`
	`end`
		MIAWs (D06)	

on rightMouseDown	`on rightMouseDown {me}`
	`    statement(s)`
	`end`
		Mouse (L09)	

on rightMouseUp	`on rightMouseUp{me}`
	`    statement(s)`
	`end`
		Mouse (L09)	

on runPropertyDialog	`on runPropertyDialog me, initialProps`
	`    return behaviorPropertyList`
	`end`
		Behaviors (L12)	D6

on startMovie	`on startMovie`
	`    statement(s)`
	`end`
		Movie Events, MIAWs (L02/ D06)	SW

on startUp	`on startUp`
	`    statement(s)`
	`end`
		Projectors, LINGO.INI (LD/ D08)	Undocumented. Table 17-1

on stepFrame	`on stepFrame me`
	`    statement(s)`
	`end`
		ActorList (L02/ L12)	

on stepMovie	`on stepMovie (Obsolete; on enterFrame is preferred.)`	Events (L02)	Obsolete

on stopMovie	`on stopMovie`
	`    statement(s)`
	`end`
		Movie Events (L02/D06)	SW, Not for MIAWs

on streamStatus	`on streamStatus url, state, [LC]`
	`    bytesSoFar, bytesTotal, error`
	`    case (state) of`
	`        "Connecting":`
	`        "Started":`
	`        "InProgress":`
	`        "Complete":`
	`        "Error":`
	`    end case`
	`end streamStatus`
	
	(See `tellStreamStatus`)
		NetLingo (D11)	D6

on timeOut	`on timeOut`
	`    statement(s)`
	`end`
		Timers (L11)	

Table 18-1: Lingo Command and Keyword Summary (continued)

Keyword	Description or Example	See	Notes

on zoomWindow	`on zoomWindow`
	`    statement(s)`
	`end`
		MIAWs (D06)	

#once	`cacheDocVerify(#once)` `if cacheDocVerify() = #once then...`	NetLingo (D11)	D6, not for SW
open (exe)	`open {whichDocument with}` `whichApplication`	External Files (L14)	Not for SW
open window	`open window whichWindow` `open the stage`	MIAWs (D06)	Not for SW
open...with	`open whichDocument with` `whichApplication`	External Files (L14)	Not for SW
openDA	`openDA whichDeskAccessory`	External files (L14)	Obsolete, Mac-only

openFile	`openFile (fileIOinstance, "fileName",`
	`mode)`
	`mode: 0=Read/Write, 1=Read, 2=Write`
		FileIO Xtra (L14)	

openResFile	`openResFile whichResFile`	External Files (L14)	Obsolete, Mac-only
#openWindow	See *call* and *on openWindow*.	MIAWs (D06)	
openXLib	`openXLib xlibFile (avoid using with` `Xtras)`	XObjects (L13)	Obsolete
optionDown	`if the optionDown then...`	Keyboard (L10)	Read-only, differs Mac/Win
or	`if (logicalExpression1) or` `(logicalExpression2) then...`	Expressions (L05)	

organizationName	`put "Your company is" && the`
	`organizationName`
	Authoring-time only, see Table 17-1. Unsupported.
		Authoring (D08)	Read-only, D5, D6

"other"	`if getErrorString(member swaMember)` `starts "other" then...`	SWA Xtra (D15)	D6, Table E-6

otherwise	`case (expression) of`
	`    value(s):`
	`    otherwise: statement(s)`
	`end case`
		Lingo (L01)	D5, D6

"outline"	`set the fontStyle of member` `fieldMember = "outline"`	Fields (D12)	Mac-only

Table 18-1: Lingo Command and Keyword Summary (continued)

Keyword	Description or Example	See	Notes
#oval	`set the shapeType of member shapeMember = #oval`	Shapes (D13)	
pageHeight	`put the pageHeight of member fieldMember`	Fields (D12)	Read-only
#palette	`if (the type of member whichMember = #palette) then...`	Palettes (D13)	
palette of member	`set the palette of member whichMember = member paletteMember`	Palettes (D13)	
PALETTE	`PALETTE=background | foreground`	HTML EMBED (DLL)	SW

[Palette]	`[Palette]`
	`Animation = 0 | 1`
	`0 Prevents palette conflicts, but slows palette fades. Default is 1.`
		DIRECTOR.INI (LD/D13)	Win-only

paletteMapping	`set the paletteMapping = TRUE | FALSE`	Palettes (D13)	
paletteRef	`set the paletteRef of member whichMember = #systemMac | #systemWin | #rainbow | #grayscale | #pastels | #vivid | #VGA | #NTSC | #metallic | #systemWinDir4`	Palettes (D13)	
param	`set someParam = param(parameterNumber)`	Lingo Arguments (L01)	
paramCount	`put the paramCount`	Lingo Arguments (L01)	Read-Only
#parent	`set the scriptType of member scriptMember = #parent`	Parent Scripts (L12)	

pass	`on mouseDown`
	`    pass`
	`end`
		Events (L02)	

pasteClipBoardInto	`pasteClipBoardInto member whichMember of castLib whichCast`	Cast (D04)	Not for SW
#pastels	`if the paletteRef of member whichMember = #pastels then...`	Palettes (D13)	
pathName	`put "This movie is in" && the pathName`	External Files, MIAWs (L14)	Read-only, SWA, URL
pattern	`set the pattern of member shapeMember = index (index = 1 to 64)`	Shapes (D13)	

Table 18-1: Lingo Command and Keyword Summary (continued)

Keyword	Description or Example	See	Notes
pause	`pause`	Score (D03)	Obsolete
pause member	`pause member` *swaMember*	SWA (D15)	D6
pausedAtStart	`set the pausedAtStart of member` *videoMember* `= TRUE | FALSE`	Video (D16)	
pauseState	`put the pauseState` (Not valid until *on startMovie* handler. See *pause* and *continue*.)	Score (D03)	Read-only
percentPlayed	`put the percentPlayed of member` *swaMember*	SWA (D15)	D6, Read-only
percentStreamed	`put the percentStreamed of member` *swaMember*	SWA (D15)	D6, Read-only
perFrameHook	`set the perFrameHook =` *object* (use *stepFrame* and *actorList*)	XObjects	Obsolete
pi pi() the pi	`set` *area* `= pi * power (`*radius*`, 2)` `set` *x* `= cos(pi())` `set` *circumference* `= 2 * the pi *` *radius*	Math (L08)	D6, Fixed in D6. 0.1
#picture	`if ilk(item, #picture) then...`	Data Types (L05)	
picture	`put the picture of member` *bitmapMember*	Graphics (D13)	Authoring only
<Picture>	`put the picture of member` *bitmapMember* `-- <Picture:1ef9108>`	Object Type (D13)	
pictureP()	`if pictureP(`*item*`) then...`	Graphics (D13)	
"plain"	`set the fontStyle of member` *fieldMember* `= "plain"`	Fields, Buttons (D12)	
platform	`"Macintosh,68k" | "Macintosh,PowerPC" | "Windows,16" | "Windows,32" | "Java` *javaVersion, browser, OS*`"` `if the platform starts "Windows" then` `  -- Do Windows stuff` `else if the platform starts "Mac"` `then` `  -- Do Macintosh stuff` `end if` (Use instead of *the machineType*)	Runtime (D07/ D08)	D5, D6, SW, Differs Mac/ Win. Tables 16-1 and 17-1

Table 18-1: Lingo Command and Keyword Summary (continued)

Keyword	Description or Example	See	Notes
play	`play whichFrame {of movie whichMovie}` See *play frame* and *play movie*.	Score (D03)	SW, URL
play done	`play done`	Score (D03)	
play frame	`play {frame} whichFrame {of movie whichMovie}`	Score (D03)	SW, URL
play member	`play member swaMember`	SWA (D15)	D6
play movie	`play {frame whichFrame of} movie whichMovie`	Score (D03)	SW, URL
Play()	Netscape: document.*html NAME tag*.Play() MIE: *html NAME tag*.Play()	Browser Scripting (D11)	D6, SW, PPC Win 95/NT
"playback device"	`if getErrorString(member swaMember) = "playback device" then...`	SWA Xtra (D15)	D6, Table E-6
playFile, sound	`sound playFile soundChannel, whichSoundFile`	Sound (D15)	
"Plugin"	`if the runMode = "Plugin" then...` See Tables 16-1 and 17-1.	Runtime (D11)	D5, D6, SW
PLUGINSPAGE	`PLUGINSPAGE="http://www.macromedia.com/shock-wave/"`	HTML EMBED (D11)	SW
#point	`ilk(item, #point) then`	Data Types (L05), Lists (L06), Coords (D05)	
point	`set the loc of sprite whichSprite = point(x, y)`	Coords (D05), Lists (L06)	
#port	`set portNum = proxyServer (#http, #port)`	NetLingo (D11)	D6, not for SW
power	`set answer = power(base, exponent)` `set area = pi * power(radius, 2)`	Math (L08)	
preLoad	`preLoad {toFrameNum}` `preLoad {fromFrameNum, toFrameNum}` `set lastFrameLoaded = the result`	Memory (D09)	
preLoad of member	`set the preLoad of member videoMember = TRUE	FALSE` (See *the preLoadRAM*)	Video (D15), Memory (D09)	
preLoadBuffer	`preLoadBuffer (member swaMember)`	SWA (D15), Memory (D09)	D6

Table 18-1: Lingo Command and Keyword Summary (continued)

Keyword	Description or Example	See	Notes
preLoadCast	`preLoadCast {cast whichMember}` (obsolete, use *preLoadMember* instead) `preLoadCast {cast fromMember, cast toMember}`	Memory (D09)	Obsolete
preLoadEventAbort	`Set the preLoadEventAbort = TRUE	FALSE`	Loading (D09)	
preLoadMember	`preLoadMember{member whichMember {of castLib whichCastLib}}` `preLoadMember{member fromMember {of castLib whichCastLib}, member toMember {of castLib whichCastLib}}` `set lastMemberLoaded = the result --` Buggy	Memory (D09)	
preLoadMode	`set the preLoadMode of castLib whichCastLib = 0	1	2`	Loading (D09), Casts (D04)	Table 16-1
preLoadMovie	`preLoadMovie whichMovie`	Memory (D09)	URL
preloadNetThing	`set netID = preloadNetThing (url)`	NetLingo (D11)	D6, SW, URL
preLoadRAM	`set the preLoadRAM = nBytes` (Default, 0. means "all available memory" if *the preLoad of member* is TRUE)	Video (D16), Memory (D09)	
preLoadTime	`set the preLoadTime of member swaMember = timeInSeconds`	SWA (D15)	
#prepareFrame	See *call* and *on prepareFrame*.	Score Events (L02)	D6
#prepareMovie	See *call* and *on prepareMovie*.	Score Events (L02)	D6
previous	`go previous`	Score (D03)	
print	See *PrintOMatic* Xtra's documentation.	PrintOMatic Xtra (L14)	
printFrom	`printFrom fromFrame {, toFrame} {, scaling}`	Printing (L14)	Table 17-1
productName	`put "You are running" && the productName` See Tables 16-1 and 17-1.	Runtime (D08)	Read-only, D5, D6, SW
productVersion	`put "This is version" && the productVersion` See Tables 16-1 and 17-1.	Runtime (D08)	Read-only, D5, D6, SW

Table 18-1: Lingo Command and Keyword Summary (continued)

Keyword	Description or Example	See	Notes
"Projector"	if the runMode = "Projector" then... See Tables 16-1 and 17-1.	Runtime (D08)	D5, D6
property	property *pVariable1* {, *pVariable2*} {, *pVariable3*}	Variables (L01), Behaviors (L12), Parent Scripts	
property...of	the *property* of *object* the *property* of *list*	Lists (L01), Behaviors (L12), Parent Scripts	
#propList	if ilk(*list*, #propList) then...	Lists (L06), Data Types (L05)	
proxyServer	proxyServer #ftp | #http, #stop proxyServer #ftp | #http, "*ipAddress*", *portNum* set *portNum* = proxyServer (#ftp | #http, #port) set *IPaddressString* = proxyServer (#ftp | #http)	NetLingo Xtra (D11)	D6, not for SW
puppet	set the puppet of sprite *whichSprite* = TRUE | FALSE (see *puppetSprite*)	Sprites, Auto-puppet (D04)	Table 17-2
puppetPalette	puppetPalette "*paletteName*" {, *speed*} {, *nFrames*}	Palettes (D13)	Table 16-1
puppetSound	puppetSound *soundChannel*, *soundMember* puppetSound *soundMember* puppetSound member *soundMember* puppetSound 0 puppetSound *soundChannel*, 0 updateStage	Sounds (D15)	Table 16-1
puppetSprite	puppetSprite *whichSprite*, TRUE | FALSE (see *puppet of sprite*)	Sprite (D04)	Table 17-2
puppetTempo	puppetTempo *framesPerSecond*	Tempos (D03)	Table 16-1
puppetTransition	puppetTransition *transitionNumCode* | member *transitionMember* {, *time*} {, *chunkSize*} {, *changeArea*}	Transitions (D03)	Table 16-1
purgePriority	set the purgePriority of member *whichMember* = 3 | 2 | 1 | 0 (Default is 3. Don't use a setting of 0)	Loading (D09)	Table 17-1
#pushButton	the buttonType of member *buttonMember* = #pushButton	Buttons (D14)	

Table 18-1: Lingo Command and Keyword Summary (continued)

Keyword	Description or Example	See	Notes
#pushButton	Also a MUI Xtra widget type, see *GetWidgetList()*	MUI Xtra (L21)	D6
put (Message window)	`put "someString"`	Debug (L01, L03)	Not for SW or Authoring
put...after	`put "someString" after field "myField"`	Fields, Strings (L07/D12)	
put...before	`put "someString" before field "myField"`	Fields, Strings (L07/D12)	
put...into	`put "someString" into field "myField"` `put "someString" into char	item |` `line	word start {to end} of` `chunkExpression` `put value into x` (I prefer using `set x = value`)	Fields, Strings (L07/D12)	
putImageIntoCast-Member	`putImageIntoCastMember (member fromBtnEdMember, "imageString", member toBitmapMember)`	Button Editor Xtra (D14)	D6, Table 16-1.
#question	`Alert(MUIinstance, [#icon: #question, ...])`	MUI Xtra (L15)	D6, Table 16-1
#quickTime	`if the digitalVideoType of member videoMember = #quickTime then...`	Video (D16)	Read-only
quickTimePresent	`if not (the quickTimePresent) then alert "Please install QuickTime"`	Video (D16)	Read-only, Unreliable
QuickTimeVersion	`if QuickTimeVersion() >= 3.000 then...`	QuickTime3 Xtra (D16/LB)	D6.5, Unreliable
quit	`quit` (See *halt* and *the exitLock.*)	Lingo	Not for SW
quote	`alert "Couldn't locate the file" && QUOTE & "myFile.doc" & QUOTE`	Strings (L07)	
#radioButton	`set the buttonType of member buttonMember = #radioButton`	Buttons (D14)	
#radioButton	Also a MUI Xtra widget type; see *GetWidgetList().*	MUI Xtra (L21)	D6
#rainbow	`if the paletteRef of member whichMember = #rainbow then...`	Palettes (D13)	
ramNeeded	`put ramNeeded (fromFrame, toFrame)`	Memory (D09)	Unreliable
random	`put random(maxRandomInteger)`	Math (L08)	
randomSeed	`set the randomSeed = integeSeedr`	Math (L08)	

Table 18-1: Lingo Command and Keyword Summary (continued)

Keyword	Description or Example	See	Notes

#range	on getPropertyDescriptionList
	    return [¬
	{#range:[#min: *minValue*, ¬
	        #max: *maxValue*] | ¬
	        [*item1*, *item2*, ...]}]
	end getPropertyDescriptionList
		Behaviors (L12)	D6, Table 16-1

"read" or "?read"	set *fileXObjInst* = FileIO (mNew, "read", *fileName*)	FileIO XObject (L14)	Obsolete
readChar	set *nextChar* = readChar (*fileIOinstance*)	FileIO Xtra (L14)	
readFile	set *remainingData* = readFile (*fileIOinstance*)	FileIO Xtra (L14)	
readLine	set *nextLine* = readLine (*fileIOinstance*)	FileIO Xtra (L14)	
readToken	set *nextToken* = readToken (*fileIOinstance*, *stringToSkip*, *stringForBreak*)	FileIO Xtra (L14)	
readWord	set *nextWord* = readWord (*fileIOinstance*)	FileIO Xtra (L14)	
#rect (data type)	if ilk(*someItem*, #rect) then... put ilk (the rect of the stage)	Coords (D05, L05)	
#rect (shapeType)	if the shapeType of member *shapeMember* = #rect then...	Shapes (D13)	
rect (*l*, *t*, *r*, *b*)	if inside (the clickLoc, rect(*left*, *top*, *right*, *bottom*)) then... set the drawRect of window *whichWindow* = rect(point(*left*, *top*), point(*right*, *bottom*))	Lists, Coords (D05, D06)	
rect of member	put the rect of member *whichMember* (settable for field castmembers only)	Casts, Coords (D04/D05)	Table 17-1
rect of sprite	set the rect of sprite *whichSprite* = rect (*left*, *top*, *right*, *bottom*)	Sprites, Coords (D04/D05)	Table 17-1
rect of window	set the rect of window *whichWindow* = rect (*left*, *top*, *right*, *bottom*) put the rect of the stage	MIAWs (D05/ D06)	
regPoint	set the regPoint of member *whichMember* = point (*x*, *y*)	Coords (D05)	

Table 18-1: Lingo Command and Keyword Summary (continued)

Keyword	Description or Example	See	Notes
(relative paths)	See @ (relative path operator).	External Files (L14)	
repeat	See *end repeat*, *exit repeat*, *next repeat*.	Lingo Loops (L01)	
repeat while	repeat while (*expression* = TRUE) *statements(s)* end repeat	Lingo Loops (L01)	
repeat with...to...	repeat with *index* = *start* to *end* *statements(s)* end repeat	Lingo Loops (L01)	
repeat with...down to...	repeat with *index* = *high* down to *low* *statements(s)* end repeat	Lingo Loops (L01)	
repeat with...in	repeat with *element* in *someList* put *element* end repeat	Lists (L01/L06)	
#resizeWindow	See *call* and *on resizeWindow*.	MIAWs (D06)	
restart	restart See Table 17-1 and Chapter 8 in *Director in a Nutshell*.	Runtime (D08)	Differs Mac/Win, not for SW
result	preLoadMember *fromMember*, *toMember* set *lastMemberLoaded* = the result	Parameters (L01)	
#RetryCancel	Alert(*MUIinstance*, [#buttons: #RetryCancel, ...])	MUI Xtra (L15)	D6, Table 16-1
RETURN	if the key = RETURN then *checkUserInput()*	Keyboard (L09), Strings (L07)	
return	on *handlerName* return {*returnValue*} end	Lingo (L01)	
Rewind()	Netscape: document.*htmlNAMEtag*.Rewind() MIE: *htmlNAMEtag*.Rewind()	Browser Scripting (D11)	D6, SW, PPC Win 95/NT
#richText	if the type of member *whichMember* = #richText then...	Text, Fields (D12)	
right of rect	put the right of the stage (same as *the stageRight*)	Coords (L06) (D05)	Read-only
right of sprite	put the right of sprite *whichSprite*	Coords (L06) (D05)	Read-only

Table 18-1: Lingo Command and Keyword Summary (continued)

Keyword	Description or Example	See	Notes
"right"	set the alignment of member *fieldMember* = "right"	Fields, Buttons (D12)	
#rightMouseDown	See *sendSprite* and *on rightMouseDown*.	Mouse (L09)	
#rightMouseUp	See *sendSprite* and *on rightMouseUp*.	Mouse (L09)	
rollOver, the rollover()	put "Mouse is currently over active sprite" && the rollOver put "Mouse is currently over active sprite" && rollOver()	Mouse (L09)	Read-only
roll-Over(*n*)(Boolean)	if rollOver(*whichSprite*) = TRUE | FALSE then...	Mouse (L09)	
romanLingo	set the romanLingo = TRUE | FALSE (default depends on OS language)	Strings, Performance (D09)	Differs Mac/Win
#roundRect	set the shapeType of member *shapeMember* = #roundRect	Shapes (D13)	
rowBytes	put the rowBytes of member *whichMember*	Graphics	Table 17-1
Run (MUI)	Run(*MUIinstance*)	MUI Xtra (L21)	D6
runMode	if the runMode = "Author" | "Plugin" | "Projector" | "Java Applet" then...	Runtime (D08)	Read-only, D5, D6, SW Tables 16-1 and 17-1.
runPropertyDialog, on	on runPropertyDialog me, *initialProps* return *behaviorPropertyList* end	Behaviors (L12)	D6
safePlayer	if not (the safePlayer) then alert "No security features in place" See Table 17-1.	Runtime (D08)	Read-only, D6, SW, unsupported
sampleRate	put the sampleRate of member *soundOrSWAmember*	Sound, SWA (D15)	Read-only, Table 16-1
sampleSize	put the sampleSize of member *soundMember*	Sound (D15)	Read-only, Table 16-1
save castLib	save castLib *whichCast* {, *fileNameWithOptionalPath*}	Casts, External Files (D04)	Not for SW
saveMovie	saveMovie {*fileNameWithOptionalPath*}	Score, External Files (D04)	Not for SW

Table 18-1: Lingo Command and Keyword Summary (continued)

Keyword	Description or Example	See	Notes
#score	`set the scriptType of member` *`scriptMember`* `= #score`	Scripts (L02)	

score	`set the score = the media of [LC]`
	 `member` *`filmLoopCastmember`*
	 `put ilk (the score)`
	 `-- #media`
		Score (D03/ D06)	

scoreColor	`set the scoreColor of sprite` *`whichSprite`* `= 0	1	2	3	4	5`	Score, Colors (D03/D13)	
scoreSelection	`set the scoreSelection =` `[[`*`startChan1, endChan1, startFrame1,`* *`endFrame1`*`] {, [`*`startChan2, endChan2,`* *`startFrame2, endFrame2`*`]} ]`	Score (D03)	Table 17-2
#script	`if the type of member` *`whichMember`* `=` `#script then...`	Scripts (L02)	

script (instance)	`set` *`newInstance`* `= new (script`
	 `"ParentScript")`
	 `put ilk (script` *`scriptMember`*`)`
		Behaviors, Parent Scripts (L12)	

script of member	`put the script of member` *`whichMember`*	Scripts (L02)	Read-only, unsupported, Table 17-1

script of menuItem	`set the script of menuItem`
	 `whichMenuItem` `of menu` *`whichMenu`* `=`
	 `"commandString"`
		Menus (D14)	

scriptInstanceList	`put the scriptInstanceList of sprite` *`whichSprite`*	Behaviors (L12)	Settable only at run-time. Table 17-1.
scriptNum	`the scriptNum of sprite` *`whichSprite`*	Scripts (L02)	Read-only
scriptsEnabled	`set the scriptsEnabled of member` *`movieMember`* `= TRUE	FALSE`	Movie Cast members (D04)	
scriptText	`set the scriptText of member` *`whichMember`* `=` *`stringContainingScripts`*	Scripts (L02)	Disabled in protected movies
scriptType	`set the scriptType of member` *`scriptMember`* `= #movie	#parent	`   `#score`	Scripts (L02)	
#scroll	`set the boxType of member` *`fieldMember`* `= #scroll`	Fields (D12)	

Table 18-1: Lingo Command and Keyword Summary (continued)

Keyword	Description or Example	See	Notes
scrollByLine	`scrollByLine member fieldMember, numLines`	Fields (D12)	
scrollByPage	`scrollByPage member fieldMember, numPages`	Fields (D12)	
scrollTop	`set the scrollTop of member textMember = newTopLine`	Fields RTF (D12)	
searchCurrent-Folder	`set the searchCurrentFolder = TRUE | FALSE (default is TRUE!)`	External Files (L14)	
searchPath	`add (the searchPath, newPath)` `deleteAll (the searchPath)`	External Files (L14)	
searchPaths	`add (the searchPaths, newPath)` `deleteAll (the searchPaths)`	External Files (L14)	
selection	`if the selection = EMPTY then alert "Please hilight something"` `put selection()` see *hilite*	Fields (L10) (D12)	Read-only
selEnd	`set the selEnd = endingCharNumber`	Fields (L10) (D12)	Buggy, Table 17-1
selStart	`set the selStart = startingCharNumber`	Fields (L10) (D12)	Buggy, Table 17-1
send	`send (object, #message) (see call)`	Messages (L02)	Unsupported, Table 17-1
sendAllSprites	`sendAllSprites (#message {, args})`	Messages (L02)	D6
sendAncestor	`sendAncestor (object, #message) (see callAncestor)`	Messages (L02) (L12)	Unsupported, Table 17-1
sendSprite	`sendSprite (whichSprite, #message {, args})`	Messages (L02)	D6
serialNumber	`put "You serial number is" && the serialNumber` Authoring-time only, see Table 17-1. Unsupported	Authoring (D08)	Read-only, D5, D6
SerialPort	`set serialPortInstance = SerialPort (mNew, portNum)`	SerialPort XObject (L13)	Mac-only
#service	`[#nameFAT:"Mix Services", #nameW32:"mix32.x32", #nameW16:"mix16.x16", #type:#service]`	XtraInfo.TXT (D10)	D6

Table 18-1: Lingo Command and Keyword Summary (continued)

Keyword	Description or Example	See	Notes

set	`set the property {of object} = value`
	`set the property {of object} to value`
	`set variable = value`
	`set variable to value`
		Variables (L01)	

setaProp (list)	`setaProp(propList, property, value)` `setaProp(linearList, position, value)`	Lists (L06)	
setaProp (object)	`setaProp (childObject, property, value)`	Parent Scripts, Behaviors (L12)	
setAt()	`setAt (list, position, value)`	Lists (L06)	
setButtonImage-FromCastMember	`setButtonImageFromCastMember (member toBtnEdMember, "imageString", member fromBitmapMember)`	Button Editor Xtra (D14)	D6, Table 16-1
setCallBack	`setCallBack XCMDname, value`	XCMDs (L13)	Obsolete

setFilterMask (Mac)	`setFilterMask (fileIOinstance, "fourCharFileType")`
	`setFilterMask (fileIOinstance, "TEXT")`
	`setFilterMask (fileIOinstance, EMPTY)` `(all files)`
		FileIO Xtra (L14)	Differs Mac/Win, Table 16-1.

setFilterMask (Win)	`setFilterMask (fileIOinstance, "description, extension")`
	`setFilterMask (fileIOinstance, "Text Files,*.txt")`
	`setFilterMask (fileIOinstance, "All Files,*.*")`
		FileIO Xtra (L14)	Differs Mac/Win, Table 16-1

setFinderInfo	`setFinderInfo (fileIOinstance, "fourCharFileType fourCharCreatorCode")`
	`setFinderInfo (fileIOinstance, "TEXT ttxt")`
	(See *getFinderInfo* and Table 16-1.)
		FileIO Xtra (L14)	Mac-only

setPosition	`setPosition (fileIOinstance, position)`	FileIO Xtra (L14)	
setPref	`setPref prefFileName, prefFileText` Valid in Directors and Projectors, but path differs from Shockwave. See Table 16-1.	Browser, External Files (D11/L14)	D6, SW, Differs at Run-time
setProp	`setProp (propertyList, property, value)`	Lists (L06)	

Table 18-1: Lingo Command and Keyword Summary (continued)

Keyword	Description or Example	See	Notes
setTrackEnabled	`setTrackEnabled (sprite videoSprite, whichTrack, TRUE | FALSE)`	Video (D06)	
"shadow"	`set the fontStyle of member fieldMember = "shadow"`	Fields (D12)	
shape	`if the type of member whichMember = #shape then...`	Shapes (D13)	
shapeType	`set the shapeType of member shapeMember = #oval	#line	#rect	#roundRect`	Shapes (D13)	
shiftDown	`if the shiftDown then...`	Keyboard (L10)	Read-only
short	`put the short date` `put the short time`	Date/Time (L11)	Read-only
showGlobals	`showGlobals`	Variables (L01)	
showLocals	`showLocals`	Variables (L01)	
showResFile	`showResFile whichResFile`	External Files (L14)	Obsolete, Mac-only
showXlib	`showXlib {XlibFileName}`	Xtras (L13)	
shutDown	`shutDown` See Table 17-1 and Chapter 8 in *Director in a Nutshell*.	Runtime (D08)	Differs Mac/Win, not for SW
sin()	`set value = sin(angleInRadians)`	Math (L08)	
size	`put the size of member whichMember`	Memory (D09)	Read-only
sort()	`sort (list)`	Lists (L06)	
#sound (member type)	`if the type of member whichMember = #sound then...`	Sound (D15)	
#sound (trackType)	`if the trackType (sprite videoSprite, whichTrack) = #sound then...` `if the trackType (member videoMember, whichTrack) = #sound then...`	Video (D16)	
sound (instance)	`put ilk (sound soundMember)`	Sound (D15)	
sound, the volume of	See *the volume of sound soundChannel*.	Sound (D15)	

Table 18-1: Lingo Command and Keyword Summary (continued)

Keyword	Description or Example	See	Notes
[Sound]	`[Sound]` `SpoolBufferAlloc = 0	1` `LowSpoolBufferMs = milliseconds` `HighSpoolBufferMs = milliseconds` `SpoolBufferCount = 2	3	4	5	6` `| 7	8	9	10` `MixMaxChannels = 1	2	3	4	5 |` `6	7	8` `MixWaveDevice = deviceID` `SoundLevel0 = n` `SoundLevel1 = n` `SoundLevel2 = n` `SoundLevel3 = n` `SoundLevel4 = n` `SoundLevel5 = n` `SoundLevel6 = n` `SoundLevel7 = n` `MixMaxFidelity = 0	1	2	99`	DIRECTOR.INI, Sound (D15/LD)	Win-only, Appendix D
sound close	`sound close soundChannel`	Sound (D15)	
sound fadeIn	`sound fadeIn soundChannel {, nTicks }`	Sound (D15)	Table 17-2
sound fadeOut	`sound fadeOut soundChannel {, nTicks }`	Sound (D15)	Table 17-2
sound of member	`set the sound of member videoMember = TRUE	FALSE`	Video (D16)	
sound playFile	`sound playFile soundChannel, whichFile` `soundChannel = 1 to 8`	Sound (D15)	URL
sound stop	`sound stop soundChannel`	Sound (D15)	

#Sound1
#Sound2
	`on cuePassed {me,} whichChannel`
	`  case (whichChannel) of`
	`  #Sound1, #Sound2:`
	`    put "Passed cue in" &&`
	`whichChannel`
	`    otherwise:`
	`      put "Passed cue in some sprite"`
	`    end case`
	`end`
		Sound, Cue Points (D15)	D6

soundBusy	`if soundBusy(soundChannel) then...`	Sound (D15)	

Table 18-1: Lingo Command and Keyword Summary (continued)

Keyword	Description or Example	See	Notes
soundChannel of member	set the soundChannel of member *swaMember* = 0 -- (0 assigns to highest unused channel)	SWA (D15)	D6
soundEnabled	set the soundEnabled = TRUE | FALSE	Sound (D15)	
soundKeepDevice	set the soundKeepDevice = TRUE | FALSE -- (Default is FALSE.)	Sound (D15)	D6, Undocumented, Table 17-1
soundLevel	set the soundLevel = 0 | 1 | 2 | 3 | 4 | 5 | 6 | 7	Sound (D15)	
SoundLevel0 SoundLevel1 SoundLevel2 SoundLevel3 SoundLevel4 SoundLevel5 SoundLevel6 SoundLevel7	[Sound] SoundLevel0 = *n* (default 0) SoundLevel1 = *n* (default 24770) SoundLevel2 = *n* (default 35030) SoundLevel3 = *n* (default 42903) SoundLevel4 = *n* (default 49540) SoundLevel5 = *n* (default 55388) SoundLevel6 = *n* (default 60674) SoundLevel7 = *n* (default 65535) *n* = 0 to 65535	DIRECTOR.INI, Sound (D15/ LD)	Win-only, Appendix D
sourceRect	put the sourceRect of window *whichWindow* See *the drawRect of window.*	MIAW (D05/ D06)	Read-only
SPACE space() the space	if the key = SPACE then... if *string* starts the space then... if *string* contains space() then...	Strings (L07), Keyboard (L10)	D6, Fixed in D6. 0.1
SpoolBufferAlloc	[Sound] SpoolBufferAlloc = 0 | 1	DIRECTOR.INI, Sound (D15)	Win-only, Appendix D
SpoolBufferCount	[Sound] SpoolBufferCount = 2 | 3 | 4 | 5 | 6 | 7 | 8 | 9 | 10	DIRECTOR.INI, Sound (D15)	Win-only, Appendix D
#sprite	put ilk(sprite *whichSprite*, #sprite)	Sprites (D04)	
sprite	put the *property* of sprite *whichSprite* set the *property* of sprite *whichSprite* = *value*	Sprites, Behaviors (L12) (D04)	
sprite...intersects	if sprite *sprite1* intersects {sprite} *sprite2* then...	Sprites, Coords (D05)	

Table 18-1: Lingo Command and Keyword Summary (continued)

Keyword	Description or Example	See	Notes
sprite...within	if sprite *sprite1* within{sprite} *sprite2* then...	Sprites, Coords (D05)	
spriteBox	spriteBox *whichSprite, left, top, right, bottom* (See *rect of sprite*.)	Coords (D05)	Obsolete
spriteNum of me	on mouseDown me set the foreColor of sprite ¬ (the spriteNum of me) = random(255) end	Sprites, Behaviors (L09)	D6
sqrt() the sqrt	put sqrt(*number*) put the sqrt of *number*	Math (D08)	
SRC (MIE)	<PARAMNAME="SRC" VALUE="*movieUrl*"	HTML OBJECT (D11)	SW
SRC (Netscape)	SRC="*movieUrl*"	HTML EMBED (D11)	SW
stage, the	*The stage* can be the target of a *tell* command: tell the stage go to frame 50 end tell	MIAWs (D06)	Read-only
stage, the	The *stage* has properties like other windows: put the rect of the stage put the drawRect of the stage put the sourceRect of the stage	Coords, MIAWs, Stage (D05) (D06)	Read-only
stageBottom	if the mouseV > the stageBottom - the stageTop then put "Now you've gone too far!"	MIAW, Coords (D05/D06)	Read-only
stageColor	set the stageColor = *colorIndex*	MIAWs, Colors (D05/D06)	
stageLeft	if the mouseH > the stageRight - the stageLeft then put "Exit, stage right."	MIAW, Coords (D05/D06)	Read-only
stageRight	set the locH of sprite *whichSprite* = the stageRight - the stageLeft	MIAW, Coords (D05/D06)	Read-only
stageTop	set the locV of sprite *whichSprite* = the stageTop	MIAW, Coords (D05/D06)	Read-only
"Started"	See *state* parameter sent to *on streamStatus*.	NetLingo (D11)	SW, D6

Table 18-1: Lingo Command and Keyword Summary (continued)

Keyword	Description or Example	See	Notes
#startMovie	See *call* and *on startMovie*.	Movie Events (L02), MIAW (D06)	SW

starts	`if string1 starts string2`
	`if the platform starts "Windows"`
	`then...`
		Strings (L07)	Appendix C

startTime	`set the startTime of sprite` `videoSprite = nTime`	Video (D16)	Table 17-1
startTimer	`startTimer (resets the timer to zero)`	Timers (L11)	

startUp	`on startUp`
	`    statement(s)`
	`end`
		Projectors, LINGO.INI (LD/D08)	Undocumented, Table 17-1

state of member	`if the state of member swaMember = 0` `| 1	2	3	4	5	9	10 then...`	SWA (D15)	D6, Table 16-1
status (FileIO)	`set lastOperation = status` `(fileIOinstance)`	FileIO Xtra (L14)	Table E-3
stepFrame	See *the actorList* and *on stepMovie*.	Events, Behaviors and Objects (L02/L12)	
stepMovie	*on stepMovie* (obsolete; *on enterFrame* is preferred)	Events (L02)	Obsolete
stillDown	`if the stillDown then...`	Mouse (L09)	Read-only
#stop (MUI))	`Alert(MUIinstance, [#icon: #stop, ...` `])`	MUI Xtra (L15)	D6, Table 16-1
#stop	`proxyServer (#ftp, #stop)`	NetLingo (D11)	D6, Table 16-1
Stop (MUI)	`Stop(MUIinstance, integerStopItem )`	MUI Xtra (L21)	D6
Stop()	Netscape: `document.html NAMEtag.Stop()` MIE: `html NAMEtag.Stop()`	Browser Scripting (D11)	D6, SW, PPC Win 95/NT
stop (member)	`stop member swaMember`	SWA (D15)	D6
stop, sound	`sound stop soundChannel`	Sound (D15)	

stopEvent	`on mouseUp me`
	`    stopEvent`
	`end`
		Events (L02)	D6

#stopMovie	See *call* and *on stopMovie*.	Movie Events (L02/D06)	SW, Not for MIAWs
stopTime	`set the stopTime of sprite` `videoSprite = nTime`	Video (D16)	Table 17-1

Table 18-1: Lingo Command and Keyword Summary (continued)

Keyword	Description or Example	See	Notes
streamName	`set the streamName of member swaMember = name`	SWA (D15)	D6
streamStatus	See *on streamStatus, tellStreamStatus*.	NetLingo (D11)	D6
stretch	if the stretch of sprite *whichSprite* then...	Sprites (D04)	
#string	`if ilk(someItem, #string) then...`	Data Types, Strings (L05)	
#string	See *getPropertyDescriptionList's* #format option.	Behaviors (L12)	D6
string()	`set newString = string(value)`	Data Types, Strings (L07)	
stringP()	`if stringP(someItem) then...`	Data Types, Strings (L07)	
#SWA	`if the type of member whichMember = #SWA then`	SWA (D15)	D6
SwapFileMeg	`[Memory]` `SwapFileMeg = megaBytes`	DIRECTOR.INI, Memory (D09)	Win-only, Appendix D
switchColorDepth	`set the switchColorDepth = TRUE |` `FALSE -- (Default is FALSE.)`	Color (D13)	Mac-only
#symbol	`if ilk (someItem, #symbol) then...`	Symbols (L05/L19)	
#symbol	See *getPropertyDescriptionList's* #format option.	Behaviors (L12)	D6
#*symbol* (used as property)	`set myList = [ #symbolName : value]`	Symbols, Lists (L06)	
symbol()	`set newSymbol =` `symbol("MakeMeASymbol")`	Symbols, Data Types (L05)	D6
symbolP()	`if symbolP (item) then...`	Symbols, Data Types (L05)	
#systemMac	`if the paletteRef of member whichMember = #systemMac then...`	Palettes (D13)	
#systemWin	`if the paletteRef of member whichMember = #systemWin then...`	Palettes (D13)	
#systemWinDir4	`if the paletteRef of member whichMember = #system WinDir4 then...`	Palettes (D13)	
TAB	`if the key = TAB then go frame` `"Elsewhere"`	Strings (L07), Keyboard (L10)	
tan	`set angleInRadians = tan(x)`	Math (L08)	

Table 18-1: Lingo Command and Keyword Summary (continued)

Keyword	Description or Example	See	Notes

tell	```tell the stage```
	  ```tell window 1```
	    ```go frame n```
	    ```end tell```
	  ```end tell```
	See *end tell, exit tell.*
		MIAWs (D06)	

tellStreamStatus	```tellStreamStatus (TRUE | FALSE)```
	```set showingStreamStatus =```
	```tellStreamStatus()```
	(Default is FALSE. See *on streamStatus.*)
		NetLingo Xtra (D11)	D6

#text (castmember type)	```if the castType of member whichMember```
	```= #text then...```
	```if the type of member whichMember =```
	```#text then... (D4 only)```
	See #field, #richText.
		Fields (D12)	D4/D5, D6

#text (track type)	```if trackType(member videoMember,```
	```whichTrack) = #text then...```
	```if trackType(sprite videoSprite,```
	```whichTrack) = #text then...```
		Video (D16)	

text	```set the text of member textMember =``` ```newText```	Fields, RichText, Buttons (D12)	
textAlign	```set the textAlign of field``` ```fieldMember = "center"	"left" |``` ```"right"``` (obsolete, use *alignment of member*)	Fields, Buttons (D12)	Obsolete
textFont	```set the textFont of field fieldMember``` ```= "fontName"``` (obsolete, use *font of member*)	Fields, Buttons (D12)	Obsolete

textHeight	```set the textHeight of field```
	```fieldMember = newHeight``` (obsolete,
	use *lineHeight of member*)
		Fields, Buttons (D12)	Obsolete

textSize	```set the textSize of field fieldMember``` ```= newSize``` (obsolete, use *fontSize of member*)	Fields, Buttons (D12)	Obsolete

textStyle	```set the textStyle of field```
	```fieldMember = newStyle``` (obsolete, use
	fontStyle of member)
		Fields, Buttons (D12)	Obsolete

the	```set the property {of object} = value``` ```put the property {of object}```	Lingo Properties, Lists, Variable (L01)	

Table 18-1: Lingo Command and Keyword Summary (continued)

Keyword	Description or Example	See	Notes

then	`if (expression) then`
	 `    statement(s)`
	 `end if`
		Lingo (L01)	

ticks	`set currentTime = the ticks`	Timers (L11)	Read-only
time	`put the {abbr{ev{iated}}} | long |` `short} time`	Timers (L11)	Read-only
#timeOut	See *call* and *on timeOut*.	Timers (L11)	
timeoutKeyDown	`set the timeoutKeyDown = TRUE | FALSE` (Default is TRUE.)	Timers (L11)	

timeoutLapsed	`if (the timeoutLapsed <`
	 `timeoutLength) then...`
	 `set the timeoutLapsed = nTicks`
		Timers (L11)	Settable. Table 17-1

timeoutLength	`set the timeoutLength = nTicks` `(Default is 10800.)`	Timers (L11)	
timeoutMouse	`set the timeoutMouse = TRUE | FALSE` `(Default is TRUE.)`	Timers (L11)	
timeoutPlay	`set the timeoutPlay = TRUE | FALSE` (Default is FALSE.)	Timers (L11)	
timeoutScript	`set the timeoutScript = "TimeOutAction"`	Timers (L11), Events	
timer	`set the timer = nTicks`	Timers (L11)	Settable. Table 17-1

timeScale of member	`put the timeScale of member`
	 `videoMember`
	 Differs with the digital video format and the platform. See Table 16-1.
		Timers, Video (D16) (L11)	Read-only, Differ Mac/Win

#title	`Alert (MUIinstance, [ #title:` `"string", ...]`	MUI Xtra (L15)	D6
title	`set the title of window whichWindow =` `"titleString"`	MIAWs (D06)	
titleVisible	`set the titleVisible of window` `whichWindow = TRUE | FALSE`	MIAWs (D06)	

to	`set variable to value`
	 `repeat with x = 1 {down} to 10`
	 `tell window whichWindow to action`
	 `put char 1 to 5 of "Macromedia"`
		Lingo, Variables, Loop, Strings (L01)	

Table 18-1: Lingo Command and Keyword Summary (continued)

Keyword	Description or Example	See	Notes
top of rect	`put the top of rect (left, top, right, bottom)`	Coords (D05)	Read-only
top of sprite	`put the top of sprite whichSprite`	Coords (D05)	Read-only
trace	`set the trace = TRUE | FALSE`	Debugging (L03)	
traceLoad	`set the traceLoad = 0 | 1 | 2`	Debugging (L03)	
traceLogFile	`set the traceLogFile = EMPTY | filePath`	Debugging (L03)	
track of member	`if the track of member videoMember = #video then...`	Video (D16)	Read-only, unsupported, Table 17-1
trackCount (member)	`put trackCount (member videoMember)`	Video (D16)	Read-only
trackCount (sprite)	`put trackCount (sprite videoSprite)`	Video (D16)	Read-only
trackEnabled (sprite)	`put trackEnabled (sprite videoSprite, whichTrack)`	Video (D16)	Read-only
tracking of sprite	`put the tracking of sprite btnEdSprite`	Button Editor Xtra (D14)	D6
trackNextKeyTime	`put trackNextKeyTime (sprite videoSprite, whichTrack)`	Video (D16)	Read-only
trackNextSample-Time	`put trackNextSampleTime (sprite videoSprite, whichTrack)`	Video (D16)	Read-only
trackPreviousKey-Time	`put trackPreviousKeyTime (sprite videoSprite, whichTrack)`	Video (D16)	Read-only
trackPreviousSam-pleTime	`put trackPreviousSampleTime (sprite videoSprite, whichTrack)`	Video (D16)	Read-only
tracks	`set trackCount = the tracks of member videoMember`	Video (D16)	Read-only, Unsupported, Table 17-1
trackStartTime (member)	`put trackStartTime (member videoMember, whichTrack)`	Video (D16)	Read-only
trackStartTime (sprite)	`put trackStartTime (sprite videoSprite, whichTrack)`	Video (D16)	Read-only
trackStopTime (member)	`put trackStopTime (member videoMember, whichTrack)`	Video (D16)	Read-only

Table 18-1: Lingo Command and Keyword Summary (continued)

Keyword	Description or Example	See	Notes
trackStopTime (sprite)	`put trackStopTime (sprite videoSprite, whichTrack)`	Video (D16)	Read-only
trackText	`put trackText (sprite videoSprite, whichTrack)`	Video (D16)	Read-only
trackType (member)	`put trackType (member videoMember, whichTrack)`	Video (D16)	Read-only
trackType (sprite)	`put trackType (sprite videoSprite, whichTrack)`	Video (D16)	Read-only
trails of sprite	`set the trails of sprite whichSprite = TRUE	FALSE`	Sprites, Inks (D13)	
#transition	`if the type of member whichMember = #transition then...`	Transitions (D03)	
transitionType of member	`set the transitionType of member transitionMember = transitionNum`	Transitions (D03)	Table 16-1
TRUE	`if (expression = TRUE) then...` `set the booleanProperty {of object} = TRUE`	Constants (L01)	
tweened	`set the tweened of sprite whichSprite = TRUE	FALSE`	Score (D03)	D6
type of member	`put the type of member whichMember {of castLib whichCastLib}` See *type of cast*	Casts (D04)	D6 vs. D4, Tables 16-1 and 17-2.
type of sprite	`set the type of sprite whichSprite = typeCode` Settable during Score Recording	Score (D03)	
"underline"	`set the fontStyle of member whichMember = "underline"` See menu item <U command	Fields, Buttons, Menu (D12)	
union	`if union (rect (left, top, right, bottom), the stageRect) = the stageRect then...`	Coords (D05)	
unLoad	`unLoad{toFrameNum}` (Unloads from current frame to specified frame, not only specified frame) `unLoad{fromFrameNum, toFrameNum}`	Memory (D09)	

Table 18-1: Lingo Command and Keyword Summary (continued)

Keyword	Description or Example	See	Notes
unLoadCast	unLoadCast {cast *whichMember*} (use *unLoadMember* instead) unLoadCast {cast *fromMember*, *toMember*}	Memory (D09)	Obsolete
unLoadMember	unLoadMember {member *whichMember* {of castLib *whichCastLib*}} unLoadMember {member *fromMember* {of castLib *whichCastLib*}, member *toMember* {of castLib *whichCastLib*}}	Memory (D09)	
unLoadMovie	unLoadMovie *whichMovie*	Memory (D09)	URL
updateFrame	updateFrame	Score (D03)	
updateLock	set the updateLock = TRUE | FALSE	Stage (D03)	
updateMovieEnabled	set the updateMovieEnabled = TRUE | FALSE	External Files (L14)	Avoid from Projectors.
updateStage	puppetSound "mySound", 2 updateStage (Redraws stage, triggers sounds, and triggers transitions.)	Stage, Puppets (D01)	
URL	set the URL of member *swaMember* = *url*	SWA (D15)	D6, URL
userName	alert "Hello" && the userName Authoring-time only; see Table 17-1. Unsupported.	Authoring (D08)	Read-only, D5, D6
value	set *myNumber* = value(*someString*)	Data Types, Math (D08)	
version	global version put version Differs during Shockwave and Authoring (see *the productVersion*).	Runtime Environment (D08/L01)	SW, Table 16-1
version (FileIO Xtra)	set *fileIOXtraVersion* = version (xtra "FileIO")	FileIO Xtra (L14)	
#VGA	if the paletteRef of member *whichMember* = #VGA then...	Palettes (D13)	
#video	if trackType(member *videoMember*, *whichTrack*) = #video then... if trackType(sprite *videoSprite*, *whichTrack*) = #video then... if the track of member *videoMember* = #video then	Video (D16)	

Table 18-1: Lingo Command and Keyword Summary (continued)

Keyword	Description or Example	See	Notes
video of member	`set the video of member videoMember =` `TRUE | FALSE`	Video (D16)	

#videoForWindows	`if the digitalVideoType of member`
	`videoMember = #videoForWindows then..`
	`.`
		Video (D16)	Read-only

videoForWindow- sPresent	`if not (the videoForWindowsPresent)` `then put "Can't play AVI"`	Video (D16)	Read-only
visibility of sprite	`set the visibility of sprite` `whichSprite = TRUE | FALSE`	Sprites (D04)	Unsupported
visible of sprite	`set the visible of sprite whichSprite` `= TRUE | FALSE`	Sprites (D04)	

visible of window	`set the visible of window whichWindow`
	`= TRUE | FALSE`
	`set the visible of the stage = TRUE |`
	`FALSE (undocumented)`
		MIAW (D06)	Table 17-1

#vivid	`if the paletteRef of member` `whichMember = #vivid then...`	Palettes (D13)	
#void	`if ilk(someItem, #void) then...`	Data Types (L05)	

VOID
void()
the void
	`set someVariable = VOID`
	`if (someVariable = the void) then...`
	`set someObject = void()`
		Data Types
		(L05)
			Fixed in D6.01

\<VOID>	Returned for uninitialized globals in D4 and D5
	To create a void value in D4 or D5
	`set voidValue = value ("<Void>")`
	or
	`global void`
	`set voidValue = void`
		Data Types
		(L05)
			Obsolete ,
			unsupported

voidP	`if voidP(item) then...`	Data Types (L05)	

volume of member	`set the volume of member swaMember =`
	`n`
	0 <= n <= 255
		SWA (D15)	D6, Table 16-1

volume of sound	`set the volume of sound soundChannel`
	`= n`
	0 <= n <= 255
		Sound (D15)	Table 16-1

Table 18-1: Lingo Command and Keyword Summary (continued)

Keyword	Description or Example	See	Notes
volume of sprite	`set the volume of sprite videoSprite = n` 0 <= n <= 255 (higher settings cause distortion)	Video (D16)	Table 16-1
volumeLevel of sprite	`set the volumeLevel of sprite quickTime3Sprite = n` 0 <= n <= 255 (higher settings cause distortion)	QuickTime3 Xtra (D16)	D6.5
when...then	`when keyDown	mouseDown then action` (Obsolete; use `on keyDown, on timeOut, on mouseDown`.)	Events	Obsolete

while, repeat	`repeat while (expression)`
	   `statement(s)`
	`end repeat`
		Lingo (L01)	

WIDTH	`WIDTH="numPixels"`	HTML (D11)	
width of member	`put the width of member whichMember`	Coords (D05)	Read-only
width of rect	`put the width of rect (left, top, right, bottom)` `put the width of the stageRect`	Coords, MIAW (D05)	Read-only
width of sprite	`set the width of sprite whichSprite = newWidth` (set *the rect of sprite* instead)	Coords (D05)	Read-only
#window	`if ilk(item, #window) then...`	MIAWs (D06)	
window	`set the property of window whichWindow = value`	MIAWs (D06)	
window	See *close window, open window, forget window, moveToFront, moveToBack.*	MIAWs (D06)	
windowList	`put the windowList` Use *open window* and *forget window* to add items to and delete items from *the windowList*. Do not add or delete items using the list functions.	MIAWs, Lists (D06)	Read-only
WindowOperation()	`WindowOperation(MUInstance, #center | #hide | #show | #tipsOn | #tipsOff | #zoom)`	MUI Xtra (L21)	D6
windowPresent	`put windowPresent("windowName")`	MIAWs (D06)	Read-only
"Windows,16"	`if the platform = "Windows,16" then..`	Runtime (D08)	Win-only

Table 18-1: Lingo Command and Keyword Summary (continued)

Keyword	Description or Example	See	Notes
"Windows,32"	`if the platform = "Windows,32" then..` `.`	Runtime (D08)	Win-only
windowType	`set the windowType of window` `whichWindow = windowType` See Chapter 6, in *Director in a Nutshell* for details on the windowTypes.	MIAWs (D06)	Differs Mac/ Win, Table 16-1
WinG	`[Graphics]` `WinG = 0 │ 1`	DIRECTOR.INI (LD)	Win 3.1, Appendix D
with	See *repeat with...to* and *repeat with. ..in.*	Lingo Loops (L01)	
within	See *sprite...within.*	Coords (D05)	
word...of	`set word firstWord {to lastWord} of` `chunkExpression = newValue`	Fields, Strings (L07)	
word...of, last	`delete the last word of` `chunkExpression` `put the last word of chunkExpression`	Fields, Strings (L07)	Can delete, but not set
words	`put the number of words in` `chunkExpression`	Strings (L07)	Read-only
wordWrap	`set the wordWrap of member` `fieldMember = TRUE │ FALSE`	Fields (D12)	
"write" or "?write"	`set fileXObjInst = FileIO (mNew,` `"write", fileName)`	FileIO XObject (L14)	Obsolete
writeChar()	`writeChar (fileIOinstance, someChar)`	FileIO Xtra (L14)	
writeString()	`writeString (fileIOinstance,` `someString)`	FileIO Xtra (L14)	
XCMDglue	XCMDglue allows Director to use XFCNs and XCMDs	XCMDs (L13)	Obsolete
xFactoryList	`xFactoryList (whichLibrary)`	XObjects (L13)	Obsolete
#xtra	`if ilk(xtra "FileIO", #xtra) then...` `if the type of member whichMember =` `#xtra then...`	Xtras, Member Types (L13)	D5, D6
xtra "*XtraName*"	`set xtraInstance = new (xtra` `"XtraName"),`	Xtras (L13)	D5, D6
xtra, name of	`put the name of xtra whichXtraNumber`	Xtras (L13)	D5, D6
<Xtra child>	`put new (xtra "FileIO")` `-- <Xtra child "FileIO" 1 21341fa>`	Object Type (L13)	D5, D6
xtras, number of	`put the number of xtras`	Xtras (L13)	D5, D6

Table 18-1: Lingo Command and Keyword Summary (continued)

Keyword	Description or Example	See	Notes
#YesNo	`Alert(`*MUIinstance*`, [#buttons: #YesNo, ...])`	MUI Xtra (L15)	D6, Table 16-1
#YesNoCancel	`Alert(`*MUIinstance*`, [#buttons: #YesNoCancel, ...])`	MUI Xtra (L15)	D6, Table 16-1
zoomBox	`zoomBox` *startSprite, endSprite* `{,` *delayTicks*`}`	Sprites, Transitions (D03)	
#zoomWindow	See *call* and *on zoomWindow*.	MIAWs (D06)	Not for SW

CHAPTER 19

The Lingo Symbol Table

Director maintains a hidden table containing every keyword or "symbol" in use. In this context, *symbol* denotes any word Director recognizes, including "true" *Lingo symbols* that begin with a pound sign (#). (Refer to Chapter 18, *Lingo Keyword and Command Summary*.) In point of fact, all recognized keywords are converted to symbols for storage in the *Symbol Table*. Thus, the keyword *mouseUp* is stored internally as *#mouseUp*. See *"Symbols"* in Chapter 5, *Data Types and Expressions*, for the party line regarding true Lingo symbols, which I will refer to as "Lingo symbols" in this chapter to indicate those items traditionally thought of as symbols.

The Symbol Table includes built-in symbols and keywords defined by Director itself, and symbols, variable names, handlers, and so on, defined by the programmer.

See the downloadable Chapter 22, *Symbol Table Archaeology*, at *http://www.zeusprod.com/nutshell/chapters/symtable.html* for many more details.

Why Do I Care?

You can use the Symbol Table for some neat stuff (which is what being a geek is all about).

- Verify whether Director recognizes a particular keyword. This is useful when there is a typographical error in the documentation. For example, the FileIO Xtra's documentation claims that it supports a method called *getOSdir*, which is actually named *getOSdirectory*. You can verify that *getOSdir* is *not* recognized by Director and therefore not a valid keyword.

- Avoid overflowing the Symbol Table (applies only to Windows 3.1). If your movie suddenly starts behaving very oddly under Windows 3.1, you may have created too many symbols.

- Examine the Symbol Table to find heretofore undocumented (and unsupported) Lingo commands to impress your friends. See Table 17-1.

- Perform some Director archaeology. The Symbol Table can tell you when a command was added to Director. For example, the *deleteAll* command documented in D6 has been around since D4.

- Finally understand why symbols don't always show up in the case that you want them to (and possibly fix individual symbols). See "Symbol Table Entries' Case."

- Make an educated guess as to whether a particular Sprite Asset Xtra (such as the Flash Asset Xtra) is installed (*the number of xtras* reports only Lingo scripting Xtras). See "Determining a Sprite Asset Xtra's Presence."

Symbol Table Entries' Case

Symbols in the Symbol Table are *case-insensitive*, so #BaNaNa is the same as #banana. The case of a given symbol is determined by the case of its first use.

Example 19-1: The Fixed Case of Symbols

If you define a symbol using:

```
set myList = [#abc: 1]
```

the symbol #abc will forever be stored in lowercase. Therefore:

```
put #ABC
-- #abc
put string (#AbC)
-- "abc"
```

See the downloadable Chapter 22 for details on changing the case of a symbol.

Entries in the Symbol Table don't actually include the pound sign (#), but Lingo thinks of them as symbols.

 The Symbol Table merely includes a list of keywords. It does not indicate the exact syntax for using the keyword, or even whether the keyword is a Lingo symbol, handler name, command, or function.

Symbol Table Entry Numbers

Entries in the Symbol Table are in chronological order. The built-in symbols come first, followed by symbols defined by Xtras and the user-defined symbols as they are declared or used. The default Symbol Table reveals Director's history as would an archaeological dig. You can determine exactly when a symbol was added based on its position in the default symbol table. See downloadable Chapter 22.

Determining the Size of the Current Symbol Table

Director defines about 750 symbols, but hundreds, even thousands, of entries may have been added beyond the built-in ones. To determine the number of symbols, test the value of a new symbol name that you know to be unique (the "+ *0*" is required to fool Director into translating a symbol to its integer position in the Symbol Table):

```
put #unusedSymbolName + 0
--1450
```

This test adds the symbol to the end of table if it is unique. In either case, for subsequent tests, you need to make up a fresh, unique symbol.

Determining a Symbol's Presence and Number

To determine an existing symbol's number, in Director 4.0 or later, use the following in the Message window :

```
put #symbolName + 0
--800
```

If the resulting integer is less than the number returned for *#unusedSymbolName,* above it is a built-in symbol. Otherwise, it is either a symbol that has been added by an Xtra or your Lingo code. Or it may be a new symbol that is added to the end of the Symbol Table (by virtue of your using it) and assigned a number one greater than the previous existing symbol. Example 19-2 determines whether a symbol exists. Keep in mind that checking whether a symbol exists also adds that symbol. This handler determines the last symbol in use when it is first called and arbitrarily uses that as the cut-off point for whether a symbol is "new."

Example 19-2: Checking If a Symbol Exists

```
on existingSymbol symbolName
  global gInitialSymbolCount
  -- Record the last symbol defined when first called
  if voidP(gInitialSymbolCount ) then
    set newSymbol = symbol ("uniqueSymbol" & the ticks)
    set gInitialSymbolCount = (newSymbol + 0)
  end if
  -- Compare the number of the new symbol to "last symbol"
  set checkSymbol = (symbol(symbolName) + 0)
  if  checkSymbol < gInitialSymbolCount  then
    return TRUE
  else
    return FALSE
  end if
end existingSymbol
```

Determining a Sprite Asset Xtra's Presence

The *showXlib* function and *the number of xtras* property show only Lingo scripting Xtras (See Chapter 13, *Lingo Xtras and XObjects*). At runtime, you can use *the netPresent* property (see Table 17-1) to determine whether the NetLingo and

NetFile Xtras are installed, but there is no Lingo command to determine if a Sprite Asset Xtra is installed.

To determine if a Sprite Asset Xtra is installed, you can try to create a cast member. If it fails, then the Xtra is not installed. (An enterprising develop could create an Xtra that queries Director for all known Xtras installed and returns a complete list including Sprite Asset Xtras.)

Example 19-3: Checking If an Asset Xtra is Installed

```
on assetXtraInstalled assetType
   -- Try to create a new cast member
   set asset = new (assetType)
   if ilk(asset) = #member then
      -- Erase it when done
      erase asset
      return TRUE
   else
      -- Failure returns error code -2147219501
      -- "MOA core error: XAsset type unknown"
      -- See MoaErrorToString() in MUI Xtra
      return FALSE
   end if
end assetXtraInstalled
```

This example checks if the Flash Sprite Asset Xtra is installed:

```
put assetXtraInstalled(#flash)
-- 1
```

This example checks if the Alphamania Sprite Xtra is installed:

```
put assetXtraInstalled(#alpha)
-- 0
```

There were some problems in D6.0 in which *new(#symbolName)* always returned *#symbolName*. You might instead try using the *existingSymbol()* handler in Example 19-2 to see if the symbols(s) used by the sprite Xtra are defined. For example, the Flash Asset Xtra creates cast members whose *type of member* property is *#flash*. If *#flash* is recognized by *existingSymbol()*, there is a good chance that the Flash Asset Xtra is installed, but only a FALSE response from *existingSymbol()* is truly reliable. It will return an erroneous TRUE value if any symbol with the same name as the asset's type has been defined elsewhere. You might try checking other unique symbols known to be used by the Xtra or multiple symbols to increase the likelihood of an accurate determination.

Symbol Table Limits and Limiting the Symbol Table

The Symbol Table is essentially unlimited on the Macintosh and in the 32-bit version of Director for Windows (Windows 95 and NT).

The Symbol Table under Windows 3.1 (and 16-bit Projectors run under Windows 95 or NT) is limited to 64 KB of data. The cumulative growth of the Symbol Table in earlier versions of Director caused this limit to be exceeded even for movies using relatively few symbols.

A large number of symbols (approximately 5000) can exceed the 64 KB limit and overflow the Symbol Table. (See "Determining the Symbols Used in a Director Movie" in Chapter 22.) For a dated explanation of overflowing the Lingo Symbol Table see *http://www.updatestage.com/previous/960927.html#item4*.

The actual number of symbols allowed depends on the length of the symbols' names (if your symbols average more than 13 characters, the limit will be less than 5000). If you have a very large project and are encountering unexpected "Index Too Big" or "Handler Not Defined" errors, try the following:

- Use fewer unique symbols
  - Delete unneeded variables, properties, and handler names.
  - Reuse names for local variables whenever possible.
  - Use integers, floats, and literal strings instead of symbols and variables.
  - Use a single global list instead of multiple, separate global variables.
  - Use property variables instead of separately named variables.
  - Remove unneeded Xtras.
- Use shorter variable, handler. and symbol names
- Clean up the movie symbol list (see Chapter 22 for details)

 Aoid using any of the keywords in Table 18-1 as *handler* names, as they could inadvertently override a built-in Lingo handler of the same name.

You *can* use variables, handlers, properties, and symbols of the same name, although doing so may be confusing to humans (but not to Director).

PART VI

Appendixes

APPENDIX A

ASCII Codes and Key Codes

Table A-1 shows the most common non-standardized characters you'll need. Table A-2 shows ASCII values only up to 127; above 127 the characters differ drastically by font and platform. Use the Macintosh *Key Caps* desk accessory or the Windows *Character Map* utility (under the Windows 95 *Start* menu under Programs►Accessories) to view various characters in different fonts. Refer to the font and character-mapping capability of FONTMAP.TXT covered in Chapter 12, *Text and Fields*, in *Director in a Nutshell*, or print out your own ASCII table as shown in Example A-1.

Table A-1: Nonstandardized ASCII Codes

Symbol	Macintosh[1]	Windows[2]	HTML[3]
Copyright (©)	Option-g or *numToChar(169)*	Alt+0-1-6-9 or *numToChar(169)*	© or ©
Registered (®)	Option-r or *numToChar(168)*	Alt+0-1-7-4 or *numToChar(174)*	® or ®
Trademark (™)	Option-2 or *numToChar(170)*	Alt+0-1-5-3 or *numToChar(153)*	&#153;
Checkmark (✓)[4]	Option-v or *numToChar(195)*	Alt+0-1-9-5 or *numToChar(195)*	N/A
Menu action (Å)[5]	Option-x or *numToChar(197)*	Alt+0-1-9-7 or *numToChar(197)*	N/A

[1] On the Macintosh you can create extended characters using the Option key.
[2] Under Windows. you can create ASCII characters by holding down the Alt key while typing in their ASCII code on the numeric keypad with *Num Lock* on (that is, Alt+6-5 will create a capital "A").
[3] The HTML codes are unrelated to Director or Shockwave, and they may not be supported by some browsers. The numeric codes are more likely to be supported than the equivalent names.

Example A-1 prints the specified portion of the ASCII table.

Example A-1: ASCII Table Printout

```
on asciiTable startNum, endNum
  if voidP(startNum) then set startNum = 0
  if voidP(endNum)  then set endNum  = 255
  repeat with n = startNum to endNum
    put n && numToChar (n)
  end repeat
end asciiTable
```

```
asciiTable (0, 127)   -- This prints chars 0 to 127
```

Example A-2 checks whether the character passed in is an alphabetic character (either uppercase or lowercase). You can use this to screen nonalphabetic characters from user input. Note that the ASCII codes for "A" to "Z" are 65 through 90 and the codes for "a" to "z" are 97 through 122.

Example A-2: Test for Alpha Character

```
on isAlpha testChar
  set asciiNum = charToNum (testChar)
  -- Uppercase A to Z
  if asciiNum >= 65 and asciiNum <= 90 then
    return TRUE
  -- Lowercase A to Z
  else if asciiNum >= 97 and asciiNum <= 122 then
    return TRUE
  else
    return FALSE
  end if
end isAlpha
```

```
set x = "a"
put isAlpha (x)
-- 1
```

See also Examples C-3 and C-4 in Appendix C, *Case-Sensitivity, Sort Order, Diacritical Marks, and Space-Sensitivity*, for details on converting between uppercase and lowercase.

Example A-3 checks whether the character passed in is a numeric character (not an integer digit). You can use this to screen non-numeric characters from user input.

Example A-3: Test for Alpha Digit

```
    on isDigit testChar
      set thisCode = charToNum (testChar)
      if thisCode >= charToNum ("0") and ¬
```

```
         thisCode <= charToNum ("9") then
      return TRUE
   else
      return FALSE
   end if
end isDigit
```

Note that the ASCII codes for the digits '0" through "9" are 48 through 57. Example A-3 is designed for readability; for speed, you should use:

```
on isDigitFast testChar
   set thisCode = charToNum (testChar)
   if thisCode >= 48 and thisCode <= 57 then
     return TRUE
   else
      return FALSE
   end if
end isDigitFast
```

In Table A-2, the column labeled *key* is the value returned by the Lingo property *the key* when a given key is pressed. The column labeled *keyCode* is the value returned by the Lingo property *the keyCode* when a given key is pressed. The column labeled *ASCII* is the corresponding ASCII value. Convert between *the key* and the ASCII code as follows:

```
set asciiCode  = charToNum(the key)
set whatsMyCode = numToChar(n)   -- where 0 <= n <= 255
put numToChar(65)
-- "A"
put charToNum("A")
-- 65
```

The following always returns 13 from the Message window because the last key pressed is the RETURN key sent when you type the command.

```
put charToNum(the key)
-- 13
```

Refer to *Tables 10-8, 10-9,* and *10-10* in Chapter 10, *Keyboard Events,* for summaries of the editing keys, numeric keypad, and function keys. Examples throughout that chapter show how to trap those keys. See also *Example 10-14,* "Your Own KeyCode Tester," to determine *the keyCode* or character returned by a specific key or key combination including modifier keys.

Table A-2: ASCII Codes and Key Codes

key	ASCII	keyCode
EMPTY or NULL	0	N/A
Ctrl-A	1	0
Ctrl-B	2	11

key	ASCII	keyCode
Ctrl-C	3	8
Enter (keypad)	3	76
Ctrl-D	4	2
Ctrl-E	5	14
Ctrl-F	6	3
g	7	5
Ctrl-H	8	4
Delete (Backspace)	8	51
Ctrl-I	9	34
Tab	9	48
Ctrl-J	10	38
Line Feed	10	N/A
Ctrl-K	11	40
Ctrl-L	12	37
Ctrl-M	13	46
Return (main keyboard)	13	36
Ctrl-N	14	45
Ctrl-O	15	31
Ctrl-P	16	35
Ctrl-Q	17	12
Ctrl-R	18	15
Ctrl-S	19	1
Ctrl-T	20	17
Ctrl-U	21	32
Ctrl-V	22	9
Ctrl-W	23	13
Ctrl-X	24	7
Ctrl-Y	25	16
Ctrl-Z	26	6

key	ASCII	keyCode
Escape	27	53
Left Arrow	28	123
Right Arrow	29	124
Up Arrow	30	126
Down Arrow	31	125
Space	32	49
!	33	18
"	34	39
#	35	20
$	36	21
%	37	23
&	38	26
'	39	39
(	40	25
)	41	29
*	42	28
+	43	24
,	44	43
-	45	27
.	46	47
/	47	44
0	48	29
1	49	18
2	50	19
3	51	20
4	52	21
5	53	23
6	54	22
7	55	26

Table A-2: ASCII Codes and Key Codes (continued)

key	ASCII	keyCode
8	56	28
9	57	25
:	58	41
;	59	41
<	60	43
=	61	24
>	62	47
?	63	44
@	64	19
A	65	0
B	66	11
C	67	8
D	68	2
E	69	14
F	70	3
G	71	5
H	72	4
I	73	34
J	74	38
K	75	40
L	76	37
M	77	46
N	78	45
O	79	31
P	80	35
Q	81	12
R	82	15
S	83	1
T	84	17

key	ASCII	keyCode
U	85	32
V	86	9
W	87	13
X	88	7
Y	89	16
Z	90	6
[	91	33
\	92	42
]	93	30
^	94	22
_	95	27
`	96	50
a	97	0
b	98	11
c	99	8
d	100	2
e	101	14
f	102	3
g	103	5
h	104	4
i	105	34
j	106	38
k	107	40
l	108	37
m	109	46
n	110	45
o	111	31
p	112	35
q	113	12

ASCII Codes

key	ASCII	keyCode
r	114	15
s	115	1
t	116	17
u	117	32
v	118	9
w	119	13
x	120	7
y	121	16
z	122	6
{	123	33
		124	42
}	125	30
~	126	50
Del (keypad)	127	117

APPENDIX B

Changes in D6 Through D6.5

New Lingo in Director 6.5

Director 6.5 was released as this book was going to press. The core application is the same as Director 6.0.2, but many new Xtras are now included.

The D6.5 upgrade is very reasonably priced, considering the boat-load of new Xtras and the features it includes (*http://www.macrome-dia.com/software/director/productinfo/newfeatures/*).

This appendix lists the Lingo for the QuickTime 3 Asset, Flash Asset, and Custom Cursor Xtras. Director in a Nutshell provides details on these Xtras, and the ActiveX (Windows only), Aftershock, Java Export, and PowerPoint Import Xtras included with D6.5. To print out a list of methods for applicable Xtras, use the following:

```
put mMessageList ("ActiveX")
put mMessageList ("JavaConvert")
put mMessageList ("QuickTimeSupport")
```

See also the Help files in HTML format that come with D6.5.

These unsupported Xtras also come with Director 6.5:

```
put mMessageList ("FileXtra")
put mMessageList ("UiHelper")
```

QuickTime 3 Sprite Asset Xtra

Table B-1 lists the QT3 Xtras you'll need for authoring and distribution. Windows 3.1 and 68K are not supported by the Xtra (and Windows 3.1 is not supported by QuickTime 3 at all). All versions require D6.5.

Table B-1: QuickTime 3 Xtras

Projectors	Xtra Name
Power Macintosh Authoring	QuickTime Asset Options PPC
Power Macintosh Distribution (Projectors or Shockwave)	QuickTime Asset PPC
Windows 32-bit Authoring	QuickTime Asset Options.x32
Windows 32-bit Distribution (Projectors or Shockwave)	QuickTime Asset.x32

Getting the Xtra to work:

- The QT3 Xtra requires at least 15 MB allocated to Director on the PPC. Although Projectors seem to work with the default allocation (< 7.5 MB) you should consider increasing it when using QuickTime 3.

- QTVR 1.0 panoramas may not work with the QT3 Asset Xtra. Update your QTVR panoramas to QTVR 2.0 or higher. On the Macintosh, Macromedia recommends deleting all old versions of QTVR and QT-related extensions and doing a clean install of QT3.

- Add the following to your DIRECTOR.INI file (or see the DIRECTOR.INI that comes with the QT3 Xtra) to use QT3's sound mixing capability under Windows.

```
[sound]
DLL = "QMix.dll"
```

 Macromedia currently advises using *DLLName* = *"Macromix.DLL"* for the sound mixer instead of *QMix.DLL*. But the *Macromix.DLL* file that shipped with D6.5 was buggy. At press time Macromedia promised a fix imminently. See Chapters 15 and 16 in *Director in a Nutshell* for the latest information.

The QT3 Asset Xtra provides new Lingo commands and properties, but all existing digital video commands (with minor exceptions noted) also work with media inserted as QuickTime 3 cast members. See the *Show Me 6_5/ QT3/qt3_showme.dir* that comes with D6.5. Also see Macromedia's Web site, and Chapter 16, *Digital Video*, in *Director in a Nutshell* for more details on the QuickTime 3 Asset Xtra's capabilities.

QuickTime 3 from Apple implements many features that are not available in the first release of the QT3 Xtra from Macromedia. See *http://quicktime.apple.com//*.

Table B-2 lists only the properties that are new for QT3 cast members or behave differently with QT3 cast members than standard *#digitalVideo* cast members. Consult Chapter 4, *CastLibs, Cast Members, and Sprites*, and Chapter 16 in *Director in a Nutshell* for details on other digital video castmember and sprite properties. See also the HTML documentation that comes with the QT3 Xtra. In Table B-2, it is implicit that each property takes the form:

        the *property* of member *qt3Member*

and/or

        the *property* of sprite *qt3Sprite*

Note that sprite properties override any member property of the same name on a per-sprite basis. The default, if any, is shown in *italics* in the *Value* column. Because QT3 imports many media types, not all commands and properties are applicable for all media types.

To create a QT3 cast member, choose `Insert`➤`Media Element` ➤`QuickTime 3`, not `File`➤`Import`.

See Chapter 16 in *Director in a Nutshell* for details on the media types that Quick-Time 3 can import (and there are many).

Table B-2: QuickTime 3 Asset Xtra Properties

Command	Value	Read-only	Member	Sprite	Notes
center	TRUE | *FALSE*		•		See *crop* = TRUE.
controller	TRUE | *FALSE*		•		See *directToStage* = TRUE.
crop	TRUE | *FALSE*		•		See *center, scale, translation*. If *crop* is FALSE, movie is scaled to sprite box
digitalVideoType	#quickTime	•	•		See *trackType, type*.
directToStage	*TRUE* | FALSE		•		See *controller, mask*.
duration	measured in ticks	•	•	•	See *mTime, movieTime*.

Table B-2: QuickTime 3 Asset Xtra Properties (continued)

Command	Value	Read-only	Member	Sprite	Notes
fileName[1]	stringPath		•		Path is absolute by default; Add "@" to file path to make it relative
frameRate of member	0 | -1 | -2 | n		•		See mRate and movieRate.
invertMask	TRUE | FALSE		•		See mask.
isVRmovie	TRUE | FALSE	•	•	•	See VRNodeType.
loop	TRUE | FALSE		•		See loopBounds.
loopBounds	[startTicks, endTicks]			•	[0, 0] indicates no loopBounds.
mask	member oneBitMember		•		Set to 1-bit cast member or zero to disable; see directToStage = TRUE
mouseLevel	#none | #controller | #all | #share			•	See VRTriggerCallback.
mRate[2]	0 - n, default is 1.0			•	Use mRate for Shockwave, instead of movieRate. See pausedAtStart.
mTime	measured in ticks			•	Use mTime for Shockwave, instead of movieTime.
movieRate[2]	0 - n, default is 1.0			•	Use mRate instead for QT3 sprites.
movieTime	measured in ticks by default			•	Use mTime instead for QT3 sprites.
regPoint	point (x,y)		•		Defaults to center.
rotation	0.0 to 360.0 degrees (default is 0)		•	•	
scale	[xScale, yScale] default is [100.0, 100.0]		•	•	See crop = TRUE.
sound	TRUE | FALSE		•		Ignored if frameRate not 0 (sync to soundtrack)
timeScale	units/second	•	•	•	Defaults to 600 for QT on Mac.
translation	[hPixels, vPixels]		•	•	See crop = TRUE.
type	#QuickTimeMedia	•	•		See digitalVideoType.

Table B-2: QuickTime 3 Asset Xtra Properties (continued)

Command	Value	Read-only	Member	Sprite	Notes
video	*TRUE* | FALSE		•		See *sound*.
volume	0 to 255 (or higher)[3]			•	Always reports 0 for QT3; see *volumeLevel*.
volumeLevel	0 to 255 (or higher)[3]			•	Replaces *volume* for QT3 sprites.
VRFieldOfView	*degrees*			•	Current field of view.
VRHotSpotEnterCallback	*#enterHotspot* | 0			•	on *enterHotspot* me, *hotSpotID* *actions* end
VRHotSpotExitCallback	*#exitHotspot* | 0			•	on *exitHotspot* me, *hotSpotID* *actions* end
VRMotionQuality	#minQuality | #maxQuality | #normalQuality			•	See *VRStaticQuality*.
VRMovedCallback	*#movedVR* | 0			•	on *movedVR* me *actions* end
VRNode	*nodeID*			•	Current node ID being displayed.
VRNodeEnterCallback	*#nodeEnter* | 0			•	on *nodeEnter* me, *nodeID* *actions* end

VRNodeExitCallback	*#nodeExit* | 0			•	on *nodeExit* me, *oldNode*, *newNode*
					    actions
					    return 0 | 1
					end
					0: cancel (not implemented)
					1: allow (go to new node)

VRNodeType	#panorama | #object | #unknown	•		•	#unknown means non-QTVR; see *isVRMovie*.
VRPan	*degrees*			•	See *VRTilt*.
VRStaticQuality	#minQuality | #maxQuality | #normalQuality			•	See *VRMotionQuality*.

Table B-2: QuickTime 3 Asset Xtra Properties (continued)

Command	Value	Read-only	Member	Sprite	Notes
VRTilt	*degrees*			•	See *VRPan*.
VRTriggerCallback	*#triggerVR* | 0			•	*MouseLevel* must be *#all* or *#share*, not *#none* or *#controller*. on *triggerVR* me, *hotSpotID* *actions* return 0 | 1 end 0: cancel (not implemented) 1: continue
VRWarpMode	#none | #partial | #full			•	See *VRStaticQuality, VRMotion-Quality*.

[1] The default *fileName* is an absolute path. Add the "@" operator to the beginning of the path in the QuickTime 3 cast member properties dialog to create a relative path.
[2] The *mRate* and *movieRate* return 0 if *the frameRate of member* is not 0 (Sync to soundtrack).
[3] Setting *the volumeLevel* or *volume* higher than 255 causes distortion.

Table B-3 lists the new and important QuickTime 3 functions. See Chapter 16 in *Director in a Nutshell* for details, and more on the track-specific commands.

Table B-3: QuickTime 3 Asset Xtra Commands and Functions

Command	Member	Sprite
CanUseQuicktimeStreaming()[1]		
IsUsingQuicktimeStreaming()[1]		
mMessageList (xtra "QuicktimeSupport")		
new (#QuickTimeMedia)		
QuickTimeVersion()[2]		
trackCount(member *qtMember*) trackCount(sprite *qtSprite*)	•	•
trackEnabled(sprite *qtSprite*), *track*)		•
trackText(sprite *qtSprite*), *track*)		•
trackType(member *qtMember, track*)) trackType(sprite *qtSprite, track*)) = #video | #sound | #text | #music | #unknown	•	•

Command	Member	Sprite
UseQuicktimeStreaming(TRUE | FALSE)[1]		
VRNudge (sprite *qtvrSprite*, #left | #upLeft | #up | #upRight | #right | #down-Right | #down | #downLeft)		•

[1] Not implemented and "extremely unsupported" in the initial release of the QT3 Xtra, according to Macromedia.

[2] Supplements *the quickTimePresent* property. *QuickTimeVersion()* returns 3.000 if QT3 is installed under Windows, or 2.0 if only prior versions are installed under Windows. On the Macintosh, it either returns 3.000 or causes an error because the QuickTime 3 Xtra doesn't load unless QT3 is installed. See Chapter 16 in *Director in a Nutshell* for complete details on detecting the installed QuickTime version(s).

QTVR 1.0 Xtra

The QT3 Sprite Xtra can import QTVR 2.0 panorama or object movies as one of its many supported media types, but it won't work with QTVR 1.0 movies nor support all platforms. The separate QTVR 1.0 Xtra supports QTVR 1.0 files on Director 5 and Director 6 (and also supports 68K Macs and Windows 3.1 but does not work with Shockwave).

The QTVR Xtra is a Lingo Scripting Xtra, not a Sprite Asset Xtra, although QT3 Asset Xtra supports importing QTVR 2.0 assets.

The QTVR Xtra's full documentation and examples can be found under the *Macromedia: QTVR Xtra* folder on the D6 CD. Table B-4 shows only a few of the commands. Notice that a QTVR 1.0 file is opened via Lingo, not stored as a cast member or used in the Score. Note that the QTVR 1.0 Xtra uses strings in many places instead of symbols, integers, and so on. For example, the QTVROpen command requires the window dimensions as a string of four integers.

Table B-4: QTVR 1.0 Xtra commands

Command	Notes
QTVREnter (xtra "QTVRXtra")	Call once to initialize the Xtra.
set *instance* = new (xtra "QTVRXtra")	Create an instance.
put mMessageList (xtra "QTVRXtra")	Display documentation.
QTVRExit (xtra "QTVRXtra")	Close the Xtra.
QTVROpen(instance, "*vrMovie.mov*", "*left,top,right,bottom*", "visible" | "invisible")	Opens QTVR in specified rectangle; returns error string, or EMPTY for success.

Flash Asset Xtra

The Flash Asset Xtra allows Director to play Flash 2 files. Support for Flash 3 files in Director has not yet been announced, although Flash 3 files can be played in a browser via the separate Shockwave for Flash plug-in. As of May 1998, the latest

Flash Asset Xtra revision is 1.0.2 (which ships with Director 6.5). It is used along with the PowerLine Xtra to import shape objects and gradients from PowerPoint and reproduce them as Flash Assets in Director.

To import a Flash 2 filet, use `Insert➤Media Element➤Shockwave Flash Movie`, not `File➤Import`.

Table B-5 lists the Xtras you'll need for authoring and distribution of Flash files (Windows 3.1 and 68K are not supported). The playback version of the Xtra is included in the recent versions of the Shockwave for Director download from Macromedia's site. D6.0.1 or later is required.

The Xtra does not create Flash files. Macromedia Flash version 2.0 or 3.0 is required separately to create .SWF files. See also the new Flash Generator.

Table B-5: Flash Asset Xtras

Projectors	Xtra Name
Power Macintosh Authoring	Flash Asset Options PPC
Power Macintosh Distribution (Projectors or Shockwave)	Flash Asset PPC
Windows 32-bit Authoring	Flash Asset Options.x32
Windows 32-bit Distribution (Projectors or Shockwave)	Flash Asset.x32

Table B-6 shows sprite and castmember properties for Flash Assets. It is implicit that each property takes the form:

> the *property* of member *flashMember*

and/or

> the *property* of sprite *flashSprite*

Note that sprite properties override any member property of the same name on a per-sprite basis. The default, if any, is shown in *italics* in the *Value* column. For details, see the HTML documentation installed along with the Flash Asset Xtra.

Table B-6: Flash Asset Properties

Command	Value	Read-Only	Member	Sprite	See Also
actionsEnabled	*TRUE* | FALSE		•	•	*buttonsEnabled*

Command	Value	Read-Only	Member	Sprite	See Also
broadcastProps	*TRUE* | FALSE		•		
bufferSize	*n* bytes (default 32768)		•		*preLoad* = FALSE, *stream()*, *streamMode*, *bytesStreamed*
buttonsEnabled	*TRUE* | FALSE		•	•	*actionsEnabled* = TRUE
bytesStreamed	*n* bytes	•	•		*bufferSize, percent-Streamed*
centerRegPoint	*TRUE* | FALSE		•		*regPoint*
clickMode	#boundingBox | *#opaque* | #object		•	•	
defaultRect	rect (*l*, *t*, *r*, *b*)		•		*flashRect, defaultRect-Mode*
defaultRectMode	*#flash* | #fixed		•		*flashRect, defaultRect*
directToStage	TRUE | *FALSE*		•	•	Set to FALSE for Shockwave playback.
eventPassMode	*#passAlways* | #pass-Button | #passNot-Button | #passNever		•	•	*buttonsEnabled, actionsEnabled*
fileName[1]	*path* | EMPTY		•		Buggy. Use *pathName* or *URL* instead.
fixedRate	*n* (default is 15)		•	•	*playbackMode* = #fixed
flashRect	rect(*l*, *t*, *r*, *b*)	•	•		*defaultRectMode*
frame	*n*			•	*frameRate, frameCount*
frameCount	set in Flash	•	•		*frame, frameRate*
frameRate	set in Flash	•	•		*frame, frameCount*
imageEnabled	*TRUE* | FALSE		•	•	*sound*
linked	*TRUE* | FALSE		•		Cannot be set to TRUE during runtime for Shockwave. See *pathName, URL, fileName.*
loop	*TRUE* | FALSE		•	•	
mouseOverButton	TRUE | FALSE	•		•	

Command	Value	Read-Only	Member	Sprite	See Also
originH	*n* (default is 0.0)		•	•	*originV, originMode = #point*
originMode	*#center* | *#topleft* | *#point*		•	•	*originH , originPoint, originV.*
originPoint	*point (x, y)* default is (0. 0, 0.0)		•	•	*originMode = #point.*
originV	*n* (default is 0.0)		•	•	*originH, originMode = #point*
pathName	*pathName*		•		*Same as URL, (avoid file-Name); see linked = TRUE.*
pausedAtStart	TRUE | *FALSE*		•	•	*play()*
percentStreamed	0.0 to 100.0	•	•		*bytesStreamed*
playBackMode	*#normal* | *#lockStep* | *#fixed*		•	•	*fixedRate*
playing	TRUE | FALSE	•		•	*play(), stop()*
posterFrame	*n* (default is 1)		•		*frame, frameCount*
preload	TRUE | *FALSE*		•		*bufferSize, streamMode*
quality	*#autoHigh* | *#autoLow* | *#high* | *#low*		•	•	
regPoint	*point (x, y)* default is center		•		
rotation	*n (0.0* to 360.0) rotates around origin		•	•	*originMode*
scale	*n* (default is 100.0) scales around point set by *originMode*		•	•	*originMode, originPoint, scaleMode, viewScale*
scaleMode	*#showAll* | *#noBorder* | *#exactFit*		•	•	*scale, viewScale*
sound	*TRUE* | FALSE		•	•	*imageEnabled*

Table B-6: Flash Asset Properties (continued)

Command	Value	Read-Only	Member	Sprite	See Also
state	-1: error 0: not loaded 1: header loading 2: header loaded 3: media loading 4: media loaded	•	•		*playing, stop(), play()*
static	TRUE | *FALSE*		•	•	Don't use if Flash sprite overlaps other sprites; see *imageEnabled.*
streamMode	#frame | #idle | #manual		•		*stream(), streamSize*
streamSize[2]	n bytes	•	•		*bytesStreamed, stream-Mode, stream()*
type	#flash	•	•		*new()*
URL	*pathName*		•		Same as *pathName,* (avoid *fileName*); see *linked* = TRUE.
viewH[3]	*horiz* (default is 0.0)		•	•	*viewPoint, viewV*
viewPoint[3]	*point* (x, y) default is (0,0)		•	•	*point* is relative to *origin-Point.*
viewScale	n (default is 100); scales from center		•	•	*scale, originPoint, origin-Mode*
viewV[3]	*vert* (default is 0.0)		•	•	*viewPoint, viewH*

[1] Setting *the fileName of member* deletes cast member in D6.0 and D6.0.1 (upgrade to D6.0.2).
[2] *StreamSize* is the size of the asset on disk.
[3] Can be set automatically by scrolling asset preview in Cast member options window.

Table B-7 shows the commands and functions supported for Flash Assets.

Table B-7: Flash Functions and Commands

Command	Member	Sprite	See Also
clearError (*member flashMember*)	•		*state, getError()*
flashToStage(sprite *flashSprite, flashPoint*)		•	*stageToFlash()*
frameReady(sprite *flashSprite, frameNum*)		•	*frame*

Table B-7: Flash Functions and Commands (continued)

Command	Member	Sprite	See Also
getError(member *flashMember*)	•		Returns FALSE | #memory | #file-NotFound | #network | #file-Format | #other.
goToFrame(sprite *flashSprite*, *frameNum*)		•	*frameCount, frame*
hitTest(sprite *flashSprite*, *point*)		•	Returns #background |#normal |#button.
hold(sprite *flashSprite*)		•	
new(#flash, member *newMember*)	•		See Chapter 19, *The Lingo Symbol Table.*
play(sprite *whichSprite*)		•	*rewind(), pausedAtStart*
rewind(sprite *flashSprite*)		•	*play()*
showProps(member *flashMember*) showProps(sprite *flashSprite*)	•	•	Requires Flash Asset Options Xtra (Authoring mode only).
stageToFlash(sprite *flashSprite*, *stagePoint*)		•	*flashToStage()*
stop(sprite *flashSprite*)		•	*play(), rewind()*
stream(member *flashMember*, *numBytes*)	•		*streamMode, streamSize*

Custom Cursor Xtra

 To create a Custom Cursor asset, use Insert➤Media Element ➤Cursor, not File➤Import.

Table B-8 lists the Xtras you'll need for authoring and distribution of Director movies using Custom Cursors (Windows 3.1 and 68K are not supported). See Chapter 14, *Graphical User Interface Components*, of *Director in a Nutshell* for details on using the Xtra.

Table B-8: Custom Cursor Xtra

Projectors	Xtra Name
Power Macintosh Authoring	CurOptPPC
Power Macintosh Distribution (Projectors or Shockwave)	CursorPPC

Table B-8: Custom Cursor Xtra (continued)

Projectors	Xtra Name
Windows 32-bit Authoring	CurOpt.x32
Windows 32-bit Distribution (Projectors or Shockwave)	Cursor.x32

Table B-9 shows sprite and castmember properties for *Custom Cursors*. It is implicit that each property takes the form:

    the *property* of member *cursorMember*

Custom cursors don't have sprite properties (they should never be used as sprites). Instead custom cursors are used to set *the cursor of sprite* property of *other* sprites:

    set the cursor of sprite *whichSprite* = [member *cursorMember*]

or to set the sustem cursor:

    cursor [member *cursorMember*]

For details, see the HTML documentation installed along with the *Custom Cursor Xtra*.

Table B-9: Custom Cursor Xtra Properties

Command	Value	Read-Only	Member
automask	TRUE | FALSE		•
castMemberList[1]	list of member references		•
cursorSize[2]	16 | 32	•	•
hotSpot[2]	point (*x*, *y*)		•
interval[1]	*milliseconds* (default is 100)		•
type	#cursor		•

[1] Use the same cast member more than once within an animated cursor to create the appearance of uneven intervals in the animated cursor.
[2] The *hotspot* can range from *point(0,0)* to *point(15,15)* for 16 x 16 pixel cursors or *point(32, 32)* for 32 x 32 pixel cursors.

Changes in Earlier Versions of D6

Refer to Table 17-2 in Chapter 17, *Changed, Undocumented, and Misdocumented Lingo,* for details on Lingo that behaves differently in D6 than in D5. Also refer to the *ReadMe* files that come with the D6, D6.0.1, D6.0.2, and D6.5 updates.

Changes for D5 to D6

Refer to "New Features in Director 6" in the *Preface* for the big picture. Here are some lesser-known technical details.

- Director 6 no longer reads Xtras from the system *Xtras* folder, as did D5. The *Xtras* folder must reside where Director is installed. D5 and D6 Projectors both access the *Xtras* folder one level down from the Projector. In D6 Xtras can be bundled into Projectors, although I advise against it.

- The D6 Authoring environment will not run under Win NT 3.5 or Windows 3. 1; it requires Windows 95 or NT 4.0. Director 5 ran under both Windows 3.1 and NT 3.5. Director 6 can still create Projectors for those platforms.

- Director 6.0 has a lot of new Lingo including all commands in the NetLingo Xtra. Refer to Table 18-1, which identifies all Lingo that is new in D6 (the online Help also has a partial listing under "*What's New.*")

- Director 6.0 used MIX (*Macromedia Import Xtras*) to import many new file types. These generally must be included, along with the MIX Services Xtra when linking to media at runtime.

- Director 6.0 supports streaming media from the Internet, which is completely separate from Shockwave. Director itself transparently accesses remote data allowing you to create "hybrid" CDs.

Changes from D6.0 to 6.0.1

The following is a summary of the most important changes from D6.0 to D6.0.1. You should upgrade to at least D6.0.2 (which is free for D6.0 and D6.0.1 users) or upgrade to D6.5 if you need any of its new Xtra-based features.

Miscellaneous

Behavior Library scripts revised to address bugs.

Clicking the "+" (new) button in the Script window while editing a score or parent script now creates a script of the same type instead of always creating a movie script. Clicking the "+" new button while editing a cast (or movie) script still creates a movie script. Use the *Script Castmember Properties* dialog to change the script type.

Opening a cross-platform file and editing fields/saving them no longer loses the font mapping.

SPACE or PI no longer become VOID when used as arguments to function calls.

The problem where sprite blend values can automatically get set to 0% has been fixed.

The *new(#SWA)* command now works.

There are many new keyboard shortcuts in Paint window. (See Chapter 14, *Graphics, Colors, and Palettes* in *Director in a Nutshell.*)

Buttons and Events

Custom Buttons now unhighlight when the mouse rolls off with button down, and Behaviors attached to Custom Buttons now receive *mouseEnter, mouseWithin*, and *mouseLeave* events.

Rollover and mouse events are no longer sent to off-stage sprites or while cursor is over an off-stage portion of a sprite (and *the mouseCast* returns −1 and *the mouseMember* returns VOID for off-stage sprites).

Sprite cursors are now ignored for invisible sprites.

A warning is issued when D5 movies containing *enterFrame* or *exitFrame* handlers attached to graphic sprites are opened (these handlers are executed in D6, but not D5). See *Goodies/Movies/Cleaner/Cleaner.dir* on the D6 CD.

See the "Mouse-Opaque Sprites" section in Chapter 9, *Mouse Events*, for details on how mouse events differ from Director 5.

Browsers, Streaming, and the Internet
 ImportFileInto now supports importing a QuickTime movie at a URL.

If the browser is already running, *gotoNetPage* opens the existing window, rather than launching a separate instance of the browser.

The *netError()* function no longer returns error 20 ("Internal error") after a successful *gotoNetMovie* command.

gotoNetPage now supports a relative URL in both Authoring and Projectors.

Linked Shockwave Audio (SWA) files now play locally in via Shockwave.

Director for Windows
 The problem with Windows 3.1 Projectors crashing on launch on some machines with SHARE.EXE installed has been fixed.

The problem where 32-bit Projectors could leave behind "Mix32.x32" in an "*Xtras*" folder when playing from locked media has been fixed.

Support for multiple monitors on Windows 98
 Director's application window can now be placed on a second monitor.

Problems with transitions on multiple monitor systems has been fixed.

The D6.0.1 and 6.5 versions of the Shockwave plug-in use completely different underlying code (the so-called "portable player" or IML (Ideal Media Layer)) than Shockwave 6.0 or Director Authority Tool or Projectors (all versions).

Changes from D6.0.1 to 6.0.2

The following is a summary of the most important changes from D6.0.1 to D6.0.2. You should upgrade to at least D6.0.2 (which is free for D6.0 and D6.0.1 users) or to D6.5. Refer to *D6.0.2 Changes.txt ReadMe* file for details.

Miscellaneous
 The machineType no longer returns outdated values.

NetLingo commands properly parse URLs containing periods (.).

Copy to clipboard now works in the Debugger.

Sprite *blend* and *loc* properties won't reset to the property stored for the previous sprite.

A potential problem with rich text cast members not appearing in Shockwave 6.0.1 has been fixed.

XtraInfo.TXT has been updated to include some third-party Xtras.

Cast Window

Swapping cast files containing sprite Xtra cast members or moving sprite Xtras cast members between casts has been fixed (Macromedia was unclear which).

Importing RTF into external casts created using the cast dialog has been fixed.

Dragging film loops from external unlinked casts has been fixed.

Projectors

Projectors can now be created on Macintosh volumes with more than 2 GB free.

Projectors will no longer potentially crash on startup under Windows NT (Macromedia's documentation is not clear whether this addresses a problem when starting a Projector under NT with drives larger than 4 GB).

JPG and other MIX Xtras can now be packaged properly into Projectors. (I still recommend against it.)

Sound and Video

QuickTime movies can not play when puppeted into empty channels.

Sound playFile with large sounds no longer will have latency problems.

Cue point times will not overflow for long sounds nor return negative values.

Problems that could prevent other applications from playing sounds on PCs and could cause a memory leak when RSX is installed have been fixed.

APPENDIX C

Case-Sensitivity, Sort Order, Diacritical Marks, and Space-Sensitivity

This appendix covers the idiosyncrasies of uppercase and lowercase characters, sort order ranking, spacing, and diacritical marks in Director.

Case-Sensitivity

For the most part, Director is case-insensitive (that is, *not* case-sensitive).

The following are all case-*insensitive*:

- Handler names
- Variable names
- String comparison using =, <>, *contains*, *starts*, or *offset()*, and clause evaluation in *case* statements.
- Symbol names (see exceptions below)
- *Symbol* lookup using *deleteOne()*, *getOne()*, *getPos()*, *findPos()*, and *findPosNear()*; refer to Chapter 6, *Lists*, and Chapter 19, *The Lingo Symbol Table*.
- External local filenames, including Lingo properties that use external files
- Macintosh hard drive names
- Castmember names
- Marker label names
- Xtras' names and methods
- XObject names and methods
- Lingo keywords
- Strings recognized by Director, such as "left," "right," and "center"
- VBScript and JavaScript using Microsoft Internet Explorer only
- HTML tags
- e-mail addresses

The following items are case-*sensitive* to some degree:

- Symbols—converting a symbol to a string using *string(#symbolName)* will always return a string with the same case with which the symbol was first declared. Refer to Chapter 19.

- *String* lookup using *deleteOne(), getOne(), getPos(), findPos(), findPosNear(),* and *sort()*; refer to Chapter 6.

- String comparisons using <, <=, >, >=, *min()*, and *max()*.

- Macintosh File Type and Creator Codes (as used in the *FileIO* Xtra's `setFinderInfo`, `getFinderInfo()`, and *setFilterMask* methods. The codes must also be *exactly* four characters and include spaces if applicable. For example, the file type for QT movies is "MooV" (note the capitalization).

- Macintosh gestalt codes (see *http://www.bio.vu.nl/home/rgaros/gestalt/*)

- The formatting codes used in menu definitions, such as <B and <I; they must be uppercase.

- Browser Scripting—use the case shown here for an *on EvalScript* handler.

- JavaScript using Netscape Navigator—use the case shown here for *Play, Rewind, Stop, GotoFrame, GotoMovie,* and *GetCurrentFrame()*.

- JavaScript string comparison and equalities.

- Variable names in Java (because when using the *Save as Java* export feature).

- ActiveX control names.

- File paths using URLs (particularly on a UNIX-based server).

- String arguments to Xtras, depending on the Xtra's internal operation (although usually *not* case-sensitive). Consult each Xtra's documentation. For example a method accepting a gestalt code would be case-sensitive.

 Case-sensitivity is usually OS-dependent. If using an OS-specific entity via an Xtra, such as a window name or a process name, it may be case-sensitive. Macintosh and Windows are usually case-insensitive. UNIX is usually case-sensitive.

Case-Sensitivity in Comparisons

Director relies on the underlying OS-dependent system calls to perform string comparisons. Therefore, the same comparison may return different results on Macintosh and Windows.

The <, <=, >, and >= operators perform *case-sensitive* string comparisons that differ cross-platform. The = and <> operators and the *offset()* contains and *starts* functions are *case-insensitive*. *All* string comparisons are *sensitive* to diacritical marks, such as accents, despite the Macromedia documentation's claims to the contrary.

Strings can be equal only if they are the same length. Use the *starts* function to compare the beginning of strings of unequal length.

Sort Order Ranking

Sorting of strings within lists is case-sensitive. Use the *max()* or *min()* function to determine which character has the higher sort order.

Director for *Macintosh* ranks alphanumeric characters as follows:

"0" < "1" < "2"...< "9" < "A" < "a" < "B" < "b"...
```
put max ("a", "A")
-- "a"
put max ("a", "b")
-- "b"
```

Director for *Windows* ranks alphanumeric characters as:

"0" < "1" < "2"...< "9" < "a" < "A" < "b" < "B"...
```
put max ("a", "A")
-- "A"
put max ("a", "b")
-- "b"
```

On Windows, *all* non-alphanumeric characters are ranked *below* the alphanumeric ones. On the Macintosh, some non-alphanumeric characters are ranked *higher* than alphanumerics, but others are ranked *lower*. Still others are ranked *between* the numeric characters and alphabetical ones! Director does *not* rank characters based solely on their ASCII codes in any case.

Example C-1 can be used to display the sort order for a given platform. It will vary on Macintosh and Windows.

Example C-1. Character Sort Order Ranking

```
on showRank startCode, endCode
  set alphaList = []
  -- Create a list using characters ("A", "B", etc.)
  -- as the property by which to sort the entries
  repeat with x = startCode to endCode
    add alphaList, numToChar(x)
  end repeat
  sort alphaList
  return alphaList
end showRank

put showRank (32, 127)
```

Example C-2 is very similar, to Example C-1 but it includes each character's ASCII value in a sorted property list. Compare its output with the ASCII table printed by Example A-1.

Example C-2. Character Sort Order Ranking Showing ASCII Values

```
on sortByAlpha startCode, endCode
  set alphaList = [:]
  -- Create a list using characters ("A", "B", etc.)
  -- as the property by which to sort the entries
  repeat with x = startCode to endCode
    addProp alphaList, numToChar(x), x
  end repeat
  sort alphaList
  return alphaList
end sortByAlpha

put sortByAlpha (0, 255)
```

Case-Insensitive Comparison

To perform case-insensitive comparison, either rely on the case-insensitive opera-tors (such as = and *starts*) or convert all characters to the same case before comparison.

The *ForceUpperCase* example under the *numToChar()* entry in the *Lingo Dictionary* is very wrong. It has the wrong range of ASCII values and corrupts or deletes some non-alphabetic characters in the string. Example C-3 converts lowercase letters to uppercase and leaves other characters unchanged.

Example C-3: Convert to Uppercase

```
on makeUpperCase upString
  repeat with x = 1 to length(upString)
    set thisChar = charToNum (char x of upString)
    -- Convert ASCII "a" through "z" to upper case
    if thisChar >= 97 and thisChar <= 122 then
      put numToChar (thisChar - 32) into char x of upString
    end if
  end repeat
  return upString
end makeUpperCase
```

Reader exercise: write a routine to convert characters to lowercase. (Hint: The ASCII values of uppercase "A" to "Z" are 65 through 90.)

Case-Sensitive Comparison

To perform case-sensitive comparison, either rely on the case-sensitive operators (such as < and >) or compare each character's ASCII value using *charToNum()*.

Example C-4 distinguishes between the uppercase "A" and lowercase "a."

Example C-4: Distinguishing Between Cases

```
on keyDown
  if charToNum(the key) = charToNum("A") then
    Alert "You hit the uppercase A"
  else if charToNum(the key) = charToNum("a") then
    Alert "You hit the lowercase a"
  end if
end
```

Don't use a *case* statement to check for case-specific keys because *case* statements are case-insensitive, too.

The TextCruncher Xtra by Yair Sageev (*http://www.itp.tsoa.nyu.edu/~student/yair/texcruncher/HTML/YairTextCruncher.html*) performs both case-sensitive and case-insensitive text manipulations.

Refer to Appendix A, *ASCII Codes and Key Codes*, for more details on ASCII values.

Reader exercise: create a routine that compares two strings in a case-sensitive manner (Hint: Use *charToNum()* on each character.)

Case-Sensitivity in Lists

The *findPos()*, *findPosNear()*, *getOne()*, *getPos()*, and *deleteOne()* list functions are case-sensitive when accessing string elements. The same functions are case-insensitive when accessing symbolic elements.

See Example 6-12, "Case-Sensitive Deletion of String Values," *Example 6-13*, "Case-Insensitive Deletion of Symbolic Values," and *Example 6-14*, "Case-Sensitive Searching of String Values."

Lists elements sorted with *sort()* obey the same sort order shown in Example C-1.

Case-Sensitivity in URLs

Remote URLs using *ftp:* and *http:* schemes in browsers are usually *case-sensitive*, especially for UNIX servers. Shockwave 6.0.1 and 6.5 performs *case-sensitive* filename comparison, except for the initial "*ftp:*" or "*http:*" and the server name, which are *case-insensitive*. (Earlier versions performed *case-insensitive* filename comparisons, which was incorrect for most remote servers.) When testing locally, in a browsers filenames including URLs with the *file:* scheme are *case-insensitive* although they are case-sensitive once uploaded to the server. If a Shockwave movie or linked media works locally, but not after uploading, check the filename's case.

Refer to Macromedia Technote 12568, *Shockwave for Director 6.0.1 Notes for Developers*, for details.

Diacritical Marks

Despite Macromedia's documentation's claims to the contrary, all Lingo string operations (including =, <>, <=, >=, *starts*, *contains*, *case*, and offset are sensitive to diacritical marks (such as accents and umlauts) on both Macintosh and Windows.

Using the *showRank* utility in Example C-1, examine the sort order for characters with diacritical marks.

```
put showRank (0, 255)
```

Even though different diacritical marks prevent two strings from being considered equal, characters that differ only by diacritical marks are adjacent in the sorted list (the sort order of diacritical marks also varies cross-platform).

Diacritical marks use nonstandard (that is, *extended*) ASCII values (those above 127) that vary with the font.

You can create characters with any ASCII value using *numToChar()* or enter the ASCII code on the Windows numeric keypad while holding down the Alt key.

Using U.S. keyboard mapping on the Macintosh, some diacritical marks are created in two steps. First, hold down the Option key and then press either "e" (for accent grave, "`"), "`" (for accent ague, "´"), "u" (for umlaut, "¨"), "i" (for circumflex, "^"), or "n" (for tilde, "~"). No character will appear yet. Release both keys, and then enter the character over which the diacritical mark should appear. For example, "é" is created using Option-e then pressing "e" again; "è" is created using Option-` (the "`" key is in the upper left corner of most keyboards) and then pressing "e" again; "ö" is created using Option-u then pressing "o," and so on. If the second character does not support the specified diacritical mark, or if the last key pressed is a space, the diacritical mark will appear as a separate character. Other characters, such as "ç" can be created using the Option key with a second character (in this case Option-c).

You can change the keyboard layout for foreign languages under the *Keyboard* Control Panel in which case keyboard mappings may be different. Use the Macintosh *Key Caps* desk accessory or the Windows *Character Map* utility (under the Windows 95 *Start* menu under Programs➤Accessories) to determine the keystrokes or ASCII code to create the desired character.

 Refer to the (*http://www.zeusprod.com/nutshell/examples.html*) for a utility that strips diacritical marks from a string. It is *very* cool.

Space-Sensitivity

Lingo code is often whitespace-*insensitive* (that is, it ignores extra Space, Tab, and Return characters). Director ignores any spaces you type at the *beginning* of a line of Lingo. It indents each line of code in the current code block (such as an *if..*

.then...else...end if statement two spaces) from the surrounding code. Use the Tab key to auto-format your Lingo code with proper indenting. Use the auto-indenting as your guide to indicate possible structural errors. (See Chapter 1, *How Lingo Thinks.*) You can add spaces within your lines and blank lines to your Lingo scripts to make them more readable.

JavaScript scripts and HTML tags also tend to be space-insensitive.

Many aspects of Lingo and Director are space-sensitive, however.

The following must *not* include any spaces:

- Handler names
- Variable names
- Symbol names
- Windows 3.1 filenames
- Windows 95 filenames can not *begin* with a space but may contain spaces elsewhere
- Xtras names and methods; the name of the external Xtras file can have spaces (except under Windows 3.1), but not the internal name by which Xtras are accessed
- XObject names and methods (see previous note for Xtras)
- Lingo keywords
- e-mail addresses
- Do not include spaces at the end of a line after the Lingo continuation character ¬.
- URLs—use %20 in lieu of spaces

The following allow spaces, but they are *space-sensitive*, including any leading or trailing spaces:

- The FileIO Xtra under Windows does not differentiate names with spaces from similar names without space.
- String comparison
- External local filenames, including Lingo properties (such as *the fileName of member*) that refer to external files on the Macintosh and Windows 95/NT
- Macintosh drive names
- Castmember names
- Marker label names
- Any string within quotes
- Macintosh File Type and Creator Codes (as used in the *FileIO* Xtra's `setFinderInfo, getFinderInfo()`, and *setFilterMask* methods are space-sensitive. The codes must also be *exactly* four characters and include spaces if applicable. For example, the file type for PDF files is "PDF " (note the trailing space).
- String arguments to Xtras, such as the QTVR Xtra, are usually space-sensitive. Consult each Xtra's documentation.

Trimming Spaces

In order to prevent the user from entering spaces into an editable text field, use the code shown in Example C-5.

Example C-5: Intercepting Spaces

```
on keyDown
  -- This prevents the SPACE key from passing through
  if the key = SPACE then
    beep
  else
    pass
  end if
end
```

Example C-6: Trimming and Deleting Spaces

```
--This removes leading and trailing spaces, but not internal spaces:
on trimSpaces inString
  set outString = inString
  repeat while char 1 of outString = SPACE
    delete char 1 of outString
  end repeat
  repeat while the last char of outString = SPACE
    delete the last char of outString
  end repeat
  return outString
end
--This removes all spaces:
on removeSpaces inString
  set outString = EMPTY
  repeat with x = 1 to length(inString)
    if char x of inString <> SPACE then
      put char x of inString after outString
    end if
  end repeat
  return outString
end
```

APPENDIX D

The DIRECTOR.INI and LINGO.INI Files

DIRECTOR.INI

The DIRECTOR.INI file, located in the folder where Director is installed, configures Director for Windows' memory, sound, and video options. (There is no such file for the Macintosh.) Each section within the file is indicated by a *section heading* enclosed in square brackets, with one of more parameters defined below it.

```
[sectionName]
param1=value
param2=value
```

See the TechNote at *http://www.zeusprod.com/technote/ini.html* for a description of the standard Windows INI file format.

The DIRECTOR.INI file contains many comments. In fact, every line is commented out with a semi-colon (;), and you need not include the DIRECTOR.INI file unless you change the defaults. Edit the DIRECTOR.INI file in a Windows text editor, such as NOTEPAD. Save as plain text if editing in a fancier word processor, such as MS-Word.

 If you make a change, delete the semi-colon (;) at the start of the line and restart Director for the change to go into effect. For distribution, the DIRECTOR.INI file must be renamed to match your Projector and placed in the Projector's folder.

For example, if the Projector is named *MYTHANG.EXE*, rename DIRECTOR.INI to *MYTHANG.INI*. The default settings shown in the DIRECTOR.INI file that ships with Director are built into the Projector. You don't need to include a custom version unless you change the defaults.

You can add the entry: *DLLName="QMix.DLL"* in the *[Sound]* section to use QuickTime 3's new audio mixing features. This feature is still buggy, as is Macromedia's current work-around using *DLLName="Macromix.DLL"*. A fix is promised imminently at press time. See Chapter 15, *Sound and Cue Points*, and Chapter 16, *Digital Video*, in *Director in a Nutshell*.

Although you would not ordinarily do so, you can read the INI file at runtime using one of the third-party Windows OS Xtras that read and write standard Windows INI files, such as Buddy API or DirectOS.

The following describes each section of the DIRECTOR.INI file and the settings within it. The most common ones to change from their default are the *Animation* setting in the *[Palette]* section, and the *SoundLeveln* and *MixMaxChannels* settings in the *[Sound]* section.

[Memory]

```
[Memory]
ExtraMemory=kiloBytes    (default is 400 KB)
SwapFileMeg=megaBytes    (default is zero, meaning half of RAM)
```

ExtraMemory option (Projectors only)

Determines the amount of swap space (in KB) a Projector should use at runtime and defaults to 400 KB. You can increase this to guarantee more memory to the Projector.

SwapFileMeg option (authoring-only)

Determines the amount of swap file space (in MB) that Director should use. It defaults to 0, indicating that disk space equal to one-half of available physical RAM should be used. Increase this as needed to, say, import more cast members before running out of memory.

Refer to Chapter 9, *Performance and Memory*, in *Director in a Nutshell* for many more details on memory usage in Director and Projectors.

[Graphics]

```
[Graphics]
WinG= 0 | 1 (default)
```

WinG is a graphics acceleration library under Windows 3.1. This may improve performance of some applications, but it may also create unforeseen conflicts. This setting is ignored under Windows 95 (and under Windows 3.1 if WinG is not installed).

0: Do not use WinG graphics accelerator.

1: (Default) Use WinG graphics accelerator software, if installed. Projector size and memory usage may increase.

[Palette]

```
[Palette]
Animation = 0 | 1 (default)
```

Any custom palette in use by Director for Windows will get "frozen" by a Windows system dialog box of any type, such as Alert boxes or File dialogs created with the *FileIO* Xtra.

0: (more compatible) prevents Director from seizing control of the palette. Director palette fades will be *much* slower, but other applications will be able to set their palettes (and therefore will look better), and the Windows system palette will not freeze out Director's custom palette.

1: (default; faster) allows Director to seize control of the palette, resulting in faster palette fades and color cycling, but potential palette conflicts.

Refer to Chapter 13, *Graphics, Color, and Palettes*, in *Director in a Nutshell* for many more details.

[Sound]

Settings in the *[Sound]* section apply to all sound cards. Refer to Chapter 15 in *Director in a Nutshell* for more information.

```
[Sound]
DLLName="MacroMix.DLL" (default) | "QMix.dll" (BuickFimez)
SpoolBufferAlloc = 0 (default) | 1
LowSpoolBufferMs = milliseconds (default 2500)
HighSpoolBufferMs = milliseconds (default 1500)
SpoolBufferCount = 2 (default) | 3 | 4 | 5 | 6 | 7 | 8 | 9 | 10
MixMaxChannels = 1 | 2 | 3 | 4 (default) | 5 | 6 | 7 | 8
MixWaveDevice = deviceID
SoundLevel0=0      (default)
SoundLevel1=24770 (default)
SoundLevel2=35030 (default)
SoundLevel3=42903 (default)
SoundLevel4=49540 (default)
SoundLevel5=55388 (default)
SoundLevel6=60674 (default)
SoundLevel7=65535 (default)
MixMaxFidelity=0 | 1 | 2 | 99 (default)
```

DLLName (defaults to "MacroMix.DLL")

This is a new setting shown in the DIRECTOR.INI file that comes with D6.5. If using QuickTime 3 (Windows 95/NT only), set the DLLName to "QMix.DLL." This feature was still buggy at press time, but Macromedia promises a fixed version of Macromix.DLL. Search the Macromedia TechNotes for more details, or see Chapters 15 and 16 in *Director in a Nutshell*.

SpoolBufferAlloc (default 0) controls when spool buffers are allocated.

0: allocate/deallocate dynamically when sound starts/stops (default).

1: allocate spool once at startup and keep for entire session (may improve performance).

LowSpoolBufferMs (default 2500)

Length of one 8-bit spool buffer, in milliseconds. Try lengthening it if 8-bit sounds are cutting off while doing other things in Director.

HighSpoolBufferMs (default 1500)

Length of one 16-bit spool buffer, in milliseconds. Try lengthening it if 16-bit sounds are cutting off while doing other things in Director.

SpoolBufferCount (default 2)

Number of spool buffers to use. Must range from 2 to 10.

MixMaxChannels (default 4)

Maximum number of channels (from 1 to 8) supported by the sound mixer. Reduce this for improved performance when using fewer than four channels.

MixWaveDevice (default 0)

DeviceID of waveOut device to use for playing sound. Default is 0 (the first device), and the max is one less than the number of devices installed.

SoundLeveln = volume (defaults shown above; volume from 0 to 65535)

The eight *soundLevel n* settings control the Windows waveOut volume corresponding to the Lingo property *the soundLevel* from 0 to 7. Volume response is logarithmic, not linear, so the lowest sound levels may be inaudible. Increase the lower end if necessary. Use a third-party Xtra to control the master volume (see *http://www.updatestage.com/Xtras*).

MixMaxFidelity (default 99)

Sounds are mixed dynamically under Windows. Improve performance by using the lowest value that meets or exceeds your audio source quality.

0: 22.050 kHz, 8-bit, mono

1: 22.050 kHz, 8-bit, stereo

2: 44.100 kHz, 16-bit, stereo

99: Switch formats on the fly. The first sound in a run of overlapping sounds determines the format for that run (default).

Other Sound Card Settings

I've never known anyone to change the sound card settings for individual types of sounds or sound cards, but it is possible. The following nine section headings each affect a different type of sound or sound card.

```
[Low Mono Default Sound]
[Low Default Sound]
[High Mono Default Sound]
[Low Mono <SoundCardName>]
[Low <SoundCardName>]
[High <SoundCardName>]
[Low Mono Override]
[Low Override]
[High Override]
```

They each support the following options:

```
MixBufferMs = milliseconds
MixBufferBytes = bytes
MixBufferCount = n (2 through 16)
MixServiceMode = 0 | 1 | 2
MixIntPeriodMs = milliseconds
MixIntResolutionMs = milliseconds
```

Refer to the comments in the DIRECTOR.INI file for more details.

LINGO.INI

The LINGO.INI file is *not* a standard Windows INI file and is supported on both the Macintosh and Windows for D5 and later. (D4 for Windows also supported it.)

The only thing that should ever be in your LINGO.INI file is an *on startUp* handler of the form:

```
on startUp
  statement(s)
end startUp
```

(You can define other handlers within your LINGO.INI file, but they are ignored unless called from the *on startUp* handler.) The *startUp* event is sent once and only once to the LINGO.INI file when Director or a Projector starts up. The file must be in the same folder as Director or the Projector (so make a copy for distribution) and is always named LINGO.INI. Edit the LINGO.INI file in a Windows text editor, such as NOTEPAD, or a Macintosh text editor, such as SimpleText. Save as plain text if editing in a fancier word processor, such as MS-Word.

Treat the LINGO.INI file as if it were a Script window, although you won't have the standard script editing tools (such as Lingo popups) at your disposal. Use the standard Lingo syntax to create scripts, including using two hyphens to create comments. The script will not auto-format in the text editor. Work in the Director Script window and copy the text into the LINGO.INI file if necessary. Any *on startUp* handler in your Director movie scripts will be ignored.

 Always include a LINGO.INI file with your Windows Projector to prevent spurious warnings that the LINGO.INI file can not be found.

The spurious LINGO.INI error is seen on some consumer machines, such as Gateways, using multimedia shells, such as "Explorer," "Navigator," (no relation to the popular browsers) or "Norton Commander," especially in low-memory situations. The user should use the standard Windows 3.1 Program Manager or Windows 95 desktop shell instead.

The spurious LINGO.INI error was also seen with some old versions of Cirrus Logic video drivers that overwrote other areas of memory. Users should update their video driver.

Your LINGO.INI file should not be empty, as that too can cause a crash. Use at least a minimal *on startUp* handler (this also prevents a potential math error):

```
on startUp
   if string(0.0)="a" then nothing
end
```

LINGO.INI for Director for Windows

The default LINGO.INI file (installed with Director 6 for Windows) contains:

```
on startup
   put "Now loading LINGO.INI"&&the date&&the time
   put "This computer is running in "&& [LC]
      the colorDepth &"-bit color depth."
   --  set the centerStage to TRUE
   -- Following line prevents crashes on Windows systems when
   -- using math functions such as power or log and passing
   -- bogus or extremely large/small values. Invoking the
   -- float->string conversion code with a valid value
   -- prevents future crashes in this routine. drs  1mar96
   if string(0.0)="a" then nothing
end startup
```

In the Director 4 and 5 for Windows LINGO.INI file you'll find the line:

```
openxlib "fileio"
```

It was used to open the FileIO DLL (XObject) under Windows (on the Macintosh in Director 4 and 5, the FileIO XObject was built into Director's resource fork). If you failed to include such a line in a LINGO.INI file with your Windows Projector, you would get an error if you tried to use the FileIO XObject's methods. In both Director 5 and Director 6, though, the FileIO XObject has been replaced by the FileIO Xtra. The latter is opened automatically if it is present in the *Xtras* folder, and so the open Xlib command is not is needed in the LINGO.INI file. See Chapter 14, *External Files*, for details.

There is no default LINGO.INI file on the Macintosh, but you can create one. I often use it to set global variables on both platforms.

Example D-1: Using LINGO.INI to Configure a Projector

```
on startUp
   global gAutoStart, gFirstMovieToPlay, gStartingFrame
   set gAutoStart = TRUE
   set gFirstMovieToPlay = the pathName & "main"
   set gStartingFrame = 50
end
```

Your Director movie would presumably make use of those globals. You shouldn't attempt to call other Lingo handlers or access the Score from the *on startUp* handler; it is called before the first movie's scripts and Score are loaded. (Technically, you can define other handlers within your LINGO.INI file and call them from your *on startUp* handler.) Notice that Example D-1 uses a hardcoded frame

---

number for the global variable *gStartingFrame* because the *label()* function won't work properly before the Score is loaded.

Inside my first Director movie, I could then use:

```
on startMovie
  global gAutoStart, gFirstMovieToPlay, gStartingFrame
  if gAutoStart then
    put "Yahoo!  It worked!"
    go frame gStartingFrame of movie gFirstMovieToPlay
  end if
end
```

Refer to Chapter 8, *Projectors and the Run-Time Environment,* in *Director in a Nutshell* and the TechNote *http://www.zeusprod.com/technote/stub.html* for details on using the LINGO.INI file to create a configurable stub Projector that need never be rebuilt.

APPENDIX E

Error Messages and Error Codes

Lingo Compiler and Runtime Error Messages

There are two broad classes of Lingo errors: those that occur when compiling scripts (compile-time) and those that occur when running Lingo (runtime). Table E-1 lists both types of errors alphabetically. Refer to Chapter 1, *How Lingo Thinks*, Chapter 2, *Events, Messages, and Scripts*, and Chapter 3, *Lingo Coding and Debugging Tips*, for many more details. See the Zeus Tech Note on Lingo Error Messages at *http://www.zeusprod.com/technote/error.html*.

Table E-1: Lingo Errors

Error Message	Cause or Solution
`<Member Type>` cast member expected	You specified a cast member as part of the command, but it was not of the expected asset type. Check its *type of member* and explicitly refer to a cast member's castLib if it is not in castLib 1.

`<Member Type>` cast member not found	You specified a nonexistent cast member either by name or by number. When using multiple castLibs, specify the castLib explicitly, such as:
	 `member 5 of castLib 2`
	
	 Adding an integer to a member reference causes an incorrect result because members and integers are different data types (See Chapter 5, *Data Types and Expressions*):
	 `put the member of sprite 5`
	 `-- (member 2 of castLib 1)`
	 `put the member of sprite 5 + 1`
	 `-- 0`
	
	 Increment *the memberNum* instead.
	 `set the memberNum of sprite 5 = ¬`
	 `  (the castLibNum of sprite 5) + 1`

Error Message	Cause or Solution
An internal error occurred	This error is returned by Adobe Acrobat when using *open... with* because it does not set the working directory. See Chapter 14, *External Files*.
<Something> expected	The Lingo command or function expects you to specify a different type of parameter than you are specifying (such as a string instead of an integer). If using a variable, check that it is not VOID or of the incorrect type, using the Debugger or an *ilk()* statement. If the incorrect value is a parameter that is being passed into your handler, verify the function call arguments in the calling routine. Verify the number, order, and type of the parameters. You can force a conversion to the desired type using *string()*, *float()*, etc. (See Chapter 5, *Data Types and Expressions*.)
At least 2 parameters expected	You specified the wrong number of parameters to a function call.
Cannot divide by zero	A math equation has zero in the divisor. A variable is uninitialized, or a calculation is unexpectedly evaluating to 0, perhaps because of integer division truncating the result to 0. See Chapter 8, *Math (and Gambling)*.
Cannot open this file because it is protected	You attempted to open a DXR or DCR file (you need the original source DIR file) or you are attempting to open a D6 movie file with D5. Launch D6 and manually open the file from within D6 using File▶Open.
Cannot perform TELL	The *tell* command was used improperly, or to execute an invalid command. See Chapter 6, *The Stage and MIAWs* in *Director in a Nutshell*.
Cannot set this property	The property is read-only and can be tested but not set. Some properties, such as the *framePalette*, can be set only during a Score recording session begun with *beginRecording*.
Cast member expected	Specify a castmember reference by name or by number, such as *member "myThing"* or *member 5 of castLib 2*.
Cast member name expected	Specify a castmember name, and ensure that the named cast member exists. If not, this test will return 0: put the number of member "*memberName*"
Cast Member not a bitmap or not black and white	Specify a bitmap cast member or use Modify▶Transform Bitmap to convert it to 1-bit.
Cast member not found	See *<Member Type> cast member not found* error.
Chunk expression expected	Specify a chunk expression, such as a string or the contents of a field. See Chapter 7, *Strings*.
Chunk specifier out of order	Check the syntax of your chunk expression command using *char, item, line,* or *word*. See Chapter 7.

Error Message	Cause or Solution
Comma expected	Make sure list elements, parameters to function calls, and arguments to handlers are separated by commas, that lists are terminated with a "]", and that nested function calls are terminated with the correct number of parentheses. Get rid of any spaces at the end of a line after a continuation character ¬.
Comma expected in Xtra interface	See *Comma expected* error.
Command not defined	Use of an invalid or nonexistent command. Check your syntax and that you are passing the command the correct types of parameters. See "Handler not defined" error.
Digital video sprite expected	When specifying digital video sprite properties, be sure that the sprite in the current frame is a digital video.
End of property list expected	A property list was not terminated properly. Check for missing commas and mismatched brackets. Look for missing ¬ continuation characters at the end of long lines.
Error...	Refer to remainder of dialog for more information on the error.
Error unpacking cast member	This error indicates a corrupted cast member within a Director movie or external castLib. Restore the cast member from a previous version, or delete it using `File ►Clear Cast Member` and re-import it.
Expected :	Check the syntax of your command, such as a *case* statement or property list.
Expected =	Use a statement of this form to assign values: `set x = 5`
Expected a variable	You're attempted to assign a value to something that isn't a variable. Lingo expected you to enter a variable name instead of a literal, such as: `set "foo" = "whatever"` *-- wrong; "foo" is not a variable* `set 5 = 7` *-- wrong; 5 is not a variable* `set x = 7` *-- right* `put the clickOn into sprite 5` *-- wrong; a sprite is not a variable*
Expected CASE clause	Refer to Chapter 1 for the format of a *value* clause following a *case* statement.
Expected END CASE	Include an *end case* statement for each *case* statement begun with *case...of*. Refer to Chapter 1 for multiline command caveats.
Expected END IF	Include an *end if* statement for each multi-line *if* statement begun with *if...then*. (I recommend always using multi-line *if* statements.) Refer to Chapter 1.
Expected end of statement	You specified more characters after Lingo thought the line was complete, such as too many square brackets at the end of a list: `set x = [#a:1, #b:2]]` *-- wrong*
Expected END REPEAT	Include an *end repeat* statement for each *repeat* statement begun with *repeat...with* or *repeat...while*. Refer to the Chapter 1 for multiline command caveats.

Error Message	Cause or Solution
Expected END TELL	Include an *end tell* statement for each multi-line *tell* statement.
Expected FIELD	Lingo expected the word *field*, as in: `put the text of field "myField"`
Expected MOVIE	Lingo expected the word *movie*, as in: `go frame 5 of` -- *wrong* `go frame 5` -- *right; assumes the current movie* `go frame 5 of movie "main"` -- *right*
Expected OF	Lingo expected the word *of*, as in: `put char 1 to 5` -- *wrong* `put char 1 to 5 of field "myField"` -- *right*

Expected THEN	You have used an *if* statement but forgot to include the *then* after the expression to evaluate:
	`if x = 5 alert "Hooray"` -- *wrong*
	`if x = 5 then alert "Hooray"` -- *right*
	`if x = 5 then`
	`  alert "hooray"`
	`end if`

Expected TO	Lingo expected you to assign a variable using *to* or "=." `set x` -- *wrong* `set x to 5` -- *right* `set x = 5` -- *right*
Expected WHILE or WITH	Use the word *with* or *while* in *repeat* commands `repeat x = 1 to 4` -- *wrong* `repeat with x = 1 to 4` -- *right* `repeat while the mouseDown` -- *right*
Expected WITHIN or INTERSECTS	You began a command with *sprite n*, and Lingo expects you to use a *sprite within* or *sprite intersects* command.
Factory name expected	This error message is obsolete; factories predated lists.
Fault in...	A general problem is called a *fault*. Read the remainder of the error message for more information.
File can not be closed since xtras are in use	Dispose of Xtra instances by setting them to 0, or close Xtras opened with *openXlib* (not recommended) using *closeXlib*
File error...	This message indicates a file error caused by a protected file, a file in use, or a file that can't be found. Refer to error dialog for more details or an error number. See Table E-3.
File read error	A problem reading the file, such as a disk error or protection violation, has occurred. See Table E-3.

Errors

Table E-1: Lingo Errors (continued)

Error Message	Cause or Solution
Floating point number expected	You specified an integer, string, or other data type when Lingo wanted a float. See the *<Something> expected* error.

Four parameters expected	You specified too few or too many parameters. Check the command syntax and the commas used to separate parameters. Rects should have four parameters, such as:
	`set the rect of sprite n = rect (l, t, r, b)`
	or two points, such as:
	`rect (point(l, t), point (r, b))`

Frame Not Defined	You have specified a frame that does not exist, such as a nonexistent or misspelled label name, incorrect frame number, or improper variable. Check for spaces in the label name, especially leading and trailing spaces, and check the value of variables in Debugger.
Function not defined	You attempted to call a nonexistent function.
Handler definition expected	Each handler in each script should start with the words: `on handlerName` and end with the word *end*.
Handler not defined	This error indicates that Director can't find or execute the handler, even though it may exist. There are *many* possible and diverse causes of this error, such as: You may be calling a non-existent Lingo command. Verify the spelling of the command or function name. (*PuppetSound* is one word, *sound playFile* is two words.) If calling a custom handler, ensure that the handler definition and the call to the handler are using the same name. Recompile all scripts so that Director recognizes new handlers. Make sure that the handler is located in a script where it can be found, such as a movie script. The first argument passed to the function is of the wrong type, such as trying to use a list function when the first argument is not a list of the correct type (such as using a linear list with *getProp*). Any command that expects a cast member, sprite, list, or object reference as the first parameter will fail if the first parameter is of an invalid type. If the error occurs only in a Projector, you are most likely missing a necessary Xtra in the Projector's *Xtras* folder (or you didn't bundle the necessary Xtras, which I advise against anyway). Check if the function requires an Xtra, such as the NetLingo commands and FileIO's *getOSdirectory()* command (refer to Table 18-1). If an Xtra doesn't load, any calls to its methods will fail. (This is a problem with the QuickTime 3 Xtra's *QuickTimeVersion()* method on the Macintosh when QT3 is not installed. See Chapter 16, *Digital Video*, in *Director in a Nutshell*.) If the handler requires an Xtra instance, instantiate the Xtra before calling the handler. See Chapter 13, *Lingo Xtras and XObjects*. It's possible that you've overflowed the Lingo Symbol Table under Windows 3.1 (see Chapter 19, *The Lingo Symbol Table*).

Error Message	Cause or Solution
Handler not found in object	You specified a function call with an object as the first parameter, and that object does not contain the specified handler. Recompile your object's parent script. Variables referring to script instances use a copy of the code that existed when the script was instantiated. You must re-initialize your variables if the underlying parent script changes.
Having trouble reading this file	This error message indicates some generic problem reading a Director movie or castLib. It should also include an error code that can be interpreted using Tables E-2 and E-3. Typically the file is the wrong format for the specified operation or the file is protected or in use.
Incorrect Preference File Extension	Preferences file used with *getPref()* and *setPref()* must have .TXT (the default) or . HTM extension (not .HTML).
Index is not positive	The index into a list must be greater than zero, such as: getAt (*myList*, *index*) -- *index* > 0
Index out of range	You are trying to access a list element using a list position that is zero, negative, or greater than the number of elements in the list, such as: getAt ([1, 3, 5], 5)
Index too big	You've exceeded the maximum number of elements in a list or overflowed the Lingo Symbol Table under Windows 3.1 (see Chapter 19).
Instance command not allowed here	Unexpected use of an Xtra instance has occurred. Check your syntax and the Xtra's documentation.

Integer expected	You specified a float, string, etc., when Lingo expected an integer or a Boolean expression.
	if (*string*) then... -- *wrong*
	if (*string* = EMPTY) then... -- *right*
	See *<Something> expected* error.
	For linear lists, *setaProp()* is identical to *setAt()* and requires an integer index as the second argument. Specifying anything else causes an "Integer Expected" error.

Integer or list expected	You specified a float, string, etc., when Lingo expected an integer or a list. See *<Something> expected* error.
Invalid palette	This error is seen in D6.5 when importing a bitmap. Remove the new PICT import/export Xtra (Mac) or Bitmap import/export Xtra (Windows). Use these only for *Save as Java* exporting.
Invalid Projector File <path>	Error occurs under Windows 3.1 running SHARE.EXE with Projectors built with D6.0 and possibly D6.0.1. Set the Projector file to read-only or rebuild it with D6.0.2 or D6.5.
Label expected	Lingo expected the name of a marker label.

Error Message	Cause or Solution
LINGO.INI file not found	You have not included a LINGO.INI file. See Appendix D, *The DIRECTOR.INI and LINGO.INI Files*.
Lingo Xtra handler requires instance	You must instantiate the Xtra first using: `set instance = new (Xtra "XtraName")` Then use the instance to access other methods in the Xtra.
List cannot be empty	The list is either an empty linear list or property list ([] or [:]) and should contain at least one element.
List expected	The command expected a list as a parameter and got something else, such as an empty variable. See *<Something> expected* error.
List must contain integer	The list used as an input to the command was expected to contain an integer.
Media expected	Lingo expected a media reference, such as the media of a film loop when using: `set the score = the media of member filmloop` See *<Something> expected* error.
Menu item not defined	You are trying to access an invalid item on a custom menu, such as: `put the name of menuItem 12 of menu 1`
Menu not defined	You are trying to access a custom menu that has not been installed, such as: `put the name of menu 1` See *installMenu*.
Message expected	You used *call()* or a similar function without specifying a message symbol using the # character, such as *call(#message)*.
Method not defined	You called a non-existent method within an object.
Misplaced ELSE	You used an *else* statement before the *if...then* or after the *end if* statement. See Chapter 1.
Misplaced END REPEAT	You used *end repeat* before the *repeat with* or *repeat while* statement or after another *end repeat* statement. See Chapter 1.
Misplaced EXIT TELL	You used *exit tell* outside of a *tell...end tell* block.
Misplaced NEXT REPEAT	You used *next repeat* outside of a *repeat* loop. See Chapter 1.

Misplaced Operator	You forgot the *set* keyword when assigning variables.
	`x = 5       -- wrong`
	`set x = 5 -- right`

Misspelled event	The event name is invalid.
More than 16 xobject parameters	XObjects can't receive more than 16 parameters. Check the XObject documentation or your parameter list.

Table E-1: Lingo Errors (continued)

Error Message	Cause or Solution
Movie cast member expected	Lingo expected a cast member whose *type of member* is #movie. See *<Member Type>* expected error.
Movie cast member not found	Lingo expected a cast member whose *type of member* is #movie. See *<Member Type>* cast member not found error.
Movie cast not found	You are trying to access *the castLib of sprite*, whereas the correct syntax is *the castLibNum of sprite*. Or the cast for a linked #movie cast member could not be found. Open the movie as Director's main movie and check *the fileName of castLib* property.
Movie name expected	Director expected the name of a movie file.

Name already used	You've declared the same handler name twice in the same script (not allowed, so delete one), such as:
	`on mouseUp`
	`  statement(s)`
	`end`
	
	`on mouseUp`
	`  statement(s)`
	`end`

Name expected	You started a line with the *on* keyword, but you have not followed it with a handler name on the same line, such as:
	`on handlerName`
	`  statement(s)`
	`end`

No XCOD resource for XObject	The loaded XObject does not have any executable code. Check for a corrupted file. Replace if possible.
Not a text cast member	Lingo expected a *field* cast member, not a rich text cast member. (In D4 fields were called "text" cast members.)
Number expected	Lingo expected an integer or floating-point number, not a VOID, string, etc. See *<Something>* expected error.
Object expected	Lingo expected a script instance, xtra instance, list, window, or other object. See *<Something>* expected error.
One parameter expected	You specified the wrong number of parameters, such as: `alert          ` *-- wrong* `alert "Hello"  ` *-- right* `alert EMPTY    ` *-- right*
Only field cast members can be used to create menus	The *installMenu* command can refer only to a field cast member, not a rich text cast member.

Errors

Table E-1: Lingo Errors (continued)

Error Message	Cause or Solution
Operand expected	The current line of Lingo ended prematurely. You've specified an operator such as "+" or a comma, but no operand to follow it: `set x = 5 +` *-- wrong* `set x = 5 + 7` *-- right* `set myList = [1,2,` *-- wrong* `set myList = [1,2,]` *-- wrong* `set myList = [1,2]` *-- right* Break up very long lines of Lingo using ¬. Get rid of any spaces at the end of a line after a continuation character as this confuses Director.
Out of memory	You're importing too many items or importing at a high bit depth. Import fewer files at once and save the Director movie between imports. You may be leaking memory or calling a Lingo handler recursively.
Out of memory for string	Director can't allocate enough memory for a large string that you've created. Use smaller strings or the FileIO Xtra.
Palette not defined	You've specified a nonexistent palette. See Table 16-1 for details on the palette types for various palette-related commands.
Picture expected	The *picture of member* property requires a picture object. See *<Something> expected*.
Point expected	The property or command expects a point, such as: `set the loc of sprite 5 = point (100, 200)` See *<Something> expected*.
Problem opening C:\ WINNT	This error occurs when starting a Projector with bundled Xtras on a Windows NT machine with a hard disk partition larger than about 4 GB. Don't bundle your Xtras into the Projector. Put them in a separate *Xtras* folder instead.
Property list did not start with property name	Specify your property list of this form: `set x = [#a: "a", #b: 12, #c: "oranges"]` See Chapter 6, *Lists*.
Property modifier expected	You've specified a property name incorrectly.
Property name expected	You've forgotten the property following the keyword *the*.
Property not found	You specified an invalid property for a member, sprite, or the system. Check the cast member or spriter asset type.
Property or value missing	You've omitted a necessary property or value.
Rect expected	The property or command expects a rect, such as: `set the rect of sprite 5 = ¬` `    rect (0, 0, 320, 240)`

Error Message	Cause or Solution
Right parenthesis expected	You have more opening parentheses than closing parentheses. Count parentheses carefully.
Script cast member expected	You've neglected to specify a script cast member for a property or command that expects one. See *<Something> expected*.
Script cast member not found	You've referred to a script by name or number than can't be found. See *<Member Type> cast member not found*.
Script runtime error...	A generic error (consult the dialog for more details) that occurs when Director tries to execute your code.
Script syntax error...	Director can not correctly interpret your code in order to compile it. This generic error should be accompanied by more details, such as "Variable used before assigned value."
Script wrong	Director could not parse or identify your script.
Shape cast member expected	See *<Member Type> cast member expected*.
Shape cast member not found	See *<Member Type> cast member not found*.
Sound cast member expected	See *<Member Type> cast member expected*. Sound cast members must be specified for *puppetSound* commands.
Sound cast member not found	See *<Member Type> cast member not found*.
Sound not defined	You are trying to access a nonexistent sound.
Sound option wrong	You are trying to set a sound property to an invalid value.
Sprite number wrong	You've specified a sprite number outside of the allowed limits of 1 to 120.
Stopped by user	The user has halted the movie, such as by using `Ctrl-Q` or `Cmd-Q`.
String does not end correctly	You've forgotten or misplaced one or more straight double quotes (") or your line of Lingo is too long. Shorten the string, and concatenate it in pieces. See Chapter 7.
String expected	See *<Something> expected*. If a command such as *alert* requires a string, you can force a conversion to a string: `alert myIntegerVariable` *-- wrong* `alert string(myVariable)` *-- right*

Errors

Table E-1: Lingo Errors (continued)

Error Message	Cause or Solution
Symbol expected	See *<Something> expected*. You may have incorrectly used parentheses after a handler declaration: `on handlerName (a, b, c)` *-- wrong* `end` `on handlerName a, b, c` *-- right* `end` For property lists, the second argument to *getaProp()* is assumed to be a property name, not an index, even if it is an integer. For rects and points, the second argument to *setaProp()* must be one of the valid rect or point properties (*locH, locV, left, top, right* or *bottom*). Use of an integer in this case causes a "Symbol expected" error.
Syntax error...	Your grammar, punctuation, or spelling somehow confused Director. Additional details should be provided on the nature of the error. Check the spelling of all commands, variables, and handlers. Confirm the syntax for the command and the number, type, and order of expected parameters. Check for missing or mismatched parentheses or quotes. Be sure you understand the use of quotes and the concatenation symbols. See Chapter 7.
Text style wrong	You've specified an invalid value for the *textStyle* or *fontStyle of member* property. See Table 16-1.
There is no disk in drive A: please insert disk into drive A:	This occurs under Windows 3.1 or NT (but not necessarily Win 95/98) when trying to read from a floppy drive with no media inserted, using perhaps FileIO, *getNthFileNameInFolder()* or *the searchPath*. See Chapter 14.
This application requires at least 3 MB of virtual memory	Windows Projectors require the Virtual Memory be turned on unless a lot of RAM (> 32 MB or so) is available. Refer to Chapter 9, *Performance and Memory*, in *Director in a Nutshell*.
This command not allowed in a method	You tried to execute an unallowed command that has been specifically disabled by Macromedia from within certain types of handlers.
Too many parameters to an XObject	You've exceeded the maximum number of allowable parameters. You've probably misplaced quotes or parentheses or added too many commas.
Too many parameters to Lingo Xtra	You've exceeded the maximum number of allowable parameters. You've probably misplaced quotes or parentheses or added too many commas.
Too many symbols	You've overflowed the Lingo Symbol Table. This is most likely to occur under Windows 3.1. See Chapter 19, *The Lingo Symbol Table*, for gory details.
Transition cast member expected	The *puppetTransition* and *frameTransition* commands require transition cast members. See *<Member Type> cast member expected*.
Unexpected end of statement	Lingo thinks it has detected the ending punctuation for a statement, but it still expected more items. Confirm the syntax of the command.

Error Message	Cause or Solution
Use of unsupported Lingo command	Command is not allowed in Shockwave. See entries marked "Not for SW" in Table 18-1. See Chapter11, *Shockwave and the Internet*, in *Director in a Nutshell*.
Value out of range	You've specified an out-of-range value for a property that allows only limited values.
Variable not defined	You've attempted to use a variable before setting a value for it or declaring it as a global or property.
Variable used before assigned a value	You've attempted to use a variable before setting a value for it or declaring it as a global or property. See Example 3-13. "Addressing a, 'Variable Used Before Assigned a Value' Error," in the "Script Error" section of Chapter 3. Also see "Common Errors" in the "*Variables and Properties*" section of Chapter 1.
Window not found	You've referred to an invalid window. Check *the windowList*. Refer to a new window by name, not number, to initialize it, such as: `set the windowType of window "newWindow" = 1` See Chapter 6, *The Stage and MIAWs*, in *Director in a Nutshell*.
Wrong number of parameters	You've specified the wrong number of arguments to a command or function.
Wrong type	Lingo expected a different type cast member or data type.
XCMD name expected	XCMD names are expected as parameters to some of XCMDglue's method.
XLib file not found	You tried to open a non-existent Xlib with *openXlib* or close one that wasn't open with *closeXlib*. Specify the complete path if necessary.
XObject callback not supported	You attempted to use a Hypercard XFCN or XCMD that uses a Hypercard-specific function.
XObject entry not found	XObject is not open or loaded. Open it with *openXlib*.
Xtra handler name expected	See <*Something*> *expected*. Director is expecting the name of a handler within an Xtra.
Xtra name expected	Specify an Xtra name in quotes of the form: `put mMessageList (xtra "XtraName")`
Xtra not found	You specified an incorrect name for an Xtra, such as: `put mMessageList (xtra "XtraName")` or the Xtra is not installed. Check *the number of xtras* and *the name of xtra* properties. Xtras may not be in the proper support folder or may not have loaded due to RAM limitations.
Zero parameters expected	You specified parameters when you should not have. Specify no parameters using two parentheses such as: `put getOSdirectory()`

Director Error Codes

On both the Macintosh and Windows, Director uses many (negative) numeric error codes that are the same as the Macintosh system error codes.

 MacErrors is a shareware utility that interprets Macintosh error codes. (Search the Web or the usual shareware sites). See *http://www.zeusprod.com/technote/winerr.html* for a long list of Windows Error codes.

Director itself often posts error messages showing the same codes as returned by the FileIO Xtra. For example, Director displays a -35 error when it can't find the Help file, and a -49 error when a file is in use. (See Table E-3.)

Director also issues positive error codes that don't match those returned by FileIO as shown in Table E-2 (which lists both positive and negative codes without regard to their sign). If you can't find an error in Table E-2, try the other tables in this chapter, especially Table E-3.

Table E-2: Director Error Codes

Code	Meaning
INF or -INF	This code, meaning, "Infinity," is usually due to an invalid math calculation or computational overflow. See Chapter 8.
NAN	This code, meaning, "Not a number," is usually due to an invalid math calculation or computational overflow. See Chapter 8.
VOID	VOID is not an error per se. It indicates "nothingness" such as an uninitialized global variable. Taking the *integer()*, *float()*, or *value()* of an invalid datum returns VOID.
11	"Type 11" error. A genereal Mac configuration error. Search the Macromedia Technotes for suggestions.
12	You are trying to use a D6 movie from a D5 Projector. Upgrade to D6, or copy and paste the assets into a D5 movie file.
-35	When launching help system on the Macintosh, the Help file must be named "Director 6.0 Help" in the *Help* folder one folder down from Director. You must have *QuickHelp* (aka the *Macromedia Help Player*) installed. The creator code of application must be "MMQ5", not "ALTH" as was used in earlier versions of Director and beta version of D6.
-45	"File locked Error," you've specified a Director movie name without the .DIR extension in a *go movie* or *play movie* command and Director is confused by Windows folder of the same name.

Code	Meaning
-49	A generic file access conflict usually caused by two programs trying to open the same file at the same time. For example, only one user can edit a Director movie stored on a file server, at any given time. Quit whatever other application may be using the file. In D5 for Windows, the Lingo *open* and *open...with* commands would permanently lock any movies that were open when the command was issued. The solution is to set the file to read-only using the File Explorer's Properties option.
-50	This error may occur when attempting to open the Macintosh online Help. It may be due to multiple versions of QuickHelp, an old desktop that needs rebuilding, or older versions of QuickHelp on MacOS 8. If all else fails, re-install Director.
100	"Having trouble reading this file - error 100" is caused by trying to open a D6 movie from the D5 authoring environment. This is usually because your Windows system is configured to open Director 5 when double-clicking a .DIR. Change the associated application to D6 using the *File Types* tab in File Explorer's View➤Options dialog box, or open the movie file using File➤Open from within D6. "Cannot open this file because it is protected". You attempted to open a DXR or DCR file. You need the original source DIR file.
-108	"Out of memory" errors occur when trying to launch a browser with *gotoNetPage* or trying to launch an external application with *open* or *open...with* when insufficient RAM exists. Zeus Productions' zLaunch utility (*http://www.zeusprod.com/products/zlaunch.html*) allows you to quit Director to free up RAM while running another applications.
-111	"Memory storage Error." This may be seen when exporting QT files if not enough memory or disk space is available.
201	"Having trouble opening this file". You've specified a non-movie file such as Projector with *go movie* or *play movie*.
-208	Sound manager error indicating corrupt or unreadable sound file.

FileIO Errors

When you instantiate either the FileIO *Xtra* or *XObject* on either Macintosh or Windows, the return value is either a successful instance or an integer error code. Refer to Chapter 14, *External Files*.

The older FileIO XObject and Xtra on both platforms return the same values, with exceptions noted in the text that follows. Other FileIO methods, such as *write-Char* and *readChar*, also return either success (0) or some negative error code.

Table E-3 shows the strings returned by FileIO's *error()* method for a given integer error code as returned by the *status()* method (column 1), such as:

```
set fileInstance = new (xtra "FileIO")
openFile (fileInstance, fileName, mode)
set errorCode = status(fileInstance)
put error (fileInstance, errorCode)
```

Similar values are returned by the *mStatus()* and *mError()* methods of the FileIO XObject. Some error codes shown are not translated by either the Xtra or XObject, but appear occasionally and can be interpreted using *MacErrors* instead. These descriptions and their likely cause are shown in parentheses.

Table E-3: FileIO Xtra and XObject Errors

Code	Xtra	XObject	Meaning
1	•		"Memory allocation failure"
0	•		"OK" (Mac and Windows Xtra) (Sucess)
0		•	"OK" (Mac FileIO XObject) (Sucess)
0		•	EMPTY (Windows FileIO XObject) (Sucess)
-1	•		"Unknown Error" (attempted to use *readChar* when already at the end of the file)
-1		•	EMPTY (Mac FileIO XObject)
-33	•	•	"File directory full" (too many files in directory)
-34	•	•	"Volume full" (disk is full)
-35	•	•	"Volume not found" (disk can not be found)
-36	•	•	"I/O Error" (used *getFinderInfo* before opening a file, or used *readWord* or *readToken* with an invalid file position as set by *setPosition*)
-37	•	•	"Bad file name" (invalid file name or EMPTY name)
-38	•	•	"File not open" (must use *openFile* before using read or write methods)
-39		•	(Logical EOF reached during operation; attempted to set file position past end of file with *mSetPosition*)
-40		•	(Tried to position to before start of file; attempted to set file position to negative number with *mSetPosition*)
-41			(Memory full)
-42	•	•	"Too many files open" (must close files when you're done)
-43	•		"File not found" (or folder not found)
-43		•	"File not found" (User clicked *cancel* in File dialog created with *mNew* command using "?read", "?write" or "?append" mode)
-44			(Disk is write protected, volume is locked)
-45			(File is locked or in use)
-46			(Volume is locked through software)
-47			(File is busy)
-48			(Duplicate filename during rename)

Code	Xtra	XObject	Meaning
-49		•	(File already open with write permission; that is, file in use. Try setting file to Read-only.)
-54			(Permission violation, insufficient privileges)
-56	•	•	"No such drive" (check your file path)
-65	•	•	"No disk in drive" (insert CD, etc.)
-120	•	•	"Directory not found" (check your file path)
-121	•		"Instance has an open file" (use *closeFile* to close the instance)
-122	•		"File already exists" (use *openFile* instead of *createFile*)
-123	•		"File is opened read-only" (*closeFile* and re-*openFile* in write or read/write mode)
-124	•		"File is opened write-only" (*closeFile* and re-*openFile* in read or read/write mode)

SWA Xtra getError(), getErrorString()

The SWA cast member's *state of member* property is set to 9 if an error occurs while a cast member is streaming into memory. (See Table 16-1.)

```
if the state of member swaMember = 9 then
   put getError(member swaMember)
   put getErrorString(member swaMember)
end if
```

Table E-4 shows the integer value returned by *getError()* and the corresponding string returned by *getErrorString()* for an SWA cast member.

This Requires the SWA Streaming Xtra.

Table E-4: SWA Member Error Codes

getError()	getErrorString()
0	EMPTY or "OK"
1	"memory"
2	"network" (or "Network software error")
3	"playback device"
99	"other"

Flash Asset Xtra getError()

The Flash cast member's `state of member` property is set to -1 if an error occurs while a cast member is streaming into memory.

```
if the state of member flashMember = -1 then
  put getError(member flashMember)
end if
```

Table E-5 shows the code returned by *getError()* for a Flash cast member.

This requires the Flash Asset Xtra.

Table E-5: Flash Asset Xtra Error Codes

getError()	Meaning
FALSE	No error occurred (Sucess).
#memory	There is not enough memory to load the cast member.
#fileNotFound	The file containing the cast member's assets could not be found.
#network	A network error prevented the cast member from loading.
#fileFormat	The file was found, but it appears to be of the wrong type, or an error occurred while reading the file.
#other	Some other error occurred.

Network Errors—netError()

The error codes returned by *netError()* depend on the environment. In Authoring and Projectors, the errors are generated from the INetURL Xtra (Macromedia's http implementation). In Shockwave, the error codes come from the browser (Netscape or MIE).

Error Handling in Shockwave versus Projectors

During Authoring and from Projectors if you attempt to *preLoadNetThing(url)* with a bad URL, *netError()* will report an error 4165, "*Requested object could not be found.*" In Shockwave the same attempt may still return a human-readable HTML page if the server name is valid, but the page is simply missing. The returned HTML text may be, "The requested object could not be found on the server." Example E-1 detects the situation properly.

Example E-1: Error Handling

```
property pUrl
property pNetId

on startDownLoad me, url
  set pUrl = url
  set pNetId = preloadNetThing(pUrl)
end startDownLoad

on checkProgress me
  -- Call this periodically
  if netDone(pNetId) then
```

Example E-1: Error Handling (continued)

```
      case (netError(pNetId)) of
        "OK", 0: importFileInto member "dynamic content", pUrl
        otherwise: alert "Error:" && netError(pNetId)
      end case
    end if
  end checkProgress
```

Table E-6 shows the *netError()* error codes. Those over 4000 appear to be TCP error codes.

Table E-6: Macromedia NetError() Codes

Code	Meaning
0	"OK"
1	Usually a memory error, but possibly a bus error.
4	"Bad MOA Class"—network Xtras may not be properly installed. Check with *the netPresent (not the netPresent() function).*
5	"Bad MOA Interface" (see "Bad MOA Class").
6	Usually a bad URL (see error 905).
20	"Internal error"—Returned by *netError()* in Shockwave if browser detected a network or internal error.
905	"Bad URL"
4144	"Failed network operation"[1]
4146	"Connection could not be established with the remote host"
4149	"Data supplied by the server was in an unexpected format"
4150	"Unexpected early closing of connection"
4154	"Operation could not be completed due to timeout"
4155	"Not enough memory available to complete the transaction"
4156	"Protocol reply to request indicates an error in the reply"
4157	"Transaction failed to be authenticated"
4159	"Invalid URL"
4164	"Could not create a socket"
4165	"Requested Object could not be found" (URL may be incorrect)
4166	"Generic proxy failure"
4167	"Transfer was intentionally interrupted by client"
4242	"Download stopped by netAbort(url)"

Code	Meaning
4836	"Download stopped for an unknown reason"—May have been a network error, or the download may have been abandoned.

[1] Error codes between 4145 and 4168 that are not shown are the same as code 4144, "Failed network operation."

MOA Errors

Table E-7 shows a few codes returned by various MOA operations that can be interpreted with the *MOAerrorToString()* function included in the MUI Dialog Xtra. The full list of MOA error codes are mainly of interest to MOA Xtra developers. Refer to *http://www.zeusprod.com/nutshell/chapters/moaerror.html* or the MOA XDK documentation for a more complete list of MOA error codes.

Table E-7: MOA Codes Error

Code	Meaning
0	"** String Not Available! **"
-2147219501	"MOA core error: XAsset type unknown"[1]
MOA Error code	Use *MOAerrorToString()* to interpret.
Non-MOA errors	"Unknown or System specific error"

[1] This error code is returned when the *new(#assetType)* command fails. See Example 19-3.

Glossary

This glossary presents key definitions pertaining to Lingo and Director. See also *http://www.zeusprod.com/glossary/*.

argument: n. A piece of data used by a function that is required when you make the function call. For example, if you were multiplying two numbers, the numbers themselves would be arguments passed to the `multiply` handler. Sometimes used synonymously with "parameter" or "operand."

asynchronous: adj. An idle loading or network operation is asynchronous because the requested data may not be available immediately. Asynchronous operations usually provide some way to check their status, such as using `netDone()`.

authoring: n. "Authoring" refers to the Director development environment. Contrasted with runtime or playback (Projectors).

Behavior : n. A Behavior script. Macromedia's name for a reusable script that can be attached to a sprite or a frame. The handlers defined in the script give it a certain behavior.

behavior: n. The way in which an item operates.

Boolean: n. or adj. A value that can be either 0 (indicating false) or nonzero (indicating true), usually represented in Lingo by the constants TRUE and FALSE, which equal 1 and 0, respectively. Not to be confused with the strings "TRUE" and "FALSE."

call: 1. v. To run a Lingo handler by typing its name in the Message window or including its name in another Lingo script. 2. n. A line of Lingo code that calls another handler (synonymous with "function call"). The function call may also require additional parameters or arguments.

calling routine: n. A routine that includes a call to another handler. When Lingo is inside a handler, the "calling routine" is the routine that sent it there.

call stack: n. The series of calling routines that have led to the current handler. The call stack is shown in the upper left pane in the Debugger window.

Cast: n. Director's database of bitmaps, sounds, text, and Lingo scripts. In Director 4 and earlier "*cast*" was synonymous with "*member*" or "*cast member*," but in D5 and later it means the Cast window or a Cast library.

Cast Library or *castLib*: n. A collection of cast members stored either internally to a Director movie or in an external cast file.

Cast member. n. An asset in the Cast window.

Castmember. adj. Pertaining to a cast member, such as a castmember property.

child object. n. An instance of a parent script. A child object has its own independent copies of any properties declared in the parent script. See Chapter 12, *Behaviors and Parent Scripts.*

code. 1. v. To program; 2. n. Lingo scripts; 3. v. To require emergency care, as during a heart attack.. See definitions 1 and 2.

comment. n. A line in a Lingo script that Director ignores but that is instructive for humans. Lingo comments begin with two hyphens "--".

command. n. A function that is built into the Lingo language. Use a command by typing its name in a script or the Message window. Commands usually perform some operation, but they do not return a value.

compile. v. To prepare a script to run. You must recompile a script before Director will be able to recognize and interpret it properly. See Chapter 1, *How Lingo Thinks.*

concatenate. v. To join two strings together to make a bigger string, using the & or && operators.

constant. n. A value that doesn't change, such as Lingo's built-in constants (TRUE, FALSE, TAB, etc.) or a fixed number or string such as 6 or "Hello."

constructor. n. The C++ equivalent of a *new()* method used to instantiate an object in Lingo.

continuation character. n. A special Lingo symbol ([LC]) that tells Director to continue a Lingo statement onto the next line. Created using Option-Return or Option-L (Mac) or Alt-Enter (Windows).

cue points. n. Notations in a sound, SWA, or digital video file that are used to synchronize the soundtrack to something else. D6 supports cue points in SWA, AIF, and QT files. D6.5 also supports cue points in WAV files. See the *on cuePassed* event handler in Chapter 15, *Sound and Cue Points*, in *Director in a Nutshell.*

D3.1.3: Director 3.1.3 for Macintosh (there was a converter for Windows).

D4: Director 4.x for Macintosh or Windows.

D5: Director 5.x for Macintosh or Windows.

D6: Director 6.x for Macintosh or Windows.

D6.5: Director 6.5 for Macintosh or Windows, shipped May 1998.

declare. v. To initialize or otherwise name a variable or handler that is to be used. You can declare variables using the *property* or *global* keywords or assign a value using *set* or *put...into*. Declare a handler with the *on* keyword.

default. adj. The initial value for a Lingo property or variable that remains in effect unless you change it.

delimiter. n. A character, such as a space, tab, or comma, that sets off one item from another. The *itemDelimiter* defaults to a comma and is used to parse text.

dynamic. adj. Can be changed at runtime, such as setting a property dynamically or creating a cast member dynamically.

explicit. adj. An explicit operation is one that you perform specifically in your Lingo code. Using the *string()* function explicitly converts an item to a string. Using the concatenation operator(s) will implicitly convert an item to a string.

event handler. n. A handler that is called automatically in response to an event such as a mouse click or key press, including, *on mouseDown, on mouseUp, on keyDown, on keyUp, on enterFrame*, and *on exitFrame*.

external asset. n. An asset that resides in a separate external file, such as digital video or audio, and is usually linked into either an internal or external castLib. See *linked.* An external sound file can be played using *sound playFile* without being linked to a particular cast member.

external castLib: n. castLib that is external to the Director movie file. Not to be confused with an external asset. It can be associated with a Director movie via `Modify` ➤`Movie`➤`Casts` or used as a standalone library. See *linked*.

field: n. A field cast member or its contents. Previously called a *text* cast member. Not to be confused for a rich text cast member.

flag: n. A Boolean variable that is used to signal an on/off condition.

Flash: n. A vector-based animation tool from Macromedia.

Flash Asset Xtra: n. An Xtra included with D6.5 that allows Director to use Flash 2 (not yet Flash 3) files.

float: n. A decimal (floating-point number), which may be negative, 0.0, or positive, such as 3.14159.

function: n. A handler that accepts arguments and/or returns a value. Often used interchangeably with "script," "handler," or "routine."

function call: n. Lingo making use of a function. The function call includes the name of the function and any parameters it requires and can be made from the Message window or from another handler by typing the function's name and required parameters.

handler: n. A collection of Lingo statements that performs some useful function. Handlers start with the words *on handlerName* where *handlerName* is arbitrarily chosen by the programmer. Once a handler is written, it can be called (i.e., executed) by typing its name in the Message window or using its name in another script. *Event handlers* are called automatically when the user presses the mouse button or a key.

handler declaration or *definition*: n. The Lingo code that makes up a handler, starting with *on handlerName* and ending with an *end* statement.

hardcoded : adj. or v. To program (code) with fixed values, rather than variables or other flexible values that can be changed at runtime.

implicit: adj. An implicit operation is performed automatically by Director or Lingo without a specific request. For example, a variable may be implicitly converted from an integer to a string before being displayed.

index: n. An integer indicating an element's position within a list. The index 1 (one) represents the first element.

instance: 1. n. An occurrence of a Behavior, Xtra, or parent script. A child object is an instance of a parent script; 2. v. To instantiate.

instantiate: v. To create an instance of a Behavior or parent script. You instantiate a parent script using the *new()* method, which creates a child object. Behaviors are instantiated automatically when they are encountered in the Score. Cast scripts and movie scripts are not instantiated.

integer: n. A whole number that can be positive, negative, or zero.

internal asset: n. An asset that is imported into either an internal or external castLib and does not make use of an external asset file. See *external*, *linked*, and *unlinked*.

internal castLib: n. A castLib that is internal to a Director movie file. An internal castLib can contain both *linked* and *unlinked* cast members. Contrast *external castLib*.

keyword: n. A word that is part of the Lingo language itself. Keywords must be typed exactly as expected by Director. See Chapter 18, *Lingo Keyword and Command Summary*.

linked asset: n. An asset for which a cast member points to an external file, such as a digital video or audio file containing the actual data. See *external*, *internal*, and *unlinked*.

linked castLib: n. External castLib that is associated with a Director movie via Modify➤ Movie➤Casts. See *external, internal,* and *unlinked.*

linking: v. To attach an external asset (external sound or video, external castLib, or internet URL) to your Director movie. The term has nothing to do with the programming sense of the word (creating an executable from object files).

list: n. A special data type that can contain a series of values of any other data type. You could have a list of integers, a list of strings, a list that contains both integers and strings, or even a list of lists! See Chapter 6, *Lists.*

literal: n. A string contained in quotes, such as "Boo Boopy Doo," or a fixed number, such as 6. Literal numbers are sometimes called *constants.*

loaded: adj. A cast member that resides in memory, rather than on disk, is said to be *loaded.*

member: n. A cast member in the Cast window.

member reference: n. A member or castmember reference identifying a cast member by name or number including an optional castLib, such as:

```
member "someMember"
member 1 of castLib 2
member "someMember" of castLib "myCastLib"
```

method: 1. n. A handler within a parent script or Behavior that performs some function. A method is just the name used for functions that are part of an object-oriented script.

MIAW: n. Movie-in-a-window.

MOA: n. Macromedia Open Architecture that allows Director to support Xtras.

movie: n. 1. A Director data file that contains the Score and an internal Cast and is played on Stage or as a Movie-in-a-Window. Movie files have nothing directly to do with QuickTime or other digital video formats. 2. A digital video movie, usually QuickTime or AVI format.

Movie-in-a-window (MIAW): n. A standard Director movie played in a subwindow instead of on the Stage.

MUI: n. Macromedia User Interface. The *MUI Dialog* Xtra creates custom dialogs.

N/A: n. Indicates that an item in a table is not applicable or not meaningful.

offset: n. The difference between two values usually indicating relative position, as opposed to absolute positions.

parameter: n. An argument received by a function. The function call's arguments are automatically equated to the parameters that are defined in the first line of the handler following the handler name. For example *a* and *b* are parameters in

```
on multiply a, b
   return a * b
end
```

parent script: n. A Lingo script, whose *scriptType* is #parent, that contains the Lingo code that defines the behavior of a child object. See Chapter 12.

parse: v. To break down into smaller pieces, such as to extract words from a long text string. See "Text Parsing" in Chapter 7, *Strings.*

preloaded: adj. A cast member that is loaded manually prior to being needed in a given frame is said to be *preloaded.*

property: 1. n. A Lingo keyword that provides information about the system setup, such as the `colorDepth`. See Chapter 1; 2. n. A type of Lingo variable used with child objects, such as the `ancestor` property. See Chapter 12; 3. A symbol used to identify an item in a property list (see Chapter 6 and Chapter 19, *The Lingo Symbol Table*).

purgeable: adj. A cast member or other asset that is eligible to be removed from memory is said to be *purgeable*.

purged: adj. A cast member that is removed from memory is said to be *purged* or *unloaded*.

QT: n. QuickTime.

QT3: n. QuickTime 3, released in May 1998. To take advantage of QT3 requires the *QuickTime3* Xtra included with D6.5.

QTW: n. QuickTime for Windows.

read-only: adj. 1. A Lingo property that can be tested but not set. 2. A file that can be read from, but not written to. 3. A nonwritable disk, such as a CD-ROM.

reference count-based garbage collection: n. The process by which Director decides whether any variables refer to a list or other object before deciding whether to free the memory allocated to the object.

reserved word: n. A keyword that is part of the Lingo's structure itself, such as the word "*on*," that identifies the beginning of a handler. Arbitrary names chosen by the programmer for variables and handler names should not conflict with Lingo reserved words.

returns: v. A function or property *returns* a value to the caller.

routine: n. A function or handler.

RSX: n. An audio sound driver under Windows 95 that interferes with Lingo substantially. See Chapter 15 in *Director in a Nutshell*.

run-time: adj. 1. Occurring when being tested from a Projector as opposed to the authoring environment; 2. Occurring when Director is running, as opposed to compile-time.

script: n. A cast member that contains Lingo statements that tell Director what to do (just as real-life actors follow a script). There are several types of script cast members (cast scripts, movie scripts, sprite scripts, and parent scripts), and a script can contain one or more Lingo handlers. See Chapter 2, *Events, Messages, and Scripts*.

Script channel: n. The channel in the Score where so-called *frame scripts* can be attached (below the Effects channels and above sprite channel 1).

scope: n. A handler's or variable's scope determines from where it is accessible. See Chapters 1 and 2.

Score: n. Director's timeline (like a giant spreadsheet) for constructing cell animations. Refer to Macromedia's *Using Director* manual and to Chapter 1, *How Director Works*, in *Director in Nutshell*.

Shockwave for Director: n. The Netscape compatible plug-in or Active-X control required to view Director content in a Web browser.

Shockwave Flash: n. The Netscape-compatible plug-in or Active-X control required to view Flash content in a Web browser. Included in Shockwave for Director download.

sprite or sprite span: n. A unified range of cells occupying a sprite channel or the script channel over one or more frames in the Score. In Director 6, a sprite is no longer a single cell as it was in previous versions of Director.

sprite channel: n. One of the channels (numbered 1 to 120) in the Score that holds sprites, such as bitmaps. *Channel* is sometimes used synonymously with the sprite in that channel.

stack: n. See call stack.

stacking order: n. The order of windows, sprites, or paint layers. Also called Z-order.

Stage: n. The window where your Director presentation plays; referred to using the Lingo property, the `stage`.

Glossary

static: adj. Fixed; the opposite of dynamic. Also used in C programming to indicate variables that persist over time, as would a Lingo global variable.

string: n. A collection of zero or more characters. A literal string is indicated with quotes, such as "Bite Me." EMPTY is a string of zero length, represented by double quotes with no contents ("").

subroutine: n. See *handler* or *function*.

SW: n. Shockwave.

SWA: n. Shockwave Audio (compressed audio streamed from disk or the Internet).

swap file or *swap space*: n. The physical file on disk used as virtual memory.

SWF: n. Shockwave Flash.

synchronous: adj. Operations that immediately return a valid result are said to be *synchronous*, as opposed to commands for which the result may not be available until some time in the future, which are said to be "*asynchronous*."

syntax: n. The form a command takes, or the rigid but simple rules that govern the acceptable form of a Lingo script. Syntax includes spelling, punctuation, spacing, and the order and number of arguments.

ticks: n. A measurement equal to 1/60th of a second. See Chapter 11, *Timers and Dates*.

unlink: v. To remove an association between two items, such as to unlink an externally linked castLib from a Director movie.

unlinked: adj. An asset imported directly into a castLib (see *internal*, contrast *linked* and *external*).

unloaded: adj. A cast member that is removed from memory is said to be *purged* or *unloaded*.

variable: n. A placeholder that contains data that can change while a program executes. Variable names are arbitrarily chosen by the programmer but should not conflict with Lingo's keywords.

VFW: n. Video for Windows, a digital video technology using AVI files.

virtual memory: n. Hard drive space used to augment real RAM to simulate memory. Virtual memory is at least several orders of magnitude slower than RAM.

void: adj. A variable containing no data whatsoever (because it has never been assigned a value) is considered "void." This is not the same as EMPTY or zero, and is represented in Lingo by the keyword VOID.

windowID: n. A *window identifier* indicates a movie-in-a-window (MIAW) or the Stage, and it can take these forms:

```
window windowNumber
window "windowName",
the stage
```

XDK: n. Xtra Developer's Kit, used for creating Xtras.

XObject: n. Precursor to Xtras prior to version 5 of Director.

Xtra: n. A plug-in for Director or other Macromedia application.

Index

Null-termination, 154
Number systems, 239–247
  conversion, 243
Numeric keypad, 531
  input, 293–294
numToChar(), 280, 556

O

object, 444
Object-oriented programming (OOP),
    29, 155, 326, 328–330, 349
  C+ comparison, 155–157
  usage, 334–335
Object-oriented scripts, 339
Object-oriented stopwatch, 330–332
Object-oriented style, 81
Objects
  class creation, 335
  death/life, 328
  references. *See* Child object
    references.
Objects of mystery, 326–338
Obsolete commands, 445
Obsolete Lingo, 442
On AlertHook, 139–142
on eventName, 77
on exitFrame handler, 74
on keyDown, 7
  handler, 155
on mouseDown handler, 136
on mouseUp, 7
  handler, 74, 76, 154
on startUp handler, 424
One-line if statements, 45
One-time initialization, 36
Online casino, 245–247
OOP. *See* Object-oriented
    programming.
Operands, 55, 164, 229
Operations, 55. *See also* Asynchronous
    operations; Points; Property lists;
    Rects.
  validity, 201, 202
Operators, 173–179. *See also* Arithmetic
    operators; Comparison operators;
    Decrement operators; Increment
    operators; Logical operators;
    String operators.

Option key, 283
Optional arguments, variation, 63–64
Optional debugging, 119
Option-Return, 11
OS, 554
OS-dependent system, 554
OS-level functions, 271, 298
OS-related functions, 376
OS-specific entity, 554
Override functions, 118

P

[Palette], 563
param(), 66
paramCount property, 65, 66
Parameter dialog, 344
Parameter types, checking, 164–166
Parameters, 27, 55–57, 152–153, 361
  error checking, 66–68
  inclusion. *See* Functions.
  lists. *See* Variable-length parameter lists.
Parent class, 156
Parent script, 156
Parent Script Lingo, 345–349
Parent scripts, 12, 80, 85, 316, 322, 326,
    328–330, 345–347
  creation, 329
Parent-child scripting, errors, 334
Parentheses, 177, 178, 179
pass, 19, 77, 108, 290
Passing arguments, 56–57
Password entry field, simulation,
    290–291
Performance, 151–152. *See also* List
    performance.
  gauging, 315
PI, 443
Pick lists, 213
Platform property, 44
Platform-independent paths, 372
Platforms, 368, 555
play, 19
play done, 19
Playback platform, 44
playSound, 63, 64
Pointers, 150
Points, 181, 212
  operations, 205–207

About the Authors

Bruce Epstein first learned Director when it became apparent that no one would fund his desire to wander aimlessly unless he was doing so in front of a keyboard. Since that time, he has become a recognized Director and Lingo expert, spouting unsolicited advice in various books, magazines, and multimedia fora. Bruce has programmed and optimized dozens of cross-platform multimedia products, such as children's edutainment titles, enhanced audio CDs, and interactive advertisements, including the Chrysler/Plymouth Virtual Auto Plaza. He writes voraciously about multimedia development, software design, and project management, and refers to himself in the third person. In his copious spare time, Bruce runs Zeus Productions (*http://www.zeusprod.com*), which offers Lingo consulting and Xtras for Director. *Lingo in a Nutshell* is Bruce's brain in a book, distilling years of Director and Lingo expertise into a concise desktop reference.

Colophon

Our look is the result of reader comments, our own experimentation, and feedback from distribution channels. Distinctive covers complement our distinctive approach to technical topics, breathing personality and life into potentially dry subjects.

The animal on the cover of *Lingo in a Nutshell* is a macaw, a usually brightly colored South American parrot. Macaws include several species, ranging in size from 12 to 40 inches long; some of the most common include the blue and gold macaw (*Ara ararauna*) and the scarlet macaw (*Ara macao*). Many of these often noisy parrots can be trained to mimic human speech.

All macaws have large beaks, with the upper portion overlapping the lower. Their diet consists mainly of seeds, nuts, and fresh fruit. They have four toes, two pointing forward and two backward. Larger macaws have a lifespan of up to 75 years.

Macaws generally nest in treeholes or crevices in rocks. One of their roles in nature is the propagation of plant life; undigested seeds are carried throughout the forest in the birds' droppings. Males and females are similarly colored. Many of the macaw species are threatened with extinction both because of their popularity as pets and the destruction of their natural habitat. Poachers regularly steal the young from nests and export birds for illegal sale.

Paula Carroll served as production coordinator. Benchmark Productions provided editorial and production services. Robert Romano created the illustrations using Macromedia FreeHand 7. Mike Sierra provided FrameMaker technical support. Benchmark Productions wrote the index, with additional index work done by Robert Saigh.

Edie Freedman designed the cover of this book, using an illustration by Susan Hart. The cover layout was produced with Quark XPress 3.32 using the ITC Garamond font. Whenever possible, our books use RepKover™, a durable and flexible lay-flat binding. If the page count exceeds RepKover's limit, perfect binding is used.

The inside layout was designed by Nancy Priest and implemented in FrameMaker 5.0 by Mike Sierra. The text and heading fonts are ITC Garamond Light and Garamond Book. This colophon was written by Nancy Kotary.

More Titles from O'Reilly

Graphics/Multimedia

Encyclopedia of Graphics File Formats, 2nd Edition

*By James D. Murray &
William vanRyper
2nd Edition May 1996
1154 pages, Includes CD-ROM
ISBN 1-56592-161-5*

The second edition of the *Encyclopedia of Graphics File Formats* provides the convenience of quick look-up on CD-ROM, up-to-date information through links to the World Wide Web, as well as a printed book—all in one package. Includes technical details on more than 100 file formats. The CD-ROM includes vendor file format specs, graphics test images, coding examples, and graphics conversion and manipulation software. An indispensable online resource for graphics programmers, service bureaus, and graphic artists.

QuarkXPress in a Nutshell

*By Donnie O'Quinn
1st Edition June 1998
546 pages, ISBN 1-56592-399-5*

This quick reference describes every tool, command, palette, and sub-menu in QuarkXPress 4, providing users with a detailed understanding of the software so they can make informed choices and reduce time spent learning by trial-and-error.

Director in a Nutshell

*By Bruce A. Epstein
1st Edition January 1999 (est.)
450 pages (est.), ISBN 1-56592-382-0*

Director in a Nutshell is the most concise and complete guide available for Director®. The reader gets both the nitty-gritty details and the bigger context in which to use the multiple facets of Director. It is a high-end handbook, at a low-end price—an indispensable desktop reference for every Director user.

Photoshop in a Nutshell

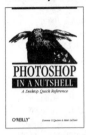

*By Donnie O'Quinn & Matt LeClair
1st Edition October 1997
610 pages, ISBN 1-56592-313-8*

Photoshop 4's powerful features make it the software standard for desktop image design and production. But they also make it an extremely complex product. This detailed reference defines and describes every tool, command, palette, and sub-menu of Photoshop 4 to help users understand design options, make informed choices, and reduce time spent learning by trial-and-error.

Web Authoring and Design

Photoshop for the Web

*By Mikkel Aaland
1st Edition April 1998
238 pages, ISBN 1-56592-350-2*

Photoshop for the Web shows you how to use the world's most popular imaging software to create Web graphics and images that look great and download blazingly fast. The book is crammed full of step-by-step examples and real-world solutions from some of the country's hottest Web producers, including *HotWired*, c|net, *Discovery Online*, *Second Story*, *SFGate*, and more than 20 others.

Web Navigation: Designing the User Experience

*By Jennifer Fleming
1st Edition September 1998
288 pages, Includes CD-ROM
ISBN 1-56592-351-0*

This book takes the first in-depth look at designing Web site navigation through design strategies to help you uncover solutions that work for your site and audience. It focuses on designing by purpose, with chapters on entertainment, shopping, identity, learning, information, and community sites. Comes with a CD-ROM that containing software demos and a "netography" of related Web resources.

Web Authoring and Design

Designing with JavaScript

By Nick Heinle
1st Edition September 1997
256 pages, Includes CD-ROM
ISBN 1-56592-300-6

Written by the author of the "JavaScript Tip of the Week" web site, this new Web Review Studio book focuses on the most useful and applicable scripts for making truly interactive, engaging web sites. You'll not only have quick access to the scripts you need, you'll finally understand why the scripts work, how to alter the scripts to get the effects you want, and, ultimately, how to write your own groundbreaking scripts from scratch.

Information Architecture for the World Wide Web

By Louis Rosenfeld & Peter Morville
1st Edition January 1998
226 pages, ISBN 1-56592-282-4

Learn how to merge aesthetics and echanics to design web sites that "work." This book shows how to apply principles of architecture and library science to design cohesive web sites and intranets that are easy to use, manage, and expand. Covers building complex sites, hierarchy design and organization, and techniques to make your site easier to search. For webmasters, designers, and administrators.

HTML: The Definitive Guide, 3rd Edition

By Chuck Musciano & Bill Kennedy
3rd Edition August 1998
576 pages, ISBN 1-56592-492-4

This complete guide is chock full of examples, sample code, and practical, hands-on advice to help you create truly effective web pages and master advanced features. Learn how to insert images and other multimedia elements, create useful links and searchable documents, use Netscape extensions, design great forms, and lots more. The third edition covers HTML 4.0, Netscape 4.5, and Internet Explorer 4.0, plus all the common extensions.

Web Programming

Dynamic HTML: The Definitive Reference

By Danny Goodman
1st Edition July 1998
1088 pages, ISBN 1-56592-494-0

Dynamic HTML: The Definitive Reference is an indispensable compendium for Web content developers. It contains complete reference material for all of the HTML tags, CSS style attributes, browser document objects, and JavaScript objects supported by the various standards and the latest versions of Netscape Navigator and Microsoft Internet Explorer.

Learning VBScript

By Paul Lomax
1st Edition July 1997
616 pages, includes CD-ROM
ISBN 1-56592-247-6

This definitive guide shows web developers how to take full advantage of client-side scripting with the VBScript language. In addition to basic language features, it covers the Internet Explorer object model and discusses techniques for client-side scripting, like adding ActiveX controls to a web page or validating data before sending it to the server. Includes CD-ROM with over 170 code samples.

Web Client Programming with Perl

By Clinton Wong
1st Edition March 1997
228 pages, ISBN 1-56592-214-X

Web Client Programming with Perl shows you how to extend scripting skills to the Web. This book teaches you the basics of how browsers communicate with servers and how to write your own customized web clients to automate common tasks. It is intended for those who are motivated to develop software that offers a more flexible and dynamic response than a standard web browser.

Web Programming

CGI Programming on the World Wide Web

By Shishir Gundavaram
1st Edition March 1996
450 pages, ISBN 1-56592-168-2

This book offers a comprehensive explanation of CGI and related techniques for people who hold on to the dream of providing their own information servers on the Web. It starts at the beginning, explaining the value of CGI and how it works, then moves swiftly into the subtle details of programming.

JavaScript: The Definitive Guide, 3rd Edition

By David Flanagan & Dan Shafer
3rd Edition June 1998
800 pages, ISBN 1-56592-392-8

This third edition of the definitive reference to JavaScript covers the latest version of the language, JavaScript 1.2, as supported by Netscape Navigator 4.0. JavaScript, which is being standardized under the name ECMAScript, is a scripting language that can be embedded directly in HTML to give web pages programming-language capabilities.

Frontier: The Definitive Guide

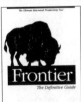

By Matt Neuburg
1st Edition February 1998
618 pages, 1-56592-383-9

This definitive guide is the first book devoted exclusively to teaching and documenting Userland Frontier, a powerful scripting environment for web site management and system level scripting. Packed with examples, advice, tricks, and tips, Frontier: The Definitive Guide teaches you Frontier from the ground up. Learn how to automate repetitive processes, control remote computers across a network, beef up your web site by generating hundreds of related web pages automatically, and more. Covers Frontier 4.2.3 for the Macintosh.

Web Server Administration

Web Performance Tuning

By Patrick Killelea
1st Edition October 1998
374 pages, ISBN 1-56592-379-0

Web Performance Tuning hits the ground running and gives concrete advice for improving crippled Web performance right away. For anyone who has waited too long for a Web page to display or watched servers slow to a crawl, this book includes tips on tuning the server software, operating system, network, and the Web browser itself.

Building Your Own Web Conferences™

By Susan B. Peck &
Beverly Murray Scherf
1st Edition March 1997
270 pages, Includes CD-ROM
ISBN 1-56592-279-4

Building Your Own Web Conferences is a complete guide for Windows® 95 and NT™ users on how to set up and manage dynamic virtual communities that improve workgroup collaboration and keep visitors coming back to your site. The second in O'Reilly's "Build Your Own..." series, this book comes with O'Reilly's state-of-the-art WebBoard™ 2.0 software on CD-ROM.

Building Your Own WebSite™

By Susan B. Peck & Stephen Arrants
1st Edition July 1996
514 pages, Includes CD-ROM,
ISBN 1-56592-232-8

This is a hands-on reference for Windows® 95 and Windows NT™ users who want to host a site on the Web or on a corporate intranet. This step-by-step guide will have you creating live web pages in minutes. You'll also learn how to connect your web to information in other Windows applications, such as word processing documents and databases. The book is packed with examples and tutorials on every aspect of web management, and it includes the highly acclaimed WebSite™ 1.1 server software on CD-ROM.

O'REILLY®

TO ORDER: **800-998-9938** • **order@oreilly.com** • **http://www.oreilly.com/**
OUR PRODUCTS ARE AVAILABLE AT A BOOKSTORE OR SOFTWARE STORE NEAR YOU.
FOR INFORMATION: **800-998-9938** • **707-829-0515** • **info@oreilly.com**

Web Server Administration

How to stay in touch with O'Reilly

1. Visit Our Award-Winning Site

http://www.oreilly.com/

★ "Top 100 Sites on the Web" —*PC Magazine*
★ "Top 5% Web sites" —*Point Communications*
★ "3-Star site" —*The McKinley Group*

Our web site contains a library of comprehensive product information (including book excerpts and tables of contents), downloadable software, background articles, interviews with technology leaders, links to relevant sites, book cover art, and more. File us in your Bookmarks or Hotlist!

2. Join Our Email Mailing Lists

New Product Releases
To receive automatic email with brief descriptions of all new O'Reilly products as they are released, send email to:
listproc@online.oreilly.com
Put the following information in the first line of your message (*not* in the Subject field):
subscribe oreilly-news

O'Reilly Events
If you'd also like us to send information about trade show events, special promotions, and other O'Reilly events, send email to:
listproc@online.oreilly.com
Put the following information in the first line of your message (*not* in the Subject field):
subscribe oreilly-events

3. Get Examples from Our Books via FTP

There are two ways to access an archive of example files from our books:

Regular FTP
- ftp to:
  ftp.oreilly.com
  (login: anonymous
  password: your email address)
- Point your web browser to:
  ftp://ftp.oreilly.com/

FTPMAIL
- Send an email message to:
  ftpmail@online.oreilly.com
  (Write "help" in the message body)

4. Contact Us via Email

order@oreilly.com
To place a book or software order online. Good for North American and international customers.

subscriptions@oreilly.com
To place an order for any of our newsletters or periodicals.

books@oreilly.com
General questions about any of our books.

software@oreilly.com
For general questions and product information about our software. Check out O'Reilly Software Online at **http://software.oreilly.com/** for software and technical support information. Registered O'Reilly software users send your questions to:
website-support@oreilly.com

cs@oreilly.com
For answers to problems regarding your order or our products.

booktech@oreilly.com
For book content technical questions or corrections.

proposals@oreilly.com
To submit new book or software proposals to our editors and product managers.

international@oreilly.com
For information about our international distributors or translation queries. For a list of our distributors outside of North America check out:
http://www.oreilly.com/www/order/country.html

O'Reilly & Associates, Inc.
101 Morris Street, Sebastopol, CA 95472 USA
TEL   707-829-0515 or 800-998-9938
       (6am to 5pm PST)
FAX   707-829-0104

International Distributors

UK, Europe, Middle East and Northern Africa (except France, Germany, Switzerland, & Austria)

INQUIRIES
International Thomson Publishing Europe
Berkshire House
168-173 High Holborn
London WC1V 7AA, UK
Telephone: 44-171-497-1422
Fax: 44-171-497-1426
Email: itpint@itps.co.uk

ORDERS
International Thomson Publishing Services, Ltd.
Cheriton House, North Way
Andover, Hampshire SP10 5BE,
United Kingdom
Telephone: 44-264-342-832 (UK)
Telephone: 44-264-342-806 (outside UK)
Fax: 44-264-364418 (UK)
Fax: 44-264-342761 (outside UK)
UK & Eire orders: itpuk@itps.co.uk
International orders: itpint@itps.co.uk

France
Editions Eyrolles
61 bd Saint-Germain
75240 Paris Cedex 05
France
Fax: 33-01-44-41-11-44

FRENCH LANGUAGE BOOKS
All countries except Canada
Telephone: 33-01-44-41-46-16
Email: geodif@eyrolles.com

ENGLISH LANGUAGE BOOKS
Telephone: 33-01-44-41-11-87
Email: distribution@eyrolles.com

Germany, Switzerland, and Austria

INQUIRIES
O'Reilly Verlag
Balthasarstr. 81
D-50670 Köln
Germany
Telephone: 49-221-97-31-60-0
Fax: 49-221-97-31-60-8
Email: anfragen@oreilly.de

ORDERS
International Thomson Publishing
Königswinterer Straße 418
53227 Bonn, Germany
Telephone: 49-228-97024 0
Fax: 49-228-441342
Email: order@oreilly.de

Japan
O'Reilly Japan, Inc.
Kiyoshige Building 2F
12-Banchi, Sanei-cho
Shinjuku-ku
Tokyo 160 Japan
Tel: 81-3-3356-5227
Fax: 81-3-3356-5261
Email: kenji@oreilly.com

India
Computer Bookshop (India) PVT. Ltd.
190 Dr. D.N. Road, Fort
Bombay 400 001 India
Tel: 91-22-207-0989
Fax: 91-22-262-3551
Email: cbsbom@giasbm01.vsnl.net.in

Hong Kong
City Discount Subscription Service Ltd.
Unit D, 3rd Floor, Yan's Tower
27 Wong Chuk Hang Road
Aberdeen, Hong Kong
Telephone: 852-2580-3539
Fax: 852-2580-6463
Email: citydis@ppn.com.hk

Korea
Hanbit Publishing, Inc.
Sonyoung Bldg. 202
Yeksam-dong 736-36
Kangnam-ku
Seoul, Korea
Telephone: 822-554-9610
Fax: 822-556-0363
Email: hant93@chollian.dacom.co.kr

Taiwan
ImageArt Publishing, Inc.
4/fl. No. 65 Shinyi Road Sec. 4
Taipei, Taiwan, R.O.C.
Telephone: 886-2708-5770
Fax: 886-2705-6690
Email: marie@ms1.hinet.net

Singapore, Malaysia, and Thailand
Longman Singapore
25 First Lok Yan Road
Singapore 2262
Telephone: 65-268-2666
Fax: 65-268-7023
Email: daniel@longman.com.sg

Philippines
Mutual Books, Inc.
429-D Shaw Boulevard
Mandaluyong City, Metro
Manila, Philippines
Telephone: 632-725-7538
Fax: 632-721-3056
Email: mbikikog@mnl.sequel.net

China
Ron's DataCom Co., Ltd.
79 Dongwu Avenue
Dongxihu District
Wuhan 430040
China
Telephone: 86-27-83892568
Fax: 86-27-83222108
Email: hongfeng@public.wh.hb.cn

Australia
WoodsLane Pty. Ltd.
7/5 Vuko Place, Warriewood NSW 2102
P.O. Box 935,
Mona Vale NSW 2103
Australia
Telephone: 61-2-9970-5111
Fax: 61-2-9970-5002
Email: info@woodslane.com.au

All Other Asia Countries
O'Reilly & Associates, Inc.
101 Morris Street
Sebastopol, CA 95472 USA
Telephone: 707-829-0515
Fax: 707-829-0104
Email: order@oreilly.com

The Americas
McGraw-Hill Interamericana Editores, S.A. de C.V.
Cedro No. 512
Col. Atlampa 06450
Mexico, D.F.
Telephone: 52-5-541-3155
Fax: 52-5-541-4913
Email: mcgraw-hill@infosel.net.mx

Southern Africa
International Thomson Publishing
Southern Africa
Building 18, Constantia Park
138 Sixteenth Road
P.O. Box 2459
Halfway House, 1685 South Africa
Tel: 27-11-805-4819
Fax: 27-11-805-3648

O'REILLY™

O'Reilly & Associates, Inc.
101 Morris Street
Sebastopol, CA 95472-9902
1-800-998-9938

Visit us online at:
http://www.ora.com/
orders@ora.com

O'REILLY WOULD LIKE TO HEAR FROM YOU

Which book did this card come from?

_____

Where did you buy this book?
- ❑ Bookstore
- ❑ Direct from O'Reilly
- ❑ Bundled with hardware/software
- ❑ Computer Store
- ❑ Class/seminar
- ❑ Other _____

What operating system do you use?
- ❑ UNIX
- ❑ Windows NT
- ❑ Other _____
- ❑ Macintosh
- ❑ PC(Windows/DOS)

What is your job description?
- ❑ System Administrator
- ❑ Network Administrator
- ❑ Web Developer
- ❑ Other _____
- ❑ Programmer
- ❑ Educator/Teacher

❑ Please send me O'Reilly's catalog, containing a complete listing of O'Reilly books and software.

Name _____   Company/Organization _____

Address _____

City _____ State _____ Zip/Postal Code _____ Country _____

Telephone _____   Internet or other email address (specify network) _____

Nineteenth century wood engraving
of a bear from the O'Reilly &
Associates Nutshell Handbook®
Using & Managing UUCP.

POST CARD

PLACE
STAMP
HERE

BUSINESS REPLY MAIL
FIRST CLASS MAIL PERMIT NO. 80 SEBASTOPOL, CA

Postage will be paid by addressee

O'Reilly & Associates, Inc.
101 Morris Street
Sebastopol, CA 95472-9902